Urban Change in the United States and Western Europe

ANITA A. SUMMERS,
PAUL C. CHESHIRE, AND
LANFRANCO SENN
Editors

Urban Change in the United States and Western Europe

Comparative Analysis and Policy

Second Edition

THE URBAN INSTITUTE PRESS
Washington, D.C.

Library of Congress Cataloging in Publication Data

Urban Change in the United States and Western Europe: Comparative Analysis and Policy, second edition/Anita A. Summers, Paul C. Cheshire, and Lanfranco Senn, editors.

Includes bibliographic references and index.

1. Cities and towns—United States—Growth—Congresses. 2. Cities and towns—Europe—Growth—Congresses. 3. Urban policy—United States—Congresses. 4. Urban policy—Europe—Congresses. 5. Community development, Urban—United States—Congresses. 6. Community development, Urban—Europe—Congresses. I. Summers, Anita A. II. Cheshire, P. C. III. Senn, Lanfranco.

HT384.U5U73   1999   98-48112
307.76'0973—dc21   CIP

ISBN 0-87766-683-0 (paper, alk. paper)

Printed in the United States of America

ACKNOWLEDGMENTS

We are grateful to the several sources of funding that made the conference and this volume possible. The Rockefeller Foundation supported all the activities at the Bellagio Study and Conference Center—with efficiency and elegance. Funding was also received from the Chamber of Commerce of Milan, the Giovanni Agnelli Foundation, the Lombard Regional Government, the Banca Popolare di Milano, the Economic and Social Research Council (United Kingdom), the Wharton Real Estate Center of the University of Pennsylvania, the Urban Institute, and the University of Glasgow.

CONTENTS

FOREWORD

Cities in the United States developed in response to profoundly different cultural, economic, and political factors than cities in Western Europe. Consequently, they occupy a different place in their country's national life. Yet cities have undoubtedly been affected by the changes sweeping both continents in the last 50 years.

Contributors to this updated edition of *Urban Change in the United States and Western Europe: Comparative Analysis and Policy* are intrigued with how urban areas have changed and what role public policy may have played in those changes. After analyzing an enormous range of factors affecting where people live and work, they have concluded that contemporary urban areas in the United States and Western Europe have similar patterns of growth and face similar problems.

Most urban areas have experienced a population shift from the central city to suburban regions. In the United States, this decentralization has resulted in large proportions of poor residents living in the inner cities. A new chapter addresses three policy strategies for alleviating this situation and suggests that improving transportation offers an effective way of improving inner-city residents' access to the new jobs available in the suburbs.

In Europe, notes the author of another new chapter, the formation of the European Union and the increase in service sector jobs in many central cities appear to be exerting a beneficial effect on decentralization. The prospects of many U.S. metropolitan areas are brightening because of very low unemployment rates, but the United States, unlike Western European countries, has historically had weak, if any, national priorities regarding its cities or urban regions.

Analysts are beginning to see recentralization in some urban areas—that is, the movement of people and jobs into the central city. London is an example. Americans should not be too quick to rejoice at this glimmer of inner-city revitalization, however. Our cities have a far higher concentration of poor residents than European cities do, and this demographic fact of life presents a major impediment to recentralization. Consider that large U.S. cities spend a walloping 30 percent of their revenues on public welfare, health, and hospitals. Consider also that public policy in the United States has tended to promote decentralization, both directly and indirectly.

What policy has done, or failed to do, policy may also be able to remedy. The United States and Western European countries are facing the challenges of an increasingly global, high-technology economy. As they do so, they can learn from each other's experiences. The contributors to *Urban Change* identify numerous areas—such as transportation, land use and zoning, business development, housing, and cultural and recreational amenities—in which national policy might fruitfully be brought to bear on urban problems.

William Gorham
President
The Urban Institute

Chapter One

URBAN AMERICA AND URBAN WESTERN EUROPE: ARE THEY DIFFERENT?

Anita A. Summers

The answer to the question posed in the chapter title is: yes, they are different, mostly because of the very different relationships between central and local governments in the United States and Western Europe. This was the answer reached in the first edition of this book (1993), and it has now been substantially reinforced by the data and analysis of urban patterns on both continents since then. This second edition takes the baseline studies of 1990, updates the data, and re-analyzes the conclusions.

The 1990 conference in Bellagio, Italy, on "Comparisons of Urban Economic Development in the United States and Western Europe, 1950–87" was an effort to improve understanding of the efficacy of urban policies by telling a cohesive tale of the cities on two continents. This conference produced the chapters for the first edition of this book, focusing on the basic question: What can be learned by a rigorous comparison of the patterns and processes of urban concentrations of residents and employment in Western Europe and the United States? Participants analyzed this issue with particular emphasis on the role and effectiveness of public policy. A wide range of methodological techniques was used—economic theory, econometrics, general economic analysis, regional science, and institutional historical analysis. Fifteen to twenty years ago, analyses of transportation and land-use issues would have dominated such a conference, but by 1990 there was full recognition of the multiplicity of factors—political, social, and economic—underlying urban location decisions. This second edition, updating the data and conclusions of most of the conference papers and, in two cases, putting in entirely new chapters, underscores that reality.

Among the striking conclusions that have emerged from the conference and this update are the following: (1) There are clear similarities in the contemporary patterns and problems of urban areas between the United States and Western Europe, but wide disparity in the intensity of the distributional problems. (2) Government has and continues to affect the patterns and problems in urban areas on both continents. (3) The policies undertaken by governments in Western Europe are very different from those taken in the United States. (4) The Europeans institutionalize the fact that they comprise many cultures and countries into models of disequilibrium among their urban areas. The Americans—though steeped in the neoclassical traditions of equilibrium—frequently see disequilibrium within theirs.

The contributions to this volume reveal three very visible commonalities in the interpretation of urban economic processes in Western Europe and the United States. Virtually all authors converge on the role and potential effectiveness of government policies in influencing the visible patterns of urban and regional growth. Almost every author sees changes—similar on both continents—in the size and structure of urban areas. And, though the Europeans and Americans differ in their intellectual traditions concerning the ability of urban areas across the map to converge in their state of economic health, they are not far apart in seeing "permanent" disequilibrium, in the absence of intervention.

ROLE OF GOVERNMENT

The reality of the dominance of market forces in influencing the location concentrations of people and jobs is recognized in this volume by analysts on both sides of the Atlantic—as is the desirability of the individual freedom of choice underlying that reality. But every author (with the exception of Edwin S. Mills, in chapter 6) agrees on the desirability of a strong role for the national government in effecting changes in the economic and social patterns of subnational governments. The Europeans argue in favor of this position because, on the whole, there is no significant economic power in the hands of local government (though Leo van den Berg, in chapter 17, advocates assigning more strength to local government), and they believe this distribution of responsibilities has served them well in many respects. The Americans (except Mills), because the absence of a strategic national urban policy has coincided with severe fiscal and social problems in the largest cities, point to the inability and failure of state and local policies to cope with central-city crises.

However, both Europeans and Americans point out the negative impact of some national policies on central cities—particularly the low-income housing concentrations that were an integral part of many national urban policies, and the fragmented fiscal structure of metropolitan areas in the United States. Anthony Downs (chapter 2), Peter D. Linneman and Anita A. Summers (chapter 4), Helen F. Ladd (chapter 11), Mark Alan Hughes and Anaïs Loizillon (chapter 13), and Dick Netzer (chapter 14) argue for national involvement with the national public good responsibilities that are now being handled by cities, and particularly those derived from the concentrations of poverty. Lanfranco Senn and Gianluigi Gorla, in chapter 8, make the same public good argument with respect to other types of benefits that would derive from collaboration among local governments.

The analyses by Ladd, Joseph Gyourko and Joseph Tracy (chapter 12), and Netzer show clearly the links between the types of population that tend to concentrate in American cities and the fiscal problems of these cities. Most of the large cities of the United States have relatively high concentrations of people in poverty, many of them immigrants. In essence, in the United States, large cities are major caretakers of the nation's poor and immigrants, enabling the rest of the country to become more removed from the disamenities of poverty. In the political economist's lingo, the nation as a whole is the beneficiary of some of the services that cities are delivering and paying for from their own tax base—but the nation is not paying for much of those costs. In Europe—as is particularly clear in the discussions by John B. Parr (chapter 7), Rainer Mackensen (chapter 10), and Duncan Maclennan (chapter 16)—the significant centralization of economic responsibility for subnational governments has been a factor in explaining why their cities have not suffered as much as those in America, though Maclennan emphasizes the recent evidence that social housing has worsened the economic strength of central cores.

The fiscal relationships among various levels of government—comprising the fiscal federalist structure—are not the only government policies emphasized in this volume as being influential and effective. Every chapter, to some degree, points to the important role of infrastructure, in terms of both amount and quality. Downs, Paul C. Cheshire (chapters 5 and 19), Parr, Maclennan, and van den Berg particularly stress this role for European nations; and Downs, Linneman and Summers, Hughes and Loizillon, and Netzer emphasize this role for the United States. Downs concludes that the influential role of infrastructure is the same on both continents, but that the relatively shabby state of American cities is, in part, due to the relatively low rates of spending on infrastructure in the past.

Other government policies are regarded as highly significant by several scholars. Peter Hall (chapter 3) argues for a set of regionally based industrial policies to foster high-tech manufacturing sectors, encourage the producer services sections, and attack factors underlying work force polarization. His policy proposals are directed at helping the winners, led by demand. Michael I. Luger (chapter 15) examines the regional development of high-tech industries in the United States and advocates a national mechanism for allocating technology assistance (a winner industry) to reduce regional disparities. Mills, on the other hand, contends that only markets, not governments, can pick winners. Van den Berg also advocates demand, led by policies.

There is considerable documentation of the attractiveness of employment in locations with a higher quality of life—Cheshire, Mackensen, and van den Berg note this for Europe, as do Linneman and Summers, and Gyourko and Tracy for the United States. Hughes argues that effective labor mobility policies can expand the employment opportunities for those living in the parts of metropolitan areas with fewer amenities.

Two American authors argue that particular types of regulatory restrictions are impediments to economic development. Downs asserts that zoning restrictions impede intrametropolitan mobility— thus keeping the poor concentrated in the central cities; Mills argues that central cities overregulate business, the effect of which is to raise costs because of production rigidities, making it more attractive for business to locate outside central cities. Cheshire, in his postscript chapter 19, argues that land use regulation in the United States has accentuated urban decentralization, whereas in the United Kingdom it has not only substantially increased land costs but has produced a form of concentrated deconcentration by generating detached high-density exurbs. Linneman and Summers were not able to establish any econometrically robust link between regulatory practices and employment. (It is noteworthy that, although elected officials and the media—particularly in the United States and the United Kingdom— assume the clear positive impact of defense procurement allocation decisions, there is little hard evidence to substantiate that view. Linneman and Summers did examine this question for American metropolitan areas, and found some evidence, though not strong, for these hypothesized positive effects.)

Though the dominant role of markets in the determination of the location of people and jobs is underscored by all the authors, confidence in the ability of government policies to influence regional economic development is expressed in most of the chapters. Some stress allocations related to the low-income concentrations in cities (Downs, Ladd, Hughes, Netzer, van den Berg); some stress the importance of infrastructure investment (Downs, Hall, Cheshire, Parr, Hughes); some stress investing in urban amenities (Cheshire, Gyourko and Tracy, van den Berg); some advocate targeted industrial assistance (Hall, Luger); and some emphasize the importance of a strategic housing policy (Downs, Netzer, Maclennan). This volume's contributors agree, in general, with the importance of the central government in implementing these policies, but several authors emphasize the importance of subnational government policy (Gyourko and Tracy, Luger, van den Berg).

A somewhat overgeneralized summary of the positions of the contributing scholars might be that the Europeans stress the efficacy of "hard" instruments for urban policy—tangible physical infrastructure such as housing and transportation networks—and that the Americans stress the efficacy of "soft" instruments—assistance in the form of welfare grants, educational expenditures, and health insurance. In terms of future planning, this is probably relevant information for both groups. In Europe, the coming of age of the European Union is bringing with it more mobility among member nations' urban areas—and with it, the increased concentrations of the poor so apparent in the United States. In chapter 10, Rainer Mackensen, taking a broad historical sweep, suggests that some of this is already visible. If so, the bitter lessons learned in America in the last few decades may provide a how-not-to-do-it textbook. The crisis state of many of the largest United States cities coincided with the decision not to have a national urban policy. On the other hand, the European success with centralized regional financing and policy making could provide a how-to-do-it textbook. It will be interesting to see how far the European proposed action plan for European cities embodies these lessons.

CHANGING STRUCTURE OF URBAN AREAS

Two major topics addressed in detail in this volume relate to the changing structure of urban areas in Western Europe and the United States. First, on both continents, the structure of these areas has changed significantly over the last few decades, as measured by employment and population characteristics. Second, the need for a functional definition of an urban area, and the lack of coincidence between legal and functional boundaries, is recognized by all the authors in one way or another. A number of chapters include conceptual and empirical discussions of measurement problems in the analyses of subnational areas that arise from this difficulty. Much commonality emerges here between the European and American experiences: population and jobs deconcentrated away from central cities in the 1960s and 1970s, and have continued to do so in many American cities; there are relatively more poor people in the central cities, though this is much more true of the United States and there are contrary cases in Europe; the standard, legally defined metropolitan areas no longer define the realities of the urban network; and government data available for regions do not allow analysis of these changed realities.

Chapters 4, 5, 9, and 10, by Linneman and Summers, Cheshire, Leven, and Mackensen respectively, provide the primary sources for the empirical analysis of the decentralization of population and employment from the urban areas in Europe and the United States. Linneman and Summers analyze 60 areas (called PMSAs, primary metropolitan statistical areas) and Cheshire analyzes 117 European urban concentrations (called FURS, functional urban regions). Both chapters document the movement away from central cities, and both of their econometric analyses support the hypotheses that the poor quality of the urban infrastructure, the concentration of employment in declining industries, and large size have been important explanations of this pattern. Cheshire emerges from the analysis somewhat optimistic about the future of many European cities because of the reduced transportation costs activated by the developing European Union. Linneman and Summers see no such basis for optimism about America's central cities; they expect smaller central cities to be fixed features of the metropolitan landscape. Several other scholars document this decentralization and the associated decline of major cities— Downs, Mackensen, Ladd, Hughes, and Netzer. The American contributors are greatly concerned with the socioeconomic implications of the changed metropolitan map—Ladd, Hughes, and Netzer, particularly. But the Europeans are also worrying—Mackensen and Maclennan, particularly. The postscript chapter by Cheshire updates the analysis further. It shows that patterns became more varied during the 1980s and early 1990s, with some relative recentralization in many cities, and absolute recentralization in some. His analysis suggests that future patterns may be more varied—although cities in the United States are likely to continue to decentralize because of their inherited characteristics and the institutional constraints within which they operate.

One element that muddies the waters of much academic and media discussion of urban issues is the absence of a meticulous designation of the area under discussion—Are we discussing a legally bound jurisdiction called a city or an analytically determined (or government-data-agency-determined) nonlegally bound metropolitan area in which the central city is a core civil division? Virtually all the contributors reach for some sort of functional definition of subnational urban areas. However, clear pragmatic considerations impede the implementation of such a concept by the compilers of statistics. Functions change over time, and this implies periodic changes in the definition of the area concerned.

The European contributors to this volume have been concerned for some time about this issue, apart from the more recent stimulus presented by the rise of the European Union. Senn and Gorla argue for the need for a wider concept of metropolitan areas and of how they interact, claiming that—because of networking benefits—the social benefits of a functionally defined metropolitan area are greater than the sum of the individual benefits. Parr argues that we are understating metropolitan area growth by using boundaries that are no longer functionally accurate—we are not including the peripheral areas that, in fact, are attached to the former core. Cheshire and van den Berg use the concept of functional urban regions. And Maclennan argues that planning policies which enable markets, not displace them, can produce a more harmonious income profile.

The American contributors, despite a growing awareness of the limitations of the PMSA unit of analysis—which does not embrace communities that are clearly large, clearly growing, and clearly attached—focus on the problems arising *within* the defined metropolitan areas. Ladd analyzes the severe fiscal problems of cities arising from their disconnected tax bases; Linneman and Summers document the very different patterns of growth and population characteristics between central cities and their suburbs and between central business districts and the rest of the central city; and Hughes documents the immobility of central city labor markets, even to the close suburban employment opportunities. Mills's analysis accepts the legal size constraints, and, given that assumption, argues that in the future the smaller metropolitan areas will fare better.

Four of the contributors, as they wrestle with these definitional concerns, actually assemble new data to match their interests. Cheshire develops a measure of local welfare primarily to inform the analysis of the processes of urban change; Gyourko and Tracy develop new local measures of the quality of life that incorporate fiscal characteristics of the community; Hughes creates measures of employment accessibility to enhance understanding of the relative immobility of some city residents; and Linneman and Summers construct disaggregated employment and population data on central business districts versus the rest of the central city and on individual suburbs, as well as measurements of the local regulatory climate for cities and suburban jurisdictions. Without question, the authors of this book fully recognize that the ability to assess the socioeconomic patterns of metropolitan areas is hampered by the various constraints on the geographic area that can be included. These constraints are imposed by the frequent unavailability of regional data, the interest in analyzing a constantly defined area over time, the constitutional definitions of boundaries and responsibilities—and perhaps, also, the slow pace at which we recognize changed realities. New communications technology and new transportation networks have expanded the size and altered the landscape of urban centers. Clearly it will be essential—if we are to understand and influence these patterns—to develop empirical bases that incorporate new areas and that are sufficiently disaggregated to allow for the required flexibility to adjust to changed and changing transactions costs.

CONVERGENCE OR DIVERGENCE IN AND AMONG METROPOLITAN AREAS

Wide differences exist in the state of economic and social health between and within metropolitan areas in the United States, and between and within metropolitan areas in Western Europe.

In the United States, annual employment growth rates among the largest PMSAs between 1980 and 1986 varied from a low of − 5.0 percent (Gary, Indiana) to a high of + 8.2 percent (Orlando, Florida); annual population growth rates between 1980 and 1987 varied from a low of − 0.7 percent (Youngstown, Ohio) to + 3.9 percent (Phoenix, Arizona); for the same periods, the median annual employment growth rates in the center cities of the sixty largest metropolitan areas were + 1.7 percent, compared with + 3.3 percent in their suburbs; and the median annual population growth rate was + 0.5 percent in the cities, in contrast to + 1.9 percent in their suburbs. These patterns were sustained ones (data from Linneman and Summers, chapter 4, this volume). In Europe, in the Benelux countries, 60 percent of the urban cores were losing population between 1971 and 1981, but only 40 percent had population losses in 1981–91; in Germany the ratios changed from 78 percent to 35 percent, in Italy from 56 percent to 17 percent, and in the U.K. from 92 percent to 89 percent—but in France, the ratios increased from 18 percent to 29 percent, and, in Spain, from 0 percent to 34 percent (data from Cheshire, chapter 19). The balance of losers to gainers shifted for reasons Cheshire analyzes, but losing was still a significant pattern.

Neoclassical analysis would lead one to conclude that, if the factors of production are mobile (as is assumed to be characteristic of market economies), the state of health of urban areas in a country should tend to converge, to equilibrate. Western Europe, of course, consists of many countries and many cultures, so the mobility of factors of production is clearly restricted. Presumably, the developing strength of the European Union will make their urban areas more similar in this respect in the long run. It is not surprising, therefore, that European analysts, steeped in the Kaldor institutionalist tradition and reinforced by recent work, see spatial disequilibrium as they study urban maps. Van den Berg's dynamic modeling of the stages of metropolitan area growth reflects acceptance of their disequilibrium character. Downs regards the relatively slow migration response in Western Europe as a major disequilibrating factor, as does Mackensen. Cheshire does not view the equilibrating process of capitalization of quality-of-life characteristics as a valid description for Europe—his analysis reveals very different degrees of adaptiveness in the 117 urban areas he studies, and this adaptiveness can be redefined as a measurement of the capacity to equilibrate. Maclennan sees minimal intraurban mobility, arguing that there will be disequilibrium without government policy, as does Hughes. Senn and Gorla regard the expanding networks among urban areas as an equilibrating force, but they also see the hierarchical characteristics of cities—their economic, political, and cultural concentrations of power—as major forces in continuing disequilibrium; Mackensen argues similarly; and Parr's reading of the evidence is that a narrow geographic definition of metropolitan areas suggests disequilibrium, but that a broader definition would not.

In the United States, on the other hand, though the neoclassical tradition has dominated, there is far from universal confidence that there can be equilibration—and in the eyes of several of this volume's contributors, that confidence has disappeared. Mills's study of the determinants of the size and growth of metropolitan areas is explicitly grounded in general equilibrium analysis; Downs sees interurban homogeneity—equilibration—but intraurban diversity; and Leven discusses the equilibrating influence of increased labor mobility in the United States. But the other writers see much disequilibrium: Hall assumes spatial disequilibrium as he argues for the need to move urban economies out of their declining sectors; Parr, as well as Linneman and Summers and Hughes, documents the spatial disequilibrium within metropolitan areas; Netzer, in arguing for a stronger role for the federal government in reducing disparities among urban areas, accepts the "stickiness" of the snapshot of their divergence; Ladd sees the need to alter federal aid and procurement policies to reduce intermetropolitan disparities, and views the fixed intrametropolitan disequilibrium as the major cause of the poor fiscal health of center cities; and Luger finds that government's support of high-technology programs has had the effect of increasing regional disparities.

European and American analysts converge in finding the strength and fixity of disequilibrium among and within metropolitan areas—though there is not unanimity. Grounded in institutional theory, the European experience continues to document the persistence of disparities. The Americans, though they are grounded in the neoclassical tradition, see the persistence of extreme disparities and their consequences.

ORGANIZATION OF THIS VOLUME

The chapters in this volume contain separate analyses by authors from different countries using different data and different theory. But despite divergencies in perspective, methodology, and conclusions, there is agreement that urban landscapes have shown deconcentration from the central cores, that widely varying socioeconomic profiles of jobs and residents emerge and persist within and among metropolitan areas, that these disparities give rise to significant socioeconomic problems, and that central government policies have the potential to have some effective impact on these patterns.

The four studies in Part I are grouped under the title "Intra- and Intermetropolitan Area Change: Evidence and Strategies." In the opening chapter, Anthony Downs's analysis of the contrasting strategies shaping metropolitan economic development in the United States and Western Europe concludes that the lesson for the United States is that economic development strategies will not solve all urban problems, and that the lesson for Europe is that the European Union may bring more interurban homogeneity. Peter Hall, in the chapter following, identifies policies that might help cities move from their declining industries to expanding ones. He integrates the view that locational decisions should be left entirely to the market, with the view that there are significant social costs to urban decline, by focusing on the desirability of supporting research and development for new industries in their innovative stage. The last two chapters are both heavily empirical analyses of urban economic development patterns. Peter Linneman and Anita Summers document the change from increased independence of suburbs from cities in the United States to greater dependence of suburbs on the health of their urban cores, as well as the need for a federal strategic urban policy. Paul Cheshire develops measurements of local welfare and explains the differences in those measures across Western European urban areas, in welfare levels, if not in form. He sees some bases for expecting more convergence among European urban areas: the European Union, the growth of service employment, and the emphasis on adaptiveness. And he sees some evidence of the reality of these expectations.

Part II, "The Dynamics of Metropolitan Area Change: Theory and Evidence," contains five chapters. Edwin Mills analyzes the determinants of the size and growth of metropolitan areas in the United States and concludes that the smaller areas are likely to function better because they can reap the efficiencies of agglomeration without the diseconomies of very large scale. John Parr's analysis focuses on the importance of considering the wider region—the metropolitan area as typically configured plus the nonmetropolitan zone surrounding it— to understand why metropolitan regions will continue to grow. Lanfranco Senn and Gianluigi Gorla's chapter encourages collaboration among regional governments, as well as the less feasible goal of reducing the concentration of power in large cities. Charles Leven examines, from a historical perspective and using two different measures, the process of regional deurbanization, concluding that the process intensified in the 1980s. Rainer Mackensen gives a broad sociological and historical perspective to European urban development, particularly Germany's. He predicts larger urban agglomerations in Europe—and a greater number of them.

Three studies comprise Part III, "Implications of Metropolitan Change." Helen Ladd studies the links between the spatial disequilibrium within America's metropolitan areas and the fiscal distress of its cities and concludes that redistributive government assistance is needed to preserve its central cities. Joseph Gyourko and Joseph Tracy analyze the links between urban quality-of-life measures and fiscal policies, incorporating the two measures into one, and conclude that cities must heed both to attract employment. Mark Alan Hughes, in a new concluding chapter to this section, analyzes the implications of metropolitan decentralization in the context of the relative immobility of the center city labor supply, and advocates government assistance to resolve the persistence of "impacted ghettos."

Part IV, "The Role of Government," contains four chapters. Dick Netzer evaluates the appropriateness of the present federalist arrangements in the United States to the problems of its cities. He concludes that giving dollars to people only is inadequate; unconditional federal aid triggered by local conditions is the policy he prefers, along with marginal cost pricing of public infrastructure. Michael Luger's analysis focuses on regional high-technology policy. He argues that government assistance has favored the high-growth areas, thereby increasing regional disparities, and that there should be a supranational mechanism for allocating technology assistance that would reduce disparities. Duncan Maclennan, concentrating on housing policy and using Glasgow as a case study, examines the role of government housing policy and concludes that housing policies directed to enabling markets to function will help central cities. Leo van den Berg argues that cities need to adopt more demand-driven policies—using marketing strategies, emphasizing accessibility, and improving amenities to attract residents.

Two chapters comprise the final section, "Summary and Conclusions." John Quigley closely examines the studies of Linneman, Summers, and Maclennan to analyze commonalities in the structure of urban economic development in the United States and the United Kingdom. He concludes that the authors agree on some diminution in the decentralization trend, and on the relevance of the macroeconomy to the health of urban areas. The final and new chapter, by Paul Cheshire, gathers together the volume's chapters by asking the question: will metropolitan decentralization continue? His conclusion is that it is no longer the necessary "fact" that it was when the first edition was published. In Europe the formation of the European Union and the increased service sector orientation of cities are having positive effects on their urban cores. In the United States, extremely low unemployment rates have helped many large cities, but the essential ingredient of well-deployed federal assistance is not in place.

Note

This chapter is the product of an intensive session among the three volume editors.

Part One

INTRA- AND INTERMETROPOLITAN AREA CHANGE: EVIDENCE AND STRATEGIES

CONTRASTING STRATEGIES FOR THE ECONOMIC DEVELOPMENT OF METROPOLITAN AREAS IN THE UNITED STATES AND WESTERN EUROPE

Anthony Downs

The economic development of U.S. metropolitan areas has occurred without much influence from overall development strategies created by governmental bodies at any level. Rather, it has resulted almost entirely from a combination of market forces plus political policies aimed at goals other than how metropolitan economies ought to develop. That is the case partly because "overall strategies" for long-range planning have long been considered almost un-American by nearly all U.S. governmental bodies.

In contrast, the economic development of most Western European metropolitan areas has occurred under the influence of explicit development strategies at both national and metropolitan-area levels. True, these strategies have not always worked as planned, but they have been implemented at least to some extent.

Comparing the results of these two fundamentally different approaches to metropolitan economic development is one of two purposes of this chapter. The other purpose is to identify and briefly analyze the major forces shaping metropolitan economic development within the United States since 1945. Since delineating these forces is a necessary prerequisite to achieving the first purpose, the chapter focuses initially on this second purpose. Owing to my specialty in urban and real estate economics, the analysis emphasizes the spatial and real estate aspects of the economic development of metropolitan areas more than, say, labor markets or macroanalysis. However, it also tries to present a broad overview of the subject. The original research for this chapter was conducted in the early 1990s. Many of the statistics in the chapter for this second edition have been updated, and the fundamental policy conclusions in the earlier edition still appear to be applicable in 1999.

MAJOR FORCES INFLUENCING U.S. METROPOLITAN-AREA DEVELOPMENT

General Approach

Economic development is a process influenced by myriad factors; thus, any selection of a few as especially important is bound to be somewhat arbitrary. Moreover, this chapter seeks to present a general overview of such factors, rather than a detailed empirical analysis of their relative significance, and is necessarily rather general in assigning relative weights to the many factors it discusses. Since the analysis also endeavors to compare U.S. and Western European experience, it focuses especially upon those factors that have exerted different influences in these two regions.

Fundamental Historical and Structural Factors

LARGE SIZE AND CULTURAL UNITY OF THE UNITED STATES

The United States contains a vastly larger spatial territory under a single national government than any Western European nation, or most such nations combined. Moreover, except for very recent immigrants, nearly all Americans speak the same language, are exposed to the same national communications media, and share one basic culture. Western Europeans, by contrast, speak many languages, are exposed to different communications media, and live under very different cultures. Hence, there is much greater population mobility within the United States than in Western Europe. Even after most economic barriers among Western European nations were removed in 1992, language and cultural factors still make it much harder for people to move from, say, Spain to Germany than from Alabama to California. This is reflected by the much higher mobility rates among American households—about 17–20 percent move each year—than among Western European households.

DIFFERENCES IN INTENSITY OF URBAN LAND USES

Another impact of the greater size of the United States, and its much lower average density of population, is a very different attitude toward the appropriate intensity of land use than in Western Europe. For centuries, the land immediately surrounding most Western European cities has been much more intensively used for agricultural or urban purposes than that around U.S. cities. This is particularly true in smaller nations, such as the Netherlands and Denmark, where there is acute competition for every available acre. Hence, the pressure to use land intensively in the process of urban development and growth is extremely strong in Western Europe, but comparatively weak in the United States.

Since Americans regard land as abundantly available, they have historically been willing to entrust considerable authority over its use to the owners of individual land parcels. In contrast, Western Europeans regard land as an extremely scarce but vital good. So they have historically wanted to exercise much tighter control over land use by political authorities entrusted with pursuit of the common good, rather than the good of individual landowners.

DIFFERENCES IN GOVERNMENTAL STRUCTURES

This variance in general attitudes has been reinforced by a fundamental difference in governmental structure between the American federal system and Western European centralized systems. The American system entrusts to the fifty states major governmental authority; in most European nations, such authority is retained by the national government, including final control over land use. Hence, the American national government has almost never exercised any direct authority over land-use decisions, or developed any coherent national policies concerning them. Western European national governments, by contrast, have retained direct authority over some land-use decisions—at least as a court of last resort. And they have often developed coherent national policies concerning land-use patterns, both among and within their major metropolitan areas.

This difference is further accentuated by greater U.S. fragmentation of authority over land use *within* individual metropolitan areas. The fifty U.S. states have delegated most of their authority over land use to individual local governments. Each major metropolitan area contains many such local governments, sometimes over one hundred. Only a handful of the more than three hundred metropolitan areas in the United States have any regional governmental body with general authority extending throughout most of the area that constitutes a unified urban economic and social entity. Instead, land-use control has been fragmented among many small, legally separate communities whose political authorities are elected by local residents. Such officials are therefore motivated to act primarily in the interest of their own communities, rather than in the interests of their metropolitan areas as wholes.

Western European nations have often delegated considerable power over land use within an entire metropolitan area to a single governmental body located there. This body may be the central city government or a regional government, but it has the authority and the power to implement a single coherent land-use planning strategy throughout most of the metropolitan area. This is not always the case, but it is far more often true in Western Europe than in the United States.

IMPACTS OF FRAGMENTED LAND-USE CONTROLS WITHIN
U.S. METROPOLITAN AREAS

The extreme fragmentation of land-use control and other governmental powers within U.S. metropolitan areas has had profound impacts upon the ways these areas have developed economically. For example, central city governments were prevented from blocking the development of new commercial areas outside their established downtowns. Those outlying retail and commercial districts—such as regional shopping malls—eventually undermined sales in previously dominant downtown shopping areas. In Western European nations, the dominance of such historic city centers was deliberately preserved. Central-city governments had the power to prevent construction of competitive outlying facilities, and they used that power to maintain the economic strength of their historic downtowns. Even now, there are very few outlying regional shopping malls in the United Kingdom or in Germany.

A second impact of fragmented land-use control in U.S. metropolitan areas has been their rapid sprawling into low-density suburban settlements outside the boundaries of the original central city. Private housing developers were able to buy sites some distance beyond the periphery of already-built-up areas and construct whole new residential subdivisions. They were motivated to do so by the low prices of such suburban land, which enabled them in turn to offer homes for sale at low prices. Local governments in those outlying areas had the power to permit such development, even when doing so undermined the market for housing closer in, within the boundaries of the central city. This permitted a leapfrog pattern of development that spread new housing widely across the landscape, leaving large intermediate areas of still-undeveloped land between that housing and the previously built-up areas around the central city.

In Western European metropolitan areas, such a leapfrog pattern was prevented by deliberate regional or national policies seeking to preserve agricultural uses for as long as possible in the territory immediately outside the densely settled portion of each urbanized area.

This policy was enforced by regional authorities who controlled land-use decisions over wide areas. They compelled all new development to occur either as in-fill within already-settled areas, or on the immediate peripheries of those areas. The result is a striking visual difference between the edges of metropolitan areas in Western Europe and the United States. In Western Europe, travelers leaving a metropolitan area suddenly pass from densely settled urbanized neighborhoods to uninterrupted, open farmland. In the United States, there is a gradual transition from the former to the latter through a broad region of scattered patchwork subdivisions and small outlying residential and commercialized areas.

Under the U.S. pattern, at least during housing boom periods from 1950 to about 1970, developers could build single-family homes on outlying land and sell them at prices many moderate-income households could afford. That fact, plus other forces such as federal insurance for home mortgages, made homeownership widely available to U.S. households. In 1940, only 43.6 percent of all U.S. households owned their own homes, but by 1960, 61.9 percent did so. (This percentage has subsequently increased much more slowly, peaking at about 64.4 percent in 1980.)

In contrast, the Western European policy of keeping new development tightly confined to the edges of existing settlements gave landowners at those edges relatively monopolistic positions in the market. This increased land prices for new housing, relative to household incomes, and kept home prices too high for most households to afford homeownership. In addition, large subsidies were made available to renters in Western European societies, for other reasons discussed later in the chapter. These factors kept homeownership percentages lower in most Western European nations than in the United States.[1]

The more tightly circumscribed development of Western European metropolitan areas also led to much higher average residential densities in those areas than in the United States. That helped sustain widespread reliance among European households upon mass transit systems supported by large-scale public subsidies. These systems usually converged upon the traditional downtown district, thereby reinforcing its dominance within the life of its metropolitan area. Conversely, U.S. low-density settlement patterns—both caused by and contributing to greater automobile ownership and use—discouraged mass transit systems. Many public transit systems in the United States were dismantled or weakened during the period after 1945, as reliance upon automobiles accelerated.

"NATIONALLY DOMINANT CITIES" IN WESTERN EUROPE BUT NOT IN THE UNITED STATES

The economic, political, and social lives of several Western European nations—and of Japan—are dominated by what happens in a single city and metropolitan area that serves as the national capital. Examples are London, Paris, Tokyo, Athens, and Stockholm. No single city or metropolitan area is similarly dominant within the national life of the United States, or that of several other Western European nations, such as Germany. In countries containing such dominant "super cities," both population and economic growth tend to concentrate in and around the metropolitan areas of those cities. This is true even if the national government adopts policies and programs designed to discourage growth in those metropolitan areas and to encourage it elsewhere. Such policies rarely work effectively.

The absence of any one such dominant city in the United States has certainly influenced the way its metropolitan areas have developed economically. Although a few major metropolitan areas have experienced much more growth than most others, none has yet attained the status within the United States as a whole of the Western European "super cities" just mentioned.[2]

IMPACT OF WARTIME DAMAGE IN WESTERN EUROPE

Another factor differentiating metropolitan-area development in these two regions was the extensive physical destruction and damage in most of Western Europe caused by World War II. After 1945, most Western European governments were faced with acute shortages of housing, food, and building materials that affected their entire societies. They were almost compelled to adopt more interventionist policies in housing markets than seemed appropriate to U.S. governments, where no wartime damage existed. These policies included publicly subsidizing large-scale housing construction and occupancy, and allocating access to the units so created through political processes rather than sheer market forces.

As a result, most Western European nations have housed much higher fractions of their households in directly subsidized units than the United States has—from 20 percent to 30 percent in Europe compared to less than 10 percent in the United States. Consequently, directly subsidized housing in Western Europe contains residents from a much broader socioeconomic spectrum of the entire population than does such housing in the United States, whose residents tend to be from society's poorest and most destitute groups.[3] This fact—plus the high concentration of black, single-parent households in U.S. public housing—has the effect of making publicly subsidized housing socially more acceptable to surrounding residents in Europe than in the United States. Hence, subsidized housing in Western Europe is spread throughout each metropolitan area, rather than heavily concentrated within central cities, as in the United States.

The devastation of World War II also created much stronger pressures within Western Europe than in the United States to establish extensive welfare programs aimed at raising the economic level of all persons in society to an acceptable minimum. This reinforced a similar tendency caused by another factor, as discussed next.

THE TRADITION OF SOCIALIST OR LABOR PARTIES IN EUROPE

The final historical difference between these two sets of regions mentioned here concerns the structure of their political parties. Beginning in the late nineteenth century, most Western European nations developed socialist or labor parties that espoused strong central governmental roles in managing their nations' economies. These parties frequently captured large fractions of the total vote and in some nations, especially Scandinavia, they were elected to office and saw many of their policies enacted. But the United States never developed a strong political movement stressing socialist themes or the rights of labor. Historically the U.S. labor movement remained weak and focused upon pragmatic economic benefits for workers, rather than ideological platforms involving strong government intervention in economic life. Even after U.S. labor unions gained more strength in the 1940s, they did not adopt anything like the economic interventionist theories typical of European labor parties. Thus, there was no American political tradition favoring national government intervention into many aspects of economic life similar to the socialist-worker party tradition in Western Europe. This difference had especially profound impacts on economic development strategies aimed at attacking poverty, rather than those explicitly aimed at spatial development patterns among or within metropolitan areas.

Population Growth and Migration Factors

Major differences in population trends in the United States and Western Europe have greatly affected the economic development of metropolitan areas in these regions. These are discussed next.

POPULATION GROWTH

The United States has experienced much greater population growth during the past few decades than has Western Europe, both absolutely and in percentage terms. In 1995, fifteen major Western European nations had a combined population of 360.7 million, compared to 263.8 million in the United States and 125.5 million in Japan. From 1980 to 1995, total population grew 36.1 million in the United States, 18.8 million in the 15 Western European nations, and 8.7 million in Japan. Percentage population gains from 1980 through 1995 are shown in the accompanying figure 2.1.[4] The United States had by far the greatest percentage increase among all the larger of these nations— 15.85 percent. Thirteen of the fifteen Western European nations showed gains of less than 10 percent. For all fifteen Western European nations in figure 2.1 combined, the growth rate for this period was only 5.2 percent, or about one-third that of the United States. Western European nations grew more slowly than the United States because of both lower fertility rates and lower immigration from abroad.

Regression analysis of the most important causes of employment growth in individual United States metropolitan areas in the 1970s

Figure 2.1 POPULATION GROWTH, 1980–95 (United States, Western Europe, and Japan)[4]

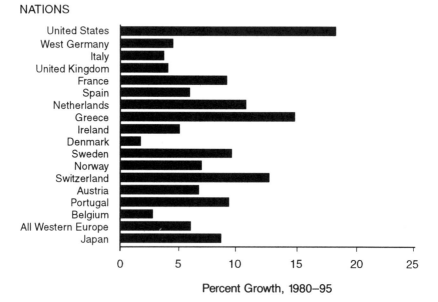

NATIONS

Percent Growth, 1980–95

has shown population increases in those areas to be the single most influential factor underlying their job growth (see Bradbury, Downs, and Small 1982: chaps. 5, 6). Hence, the greater growth of population in the United States compared to that in Western Europe has undoubtedly stimulated stronger economic growth in United States metropolitan areas than in such areas in Western Europe. This inference is confirmed by total employment data for selected nations for the period 1980–93. The United States had a net gain of 20.0 million jobs, or 20.1 percent, in those thirteen years. In contrast, West Germany gained only 1.7 million jobs, or 6.4 percent; Italy gained 1.0 million, or 5.0 percent; the United Kingdom gained 0.5 million, or 2.0 percent; and France gained 0.3 million, or 1.4 percent. Even dynamic Japan had a net gain of 9.2 million jobs, or 16.9 percent. Thus, there was an immense disparity between the employment dynamism of the United States and that of Western Europe in this period. It is not possible in this chapter to analyze the reasons for this disparity. However, greater dynamism in the United States economy surely stimulated the economic development of its metropolitan areas.

That development has also been greatly affected by four major population migration trends since 1945, discussed next.

MIGRATION FROM RURAL TO METROPOLITAN AREAS

In the 1940s, a massive movement of rural Americans into major metropolitan areas was begun as part of the recruitment of workers for wartime industries. Because housing production was essentially suspended during the war, this migration generated extensive overcrowding in the housing stocks of most major cities. After about 1950, production of new housing accelerated sharply, enabling a "decanting" of overcrowded households into new housing units, especially those built in suburbs outside central cities.[5] At the same time, the mechanization of cotton farming in the South and of farming in general created huge labor surpluses in rural areas. Millions of poor rural residents moved into metropolitan areas to find jobs in burgeoning postwar industries. This movement continued at high levels until about 1965.

Because most of the newcomers were quite poor, and many were black, this movement aggravated racial segregation patterns in many metropolitan areas, especially in the Northeast and Midwest. Black newcomers moved into neighborhoods already dominated by black households, because racial segregation and discrimination by whites prevented them from moving into mainly white areas. This generated more overcrowding in poor black neighborhoods. After the U.S. Supreme Court ruled in 1948 that racially restrictive private covenants were not enforceable, blacks began moving into previously white areas on the edges of overcrowded all-black neighborhoods. This caused most whites there to withdraw, resulting in a massive transition from white to black occupancy. As this process continued, most large U.S. central cities had rising black populations and declining white populations. Many of their white residents moved out to mainly white suburbs. Over a period of forty years, from 1950 to 1990, this process caused many of the largest U.S. central cities to shift from a largely white population composition to a largely or even mainly black composition. Moreover, the black population in these cities is much younger than the white population, on the average, and many white children attend private schools. Consequently, a majority of public school children in nearly all of the nation's twenty-five largest central cities consists of minority-group children, mostly black. These race-related processes were mostly absent from Western European cities, or occurred on a much smaller scale with immigrant groups of different racial backgrounds from the nationally predominant ethnic group. Thus, some such phenomena took place in London with West Indians and Pakistanis; in West Berlin with Turks; in Amsterdam with Indonesians; and in Paris with Algerians. But few Western European cities were so profoundly affected by racial segregation and transition as were a majority of the largest American cities.

MIGRATION FROM ABROAD INTO AMERICAN CITIES

Immigration from abroad has been a major source of U.S. urban development throughout the nation's history. During the past two decades, such immigration has markedly accelerated and changed in nature. Whereas most immigrants to the United States before about 1960 were from various parts of Europe, a large majority of those arriving during the 1970s and 1980s were from Latin America and Asia, most entering the United States through the West Coast and the Mexican border. Over 7.3 million legal immigrants *net* entered the United States during the 1980s; the total including illegal entrants may have been closer to 10 million.

This large inflow of newcomers markedly affected the population composition of certain metropolitan areas, especially those that already contained large numbers of Hispanics. The New York, Los Angeles, Miami, Chicago, Washington, D.C., San Diego, San Francisco, Orange County (Calif.), San Jose, Oakland, and Boston metropolitan areas each received over ten thousand immigrants from abroad in the year 1987. Children attending public schools in the city of Los Angeles come from homes in which over one hundred different languages are spoken as "native tongues." This cultural and linguistic diversity poses an extremely difficult challenge for educators and other public officials in such communities. That challenge is absent from most Western European nations, or is at least present to a much lesser degree.

MOVEMENT OUT OF CENTRAL CITIES INTO SUBURBS

From about 1950 onward, a massive shift of population and economic activities out of central cities into surrounding suburbs occurred within U.S. metropolitan areas. This movement had actually started in the 1920s, but was interrupted by the great Depression of the 1930s and World War II in the 1940s. It was accelerated after 1950 by several key public policies. One such policy made federal mortgage insurance available to millions of homebuying households. A second policy, the Interstate Highway System program, which started in 1956, created a nationwide network of limited-access, high-speed, high-capacity roadways. These highways not only linked together most major metropolitan areas but also provided both radial and circumferential arteries within most of them. This opened up accessibility to immense areas of vacant land on the outskirts of most major cities. In addition, the federal government provided urban renewal funds to redevelop large portions of older cities, and infrastructure funds to build sewer and water systems in growing suburban areas. Large-scale construction and sale of automobiles and trucks increased the mobility of both households and business firms so they could effectively spread out over the landscape without becoming economically inefficient.

All these forces, together with huge population inflows of poor rural residents into central cities themselves, generated massive movements of households and business firms out of central cities and into the suburbs. At the same time, in the nation as a whole, more new housing units were being built each year after 1960 than new households were being formed, mostly in suburban areas. By 1965, this construction had generated a sufficient overall surplus of available housing within each metropolitan area as a whole to cause some abandonment of the worst-quality structures within central cities.[6]

This suburbanization had profound impacts upon the economic development of U.S. metropolitan areas. Manufacturing and wholesaling shifted out of older, multistory, congested neighborhoods in central cities into spacious new one-story buildings located along expressways in the suburbs. This reduced the tax bases of central cities but increased those of the suburbs. Downtown areas formerly dominated by a combination of retailing, manufacturing, and whole-saling were largely abandoned by the last two, and suffered from increasing competition from outlying shopping centers. This greatly weakened their economic viability until the office-space boom of the 1970s and 1980s restored vitality to many such central business districts. The loss of millions of middle- and upper-income households to the suburbs caused central cities to shift toward greater economic, social, and political dominance by low-income groups. Their governments were increasingly squeezed fiscally by rapidly rising demands for services but only slowly rising tax bases. Large portions of some older midwestern and northeastern central cities cleared by urban renewal programs remained vacant for decades. No viable enterprises or households wanted to move there because these sites were surrounded by neighborhoods dominated by poverty and the many adverse conditions associated with it, including high rates of crime, delinquency, drug abuse, broken families, unemployment, and mental health difficulties. This situation persists in such cities as Chicago, Detroit, New York, Philadelphia, Washington, D.C., Gary, and Cleveland.

MIGRATION OF PEOPLE AND BUSINESSES TO THE SOUTH AND WEST

The fourth major migration flow in the postwar United States has been a steady domestic movement (not counting immigratiion from abroad) of both households and business firms out of the Northeast and Midwest and into the South and West. In the early postwar period, migration from the rural South to the Northeast and Midwest caused net outflows from the South. But after 1960, these flows reversed. In the 1970s, the Northeast had net outmigration of at least 2.9 million persons, and the Midwest, 2.7 million. At the same time, the South had net immigration of at least 6 million, and the West, 4.1 million. From 1984 to 1993, the figures were − 2.9 million for the Northeast, − 296,000 for the Midwest, + 2.2 million for the South, and + 1.2 million for the West.[7]

It is not clear exactly why these migration flows have occurred. Living costs are generally lower in the South than in the Northeast or the Midwest, as are wage levels. But living costs and wage levels are relatively high in California, which has consistently had the greatest net immigration of any state. In fact, just three states—California, Florida, and Texas—captured 41.7 percent of the nation's total population growth during the 1970s and 54.3 percent during the 1980s. Yet they contained only 24 percent of the nation's total population as of 1990. Mean January temperatures are positively correlated with metropolitan area population growth rates and are statistically significant in regressions seeking to "explain" those rates (see Bradbury et al. 1982: chaps. 5, 6). So warmer climate is undoubtedly one factor luring people out of the Northeast and Midwest. Some economists have speculated that many business firms have moved out of the Midwest and Northeast and into the South to escape from high-wage and highly unionized labor markets. However, that is hard to prove statistically. Nevertheless, there is no doubt that this basic migration flow has immensely influenced economic development patterns among U.S. metropolitan areas.

DIFFERENCES BETWEEN U.S. AND WESTERN EUROPEAN MIGRATION PATTERNS

Several Western European nations have experienced population migration patterns since 1945 similar to those just described in the United States. A significant movement out of rural areas and into metropolitan areas has occurred in most Western European nations since 1945. (However, the timing of such migration has differed greatly among Western European nations; for example, it happened much earlier in the United Kingdom than in Spain.) And there has been notable suburbanization of population around most major Western European cities. But both of these movements have been smaller, relative to the total size of the central cities involved, than in the United States.

In addition, there has been sizable immigration into several Western European nations by members of ethnic groups other than the traditionally dominant groups in those nations, as pointed out earlier. However, as stated previously, such immigration has also been much smaller, in relation to the dominant group, than the immigration of either blacks or Hispanics into U.S. metropolitan areas. Hence, far less "massive racial transition" occurred in Western European cities than in U.S. cities.

The last U.S. migration trend—movement from the Northeast and Midwest to the South and West—also has some analogue in Western Europe. In the United Kingdom, economic growth has been much stronger in the South than in the North; hence, there has been some movement from Scotland and the northern regions of England into the area around London and the South. Similarly, in Germany, jobs in the industrial Ruhr area have grown much more slowly than those in industrial cities in the southern part of the country; thus, there has been another north-to-south migration flow there. And in Italy, northern regions have generated far more new jobs than southern regions; so some migration flows from the South to the North have taken place.

Nevertheless, in all three instances, internal migration flows in Western Europe have been much smaller than those in the United States. (However, West Germany twice received very large inflows of immigrants from East Germany: once soon after 1945, and again immediately preceding unification.) European citizens appear much more rooted to subregions within their nations than do Americans, probably because of greater subregional cultural and other differentiation within Western Europe than within the United States, and perhaps because of longer periods of family history and connections in the former.

Also, large housing price disparities between economically stagnant and economically growing regions make it hard for homeowning households to move from the former to the latter. For example, a homeowning household in northern England that sells its home receives a relatively low price and must pay a much higher price for a similar home in southern England. This clearly discourages migration among homeowners from northern to southern England, or similarly, from the Ruhr to the southern states of Germany, even though in each case there are far more jobs available in the latter region than in the former. The people who make such moves are mainly young people unencumbered either by long-established social ties to their "native" communities or by homeownership. True, since about the mid-1970s, similar housing price disparities have developed among U.S. metropolitan areas. They may have similar impacts upon internal U.S. migration in the long run, but that has not yet been clearly established.

Technological Factors

At least four major technological forces have affected the economic development of U.S. metropolitan areas since 1945. Most of these factors have had a *centralizing* impact upon the location of economic activities in metropolitan areas compared to nonmetropolitan areas, but a *decentralizing* impact upon the location of such activities within metropolitan areas.

CREATION OF MAJOR HIGHWAY NETWORKS AND EXPANDED USE OF
AUTOMOTIVE VEHICLES

The building of the Interstate Highway System and related vehicle expressways linking major metropolitan areas has already been described. It was accompanied by an "explosion" in the U.S. automotive vehicle population. From 1980 to 1993, the human population of the United States rose by 30.1 million, or 13.2 percent. But the population of cars, trucks, and buses in use skyrocketed by 46.6 million, or 33.3 percent. From 1983 to 1988, the United States was annually adding more than twice as many vehicles as people. Regardless of whether these forces should be considered technological or economic, they revolutionized the economic development of U.S. metropolitan areas.

Automotive vehicles became the overwhelmingly dominant form of transportation for both people and goods. This had a sharply decentralizing impact upon the way U.S. metropolitan areas developed, both internally and among regions. Business firms were more able to locate almost anywhere near a major expressway. Vacant land near such roads became available for new residential subdivisions, even though they were many miles from established downtown areas. Employment within each metropolitan area scattered widely around its periphery. In consequence, all established downtowns—even though most downtowns added more jobs absolutely—declined relatively as employment centers vis-à-vis their suburbs.

These forces also weakened U.S. reliance upon public transit of all types for movements *within* metropolitan areas. The percentage of workers commuting daily by mass transit, as well as the percentage of all types of trips on mass transit, declined sharply after 1945 and has remained much lower than in Western European nations.

TELECOMMUNICATIONS AND COMPUTER INNOVATIONS

Rapid technical advances in telecommunications and computers enabled firms to integrate their operations closely in function, even though they were widely separated in space. This had ambiguous impacts upon the location of economic activity. It enabled firms that wanted to more fully centralize control over spatially scattered operations to do so. But it also enabled firms to separate spatially operations that had formerly been considered too functionally linked to be located apart from each other. Because other forces in society and the economy more strongly favored decentralization than centralization, the net impact of telecommunications and computer innovations has surely been a decentralizing one.

EXPANSION OF AIR TRANSPORTATION AND AIRPORTS

U.S. air travel expanded tremendously in the postwar period, partly because of such technical innovations as jet engines, much larger aircraft, and improved radar control of flight movements. Whereas the total population of the U.S. increased 35 percent from 1960 to 1987, total passenger revenue miles flown rose from 39 billion in 1960 to 163 billion in 1975, 404 billion in 1987, and 489 billion in 1993—

more than a twelve-fold increase. Major airports became much more important modal-transfer points than railroad passenger stations, which served fewer and fewer people. By 1993, the number of passengers traveling through specific airports each year had risen to huge levels: 29 million in Chicago's O'Hare Field, 25 million in Dallas–Fort Worth International, 22 million in Atlanta, and 18.5 million in Los Angeles International.[8] Airports consume considerable space for runways, taxiways, hangars, terminal facilities, and access roads; hence, they are usually built on the edges of metropolitan areas where large vacant sites are available, rather than near traditional downtown centers. As the importance of airports rose, other facilities to serve them grew up around them, including hotels, apartment clusters, industrial parks, restaurants, and office complexes.

Air travel thus had a doubly decentralizing impact upon economic activity in U.S. metropolitan areas. It enabled firms to locate branch activities in metropolitan areas distant from their main offices while still allowing them to reach those offices quickly. Hence, this dispersed economic activity more widely across the nation. In addition, the rising importance of airports *within* metropolitan areas created outlying clusters of activities rivaling traditional downtowns.

PRODUCTIVITY INCREASES IN MANUFACTURING AND AGRICULTURE

In the period from about 1950 to 1973, productivity rose rapidly in both manufacturing and agriculture, not only in the United States but around the world. As a result, the number of workers required per million dollars of output in both these economic sectors declined, compared to the analogous number in other sectors—notably both private and government services. This was a major cause of the population migration from rural to metropolitan areas already described. In 1950, 12.5 percent of all employed workers were in agriculture and 25.9 percent in manufacturing. By 1975, these fractions had declined to 3.9 percent and 22.7 percent, respectively, and by 1994, they were 2.7 percent and 16.4 percent, respectively. In 1950, agriculture comprised 7.2 percent of gross domestic product (GDP) and manufacturing comprised 30.9 percent of GDP. In 1975, these fractions were 3.4 percent and 25.1 percent, respectively; by 1992, they were 1.9 percent and 17.6 percent. Thus, the shares of the workforce in these sectors had declined more than their shares of total value of output, though the latter also declined. One of the results of these changes was a marked shift in the location of jobs from farms and agricultural industries, and from manufacturing plants, into offices of all types, as service employment became a rising share of an expanding labor force.

Accompanying this was a sharp increase in the need for office space, which fueled an enormous development of such space, especially after the recovery period of 1976–79 began. The biggest "explosion" of office space occurred in the 1980s under the dual impact of rising numbers of office workers and overflowing availability of investment capital for real estate development, as discussed later.

These factors stimulated rapid economic growth in those metropolitan areas well situated as locations for international, national, or regional office headquarters for firms of all types. A virtual "headquarters hierarchy" of metropolitan areas developed in U.S. office space markets. At the top of this pyramid were the "international headquarters" cities of New York, Washington, D.C., Los Angeles, and Chicago. At a slightly lower level were the "regional headquarters or gateway" cities of Atlanta, Dallas, Minneapolis, Boston, San Francisco, Miami, and Seattle. Still farther down were "industrial headquarters" cities for specific industries, such as Houston for oil and energy, and Detroit for automobiles. Their economic fate depended heavily upon what happened in their industries. But every major city enjoyed some office-space boom in the 1980s.

Although more office space was built in the suburbs than in central cities in total, the concentration of large amounts of new office space within traditional downtowns helped stimulate their revival in most of the cities just mentioned in the 1970s and especially in the 1980s. New downtown offices were accompanied by new hotels, restaurants, convention centers, stadiums, performing arts facilities, and public buildings. These injections of both capital and jobs helped offset the continuing loss of retail, wholesale, and manufacturing jobs from downtown areas.

DIFFERENCES BETWEEN THE UNITED STATES AND WESTERN EUROPE

Many of the same technological factors that influenced the economic development of U.S. metropolitan areas also occurred in Western Europe. The biggest difference between such factors in these two major regions concerned automotive transportation. Western European nations did not experience nearly so great an expansion of either highway facilities or ownership and use of automotive vehicles as did the United States. Instead, their public policies deliberately emphasized continued reliance upon extensive networks of railroads and local mass transit systems, financing the large losses of such systems through public subsidies.[9] This reinforced the basic Western European urban development strategy of strengthening traditional downtown or other established shopping districts, encouraging relatively high-density residential living, and limiting suburban sprawl.

Moreover, Western European metropolitan areas did not experience nearly so great an increase in office space development as most U.S. metropolitan areas. This was true because of much tighter local government planning controls over new development in Western Europe, as well as two other factors discussed later in the chapter: less readily available financing for new office development and slower creation of new jobs.

Sociological Factors

At least four major sociological factors influenced economic development patterns in U.S. metropolitan areas. One factor was racial segregation and discrimination, discussed previously under population migration. A second factor was the increasing tendency of women, both single and married, to work outside the home. This tendency accelerated after 1973 because of the sudden cessation of real wage increases that had previously been sizable; more and more married women had to work to support increases in their families' standards of living, since their husbands' real wages stopped rising and even declined. Moreover, divorce rates rose sharply in the 1950s and 1960s, partly because of liberalized divorce laws. Thus, as more and more women became heads of households, they were required to support themselves and their children.

As more women took jobs outside the home, the commuting patterns of households changed. Many more households contained multiple workers who traveled to work simultaneously, but to jobs in different locations. This was a major factor causing increased use of automotive vehicles. Today, over 50 percent of all U.S. households own more than one such vehicle.

Another major sociological force was the U.S. baby boom—a period of unusually high birthrates from about 1950 to about 1965. A huge bulge in the previously "normal" age distribution was generated by this surge in births. This bulge gradually moved through succeeding ages, causing dislocations in public facilities and shifts in cultural emphasis within the entire nation. Thus, the 1960s saw a big increase in the number of school-aged children and teenagers, which produced a strong emphasis upon youth in American culture. In contrast, as the 1990s began, this bulge was entering middle age; the first baby boomers were passing their fortieth birthdays, and the last ones were passing their twenty-fifth birthdays. The ensuing drop in numbers of young households being formed reduced the demand for new housing in the 1990s, compared to the high levels of demand caused by the baby boomers in the past, especially in the 1970s, when they were entering household-formation ages.

The last sociological factor to be discussed here is the declining effectiveness of the U.S. educational system, compared to analogous systems in other nations. Dropout rates among high school students, especially in big-city public school systems, are much higher in the United States than in most other economically developed nations. Also, American students get lower scores on international tests of knowledge and ability than students from most other developed nations. Although the United States has been discussing "school reform" for over a decade, and has greatly increased spending on education, these factors have not produced any measurable improvement in the performance of U.S. schools as a whole.

This last trend could have profound impacts upon the economic development of U.S. metropolitan areas in the future, if it is not changed. Business firms that cannot hire young workers well educated enough to perform the tasks required in a high-technology society will move to other locations where such people are available. This implies further movement out of central cities to alternative locations. It also implies that business firms may have to spend large amounts training new workers to bring their capabilities up to company standards.

In Western European nations, fewer students attend higher educational institutions than in the United States, but a higher percentage of students complete secondary school educations. Moreover, in contrast to American students, students in most developed nations spend more time in school each year, spend more time in class each day studying academic material, and do more homework each day, on average. Therefore, the quality of education received by Western European students is probably better, on average, than that received by U.S. students at any stage of the learning process up to the end of secondary school.

Financial and Economic Factors

Hundreds of financial and economic factors, other than those previously mentioned, have affected the way U.S. metropolitan areas developed since 1945. This chapter arbitrarily focuses on just a few that seem especially important.

The 1970s were a decade of multiple economic shocks throughout the world. Two major oil price increases, in 1973 and again in 1979, radically changed the financial balance between oil-importing and oil-producing nations. There was also a food shortage in the early 1970s that drove agricultural prices up sharply. Those factors produced rampant inflation around the world. And there were two significant recessions—one in 1974–75 and another at the end of the 1970s.

For these reasons, and others that economic analysts have been unable to identify, the growth of U.S. economic productivity that had been so strong in the 1950s and 1960s suddenly slowed and almost stopped after 1973. Average real wages per hour were actually lower in 1990 than in 1973—seventeen years earlier. So were average weekly earnings. In 1987, median household income in 1987 dollars was $25,986, only 1 percent higher than in 1970 (U.S. Bureau of the Census 1989: 440).

Households that had become accustomed to rising standards of living before this "plateau" arrived sought to maintain their consumption increases in spite of falling real wages. They did so by (1) saving less out of their current incomes, (2) having more members work outside the home—notably women, and (3) having fewer members on the average—notably fewer children. Hence, private savings rates out of disposable income declined, especially in the 1980s, a drop that was aggravated by huge federal budget deficits in the 1980s. The overall U.S. savings rate declined sharply, and the economy became dependent upon massive borrowing from abroad to maintain the consumption standards enjoyed by U.S. citizens.

These developments had several impacts upon the economic development of U.S. metropolitan areas. Economic pressures on households in the 1970s helped cause a "taxpayers' revolt" against rising expenditures by state and local governments to accommodate metropolitan area growth. Voters in several states adopted limits on the ability of both state and local governments to raise property and other taxes, or increase expenditures. At the same time, the federal government—under pressure from rising budget deficits—cut back on financial assistance to local governments for creating new low-income housing and infrastructures. This put a double squeeze on local governments in areas experiencing rapid population growth, as in Florida and California. They had to seek new sources of revenue to build the roads, schools, sewers, water systems, and other infrastructures necessary to accommodate such growth. So they adopted "impact fees" and other taxes placed on new developments themselves to finance such improvements.

These fees helped raise the prices of newly built homes in certain fast-growth areas to very high levels. That in turn prevented low- and moderate-income households from moving into suburban new-growth subdivisions in such metropolitan areas. The result was a reinforcement of the spatial separation of low- and moderate-income households from middle- and upper-income households in most U.S. metropolitan areas, compared to most of those in Western Europe.

Another impact of the worldwide economic dislocations of the 1970s was a dramatic gyration in oil prices. A huge increase occurred from 1973 through 1979, stimulating an immense economic boom in those U.S. metropolitan areas specializing in energy exploration and processing, such as Houston, Tulsa, Oklahoma City, New Orleans, Anchorage, and Denver. Massive capital spending occurred in those cities, rapidly expanding office space and other properties in anticipation of further long-run increases in oil prices. Then oil prices suddenly collapsed in the mid-1980s under pressure from a worldwide glut of supply and conservation-generated limits on demand. The economies of those cities that had expanded rapidly in anticipation of a long-term energy-related boom were suddenly plunged into a major recession. The Houston metropolitan area, for example, lost over 200,000 jobs in less than three years. Real estate markets in these cities were devastated by these gyrations in oil prices and the fortunes of energy industries. Office vacancy rates in the cities mentioned soared to around 30 percent and stayed high for many years. Thus, a "regional recession" gripped many large U.S. metropolitan areas in the mid-1980s, in spite of overall general prosperity in the nation.

IMPACTS OF SUSTAINED PROSPERITY

The longest peacetime economic expansion in U.S. history began in 1983 with recovery from the severe recession of 1980–82. This recovery sustained itself for a record seven years, and continued into 1990. It was initially fueled by heavy federal defense spending and large federal budget deficits. In those metropolitan areas that have experienced both sustained economic prosperity and rapid population growth, residents of many communities have developed strong anti-growth attitudes that are influencing the way growth occurs there. Specifically, those attitudes cause local governments to slow down housing and commercial real estate development, raising the prices of both types. This usually does not reduce the overall growth of the entire metropolitan area concerned, even if it does reduce that of the particular communities involved. But it pushes housing prices upward and spreads development out farther over the landscape. In metropolitan areas experiencing large-scale immigration, antigrowth attitudes also create pressure on low-income households to occupy illegally overcrowded facilities, since they cannot afford to pay high housing prices.

FINANCIAL PRESSURES FOR OVERBUILDING

During the 1980s, several developments in capital markets created a "bias" favoring more investment in real estate than was economically justifiable on the basis of its competitive yields alone. This bias led to systematic overbuilding of real properties of all types, except perhaps of single-family residences. The result was a stimulation of the construction and real estate development industries, and of land prices, that greatly affected the economic development of U.S. metropolitan areas.

One element generating overinvestment in real estate markets was the Tax Act of 1981, which provided generous tax benefits for such investment. It shortened depreciation periods compared to their past lengths, thereby creating large accounting losses for new real estate projects in their early years. This permitted persons in high income-tax brackets to shield their wage and other incomes from taxes by offsetting paper real estate losses against those incomes. Syndication firms were able to raise large amounts of money from investors seeking tax shelter to invest in creating new buildings, almost regardless of whether there was an economic or space-requirement-related need for such buildings. This condition resulted in syndicators financing development of many buildings for which there was little or no market demand. This condition persisted until the Tax Reform Act of 1986 eliminated most of the tax-shelter benefits involved.

A second stimulus to overbuilding was deregulation of the banking and savings and loan industries, which reached its most complete stage in 1983. At that time, previous ceilings on the interest rates they could pay depositors were eliminated. This kept money in those institutions at all points during the business cycle, putting pressure on them to invest the money almost regardless of the prevailing supply-and-demand balance in space markets.

At the same time, savings and loans were able to use higher interest rates to attract massive inflows of deposits that enabled the most adventuresome to grow with astonishing speed. Depositors did not have to worry about whether their funds would be wisely invested, because federal deposit insurance guaranteed no losses for accounts up to $100,000. So risk-oriented operators of savings and loans raised the rates they paid depositors above the prevailing levels and expanded their liabilities to enormous levels. This put them under big pressure to make investments that would presumably pay high yields. But high-yield investments are usually riskier than lower-yield ones.

Under these conditions, many savings and loans—which had formerly invested mainly in mortgage loans for single-family homebuyers—shifted to investing large amounts in risky commercial real estate ventures, including purchase of vacant land and equity positions in new office buildings, hotels, and shopping centers. This was the second major source of "bias" toward overinvestment in real estate, since savings and loans essentially had to focus most of their investments on real estate, rather than other things.

During this same period, both foreign investors and U.S. pension funds also greatly expanded their funding of real estate projects. They were motivated by the relatively strong performance of real estate equities in the 1970s, when the stock and bond markets were languishing under the pressure of inflation and rising interest rates. So they put money into real estate to diversify against excessive concentration on stocks and bonds.

The result was an immense flow of capital into real estate markets from multiple sources. Developers had access to great amounts of money that they could "finance out" of their projects—that is, obtain more than the real cost of those projects from other investors, either as loans or equity shares. With no money of their own at stake, but able to collect large development fees, they were motivated to flood the space market with new buildings. And so they did. The prevailing vacancy rate in office space markets in major metropolitan areas rose steadily, from under 5 percent in 1981 to over 20 percent in 1986, and stayed that high for several years thereafter.

This stimulated a huge boom in real estate development, and greatly expanded the properties present in both established downtowns and outlying commercial areas. During ten of the twelve years from 1978 through 1989, over 900 million square feet of new commercial and industrial space were placed under construction contracts annually— even though that had happened in only one previous year in U.S. history. This boom accelerated the development of outlying retail centers that expanded into multiuse "new cities" on the edges of many large metropolitan areas.

To some extent, similar overbuilding of commercial real properties occurred in parts of Western Europe, especially in the United Kingdom and France. The long period of general economic growth in the 1980s, combined with ready availability of capital to finance new development, created booms in new commercial space development in London, Paris, and several other major Western European cities.

THE COLLAPSE OF REAL ESTATE VALUES IN THE EARLY 1990S

Massive overbuilding of U.S. commercial space markets of all types in the late 1980s eventually generated a collapse of real property values in the early 1990s. This debacle began when the Comptroller of the Currency issued regulations early in 1990 virtually forbidding banks from making any more real estate loans. Insurance companies also stopped making real estate loans, essentially drying up all traditional sources of credit for property developers and owners. When the latter could not borrow any more to cover their debt services, which they could no longer finance out of current incomes because of falling rents and occupancy, precipitous declines occurred in commercial property values and rents of between 30 percent and 50 percent, depending on the type of property involved. Nearly all developers were unable to keep repaying all of the highly leveraged loans they had made; most suffered serious losses of equity or had to turn their properties back to their lenders. The ensuing depression in commercial development stopped new construction dead for at least three years (except for retail projects) in both the U.S. and Western Europe. Recovery began only in late 1993 after the general U.S. economy had been expanding for two years from its recession low point in February 1991. By 1996, a combination of rising demands for space of all types generated by the continuing general economic expansion, plus a dearth of new construction, stimulated a strong recovery in both rents and values of most types of commercial properties. Yet the real estate depression of the early 1990s left its mark on urban areas throughout the U.S. and Western Europe. It wiped out a whole generation of former developers, stimulated a shift from traditional financing to funding through the stock market in the form of real estate investment trusts, and accelerated the dominance of suburban office markets over downtown markets almost everywhere.

RESULTS OF STATISTICAL ANALYSES OF METROPOLITAN AREA DEVELOPMENT

Two statistical analyses of sources of metropolitan area growth have been conducted by myself and colleagues. The first was an in-depth analysis of 121 U.S. metropolitan areas conducted for the book *Urban Decline and the Future of American Cities* (Bradbury et al. 1982: chaps. 5, 6). Two multiple regression analyses of these areas were carried out, using employment growth from 1960 to 1970 and from 1970 to 1975 as dependent variables. A number of independent variables were used that had been derived from various theories about why urban decline might occur. The analysis treated central city growth separately from suburban growth, but only the results for entire metropolitan areas are cited here.

When percentage change in metropolitan area employment for 1970–75 was the dependent variable, the statistically significant factors found to influence it were (1) percentage change in metropolitan area population from 1970 to 1975, (2) a local industry mix containing fast-growing industries, (3) whether or not the area contained a state capital (if so, it enhanced job growth), (4) an estimated cost-of-living index for the metropolitan area (the higher the living cost, the slower the job growth rate), (5) the percentage change in the cost-of-living index from 1970 to 1985 (the greater the change, the slower the job growth rate), (6) metropolitan area income per capita in 1970 (the higher the income, the faster the job growth rate), (7) the percentage change in metropolitan area income per capita from 1970 to 1975 (the greater the rise, the faster the job growth rate), and (8) a measure of the total size of employment there in 1970 (the larger the total number of jobs, the slower the job growth rate). The R-square of this regression was 0.74.

A similar regression using the percentage change in metropolitan area jobs from 1960 to 1970 as the dependent variable produced similar results, with a few changes. Living costs did not have a significant impact, nor did whether the area contained a state capital or the absolute size of the area's total employment at the start of the period. But both population density per square mile and a measure of local government taxes per capita had negative impacts upon the rate of job growth. This regression had an R-square of 0.88.

Other regressions using population growth rates as dependent variables showed that job growth and population growth were highly interdependent. Each was the single most important factor influencing the other. People follow jobs *among* metropolitan areas, but not so much *within* metropolitan areas, as separate regressions for central cities and suburbs showed. Central-city prosperity would thus be better served by retaining residents than business firms. Using percentage change in metropolitan-area population from 1970 to 1975 as the dependent variable showed that the following factors influence that variable: (1) percentage change in metropolitan area population due to natural increase, (2) percentage change in metropolitan area job growth, (3) the metropolitan-area unemployment rate (the higher the rate, the slower the population growth rate), (4) the percentage of population in the metropolitan area's largest city consisting of Hispanics (the higher the percentage, the faster the population growth rate), and (5) the mean January temperature (the higher the temperature, the faster the population growth rate). This regression had an R-square of 0.67.

Another regression analysis was conducted in 1989 as part of a study of housing prices in different metropolitan areas (Downs 1989).[10] This study focused on levels and changes in median prices of existing homes sold as the dependent variable. But job and population growth in the sixty metropolitan areas concerned were independent variables, so they could be shifted to dependent variable status easily, thanks to computer analysis. When the absolute rise in population from 1980 to 1988 is the dependent variable, the statistically significant independent variables were (1) the median home price (the higher the price, the greater the growth), (2) median income in 1988 (the lower the income, the greater the growth), (3) the number of housing units authorized from 1980 to 1988 (the greater the number, the greater the growth), and (4) the number of units granted permits per 1,000 households (the smaller the number, the greater the growth). This regression had an R-square of 0.85. When the percentage change in nonagricultural employment from 1980 to 1987 was the dependent variable, the statistically significant independent variables were (1) the median home price (the higher the price, the lower the job growth rate), (2) the percentage increase in total population from 1980 to 1988 (the greater the percentage, the higher the job growth rate), and (3) the per capita income in the metropolitan area (the higher the income, the greater the job growth rate). This regression had an R-square of 0.92.[11]

I am unaware of similar analyses performed for Western European metropolitan areas. Therefore, no comparisons of these findings with analogous ones for Western Europe are presented here.

BASIC STRATEGIES FOR METROPOLITAN-AREA ECONOMIC DEVELOPMENT

Three Types of Possible Economic Development Strategies

Governments could conceivably develop at least three different types of economic development strategies affecting metropolitan areas. One strategy would aim at affecting *the regional allocation of resources across the nation.* Such a strategy would therefore have to be created at the national level, with the goal of influencing the relative prosperity of each whole metropolitan area compared to that of other whole metropolitan areas.

A second strategy would aim at *the allocation of resources within individual metropolitan areas.* It could be created at either the national, regional, or individual metropolitan-area level. Its goal would be to influence how development occurred among different parts of a single metropolitan area, such as the central city compared to the suburbs.

A third possible strategy would aim at *the allocation of resources among certain groups within society, regardless of their locations.* Reducing poverty and decreasing existing income distribution inequalities would be two examples of such strategies. They would aim at goals that were not inherently linked to differences among metropolitan areas or among parts of individual areas—although some such linkages might exist "accidentally." Thus, poverty might be concentrated more in certain regions, like Southern Italy, or in certain parts of metropolitan areas, like older central city neighborhoods, than in others.

The remaining analysis in this chapter examines how these three types of strategies have affected metropolitan-area economic development in the United States and Western Europe.

The American Strategy—or Lack Thereof

To speak of an "American strategy" for the economic development of metropolitan areas is almost to coin an oxymoron. Americans have traditionally never employed any public policy strategies for urban economic development. This dearth of long-range conceptualizing has prevailed at all levels of government. In fact, as mentioned earlier, "strategies" of any kind—that is, long-range plans concerning how to achieve basic goals—are considered fundamentally un-American in most spheres of public policy, and certainly in the realm of urban development patterns. The basic American approach is to leave the allocation of resources that affect urban and metropolitan-area development to the operation of both "free" private markets and public policies aimed at entirely different goals. So the economic development patterns that arise among and within U.S. metropolitan areas are essentially accidental or random results, generated by actions taken by myriad private-sector and public-sector actors pursuing goals not explicitly related to overall economic development per se.

NATIONAL STRATEGIES FOR ALLOCATING RESOURCES AMONG METROPOLITAN AREAS

An example of this lack of an overall, integrated strategy is that of federal defense expenditures, which have huge impacts upon the economies of different metropolitan areas across the nation. But these expenditures are almost never explicitly aimed at assisting economically weak areas, or aimed away from booming areas to avoid aggravating their overheated economies. True, defense expenditures are greatly affected by the relative political power of individual members of the U.S. Congress who occupy key committee positions. But all such politicians invariably seek to steer more spending into their own districts or states, regardless of economic conditions there. In this respect, all members of Congress are totally locally oriented, rather than concerned with overall national patterns of defense spending impacts.

In the 1960s, the federal government created an agency called the Economic Development Administration (EDA) whose ostensible purpose is to help economically depressed areas improve their levels of employment and other productive activity. But this agency was created at a time when the thrust of nearly all federal policies was to stimulate massive movements of both people and jobs out of rural districts and into metropolitan areas. Rather than reshape all those other policies to change this impact, Congress created the EDA as an expression of concern for the rural areas that were being depopulated, partly through the impacts of all its other policies. This agency was deliberately given too few resources to stem the tide of other policies causing flight from rural areas. Hence, it was kept essentially ineffective, a symbolic gesture to show that Congress "cared" about the areas its other policies were undermining.

The U.S. federal government has also adopted many programs during the past forty years aimed at improving economic conditions within large cities and other areas. Examples are the urban renewal, public housing, model cities, community block grant, and antipoverty programs. However, these programs did not form any coherent overall strategy for allocating resources among metropolitan areas to benefit the weakest disproportionately. Rather, they were a series of ad hoc responses to specific problems, coordinated at neither the federal, state, nor metropolitan-area levels—and often not even at the local level by the receiving governments.

REGIONAL STRATEGIES FOR ALLOCATING RESOURCES WITHIN INDIVIDUAL METROPOLITAN AREAS

Within individual U.S. metropolitan areas, there is also a nearly universal dearth of anything resembling a meaningful economic development strategy. One major reason is that no governmental body has authority over the general welfare of an entire metropolitan area, except in about a dozen areas that have true regional or semiregional governments. General governmental authority is fragmented among dozens or even hundreds of local governments, as discussed earlier. Many state governments have indeed created economic development agencies. But they focus on each state as a whole, not on individual metropolitan areas as wholes.

As a result, the basic American strategy for economic development within individual metropolitan areas has been to permit private firms, entrepreneurs, real estate developers, and landowners to do whatever they want, within a set of rules established by local governments for the parochial benefit of their own citizens. Hence, the way resources are allocated within metropolitan areas is basically determined by private market forces. However, the governmental rules within which such development must occur have steadily grown more complex, more restrictive, and more difficult to conform to in areas that have experienced sustained economic prosperity. In contrast, those rules have become more permissive in those areas that have experienced severe economic recessions, such as many energy-oriented metropolitan areas.

ECONOMIC DEVELOPMENT STRATEGIES AIMED AT SPECIFIC GROUPS

Concerning the third basic type of economic development strategy identified earlier—that of focusing upon assisting population groups in need rather than aiding spatial areas—the United States has adopted a relatively disjointed and partial approach. This approach is much more extensive than that of doing nothing, but much less extensive than the approaches adopted by many Western European nations. The federal government supports a series of assistance programs that provide mainly in-kind benefits to certain groups, except for extensive cash assistance to the elderly, to some disabled persons, and to very low-income mothers with children. The in-kind benefits include entitlement programs for all very low-income households, which provide them with medical assistance and food aid, plus housing aid furnished to only those households meeting eligibility requirements. These programs have different eligibility standards and are operated by several different federal departments, rather than being combined into a single coherent welfare program.

These programs have waxed and waned over time, depending upon which party has controlled the presidency and upon general economic conditions. During the administration of Lyndon Johnson in the late 1960s, antipoverty programs were greatly expanded. Several programs delivering federal financial aid to large cities containing high percentages of poor residents were passed and funded at notable levels. These programs were continued until the presidency of Ronald Reagan in the 1980s, when all federal aid to cities and states was drastically reduced. Programs aiding states and cities that redistributed incomes were especially hit by cutbacks.

The net result is that in 1993, around 15.1 percent of all U.S. residents, or 39.3 million persons, still had annual cash incomes below the official "poverty level." That level is defined as the money cost of a minimally adequate diet multiplied by three. The fraction of all U.S. children under age 18 living in households with incomes below the poverty level has steadily risen over the past two decades. In 1993, it was 22 percent for all children, 46 percent for black children, and 40 percent for Hispanic children.[12] The percentages of all households, persons, and children with analogously low incomes in Western European nations are generally considerably lower than those prevalent in the United States.

SPATIAL DISTRIBUTION OF SOCIOECONOMIC GROUPS WITHIN
METROPOLITAN AREAS

Another aspect of American economic development strategies for metropolitan areas involves the spatial distribution of socioeconomic groups within these areas. Although no centralized authority has deliberately devised and carried out any coherent strategy concerning where such groups will live, a de facto strategy has emerged from the disjointed decisions of individual local governments. These decisions reflect two widely held values of American households: (1) the desire to live in a neighborhood where most other residents are similar to oneself in income and social status and (2) the moral and legal right of households in each community to protect themselves from forces they believe might reduce either their property values or the social status of that community.

The application of these principles by local governments is accomplished through their adoption of specific zoning regulations, subdivision regulations, building codes, and housing occupancy codes. These regulations are usually designed to prevent construction within each community of any housing with a market value substantially less than the homes now located there. One reason for this practice is that most local governments believe low-income residents are "fiscal liabilities" because they require services that cost more than the tax revenues such residents generate. In many areas containing predominantly single-family homes, this means either total or substantial exclusion of multifamily housing. Such exclusionary policies are only possible within suburbs, since most central cities already contain large amounts of both relatively low-valued housing and multifamily housing. However, central cities maintain some differentiation of specific neighborhoods by socioeconomic group through a combination of market forces that affect housing prices and differential enforcement of building and other local codes.

The result of this highly decentralized process is creation within each metropolitan area of a rough and informal but nonetheless real socioeconomic hierarchy of residential neighborhoods. In this hierarchy, the wealthiest households live in high-priced neighborhoods occupied mainly by very high-income households; middle-income households live in not-quite-so-high-priced areas occupied mainly by middle-income households; and moderate-income households live in neighborhoods occupied mainly by moderate-income households. For members of these three groups, this hierarchy works well, providing them with neighborhoods that conform to the two values just mentioned, and thereby meeting their basic residential needs.

But this hierarchy has a devastating impact upon the poorest and most destitute households in each metropolitan area. Because members of such households are excluded from most parts of the hierarchy, they are compelled to live together in the oldest, most deteriorated areas. These areas are found mostly within central cities or in older, close-in suburbs. Moreover, these areas often become dominated by conditions associated with severe poverty, such as high rates of crime, delinquency, drug abuse, child abuse, broken families, unemployment, and mental illness. And the quality of education provided in these areas is markedly inferior to that provided in other parts of the hierarchy, partly because most of the children in schools there come from such destitute families. Thus, the poorest households are forced to live in a social, physical, and economic environment that offers nothing remotely approaching the "equality of opportunity" that is part of the American mythos.[13] In recent years, some sociologists have even argued that these neighborhoods are producing an "underclass" containing many members who remain in poverty from one generation to the next.[14]

The development of such a neighborhood hierarchy is not the result of a deliberate, centralized plot by a cabal of local government officials from relatively affluent suburbs. But it is not wholly accidental, either. The officials concerned are by now well aware of the collective impact of their exclusionary behavior upon the welfare of the poorest residents of each metropolitan area. But they are elected by nonpoor residents of specific communities who do not want to have poor people living near them. And no political officials are responsible for the overall welfare of each metropolitan area as a whole. Hence, each local government adopts an essentially parochial view when it comes to deciding what land-use regulations to permit. So, the emergence of this neighborhood hierarchy is thus a direct result of the basic American strategy of having mainly fragmented governments determine how metropolitan areas should develop.

Western European Strategies

No single set of strategies for the economic development of metropolitan areas has been adopted by all the countries of Western Europe. Indeed, many diverse strategies have been employed in this regard. Nevertheless, many Western European nations have created and tried to implement certain basic and roughly similar approaches to metropolitan-area economic development, which are highlighted here. Most of these approaches have not been followed in the United States.

NATIONAL STRATEGIES FOR ALLOCATING RESOURCES AMONG METROPOLITAN AREAS

Several European nations have adopted national strategies to influence the allocation of economic resources within and among their subregions. These subregions are not usually equated with individual metropolitan areas, but rather with larger territories encompassing several such areas. For example, the United Kingdom instituted several policies aimed at encouraging private firms to locate plants and other facilities in Scotland, Wales, and the North, rather than near London or in the South. Similarly, Italy adopted policies giving tax and other preferences to firms that located facilities in the South, rather than the North. A 1982 compilation by the Commissions of the European Communities of measures providing development assistance for "depressed" regions listed measures for Belgium, Denmark, West Germany, France, Ireland, Italy, Luxembourg, the Netherlands, and the United Kingdom (McAllister 1982: 72–75). Most of these measures consisted of financial aids and incentives for locating plants and other facilities in designated regions experiencing slower-than-average employment growth. Some consisted of assistance to regional or local governments to improve infrastructures in such regions.

Almost every analysis of the impacts of such regional development strategies arrives at the same two basic conclusions: First, the "depressed" regions being assisted still have demonstrably less-dynamic economies than the rest of the nation, so such strategies have failed to "solve" the fundamental problem at which they were aimed. Second, these strategies have nevertheless probably enhanced the economic situation in those regions beyond what it would have been had they not been instituted, although this supposition is hard to measure or prove. Even if public spending produces added jobs in the target regions, to what extent is this simply a diversion of jobs from other parts of the nation? True, an important goal of regional programs is to shift the overall distribution of jobs among regions. But this should preferably occur through net gains to society as a whole—not at the cost of offsetting reductions in jobs in other regions. After all, that spending has to be financed, presumably by taxing someone else. If the spending is financed by government deficits, that might increase the inflation rate, thereby producing an offsetting cost for society as a whole. Bryan Ashcroft (1979: 231–94) conducted an exhaustive evaluation of the major studies of regional growth strategies in the United Kingdom up to 1978. He concluded that (1) about 220,000 additional jobs had been created by regional development programs in "development areas" from 1963 to 1970; (2) capital investment in those areas was stimulated by these programs; (3) the national government received a net financial gain from these programs because they increased property and other taxes and reduced social expenditures more than they cost; and (4) the programs produced a significant net benefit to society as a whole, as well as to the national government. However, he also admitted that the last two of these findings rest on complex theoretical assumptions that are impossible to confirm with much reliability.

Thus, whether regional economic development policies like those used throughout Western Europe are worthwhile from the viewpoint of society as a whole has not yet been conclusively demonstrated. However, the two previously stated conclusions have been demonstrated, namely, that such policies do not remove the regional disparities at which they are aimed, but they do provide some positive benefits to at least some of residents of the "depressed" regions involved.

REGIONAL STRATEGIES FOR ALLOCATING RESOURCES WITHIN INDIVIDUAL
METROPOLITAN AREAS

As noted earlier, most Western European nations have tried to confine new real estate development within their metropolitan areas to either in-fill sites or the immediate periphery of the already-built-up portions of those areas. In some cases, they have also permitted creation of planned "new cities" near large metropolitan areas, but separated from them by "greenbelts" of open space. More often, they have encouraged the expansion of existing communities separated from nearby large cities by "greenbelt" zones. Moreover, they have sought to protect the commercial dominance of established downtowns and other retail centers by prohibiting construction of major new automobile-oriented shopping centers in outlying locations. And they have supported extensive networks of public mass transit within their metropolitan areas to inhibit increases in the use of automotive vehicles.

In addition, the United Kingdom has attempted to stimulate economic development within older, inner-city areas through the creation of "enterprise zones." From 1981 through 1986, the national government spent about 400 million pounds for land acquisition, tax relief, and infrastructure improvements within twenty-three such zones in all parts of the United Kingdom. Barry Moore (1989) estimated that in 1986, enterprise zones contained 2,800 establishments employing 63,300 workers, 56 percent in manufacturing. However, only 35,000 of these jobs were there as a consequence of the enterprise zone policy; the rest would have located there anyway. Moreover, 29,600 of those 35,000 jobs were essentially transferred from other parts of the local economy, so they are not net gains even to the local economy. But 7,400 jobs were generated by linkages with these zones. Hence, a total net gain of 12,900 jobs was generated by this program for the local economies involved. The public cost *per job in enterprise zones* was 8,500 pounds, but the public cost *per job gained net by the local economy* was 23,000 pounds. In addition, enterprise zones produced notable nonemployment benefits, such as removal of derelict properties and improvements in the environment. Two-thirds of company representatives interviewed by Moore both in and outside the zones thought they were a positive catalyst to the local economy.

Western European economic development strategies *within* metropolitan areas have produced several important results that differ from what has happened in U.S. metropolitan areas. The economic viability of established downtowns and traditional retail districts has been more successfully sustained, especially concerning retailing. As stated, expansion of metropolitan areas has been confined mainly to in-fill sites, the immediate periphery of already-built-up areas, and planned "new cities," with one exception. There has also been substantial peripheral growth of many smaller towns and villages near major metropolitan areas, from which the new residents commute by car or train to those areas. This is the case in the south of the United Kingdom, for example.

However, not all the results of these strategies have been beneficial. Tightly confining peripheral expansion of existing metropolitan areas has increased land values within them more than in the United States on the average. Hence, the cost of becoming a homeowner is higher, relative to median incomes, in many Western European nations than in most of the United States, and homeownership percentages are lower. Also, tighter planning controls on all new development have prevented as much relative construction of new commercial space as in U.S. metropolitan areas. So vacancy rates are lower and commercial rents are much higher in many Western European cities, even though they have not experienced nearly so much population or job growth as many U.S. metropolitan areas. This benefits the owners of such properties, but not the tenants.

Also, vehicle ownership has expanded in many Western European nations much faster than the road capacity to handle those added vehicles. This results partly from the Western European strategy of discouraging use of private cars compared to public mass transit. Consequently, traffic congestion and its resultant delays are even worse in many Western European metropolitan areas—both large and small—than in most U.S. metropolitan areas. This is true even though congestion has recently increased substantially in the latter as well.

ECONOMIC DEVELOPMENT STRATEGIES AIMED AT SPECIFIC GROUPS

Most Western European nations have adopted more extensive welfare systems that support living standards among the poor than has the United States. As a result, the percentage of citizens with incomes below the poverty level is lower in most of those nations than in the United States, on average. This is especially true concerning children, because the United States is the only major developed nation that does not provide some type of children's allowance to *all* households with children.

A recent study using data from the years 1979 to 1982 compared the percentages of persons with incomes below the equivalent of the U.S. poverty line in the United States and five Western European nations (Smeeding, Torrey, and Rein 1988).[15] Its measure of income was after taxes and transfer payments. Concerning poverty among children, the United States, at 17.1 percent in 1979, had the highest fraction among these six nations, with the United Kingdom second highest, at 10.7 percent in 1979. Sweden and Switzerland had the lowest poverty shares for children, at 5.1 percent each, but they are very small nations. However, West Germany had only 8.2 percent of its children at that income level, and it had the largest population of any Western European nation.[16] Concerning the elderly, the United Kingdom had by far the highest fraction of elderly with poverty-level incomes, at 37 percent. Norway was second highest at 18.7 percent, the United States next with 16.1 percent, and West Germany next with 15.4 percent. Lowest were Sweden and Switzerland, with 2.1 percent and 6.0 percent, respectively. Since those data were gathered, the percentage of persons with incomes at or below the poverty level in the United States has risen among children, but declined among the elderly. I do not have more recent data with respect to these percentages in Western European nations.

Spatial Distribution of Socioeconomic Groups within Metropolitan Areas

Most Western European nations have adopted extensive housing subsidy programs that are used by sizable fractions of their renter populations. Moreover, they have built subsidized rental housing in all portions of their major metropolitan areas, including the suburbs. Hence, their low-income populations are not as highly concentrated in older, close-in, often deteriorated neighborhoods as in the United States. In fact, the relative scatteration of subsidized housing throughout Western European metropolitan areas has reduced the extent to which a spatial, socioeconomic neighborhood hierarchy has developed there compared to the United States.

This does not mean there is no differentiation of Western European urban neighborhoods by income and socioeconomic status. There are definite high-status, high-income neighborhoods and low-status, low-income ones in Western European cities and metropolitan areas—in fact, throughout the world's urban areas. However, the high-status neighborhoods are not so separated in distance from major downtown areas in Western Europe as in the United States. In Western European cities, many of the highest-income, highest-status neighborhoods are right next to the traditional downtown. That happens in a few U.S. metropolitan areas, too, such as the Near North Side in Chicago and the Upper East Side of Manhattan. But in general, the wealthiest households in U.S. metropolitan areas live in relatively distant suburbs, while the poorest ones live in relatively close-in central-city neighborhoods. In Western European cities, either there is no such differentiation among income groups by distance from the center, or the wealthier households live close in and the poorer ones live in newer subsidized housing on the outskirts of the metropolitan area.

Furthermore, because so much higher fractions of the total population in most Western European nations receive housing subsidies, directly subsidized housing projects there contain households from a much broader income spectrum than do those in the United States. Hence, there is less tendency in Western Europe than in the United States to isolate the poorest households together in housing projects separated from other income groups. Such projects are consequently not considered such undesirable living environments as they are in the United States. That is one reason why neighborhood political resistance to building them nearby is much less intense in Western Europe than in America.

Relevance of Strategies to Major U.S. Metropolitan Area Problems

What difference has the absence of strategies for the economic development of U.S. metropolitan areas made to the welfare of these areas, compared to what might have happened if strategies like those in Western Europe had been used? One way to approach this difficult question is to examine key existing problems in U.S. metropolitan areas, and to try to guess whether they would have been less severe if the United States had adopted strategies like those in Western Europe. For this purpose, I have identified what I believe are the nine most serious problems in U.S. metropolitan areas relevant to their economic development. These are as follows (not necessarily in order of relative importance):

1. Regionally uneven prosperity across different metropolitan areas
2. Decaying inner-city areas that create unequal opportunities for their residents, combined with suburban labor shortages
3. Failures of the public education system, especially in big cities
4. Continuing poverty among large numbers of residents, especially children
5. Inability to cope with regionally generated problems by adopting coherent regionwide remedies
6. The physical decay of much infrastructure, such as highways and bridges

7. Low productivity growth, causing a very slow real wage rate increase
8. A shortage of low-rent housing, and a rising housing affordability problem among low-income households
9. Rising automotive traffic congestion

The first of these problems is more common in Western Europe than in the United States. Hence, it is not likely that adopting national strategies for allocating resources among metropolitan areas would have alleviated this problem in the United States. Decaying inner-city areas, the second problem, are also found in some Western European cities, but not nearly so extensively as in U.S. cities, nor as tied to racial segregation and discrimination. The United States has suffered a worse incidence of this problem in part because it had no strategy for dealing with it. But the problem would undoubtedly have been worse in the United States even if Americans had adopted such a strategy, because of basic differences between urban areas in these two regions.

The next two problems—poor education and continuing poverty—are worse in the United States than in Western Europe. However, they result more from failures of welfare strategies aimed at specific groups than from spatial strategies aimed at metropolitan areas per se.

The fifth problem, lack of regional coordination, results from the fragmented nature of governance in U.S. metropolitan areas, and is much less prevalent in Europe. The problem would have been much less severe if the United States had adopted an effective strategy for allocating resources *within* individual metropolitan areas.

The poor state of American infrastructures, the sixth problem, is not caused by the absence of suitable economic development strategies, but by the unwillingness of American governments to pay for the required improvements. Similarly, regarding the seventh problem, no one knows precisely what has caused low productivity growth, but it cannot be blamed on lack of suitable economic development strategies for metropolitan areas.

The shortage of low-rent housing and related housing affordability problems—the eighth problem—are caused by two main factors. One is the unwillingness of the U.S. federal government to finance housing subsidies for very poor households, as most Western European governments do. Hence, this is a failing of welfare-oriented strategy in the United States, compared to that in Western Europe. The second factor is the restrictive laws adopted by local governments that force housing prices upward. This factor results mainly from the fragmentation of governmental authority within U.S. metropolitan areas, which blocks development of any effective strategy for economic and other development within those areas.

The last problem is just as prevalent in Western Europe as in the United States, but for a different reason. In Western Europe, the unwillingness of national governments to finance additional highways is a major cause of traffic congestion. It is true that greater highway construction alone would not totally eliminate traffic congestion, and that European strategies of supporting more extensive public transit systems than in the United States have other advantages (such as generating less air pollution and consuming less open space). Nevertheless, the lack of expressway networks in many big Western European metropolitan areas surely contributes to intense traffic jams within them. That represents a shortcoming in their own national strategies for allocating resources both among and within metropolitan areas. In the United States, the national government is similarly unwilling to finance infrastructure improvements. But traffic congestion in U.S. metropolitan areas is also caused by the unwillingness of local governments to shift some of their powers upward to regional or state planning and governance bodies. Since automobile traffic is generated at the regional level, not at the local level, it cannot be dealt with effectively by purely local governmental policies. Hence, the absence of any strategy for dealing with resource allocation *within* metropolitan areas contributes to this problem. However, in both the United States and Western Europe, another factor generating traffic congestion is political unwillingness to impose peak-hour roadway pricing upon travelers. This results from a failure of political will more than a lack of any strategy.

In summary, the absence of strategies for metropolitan area economic development in the United States has probably contributed significantly to several major U.S. metropolitan area problems, though not to all of them. The failure of the United States to adopt an effective welfare strategy to aid its most deprived citizens is especially important in generating U.S. urban problems. Somewhat less central is the unwillingness of both the national government and state governments to fund major physical improvements—such as repairing highways and bridges—that would help all metropolitan areas develop more effectively. Finally, the fragmentation of U.S. government authority within metropolitan areas clearly contributes to several major problems in these areas.

On the other hand, adopting strategies for the economic development of metropolitan areas would not eliminate all of the problems in these areas, as experience in Western Europe shows. Even so, Americans should at least consider a more strategic approach to metropolitan area economic and other development, especially in those fast-growing metropolitan areas particularly plagued by intra-metropolitan difficulties.

Notes

The views in this article are solely those of the author and are not necessarily those of the Brookings Institution, its trustees, or its other staff members.

1. The relatively recent policy of selling publicly owned housing units to their occupants, adopted in the United Kingdom under then-Prime Minister Margaret Thatcher's leadership, raised the homeownership percentage much closer to that in the United States. But homeownership rates in most other Western European nations are markedly below those in the United States.

2. The fastest economic growth in the United States *in absolute jobs* during the 1980s was in the Los Angeles and Washington, D.C., metropolitan areas.

3. The American Housing Survey (U.S. Departments of Commerce and Housing and Urban Development 1989) reported 32.724 million renter-occupied housing units in the United States in 1987. The median income of households in those units was $16,233, and 31.7 percent had incomes below $10,000. These units included 2.301 million owned by public housing authorities—7 percent of the total. The median income of households in public housing units was $6,821, and 71.8 percent had incomes below $10,000. About 41 percent of the public housing units were occupied by black households, compared to 16 percent of nonpublic-housing renter-occupied units. About 38 percent of all nonblack renter households were headed by females, compared to 53 percent of all black renter households.

4. Data taken from the *Statistical Abstract of the United States: 1995*, pp. 845–47.

5. In U.S. Census terminology, a *central city* is a single incorporated community acting as the heart of an economically integrated region containing at least 40,000 persons. These regions are referred to as *metropolitan statistical areas* (MSAs) and consist of those entire counties that are closely integrated around a central city. The areas within an MSA but outside of the central city are referred to as *suburbs* in this chapter. As of 1990, there were about 333 MSAs in the United States.

6. Abandonment of housing was also related to the deteriorated nature of the worst-quality structures and to their locations in neighborhoods exhibiting extreme poverty and high rates of crime, delinquency, unemployment, broken families, and other undesirable traits.

7. *Statistical Abstract of the United States: 1995*, p. 32.

8. *Ibid.*, p. 656.

9. Some economists consider public funding of highways to be a form of subsidy similar to public funding of the deficits from bus systems and fixed-rail transit systems. But in the United States, most highway construction and repairs are financed through taxes on gasoline and vehicle license fees; hence, they are paid for through what can

reasonably be considered "user fees." That is not true of public funds provided to cover the deficits of mass transit systems.

10. Only parts of the Downs (1989) regression analysis were included or described in this study; the rest has not been published.

11. Since these regressions were adaptations from a regression designed to analyze housing prices, they did not include all the variables that might be relevant to population growth and job growth, but not housing prices. For example, they did not include mean January temperature as a tested independent variable. Hence, these results can be viewed as only approximate and partial.

12. *Statistical Abstract of the United States: 1995*, p. 480.

13. For a more complete analysis of this situation, see Downs (1981, esp. chap. 4).

14. For example, see Wilson (1987).

15. There were eight nations in Smeeding et al.'s (1988) study, but only the United States and those in Western Europe are included in this analysis.

16. Population size may be significant, because large size is usually accompanied by greater ethnic diversity. It is politically easier to end poverty in an ethnically homogeneous nation than a diverse one, since support for income redistribution to the poor is backed by more social solidarity in the former than the latter. True, Switzerland contains several different major ethnic groups. But its diversity is small compared to that of the United States.

References

Ashcroft, Bryan. 1979. "The Evaluation of Regional Economic Policy: The Case of the United Kingdom." In *Balanced National Growth*, edited by Kevin Allen (231–94). Lexington, Mass.: Lexington Books.

Bradbury, Katharine L., Anthony Downs, and Kenneth A. Small. 1982. *Urban Decline and the Future of American Cities*. Washington, D.C.: Brookings Institution.

Downs, Anthony. 1981. *Neighborhoods and Urban Development*. Washington, D.C.: Brookings Institution.

————. 1989. *What Will Happen to Home Prices in the 1990s?* New York: Salomon Bros.

McAllister, Ian. 1982. *Regional Development and the European Community: A Canadian Perspective*. Montreal: Institute for Research on Public Policy.

Moore, Barry. 1989. "Enterprise Zones: An Evaluation of the Experiment in the U.K." In *Policy Innovation and Urban Land Markets* (30–46). Paris: Organization for Economic Cooperation and Development, Urban Affairs Programme.

Smeeding, Timothy, Barbara Boyle Torrey, and Martin Rein. 1988. "Patterns of Income and Poverty: The Economic Status of Children and the

Elderly in Eight Countries" (95–99). In *The Vulnerable*, edited by John L. Palmer, Timothy Smeeding, and Barbara Boyle. Washington, D.C.: Urban Institute.

U.S. Bureau of the Census. 1995. *Statistical Abstract of the United States: 1995*. Washington, D.C.: U.S. Government Printing Office.

————. 1989. *Statistical Abstract of the United States: 1989*. Washington, D.C.: U.S. Government Printing Office.

U.S. Departments of Commerce and Housing and Urban Development. 1989. *American Housing Survey for the United States, 1987.* Pub. no. H-150-87. Washington, D.C.: U.S. Government Printing Office.

Wilson, William Julius. 1987. *The Truly Disadvantaged: The Inner City, the Underclass, and Public Policy.* Chicago: University of Chicago Press.

Chapter Three

PRIORITIES IN URBAN AND ECONOMIC DEVELOPMENT

Peter Hall

This chapter first identifies two key trends underlying all attempts to develop priorities for local urban and economic development. It then argues that the overall policy must be to help local economies move from declining to expanding activities and outlines a number of key sectoral/spatial policies to help achieve that end. It goes on to identify a number of key policy levers, and ends by suggesting that the new locational logic creates an open field for policy.

TWO KEY TRENDS

Before one can establish priorities for development, one must define the key trends that shape them. Two such trends are identified here: the globalization of the economy, especially of production; and the shift in advanced countries from a goods-handling to an information-handling economy.

Globalization of the Economy

During the 1970s and 1980s the globalization of the capitalist economy led to a profound spatial resorting of the economy on a worldwide scale, whereby entire processes and industries were progressively relocated in newly industrializing countries. As Manuel Castells has put it, "The growing internationalization of the American economy reshapes cities and regions following the logic of the space of flows" (1989: 344). American companies have reacted to global challenges by relocating a large part of their operations offshore and in low-wage regions like the South. Four consequences have followed: increasing internationalization within corporations; the further decline of the manufacturing belt; the growth of a Mexican border economy; and the industrialization of the South (Castells 1989: 345). Yet, worldwide capital flows concentrate the processing operations in the cores of a few global cities, notably New York.

In the 1990s this process of globalization is, if anything, likely to accelerate in Europe, because of the economic transformation of its eastern countries. Most of these countries have long industrial traditions, including a specialization in high-technology knowledge-based industries. They have fallen steadily behind in their application of information to production—which, indeed, viewed in the broadest historical sense, may have constituted the gigantic Marxian contradiction that brought their regimes down. Since they do, however, possess a reasonable physical infrastructure and a rather better than reasonable educational one, their prospects for rapid transformation appear good. But because they are relatively backward in the use of information, it is virtually certain that they will be rapidly colonized by international capital. The contradiction between those forces and the national spirit of self-determination that has helped shape the revolutionary transformation should be acute.

Shift to the Informational Economy

The second trend can variously be termed the "tertiarization" of the economy, or the shift to the information economy, or the transition to the informational mode of production (Hall 1987c). Colin Clark's half-century-old argument—that there is a very long term trend in all advanced industrial economies for the proportion of workers in manufacturing occupations and industries to fall, and for the proportion in service industries and occupations to rise—has continued to prove true (Clark 1940). Though after World War II some countries managed to increase their manufacturing proportions or at least to hold constant the proportions, since the 1960s the declining tendency has been universal. Typically, in the most advanced economies today, between 65 percent and 75 percent of all employment does not involve the handling of goods at all. As is well known, the shift arises largely from the fact of productivity gains in production processes, while more and more workers have been needed in ancillary processes such as planning, finance, and marketing. The quintessence of this process is the robotized factory, monitored by technicians hundreds of miles away, and owned and controlled by a company in another continent.

Some observers have argued that within a true accounting matrix, these jobs should indeed be treated as part of manufacturing (Cohen and Zysman 1987; Gershuny and Miles 1983). But Castells (1989) has recently suggested the radical hypothesis that we are witnessing the second great economic transformation of modern times: from the industrial to the informational mode of production, in which the fundamental inputs are no longer material, but are knowledge based. This informational mode is not simply the product of new technologies, nor are the technologies a mechanical response to the demands of the new organizational system; rather, it is the convergence between these two processes that changes the technical relationships of production, giving rise to a new mode of development. It is this fundamental shift, so Castells argues, that has underlain some key economic changes of the 1980s—including the globalization of the economy.

FOUR PRIORITY AREAS

Against this background, one overarching priority emerges: to move urban and regional economies out of declining sectors and into expanding ones, while preparing their workers to make the transition into the new occupations that this will involve. To accomplish this, specific action will be necessary in four priority areas: fostering that part of the residual manufacturing sector which produces goods embodying science and technology (high-technology manufacturing); developing, in parallel, the producer services sector; exploiting the changing desirable locations for both these key sectors, and thus for economic activity in general; and tackling the growing polarization of the work force, represented by the phenomena of labor market mismatch and the associated urban underclass.

Promoting High-Technology Manufacturing

As a result of the shift of production to services, percentages of the total work force in manufacturing are already down to some 20–25 percent in most advanced industrial countries, and may be as low as 5–10 percent by the early twenty-first century (Hall 1987a). Generally, manufacturing employment is static or declining, though production may still be increasing; the reasons are familiar. However, within this framework some countries—especially the United States and Japan—have recorded gains in high-technology employment; and even those countries that have failed to do so (e.g., the United Kingdom) have recorded sharp geographical shifts in such employment.

Recent work (Buswell and Lewis 1970; Hall 1987a, c; Hall and Preston 1988; Hall, Breheny, McQuaid, and Hart 1987; Howells 1984; Malecki 1980b; Markusen, Hall, and Glasmeier 1986; Markusen et al. 1990; Oakey, Thwaites, and Nash 1980; Saxenian 1985c, 1994; Scott 1986, 1993; Thwaites 1982) suggests the following common features of high-tech manufacturing locations.

1. They are highly concentrated in a few zones in each country.

2. Some are relatively new, but some are in old, established industrial areas with long traditions of science-based industry (e.g., London, Boston).

3. Invariably, these areas have a well-developed business infrastructure, both physical (major airports, motorways) and organizational (headquarters offices, business services, educational services).

4. Within these zones, there has been a pronounced pattern of outward diffusion to the urban periphery (e.g., Highway 128, Orange County, California, the so-called M4 Corridor west of London).

5. Some factors (such as climate, educational quality and spending, and the presence of major company headquarters and business services) are important in long-term location, whereas others (wage rates, unionization) appear unimportant.

6. A critical factor is the presence of organized research and development, meaning that access to a major university, city, or government research establishment—especially government-funded, defense-based research—can prove important.

7. The precise pattern of localization seems to depend a great deal on historical circumstance, but the pattern of defense contracting appears to have been crucial for high-tech industry in both the United Kingdom and the United States. Particularly important here seem to have been decisions made under pressure during World War II and in the Cold War buildup of 1951–55, when some of the most important complexes came into being.

8. Why these contracts went to cities outside the traditional manufacturing areas and not to older industrial cities is not easily explained; for a variety of reasons, entrepreneurs set up business in new locations like Los Angeles and Seattle, and once established, they proved hard to dislodge.

9. The so-called innovative milieu seems critically important (Aydalot 1986a, b, 1988; Aydalot and Keeble 1988a, b), a concept further developed by Åke Andersson (1985a, b) and Andersson and Strömqvist (1988) in their work on creativity as the key to the metropolis. Certain places, at certain times, prove uniquely innovative in terms of

technology or industrial organization, and thereby generate new industrial traditions. They may be older industrial centers, which thus revitalize themselves, but they are often new centers. The circumstances of their gestation are not entirely clear, but a key role seems to be played by synergy between individuals and organizations. Such synergy may arise more easily in certain types of economic environment—for instance, in cities with many small workshops—than in others.

Key Role of Producer Services

The shift to the informational mode of development also entails an equally fundamental reappraisal of the role of service industries in regional and urban development. Until the late 1960s, following the classic work of Christaller and Lösch on central place theory, service industries were viewed primarily as catering to local consumer demand. More recently, as already noticed, it has been strongly argued that much output and employment within the service sector should properly be regarded as generated by manufacturing demand (Cohen and Zysman 1987; Gershuny 1978; Gershuny and Miles 1983). At the same time, a series of studies has produced a new classification of services (Noyelle and Stanback 1984; Singelmann 1978; Stanback 1979, 1985; Stanback and Knight 1970; Stanback and Noyelle 1982; Stanback et al. 1981): distributive services, including the complex of transportation, communications, and public utilities (TCU) and wholesaling; retailing and consumer (personal) services; and producer services, the latter of which includes the corporate headquarters complex, the FIRE (finance, insurance, and real estate) group, and the corporate services group (all other producer services except FIRE); and nonprofit services and government. The first two have seen extensive substitution of capital for labor, though with some employment growth in the second case; the third has grown massively; the fourth expanded in the 1960s and 1970s but not (owing to policy reversals) in the 1980s.

So there has been increasing emphasis on the producer and social (nonprofit) services because they have exhibited rapid gains in employment while traditional sectors (manufacturing and distributive services) have been contracting. Indeed, the two processes may be symbiotic, with gains in productivity in the manufacturing and distributive sectors and an increasing emphasis on the specialist producer-service functions, including research and development, technical consultancy, marketing and advertising, management consultancy, legal and accountancy services, data processing, and other information services.

Robert Reich has suggested a division of the work force into three groups: the residual production sector, consumer services, and what he calls the manipulation of symbols (Reich 1991). This division is close to, but not identical to, the conventional division between producer and consumer services, and is also similar to another division: between goods-handling services and information-handling services. All these ways of looking at the services are useful and important. But in many ways the crucial and elusive activity is what can be called, alternatively, information handling, or symbol manipulating, or producer-service provision. It includes the work of bankers and lawyers and accountants and computer technicians, although some of the work of all these could also be classified under consumer services—just as the work of physicians and educators has the same ambiguous quality.

The role of producer services is intimately connected with the increasing scale and complexity of modern corporate organizations, in which the growing need for producer-service functions may increasingly be met in-house by a substantial nonproductive work force. But such a process is not automatic, nor is it a simple function of the size of the corporation. Large companies may internalize their more standard service functions while buying more specialized services such as marketing. Recent research, based on the concept of flexible specialization developed by Piore and Sabel, suggests that a more important trend is to contract out many specialized services (Daniels 1983; Howells and Green 1986; Marshall 1988; Piore and Sabel 1984).

These changes have profound consequences for the location of economic activity. The classic early work on producer services in New York City (Haig 1926; Hoover and Vernon 1959), assumed that such services tended to agglomerate in the central business districts of a few very large metropolitan areas. Later research—by Törnqvist (1970) in Sweden, Goddard (1975) in Great Britain, and Pred (1977) in the United States—focused on control functions and information flows, suggesting that routine functions could be decentralized while top-level decision making and control must remain in a few centers.

Significantly, it appears that, despite drastic reductions in the cost of long-distance telecommunications, far greater than in that for equivalent personal travel, the curves of telecommunications and personal traffic have moved in parallel over a long period; the implication is that the two are complementary, rather than substitutional (Graham and Marvin 1995). Improvements and drastic cost reductions in telecommunications have powerfully aided routine decentralization, whereas face-to-face contact is still thought essential for higher-level functions. Simultaneously, the idea of independent development has been extended to the regional level within developed countries, suggesting that traditional policies to favor less-developed regions have mainly resulted in the establishment of branches lacking the potential for creating regional multipliers.

The state of research on producer service industries, on both the theoretical and empirical sides, can be summed up in the following general propositions.

1. Higher-level producer services remain concentrated in the cores of the most highly developed central metropolitan areas of the most highly developed national economies (London, Paris, New York). The recent recovery of the New York City economy, based on successful transition to a service-based economy, seems to confirm this.

2. Such services may be either separate or internalized in headquarters offices or specialist subdivisions of large corporations. If the latter, they may decentralize a very short distance from headquarters (e.g., research laboratories in a semirural location on the urban fringe.)

3. More routine producer services (e.g., some financial services such as insurance or credit card operations) may decentralize some distance to "back offices" in smaller centers with lower costs, though they may still be within easy traveling distance of the major metropolitan center (e.g., Croydon or Reading in Southeast England; the Paris new towns; Stamford, Connecticut; Tysons Corner, Virginia; Concord-Walnut Creek-San Ramon-Pleasanton-Dublin, California). The dominant reason for this decentralization appears to be the search for lower rents and for a supply of the right kind of nonorganized, fairly docile, reasonably well-educated female clerical labor (Baran 1985; Mills 1987; Nelson 1986). This development might have occurred without technological advancement, but has been powerfully aided by data processing and communications technologies.

4. There is an important open question of whether certain types of "head office" activity are now decentralizing also. Recent statistics indicate a decline in headquarters-type employment in some major cities, such as San Francisco, accompanied by continued rapid suburban growth (compare Beers 1987, for a popular account). Experts suggest that the United States may be witnessing the development of "polynucleated" cities on the Los Angeles model, in which the traditional downtown is only one of a number of major information technology (IT) processing centers. Improved IT could, of course, contribute powerfully to this process.

5. Older industrial cities may fail to develop significant producer-service concentrations; and, indeed, their existing concentrations may weaken as a result of contracting demand from the local productive sector, coupled with increasing takeover of productive plants and the development of a branch plant economy. This process may particularly affect second-order cities within the national settlement hierarchy (the "provincial capitals"), leading to a contraction of productive employment there. In Europe such cities tend to be concentrated in a narrow band, from Genoa and Turin through eastern and northern France, the Saar and Ruhr and southern Belgium to the Midlands, northwest and northeast England, and finally north to Glasgow and Belfast (Cheshire and Hay 1989). These areas have suffered massive deindustrialization and have failed to develop compensating service functions (Gillespie and Green 1987; Green and Howells 1987; Hall 1987a). Most of these places—including Essen and Dortmund, Liverpool and Manchester— are the European equivalents of the American functional-nodal centers identified by Stanback and Noyelle, which are similarly concentrated in the Mid-Atlantic and East North Central divisions.

6. In contrast, the equivalents of these areas' regional-nodal cities— strong provincial cities like Munich or Frankfurt, Grenoble or Norwich, and smaller national capitals like Brussels or Copenhagen—are performing conspicuously well in the same sector.

7. London is an anomaly: a national-nodal—in fact an international-nodal—city that nevertheless saw economic decline in much of the 1980s, reversed only toward the end of that decade, and with another steep fall in employment during the early 1990s. Overall, the city recorded jobless growth, with big increases in gross domestic product, but not in employment (Great Britain Government Office for London 1996a, 1996b). However, recent analysis confirms a paradoxical feature of the London economy in decline: there has been virtually no differential effect on overall unemployment rates, which have remained marginally below the national average. Because the labor force has proved very mobile, the decline in the work force has kept in step with the decline in jobs. People have moved out of London for housing reasons, but once out of the city, many eventually find jobs there (Buck, Gordon, and Young 1987: 97).

Exploiting the New Locational Logic

The resulting picture of locational change is dominated by the controlling producer-services and corporate headquarters cities. These world cities increasingly relate more to each other than to the rest of the world: London, New York, Tokyo. They sit in the centers of vast and spreading metropolitan regions, within which more routine informational functions are constantly banished to more peripheral low-cost suburban locations. Even more routine functions, like service delivery and information distribution and retrieval, can be standardized and spread across the entire national and international space, driven by the new information technologies. These technologies thus permit the spread of control of the leading centers, and cement their power (Castells 1989: 151, 169; Sassen 1991: passim).

Noyelle and Stanback have shown that within the American urban system, the global cities—the national nodal centers, only four in number (New York, Chicago, San Francisco, Los Angeles)—have continued to augment their service functions, though less rapidly than the next level of the hierarchy, which the authors label regional nodal centers (Boston, Philadelphia, Atlanta, Houston, Minneapolis, Phoenix); the traditional manufacturing headquarters cities (like Pittsburgh and Detroit), which they term "functional-nodal" centers, have lost ground badly (Noyelle and Stanback 1984; Stanback 1985). Other evidence, on a regional level, suggests that during the late 1970s and 1980s the older Frostbelt industrial regions performed poorly overall in substituting informational for goods-handling jobs (Hall 1988b).[1]

Noyelle and Stanback's (1984) conclusions, though interesting, apply to an open continental-scale economy. There is now some important parallel work on the producer-service sector in Britain and, to some degree, in Europe (Cheshire and Hay 1989; Daniels 1985, 1986; Daniels and Holly 1983; Evans 1973; Gillespie and Green 1987; Goddard 1975; Goddard and Morris 1975; Goddard and Smith 1975; Green and Howells 1987; Howells and Green 1986; Marshall 1982, 1988; Westaway 1974a,b). One could speculate that in Europe, national frontiers will still exert a major influence on the hierarchy of centers and so on the pattern of service employment growth; clearly, by definition, Europe has many more national-level service centers than the four identified for the United States by Noyelle and Stanback. In 1992, the year of the Single European Market, Europe still had a series of distinct urban hierarchies that reflected two millennia of evolution. Britain and France still have their dominant national capitals, which are now each the centers of giant metropolitan regions: a heavily primate urban hierarchy, as the geographers call it. Spain and Italy and Germany still have their flatter urban hierarchies, which reflect the long and tortuous history of national unification. But certain features—the

poor performance of the pure production centers and specialized nodal centers—are very likely, from the evidence so far, to be similar in
Europe.

The work by Cheshire and Hay (1989) on the European urban system
concludes that some of the best performers are either second-rank
cities in the bigger countries—places like Bristol, Toulouse, Florence,
or Stuttgart—or the smaller national capitals like Brussels, Amsterdam, or Copenhagen. But there is an exception: older industrial and
port cities that served as provincial capitals for old industrial regions,
like Glasgow or Liverpool or Dortmund, did not do well at all. Probably, too, the behavior of urban hierarchies differs from one nation-
state to another. Very partial evidence suggests that Liverpool and
Manchester, two of the United Kingdom's major regional service sectors, have suffered a serious loss in producer-service employment
(Cheshire and Hay 1989; compare Tym and Partners 1981); more extended analysis shows that a number of major British provincial centers did rather badly in substituting informational services for lost
goods-handling jobs during the 1970s, though a few (Bristol, Cardiff,
Edinburgh) did relatively well (Hall 1987a); an even wider analysis
indicates that both London and the major provincial cities were decentralizing producer-service jobs to surrounding subdominant centers (Gillespie and Green 1987). This underlines the strong growth of
such services in certain centers at the next-lower level of the British
urban hierarchy.[2]

It appears doubtful that this feature is replicated elsewhere in Europe; the Cheshire-Hay case studies suggest that it is not true of such
functional urban regions (FURs)[3] as Dortmund, Essen, Liège, Nancy,
or Saarbrücken, which are comparable regional centers to Birmingham, Liverpool, Manchester, or Glasgow.

Below these medium-sized metropolitan areas, Europe has over 100
smaller places with less than a quarter of a million people, many of
them administrative centers for rural areas, or resort and retirement
towns. Cheshire and Hay (1989) have shown that nearly three-quarters
of these areas gained people in the 1970s; more than two in five had
gains of 5 percent or more. The fastest-growing metropolitan areas,
whether small or medium-sized, tend to be semirural but not remote:
they are often close to the biggest metropolises, which are losing
people and jobs. There is thus a process of recentralization of jobs in
these smaller places, with local concentrations of residential populations in relatively small and compact areas where they live and work.

Southeast England provides an excellent example of these processes. Over a period of nearly three decades, London has been losing

both population and employment, with a limited reversal in the late 1980s. A ring of about twenty metropolitan areas around it has shown big gains. The wave of growth has progressively spread, to engulf places 80 and 100 miles (130 to 160 km) from London. These are all medium-sized towns in rural counties. Research clearly indicates that people move first, in search of affordable housing; then, after a time lag, the local economy expands to employ more and more of them. The same story could doubtless be replicated around Paris, Frankfurt, Milan, and a number of other urban centers.

Part of this transformation can be explained by the Castells (1989) schema: firms decentralize their more routine operations to the fringes of the global metropolises, in search of lower-cost labor and lower rents. However, Southeast England also includes innovative milieux like the so-called M4 Corridor west of London or the Cambridge area, which constitute independent sources of growth. The origins of these milieux prove complex and elusive: whereas the M4 Corridor seems to have resulted from long-distance relocation out of London coupled with defense contracting, the so-called Cambridge phenomenon was an indigenous spin-off from university research that somewhat resembles its transatlantic cousin.

Tackling Polarization and Mismatch in the Labor Market

With the shift from manufacturing to services, there is also a shift from goods-handling to information-handling occupations. One consequence is that education, at least up to the minimum level represented by a high school diploma, becomes increasingly a prerequisite for employment. A second consequence is that bodily strength and muscular power are no longer significant in employment; consequently, for most occupations women can potentially compete on the same terms as men, though they may find themselves constrained by traditions and by accumulated power. These in combination help explain the paradox, in every advanced country, of the vast recruitment of middle-level-skill women into the labor force at a time when male employment is stagnant or even declining.

Since in the United States and some Western European countries the traditional pattern of socioeconomic segregation leaves low-skill workers trapped in the inner city, this gives rise to serious spatial as well as social inequalities. Low-skill, minimum-education workers, who previously could always find casual work at some equilibrium wage, may no longer be able to do so; these jobs have disappeared. Thus, attempts to revive inner-city economies may simply attract commuters who have the right skills, while local residents remain unemployed. The archetypal victim of this process is the young, often minority, high school dropout (Kasarda and Friedrichs 1986).

Castells, characterizing New York and Los Angeles, has described "a sharply stratified, segmented social structure that differentiates between upgraded labor, downgraded labor and excluded people," resulting from "increasing differentiation of labor in two equally dynamic sectors . . . the information-based formal economy, and the down-graded labor-based informal economy" (1989: 225). In the United States, determined attempts have been made over a long period to regenerate the urban economies, to provide comprehensive education and training, and to fight racial discrimination. Despite this, the percentage of blacks in poverty has begun again to increase. In fact America's black population has itself become polarized: part has rapidly raised itself into the middle-class salariat, whereas part has sunk ever deeper in the urban underclass (Farley 1984; Wilson 1978, 1996). This became apparent during the second half of the 1970s, a period when the American economy, too, was in recession.

Some American observers believe that this is a structural, not a cyclical phenomenon. As long ago as 1968, the economist Charles C. Killingworth identified a phenomenon that he labeled the "twist" in labor demand. He claimed that there had been a long-term fall in demand for low-skill, unqualified, poorly educated labor and a long-term rise in demand for high-skill, well-educated labor, and that these shifts were occurring faster than the corresponding shifts in the supply of labor. Demographic phenomena, the result of the baby boom in the United States from 1946 to 1958 and in the United Kingdom from 1955 to 1965, may have exacerbated this, some believe, by leading to a secular fall in educational quality and the development of a youth culture inimical to learning, on top of a previous glut of these low-skill jobs, which have been destroyed most rapidly in the inner urban areas because so many were in industries like manufacturing and warehousing, which have suffered particularly grievous losses in the inner cities. Wilson's studies of the American urban underclass show that during the 1980s there was a major shift in the economies of central cities, which lost huge numbers of manual jobs and gained white-collar jobs requiring at least a high school education.[4] And very similar evidence is emerging in both New York and London (Yaro and Hiss 1995; Fainstein et al. 1992; Great Britain Government Office for London 1996a).

If the problem is long-term and structural, then even the reflation of the economy will not deal with it. The United States offers a strong suspicion of this, where in the mid-1980s a fairly buoyant national economy continued to contain pockets of stubborn urban unemployment. Kasarda and Friedrichs, in comparing these phenomena in the New York region and in German cities, have confirmed a problem of mismatch between labor demand and supply: the urban economies, they argue, are no longer supplying the entry-level jobs that could be performed by an unskilled, unqualified labor force (Kasarda and Friedrichs 1986).

Thus there develops, in typical urban labor markets, the phenomenon of simultaneous high rates of unemployment, concentrated in certain groups, and high numbers of job vacancies: the one in no way matches the other. Another key indicator, very evident in London in recent years, has been huge variations in local residential unemployment rates between inner and outer boroughs sometimes not far apart (SERPLAN 1987). We are dealing here with segmented labor markets.

There is no expert agreement as to appropriate policy responses. "Chicago School" economists suggest that the remarkable success of the American economy in job creation, even in urban locations, is due to the effective operation of an equilibrium-wage labor market with relatively weak welfare underpinnings (Butler and Kondratas 1987). However, "radical" economists argue that the result is large numbers of people in dead-end, low-skill, "McDonald's"-type jobs, and point to evidence suggesting that the net change has been dominated by increases in low-wage jobs (Bluestone and Harrison 1987). Others disagree on the interpretation of the evidence, pointing out that in fact much of the growth in service jobs, even in the noninformation sectors, has been in relatively high-income jobs (gourmet restaurants rather than fast-food outlets).

An additional complication is that in the United States many of the low-income entry-level jobs have been filled by new immigrants, many illegal, who have been willing to accept the low wages and sometimes poor working conditions involved. This, of course, may be because they entirely lack a welfare floor. In any event, low-skill indigenous labor appears often unwilling to take such work, for reasons that are obscure and even controversial. Thus a paradox exists, especially in certain high-immigration American cities (e.g., Los Angeles, San Francisco), where immigrants may overtake the lower strata of the indigenous minority population.

The spatial implications of these mismatches are fairly clear. In general, the largest supplies of qualified labor are found in the middle-class suburbs. Long-continued suburbanization of population, which has been observable in the United States and Great Britain since the

1950s and progressively extended to the other countries of Western Europe during the 1960s and 1970s, has meant that these suburbs have become more and more separated from the historic downtown business cores (Cheshire and Hay 1989; Hall and Cheshire 1987). It is small wonder that large-scale decentralization of information-sector functions has been the eventual result; indeed, the surprise is rather that it did not occur earlier. As a study of London put it, there is thus "a growing polarization of society characterized by concentrated poverty, dependence, unemployment, and deterioration of the built environment for those left behind in the cities," wherein "secular stagnation of the economy accentuates the results of the current redistributions, designating places and people within them as either 'winners' or 'losers'" (Begg, Moore, and Rhodes 1986: 36).

Kasarda and Friedrichs have concluded that "under conditions of sustained national economic growth, a locality with a moderate amount of unemployment has much better prospects of economically rebounding and further reducing its unemployment rate than a locality with substantially larger portions of its labor force unemployed" (1986: 245). This assertion is challenged, however, by parallel British research on a relatively successful urban economy, that of Bristol. Here, the high-risk groups—the less-qualified young, the minorities— fail to get the jobs; employers are free to pick and choose, and they pick those whom they find suitable not merely in technical but also in social terms. The result is that the Bristol labor force, too, is polarized (Boddy, Lovering, and Bassett 1986: 207–12). Nevertheless, the fact remains that these high-risk groups have a better chance of a job in a growth area such as Bristol, or a new town, or one of the faster-growing towns around a metropolis (Buck and Gordon 1987).

The hope may paradoxically lie in a process now much noticed both in the United States and in Europe: the gentrification of the city, coupled with the conversion of old buildings to new uses, sometimes called Rousification, as exemplified by Quincy Market in Boston, South Street Seaport in New York, the Inner Harbor in Baltimore, and Covent Garden in London (Hall and Cheshire 1987). This process creates consumer-led service employment and associated construction, which may provide the basis for broad-based economic revival with jobs for a wide spectrum of skills and talents. The question must be: How many such cities can join in the process, and on what basis? Some evidence suggests that in America, more cities are joining, including some earlier identified as problem cities (such as St. Louis). But what will count, more than ever, is the general cultural and physical environment.

LESSONS FOR POLICY

During the late 1970s and early 1980s, the advanced industrial countries experienced a process of massive deindustrialization that had a profound impact on traditional spatial policy instruments (Bluestone and Harrison 1982; Massey and Meegan 1982). As firms in the declining older-established industries become more cautious about large-scale investment, traditional governmental inducements have lost appeal; and, because of the new emphasis on productivity, their payoff in terms of employment may be small. Newer high-technology and service jobs have helped compensate, but at rates that vary greatly from country to country and from region to region within the same country. It is small wonder that governments have become obsessively concerned with the encouragement of these newer sectors.

These structural changes have very clear spatial implications for regional and urban policies within the advanced industrial countries. The older industries are disproportionately concentrated in certain regions and certain cities: particularly, the specialized industrial centers that resulted from previous waves of technological innovation in the nineteenth and early twentieth centuries. As stated, in both the United States and Europe, the decline of manufacturing has been heavily concentrated in the old industrial heartlands (Bluestone and Harrison 1982; Cheshire and Hay 1989; Hall 1987a; Hall and Cheshire 1987). In sharp contrast, Sunbelt cities in states such as Texas and California have attracted new industrial activity. In Europe, growth in areas like the London-Bristol or Stuttgart-Munich corridors illustrates the same contrast: the newer industries are attracted to areas distant from the regions and cities of industrial decline (Hall, Breheny, et al. 1987).

Despite the demand for fresh regional/urban policies induced by structural changes in production, there is now a disjuncture between such policies and the reality of development; and this raises the question, how effective can government actions be? In the United Kingdom, a country that traditionally attempted a vigorous policy of regional development to steer growth into declining older industrial areas, other government programs—in science, education, and defense policy—were busy steering growth into quite different areas, ironically often to the areas targeted for diversion of growth by the other policy. And these latter, indirect, policies appear to have been massively more successful than the direct one.

The United States never had a regional policy on this scale. But, even there, while funds went into the regeneration of depressed rural areas like Appalachia, and other policies—Lyndon Johnson's Model Cities, Jimmy Carter's National Urban Policy—tried to shore up the troubled cities of the nation's manufacturing belt, defense/research policy diverted federal money into quite different areas.

Without new positive policies—perhaps even with them—the future will probably resemble the recent past. The growing high technology and service activities are unlikely to seek the same locations as the activities of the recent past, except for a few favored locations—such as Boston and Pittsburgh—that successfully promoted their universities as the basis of economic development. Recent evidence forcefully suggests, for instance, that in the United States, the biotechnology industry is strongly concentrating in a few major research centers like the San Francisco Bay Area and the Greater Boston area, which a generation before became the leading locations for the manufacture of information technology (Hall 1987a; Hall, Webber, et al. 1987, 1988).

Two contradictory prescriptions can be drawn from this analysis. One stresses the locational preferences of the new industries, and concludes that the right policy should be to encourage their growth almost wherever they may be. The other stresses the social costs to the older industrial regions, and concludes that there should be a new integration of regional-urban and educational-scientific policies to help such regions acquire a brand-new technological and business culture base. The two policies appear to point in different directions, with spatially different consequences. Nevertheless, it is possible to integrate them to some degree.

The limited evidence suggests that government policies can be crucial for certain kinds of industry at certain stages in their development: in particular, for defense-related industries at any time, and for many high-technology industries in their early stages (when they are most likely to be defense dependent). Assuming a positive industrial policy to divert research and development from defense into new global challenges, such as the environment, the same rules would appear to apply. It may be impossible to replicate this influence at later stages of development, because by then individual units have become large and have begun to enjoy internal economies of scale and agglomeration. But in the early stages, when firms are small and greatly dependent on outside procurement contracts, it may prove critical. The Silicon Valley, California, experience, in particular, suggests that research and development contracts can be used to create a major center of innovative research, which can then be spun off in the form of new firm creations grouped around a campus or other center of basic research (Saxenian 1985a, b, c).

Identifying the New Growth Sectors

All this suggests that it will be crucial to try to identify new industries in their innovative stage: the stage that electronics had reached in the late 1940s. There are some promising candidates:

1. commercial applications in biotechnology are emerging in increasing numbers, especially in agriculture, and

2. superconductivity, undoubtedly one of the major scientific breakthroughs of the century, seems to promise very rapid commercial applications (Mensch's "wagon train" effect) (Mensch 1989). The most important of these seem likely to be in the generation and transmission of electricity, promising much cheaper electricity generated by relatively benign sources of renewable energy (hydroelectric, solar) which may be transmitted over long distances; remarkable advances in computing power and in power-to-size and power-to-cost ratios; and development of new transportation systems based on magnetic levitation.

The implications of these for urban development are by no means clear. But two points can be made. First, in the past, the eventual major application of new scientific advances has seldom been grasped. In particular, the contribution of the steam engine and the internal combustion engine to locomotion was not appreciated at first. The same may well be true here. Second, major scientific/technological advances in the past have invariably involved the creation of a new infrastructure system that has proved to be the basis of an upswing in the world economy. This was true of railroads in the 1840s and 1850s, electrical power and telephone systems in the 1890s, and motorways and airports in the 1950s and 1960s.

One guess—it can be no more than that—is that superconductivity will result in a new system of transportation for people and goods, especially for longer-distance intercity travel. This will not take the form of magnetic-levitation trains, as now discussed, but of individual vehicles capable of being driven onto magnetic levitation paths. Such vehicles would need to be dual-mode with respect to power (internal combustion/electricity), roadbed (tires on road/magnetic levitation), and control (individual/automatic). These would require a totally new infrastructure either supplementing or replacing the motorway systems created in the 1950s and 1960s. A major question, which at present seems impossible to resolve, is whether or how far such a system could be extended to operate on ordinary city streets.

Whatever the case, such a system could presage an enormously extended deconcentration of cities, since it would combine the characteristics of very high speed and very low cost travel. This would provide a perfect complement to a low-cost informational economy based on the development of a true IT infrastructure network, as discussed earlier.

Identifying Relevant Policy Levers

For such promising developments, government scientific policies in each country would identify, for each major research and development area, a major university or research center in a region needing regional aid, and would concentrate research contracts there. The center would thus be assisted to attract the best research talent in the field. Such a center could not easily be built from scratch; it should already be an established center of excellence in its field, and furthermore it should preferably be well located in relation to national and international transportation and communication linkages. Then, a systematic effort would be made to build up small infant industries via a spin-off process, using small business policies specially tailored to provide incentives to set up close to the research center. Planned facilities for such new enterprises, in the form of science parks, may have some role here, but their role should not be exaggerated and they are certainly not sufficient in themselves (compare Taylor 1985; Worthington 1982); most importantly, they need to be planned in relation to the overall thrust of the scientific effort.

The producer-service sector does not appear to be as readily susceptible to any form of government influence; ill-judged regional subsidies may merely assist existing employers who do not necessarily need the support. Rather, policy should recognize that such services grow up in response to the demands placed by other sectors—as, for instance, by high-technology firms for services like accounting and legal services. Work by researchers at the British Department of Employment (Robertson, Briggs, and Goodchild 1982) suggests that some one-fifth of jobs in what they call miscellaneous services, including producer services and some consumer services, are derived from demand in the manufacturing sector. Locally, of course, these effects might be stronger. Well-conceived regional planning policies, including transportation and land-use planning policies, may be relevant here in encouraging the development of one city in the region as the best-favored producer service center, servicing a cluster of manufacturing firms in the surrounding area.

Certain kinds of producer services, analysis suggests, are not so immediately dependent on local regional demand. But these tend to locate in the highest-level international centers that are least susceptible to national policy intervention. The most that might be possible here is to encourage international transportation and communications linkages—such as the development of an international airport, or the concentration of high-quality telecommunications services—as an incentive to firms in the international business sector, which may be amenable to this kind of service. Two recent policy reports on the development of northern England, for instance, have suggested that the city of Manchester, traditionally the region's strongest independent commercial center and the location of its busiest international airport, should be built up in this way, by the establishment of a very high-speed train service from London, the development of regional transit systems, and the creation of a "wired city" for top-quality telecommunications (Breheny, Hall, and Hart 1987; Town and Country Planning Association 1987). This is speculative, since relatively little is known about the factors that may influence the higher-level producer service industries. But the experience of two of Britain's most successful second-order cities, Bristol and Cardiff, in attracting financial services suggests that a strategy of this kind could be successful.

One sector that has recently attracted attention is the cultural and creative industries, including both live arts (galleries, museums, theatres, concerts) and the electronic and print media (Hall 1995; Landry and Bianchini 1995a, 1995b; Landry et al. 1995). Evidence suggests that they were a major contributor of new jobs to the London economy in the 1980s (London Planning Advisory Committee 1991). The likelihood now is that there will be increasing convergence of these activities with high-technology manufacturing, in the form of multimedia. Significantly, in California, the two major centers of the new industry are the Los Angeles area, around the old Hollywood studios and the so-called "Aerospace Alley," and the San Francisco Bay Area, not only in the Silicon Valley, but in downtown San Francisco (Scott 1995).

Policies to affect such developments are likely to have effect, if at all, only in the medium term. Evidence from past history suggests that triggering impulses, of the sort that promote the development of new industries in new industrial regions, may take some 15 to 20 years to have a major effect: witness the development of Detroit as an automobile center between 1895 and 1915, or the parallel development of the Silicon Valley between 1940 and 1960. This is consistent with the notion of 55-year Kondratieff cycle that begins in the trough of each major depression. If today's policies bear fruit, they are likely to do so in the early twenty-first century at the earliest.

The Role of Technology

There are likely to be two major technological developments in the 1990s, which should have a particular impact on the location of economic activity. The first is *the convergence of computing and telecommunications into an integrated user-friendly system* offering a great variety of informational services from a variety of standardized entry points (Mitchell 1995; Negroponte 1995). These services will include the development of multimedia systems combining computer and advanced television services (Scott 1995), and the increasing use of electronic notebooks linked to a variety of personalized telephone systems. Theoretically, such a system would permit the almost infinite dispersion of informational activities across nations and continents, including the spread of homework and telecommuting. Practically, however, all the empirical evidence so far points to the opposite: technical advance will be most rapid in the existing centers of informational exchange, above all in the world cities, where demand produces a response in the form of rapid innovation and high-level service competition; conversely, peripheral regions will remain locked into a vicious circle of low demand and low innovation. So the most likely outcome is further development of the Castells (1989) schema: an exceptionally high level of concentrated control from the global centers and the innovative milieux, core-to-ring dispersion within these leading regions, and a limited degree of longer-distance decentralization to new regional centers, especially in fast-developing regions of the world.

The other development will be the spread of *high-speed train systems*. The pioneers were the Japanese, with the original Tokaido Shinkansen of 1964; but during the 1980s the Europeans, especially the French, have taken a leading role. It seems virtually certain that the 1990s will see completion of at least a skeletal European network linking the national capitals and leading provincial cities, and taking much of the present air traffic up to a critical limit of about 500 miles, as has already been observed on the first TGV (*Train à Grande Vitesse*) line from Paris to Lyons. Meanwhile the Japanese are working on their alternative linear motor technology, which, unlike the European system, demands a completely new dedicated infrastructure.

The outcome of the competition will clearly depend on a host of factors including speed, cost, the capacity of the existing system for upgrading, and the degree of existing congestion. At present, the first factor is highly uncertain. The latest TGV technology has achieved 320 miles (over 500 km) per hour on test and 188 miles per hour in regular service; indications are that it might eventually run at up to 240 miles per hour. The Japanese plan to operate their linear motor car at 300 miles per hour, perhaps more. Because conditions are so different, it seems likely that the Japanese technology will be used there but not in Europe. A critical unknown is whether the United States—so far virgin territory for the new train technologies—will buy either technology, or both. Several critical factors make the situation in the United States different from either Japan or Europe: average distances between cities are much greater, so that a single national high-speed system is unlikely; airline deregulation may create fiercer competition for the trains; and there are strong political pressures for an indigenous American maglev initiative. The first winner, in spring 1990, appears to have been the French TGV technology, which has been the successful bidder for the proposed Texas system.

These systems will boost the fortunes of the cities they serve, particularly those that gain early connection. Both Shinkansen and the TGV seem to have aided their terminal cities (Tokyo/Osaka, Paris/ Lyons) while weakening intermediate cities (Nagoya). The general likelihood is that the trains will disproportionately assist the major centers, particularly those that permit direct and easy transfers with air for long-distance trips. Several European cities, led by Paris, are actively working on such links. So the new rail technologies will boost the fortunes of the global metropolises, while perhaps further aiding the development of subcenters at accessible points within their regions, as has already occurred at Reading, 40 miles (60 km) west of London and Omiya, 20 miles (35 km) northwest of Tokyo, which are the first stopping-points in Britain and Japan's respective high-speed train lines.

Overall, therefore, the new technologies are likely to promote concentration at the top of the urban hierarchy rather than the reverse. But the exact mode of their operation will depend, as previously throughout urban history, on the fortunes that shape that hierarchy.

This means that the form of the high-speed network, and in particular its hub points, will be crucial for competitiveness in the informational age. A special role is almost certain to be played by the relatively few interconnection points between the rail and intercontinental air services. In Europe, where this is understood well, the French are already planning a megadevelopment around Paris's Charles de Gaulle airport, and the Germans are seriously contemplating moving the main Frankfurt train station to the airport. These two cities are likely to compete with each other, and with Brussels, for the title of the top informational cities of Europe. The French have also routed their TGV Nord line—the future European trunk line—with a major interchange at Lille, that somewhat deindustrialized industrial capital of the Nord–Pas de Calais region, thus launching it into the informational age.

Less clear is the impact of changes in *information technologies*. The overwhelming evidence, from the research so far, is that something like a process of circular and cumulative causation occurs here. Areas with existing concentrations of informational industries make the heaviest demands for information technology. Within the European Union, for instance, there are big variations even in telephone subscribers per 100 inhabitants: in the United Kingdom between London (42) and Northern Ireland (23); in Germany, between West Berlin (53) and Regensburg (24); in France between Paris (42) and Franche Comté or Lorraine (23). Even more extreme differences exist for Telex and Prestel (Goddard and Gillespie 1988: 137–39). Within Britain, the ratio of international to local calls (UK = 100) for the South East is 211, for the North, 36. Even at the consumer level, semi-anecdotal evidence suggests that personal computer ownership in Great Britain—overall, by far the highest in Western Europe—may vary from 35–41 percent in the Southeast, to 7–18 percent in the North, 7–9 percent in Wales, and as little as 1–7 percent in Scotland (Batty 1988: 162; Steinle 1988: 82–83). So services are most heavily concentrated in the Southeast, and innovations will occur there first, even if they spread fairly rapidly to other parts of the country. Further, specialized technical services are always more readily available there. And in turn, this encourages the development of yet more specialized firms, both in the provision of hardware and software and in the production of information based on that foundation.

Thus, the information-rich regions—London, Paris, Frankfurt—get even richer, while the poor regions become relatively ever poorer. This is paradoxical, because it flies in the face of the technological forecasting literature, which suggests that IT brings a diffusion and an evening-out of advantage across the whole territory.[5] That would be true only if the process of technological adoption were supply-led; but research suggests that it appears to be demand-led. So there is an accelerating center-periphery contrast. And this feeds back into transportation investments: the new high-speed trains will connect these major business centers, which also happen to be the location of the major hub airports; this, in turn, will reinforce the position of these centers as the critical nodes in the international system of information generation and exchange.

The research stresses, however, that there is one major exception to this rule. Within the information-rich regions, firms are sensitive to costs—both of rents and of salaries. So, unless their activities have a pressing need to locate in the very core, they will tend to migrate to the periphery of those regions in search of lower rents and easier access to their labor force, which disproportionately consists of middle-skill, middle-income women in suburban homes. This explains the phenomenon of local decentralization, to which I referred earlier. Here, technological innovation does play an important role in deconcentration, by allowing easy interconnection and exchange of information between a number of office centers, both central and peripheral.

The critical question is just how widely this process of deconcentration may go, and here the evidence is as yet ambiguous. Overwhelmingly the main beneficiaries, so far, have been the kinds of suburban centers earlier quoted. But in England there is evidence of wider diffusion of some of these routine processes, such as credit card payments, to more distant locations; and in the United States some such operations are being moved to very remote locations like the Dakotas, where a supply of well-educated small-town women exists. There is also the much-cited movement of operations like airline ticket checking to the Caribbean, which may be the start of a wider trend.

The critical limitation here, however, is not the technology—800-style telephone numbers, free to the caller, now operate internationally—but the supply of suitable labor. True, Best Western reservations are made from the Arizona Female Penitentiary, but this is unusual; generally, the kind of labor that is needed is especially concentrated in suburban locations. So, most likely, the prospect is that the higher-level informational industries will continue to be concentrated in the highest-level metropolitan areas—the so-called world cities—but that there will be a crucial differentiation: contact-intensive activities will continue to concentrate in the core, while the more routine activities will disperse to the edge and will, paradoxically, reconcentrate there.

There could be a change in this, if information technology—such as videoconferencing—allowed these contact-intensive activities, too, to escape from the central cores. But there is no hint that this is happening. On the contrary, in many world cities, central office rents have escalated because of the competition for space; the rent gradient between the central core and a location in the near suburbs only half a mile to a mile distant is now about 4:1 in London; beyond that point, it flattens, so that major decentralization sites like Reading, 40 miles

(60 km) distant, may command rents as high as the London suburbs. The most likely explanation is the one proffered by John Goddard (1975) in his earlier work more than two decades ago: that unprogrammed decisions, requiring random information not gleaned through information technology, are the ones that will stay in the center and are the really important ones.

Another illustration of the rule of metropolitan concentration of IT is the growth of the professional conference or convention center. If information technology were truly capable of what its proponents allege, there would be no need for gatherings of professionals at all. But, as we all know, this is one of the most dynamic forms of business tourism, which in turn is one of the most dynamic forms of tourism. One can conclude that people have an almost insatiable need for the kind of information they get in prepublished form as well as in the corridors and bars: the informal part of the formal informational economy. The location of the leading business conferences would be an important subject for research. It is, of course, constrained by the availability of hotel accommodations, which favors major business cities or major resorts.

From the foregoing, one can conceive of the outlines of a new urban hierarchy on an international and a national scale, one no longer based primarily on the production and exchange of goods but on the production and exchange of information. Particularly notable are two facts: first, in most parts of the world, nation-states so far persist,[6] which gives their capital cities disproportionate importance compared with a continental-scale nation-state like the United States; second, the accidents of national unification may produce skewed urban hierarchies like those of Italy or Spain, where two or three metropolitan areas compete for primacy. An especially important question for Europe is whether achievement of the Single European Act in 1992, coupled with the development of the new high-speed train network, radically reshapes the urban hierarchy along continental rather than national lines. The major developers are presumably betting that this will happen; hence, their obsessive interest in megaprojects within some cities.

CONCLUSION: NEW RULES OF THE GAME

My main conclusion is that there is some hope everywhere. Every city can try. The iron laws of location, which gave us the Weberian locational triangle, are no longer so unmalleable. And the new informational industries respond to quite different rules—rules that are more flexible. The transition from the goods-handling to the information-handling economy is creating something like laissez-faire competition among cities.

The changes are not equal. But the disadvantages are no longer of the permanent, immutable kind: they can be changed by public and by collective private action. A new or enhanced university system; a new airport or a new high-speed train link; or a decision to create a major entertainment or cultural complex in a decayed port or warehouse area can transform at least part of a city's economy, and this will create multiplier effects that will spread to some degree through the urban economy. But not entirely: the uneven quality of these impacts, particularly their failure to reach the most deprived and the most excluded, is the remaining enigma to which policy has as yet no answer.

Notes

1. That conclusion, however, may have been biased by being based on data for 1970–80, a decade when New York was in severe travail while places like Houston and Denver boomed; the 1980s record may look very different.

2. These were the centers that Smith (1967) called grade 3A as distinct from the grade 2 (regional centers).

3. The functional urban region is a concept similar to the metropolitan statistical area used in American statistics. First used by Hall and Hay (1980), the FUR is the basis of the analysis in Cheshire and Hay (1989). For a fuller explanation, see Cheshire's chapter 5 in this volume.

4. New York City lost 600,000 manual jobs and gained 700,00 white-collar jobs; corresponding figures for Philadelphia were 280,000 and 178,000; for St. Louis, 127,000 and 51,000 (Wilson 1987: 102).

5. It is notable, however, that even the greatest technological enthusiasts still admit that face-to-face contact in central cities will remain significant (Mitchell 1995, for example).

6. Indeed, since this paper was originally written, there is dramatic evidence that nationalism is leading to the breakup of formerly monolithic units.

References

Andersson, Å. E. 1985a. "Creativity and Regional Development." *Papers of the Regional Science Association* 56: 5–20.

————. 1985b. *Kreativitet: StorStadens Framtid*. Stockholm: Prisma.

Andersson, Å. E., and U. Strömquist. 1988. *K-Samhällets Framtid*. Stockholm: Prisma.

Aydalot, P., ed. 1986a. *Milieux Innovateurs en Europe*. Paris: GREMI (privately printed).

————. 1986b. "Trajectoires technologiques et milieux innovateurs." In *Milieux Innovateurs en Europe*, edited by P. Aydalot (345–61). Paris: GREMI (privately printed).

————. 1988. "Technological Trajectories and Regional Innovation in Europe." In *High Technology Industry and Innovative Environments: The European Experience*, edited by P. Aydalot and D. Keeble (22–47). London: Routledge and Kegan Paul.

Aydalot, P., and D. Keeble, eds. 1988a. *High-Technology Industry and Innovative Environments: The European Experience*. London: Routledge and Kegan Paul.

————. 1988b. "High-Technology Industry and Innovative Environments in Europe: An Overview." In *High Technology Industry and Innovative Environments: The European Experience*, edited by P. Aydalot and D. Keeble (1–21). London: Routledge and Kegan Paul.

Baran, B. 1985. "Office Automation and Women's Work: The Technological Transformation of the Insurance Industry." In *High Technology, Space, and Society. Urban Affairs Annual Reviews* 28, edited by M. Castells. Beverly Hills, Calif., and London: Sage Publications.

Batty, M. 1988. "Home Computers and Regional Development: An Exploratory Analysis of the Spatial Market for Home Computers in Britain." In *Informatics and Regional Development*, edited by M. Giaoutzi and P. Nijkamp (147–65). Aldershot, England: Avebury.

Beers, D. 1987. "Tomorrowland: We Have Seen the Future and It is Pleasanton." *Image (San Francisco Chronicle/Examiner Sunday Magazine)*, Jan. 18.

Begg, I., B. Moore, and J. Rhodes. 1986. "Economic and Social Change in Urban Britain and the Inner Cities." In *Critical Issues in Urban Economic Development*, vol. 1, edited by V.A. Hausner (10–49). Oxford: Oxford University Press.

Bluestone, B., and B. Harrison. 1982. *The Deindustrialization of America: Plant Closings, Community Abandonment, and the Dismantling of Basic Industry*. New York: Basic Books.

————. 1987. "The Grim Truth about the Job 'Miracle.'" *New York Times*, Feb. 1.

Boddy, M., J. Lovering, and K. Bassett. 1986. *Sunbelt City: A Study of Economic Change in Britain's M4 Growth Corridor*. Oxford: Oxford University Press.

Breheny, M., P. Hall, and D. Hart. 1987. *Northern Lights: A Development Agenda for the North in the 1990s*. Preston, England: Derrick, Wade and Waters.

Brotchie, J., P. Hall, and P. Newton, eds. 1987. *The Spatial Impact of Technical Change*. London: Croom Helm.

Buck, N., and I. Gordon. 1987. "The Beneficiaries of Employment Growth: An Analysis of the Experience of Disadvantaged Groups in Expanding Labour Markets." In *Critical Issues in Urban Economic Development*, vol. 1, edited by V.A. Hausner (77–115). Oxford: Oxford University Press.

Buck, N., I. Gordon, and K. Young. 1987. *The London Employment Problem*. Oxford: Oxford University Press.

Buswell, R. J., and E. W. Lewis. 1970. "The Geographical Distribution of Industrial Research Activity in the United Kingdom." *Regional Studies* 4: 297–306.

Butler, Stuart M., and A. Kondratas. 1987. *Out of the Poverty Trap: A Conservative Strategy for Welfare Reform*. New York: Free Press.

Castells, M., ed. 1985. *High Technology, Space, and Society. Urban Affairs Annual Reviews* 28. Beverly Hills, Calif., and London: Sage Publications.

———. 1989. *The Informational City: Information Technology, Economic Restructuring, and the Urban-Regional Process*. Oxford: Basil Blackwell.

Cheshire, P. C., and D. G. Hay. 1989. *Urban Problems in Western Europe: An Economic Analysis*. London: Unwin Hyman.

Clark, C. 1940. *The Conditions of Economic Progress*. London: Macmillan.

Cohen, S. S., and J. Zysman. 1987. *Manufacturing Matters: The Myth of the Post-Industrial Economy*. New York: Basic Books.

Daniels, P. W. 1985. *Service Industries: A Geographical Appraisal*. London: Methuen.

———. 1986. "Producer Services and the Post-Industrial Space Economy." In *The Geography of De-Industrialisation*, edited by R. L. Martin and R. Rowthorn (291–321). London: Macmillan.

Daniels, P. W., and B. P. Holly. 1983. "Office Location in Transition: Observations on Research in Great Britain and North America." *Environment and Planning* A (15): 1.

Evans, A. W. 1973. "The Location of the Headquarters of Industrial Companies." *Urban Studies* 10: 387–96.

Ewers, H.-J., H. Matzerath, and J. B. Goddard, eds. 1986. *The Future of the Metropolis: Economic Aspects*. Berlin: de Gruyter.

Fainstein, S., I. Gordon, and M. Harloe, eds. 1992. *Divided Cities: New York and London in the Contemporary World*. Oxford: Blackwell.

Farley, R. 1984. *Blacks and Whites: Narrowing the Gap*. Cambridge, Mass.: Harvard University Press.

Gershuny, J. 1978. *After Industrial Society? The Emerging Self-Service Economy*. London: Macmillan.

Gershuny, J., and I. Miles. 1983. *The New Service Economy: The Transformation of Employment in Industrial Societies.* London: Frances Pinter.

Gillespie, A. E., and A. E. Green. 1987. "The Changing Geography of Producer Services Employment in Britain." *Regional Studies* 21: 397–411.

Goddard, J. B. 1975. *Office Location in Urban and Regional Development.* Oxford: Oxford University Press.

Goddard, J., and A. Gillespie. 1988. "Advanced Telecommunications and Regional Economic Development." In *Informatics and Regional Development,* edited by M. Giaoutzi and P. Nijkamp (121–46). Aldershot, England: Avebury.

Goddard, J. B., and D. Morris. 1975. *The Communications Factor in Office Decentralization.* Oxford: Pergamon Press.

Goddard, J. B., and I. J. Smith. 1975. "Changes in Corporate Control in the British Urban System, 1972–1977." *Environment and Planning A* (10): 1,073–84.

Great Britain Government Office for London. 1996a. *London in the U.K. Economy: A Planning Perspective.* London: G.O.L./D.O.E.

————. 1996b. *Four World Cities: A Comparative Analysis of London, Paris, New York and Tokyo.* London: Llewelyn Davies Planning.

Green, A. E., and J. Howells. 1987. "Spatial Prospects for Service Growth in Britain." *Area* 19: 111–22.

Haig, R. M. 1926. "Toward an Understanding of the Metropolis." *Quarterly Journal of Economics* 40: 179–208, 402–34.

Hall, P. 1987a. "The Anatomy of Job Creation: Nations, Regions and Cities in the 1960s and 1970s." *Regional Studies* 21: 95–106.

————. 1987b. "The Geography of High-Technology Industry: An Anglo-American Comparison." In *The Spatial Impact of Technical Change,* edited by J. Brotchie, P. Hall, and P. Newton (141–56). London: Croom Helm.

————. 1987c. "Perspectives on Post-Industrial Society: Britain, America, and the World." In *The Spatial Impact of Technical Change,* edited by J. Brotchie, P. Hall, and P. Newton (3–17). London: Croom Helm.

————. 1991. "Moving Information: A Tale of Four Technologies." In *Cities in the 21st Century,* edited by J. Brotchie, M. Batty, and P. Hall. London: Unwin Hyman.

————. 1995. "The Roots of Urban Innovation: Culture, Technology and the Urban Order." *Urban Futures* 19: 41–52.

Hall, P., and P. C. Cheshire. 1987. "The Key to Success for Cities." *Town and Country Planning* 56: 50–51.

Hall, P., and D. Hay. 1980. *Growth Centres in the European Urban System.* London: Heinemann Education.

Hall, P., and P. Preston. 1988. *The Carrier Wave: New Information Technology and the Geography of Innovation 1846–2003.* London: Unwin Hyman.

Hall, P., M. Breheny, R. McQuaid, and D. Hart. 1987. *Western Sunrise: The Genesis and Growth of Britain's Major High Tech Corridor.* London: Allen and Unwin.

Hall, P., M. M. Webber, L. Bornstein, and R. Grier. 1987. "Where Biotechnology Locates." *Built Environment* 13: 152–56.

―――. 1988. *Biotechnology: The Next Industrial Frontier.* Working Paper 474, Institute of Urban and Regional Development. Berkeley, Calif.: Institute of Urban and Regional Development.

Hausner, V. A. 1986. *Critical Issues in Urban Economic Development,* vol. 1. Oxford: Oxford University Press.

―――. 1987. *Critical Issues in Urban Economic Development,* vol. 2. Oxford: Oxford University Press.

Hoover, E. M., and R. Vernon. 1959. *Anatomy of a Metropolis: The Changing Distribution of People and Jobs within the New York Metropolitan Region.* Cambridge: Harvard University Press.

Howells, J. R. L. 1984. "The Location of Research and Development: Some Observations and Evidence from Britain." *Regional Studies* 18: 13–29.

Howells, J., and A. E. Green. 1986. "Location, Technology and Industrial Organisation in U.K. Services." *Progress in Planning* 26 (pt. 2). Oxford: Pergamon Journals.

Kasarda, J., and J. Friedrichs. 1986. "Comparative Demographic-Employment Mismatches in U.S. and West German Cities." In *The Future of the Metropolis: Economic Aspects,* edited by H.-J. Ewers, H. Matzerath, and J. B. Goddard (221–49). Berlin: de Gruyter.

Killingworth, C. M. 1969. "The Continuing Labor Market Twist." *Monthly Labor Review* 91(9): 12–17.

Landry, C., and F. Bianchini. 1995a. *The Creative City.* London: Demos/Comedia.

―――. 1995b. "Creativity: Unleashing a Resource for Urban Management." *Urban Futures* 17: 53–67.

Landry, C., F. Bianchini, K. Künzman, R. Ebert, and F. Guad. 1995. *The Creative City in Britain and Germany.* London: Anglo-German Foundation.

Malecki, E. J. 1980a. "Corporate Organization of R and D and the Location of Technological Activities." *Regional Studies* 14: 219–34.

―――. 1980b. "Science and Technology in the American Urban System." In *The American Metropolitan System: Past and Future,* edited by S. D. Brunn and J. O. Wheeler. London: Edward Arnold.

―――. 1981. "Government-Funded R & D: Some Regional Economic Implications." *Professional Geographer* 33: 72–82.

Markusen, A., P. Hall, and A. Glasmeier. 1986. *High-Tech America: The What, How, Where and Why of the Sunrise Industries.* Boston: Allen and Unwin.

Markusen, A., P. Hall, S. Campbell, and S. Deitrick. 1990. *The Rise of the Gunbelt: The Military Remapping of Industrial America.* New York: Oxford University Press.

Marshall, J. N. 1982. "Linkages between Manufacturing Industry and Business Services." *Environment and Planning A* (14): 1,523–40.

————. 1988. *Services and Uneven Development.* Oxford: Oxford University Press.

Martin, R. L., and R. Rowthorn, eds. 1986. *The Geography of De-Industrialisation.* London: Macmillan.

Massey, D., and Meegan, R. 1982. *The Anatomy of Job Loss: The How, Why and Where of Employment Decline.* London: Methuen.

Mensch, G. 1989. *Stalemate in Technology: Innovations Overcome the Depression.* Cambridge, Mass.: Ballinger.

Mills, E. 1987. "Service Sector Suburbanization." In *America's New Economic Geography: Nation, Region, and Central City,* edited by G. Sternlieb. New Brunswick: Rutgers University, Center for Urban Policy Research.

Mitchell, W. J. 1995. *City of Bits: Space, Place, and the Infobahn.* Cambridge, Mass.: MIT Press.

Negroponte, N. 1995. *Being Digital.* London: Hodder & Stoughton.

Nelson, K. 1986. "Labor Demand, Labor Supply and the Suburbanization of Low-Wage Office Work." In *Production, Work, Territory: The Geographical Anatomy of Industrial Capitalism,* edited by A. J. Scott and M. Storper. Boston: Allen and Unwin.

Noyelle, T. J., and T. M. Stanback. 1984. *The Economic Transformation of American Cities.* Totowa, N.J.: Rowman and Allanheld.

Oakey, R. P., A. T. Thwaites, and P. A. Nash. 1980. "The Regional Distribution of Innovative Manufacturing Establishments in Britain." *Regional Studies* 14: 235–53.

Piore, M. J., and C. F. Sabel. 1984. *The Second Industrial Divide: Possibilities for Prosperity.* New York: Basic Books.

Pred, A. 1977. *City-Systems in Advanced Economies: Past Growth, Present Processes and Future Development Options.* London: Hutchinson.

Reich, R. 1991. *The Work of Nations: Preparing Ourselves for 21st Century Capitalism.* New York: Random House.

Robertson, J. A. S., J. M. Briggs, and A. Goodchild. 1982. *Structure and Employment Prospects of the Service Industries,* Department of Employment Research Paper 3. London: Department of Employment.

Sassen, S. 1991. *The Global City.* Princeton: Princeton University Press.

Saxenian, A. 1985a. "The Genesis of Silicon Valley." In *Silicon Landscapes,* edited by P. Hall and A. Markusen. Boston: Allen and Unwin.

————. 1985b. "Innovative Manufacturing Industries: Spatial Incidence in the United States." In *High Technology, Space, and Society,* edited by M. Castells. *Urban Affairs Annual Reviews* 28: 55–80. Beverly Hills, Calif., and London: Sage Publications.

————. 1985c. "Silicon Valley and Highway 128: Regional Prototypes or Historic Exceptions?" In *High Technology, Space, and Society,* edited by M. Castells. *Urban Affairs Annual Reviews* 28: 81–105. Beverly Hills, Calif., and London: Sage Publications.

————. 1994. *Regional Advantage: Culture and Competition in the Silicon Valley and Route 128.* Cambridge, Mass.: Harvard University Press.

Scott, A. J. 1986. "High Technology Industry and Territorial Development: The Rise of the Orange County Complex, 1955–1984." *Urban Geography* 7: 3–45.

————. 1993. *Technopolis: High Technology Industry and Regional Development in Southern California.* Berkeley, Calif.: University of California Press.

————. 1995. *From Silicon Valley to Hollywood: Growth and Development of the Multimedia Industry in California.* Lewis Center for Regional Policy Studies Working Paper 13. Los Angeles, Calif.: University of California, Los Angeles.

Scott, A. J., and M. Storper, eds. 1986. *Production, Work, Territory: The Geographical Anatomy of Industrial Capitalism.* Boston: Allen and Unwin.

SERPLAN [London and South East Regional Planning Conference]. 1987. *Regional Trends in the South East: The South East Regional Monitor, 1986–87 (RPC 800).* London: SERPLAN.

Singelmann, J. 1978. *From Agriculture to Services: The Transformation of Industrial Employment.* Sage Library of Social Research, vol. 69. Beverly Hills, Calif.: Sage Publications.

Smith, R. D. P. 1967. "The Changing Urban Hierarchy." *Regional Studies* 2: 1–19.

Stanback, T. M. 1979. *Understanding the Service Economy: Employment, Productivity, Location.* Baltimore: Johns Hopkins University Press.

————. 1985. "The Changing Fortunes of Metropolitan Economies." In *High Technology, Space and Society,* edited by M. Castells. *Urban Affairs Annual Reviews* 28. Beverly Hills, Calif.: Sage Publications.

Stanback, T. M., and R. V. Knight. 1970. *The Metropolitan Economy: The Process of Employment Expansion.* New York: Columbia University Press.

Stanback, T. M., and T. J. Noyelle. 1982. *Cities in Transition: Changing Job Structures in Atlanta, Denver, Buffalo, Phoenix, Columbus (Ohio), Nashville, Charlotte.* Totowa, N. J.: Allanheld, Osmun.

Stanback, T. M., P. J. Beare, T. J. Noyelle, and R. A. Karsach. 1981. *Services: The New Economy.* Totowa, N.J.: Allanheld, Osmun.

Steinle, W. J. 1988. "Telematics and Regional Development in Europe: Theoretical Considerations and Empirical Evidence." In *Informatics and Regional Development,* edited by M. M. Giaoutzi and P. Nijkamp (72–89). Aldershot, England: Avebury.

Taylor, T. 1985. "High-Technology Industry and the Development of Science Parks." In *Silicon Landscapes,* edited by P. Hall and A. Markusen (134–43). Boston: Allen and Unwin.

Thwaites, A. T. 1982. "Some Evidence of Regional Variations in the Introduction and Diffusion of Industrial Processes within British Manufacturing Industry." *Regional Studies* 16: 371–81.

Törnqvist, G. 1970. "Contact Systems and Regional Development." *Lund Series in Geography*, series b (35). Lund: Gleerup.

Town and Country Planning Association. 1987. *North-South Divide: A New Deal for Britain's Regions.* London: Town and Country Planning Association.

Tym, Roger, and Partners. 1981. *Capital of the North: The Business Service Sector in Inner Manchester/Salford.* Report to the Manchester/Salford Inner City Partnership. London: Author.

Westaway, J. 1974a. "Contact Potential and the Occupational Structure of the British Urban System, 1961–66: An Empirical Study." *Regional Studies* 8: 57–73.

_____. 1974b. "The Spatial Hierarchy of Business Organizations and Its Implications for the British Urban Systems." *Regional Studies* 8: 145–55.

Wilson, William Julius. 1978. *The Declining Significance of Race: Blacks and Changing American Institutions.* Chicago: University of Chicago Press.

_____. 1987. *The Truly Disadvantaged: The Inner City, the Underclass, and Pubic Policy.* Chicago: University of Chicago Press.

_____. 1996. *When Work Disappears: The World of the New Urban Poor.* New York: Knopf.

Worthington, J. 1982. "Industrial and Science Parks—Accommodating Knowledge Based Industries." In *Planning for Enterprise, Proceedings of a Council of Europe Urban Policies Seminar.* Swansea: City of Swansea.

Yaro, R. D., and A. Hiss. 1996. *A Region at Risk: The Third Regional Plan for the New York-New Jersey-Connecticut Metropolitan Area.* Washington, D.C.: Island Press.

Chapter Four

PATTERNS AND PROCESSES OF EMPLOYMENT AND POPULATION DECENTRALIZATION IN THE UNITED STATES

Peter D. Linneman and Anita A. Summers

The decentralization of urban employment and of population has occurred steadily in the United States at least since the turn of the century. These decentralization processes occurred both within and between metropolitan areas. There has been movement from the central city to the suburbs, and from the older, densest urban areas in the Northeast and Midwest to the newer urban centers of the South and West. These decentralization patterns have been particularly pronounced in the post–World War II period. This chapter documents this process and examines its course.

During the last forty years, many developments have tipped the balance in favor of this decentralization process. Modern interstate highways, and particularly their suburban circular beltways, have combined with mass automobile ownership to enable choice in the concept of urban accessibility. Formerly, nearness to the central city core had been the primary option. Now access to good highway connections was added. Further, as automobile ownership has risen to more than one car per family for the majority of Americans, members of suburban households no longer have to work in a single location or to rely on publicly provided transportation (as opposed to publicly provided road surfaces). Airplanes have become the major long-distance intercity "people movers," particularly since the deregulation of the late 1970s. However, due to noise considerations and the land requirements of modern airports, these facilities have almost without exception been located at ever greater distances from the core of the central city. Just as the great train stations were once powerful magnets for those with intercity business and vacation travel demands, distant suburban airports now beckon both employers and residents to move outward for convenient intercity travel.

Also fueling suburbanization have been the evolution of refrigeration and the advent of frozen and convenience foods. Households no longer need to "go to the market" each day to obtain quality food. Instead, less frequent visits to conveniently located supermarkets allow shoppers to "load up" on food products that are then transported home in their cars. The technological revolution of food processing has freed urban dwellers from the need to be near smaller neighborhood markets and has encouraged the employment decentralization of production processes such as meat packing. Similarly, to serve the suburbanizing population, new shopping centers, resembling enclosed and modernized versions of traditional downtowns, were developed to satisfy retail needs. These new shopping centers were technologically designed to deal with the preferences of modern consumers and are more efficient in satisfying these preferences than the more dated downtown shopping areas of the central city.

The movements to the southern and western parts of the United States were greatly spurred in the post–World War II period by a number of technological innovations, including air conditioning, modern water service technology, mass airplane travel, and modern telecommunications. The evolution of high-speed air travel for mass intercity transportation has meant that no pair of cities in the United States is more than about five hours apart. Similarly, modern telecommunications allow people to remain in close contact for personal or business exchanges even though separated by hundreds, or thousands, of miles. The spread of television, cablevision, and video recorders means that most popular forms of entertainment and culture are now available to relatively distant parts of urban areas, as well as to remote parts of the country. Thus, moving away from the core of the city and its "culture" no longer translates into missing performances by the Philadelphia Symphony, the Philadelphia Eagles, or the hot new theatrical release. The enjoyment of these formerly exclusively central-city urban amenities is now available to almost all consumers in the country, albeit not as a perfect substitute, wherever they work or live.

In view of these changing technological factors, it is not surprising that despite many offsetting, focused efforts to invigorate central cities, massive employment and population decentralization have occurred. Residents, particularly high-income households, have long struggled with the fact that, if they live in the city, they face severe trade-offs such as convenience to work, and cultural and market diversity, against the disamenities of noise, congestion, dirt, and crime. These trade-offs are not new. Jackson (1985) noted that a clay tablet dating back to 539 B.C. reads: "Our property seems to me to be the most beautiful in the world. It is so close to Babylon that we enjoy all the advantages of the city, and yet when we come home we are away from all the noise and dust."[1] Although our cities are, it is hoped, cleaner and less disease-ridden than Babylon in 539 B.C., they are noisier, more congested, and more crime-ridden (particularly in terms of violent crime) than ever before. At the same time, suburban locations are more accessible, more convenient, and better developed than ever before. Increasingly, employment sites, sports complexes, cultural facilities, and shopping facilities have moved out to the mass consumption markets of the suburbs. All of these factors have greatly reduced the vibrancy of our urban cores as places to live. In addition, the emergence of "street people" on the main thoroughfares of our urban cores (as opposed to the institutions and "skid row" locations to which they had been relegated) only adds to the unattractiveness of living, visiting, shopping, or working in our central cities. There has, however, been a growing body of evidence on the economic interdependencies between cities and suburbs (Downs 1994; Voith 1992 and 1994; Orfield 1995; Adams 1994; Brooks and Summers 1997; Persky and Wiewel 1997). Together, these studies show that, though metropolitan area suburbs grow as their central cities decline, they grow less if their core declines more. There are significant externalities associated with declining cities, and that effect became pronounced during the 1980s.

The legal structure of the U.S. political system has also exacerbated the relative decline of our cities, as it provides a great deal of autonomy to local governments. As a result, higher-income families are able to leave our central cities, move to the suburbs, and then establish statutes that make it increasingly difficult for new residents to move into these areas, unless any potential new residents are willing to pay more in local taxes than they cost in terms of local public services. Families who are "fiscal deficits" find themselves locked into their current central city locations, partially because of these zoning constraints and partially by the relatively high costs of construction. Over time, the central cities have lost some of their tax bases, as well as their diversity, through an adverse selection process that allows a central city's "fiscal surplus" families to choose the suburbs, while forcing its "fiscal deficit" families to elect a city location. This process increases the per capita tax burden in the central cities—further accelerating the process. Recent estimates of the magnitudes of the costs of poverty that cities are bearing from their own-source revenues show them to be very sustantial (Pack 1995; Summers and Jakubowski 1996; Summers and Ritter 1996; Gyourko 1997). The buoyancy of the American economy has, on a superficial level, mitigated the fiscal problems of the troubled cities in the last few years. But the failure to respond to their structural problems—the extent to which they are caretakers of the nation's poor and immigrants—continues to show up in population declines.

As Anthony Downs pointed out in chapter 2 of this volume, another peculiarly American problem that has interacted with the preceding factors to accelerate the relative decline of central cities is the location of low-income public housing projects. In many cities throughout the world these projects are scattered and placed at the distant fringes of the city. In the United States, however, these large public housing projects are generally located in the core areas of our cities, so that the downtowns service large numbers of the poorer populations, rather than the broader urban population base—people tend to shop where they live. Further, the large number of "fiscal deficit" families in these public housing projects have, in a sense, been given incentives to live in the most central parts of our cities. This contributes to the frequency with which cities face the financial crises described by Helen Ladd in chapter 11 of this volume. If crime and other forms of social dysfunction that are associated with low income are added to the description, some negative impacts on the vitality of cities of locating public housing projects in the inner core become clear. (This stands in sharp contrast to the location decisions made in European cities, described by Duncan Maclennan in chapter 16 of this volume.)

These are the overall, pervasive trends. But there are significant differences among and within urban areas in the emergent patterns. This chapter explores the patterns of urban population and employment decentralization over the period 1970–87. The analysis is divided into two subperiods for population—1970–80 and 1980–87—and two subperiods for establishment-based job growth—1976–80 and 1980–86. Specifically, the annualized percentage change of both establishment-based employment and population for several distinct geographic categories is studied: the central business district (CBD), the rest of the legally defined central city (RCC), and the individual suburbs that constitute the area outside of the central city (OCC). Together, these geographical units comprise the metropolitan statistical area (MSA). The analysis reveals that simple statements about cities versus suburbs can be misleading. All parts of the city are not alike—in particular, the distinction between the CBD and the RCC is considered. Similarly, all suburban communities are not alike—the distinction among different suburban communities is a key part of our analysis. The exploitation of these geographical distinctions distinguishes our work from the preceding literature.

The next section of this chapter describes the massive data collection task supporting our analysis. The third section examines the patterns of employment growth for each major component of the largest U.S. metropolitan areas between 1976–80 and 1980–86. The fourth section presents the patterns of urban population decentralization, followed, in the fifth section, by an exploratory econometric analysis of the determinants of both population and employment growth. The chapter ends with a summary and conclusions.

THE DATA

Differing research strategies may be used to combine theory with data. Some regard theory as the only path to molding empirical observations into an understanding of economic phenomena; others believe data are there to be learned from. We align ourselves in the latter camp with Sherlock Holmes, who stated, "It is a capital mistake to theorize before one has data. Insensibly one begins to twist facts to suit theories, instead of theories to suit facts" (Doyle 1967).

Many elaborate theories model the spatial concentration of people and jobs within a metropolitan area. One major set of these theories, focused on population location, examines the relationships between land costs and accessibility, and the implied rent gradients. Another explores the impacts of agglomeration economies on employment location. Empirical tests of the first set of theories have concentrated on housing costs and distance measures from the central city, whereas empirical tests of the second set of models have explored manufacturing employment location. Undoubtedly, the easy availability of data on housing, distances, and the manufacturing industry has played an important role in the design of these studies. However, everyone realizes that there is nothing smoothly concentrated about the way people and jobs cluster around central cities. Further, a number of major influences are omitted from these empirical studies, including quality of the labor force, quality of public services, tax burdens, and government regulations. For the research reported here, many of the resources were devoted to increasing the availability of microdata for the analysis of changing urban employment and population patterns in the United States.

Special Features of Wharton's Database

Specifically, an employment database was developed at the Wharton School of the University of Pennsylvania that is location specific in several useful ways:

☐ The employment data describe the number of people employed in a specific location (establishment-based), not the number of people living in a specific location who are employed anywhere (residence-based).

☐ Central city (CC) employment data are divided into two geographic units—the central business district (CBD) and the rest of the legally defined central city (RCC).

☐ Establishment-based employment data have been assembled for individual suburban jurisdictions outside the central city (OCC), in contrast to the usual treatment of a single suburban aggregate.

A previously unexplored aspect of urban growth is the impact of local land-use restrictions. These restrictions are employed by communities, particularly suburban communities, to restrict the growth in the supply of housing. As a result, growth in a community may be supply-side constrained. These growth restrictions have been used in particularly aggressive ways by high-growth suburban communities during the 1980s, as Downs documents in this volume, chapter 2. The absence of data on local land-use practices has made it impossible to systematically examine the impact of such variables. To remedy this situation, we conducted a survey of city planning directors that asked a wide range of questions about local land-use practices and how these have changed over time. The survey instrument was sent to over three thousand communities in the sixty metropolitan areas covered in this study and generated a complete set of central city responses, as well as approximately one thousand usable suburban community responses. This local regulatory database is described in Linneman and Summers (1993).

The basic source for our employment data was a dataset (USEEM) compiled by the U.S. Small Business Administration (SBA) of the Department of Commerce.[2] In conjunction with Dun & Bradstreet, the SBA has conducted, since 1976, a virtual biannual census of establishment-based employment of U.S. firms and their constituent establishments. Their files have mailing addresses, so that zip codes and postal city names were available.

The data were coded at the county level. To transform these data to the level of disaggregation we were interested in, and to meet the confidentiality agreements Dun & Bradstreet has with its survey respondents and others, we used an SBA data contractor, Social Scientific Systems (SSS). In a "blind" partnership, SSS pulled the establishment level data out of the USEEM database for all the counties in the sixty largest metropolitan areas for 1976, 1980, and 1986.

The 1970 and 1980 Censuses of Population, supplemented by the "Minidoris" data produced by CACI for 1987, were the prime sources of the population variables. These were the most recently available data when the study started.

This analysis of decentralization patterns in the United States is focused on several geographic units, central cities, their central business districts, the remainder of the legally defined central cities, and the surrounding suburban jurisdictions. To aggregate these geographic units, a basic unit of observation had to be chosen. Census tracts were an obvious choice, but presented several major limitations: the data are only available at ten-year intervals, the most recent Census data available were ten years old, and the 1970 Census reports had only residence-based employment data. Zip codes were another alternative, and were, indeed, the units of choice. CACI produces estimates for a wide variety of Census data for recent years by zip codes, the U.S. Bureau of the Census had a 1970 data file at the zip-code level, and the USEEM basic employment data were accessible by zip codes.

Geographic Units of Observation

MSA

In the United States, the largest standard unit for analyzing urban concentrations is the metropolitan statistical area (MSA), reflecting the definition of a labor market area: "a geographic area consisting of a large population nucleus together with adjacent communities having a high degree of economic and social integration with that nucleus" (U.S. Office of Management and Budget 1983). The title of these areas changed over time from standard metropolitan statistical areas (SMSAs) to primary metropolitan statistical areas (PMSAs), and the geographic coverage also changed. The data used in the study are standardized on the basis of the 1982 metropolitan area specifications. This simplified the use of the 1980 Census data while minimizing the loss of counties in the 1970 Census data. The analysis is limited to the sixty largest metropolitan statistical areas.

CC

Central cities are clearly defined by legal city boundaries, but are not as precisely defined by either census tracts or zip codes: both units may cover part of a central city and part of one or more suburban jurisdictions. An elaborate system for allocating across the boundaries between CCs and their OCCs, and across the boundaries between adjoining suburbs, was developed (Buist 1989).

CBD

People know where to find a central business district, but defining it precisely in terms of exact zip codes is more difficult. In the past, the Census Bureau defined CBDs by specified census tracts, though it discontinued this in the 1990 Census. The 1980 census tract definitions of the CBD for each city are used in the database, after being imposed on postal zip-code maps for each of the central cities. In addition, the CBD boundaries were verified by telephone calls to each central city's planning department. In some cases, zip codes crossed over CBD boundaries. If the crossover was substantial, the area was excluded from the CBD and put into the RCC. In other cases, the USEEM data had employment numbers associated with post office designations (P.O. box numbers), rather than geographically identified employment locations. Addresses in telephone books were used to determine the geographic location in each case.

RCC

The CC units minus their CBD units constitute the RCC units.

OCC

The MSA units minus their CC units define the OCC units (in the aggregate). In general, individual observations in the OCCs coincide with political jurisdiction. However, there are many exceptions to this rule. There are townships, municipalities, communities (unincorporated areas), and some geographic areas that are neither political units nor legal communities. Observations were created for all these residual areas outside the CCs, but within the MSAs. However, not all of these observations—referred to subsequently as jurisdictions—necessarily exist as political entities. There are 3,408 of these jurisdictions in the data, the majority of which are well-defined legal entities.

PATTERNS OF EMPLOYMENT DECENTRALIZATION

The term "urban decline" has, in the United States, frequently been used to describe employment decline in an ambiguous geographic delineation. With the sole exception of Youngstown, Ohio, employment in all sixty of America's major metropolitan areas grew over the 1976–86 decade. During this decade, "urban decline" is not an accurate absolute or relative description of employment behavior in metropolitan areas in the United States—when an area is described as the sum of its central city and adjoining jurisdictions. But the phrase does accurately describe many of the identifiable parts of these metropolitan areas.

Urban America—the sixty largest central cities and their surrounding communities—experienced employment levels that grew more rapidly than the nation as a whole over the 1976–86 period. The average annual growth rate in the major metropolitan areas dropped from 4.4 percent per year between 1976 and 1980, to 2.7 percent per year between 1980 and 1986, but national employment growth rates were running at the lower rates of 3.7 percent and 2 percent. Thus, the concentration of employment within large metropolitan areas increased.

Table 4.1 displays the average annual growth rates in employment for these two time periods, for each of these sixty metropolitan areas, for the PMSAs as a whole, and for their component parts—the central cities (CCs), the two parts of the CCs—the CBD and the RCC—and the suburban jurisdictions (OCCs). There are several striking patterns in these data:

☐ There are wide disparities in the employment growth rates among these sixty PMSAs.
☐ There are wide disparities in the employment growth rates within individual PMSAs.
☐ There are wide disparities in the differential growth rates among the parts of PMSAs across the country.

Employment Growth Rates of PMSAs

Between 1976 and 1980, Salt Lake City's metropolitan area employment grew at the astonishing rate of 11.2 percent per year, while that in Youngstown was declining at 5 percent per year. Between 1980 and 1986, Orlando's employment grew at 8.2 percent per year, but Gary's was declining at 5 percent per year. The big "winners" and "losers" in each time period are shown in tables 4.2 and 4.3, respectively. The big relative winners (table 4.2) were, with few exceptions, in the South and the West in both time periods. The big relative losers (table 4.3), in the early period, were the old industrial centers of the North

Table 4.1 AVERAGE ANNUAL GROWTH RATES IN EMPLOYMENT IN SIXTY LARGEST METROPOLITAN AREAS IN THE UNITED STATES: 1976–80 AND 1980–86 (PERCENTAGE POINTS)

	1976–80					1980–86				
	PMSA	CC	CBD	RCC	OCC	PMSA	CC	CBD	RCC	OCC
1. Akron	3.4	1.0	-1.8	1.6	6.2	0.8	0.6	0.4	0.6	1.2
2. Albany	3.2	5.3	-0.4	7.2	2.2	1.8	3.0	3.6	3.0	1.2
3. Allentown	1.4	1.1	-1.8	3.4	1.8	1.4	2.8	-6.0	7.6	0.6
4. Anaheim	9.8	4.2	-6.2	9.4	11.2	5.0	5.0	6.0	4.4	5.0
5. Atlanta	3.6	1.6	4.2	0.2	6.2	6.0	3.0	-1.4	5.2	8.8
6. Baltimore	3.2	1.6	4.6	0.6	6.6	3.6	1.8	4.0	0.8	6.6
7. Birmingham	4.2	4.2	1.4	7.8	4.2	0.2	1.4	-0.8	3.6	-2.8
8. Boston	2.8	1.2	1.4	1.0	3.6	3.4	3.2	4.2	2.6	3.6
9. Buffalo	1.2	-0.3	-4.2	2.4	3.0	-0.6	-0.2	-0.6	0.0	-1.2
10. Charlotte	3.8	3.6	-1.8	6.4	4.6	4.2	4.4	3.0	5.0	3.6
11. Chicago	1.0	-1.1	0.4	-2.2	3.0	1.0	-0.6	1.2	-2.2	2.4
12. Cincinnati	4.0	2.4	-1.4	4.2	8.4	1.2	1.0	0.2	1.2	1.6
13. Cleveland	3.0	2.0	-1.2	4.2	5.0	0.4	-0.4	-1.4	0.0	1.8
14. Columbus	2.6	2.1	3.0	1.8	4.0	5.2	5.2	2.8	5.8	5.6
15. Dallas	6.8	5.5	1.2	6.2	8.4	5.4	3.8	3.6	4.0	6.8
16. Dayton	3.0	1.7	1.6	1.8	5.0	0.4	-1.0	-2.6	0.8	2.8
17. Denver	7.8	6.8	4.4	7.8	9.4	4.4	2.0	4.0	1.4	7.2
18. Detroit	1.2	0.8	3.2	0.0	1.4	0.8	-2.6	-1.8	-2.8	2.2
19. Fort Lauderdale	6.6	7.0	10.0	6.4	6.2	4.4	3.4	-0.8	4.2	5.2
20. Gary	5.2	-2.2	-1.0	-6.2	8.0	-5.0	0.0	1.8	-8.6	-6.8
21. Grand Rapids	5.6	4.1	0.4	7.6	8.0	2.8	2.4	0.8	3.4	3.4
22. Greensboro	3.2	8.4	1.4	15.6	1.2	1.4	-2.0	-3.6	-1.0	2.6
23. Hartford	7.0	5.1	7.4	-2.2	8.0	4.4	4.4	5.6	-1.2	4.4
24. Honolulu	5.4	5.5	2.4	7.0	4.8	0.8	0.6	-1.4	1.4	2.0
25. Houston	7.0	5.8	1.8	7.6	13.0	2.6	1.6	-1.6	2.8	6.4
26. Indianapolis	2.6	2.1	16.0	-2.4	5.4	1.2	0.8	-2.4	2.2	3.4
27. Kansas City	5.8	4.1	2.0	5.2	8.8	1.8	1.0	-3.0	2.6	3.2
28. Los Angeles	4.8	3.8	4.0	3.8	5.6	1.6	0.2	0.4	0.2	2.8
29. Louisville	4.0	3.0	-3.6	8.0	7.0	-0.2	-1.0	-4.8	0.8	2.0
30. Memphis	5.0	4.8	1.4	6.0	6.6	2.2	1.8	0.6	2.2	4.2

31. Miami	3.4	2.5	4.8	12.0	4.0	1.6	2.4	-1.4	13.0	1.2
32. Milwaukee	2.4	1.3	0.0	2.0	4.8	0.8	0.4	2.8	-1.2	1.8
33. Minneapolis	4.8	4.7	2.8	5.4	4.8	4.6	3.4	6.6	1.8	5.6
34. Nashville	2.6	1.2	-4.4	4.2	6.2	5.4	4.8	5.2	4.8	6.6
35. New Orleans	4.0	2.7	1.0	4.2	6.0	1.0	0.8	2.2	-0.6	1.2
36. New York	-0.4	-1.2	-0.8	-1.6	3.4	1.6	1.4	1.2	1.4	2.8
37. Newark	1.8	-3.6	-4.8	-2.8	3.0	3.0	0.6	2.2	-0.4	3.4
38. Oklahoma City	8.0	8.0	3.6	9.4	8.0	1.0	0.6	4.0	-0.6	2.2
39. Orlando	10.4	9.7	7.2	10.4	11.4	8.2	7.8	4.0	8.8	8.8
40. Philadelphia	0.0	-2.1	0.0	-2.8	1.8	2.4	0.6	1.6	0.2	3.4
41. Phoenix	8.6	7.4	5.4	7.8	12.0	7.6	7.4	3.8	8.0	8.2
42. Pittsburgh	1.4	1.1	2.2	0.4	1.6	-0.6	1.2	1.6	0.8	-2.0
43. Portland	6.0	4.8	3.2	5.6	8.0	2.0	0.4	-0.4	0.8	4.2
44. Providence	2.0	0.3	-3.2	3.2	2.8	0.8	0.2	-0.6	0.6	1.2
45. Richmond	4.8	4.0	4.6	3.6	8.4	4.2	3.6	4.6	3.0	6.0
46. Rochester	0.0	-1.9	-12.2	2.2	4.2	4.0	5.0	2.8	5.6	1.4
47. Sacramento	5.4	2.4	-7.4	7.2	11.6	7.4	5.6	1.8	6.8	10.0
48. Salt Lake City	11.2	11.2	10.0	12.2	11.0	4.4	4.0	1.4	5.6	5.2
49. San Antonio	7.4	7.3	5.8	7.8	9.2	5.0	4.8	-2.4	6.2	6.6
50. San Diego	6.0	5.1	2.0	6.0	8.0	6.0	5.8	2.4	6.8	6.4
51. San Francisco	3.2	1.2	3.2	-0.4	4.6	3.6	2.8	0.4	4.6	4.0
52. San Jose	6.0	5.3	1.6	6.8	6.4	5.4	6.8	7.6	6.6	4.6
53. Seattle	11.0	7.0	13.6	3.6	16.8	0.8	0.0	-2.8	1.6	1.6
54. St. Louis	5.0	1.8	0.6	2.8	8.0	1.6	1.0	3.4	-1.0	2.2
55. Syracuse	4.0	2.0	5.0	0.4	6.4	3.8	5.0	2.8	6.2	2.2
56. Tampa	7.8	5.7	1.8	6.6	9.4	4.6	4.8	1.6	5.4	4.6
57. Toledo	2.2	0.3	1.4	-0.2	6.0	0.6	0.2	-3.6	1.6	1.6
58. Tulsa	5.6	4.8	2.4	5.8	9.8	2.0	2.0	1.4	2.0	3.0
59. Washington, D.C.	7.0	5.8	6.4	5.2	8.0	5.0	1.2	2.6	0.0	7.0
60. Youngstown	-5.0	-5.0	-9.2	-0.6	-5.0	1.4	0.2	-6.0	4.2	2.0
Mean	4.4	3.1	1.6	4.1	6.3	2.7	2.2	1.0	2.5	3.4
Median	4.0	2.8	1.6	4.2	6.2	2.1	1.7	1.4	2.1	3.3

Note: See text for translation of abbreviations in column headings.

Table 4.2 METROPOLITAN AREAS WITH LARGEST EMPLOYMENT GROWTH
RATES: 1976–80 AND 1980–86 (ANNUAL RATES)

1976–80		1980–86	
Salt Lake City	11.2	Orlando	8.2
Seattle	11.1	Phoenix	7.7
Orlando	10.4	Sacramento	7.3
Anaheim	9.8	Atlanta	6.1
Phoenix	8.7	San Diego	6.0
Oklahoma City	8.0	Dallas	5.4
Denver	7.9	Nashville	5.4
Tampa	7.7	San Jose	5.4
San Antonio	7.5	Columbus	5.2
Houston	7.1	Washington, D.C.	5.0

Table 4.3 METROPOLITAN AREAS WITH LOWEST EMPLOYMENT GROWTH
RATES: 1976–80 AND 1980–86 (ANNUAL RATES)

1976–80		1980–86	
Youngstown	− 5.0	Gary	− 5.0
New York	− 0.3	Buffalo	− 0.7
Rochester	0.0	Pittsburgh	− 0.6
Philadelphia	0.1	Louisville	− 0.2
Chicago	1.0	Birmingham	0.2
Detroit	1.3	Cleveland	0.5
Buffalo	1.3	Dayton	0.5
Pittsburgh	1.4	Toledo	0.7
Allentown	1.5	Seattle	0.7
Newark	1.8	Honolulu	0.8

and Midwest. But the big losers of the 1980–86 period are less clearly
defined, although most were still the old manufacturing centers of the
Midwest. Understanding these patterns, however, requires looking at
the disparate behavior within these metropolitan areas.

Employment Growth Rates within PMSAs: CCs and OCCs

Substantial differences existed in the patterns of employment growth
within urban areas between 1976 and 1986. Indeed, this is the most
striking characteristic of the data in table 4.1. Overall, growth rates in
the central cities averaged 3.1 percent in the 1976–80 period, about
half that of the outlying suburban areas (6.3 percent) (see table 4.1).
In the early 1980s, the suburbs continued to grow substantially more

than the cities (3.4 percent, compared with 2.2 percent). The lower rates in the 1980s reflect the national recession and the fact that 1976 was a recessionary low point.

In many cases, the percentage point differences in growth rates between the CC and the OCC were extraordinarily large. Table 4.4 lists the differentials in growth rates for both 1976–80 and 1980–86, sorted by size. Only eight of the PMSAs did not experience employment decentralization in the early period; only two, Greensboro and Albany, had central cities that grew significantly more than their suburbs. In the later period, thirteen cities did not decentralize, but all of these—except Albany—had done so in the earlier period. The largest and the smallest of these sixty metropolitan areas, whether they were in the high-growth Sunbelt regions or the sluggish regions of the Northeast and Midwest, deconcentrated their employment. This is a key pattern to be reckoned with.

Employment Growth among the Suburbs

Urban analysts have not generally recognized that not all suburban communities have been flourishing. In the sample of over three thousand suburbs that comprise "the suburbs" of our largest sixty PMSAs, some grew extremely rapidly while others declined. Many suburban communities have had to deal with decreasing employment over this period—22 percent had declining employment between 1976 and 1980, and 27 percent had declining employment from 1980 to 1986. A sense of the widely varying characteristics of the communities, blithely labeled "the suburbs" and usually treated as a monolith, is gained from the data presented in table 4.5. The means and standard deviations for a set of socioeconomic descriptors of the suburban jurisdictions in the sample are shown.[3]

Even with extreme outliers removed, the range of suburban experience was considerable. Approximately two-thirds of suburban jurisdictions experienced annual employment growth rates between − 0.4 percent and + 11.4 percent in the 1976–80 period, and an even greater range of − 4.6 percent to + 11.0 percent was observed in the 1980–86 period (table 4.5). Similarly, two-thirds of the suburban communities had between 33 percent and 70 percent of their residential structures built before 1960; and the variation in their industrial structures is partially captured by the fact that their percentage of employment in manufacturing varied from 7 percent to 53 percent in 1980. Minimum and maximum values, of course, show even more dramatic differences. There were communities with all adults having high school

Table 4.4 DIFFERENCES IN CENTER CITY (CC) TO SUBURBAN (OCC)
ANNUALIZED EMPLOYMENT GROWTH RATES IN SIXTY LARGEST
PMSAs IN THE UNITED STATES: 1976–80 AND 1980–86 (PERCENTAGE
POINTS)

CC–OCC, 1976–80		CC–OCC, 1980–86	
Greensboro	7.2	Gary	6.7
Albany	3.0	Birmingham	4.2
Fort Lauderdale	0.8	Rochester	3.6
Honolulu	0.7	Pittsburgh	3.0
Salt Lake City	0.1	Syracuse	2.8
Youngstown	0.1	San Jose	2.3
Birmingham	0.0	Allentown	2.2
Oklahoma City	0.0	Albany	1.8
Minneapolis	− 0.2	Miami	1.2
Pittsburgh	− 0.5	Buffalo	0.9
Allentown	− 0.7	Charlotte	0.8
Detroit	− 0.7	Tampa	0.3
Charlotte	− 1.1	Anaheim	0.0
San Jose	− 1.1	Hartford	− 0.1
Miami	− 1.4	Boston	− 0.4
Los Angeles	− 1.7	Columbus	− 0.5
Orlando	− 1.7	New Orleans	− 0.5
San Antonio	− 1.8	San Diego	− 0.6
Columbus	− 1.9	Cincinnati	− 0.6
Memphis	− 1.9	Akron	− 0.7
Washington, D.C.	− 2.1	Phoenix	− 0.9
Boston	− 2.4	Orlando	− 1.0
Providence	− 2.5	Providence	− 1.0
Denver	− 2.7	Tulsa	− 1.0
Hartford	− 2.8	Salt Lake City	− 1.1
San Diego	− 2.9	San Francisco	− 1.1
Cleveland	− 3.0	Grand Rapids	− 1.2
Dallas	− 3.0	St. Louis	− 1.3
Portland	− 3.1	Honolulu	− 1.4
Buffalo	− 3.2	Milwaukee	− 1.4
Dayton	− 3.4	Toledo	− 1.4
Indianapolis	− 3.4	New York	− 1.5
New Orleans	− 3.4	Seattle	− 1.5
Milwaukee	− 3.5	Oklahoma City	− 1.7
San Francisco	− 3.5	Nashville	− 1.7
Tampa	− 3.7	Fort Lauderdale	− 1.8
Philadelphia	− 3.8	Youngstown	− 1.8
Grand Rapids	− 3.9	San Antonio	− 1.8
Louisville	− 4.1	Minneapolis	− 2.2
Chicago	− 4.2	Richmond	− 2.2
Richmond	− 4.3	Cleveland	− 2.3
Syracuse	− 4.4	Memphis	− 2.4
Atlanta	− 4.5	Kansas City	− 2.4
New York	− 4.5	Los Angeles	− 2.6
Phoenix	− 4.6	Indianapolis	− 2.6

(continued)

Table 4.4 DIFFERENCES IN CENTER CITY (CC) TO SUBURBAN (OCC)
ANNUALIZED EMPLOYMENT GROWTH RATES IN SIXTY LARGEST
PMSAs IN THE UNITED STATES: 1976–80 AND 1980–86 (PERCENTAGE
POINTS) (continued)

CC–OCC, 1976–80		CC–OCC, 1980–86	
Kansas City	− 4.7	Philadelphia	− 2.8
Nashville	− 4.9	Louisville	− 2.9
Tulsa	− 4.9	Chicago	− 2.9
Baltimore	− 5.1	Newark	− 2.9
Akron	− 5.3	Dallas	− 3.0
Toledo	− 5.6	Portland	− 3.7
Cincinnati	− 5.9	Dayton	− 3.8
Rochester	− 6.2	Sacramento	− 4.4
St. Louis	− 6.2	Greensboro	− 4.7
Newark	− 6.7	Detroit	− 4.7
Anaheim	− 7.0	Houston	− 4.7
Houston	− 7.2	Baltimore	− 4.9
Sacramento	− 9.2	Denver	− 5.2
Seattle	− 9.7	Atlanta	− 5.7
Gary	− 10.2	Washington, D.C.	− 5.8

Table 4.5 RANGE OF SOME SUBURBAN JURISDICTION VARIABLES
(5 PERCENT TAILS REMOVED)

Variable	Mean	Standard Deviation	Minimum Value	Maximum Value
Percentage not high school graduates, 1980	29.96	12.23	0.00	74.49
Percentage black population, 1980	3.81	8.16	0.00	82.95
Annual percentage change in employment, 1976–80	5.55	5.93	− 7.42	22.64
Annual percentage change in employment, 1980–86	3.23	7.77	− 46.68	106.41
Annual percentage change in population, 1980–87	1.16	1.51	− 2.03	11.24
Annual percentage change in population, 1976–80	3.93	18.31	− 41.81	488.73
Percentage of residential structures built before 1960	51.44	18.84	2.00	99.30
Percentage employed in manufacturing, 1980	29.89	22.67	0.00	99.44

Note: For definitions of variables, see appendix.

degrees, as well as communities where 74 percent did not! There were communities with no black population and communities where 83 percent were black. Simply stated, there is nothing homogeneous about the set of communities that most urban studies and most government data cavalierly treat as a single entity called the suburbs.

Employment Growth Rates within Central Cities: CBDs and RCCs

Within central cities there were also notably different rates of growth. During the 1976–80 period, CBDs in the sixty largest PMSAs had much lower annual employment growth rates than the RCCs—1.6 percent compared with 4.1 percent, respectively (table 4.1). The same pattern also held for the period 1980–86—1 percent annual growth rates in the CBDs compared with 2.5 percent in the RCCs. But, again, these broad averages cloak very different patterns across the urban areas.

Table 4.6 displays the differences in employment growth rates between the component parts of central cities, listed in order of declining differences between the CBD and RCC. The varying patterns within the sixty central cities are organized by four groupings, shown in tables 4.7–4.10. Table 4.7 shows the cities that, in both periods, had employment growth in the CBD larger than that in the rest of the city. It is a short list, but it does contain most of the cities generally regarded as in the "most troubled" category. The cities that, in both periods, had employment growth in the outer regions of the city larger than those in the CBD are listed in table 4.8. This is a long list—about half the cities in our study, though not the very largest, are on it. Table 4.9 identifies the cities with CBDs that grew relative to their RCCs in 1980–86 but had a reverse pattern in 1976–80. Finally, table 4.10 identifies the cities in which CBDs grew relatively more than their RCCs in the earlier period, but in which the relative growth was reversed in the later period.

Summary: Employment Decentralization

Several trends are clear from these data:

☐ Employment growth was strong in the sixty largest metropolitan areas, relative to the rest of the nation.
☐ Urbanized areas of the nation expanded relatively.
☐ Employment growth was relatively slow in the central cities—the core of these urban areas.

Table 4.6 DIFFERENCES BETWEEN CENTRAL BUSINESS DISTRICT (CBD) AND
REST OF CENTRAL CITY (RCC) ANNUALIZED EMPLOYMENT GROWTH
RATES IN SIXTY LARGEST PMSAs IN THE UNITED STATES: 1976–80
AND 1980–86 (PERCENTAGE POINTS)

CBD–RCC, 1976–80		CBD–RCC, 1980–86	
Indianapolis	18.4	Gary	10.4
Seattle	10.1	Hartford	6.7
Hartford	9.5	Minneapolis	4.8
Gary	5.2	Oklahoma City	4.6
Syracuse	4.7	St. Louis	4.3
Baltimore	4.2	Milwaukee	3.9
Atlanta	4.0	Chicago	3.4
San Francisco	3.8	Baltimore	3.2
Fort Lauderdale	3.5	New Orleans	3.0
Detroit	3.2	Washington, D.C.	2.6
Philadelphia	2.9	Newark	2.6
Chicago	2.6	Denver	2.6
Pittsburgh	1.9	Richmond	1.8
Toledo	1.5	Boston	1.6
Columbus	1.3	Anaheim	1.6
Washington, D.C.	1.2	Philadelphia	1.3
Richmond	0.9	Detroit	1.0
New York	0.7	San Jose	1.0
Boston	0.5	Albany	0.7
Los Angeles	0.1	Pittsburgh	0.6
Dayton	−0.2	Nashville	0.4
Milwaukee	−1.9	Los Angeles	0.2
Newark	−1.9	New York	−0.2
San Antonio	−2.0	Akron	−0.3
Salt Lake City	−2.1	Dallas	−0.4
St. Louis	−2.2	Buffalo	−0.5
Phoenix	−2.3	Tulsa	−0.6
Portland	−2.4	Cincinnati	−1.0
Minneapolis	−2.6	Portland	−1.2
New Orleans	−3.1	Providence	−1.3
Denver	−3.2	Cleveland	−1.5
Orlando	−3.2	Memphis	−1.7
Kansas City	−3.3	Charlotte	−2.0
Tulsa	−3.3	Grand Rapids	−2.5
Akron	−3.4	Honolulu	−2.7
San Diego	−3.9	Greensboro	−2.7
Memphis	−4.5	Rochester	−3.0
Honolulu	−4.7	Columbus	−3.1
Tampa	−4.8	Dayton	−3.3
Dallas	−5.1	Syracuse	−3.4
Allentown	−5.3	Tampa	−3.8
San Jose	−5.3	Phoenix	−4.1
Cincinnati	−5.5	Seattle	−4.3
Cleveland	−5.5	San Francisco	−4.3

(continued)

Table 4.6 DIFFERENCES BETWEEN CENTRAL BUSINESS DISTRICT (CBD) AND
REST OF CENTRAL CITY (RCC) ANNUALIZED EMPLOYMENT GROWTH
RATES IN SIXTY LARGEST PMSAs IN THE UNITED STATES: 1976–80
AND 1980–86 (PERCENTAGE POINTS) (continued)

CBD–RCC, 1976–80		CBD–RCC, 1980–86	
Oklahoma City	5.7	Salt Lake City	4.3
Houston	5.8	San Diego	4.3
Birmingham	6.4	Birmingham	4.3
Providence	6.4	Houston	4.5
Buffalo	6.6	Indianapolis	4.7
Miami	7.1	Orlando	4.8
Grand Rapids	7.3	Fort Lauderdale	5.0
Albany	7.6	Sacramento	5.1
Charlotte	8.2	Toledo	5.2
Nashville	8.7	Kansas City	5.6
Youngstown	8.7	Louisville	5.6
Louisville	11.6	Atlanta	6.7
Greensboro	14.0	San Antonio	8.6
Rochester	14.4	Youngstown	10.2
Sacramento	14.6	Allentown	13.6
Anaheim	15.6	Miami	14.5

Table 4.7 CITIES WITH CBD EMPLOYMENT GROWTH GREATER THAN THAT OF
RCC IN 1976–80 AND 1980–86 (DIFFERENCES IN ANNUALIZED PERCENTAGES)

	1976–80 CBD–RCC	1980–86 CBD–RCC
Baltimore	4.2	3.2
Boston	0.4	1.6
Chicago	2.6	3.4
Detroit	3.2	1.0
Gary	5.2	10.4
Hartford	9.4	6.8
Los Angeles	0.2	0.2
Philadelphia	2.8	1.4
Pittsburgh	2.0	0.6
Richmond	1.0	1.8
Washington, D.C.	1.2	2.6

☐ The suburban areas surrounding the central cities experienced the
greatest growth in employment.

☐ Within the relatively declining central cities, the relative strength
of the central business districts waxed in some cities and waned
in others—and within a city, waxed in one period and waned in
another.

Table 4.8 CITIES WITH CBD EMPLOYMENT GROWTH LESS THAN THAT OF RCC
IN 1976–80 AND 1980–86 (DIFFERENCES IN ANNUALIZED PERCENTAGES)

	1976–80 CBD–RCC	1980–86 CBD–RCC
Akron	− 3.4	− 0.2
Allentown	− 5.2	− 13.6
Birmingham	− 6.4	− 4.4
Buffalo	− 6.6	− 0.4
Charlotte	− 8.2	− 2.0
Cincinnati	− 5.6	− 1.0
Cleveland	− 5.4	− 1.4
Dallas	− 5.2	− 0.4
Dayton	− 0.2	− 3.2
Grand Rapids	− 7.2	− 2.6
Greensboro	− 14.0	− 2.8
Honolulu	− 4.8	− 2.8
Houston	− 5.8	− 4.4
Kansas City	− 3.4	− 5.6
Louisville	− 11.6	− 5.6
Memphis	− 4.6	− 1.6
Miami	− 7.2	− 14.6
Orlando	− 3.2	− 4.8
Phoenix	− 2.4	− 4.0
Portland	− 2.4	− 1.2
Providence	− 6.4	− 1.2
Rochester	− 14.4	− 3.0
Sacramento	− 14.6	− 5.0
Salt Lake City	− 2.2	− 4.2
San Antonio	− 2.0	− 8.6
San Diego	− 4.0	− 4.2
Tampa	− 4.8	− 3.8
Tulsa	− 3.4	− 0.6
Youngstown	− 8.6	− 10.2

☐ Within the clump of communities surrounding central cities, most waxed, but many waned.

What factors underlie these patterns? What socioeconomic and policy factors explain the strong suburban development? What factors explain the different patterns across the suburban jurisdictions? And what factors account for the different economic development patterns within the central cities? These questions are explored in the regression analysis of the fifth section of this chapter. The next section examines patterns of urban population decentralization.

Table 4.9 CITIES WITH CBD EMPLOYMENT GROWTH LESS THAN THAT OF RCC
IN 1976–80 BUT GREATER THAN THAT OF RCC IN 1980–86 (DIFFERENCES
IN ANNUALIZED PERCENTAGES)

	1976–80 CBD–RCC	1980–86 CBD–RCC
Albany	− 7.6	0.6
Anaheim	− 15.6	1.6
Denver	− 3.2	2.6
Milwaukee	− 1.8	4.0
Minneapolis	− 2.6	4.8
Nashville	− 8.6	0.4
New Orleans	− 3.0	3.0
Newark	− 2.0	2.6
Oklahoma City	− 5.8	4.6
St. Louis	− 2.2	4.2
San Jose	− 5.2	1.0

Table 4.10 CITIES WITH CBD EMPLOYMENT GROWTH GREATER THAN THAT OF
RCC IN 1976–80 BUT LESS THAN THAT OF RCC IN 1980–86
(DIFFERENCES IN ANNUALIZED PERCENTAGES)

	1976–80 CBD–RCC	1980–86 CBD–RCC
Atlanta	4.0	− 6.6
Columbus	1.2	− 3.0
Fort Lauderdale	3.6	− 5.0
Indianapolis	18.4	− 4.6
New York	0.8	− 0.2
San Francisco	3.8	− 4.4
Seattle	10.0	− 4.4
Syracuse	4.6	− 3.4
Toledo	1.6	− 5.2

PATTERNS OF POPULATION DECENTRALIZATION

The 1970s witnessed major changes in the patterns of urban population locations. The decade began with a period of rapid urban decay,
fueled by the race riots of the late 1960s. By 1976, several major cities
were on the brink of bankruptcy, as the continued white flight to the
suburbs combined with a major national recession to bring cities to
their knees. At the same time, new suburbs were flourishing, while
older suburbs generally remained strong.

Just as many observers were "writing off" American cities, a major turnaround began in the late 1970s. By the end of the 1970s many cities were on a road (albeit pothole-laden) to recovery, particularly in central business districts that possessed initially strong CBD population bases. Table 4.11 reports the annual percentage changes in population for the sixty largest PMSAs and their CCs, CBDs, RCCs, and OCCs. Means and medians for these cities are reported at the bottom of each column.

An analysis of table 4.11 reveals that there was essentially no change (on average) in central-city populations during the 1970s, whereas during the 1980s these cities experienced a modest 0.4 percent annual increase in population. However, in both periods, the average population in central business districts declined, while the population of the rest of the central city grew. The decline was smaller for CBDs in the earlier period than in the later period, whereas the growth in the RCCs was greater in the 1980s than it was in the 1970s. The differential growth rate between CBDs and RCCs fell from 1.56 percent in the 1970s to 0.55 percent in the 1980s.

While the central cities were exhibiting little growth in the 1970s, the suburbs (in aggregate) of these sixty major U.S. cities were growing at a rate of more than 2 percent a year (see table 4.11). In the 1980s, these suburbs continued to markedly outgrow the central cities, although they grew at a much slower 1.4 percent annually. This lower growth rate primarily reflects the mature nature of the suburbs after the decade of rapid growth in the 1970s.

In all metropolitan areas except San Jose, the suburbs experienced higher population growth rates than the central city in both the 1970s and the 1980s. However, the relationships between the growth in the CBD relative to the growth in the RCC show divergent patterns. Specifically, in 65 percent of the metropolitan areas, the CBD experienced lower population growth rates in both the 1970s and the 1980s than did the RCC. However, in 27 percent of the CBDs, population grew faster in both periods than did the RCC. These more rapidly growing CBDs include the "traditional" central business districts of Boston, New York City, San Francisco, Philadelphia, Chicago, and Minneapolis, as well as more "modern" cities such as Los Angeles, Atlanta, and Seattle.

In 88 percent of the metropolitan areas, central business districts experienced lower population growth rates than their suburbs in both the 1970s and the 1980s. However, the CBDs of Boston, Los Angeles, New York City, and Rochester grew more rapidly than their suburbs

Table 4.11 AVERAGE ANNUAL GROWTH RATES IN POPULATION IN SIXTY LARGEST METROPOLITAN AREAS IN THE UNITED STATES: 1970–80 AND 1980–87 (PERCENTAGE POINTS)

	1970–80					1980–87				
	PMSA	CC	CBD	RCC	OCC	PMSA	CC	CBD	RCC	OCC
1. Akron	0.3	-1.2	-2.8	-1.2	1.2	-0.2	-0.9	-0.8	-0.9	0.2
2. Albany	0.3	-0.1	-2.4	-0.1	0.4	0.2	-2.7	-1.1	-0.2	0.3
3. Allentown	0.8	-0.1	-2.8	0.0	1.0	0.5	-0.0	-0.9	0.0	0.6
4. Anaheim	3.0	2.3	0.7	2.6	3.1	1.8	1.4	0.6	1.5	1.8
5. Atlanta	2.4	-0.8	-0.3	-0.9	4.4	2.7	0.7	0.8	0.7	3.5
6. Baltimore	0.6	-0.9	-1.6	-0.8	3.1	0.5	-0.4	-0.7	-0.4	1.7
7. Birmingham	1.0	0.3	-5.4	0.4	2.0	0.5	0.2	-1.3	0.2	0.9
8. Boston	-0.2	-1.3	0.6	-1.4	0.1	0.2	0.3	1.2	0.3	0.2
9. Buffalo	-0.8	-1.8	-2.2	-1.8	0.1	-0.6	-1.1	-1.1	-1.1	-2.8
10. Charlotte	1.4	0.3	-3.8	0.5	2.4	1.4	1.1	-0.5	1.1	1.7
11. Chicago	0.2	-1.1	-0.4	-1.1	1.4	0.4	-0.3	0.3	-0.3	0.9
12. Cincinnati	0.4	-0.6	-3.9	-0.6	1.5	0.3	-0.3	-1.4	-0.2	0.8
13. Cleveland	-0.9	-1.7	-3.0	-1.7	0.7	-0.4	-0.8	-0.6	-0.8	0.2
14. Columbus	0.8	-0.3	-3.0	-0.2	2.4	0.7	0.3	-0.8	0.3	1.1
15. Dallas	2.2	0.6	-2.1	0.6	3.1	2.7	1.6	0.1	1.6	3.2
16. Dayton	-0.4	-1.1	-3.3	-1.1	0.5	-0.3	-0.6	-1.2	-0.6	0.0
17. Denver	2.8	0.2	-2.1	0.3	4.6	2.3	1.0	-0.3	1.0	3.0
18. Detroit	-0.1	-2.2	-6.2	-2.2	0.8	-0.4	-1.5	-1.3	-1.5	-0.1
19. Fort Lauderdale	5.1	5.0	-0.1	5.2	5.2	1.9	1.9	-0.1	2.0	1.9
20. Gary	0.1	-1.5	-0.7	-1.7	0.9	-0.4	-1.2	-0.6	-1.3	-0.2
21. Grand Rapids	1.2	0.3	-2.0	0.6	2.0	1.0	0.6	-0.5	0.8	1.4
22. Greensboro	1.3	0.9	-1.2	1.2	1.4	0.7	0.4	-0.6	0.5	0.8
23. Hartford	0.1	-0.1	-0.1	-0.1	0.2	0.5	0.4	0.3	0.4	0.5
24. Honolulu	1.9	1.1	0.6	1.1	2.9	1.2	0.9	0.6	0.9	1.6
25. Houston	3.8	2.8	-3.6	2.8	5.9	3.2	2.8	0.5	2.8	4.0
26. Indianapolis	0.5	-0.4	-1.7	-0.4	1.9	0.5	0.2	-0.8	0.3	0.8
27. Kansas City	0.5	-0.9	-3.8	-0.8	1.5	0.7	-0.3	-1.2	-0.3	1.3
28. Los Angeles	0.7	0.6	3.8	0.6	0.8	1.4	1.3	2.5	1.3	1.4
29. Louisville	0.6	-0.3	-0.8	-0.3	2.1	0.2	-0.1	-0.6	-0.1	0.8

30. Memphis	0.9	-0.2	-1.1	-0.2	3.5	0.8	0.2	-0.3	0.2	1.9
31. Miami	2.5	2.1	-1.7	2.1	4.0	1.2	1.1	0.5	1.1	1.6
32. Milwaukee	-0.0	-1.0	-1.1	1.0	1.8	-0.1	-0.6	-0.6	-0.6	0.6
33. Minneapolis	0.8	-0.8	-0.5	-0.8	1.7	1.0	-0.1	1.7	-0.2	1.6
34. Nashville	2.1	0.0	-1.9	0.1	3.6	1.3	0.3	-0.1	0.3	1.9
35. New Orleans	1.2	-0.6	-1.9	-0.5	3.1	1.0	0.0	-0.6	0.1	1.7
36. New York	-0.9	-1.1	-0.0	-1.2	-0.1	0.3	0.4	0.8	0.3	0.1
37. Newark	-0.5	-1.5	-1.4	-1.5	-0.2	0.1	-0.5	0.2	-0.5	0.2
38. Oklahoma City	1.8	0.4	-5.2	0.4	3.7	2.1	1.4	-0.7	1.4	2.8
39. Orlando	4.3	3.4	0.3	3.5	4.9	3.8	3.1	1.5	3.1	4.2
40. Philadelphia	-0.2	-1.4	0.2	-1.5	0.6	0.3	-0.5	0.6	-0.6	0.8
41. Phoenix	4.5	2.7	-0.6	2.9	6.6	3.9	2.4	-0.2	2.5	5.1
42. Pittsburgh	-0.5	-1.4	-3.1	-1.4	0.0	-0.6	-1.0	-1.3	-1.0	-0.4
43. Portland	2.1	-0.3	-1.0	-0.3	4.1	1.0	-0.0	-0.2	-0.0	1.6
44. Providence	0.0	-0.2	-0.2	-0.2	0.1	0.4	0.2	0.2	0.2	0.4
45. Richmond	1.3	0.3	-0.3	0.3	2.6	1.2	0.8	-0.3	0.8	1.7
46. Rochester	0.1	-0.9	5.5	-0.9	1.2	0.3	-0.3	1.2	-0.3	0.8
47. Sacramento	2.4	1.5	0.1	1.5	3.2	2.5	2.1	1.2	2.2	2.8
48. Salt Lake City	2.9	1.5	-3.0	1.7	4.3	2.4	1.7	-0.2	1.7	3.0
49. San Antonio	1.9	1.7	-0.8	1.7	3.3	2.4	2.3	0.8	2.3	3.3
50. San Diego	3.4	2.5	0.4	2.5	4.4	2.6	2.1	1.0	2.2	3.0
51. San Francisco	0.5	-0.5	0.0	-0.6	0.8	1.2	1.1	1.3	1.1	1.2
52. San Jose	2.1	2.9	-0.2	3.3	1.4	1.5	1.8	0.3	1.9	1.2
53. Seattle	1.2	-0.7	0.3	-0.7	2.7	1.4	0.1	0.5	0.1	2.1
54. St. Louis	-0.2	-2.3	-1.3	-2.3	1.1	0.2	-1.2	-0.5	-1.2	0.9
55. Syracuse	0.1	-1.3	-2.1	-1.3	0.6	0.3	-0.6	-0.3	-0.6	0.6
56. Tampa	3.8	1.8	-1.5	1.9	4.6	2.6	2.2	0.0	2.2	2.8
57. Toledo	0.4	-0.6	-2.6	-0.5	1.3	-0.3	-0.6	-1.1	-0.6	0.0
58. Tulsa	2.0	0.9	-2.9	1.0	2.8	1.6	1.3	-0.4	1.3	1.8
59. Washington, D.C.	0.5	-1.7	-2.3	-1.6	1.2	1.3	-0.2	-0.4	-0.2	1.7
60. Youngstown	-0.0	-0.9	-5.9	-0.9	0.4	-0.7	-1.0	-2.1	-1.0	-0.5
Mean	1.2	0.0	-1.5	0.1	2.2	1.0	0.4	-0.1	0.4	1.4
Median	0.8	-0.3	-1.5	-0.2	1.8	0.9	0.5	-0.2	0.2	1.9

in both the 1970s and the 1980s (see table 4.11). Thus, although there are clearly general patterns of urban decentralization at work, it is equally clear that these patterns contain notable differences in the parts of metropolitan areas.

Table 4.12 reports the annualized percentage changes in population over both time periods for the fastest and slowest growing central cities. Sunbelt cities (such as Orlando, Houston, and Phoenix) experienced the strongest central-city growth in both periods, whereas Rustbelt cities (such as Detroit, St. Louis, and Buffalo) were the weakest central cities. The correlation between the population growth rates for central cities in the 1970s and in the 1980s was 0.89. Thus, central cities that did well in the 1970s also tended to do well in the 1980s, whereas central cities that experienced weak population growth in the 1970s tended to experience further weak population growth in the 1980s.

Tables 4.13 and 4.14 decompose these population growth patterns into their component geographic parts—CBDs and RCCs. Again, the correlation coefficients of the growth rates between the two time periods for each of these geographic areas were quite high. In addition, CBDs generally experienced lower growth rates than did the rest of the central city in both periods. However, a number of central business districts grew substantially in both the 1970s and the 1980s. In particular, the Los Angeles and Boston CBDs experienced strong growth in both decades. In contrast, the downtowns of Detroit, Youngstown, Birmingham, and Cincinnati were devastated in terms of their popu-

Table 4.12 ANNUALIZED PERCENTAGE CHANGE IN POPULATION IN SELECTED CCs IN THE UNITED STATES: 1970–80 AND 1980–87

1970–80		1980–87	
Fort Lauderdale	5.0	Orlando	3.1
Orlando	3.4	Houston	2.8
San Jose	2.9	Phoenix	2.4
Houston	2.8	San Antonio	2.3
Phoenix	2.7	Tampa	2.2
60-city mean	0.0	60-city mean	0.4
Percentage positive	40.0	Percentage positive	60.0
Washington, D.C.	−1.7	Youngstown	−1.0
Cleveland	−1.7	Buffalo	−1.1
Buffalo	−1.8	Gary	−1.2
Detroit	−2.2	St. Louis	−1.2
St. Louis	−2.3	Detroit	−1.5

Note: Correlation coefficient between 1970–80 and 1980–87 growth rates equals 0.9.

Table 4.13 ANNUALIZED PERCENTAGE CHANGE IN POPULATION IN SELECTED
CBDs IN THE UNITED STATES: 1970–80 AND 1980–87

1970–80		1980–87	
Rochester	5.5	Los Angeles	2.5
Los Angeles	3.8	Minneapolis	1.7
Anaheim	0.7	Orlando	1.5
Boston	0.6	San Francisco	1.3
Honolulu	0.6	Boston	1.2
60-city mean	− 1.5	60-city mean	− 0.1
Percentage positive	18.0	Percentage positive	42.0
Cincinnati	− 3.9	Birmingham	− 1.3
Oklahoma City	− 5.2	Pittsburgh	− 1.3
Birmingham	− 5.4	Detroit	− 1.3
Youngstown	− 5.9	Cincinnati	− 1.4
Detroit	− 6.2	Youngstown	− 2.1

Note: Correlation coefficient between 1970–80 and 1980–87 growth rates equals 0.8.

Table 4.14 ANNUALIZED PERCENTAGE CHANGE IN POPULATION IN SELECTED
RCCs IN THE UNITED STATES: 1970–80 AND 1980–87

1970–80		1980–87	
Fort Lauderdale	5.2	Orlando	3.1
Orlando	3.5	Houston	2.8
San Jose	3.3	Phoenix	2.5
Phoenix	2.9	San Antonio	2.3
Houston	2.8	Tampa	2.2
60-city mean	0.1	60-city mean	0.4
Percentage positive	43.0	Percentage positive	58.0
Gary	− 1.7	Youngstown	− 1.0
Cleveland	− 1.7	Buffalo	− 1.1
Buffalo	− 1.8	St. Louis	− 1.2
Detroit	− 2.2	Gary	− 1.3
Saint Louis	− 2.3	Detroit	− 1.5

Note: Correlation coefficient between 1970–80 and 1980–87 growth rates equals 0.9.

lation bases during both the 1970s and the 1980s. The strongest growing RCCs were, not surprisingly, in the Sunbelt region.

In aggregate, the suburbs of these metropolitan areas experienced
startling growth in both the 1970s and the 1980s. Our data (table 4.15)
show that in the 1970s only the suburbs of Newark and New York City
experienced declines in population. Similarly, in the 1980s only 7
percent of the metropolitan areas in the country experienced population declines in their suburbs. Not surprisingly, the weakest subur-

Table 4.15 ANNUALIZED PERCENTAGE CHANGE IN POPULATION IN SELECTED
SUBURBS IN THE UNITED STATES: 1970–80 AND 1980–87

1970–80		1980–87	
Phoenix	6.6	Phoenix	5.1
Houston	6.0	Orlando	4.2
Fort Lauderdale	5.2	Houston	4.0
Orlando	5.0	Atlanta	3.5
Tampa	4.6	San Antonio	3.3
60-city mean	2.2	60-city mean	1.4
Percentage positive	97.0	Percentage positive	93.0
Boston	0.1	Detroit	− 0.1
Buffalo	0.1	Gary	− 0.1
Providence	0.1	Buffalo	− 0.3
Pittsburgh	0.0	Pittsburgh	− 0.4
New York	− 0.1	Youngstown	− 0.5
Newark	− 0.2		

Note: Correlation coefficient between 1970–80 and 1980–87 growth rates equals 0.9.

ban population growth was in the traditional Rustbelt metropolitan
areas, while the strongest suburban population growth, in both time
periods, occurred in the Sunbelt. Particularly strong population
growth was found in the suburbs of Phoenix, Houston, and Orlando.
Again, the past was a good predictor of the future. The correlation
coefficient between these two time periods in suburban population
growth was 0.89.

The differential performance of the CBDs, the RCCs, and the suburbs has been quite striking. In spite of the fact that 40 percent of the
central cities experienced population growth in the 1970s, for example, only San Jose and Los Angeles experienced greater population
growth within their city limits than in their suburbs. In the 1980s,
three central cities grew faster than did their suburban areas: San Jose,
New York, and Boston. The correlation coefficient of these differential
city and suburban growth rates between the two time periods was
0.87, again demonstrating the continued pattern of population decentralization.

A high correlation pattern is also exhibited over time between the
differential growth rates of the CBD and the RCC. This is reflected in
both the high correlation coefficient and in the fact that the top cities
stayed at the top and the bottom cities stayed at the bottom in both
time periods. In particular, the CBDs of Rochester, Los Angeles, Boston, and Philadelphia exhibited strong growth relative to the rest of
their central cities, while the CBDs of Houston, Fort Lauderdale, and

Oklahoma City were very weak compared to the rest of their central cities.

There were differences in the population growth rates for both time periods between central business districts and their suburbs. It is not unexpected that suburban areas generally grew much more rapidly than did their CBDs in terms of population. However, it is surprising to note that, in both periods, several CBDs grew more rapidly than their suburbs—Rochester, Los Angeles, Boston, and New York. Once again, these differential growth rates were highly correlated over time, and were generally smaller in the 1980s than in the 1970s. An important question here is whether or not these differentials reflect specific efforts by local governments to direct resources to CBDs.

Table 4.16 presents summary statistics for a number of characteristics of these urban areas over the period 1970–87. Real income levels of suburban communities grew throughout this period (table 4.16, section *a*), while the incomes of families in the CBDs and RCCs declined from 1970 to 1980, then rebounded in the 1980s. As a result, the average real family income of CBDs was lower by about 3 percent in 1987 than it was in 1970, whereas the average family income in the rest of the central city was about 5 percent higher in 1987 than in 1970. In marked contrast, the average real family income in the suburbs was up by 12 percent from 1970 in 1987.

The pattern of real income growth (table 4.16, section *b*) was quite different in the 1970s than in the 1980s for central cities. Specifically, in the 1970s only 20 percent of the CBDs and 15 percent of the RCCs experienced positive growth in average real family income. However, in the 1980s 92 percent of the CBDs and 98 percent of the RCCs experienced growth in average real family income. In contrast, 66 percent of the individual suburban communities in the sixty largest metropolitan areas experienced increased average real family incomes in the 1970s, while 94 percent of these individual suburbs experienced rising real incomes in the 1980s. By any measure, the 1980s were notably better—or at least, less "bad"—for central cities than were the 1970s. However, during this entire period suburban areas significantly outperformed central cities in terms of real income growth. This pattern has substantial long-run ramifications, as these declining central-city real income levels place an additional fiscal burden on the remaining residents.

The data also reveal (table 4.16, section *c*) that the central cities had much higher proportions of black populations than did their suburbs. This is particularly true of the CBDs, which were on average approximately one-third black by 1987. Although suburbs were becoming

Table 4.16 SELECTED CHARACTERISTICS OF THE SIXTY LARGEST
METROPOLITAN AREAS IN THE UNITED STATES: 1970–87

	CBDs	RCCs	Suburbs
a. *Average Family Income*			
(1990 dollars)			
1970	33,618	43,718	44,988
1980	30,136	41,277	45,176
1987	32,877	45,985	50,414
b. *Percentage with Rising*			
Average Real Family Income			
1970–80	20	15	66
1980–87	92	98	94
c. *Percentage Black Population*			
1970	25.4	17.9	4.2
1980	29.8	21.7	4.6
1987	30.3	22.0	6.3
d. *Percentage of Establishment-*			
Based Employment in Manufacturing			
1970	28.5	28.0	26.9
1980	26.0	25.6	26.3
e. *Percentage of Dwelling Units*			
Built before 1960			
As of 1970	69.8	61.3	48.8
f. *Percentage of Dwelling Units*			
Built between 1970 and 1980			
As of 1980	14.5	19.2	31.6
g. *Annualized Percentage Change*			
in Establishment-Based Employment			
1976–80	1.6	4.1	6.7
1980–86	1.0	2.6	3.7

more racially mixed in the 1980s, only about 6 percent of suburban populations were black by 1987.

Surprisingly, the percentage of establishment-based employment represented by manufacturing jobs (table 4.16, section *d*) did not differ significantly either over time or across CBDs, RCCs, and suburbs.

The percentage of dwelling units built before 1960 (table 4.16, section *e*) was higher for CBDs than for RCCs and suburbs, respectively. Similarly, as of 1980 (table 4.16, section *f*), approximately one-third of all suburban housing units had been built in the preceding decade, much higher than the 19 percent of the RCC housing stock, and 15 percent of the CBD housing stock.

The final section in table 4.16, section g, reflects annualized percentage change in employment for CBDs, RCCs, and the suburbs, respectively. It is noteworthy that in spite of the fact that CBDs experienced significant declines in their population base in the 1970s, their employment base grew from 1976 through 1980. Similarly, although the RCCs experienced little growth in population during the 1970s, they experienced significant growth during the 1970s as spouses went to work at local work sites. For the same reason, the growth rate of suburban employment exceeded the suburban population growth rate during both the 1970s and the 1980s. The pattern of positive CBD employment growth, coinciding with declining CBD population, continued into the 1980s, as did the pattern of modest population growth in RCCs combined with significant employment growth in RCCs.

Summary: Population Decentralization

Taken together, the picture that emerges in terms of urban population growth patterns during the 1970s and 1980s is:

□ increased decentralization toward the suburbs;
□ increased deconcentration toward Sunbelt regions;
□ declining central business districts, both in terms of population and real income;
□ modest population growth in the rest of the central city;
□ diminished income performance of the RCCs in the 1970s followed by stronger economic growth in the 1980s;
□ booming suburban communities in both the 1970s and 1980s in terms of both real income and population growth;
□ substantial racial imbalance between the central cities and suburbs; and
□ stronger central-city population performance in the 1980s than in the 1970s.

The next section explores, through the use of multiple regression analysis, the determinants of the population and employment decentralization patterns for four units of observation—CCs, CBDs, RCCs, and individual suburban communities.

REGRESSION ANALYSIS: DETERMINANTS OF EMPLOYMENT AND POPULATION GROWTH

To more fully understand the determinants of employment and population growth, the annualized growth rates for these variables were regressed upon a series of variables for the previously described time periods. This analysis was conducted on the sixty CBDs, the sixty RCCs, the sixty CCs, and a sample of over 2,400 individual suburban communities surrounding these sixty major cities for the 1970s and nearly one thousand suburban communities for the 1980s.

The independent variables are derived from a number of sources. They reflect six broad categories of urban influences: base-period resident population traits, base-period industrial structure, the quality of the local infrastructure, governmental policies, local quality of life, and contemporaneous urban growth.

The base-period resident population traits include a number of socioeconomic variables. Beginning-of-the-period real average family income, percentage black in the community, and percentage high school graduates in the community are variables designed to determine if base-period socioeconomic characteristics of a community have systematic impacts on population and employment growth.

The base-period industrial structure is hypothesized to have an effect on subsequent population and employment growth. The specific hypothesis is that communities with relatively high proportions of their employment in manufacturing would suffer most—that the nation's difficult world competitive position in manufacturing would translate into local difficulties. This hypothesis is also explored by Paul Cheshire in chapter 5 of this volume.

A commonly employed surrogate for the age and quality of the infrastructure in a community is used: the proportion of residential units built before 1960. A negative relationship with both employment and population growth is hypothesized.

Many governmental policies—local, state, and federal—are undertaken with a view toward improving local economies or, at a minimum, are expected to have an impact on them. We have a rich collection of local regulatory data for the later period from our survey. Whether positive or negative coefficients should be expected for variables capturing restrictiveness is not obvious. There is reason to theorize that there will be lower rates of development where regulatory stringency is greatest, because restrictiveness acts as a quantity limitation and raises building costs. But there are also good reasons to theorize that there will be higher rates of development where regulatory severity is greater. If the regulations are limited to rectifying the impact of externalities and other market imperfections—if they are reactions to the costs of past and future growth—then high-growth areas will have more restrictive land-use regulations. A measure of the state business policy environment can be found in a study by

Michael Luger (1987). Four of his measures of state policies that are directed at being hospitable to business were selected and assembled into an index for both 1976 and 1980. Clearly, the hypothesis here is for positive coefficients.

Much can be done to examine the role of federal policies. The models used here have data on the dollars spent through defense contracts in each county or central city. Each part of a central city is regarded as potentially benefiting from the procurement dollars coming to the city as a whole; and each suburban jurisdiction is regarded as the potential beneficiary of procurement dollars coming to the county in which it is located. The extent to which U.S. policy directs these contracts on a least-cost basis or on a local economic need basis is ambiguous. Either way, if there are very different levels of defense spending flowing to different parts of the country, some effects should be anticipated—the larger the dollar amounts, the larger the employment effect.

A quality-of-life measure, based on a variety of criteria in the metropolitan area—recreation facilities, housing availability, crime, educational quality, arts facilities, climate, health care, and transportation facilities—is also included. The data are derived from Rand McNally's *Places Rated Almanac* (Boyer and Savageau 1981). Clearly, one expects better amenities to be an attraction. Though many are located in central cities, the hypothesis is that suburban communities also benefit.

Contemporaneous measures of employment and population growth within each jurisdiction and across parts of each metropolitan area are examined. Whether initial levels of employment and population affect subsequent growth and the nature of the relationships between employment growth and population growth are also analyzed. Population growth rates reflect the interaction of migration, family formation, and the net of births and deaths. Employment growth rates reflect migration and labor-force participation decisions. One expects these growth rates to be positively correlated, but it is not a certainty. There are clear multiplier effects from population growth that are hypothesized to produce subsequent employment growth. And there are clear labor demand effects from employment growth that lead one to the expectation of population growth. But other factors—immobility of labor, transportation accessibility, fiscal constraints—may negate those effects. In each case, the contemporaneous employment or population growth rates for the community are entered as independent variables—as are the contemporaneous employment or population growth rates in other parts of the metropolitan area.

Factors Associated with Employment Growth

Table 4.17 displays the results of simple OLS regressions on the annual employment growth rate over the 1976–80 period. The first column presents the results for the sample of sixty central cities, the second column for the sixty CBDs, the third column for the sixty RCCs, and the final column for the individual suburban jurisdictions. Similarly, table 4.18 reports the results for the same four geographic groupings for the 1980–86 period. The 1980–86 analyses include four additional variables that were not available for the earlier sample period. These variables are: an adjusted version of the Rand McNally *Places Rated* quality of life index (Boyer and Savageau 1981); a measure of whether the local jurisdiction had a significant increase in the amount of time required for the local planning authorities to approve a standard new building from the period 1984–89; the percentage of zoning variance applications approved by the local planning authorities in 1989; and a dummy variable indicating whether the local jurisdiction utilized impact fees in 1989. These local regulatory variables were obtained from the 1989 survey that was conducted for this project for all local jurisdictions in the sixty major metropolitan areas. Note that the 1980–86 suburban regression is based upon a smaller sample than that used in the earlier period, since these regulatory data were used as variables, and survey responses were not obtained from all jurisdictions. In fact, only one-third of all the suburban jurisdictions responded to the regulatory survey. However, the responding surveys represented approximately 55 percent of all employment in these sixty metropolitan areas. Further, when the suburban regressions for 1976–80 were re-estimated using only the nearly one thousand suburban communities that responded to the land-use survey, the results were qualitatively unchanged from those reported in table 4.17. Finally, two pure control variables (not displayed in the tables) were included in the regressions to adjust for measurement errors arising from the imperfect allocation of zip code data to jurisdictional observations, and for the measurement error in SBA employment data. Brief definitions of all variables used in this analysis are reported in the appendix.

Several broad results concerning the determinants of employment growth are apparent from an examination of tables 4.17 and 4.18. The impact of contemporaneous population growth in the community is associated with a positive impact on local employment growth rates. During the early period, this result is significant with a 90 percent confidence level for only one subset of metropolitan areas—the RCCs.

The results for the 1980s are much greater in magnitude and statistical precision, except for the CBDs. This result reflects the fact that during the late 1970s much of the employment growth was driven by an increased number of spouses going to work in local markets, rather than by larger numbers of residents. By the middle of the 1980s, however, this engine of employment growth had had its biggest impact, and significant employment growth was mostly obtained via some population growth occurring in the local community—hence, the robust positive coefficients for central cities and suburbs in the 1980s.

The base-period employment level was negative in its influence in both time periods, for all jurisdictions. This result was particularly strong for suburban areas in the late 1970s, reflecting the fact that the greatest employment growth rates were achieved by quite small communities experiencing moderate absolute job growth—in some sense, a statistical artifact. As these communities matured, this impact diminished. The results for the 1980s, which indicate that the central cities (particularly their RCCs) that had large employment bases experienced significantly lower employment growth rates, is a particularly interesting observation. A reasonable conjecture is that this reflects the erosion of the traditional employment base found in these metropolitan areas. The economies of agglomeration are not apparent in these results. In fact, it is the net diseconomies of agglomeration in central cities, and in the older, bigger suburbs, that emerges.

Communities that had a relatively high proportion of their housing units built before 1960 experienced lower growth rates in both the 1970s and 1980s. In both time periods this result was particularly strong for suburban communities, again reflecting the facts that not all suburbs are alike and that older suburbs experienced much lower growth rates than their new counterparts.

The employment structure of the community displayed two interesting patterns. First, in the 1970s, communities that had relatively high proportions of their employment in retail trade tended to experience higher growth rates in the subsequent period. This result was largest and most significant in each part of the central cities, and was particularly strong in the RCCs, indicating that central cities that had viable retail centers in the 1970s experienced greater employment growth than communities that had already lost their retail activity. However, in the 1980s, the importance of retail employment in the central city had diminished considerably. Suburban communities with high proportions in retail employment had some tendency to experience higher growth rates in both periods, reflecting the coming of age of suburban shopping communities as major employment sites.

Table 4.17 REGRESSION RESULTS: DETERMINANTS OF ANNUAL EMPLOYMENT GROWTH RATES IN PARTS OF SIXTY LARGEST PMSAs, 1976–80

Variable	CC	CBD	RCC	Suburbs
Constant	9.81 (2.49)	−3.54 (0.63)	10.24 (2.54)	15.25 (11.07)
Annual percentage change in population, 1976–80	0.06 (0.43)	0.06 (0.20)	0.55 (2.45)	0.01 (0.41)
Total employment, 1976	−6.42E-07 (1.04)	−2.74E-06 (0.98)	−1.30E-06 (0.62)	−5.08E-05 (2.23)
Percentage of residential units built before 1960	−0.04 (1.97)	0.05 (1.26)	−0.06 (1.66)	−0.11 (8.32)
Percentage employed in manufacturing, 1976	−0.10 (3.11)	−0.07 (1.46)	−0.02 (0.65)	−0.04 (3.52)
Percentage employed in retail, 1976	0.10 (0.86)	0.34 (1.90)	0.18 (2.87)	0.02 (1.22)
Percentage change in CBD employment, 1976–80			−0.11 (1.30)	0.01 (0.12)

Percentage change in RCC employment, 1976–80	0.31 (4.01)	−0.05 (0.30)	0.21 (3.24)
Percentage change in OCC employment, 1976–80	0.01 (0.08)	0.48 (2.83)	0.17 (1.28)
Luger index, 1976	1.15E-07 (1.60)	0.21 (0.95)	−0.11 (1.06)
Federal defense procurements, 1970–79	−0.01 (0.25)	2.09E-07 (1.31)	5.25E-08 (0.80)
Percentage of black population, 1970	−0.08 (1.67)	0.10 (0.33)	−0.02 (0.62)
Percentage of adults not high school graduates, 1970		−0.08 (1.27)	−0.05 (2.56)
Adjusted R-squared	0.72	0.30	0.07
N	60	60	2474

Notes: Absolute t-values are in parentheses. For definition of variables, see appendix.

Table 4.18 REGRESSION RESULTS: DETERMINANTS OF ANNUAL EMPLOYMENT GROWTH RATES IN PARTS OF SIXTY LARGEST PMSAs, 1980–86

Variable	CC	CBD	RCC	Suburbs
Constant	-5.76	2.28	-7.57	4.62
	(1.08)	(0.34)	(1.09)	(1.58)
Annual percentage change in population, 1980–87	1.15	0.61	1.21	1.03
	(2.37)	(0.90)	(2.05)	(4.53)
Total employment, 1980	-1.92E-06	-2.13E-06	-5.74E-06	-1.55E-05
	(2.12)	(0.84)	(2.52)	(1.09)
Percentage of residential units built before 1960	-4.89E-03	-0.03	-0.05	-0.10
	(0.17)	(0.99)	(1.26)	(5.37)
Percentage employed in manufacturing, 1980	0.03	7.22E-03	0.07	-0.06
	(0.88)	(0.19)	(1.94)	(4.43)
Percentage employed in retail, 1980	0.05	0.02	0.02	0.03
	(0.55)	(0.18)	(0.14)	(1.18)
Percentage change in CBD employment, 1980–86			-0.19	0.03
			(1.82)	(0.30)
Percentage change in RCC employment, 1980–86		-0.10		-0.01
		(0.66)		(0.16)
Percentage change in OCC employment, 1980–86	0.26	0.23	0.30	
	(2.43)	(1.29)	(2.16)	

Luger index, 1980	0.31	0.27	0.43	0.15
	(2.96)	(1.52)	(3.31)	(1.29)
Federal defense procurements, 1980–86	7.02E-09	5.32E-08	1.95E-09	1.28E-08
	(0.30)	(1.17)	(0.06)	(0.72)
Percentage of black population, 1980	-0.02	0.03	-0.05	0.03
	(1.12)	(1.35)	(1.81)	(0.86)
Percentage of adults not high school graduates, 1980	6.63E-03	-0.09	-0.03	-0.02
	(0.13)	(2.11)	(0.41)	(0.99)
Project approval time increased	-0.04	-0.22	0.41	-0.47
	(0.07)	(0.22)	(0.56)	(0.96)
Percentage of zoning variances approved	5.13E-04	0.02	-3.28E-03	-0.01
	(0.04)	(0.76)	(0.19)	(1.67)
Uses impact fees	-0.38	0.85	-0.41	-0.28
	(0.68)	(0.86)	(0.50)	(0.59)
Places Rated quality of life, 1981	7.02E-04	-3.58E-04	1.95E-03	1.20E-03
	(0.73)	(0.27)	(1.57)	(2.38)
Adjusted R-squared	0.50	0.13	0.59	0.19
N	60	60	60	1126

Notes: Absolute t-values are in parentheses. For definition of variables, see appendix.

In contrast, those jurisdictions that had relatively high proportions of their employment in manufacturing experienced distinctly lower employment growth rates in the 1970s. This result was true in both the central cities and suburbs. Interestingly, this pattern continued for suburban jurisdictions into the 1980s. In fact, both the magnitude and precision of this effect are almost identical in the two time periods for suburban employment growth. In contrast, RCC employment growth rates in the 1980s were significantly and positively correlated with base proportions of manufacturing employment in the 1980s, presumably reflecting the regeneration of central-city light manufacturing that left downtown areas in the early 1980s, moving toward the city borders.

Two measures of the social composition of the community were included in the analysis. Apart from any effects already incorporated in population flows, the percentage of black families in the community showed no statistically significant relation with employment growth rates in the 1970s in any part of the metropolitan areas. However, in the 1980s, central cities with relatively high proportions of black families experienced lower growth rates in employment, particularly in the RCC areas. But a higher proportion of black households in the community had no notable statistical impact on suburban employment growth rates in the 1980s. The quality of the local work force as measured by the base-period percentage of adults who had not graduated from high school indicates a negative influence on local employment growth rates. This influence is found in both time periods, and the result was particularly clear in the suburbs in the 1970s and in the CBDs in the 1980s. The presence of a poorly qualified local work force inhibited local growth during the active suburbanization period of the 1970s, and the steady deterioration of educational performance has made central cities increasingly less attractive places to locate.

Several variables were utilized to explore the impact of very specific measures of some governmental policies on local employment growth rates. The Luger index measures the pro-business attitude of the state legislature. In the 1970s this variable failed to reveal any statistically significant impact at normal confidence levels. However, in the 1980s, these policies did translate into employment growth. Across the parts of urban areas, communities located in states that adopted more pro-business policies grew at relatively more rapid rates, responding to the incentives and flexibility. This was particularly true of central cities and of each of their component parts, and somewhat less so for suburban jurisdictions. The increased impact of these efforts may well reflect the greater degree of sophistication utilized by state officials to spur business competitiveness in response to more mobile businesses. It suggests that some state-related business policies can enhance employment growth, though it does not indicate, of course, whether the benefits of the policies are greater or less than their costs over the long run.

As a measure of federal governmental incentives for employment growth provided to local communities, the cumulative defense procurements in the county in which the jurisdiction is located were included as a variable. In both periods, the effect of increased federal procurement expenditures was positive in all communities. Though these results were not statistically significantly different from zero at 90 percent confidence levels, there is a strong suggestion of positive effects on CBDs in the 1970s and 1980s. This was not true for the suburbs. The pattern and magnitude of these results suggest that federal procurement expenditures may act as a "pump primer" to city employment growth, but they do not play any discernible role in suburban growth. Again, the results do not indicate whether the costs of such "pump priming" exceed the benefits over the long run.

The final set of public policy variables included in the analysis reflects the local communities' attitude toward development—whether the community uses impact fees (an anti-development attitude), the proportion of zoning variance requests approved (an indicator of a pro-development attitude), and whether the time required for local planning officials to approve a standard development project significantly increased from 1984 to 1989 (indicating an anti-development attitude). These variables are available only for the 1980s and, in fact, reflect a survey period somewhat after the growth period covered by the employment data. It is clear that none of these local regulatory variables reveals any consistent statistically significant relationships with employment growth rates. No pattern of any type emerges from these variables as a group.

The quality-of-life variable indicates that, in the 1980s, suburbs located in high-quality-of-life metropolitan areas experienced high employment growth rates. This result was also true for RCCs, though this result is somewhat less precise. Since this index reflects general metropolitan quality of life, this finding is significant in that it indicates that suburban areas appear to experience employment growth benefits from factors, such as the presence of sports franchises, major educational institutions, cultural centers, and major health care facilities—all enterprises that are located primarily in the central cities.

These regressions also explore, in a nonsimultaneous way, the interactions between contemporaneous employment growth in other parts of the metropolitan area. In both periods, we clearly found that suburban employment growth is uncorrelated with contemporaneous employment growth in the central business district, reflecting the increasing independence of suburban employment bases from the city's traditional employment base. In particular, this reflects the fact that much of the employment growth in suburban communities is in sectors of the economy that are not represented in central business districts, and that much of the growth of these sectors is derived from the increased employment of spouses who live in the suburbs. In contrast, the central city gained significantly from increased suburban employment in both time periods. The CBD was the prime beneficiary in the 1970s, the RCC in the 1980s. This reflects a reversal of the traditional notion that central-city employment growth drives suburban employment growth. Instead, we found that suburban employment growth spurs central city employment growth, probably because suburban employment utilizes the services of central-city-based agents such as banks, lawyers, accountants, and consultants. However, a recent simultaneous equations study, using three-stage least squares regressions (Brooks and Summers 1997), was directed at disentangling the endogeneity problems in analyzing the relationships between cities and their suburbs. The finding that emerged does not support this reversal. Rather, it supports the view of interdependence over the decade of the 1980s, but independence over the 1970s, with the primary beneficiary being stronger suburban employment growth due to a healthier central city—a view supported by a number of recent studies cited earlier.

The relationship between the parts of the city is particularly important to city economic development policies. Increased CBD employment growth leads to diminished RCC employment growth. There appears to be competition between the CBD and the RCC as to where employment will locate in the city. Most likely, this is particularly descriptive of the competition for location in the extreme fringes of the RCC that are nearest the suburban employment growth. However, CBD employment growth is unrelated in both time periods to changes in RCC employment growth rates, and is more related to population characteristics and to state and federal government policies.

Not surprisingly, the explanatory power of the regression equation was much higher for the central cities than for the suburban communities. There were many more, and much more diverse, suburban communities than cities included in the analysis. The fact that the R^2

for CBDs declined considerably from the 1970s to the 1980s suggests that these areas are becoming more diverse over time. This may reflect the results of the Reagan administration's policies of reduced national aid to cities, leaving cities more to their own devices to compete. This increasing diversity would suggest that not all cities adopted similar ways of competing, and that cities have very different demands by their populations on the public purse. In contrast, the higher R^2 for suburban communities (adjusted for sample size and additional variables) in the 1980s suggests that suburban communities are maturing and becoming more homogeneous, at least in the sense that they are more urban in their characteristics.

Taken together, these results provide a simple, yet rich, picture of the determinants of local employment growth. It remains for future work to further explore these relationships, as well as to model the simultaneities between employment growth in different parts of the metropolitan area and contemporaneous population growth in the community.

Factors Associated with Population Growth

Tables 4.19 and 4.20 display the results of the OLS regressions on the annual population growth rates for 1970–80 and 1980–87, respectively. As in the case of the employment growth regressions, the 1980–87 time frame includes the four additional regulatory variables that were not available for the earlier sample period. Again, the regression results for the suburban communities that responded to the local regulatory survey yielded results for the 1970–80 period that are qualitatively identical to those obtained using the full suburban community sample.

Examination of tables 4.19 and 4.20 reveals a number of population decentralization influences. First, the impact of contemporaneous employment growth in the city was small and insignificant in the 1970s, though there was some positive association in the population and employment movements in the suburbs. In the 1980s this impact was positive and precisely estimated, especially for the RCC part of the city and the suburbs. These findings are consistent with those found in the regressions explaining employment growth. Taken together, the regressions indicate that employment and population growth within communities move hand in hand—particularly in the growing suburbs. They also indicate that population growth drives employment growth more than the reverse—the coefficients of population on

Table 4.19 REGRESSION RESULTS: DETERMINANTS OF ANNUAL POPULATION GROWTH RATES IN PARTS OF SIXTY LARGEST PMSAs, 1970–80

Variable	CC	CBD	RCC	Suburbs
Constant	5.27 (2.80)	7.34 (2.28)	6.41 (3.53)	7.93 (22.49)
Population, 1970	2.31E-08 (0.26)	1.16E-06 (0.41)	7.28E-09 (0.08)	-2.02E-05 (10.43)
Population squared, 1970				4.12E-11 (6.99)
Average real family income, 1970	-1.76E-04 (1.80)	-1.94E-04 (1.55)	-2.31E-04 (2.30)	-3.43E-05 (2.19)
Percentage of residential units built before 1960	-0.07 (8.03)	-0.05 (2.90)	-0.07 (7.53)	-0.11 (55.07)
Percentage employed in manufacturing, 1976	-0.01 (1.17)	3.78E-03 (0.23)	1.32E-03 (0.20)	-3.00E-03 (1.72)
Percentage employed in retail, 1976	0.03 (0.74)	0.01 (0.21)	9.53E-03 (0.67)	-6.70E-03 (2.54)
Percentage change in employment, 1976–80	0.02 (0.43)	-0.06 (1.03)	0.03 (0.91)	5.39E-03 (1.83)
Percentage change in CBD population, 1970–80			0.03 (0.58)	-6.59E-03 (0.38)
Percentage change in RCC population, 1970–80		0.09 (0.43)		
Percentage change in OCC population, 1970–80	0.12 (1.45)	0.02 (0.08)	0.14 (1.66)	0.15 (4.68)
Federal defense procurements, 1970–79	2.20E-08 (2.16)	7.21E-08 (2.92)	1.86E-08 (1.63)	1.53E-09 (0.42)
Percentage of black population, 1970	-0.02 (2.86)	-6.91E-03 (0.55)	-0.02 (1.83)	-0.02 (4.90)
Percentage of adults not high school graduates, 1970	0.02 (1.20)	-0.07 (1.95)	5.11E-03 (0.29)	0.02 (4.60)
Adjusted R-squared	0.83	0.31	0.83	0.64
N	60	60	60	2474

Notes: Absolute t-values are in parentheses. For definition of variables, see appendix.

employment are larger than the coefficients of employment on population.

The base-period population level was not generally statistically significantly related to subsequent population growth rates for cities in the 1970s. In the 1980s, however, the cities that had weathered the 1970s, and stayed relatively large, grew more. In contrast, larger suburban communities experienced declining population growth rates. The positive impact of the level of population on population growth rates in the 1980s in the CCs reflects the baby boom regentrification of central cities that occurred in the largest cities of the United States. The negative effect of base-period population in the suburban communities reflects the statistical artifact that for larger communities a given population increase equals a lower growth rate than for smaller communities.

New housing accompanied new population. Communities having a relatively large proportion of housing units built before 1960—a variable that is both descriptive of the housing stock and a surrogate for the age of the infrastructure—consistently experienced large and statistically significant lower population growth rates. This was particularly true in suburban communities. This result, which is consistent with the earlier findings for employment growth rates, indicates that population was drawn to and shifted—even among suburban communities—to newly created areas. This movement away from the older infrastructure epitomizes the decentralization process that has occurred during the past two decades, if not longer.

The employment structure of the community influenced local population growth rates. First, communities with high proportions of their local job base in the manufacturing sector tended to experience relatively low population growth rates in the 1970s. This was particularly true for suburban areas. In the 1980s, population had already left these areas, and the manufacturing base had no influence on suburban population growth. In the cities, however, manufacturing was a deterrent to both RCC and CC population growth. The population exodus from manufacturing centers largely took place in the 1970s in the suburbs, but, in the 1980s, manufacturing concentrations were still driving people from cities. Suburban population growth rates were found to be strongly and negatively related to the proportion of the employment in the community focused on retailing in the 1970s. This probably reflects the fact that major suburban retail areas (such as King of Prussia in Pennsylvania, Schaumberg in Illinois, and Tysons Corner in Virginia) developed into major employment nodes for all types of activity during this period. As a result of the increases

Table 4.20 REGRESSION RESULTS: DETERMINANTS OF ANNUAL POPULATION GROWTH RATES IN PARTS OF SIXTY LARGEST PMSAs, 1980–87

Variable	CC	CBD	RCC	Suburbs
Constant	4.27	−2.69	3.41	2.78
	(2.88)	(1.77)	(2.04)	(6.57)
Population, 1980	2.12E-07	−1.14E-06	1.63E-07	−4.15E-06
	(2.42)	(1.06)	(1.65)	(3.32)
Population squared, 1980				9.96E-12
				(2.86)
Average real family income, 1980	−5.92E-05	9.14E-06	−7.98E-05	−7.47E-06
	(0.86)	(0.17)	(1.18)	(0.48)
Percentage of residential units built before 1960	−0.03	−0.02	−0.03	−0.05
	(3.52)	(3.32)	(3.55)	(28.11)
Percentage employed in manufacturing, 1980	−0.02	−2.77E-03	−0.01	1.54E-03
	(3.03)	(0.40)	(1.57)	(0.91)
Percentage employed in retail, 1980	−0.04	5.95E-03	−0.01	2.79E-04
	(1.85)	(0.21)	(0.56)	(0.09)
Percentage change in employment, 1980–86	0.06	0.04	0.04	0.01
	(1.69)	(1.25)	(1.78)	(3.59)
Percentage change in CBD population, 1980–87			0.25	0.17
			(2.73)	(4.01)
Percentage change in RCC population, 1980–87		0.47		0.49
		(3.11)		(13.10)
Percentage change in OCC population, 1980–87	0.36	−0.06	0.33	
	(4.75)	(0.43)	(4.30)	

Federal defense procurements, 1980–86	5.86E-09	1.32E-08	8.12E-10	-1.04E-08
	(0.99)	(1.63)	(0.13)	(4.14)
Percentage of black population, 1980	-0.01	-0.01	-8.57E-03	-0.01
	(2.55)	(2.60)	(1.46)	(3.28)
Percentage of adults not high school graduates, 1980	7.83E-03	0.01	6.46E-03	0.01
	(0.58)	(0.89)	(0.44)	(3.39)
Project approval time increased	0.04	0.35	-0.05	0.20
	(0.29)	(1.99)	(0.37)	(3.32)
Percentage zoning variables approved	-8.22E-04	-5.33E-03	2.34E-03	4.18E-05
	(0.24)	(1.20)	(0.68)	(0.05)
Uses impact fees	0.09	-0.03	0.13	-3.90E-03
	(0.66)	(0.18)	(0.88)	(0.07)
Places Rated quality of life, 1981	-2.75E-04	9.07E-04	-2.12E-04	9.07E-05
	(1.14)	(3.95)	(0.82)	(1.32)
Adjusted R-squared	0.85	0.64	0.86	0.66
N	60	60	60	1126

Notes: Absolute *t*-values are in parentheses. For definition of variables, see appendix.

in land prices brought about by this major employment growth, population was "squeezed out" from these dominant retailing areas. This is consistent with the earlier findings that high suburban retail employment proportions led to higher total employment growth rates in both periods.

The social composition of the community was found to be relatively important as a determinant of its population growth rate. Specifically, communities with high proportions of black households were found to grow significantly more slowly in both the 1970s and 1980s—in cities and in suburbs. The effect was particularly strong in the suburbs. This result indicates that during the 1970s and 1980s, population continued a flight pattern away from communities comprising relatively high proportions of black households. Note that this is true for both the city and suburban communities. The proportion of the adult population lacking a high school degree did not seem to have much effect on population growth in the central cities. Surprisingly, however, this is not the case for suburban communities. In fact, the results indicate the somewhat perverse conclusion that suburban communities with relatively high levels of high school nongraduates grew significantly more rapidly than other communities. A reasonable conjecture is that this reflects the conversion of formerly rural communities (with relatively low rates of high school completion) to new suburban communities—that is, it reflects a changing land-use pattern, rather than a fundamental socioeconomic influence. But this is a conjecture; further work on this question is clearly called for.

Communities with relatively high real family incomes experienced lower population growth rates in the 1970s. This probably reflects an arbitrage process, whereby jobs and people moved from relatively high-cost communities to relatively low-cost communities, and the relatively high birth rates in low-income households. It is interesting to note that this process occurred primarily in the 1970s. There are no discernible influences of real family income on local population growth rates in the 1980s.

There is evidence to suggest that federal government expenditures provide some incentives for local population growth in central cities, with CBDs the primary beneficiaries. Cumulative defense procurement expenditures in the county where the jurisdiction was located were found to exert significantly positive impacts on population growth in the CBDs in both the 1970s and 1980s. This was not true for suburban communities. In fact, these expenditures had a negative effect on suburban population growth in the 1980s, probably the result of large growth rates in the least-developed communities.

The local community attitudes toward development, as measured by the variables from the local regulatory survey, failed to reveal any clear-cut pattern. The only notable result is that CBD and suburban population growth rates tended to rise as the community experienced an increase in the time necessary for project approval (from 1984 to 1989). This result obviously reflects the fact that those communities with rapidly growing population frequently found themselves attempting to slow growth rates, or were simply overwhelmed with the growth approval process; and they, therefore, experienced increasing approval delays. The suggestion, in other words, is that the causation runs from population growth rate being high to increases in zoning approval delays, rather than in the other direction. The fact that the regulatory approval data are based on the period 1984–89 underscores this view.

The quality-of-life index confirms the view that communities located in more desirable metropolitan areas tended to experience higher population growth rates. This was especially true for CBDs and suburbs. It is not surprising that this result is particularly strong for these two types of areas, since the amenities composing the index tend to be provided in the CBD, and are disproportionately consumed by high-income suburban residents. As in the case of the employment regressions, the results indicate that suburban growth is affected by central-city amenity levels.

Finally, in general, we found that the population growth rates in one part of the metropolitan area have positive spillover effects on other portions of the metropolitan area. In the 1970s, high suburban population growth rates tended to induce high RCC growth rates (and vice versa). No particular interrelation was found between CBD population growth rates in the 1970s and the growth rates for this period in either the RCC or suburban populations. For the 1980s, a full set of positive interactions was found. That is, suburban growth rates were higher in those metropolitan areas experiencing higher CBD and higher RCC population growth rates, whereas the central-city areas, particularly their RCCs, experienced higher population growth rates if their suburban counterparts were also growing relatively rapidly. In fact, even within the city, communities with high-growth RCCs tended to have higher-growing CBDs. Population growth is attracted to a metropolitan area, and then dispersed throughout the region, depending on the competitive advantages of the different component parts of the metropolitan area. These results reflect a greater degree of positive spillover benefits than was found for employment, and merit greater attention in future research.

SUMMARY

This chapter has presented an analysis of the decentralization patterns of urban population and employment that occurred in the 1970s and 1980s. It documents a strong pattern of deconcentration toward the Sunbelt and toward the suburbs, though this pattern was not found to be identical for all cities and suburbs. In particular, there were notably different growth patterns within suburbs, as well as within component parts of the central city. These differences have been generally ignored in previous research and deserve considerably more study in the future if we are to understand metropolitan area processes.

This analysis reveals a number of discernible characteristics of the intrametropolitan area decentralization process in the United States.

☐ Cities and their suburbs are characterized by quite interdependent population growth, but less interdependent employment growth. More specifically: (1) suburban employment growth translated into city employment growth in the late 1970s—and continues to do so; (2) city employment growth translates into suburban employment growth; it did so in the late 1970s, not in the early 1980s, but recent studies show strong effects for the decade of the 1980s; and, (3) population growth in the city and suburbs go hand in hand. It would appear that cities with declining populations would have declined more if their suburbs had not been expanding as rapidly—and suburban areas would have expanded more rapidly if their central cities had not experienced population losses.

☐ Contemporaneous population growth is, in recent years, associated with employment growth. The evidence suggests that population growth drives employment growth more than the reverse.

☐ The larger the employment center, the less the subsequent rate of growth. Large-city population centers continue to have large population growth, but large suburban population centers have small population growth.

☐ Communities with older infrastructure (more houses built before 1960) had lower rates of employment and population growth. Newness, and undoubtedly, the availability of land, acted as the magnets.

☐ Viable retail centers have attracted employment in the city and the suburbs—but, in the 1980s, this effect has diminished in central cities. The larger this sector is in a suburban community, however, the greater the population exodus.

☐ Large concentrations of black population were not related to employment growth in the 1970s in any part of metropolitan areas— but they were associated with employment declines in the cities in the 1980s. Population growth, however, was affected negatively in both periods—there was white flight. A less-educated population has been a deterrent to employment growth in all parts of urban areas, and a deterrent to central-city population growth.

☐ Government policies are not without their impact: (1) cities that receive more federal procurement dollars benefit in employment and population, but only in their CBDs; the policies are not a significant factor for suburbs; (2) local regulatory activity does not seem to be associated with employment or population growth— though there were more zoning approval delays in jurisdictions with more population growth; and, (3) state pro-business activities stimulated employment growth, particularly in cities.

☐ Communities located in metropolitan areas with more amenities— including sports franchises, educational institutions, cultural activities, health care facilities—are more attractive to people and jobs. Suburban communities are clearly beneficiaries of many of these quality-of-life factors, most of which are located in central cities.

CONCLUSIONS

There are, of course, policy implications to these results:

1. Communities interested in employment growth also need to be interested in population growth. For some suburban communities, the policy implication is that if the community does not want job growth, it must also restrict its population growth. For cities, successful gentrification has economic benefits in employment.
2. Aged infrastructure already took its toll on suburban communities, but, more recently, it is taking its toll on cities. Repair of CC infrastructure is an important aspect of improved employment.
3. The old manufacturing suburban communities are growing relatively slowly. Policies to increase the labor mobility of the population in these communities or to change their industrial structures will be vital to their economic improvement. Policies that continue to support noncompetitive manufacturing operations do not ultimately benefit the community. (Paul Cheshire's findings for Rotter-

dam, Birmingham, and Glasgow confirm this position. See chapter 5 of this volume.)

4. Regionalism—meaning policies such as regional taxation—predictably, had a hard time in the state legislatures in the early 1980s, given the evidence in this study that central cities benefitted from suburban employment expansions, but suburbs did not benefit much from city employment expansion. There appears to be a resurgence of interest in exploring regional collaborations, possibly because the evidence of the late 1980s is that suburbs are beneficiaries of healthier central cities. These results suggest that it is in the interest of suburbanites to strengthen the economies of their core cities.

5. The quest for regional taxation is solidly based on the empirical findings of the significant effect that quality-of-life characteristics of cities have on suburban growth. It is a policy to be pursued by cities with vigor.

6. Central cities, if newspaper reports are accurate, have become increasingly disenchanted with the assistance they have received from their state governments. They should review that reaction. There is considerable evidence that the policies states have undertaken to make the state business climate more hospitable have been helpful to them. The cities' representatives in the state legislatures should support these policies.

Employment decentralization has been a powerful movement in the United States—from central cities to the suburbs. There is every evidence that it has been brought about by the strong preferences of people to live and work in less dense areas, the difficulties of American manufacturing industries in competing abroad, and a variety of transportation and other technological changes. There is nothing to suggest a reversal of this pattern.

In fact, using population movement as a major predictor, there are strong reasons for expecting central city decline to continue. The already strong development of major employment and population nodes at the edges of metropolitan areas raises increased concern for the fate of our central cities. And the substantial poverty burden carried by the tax base of the large old cities saddles them with the need to reduce services and/or raise taxes—continuing the cycle of decline. A strong macroeconomy can paper over these issues, but it does not change the structural problem. Cities are paying for nationally mandated services.

A "neoconservative" argument would be that no policy is necessary to address this fate—that cities should compete like firms and that markets will equalize wages and employment. But the fixed disparities in regional and intraregional unemployment rates stare us in the face, casting doubt on the efficacy of equilibration. And the need for increased services to the central city needy places even greater pressures on cities.

A "liberal" argument would be that markets are far from perfect—there are public good concentrations in cities (cultural activities, processing of immigrants) and factor immobility (evidenced by very different unemployment rates in central cities and their suburbs)—and government policy should strive to save its investments in the urban infrastructure. The question facing urban policymakers in the United States is, given the powerful decentralizing forces resulting mostly from market factors, What, if anything, should be done with the central cities, and by whom?

America's old cities are the location for the nation's poor—they enable suburbanites and others to be shielded from the antisocial manifestations of poverty. America's old cities are the center of the cultural and historical heritage of the nation. Throughout the world, art and music and dance incubate and develop in large cities—but these are activities that cannot support themselves through their own revenues. And many of our old cities are the prime location for immigrants. Immigrants enter our cities in accordance with the will of national legislation, not because individual cities have invited them. Processing foreign-born persons into the country—socially, educationally, politically—is a costly activity. Cities bear much of those costs for the nation. The removal of cities from the national agenda in the early 1980s appears to have imposed an insupportable burden on them. The future viability of cities is dependent on the return of a national urban policy. However, central cities must also improve the efficiency and accountability of their governments and service delivery mechanisms if they are to survive.

States, too, benefit from the health of their cities. If the infrastructure of cities is allowed to deteriorate, if their children are not well educated, and if their criminal justice system is not well supported, the state loses its relative attractiveness to people and jobs. States are the beneficiaries of a well-maintained highway system and a well-educated labor force. Residents of the region around central cities—suburbanites—must recognize that, although businesses and residents may no longer be gravitating to the city, their population and employment growth is not unrelated to the health of the city. They have a direct stake in reducing the disamenities of the city if their access to urban living is not to be diminished. And they are the beneficiaries of many of the amenities.

A healthier urban America requires a restructuring of the major federal block grants to state and local governments. There should be a reallocation of the funding based on the share of the nation's poverty each cares for, the share of the nation's recent immigrants each cares for, and the relative efficiency with which the city operates. Leveling the playing field between cities and suburbs by having the nation pay for its services to the poor and by creating strong incentives for efficient use of public funds is a win-win strategy. No additional funding is required, cities will be much more viable, and their suburbs will benefit from their health.

APPENDIX: DESCRIPTION AND SOURCES OF VARIABLES

Education

% NOT HS GRAD 70: Percentage of adults not high school graduates in 1970 for CC, CBD, RCC, and OCC. Source: U.S. Bureau of the Census. 1970. *Census of Population and Housing, 1970: Fifth Count Summary Tape* [machine-readable data file]. Washington, D.C.: U.S. Department of Commerce.

% NOT HS GRAD 80: Percentage of adults not high school graduates in 1980 for CC, CBD, RCC, and OCC. Source: CACI, Inc. 1989. *"Minidoris" Datafile Extract.* Produced by CACI for the Wharton Urban Decentralization Project. Fairfax, Va.: CACI.

Employment

TOTAL EMP 76: Total number employed in all nongovernment industrial sectors in 1976 for CC, CBD, RCC, and OCC. Source: U.S. Small Business Administration. 1976, 1980, 1986. *USEEM Employment Extract, 1976, 1980, 1986.* Wharton Urban Decentralization Project. Bethesda, Md.: Social and Scientific Systems.

TOTAL EMP 76 SQUARED: Total number employed in all nongovernment industrial sectors in 1976 squared for CC, CBD, RCC, and OCC. Source: See TOTAL EMP 76.

TOTAL EMP 80: Total number employed in all nongovernment industrial sectors in 1980 for CC, CBD, RCC, and OCC. Source: See TOTAL EMP 76.

TOTAL EMP 80 SQUARED: Total number employed in all nongovernment industrial sectors in 1980 squared for CC, CBD, RCC, and OCC. Source: See TOTAL EMP 80.

ANN CHG EMP 76–80: Annual percentage change in employment from 1976 to 1980 for CC, CBD, RCC, and OCC. Source: See TOTAL EMP 76.

ANN CHG EMP 80–86: Annual percentage change in employment from 1980 to 1986 for CC, CBD, RCC, and OCC. Source: See TOTAL EMP 76.

% IN MANUF 76: Percentage employed in manufacturing in 1976 for CC, CBD, RCC, and OCC. Source: See TOTAL EMP 76.

% IN MANUF 80: Percentage employed in manufacturing in 1980 for CC, CBD, RCC, and OCC. Source: See TOTAL EMP 76.

% IN RETAIL 76: Percentage employed in retail sector in 1976 for CC, CBD, RCC, and OCC. Source: See TOTAL EMP 76.

% IN RETAIL 80: Percentage in retail sector in 1980 for CC, CBD, RCC, and OCC. Source: See TOTAL EMP 76.

% IN TCPU/WHOLESALE 76: Percentage employed in transportation, communications, and public utilities sectors and wholesale sector in 1976 for CC, CBD, RCC, and OCC. Source: See TOTAL EMP 76.

% IN TCPU/WHOLESALE 80: Percentage employed in transportation, communications, and public utilities sectors and wholesale sector in 1980 for CC, CBD, RCC, and OCC. Source: See TOTAL EMP 80.

Federal Funds

DEF DPT PROCRMNT 1: Sum of U.S. Department of Defense procurement contracts to SMSA (in millions of dollars) for FY 1977 and FY 1980. Source: U.S. Bureau of the Census. 1979 and 1982. *State and Metropolitan Area Data Book*. Washington, D.C.: U.S. Department of Commerce.

DEF DPT PROCRMNT 2: Sum of U.S. Department of Defense procurement contracts to SMSA (in millions of dollars) for FY 1984–86. Source: U.S. Bureau of the Census for the Office of Management and

Budget. 1984, 1985, 1986. *Consolidated Federal Funds Report: Volume II: Subcounty Areas.* Washington, D.C.: U.S. Department of Commerce.

Income

AVG FAMILY REAL INC 75: Average family income deflated by urban family price index in 1975 for CC, CBD, RCC, and OCC (in dollars). Source: U.S. Bureau of the Census. 1976. *General Revenue Sharing 1976 Population Estimates* [machine-readable data file]. Washington, D.C.: U.S. Department of Commerce; distributed by Intra-University Consortium for Political and Social Research (ICPSR), Ann Arbor, Mich., 1989; see also Weir, Paula. *Urban Family Budgets Updated to Autumn 1975. Monthly Labor Review* 99 (7): 40–47.

Infrastructure

% UNITS BUILT < 60: Percentage of existing single-family dwelling units built before 1960 for CC, CBD, RCC, and OCC. Source: See % NOT HS GRAD 80.

% UNITS BUILT 60–75: Percentage of existing single-family dwelling units built during the period 1960–75 for CC, CBD, RCC, and OCC. Source: See % NOT HS GRAD 80.

% UNITS BUILT 70–80: Percentage of existing single-family dwelling units built during the period 1970–80 for CC, CBD, RCC, and OCC. Source: See % NOT HS GRAD 80.

Local Regulations

CHG IN DEVELOP COSTS: Estimated percentage increase in cost of lot development (including subdivision) from 1983 to 1988. Source: Wharton Urban Decentralization Project. 1989. *Development Regulation Survey Questionnaire.*

CHG IN ZONING APPR TIME: Estimated change in zoning approval time from 1983 to 1988 (1–5 rating scale: 1 = shortened considerably, 5 = increased considerably).

FEES IMPORTANT (= 1): Reply to survey question asking to rate the effectiveness of impact fees in controlling growth in the respective community. Source: See CHG IN DEVELOP COSTS.

< ADEQUATE INFRA PROV: Quantitative rating by survey respondent of adequacy of provision of infrastructure for growth in the respective community. Source: See CHG IN DEVELOP COSTS.

MOS TO SUBDVN APPR < 50: Estimated number of months between application for subdivision approval and issuance of building permit (assuming proper zoning in place) for development of a subdivision of less than 50 single-family units. Source: See CHG IN DEVELOP COSTS.

MOS TO SUBDVN APPR > 50: Estimated number of months between application for subdivision approval and issuance of building permit (assuming proper zoning in place) for development of a subdivision of more than 50 single-family units. Source: See CHG IN DEVELOP COSTS.

NEW RESIDENTS PAY: Opinion of survey respondent as to whether or not new residents should pay for roads, sewers, and schools when a new residential development is built (1 = new residents should pay). Source: See CHG IN DEVELOP COSTS.

% ZONING APPROVED: Estimated percentage of applications for zoning changes approved during past 12-month period. Source: See CHG IN DEVELOP COSTS.

USE FEES = 1/NONE = 0: Flag denoting usage of impact fees on a local level. Source: See CHG IN DEVELOP COSTS.

Population

POP 76: Total population in 1976 for CC, CBD, RCC and OCC. Population figures for CBD and RCC were derived from estimates of the CC population in *General Revenue Sharing, 1976 Population Estimates* (U.S. Bureau of the Census 1976). Figures for these areas were derived by this formula:

$$\frac{\text{Population of CBD 1980}}{\text{Population of CC 1980}} \times \text{Population CC 1976}$$

$$= \text{Population CBD 1976} \quad (4.A.1)$$

Source: See AVG FAMILY REAL INC 75.

POP 76 SQUARED: Total population in 1976 squared for CC, CBD, RCC, and OCC. Source: See AVG FAMILY REAL INC 75.

POP 80: Total population in 1980 for CC, CBD, RCC, and OCC. Source: See % NOT HS GRAD 80.

POP 80 SQUARED: Total population in 1980 squared for CC, CBD, RCC, and OCC. Source: See % NOT HS GRAD 80.

ANNUAL CHG POP 76–80: Annual percentage change in population, 1976–80 for CC, CBD, RCC, and OCC. Source: See AVG FAMILY REAL INC 75 and % NOT HS GRAD 80.

ANNUAL CHG POP 80–87: Annual percentage change in population, 1980–87 for CC, CBD, RCC, and OCC. Source: See % NOT HS GRAD 80.

% BLACK POP 70: Population of blacks as percentage of total population in 1970 for CC, CBD, RCC, and OCC. Source: See % NOT HS GRAD 70.

% BLACK POP 80: Population of blacks as percentage of total population in 1980 for CC, CBD, RCC, and OCC. Source: See U.S. Bureau of the Census. 1989. *Census of Population and Housing, 1980: Fifth Count Summary Tape* [machine-readable data file]. Washington, D.C.: U.S. Department of Commerce.

Quality of Life

PLACES RATED INDEX 81: Total of normalized scores that measure certain amenities of the sixty SMSAs. The eight categories used were recreation, housing, crime, education, arts, climate, health care/environment, and transportation. The raw scores were obtained from the 1981 Rand-McNally *Places Rated Almanac* and normalized by the Wharton Urban Decentralization Project. Source: Boyer and Savageau (1981).

State Regulations

LUGER INDEX 76: Sum of number of state industrial development programs for businesses in 1976. Data indicate presence of state industrial development programs in four categories: debt and equity programs, tax programs, regulatory climate, and research and development support. The numbers can range from 0 to 19. Source: Conway Publications. 1976. *11th Annual Report of Legislative Climate. Industrial Development*. Atlanta, Ga.: Author. November.

LUGER INDEX 80: Sum of number of state industrial development programs for businesses in 1980. Data indicate presence of state industrial development programs in four categories: debt and equity programs, tax programs, regulatory climate, and research and development support. The numbers can range from 0 to 19. Source: Conway Publications. *15th Annual Report of Legislative Climate. Industrial Development*. Atlanta, Ga.: Author. March.

Statistical Corrections

CENSUS EMP > SBA EMP: Flag denoting central cities in which 1980 CC employment as measured by the 1980 Census is greater than 1980 CC employment as measured by U.S. Small Business Administration. Sources: See TOTAL EMP 76 and % BLACK POP 80.

% NOT COVERED BY ICMA: 1—percentage of SMSA's population covered by the survey. Source: Computed by Wharton Urban Decentralization Project, The Wharton School, University of Pennsylvania.

STATE CAPITAL: Flag denoting SMSA that has a central city that is a state capital. Source: DEF DPT PROCRMNT 1.

Notes

We appreciate the detailed and discerning comments and suggestions of Professor Paul Cheshire of the University of Reading and Professor William Grigsby of the University of Pennsylvania. Almost all of their recommended changes were incorporated into the revision of this paper.

1. We are indebted to A. Alfred Taubman, Chairman of the Taubman Companies, for bringing this citation to our attention.

2. A more detailed description of this database and its construction is provided in Buist (1989).

3. The full set of 3,408 units was reduced by cutting off a 5 percent tail at either end of the employment growth calculations. For very small communities, growth rates can be misleadingly large in either direction.

References

Adams, Charles, H. B. Fleeter, M. Freeman, and Y. Kim. 1994. "Flight from Blight Revisited." Mimeo. School of Public Policy and Management. Columbus, Ohio: Ohio State University.

Boyer, Richard, and David Savageau. 1981. *Places Rated Almanac*. Skokie, Ill.: Rand McNally.

Brooks, Nancy, and Anita A. Summers. 1997. "Does the Economic Health of America's Largest Cities Affect the Economic Health of Their Suburbs?" Wharton Real Estate Center, Working Paper No. 263. Philadelphia, Pa.: University of Pennsylvania.

Buist, Henry, III. 1989. The Wharton Urban Decentralization Project Database Technical Report. Philadelphia, Pa.: Wharton School of the University of Pennsylvania.

Downs, Anthony. 1994. New Visions for Metropolitan America. Washington, D.C.: The Brookings Institution and the Lincoln Institute of Land Policy.

Doyle, A. Conan. [1891] 1967. A Scandal in Bohemia. In The Annotated Sherlock Holmes, vol. 1, edited by W. S. Baring-Gould. New York: Clarkson N. Potter.

Gyourko, Joseph. 1997. "Place vs. People-Based Aid and the Role of an Urban Audit in a New Urban Strategy." Wharton Real Estate Center, Working Paper No. 225. Philadelphia, Pa.: University of Pennsylvania.

Jackson, Kenneth J. 1985. Crabgrass Frontier. New York: Oxford University Press.

Linneman, Peter D., and Anita A. Summers. 1993. "Patterns and Processes of Urban Population Decentralization in the U.S., 1970–87." Urban Change in the United States and Western Europe. Washington, D.C.: The Urban Institute Press.

Luger, M. I. 1987. "The States and Industrial Development: Program Mix and Policy Effectiveness." In Perspectives on Local Public Finance and Public Policy, edited by John M. Quigley. Greenwich, Conn.: JAI Press.

Orfield, Myron. 1995. "Philadelphia Metropolitics: A Regional Agenda for Community and Stability." Report to the Pennsylvania Environmental Council, Philadelphia, Pa.

Pack, Janet R. 1995. "Poverty and Urban Expenditures." Wharton Real Estate Center Working Paper No. 197. Philadelphia, Pa.: University of Pennsylvania.

Persky, J., and W. Wiewel. 1995. "Brownfields, Greenfields: The Costs and Benefits of Metropolitan Employment Decentralization." Mimeo, Great Cities Institute. Chicago, Ill.: University of Illinois at Chicago.

Summers, Anita A., and Lara Jakubowski. 1996. "The Fiscal Burden of Unreimbursed Poverty Expenditures in the City of Philadelphia, 1985–1995." Wharton Real Estate Center, Working Paper No. 238. Philadelphia, Pa.: University of Pennsylvania.

Summers, Anita A., and Garrett Ritter. 1996. "The Costs to Large Cities of Educating Poor Children." Wharton Real Estate Center, draft working paper. Philadelphia, Pa.: University of Pennsylvania.

U.S. Office of Management and Budget, Office of Information and Regulatory Affairs, Executive Office of the President. 1983. Metropolitan Statistical Areas. Washington, D.C.: GPO.

U.S. Small Business Administration, Office of Advocacy, Economic Research Division. 1988. *1976–1986 Linked USEEM Users Guide.* Washington, D.C.: GPO.

Voith, Richard. 1992. "City and Suburban Growth: Substitutes or Complements." *Business Review.* Philadelphia, Pa.: Federal Reserve Bank of Philadelphia.

Voith, Richard. 1993. "Does City Income Growth Increase Suburban Income Growth, House Value Appreciation and Population Growth?" Federal Reserve Bank of Philadelphia Working Paper. Philadelphia, Pa.: Federal Reserve Bank of Philadelphia.

Voith, Richard. 1994. "Do Suburbs Need Cities?" *Business Review.* Philadelphia, Pa.: Federal Reserve Bank of Philadelphia.

Chapter Five

SOME CAUSES OF WESTERN EUROPEAN PATTERNS OF URBAN CHANGE

Paul C. Cheshire

This chapter seeks to arrive at a clearer understanding of the causes of urban change, as well as of those factors that make cities better places for their citizens to live and work, or more successful urban economies. As an essential prerequisite to this analysis, it is necessary to consider the reason for constructing measures of local "welfare," "quality of life," or "urban problems."[1] Following a discussion of possible approaches to this question, a methodology is suggested that can yield practical results for the major functional urban regions (FURs)[2] of the European Union (EU) of twelve member states (EU12).[3] If the effect of systematic factors on urban change can be quantified, then the scope for local policy can be evaluated, and, it is argued, some quantitative indication of local policy effects can be suggested.

MEASUREMENT OF LOCAL WELFARE

There would seem to be three major reasons for measures of local welfare. The first may be mainly to satisfy curiosity about the comparative standing of different local economies and social systems. Although this is not per se a futile activity, it tends at best to be descriptive and is inevitably used to produce league tables of cities, regions, or whatever units are represented. Since no measures have yet been devised that are likely to be universally accepted as correct, such efforts are greeted with skepticism by those who do not like the outcomes, and are equally frequently misrepresented by those who do like the outcomes.

The second use for measures of local welfare—to guide policy interventions—is an extension of the first. The European Commission, for example, published a measure for fifteen years known as the "synthetic index" for the administrative regions of the EU, which was used to guide the intervention of the structural funds. In reality, the "synthetic index" was no more than a weighted average of regional unemployment rates and gross domestic product (GDP) per capita, with the weights determined arbitrarily as 1. An alternative reading of the synthetic index is that it was, in fact, a political device, since Northern European countries appeared more deserving of help if unemployment was used alone as a measure of regional inequalities, and Southern European countries would benefit more if per capita GDP was used alone. The 1988 reform of the EU's structural funds substituted more complicated formulas and introduced two further measures, the proportion of regional employment in industry and the average rate of decline of that employment. The result was still, of course, to inform the political bargaining process. The map of regions actually qualifying for aid corresponds only approximately to the map of those that technically should qualify if the stated measures of regional welfare were actually followed (see Cheshire et al. 1991).

The third use to which measures of local welfare variation may be put is more purely intellectual—to improve our understanding of the causes of change in local economies and societies. For example, if we want to understand processes of urban or regional economic growth or to test growth models, we need measures of local economic activity. If our interest is somewhat wider—in the processes of change and in welfare more widely defined to include some elements not reflected, for instance, in measured GDP[4]—then we may need some measure that captures not only economic factors but also some aspects of local quality of life and environmental amenities.

There are three basic methods for calculating indicators of spatial welfare differences (which the "problem indicator" used here essentially is, although with the reverse sign). Some have simply counted the numbers of "inputs" into local welfare, usually in a mindless way, and arbitrarily aggregated the result. Perhaps the best known form of this type of index is that reported by Rand McNally in their *Places Rated Almanac* for U.S. cities (Boyer and Savageau 1985). Apart from obvious problems such as choosing the appropriate weighting system, avoiding double counting, and scaling for city size, there are other insuperable objections to such an "input"-based system. It is not the value of possible inputs into welfare that is important but the level of welfare that results (it is not the number of concert hall seats that is important but the enjoyment that those seats create). Equally, some indicators have uncertain signs. Other things being equal, for example, less pollution and congestion are obviously better. But measured pollution and congestion levels may be low because of successful abatement measures, or for other reasons that mean low values are positively associated with welfare; or low values of congestion and pollution may be the result of the collapse of the local economy and thus be associated with very high unemployment and outmigration, and so be negatively correlated with local welfare.

A second approach for computing indicators of spatial welfare differences is the "quality-of-life" measure. This measure has been associated with U.S. economists such as Rosen (1979) and Roback (1982) and has been developed by Blomquist, Berger, and Hoehn (1988) and others. Gyourko and Tracy, in chapter 12 of this volume, provide a fine example of this approach, which is theoretically rigorous and consistent, although it does make heroically strong assumptions and is exceptionally demanding on data. Essentially, the assumption is that we observe spatial equilibrium. If this is the case, it can be argued that local variations in the quality of life are capitalized into property values, or reflected in wage rates. If, therefore, we can explain all such wage and price variations that are associated with differences in the nature of the housing stock, local amenities, the environment, the supply of public goods, and the quality of labor, we can infer the marginal value to be placed on local quality-of-life differences. Although theoretically rigorous and technically sophisticated, the assumption of spatial equilibrium—even in the U.S. context—is extreme and, in the context of the EU, with its barriers to spatial adjustment, patently absurd. Furthermore, we may be as interested in average as in marginal welfare differences between major FURs. The assumption of spatial equilibrium implies equalization on the margin, but not that average values are necessarily equalized. Finally, in the EU context, the data necessary to estimate reasonable labor and housing market hedonic equations are simply unavailable.

These criticisms do not invalidate the approach or efforts to improve its theoretical rigor and practical applicability. They do, however, mean that if we wish actually to construct a measure of local welfare in the context of the EU, some alternative methodology is essential. The difference is perhaps between designing rainbows and building bridges which stand up.

I have developed and applied such a methodology in a range of publications (most comprehensively in Cheshire and Hay 1989 but also in Cheshire, Carbonaro, and Hay 1986 and Cheshire 1990). The measure is briefly summarized in the appendix to this chapter; it is an output-, not an input-based, measure resting, perhaps a little awkwardly, on the idea of revealed preference.

Not only do we have to decide how best to measure local per capita welfare, but there is the additional problem of what definition of *local* is most appropriate for purposes of welfare measurement and analysis. This further practical problem has limited the usefulness and reliability of some previous efforts—for example, those of the Department of the Environment (1983) in the United Kingdom. Because of systematic patterns of social segregation and of variations in such patterns between cities and countries, a broad definition of *city* that captures the complete socioeconomic system of the urban area is essential. If a narrow definition—such as individual local governmental units, the administrative core, or even the built-up area—is applied, then measured differences are a product of both actual differences in mean per capita welfare between individual "cities" and differences in the proportion of different income and socioeconomic groups that particular urban definitions capture. Use of administrative definitions is particularly prone to this problem when the measures are compared internationally, because of the great range of variation between countries (and even within countries) in the relationship between functionally defined cities and administratively defined cities. In addition, if we also want to throw light on patterns of urbanization and decentralization, the term *cities* must be defined broadly enough to include areas to which activity may be decentralizing, or from which the urban economy may be drawing. Finally, if there is a policy interest, economic self-containment is important, since otherwise the effects of interventions will not be confined to the particular "local area" to which they are targeted. These arguments point toward using as the observational units broadly defined functional urban areas. The study described in this chapter uses the FURs originally defined in Hall and Hay (1980).

Having selected what are thought to be relevant output-type variables, there remains a weighting problem. To resolve this, and also to select technically efficient variables, the work on which this chapter draws used discriminant analysis. The weight to be attached to different variables was estimated from the data for training sets of FURs nominated by a team of advisers from each EU country to represent the range of "good" and "bad," or healthy and unhealthy, European urban regions.[5] This also allowed normal tests of statistical significance to be applied in the selection of variables.

Given the constraints imposed by the general availability of comparable data for EU countries, the range of data available was very limited. Variables, which in the context of welfare were thought to represent outputs, were chosen, reflecting adjustment problems or revealed preferences. On the margin, if people migrate to a city, it is presumed that this is because they are better off there; similarly, a proxy for the volume of travelers' spending in a city was used, since this was thought to reflect both the range of business opportunities in the city and the quality of the urban environment. Conceptual problems remained with the use of net inmigration: for example, there is no measure of intervening opportunities. It can be argued, however, that this is not very important in practical terms, because only the largest FURs in the EU were included, so, with some exceptions, intervening opportunities are fairly evenly spread. In addition, two economic variables, GDP per capita and the standardized unemployment rate for the urban region, were included. This meant that there were four "families" of variables: GDP per capita in purchasing power parity units, net inmigration, the unemployment rate derived from the labor force survey, and an index of travel demand. Each variable related to the area of the FUR as a whole and was available for a range of dates, from 1971 to 1988. In addition to values for different years and subperiods, change and percentage change values were calculated for all variables except net inmigration. The methodology is discussed in greater detail in the appendix to this chapter.

RESULTS

The analysis was done only for those FURs that had a population of more than a third of a million in 1981 and a core city that, at some date since 1951, had had a population of 200,000 or more. There are 122 of these in the EU12, but five of them—Athens, Salonica, Lisbon, Oporta, and Aarhus—had to be discarded because of lack of data. One smaller FUR, Norwich, which, although it has a total population of more than a third of a million, has a core city of less than 200,000, was included because it was a member of the training set. Two of these smaller FURs had been intentionally included in the training sets, but Cosenza, the other, had to be excluded from the time-series analysis—the focus of this chapter—because of data problems.

A time series for our local per capita welfare measure (the higher the score, the lower the welfare) was constructed by fitting a discriminant function to the data for the FUR as it related to the immediate period around 1975–83 (the training sets were nominated in mid-1984, so this was the period most likely to have determined perceptions), and the resulting estimated coefficients were applied to identically scaled data for each available subperiod. The periods over which particular variables could be measured were restricted by the nature of the sources used. Thus, inmigration data could only be estimated and measured for two periods, 1971–75 and 1976–81, because the estimates relied on census of population sources, with registration data used for the mid-decade estimate. Unemployment could be measured over any sets of years from 1977 to 1987, and the travel demand index could be measured for any year or sets of years, from 1973. This latter index is assumed to be a transformation of total travelers' expenditure plus a random error term. The discriminant analysis generated the following basic equation:

$$\text{Score 2} = -4.187 + 1.032U_1 - 0.276M_2 - 0.449T_2 \quad R^2 = 0.78, \quad (5.1)$$

"F" values   (24.95)   (2.42)   (39.32)

where the subscripts refer to sequential subperiods for individual variables:

U_1 = mean unemployment rate, 1977–81;
M_2 = estimated FUR net inmigration rate, 1976–81; and
T_2 = travel demand index, 1983.

The net inmigration rate was significant only at the 15 percent level, but the other two variables were significant at 1 percent. No training set cities were misclassified by the discriminant function. These estimated coefficients were then applied to generate appropriate scores for each subperiod as follows:

$$\text{Score 1} = f(U_1, M_1, T_1) \quad (5.2)$$
$$\text{Score 2} = f(U_1, M_2, T_2) \quad (5.3)$$
$$\text{Score 3} = f(U_2, M_2, T_3) \quad (5.4)$$
$$\text{Score 4} = f(U_3, M_2, T_4), \quad (5.5)$$

where:

M_1 = estimated FUR net inmigration rate, 1971–75;
U_2 and U_3 = mean FUR unemployment rate, 1983–84
         and 1985–87, respectively; and
T_1, T_3 and T_4 = travel demand index for 1974, 1984,
         and 1988, respectively.

The change in problem score for each subperiod was then calculated as:

$$\text{Subperiod 1} = \text{Score 2} - \text{Score 1} \quad (5.6)$$
$$\text{Subperiod 2} = \text{Score 3} - \text{Score 2} \quad (5.7)$$
$$\text{Subperiod 3} = \text{Score 4} - \text{Score 3} \quad (5.8)$$

The aggregate of these changes was taken as the indicated change in problem score for the whole period, 1971–88.

What we are doing essentially is constructing a moving average per capita welfare measure for these FURs, using constant coefficients, as estimated from the data nearest to the date at which the training sets were selected, but substituting the values for those data for earlier and later subperiods. As previously stated, this procedure implies that a given variable—say, unemployment—makes a constant contribution to welfare through time. The resulting composite index is subjective in the sense that the training set cities used to estimate the discriminant function were subjectively selected. Given those two training sets—of cities where per capita welfare was presumed to be high and low—then the weights are objective, as is the selection of variables from those available. These weights applied to these variables were the most statistically efficient at separating the "good" from the "bad" cities. Of course, other data might have performed better, but such data were not available. The GDP per capita data did not contribute significantly to the separation of the training sets and were therefore excluded. This failure of the GDP data to contribute to the index may have been because it was inaccurately measured in the data available, or because of problems of converting national currencies to a common unit, or because it was correlated with other, included, variables; probably all three explanations are valid.[6]

The value of the resulting welfare index—identified here as Score 2—ranged from a high of (−)18.24 in Frankfurt to a low of (+)12.59 in Sunderland, and is an arbitrary number[7] in that values relate only to this index; however, it is real in the sense that it is a transformation of the component variables—the rate of net inmigration, the unemployment rate, and the index of travel demand.

Table 5.1 shows the change in the value of the problem score for each FUR and each subperiod, and the aggregate change for the whole period 1971 to 1988. The focus of this table is, therefore, on the changing incidence of urban problems as measured by the welfare index. The individual subperiod scores and the resulting change values provide a measure of changing conditions. A point worth emphasizing, however, is that the aggregated measure of total change over the whole period is more reliable than that for the individual subperiods. The net inmigration data for 1971–75 and 1976–81 are less reliable than those for the intercensual decade as a whole because they rest on comparing census and registration data. In addition, variation in unemployment over short periods is subject to cyclical factors. These effectively net out when the changes between subperiods are aggregated. There is cause for the most reservation about the change measured between Score 1 and Score 2, because that is the subperiod affected by the change in net inmigration, with M_2 substituted for M_1.

CAUSAL FACTORS IN CHANGING WELFARE

Can these changes in the incidence of urban problems over the period 1971–88 be explained in terms of the characteristics of the FURs? Apart from being interested in measurements of local welfare and changes in them in order to compare urban areas and identify policy targets, there is clearly a strong interest in explaining the variation. If some systematic explanation of the behavior of the index through time can be offered, then this would tend to confirm that these measures do, in some real sense, reflect the incidence of problems or local welfare levels in the major FURs of the EU and are not just some elaborate statistical artifact.

To offer a complete theory of urban change, and a testing of it here, would require a fully operational model of urban equilibrium development, and the data to calibrate that model. What is provided here is far more ad hoc but, it is hoped, still affords useful insights as well as more rigorous tests of the hypotheses that have been suggested to explain urban development patterns than have been previously possible. The underlying conceptualization is elaborated in more detail in Cheshire and Hay (1989). Urban problems are seen as the symptoms of adjustment, resulting from changing conditions in cities and changes in cities' functions, interacting with the adaptive capacity of those cities' economies and social fabrics. In explaining the changing incidence of those problems, therefore, we should seek measures of the forces generating change as well as of the adaptive capacity of the urban economy. The choice of such variables is, however, necessarily constrained by data availability.

The simplest approach is to use regression analysis, with the dependent variable being the observations of the change in index score (or per capita welfare) shown in table 5.1 and the explanatory variables being measures of the characteristics of the FURs themselves or of the wider, Level 2 regions[8] within which the FURs are located. At this stage, the analysis is restricted to the aggregate score change, shown in the last column of table 5.1, since there are reasons, already discussed, for expecting this to be the most accurate measure of the change in welfare. The changes between the component subperiods are discussed in the paragraphs following. Various specifications and functional forms were tried, but from most points of view the mainly linear version presented in table 5.2 performed best. The overall pattern of results, including the pattern of residuals, proved very robust, and the R^2 associated with the version presented in table 5.2, at 0.80, was the highest.

The analysis indicates that, other things being equal, larger cities have done better than smaller ones over the past seventeen years or so. To the British reader, this may conflict with conventional wisdom—although that wisdom may be anglocentric and derived primarily from the very poor performance of London during the 1970s and the early 1980s (see the residuals in table 5.5). As is often the case, the conventional wisdom, however, is somewhat inconsistent. The general belief is also that the large service centers have done better, a view that is consistent with the general relationship found between larger size and improvement—take, for example, the comparative performances of Sunderland and Newcastle, Valenciennes and Lille, St. Etienne and Lyon, or Wiesbaden and Frankfurt. It should also be pointed out that the medium-sized and smaller cities—those with core populations of less than 200,000—are entirely excluded (with the exception of Norwich), so that the overall distribution is truncated. The measure of FUR size is the log of total population in 1981; there was an a priori expectation that, if significant, the log of urban size would be the most appropriate measure because of the extensive literature on the rank size rule. A stepwise procedure provided strong statistical confirmation of this expectation. The finding is consistent with the view that the adaptive capacity of larger urban regions is superior to that of smaller ones.

The other variables were selected as measures of characteristics that have determined the extent to which a particular city's functions were changing, or to which its economy and social fabric were having to adjust, although some conclusions can be drawn also about factors affecting adaptive capacity. The second independent variable (table 5.2) is a measure of the change in economic potential brought about by a combination of economic integration in Western Europe and falling transport costs. The argument has been advanced elsewhere that the effects of European economic integration have long, and consistently, favored the more central regions and have intensified the problems in more peripheral regions or in regions that have become more peripheral as a result of European integration. Tables 5.3 and 5.4 show, for example, patterns of trade through the ports of the United Kingdom and Spain, respectively. The redirection of trade in Great

Table 5.1 CHANGES IN INCIDENCE OF URBAN PROBLEMS FOR 117 EUROPEAN FURs, SUBPERIODS 1971–88 AND OVERALL

Rank, FUR	Score 81–Score 74	Rank, FUR	Score 84–Score 81	Rank, FUR	Score 88–Score 81	Rank, FUR	Total Change
1. Frankfurt	−4.30	1. Lille	−2.35	1. Brighton	−3.75	1. Bruxelles/Brussels	−5.09
2. Bruxelles/Brussels	−3.95	2. Roma	−1.44	2. Birmingham	−3.34	2. Frankfurt	−3.56
3. Bologna	−3.86	3. Toulouse	−1.11	3. Coventry	−2.86	3. Verona	−2.66
4. Granada	−2.97	4. Paris	−1.08	4. Antwerpen	−2.79	4. Bologna	−1.92
5. Strasbourg	−2.94	5. Nice	−0.90	5. Nürnberg	−2.52	5. Nice	−1.37
6. Antwerpen	−2.58	6. Rennes	−0.43	6. Utrecht	−2.37	6. Bordeaux	−1.31
7. Bordeaux	−2.37	7. Bordeaux	−0.24	7. Bruxelles/Brussels	−2.22	7. Paris	−0.98
8. Düsseldorf	−2.30	8. Marseille	−0.18	8. Amsterdam	−1.87	8. Antwerpen	−0.89
9. Norwich	−2.12	9. Lyon	−0.15	9. Barcelona	−1.83	9. Roma	−0.88
10. Amsterdam	−2.11	10. Genova	−0.03	10. München	−1.79	10. Strasbourg	−0.61
11. Hannover	−2.10	11. Verona	0.32	11. Padova	−1.74	11. Lyon	−0.39
12. Montpellier	−1.85	12. Taranto	0.32	12. Rotterdam	−1.72	12. Amsterdam	−0.22
13. Lyon	−1.84	13. Grenoble	0.41	13. Verona	−1.66	13. Birmingham	−0.00
14. Rennes	−1.80	14. Palermo	0.62	14. Mönchengladbach	−1.54	14. Lille	0.02
15. Birmingham	−1.75	15. Clermont-Ferrand	0.66	15. Edinburgh	−1.42	15. Toulouse	0.04
16. Bari	−1.72	16. Stuttgart	0.68	16. Firenze	−1.35	16. Stuttgart	0.10
17. Derby	−1.50	17. Valenciennes	0.70	17. Cardiff	−1.27	17. 's-Gravenhage	0.19
18. Essen	−1.45	18. Montpellier	0.86	18. Bologna	−1.18	18. Rennes	0.27
19. Vigo	−1.44	19. Southampton	0.93	19. 's-Gravenhage	−1.08	19. Nürnberg	0.41
20. Berlin	−1.44	20. Mulhouse	0.96	20. Manchester	−1.05	20. Derby	0.49
21. Toulon	−1.41	21. Orléans	1.01	21. London	−0.89	21. Rotterdam	0.69
22. La Coruña	−1.32	22. Edinburgh	1.02	22. Wuppertal	−0.88	22. Edinburgh	0.87
23. Verona	−1.32	23. Brescia	1.03	23. Karlsruhe	−0.79	23. Genova	0.95
24. Newcastle	−1.27	24. Bruxelles/Brussels	1.08	24. Köln	−0.77	24. Taranto	1.08
25. Stoke	−1.22	25. Nancy	1.09	25. Frankfurt	−0.62	25. Clermont-Ferrand	1.12
26. Nottingham	−1.16	26. Venezia	1.12	26. Augsburg	−0.61	26. Norwich	1.18
27. Nice	−1.09	27. Liège	1.22	27. Sunderland	−0.57	27. Hannover	1.25
28. 's-Gravenhage	−1.06	28. Charleroi	1.28	28. Berlin	−0.50	28. Glasgow	1.26
29. Wiesbaden	−1.06	29. Frankfurt	1.35	29. Stuttgart	−0.45	29. Karlsruhe	1.29

30. Aachen	−1.00	30. Toulon	1.38	30. Zaragoza	−0.37	30. Brescia	1.31
31. Roma	−0.99	31. Nantes	1.39	31. Newcastle	−0.32	31. Newcastle	1.51
32. Glasgow	−0.99	32. Bristol	1.44	32. Bremen	−0.32	32. Bari	1.54
33. Nantes	−0.95	33. Firenze	1.46	33. Valladolid	−0.25	33. Cardiff	1.58
34. Paris	−0.94	34. St. Etienne	1.47	34. Mannheim	−0.22	34. Mönchengladbach	1.59
35. Rouen	−0.94	35. Strasbourg	1.53	35. Plymouth	−0.16	35. Milano	1.66
36. Dijon	−0.87	36. Le Havre	1.53	36. Palma de Mallorca	−0.13	36. Brighton	1.69
37. Clermont-Ferrand	−0.85	37. Plymouth	1.54	37. Bielefeld	−0.12	37. Utrecht	1.69
38. Dortmund	−0.73	38. Rouen	1.54	38. Hull	−0.09	38. Firenze	1.80
39. Catania	−0.66	39. Milano	1.61	39. Brescia	−0.05	39. Wuppertal	1.83
40. Wuppertal	−0.52	40. Napoli	1.71	40. Milano	−0.01	40. Bristol	1.93
41. Teesside	−0.50	41. München	1.72	41. Münster	−0.00	41. Mulhouse	1.95
42. Utrecht	−0.46	42. Dijon	1.73	42. Aachen	0.03	42. Berlin	1.96
43. Duisburg	−0.43	43. Glasgow	1.74	43. Derby	0.04	43. Coventry	1.98
44. Hull	−0.41	44. Wiesbaden	1.92	44. Kassel	0.05	44. Venezia	2.02
45. Bochum	−0.41	45. Derby	1.95	45. Leeds	0.10	45. Rouen	2.16
46. Murcia	−0.41	46. Bonn	2.10	46. Bristol	0.11	46. Grenoble	2.35
47. Orléans	−0.41	47. Rotterdam	2.22	47. Krefeld	0.13	47. Nottingham	2.38
48. Saarbrücken	−0.39	48. Karlsruhe	2.27	48. Madrid	0.21	48. Nantes	2.41
49. Mönchengladbach	−0.37	49. 's-Gravenhage	2.33	49. Braunschweig	0.22	49. Mannheim	2.52
50. Cardiff	−0.34	50. Norwich	2.33	50. Bari	0.23	50. Montpellier	2.52
51. Sheffield	−0.32	51. Mannheim	2.34	51. Liverpool	0.24	51. Augsburg	2.60
52. Sevilla	−0.24	52. Krefeld	2.36	52. Leicester	0.46	52. Krefeld	2.71
53. Nancy	−0.22	53. Düsseldorf	2.43	53. Genova	0.48	53. Padova	2.73
54. Mulhouse	−0.19	54. Portsmouth	2.44	54. Bochum	0.49	54. Köln	2.74
55. Karlsruhe	−0.18	55. Augsburg	2.46	55. Toulouse	0.49	55. Toulon	2.80
56. Stuttgart	−0.14	56. Nürnberg	2.48	56. Glasgow	0.51	56. Dijon	2.82
57. Córdoba	−0.13	57. Belfast	2.51	57. Nice	0.62	57. Aachen	3.08
58. Kassel	−0.13	58. Torino	2.54	58. Hannover	0.66	58. Nancy	3.10
59. Le Havre	−0.09	59. Brighton	2.66	59. Dortmund	0.67	59. München	3.29
60. Taranto	−0.05	60. Hannover	2.68	60. Saarbrücken	0.68	60. Hull	3.31
61. Valencia	−0.05	61. London	2.76	61. Portsmouth	0.68	61. Orléans	3.36

(continued)

Table 5.1 CHANGES IN INCIDENCE OF URBAN PROBLEMS FOR 117 EUROPEAN FURs, SUBPERIODS 1971–88 AND OVERALL (continued)

Rank, FUR	Score 81–Score 74	Rank, FUR	Score 84–Score 81	Rank, FUR	Score 88–Score 81	Rank, FUR	Total Change
62. Lille	0.03	62. Nottingham	2.77	62. Nottingham	0.77	62. Le Havre	3.40
63. Hamburg	0.05	63. Leicester	2.87	63. Strasbourg	0.80	63. Kassel	3.53
64. Milano	0.06	64. Köln	3.02	64. Hamburg	0.81	64. Münster	3.60
65. Venezia	0.09	65. Bari	3.03	65. Taranto	0.81	65. Leicester	3.66
66. Barcelona	0.15	66. Bologna	3.12	66. Venezia	0.81	66. Plymouth	3.67
67. Grenoble	0.16	67. Newcastle	3.16	67. Duisburg	0.94	67. St. Etienne	3.71
68. Manchester	0.16	68. Cardiff	3.19	68. Norwich	0.97	68. Saarbrücken	3.71
69. Braunschweig	0.18	69. Cagliari	3.23	69. Torino	1.00	69. Portsmouth	3.77
70. Rotterdam	0.19	70. Wuppertal	3.24	70. Paris	1.02	70. Stoke	3.80
71. Münster	0.22	71. Leeds	3.38	71. Belfast	1.03	71. Manchester	3.80
72. Krefeld	0.22	72. Münster	3.38	72. Stoke	1.14	72. Marseille	3.85
73. Brescia	0.32	73. Catania	3.39	73. Mulhouse	1.17	73. Leeds	3.86
74. St. Etienne	0.33	74. Saarbrücken	3.42	74. Sheffield	1.24	74. London	3.92
75. Leicester	0.33	75. Mönchengladbach	3.51	75. Bordeaux	1.30	75. Belfast	4.01
76. Bristol	0.38	76. Liverpool	3.59	76. Clermont-Ferrand	1.31	76. Düsseldorf	4.06
77. Leeds	0.38	77. Kassel	3.61	77. Messina	1.33	77. Wiesbaden	4.21
78. Mannheim	0.39	78. Padova	3.64	78. Bonn	1.46	78. Liverpool	4.23
79. Liverpool	0.40	79. Amsterdam	3.77	79. Liège	1.49	79. Charleroi	4.24
80. Belfast	0.40	80. Hull	3.82	80. Essen	1.51	80. Braunschweig	4.28
81. Napoli	0.40	81. Hamburg	3.85	81. Roma	1.55	81. Southampton	4.37
82. Nürnberg	0.44	82. Braunschweig	3.88	82. Rouen	1.56	82. Torino	4.46
83. Köln	0.49	83. Stoke	3.88	83. Lyon	1.60	83. Bremen	4.48
84. Genova	0.50	84. Berlin	3.90	84. Valencia	1.79	84. Essen	4.51
85. Bremen	0.52	85. Aachen	4.05	85. Grenoble	1.79	85. Catania	4.53
86. Bielefeld	0.56	86. Messina	4.20	86. Catania	1.79	86. Hamburg	4.70
87. Madrid	0.58	87. Dublin	4.20	87. Teesside	1.83	87. Bielefeld	4.76
88. Coventry	0.61	88. Coventry	4.24	88. St. Etienne	1.91	88. Bonn	4.89
89. Palermo	0.62	89. Sunderland	4.25	89. Dijon	1.96	89. Palermo	4.97

#	City		#	City		#	City		#	City	
90.	Toulouse	0.66	90.	Bremen	4.27	90.	Le Havre	1.96	90.	Napoli	5.11
91.	Portsmouth	0.70	91.	Bielefeld	4.31	91.	Nantes	1.96	91.	Duisburg	5.37
92.	Augsburg	0.74	92.	Essen	4.46	92.	Southampton	1.97	92.	Liège	5.45
93.	Málaga	0.79	93.	Antwerpen	4.49	93.	Bilbao	2.03	93.	Bochum	5.52
94.	Padova	0.83	94.	Utrecht	4.52	94.	La Coruña	2.03	94.	Dortmund	5.62
95.	Charleroi	0.92	95.	Manchester	4.70	95.	Charleroi	2.04	95.	Sheffield	6.06
96.	Torino	0.92	96.	Duisburg	4.85	96.	Nancy	2.24	96.	Sunderland	6.09
97.	Valladolid	0.92	97.	Birmingham	5.09	97.	Vigo	2.24	97.	Valenciennes	6.68
98.	Valenciennes	1.10	98.	Sheffield	5.14	98.	Lille	2.39	98.	Messina	7.44
99.	Edinburgh	1.28	99.	Bochum	5.44	99.	Rennes	2.51	99.	Teesside	7.69
100.	Marseille	1.31	100.	Dortmund	5.69	100.	Alicante	2.62	100.	Cagliari	8.34
101.	Bonn	1.33	101.	Teesside	6.37	101.	Marseille	2.72	101.	Vigo	9.04
102.	Southampton	1.45	102.	Murcia	8.11	102.	Orléans	2.76	102.	Madrid	9.20
103.	Avilés/Gijón	1.62	103.	Palma de Mallorca	8.28	103.	Toulon	2.82	103.	La Coruña	10.15
104.	Firenze	1.70	104.	Vigo	8.29	104.	Napoli	3.00	104.	Zaragoza	10.21
105.	Cagliari	1.78	105.	Málaga	8.37	105.	Dublin	3.28	105.	Valladolid	10.81
106.	Bilbao	1.89	106.	Madrid	8.41	106.	Cagliari	3.32	106.	Murcia	11.12
107.	Messina	1.91	107.	Zaragoza	8.44	107.	Wiesbaden	3.35	107.	Dublin	11.12
108.	London	2.06	108.	Avilés/Gijón	8.48	108.	Murcia	3.42	108.	Granada	12.11
109.	Zaragoza	2.14	109.	Córdoba	9.35	109.	Montpellier	3.52	109.	Valencia	12.23
110.	Plymouth	2.29	110.	La Coruña	9.42	110.	Palermo	3.73	110.	Barcelona	12.84
111.	Sunderland	2.42	111.	Valladolid	10.14	111.	Düsseldorf	3.94	111.	Palma de Mallorca	12.96
112.	Liège	2.74	112.	Granada	10.87	112.	Sevilla	4.21	112.	Avilés/Gijón	14.49
113.	Brighton	2.78	113.	Valencia	11.12	113.	Granada	4.30	113.	Bilbao	15.09
114.	München	3.38	114.	Alicante	11.48	114.	Valenciennes	4.90	114.	Málaga	16.11
115.	Alicante	4.15	115.	Bilbao	12.20	115.	Avilés/Gijón	4.95	115.	Sevilla	16.70
116.	Dublin	4.63	116.	Sevilla	13.45	116.	Málaga	7.50	116.	Alicante	17.37
117.	Palma de Mallorca	6.44	117.	Barcelona	14.68	117.	Córdoba	9.20	117.	Córdoba	18.20
									117.	Córdoba	18.37

Note: The higher the negative score, the greater the reduction in the incidence of urban problems. Cities at the top of columns have had the greatest reduction. Cities with positive signs have had an increase in the incidence of urban problems. For definitions, see the text.

Table 5.2 CHANGING INCIDENCE OF URBAN PROBLEMS FOR 117 EUROPEAN
FURs, 1971–88: EXPLANATORY FACTORS

Dependent variable: Total change in problem score, 1971–88
N = 117

Independent Variable	Estimated Coefficient
Intercept	17.2972**
	(3.39)
Log total population, 1981	−0.9676**
	(−2.99)
Change in economic potential[a]	−4.9381**
	(−5.51)
Percentage of labor force in industry	0.0697*
in 1975 in wider Level 2 region	(2.24)
Percentage of labor force in agriculture	0.1745
in 1975 in wider Level 2 region	(1.94)
Percentage of labor force in agriculture	−0.0060**
in 1975 in wider region squared	(−2.65)
Dependence of local economy on coal[b]	1.2602**
	(3.55)
Dependence of local economy on port[c]	0.6274**
	(3.87)
Rate of natural population change	0.1598**
	(2.57)
Country dummy: Spain	4.4179**
	(3.83)
Italy	−3.6114**
	(−4.36)
United Kingdom	−3.6933**
	(−4.61)
France	−3.4304**
	(−5.09)
Adjusted R²	0.80

Notes: T statistics are in parentheses. One asterisk (*) = significant at 5 percent; two
asterisks (**) = significant at 1 percent. A negative change in the problem score
implies a reduction of measured problems. Since all explanatory variables are positive, a negative sign means that improvement of the problem index was associated
with a more positive value of the explanatory value.

[a]Derived from Clark, Wilson, and Bradley (1969) and Keeble, Offord, and Walker
(1988). Measures the change in economic potential in the wider Level 2 region generated by the formation and enlargement of the European Economic Community
(originally formed following the treaty of Rome in 1957) and by lower transport costs.

[b]A dummy variable with values 0, 1, and 2; 1, where territory of FUR includes a
coalfield area; 2, where whole FUR is within a coalfield.

[c]A dummy variable with values 0 to 4 scaled strictly to volume of seaborne trade
through port in 1966, except for inland port of Duisburg, the largest on the Rhine.
The source of the data for both the "coal" and "port" dummies is Oxford Regional
Economic Atlas: Western Europe (1971).

Table 5.3 CHANGING TRADE FLOWS: UNITED KINGDOM (UK), 1965–83

	Total Weight of Imports and Exports as Percentage of UK Trade				
	1965	1970	1975	1980	1983
Percentage total UK trade with EU	18.2	20.5	34.1	39.7	44.7
Percentage UK trade via:					
Liverpool	18.5	12.8	8.8	3.8	2.8
Dover	1.7	2.8	7.1	11.1	12.1
Felixstowe	3.2	3.5	5.8	6.2	9.1

Note: Trade flows are measured in value terms.

Table 5.4 CHANGING TRADE FLOWS: SPAIN, 1970–82

	Total Weight of Imports and Exports as Percentage of Spanish Trade			
	1970	1975	1980	1982
Western ports	23.8	17.4	16.2	15.5
Southwest[a]	16.6	12.2	11.2	11.6
Northwest[b]	7.2	5.2	5.0	3.9
Eastern ports	15.9	25.8	33.1	36.9
Sea[c]	14.3	22.4	29.1	29.6
Land[d]	1.6	3.4	4.0	7.3

[a]Southwest: Huelva, Cadiz, and Algeciras.
[b]Northwest: La Coruña and Vigo.
[c]Eastern sea: Barcelona, Bilbao, and Tarragona.
[d]Eastern land: Irún and La Junquera.

Britain since 1965 has been very strong indeed, with Dover by 1983 having secured almost the relative dominance that Liverpool held in 1965. Because of the absolute growth in trade, Dover in 1983 was, in absolute terms, more important as a port than Liverpool was in 1965. Because of the changes in the nature of the trade, however, Liverpool's losses were not equaled by local economic gains in Dover. For reasons discussed in the wider context of the problems of port cities, Dover remains an unimportant city, with the gains distributed all over southern Britain. The change in Spain has had even less positive effects on urban growth than in Britain. There was virtually no employment growth associated with the growth in land traffic into and from France, compared to the decline in the western ports. A further point is that not only did the changes occur continuously over a long period, but in both countries they preceded entry into the EU. The effects of

European integration are not confined to members of the EU. This also holds a message for further integration and enlargement of the EU and the relaxation of barriers between Eastern and Western Europe. The impacts on patterns of spatial development are likely to be continuous and to occur over a long period. Indeed, much anecdotal evidence indicates that these impacts are already being anticipated, and that adjustments will continue to occur well into the next century.

The impact of European integration on urban economies can, however, be measured and estimated more systematically. The second independent variable (table 5.2) is such a measure.

A previous analysis (Cheshire and Hay 1989), albeit confined to the nine countries of the EU before the accession of Greece, showed that a similar measure, derived from the estimates of Clark, Wilson, and Bradley (1969), was a significant explanatory variable in differential rates of urban population growth in both the 1960s and 1970s. For each decade the measure of changing economic potential most appropriate a priori was statistically the most significant. The form of the variable used here is the estimated change in economic potential associated with the move from there being no EU to there being an EU of twelve nations with reduced transport costs. The values for FURs in all countries except Spain (the major Greek and Portuguese FURs were eliminated for lack of other data) are calculated directly from Clark et al. (1969). Those for Spain had to be estimated using the results reported in Keeble, Offord, and Walker (1988). This was not difficult, since visual inspection of Keeble et al.'s results shows that all the major Spanish FURs, with the exception of Barcelona, Bilbao, Madrid, and Zaragoza, are in the smallest increase category. As a check, the equations were estimated separately, excluding observations for Spain, and very similar results were obtained. There is thus now strong statistical evidence confirming the fact that, ceteris paribus, European economic integration over the period 1960 to 1988 was of much greater benefit to the more central regions of Europe than to the more peripheral ones; and that those peripheral regions, especially when changes, not levels, of peripherality are examined, are not just in Southern Europe but in Northeastern and particularly Northwestern Europe. Ireland, western Scotland, and northwestern England were some of the worst affected. As further confirmation of the effects of the impact of European integration, it should be noted (from the residuals in table 5.5) that Brussels—the city that gained most from the growth of Eurocracy—shows one of the largest "unexplained" relative improvements of any FUR, and that Strasbourg—

which has also gained European institutions—shows one of the larger such residuals.

The next four variables (table 5.2) relate to the economic structure of the FUR or the wider region in which it is situated. The first two are the percentage of employment in industry and the percentage of employment in agriculture in the wider Level 2 region in 1975; the third is a dummy variable measuring the extent to which the FUR is coincident with a coalfield; and the fourth is a dummy reflecting the volume of port traffic in 1966. All except the importance of agriculture in the wider region relate, in part, to the deindustrialization debate and to the association of deindustrialization with "urban decline." Even the importance of agriculture—since "deagriculturalization" was more important than "deindustrialization" over much of Europe—relates to the wider question of economic transformation. The way in which the measure of the importance of the coal industry was formulated was deliberately intended not to reflect just the direct economic dependence of the urban region on the coal industry at the start of the period but also the environmental influence of the coal industry. This formulation was chosen partly in recognition of the arguments presented by Fothergill and Gudgin (1982) that a factor influencing patterns of industrial location in the relevant period was environmental quality; and also based on the knowledge that, even by 1971, the direct economic contribution of the coal industry to many of the urban areas that appeared to have fared worst over the period had already considerably declined or even disappeared.

The problems faced by port cities since the introduction of roll-on, roll-off ferries and containerization have been surprisingly neglected. The results presented here suggest that a dependence on port activity is statistically more closely associated with an increasing incidence of urban problems than is specialization in industrial activity or agriculture. The problem for ports, even very successful ports such as Rotterdam, is not only that capital-labor substitution has meant they have lost direct employment, but that they have lost their locational attractions to processing industries because of containerization. As the example of Dover shows, a container can be unpacked and its contents distributed or reprocessed virtually anywhere, whereas traditional cargo-handling methods meant that ships had to be unpacked at the dockside.

The extent to which the economy of the wider region in which the FUR was located specialized in industry was associated with a worsening of urban problems, but at only the 5 percent level of significance.

Table 5.5 RESIDUALS FROM REGRESSION EQUATIONS: UNEXPLAINED VARIATION IN CHANGING INCIDENCE OF URBAN PROBLEMS FOR 117 EUROPEAN FURs, 1971–88, AND FOR THREE COMPONENT SUBPERIODS

Whole Period Equation, 1971–88		Subperiod 1		Subperiod 2		Subperiod 3	
Rank, FUR	Residual	Rank, FUR	Residual	Rank, FUR	Residual	Rank, FUR	Residual
1. Frankfurt	−5.076	1. Frankfurt	−4.427	1. Lille	−3.168	1. Birmingham	−3.328
2. Verona	−4.471	2. Bologna	−3.695	2. Stuttgart	−2.594	2. Nürnberg	−2.961
3. Valladolid	−4.199	3. Norwich	−2.557	3. Avilés/Gijón	−2.229	3. Valladolid	−2.791
4. Glasgow	−3.101	4. Venezia	−2.380	4. Roma	−2.113	4. Coventry	−2.581
5. Murcia	−3.027	5. Bruxelles/Brussels	−2.313	5. Glasgow	−2.112	5. Brighton	−2.533
6. Taranto	−2.858	6. Amsterdam	−2.226	6. Genova	−2.023	6. Antwerpen	−2.493
7. Derby	−2.785	7. Strasbourg	−2.193	7. Southampton	−1.713	7. Toulouse	−1.862
8. Bologna	−2.760	8. Antwerpen	−1.777	8. Taranto	−1.709	8. Vigo	−1.852
9. Bordeaux	−2.658	9. Derby	−1.672	9. Murcia	−1.610	9. Mönchengladbach	−1.769
10. Nice	−2.649	10. Stoke	−1.578	10. Málaga	−1.595	10. Catania	−1.769
11. Mönchengladbach	−2.551	11. Hannover	−1.540	11. Charleroi	−1.471	11. Cardiff	−1.745
12. Bruxelles/Brussels	−2.413	12. Sevilla	−1.510	12. Krefeld	−1.410	12. Barcelona	−1.555
13. Lyon	−2.370	13. Nottingham	−1.430	13. Verona	−1.409	13. Utrecht	−1.527
14. La Coruña	−2.230	14. Bari	−1.426	14. Palermo	−1.362	14. Wuppertal	−1.475
15. Newcastle	−2.194	15. Düsseldorf	−1.395	15. Marseille	−1.318	15. La Coruña	−1.419
16. Antwerpen	−2.182	16. Verona	−1.381	16. Zaragoza	−1.284	16. Manchester	−1.373
17. Nürnberg	−2.090	17. Newcastle	−1.339	17. Bristol	−1.226	17. Messina	−1.343
18. Madrid	−2.007	18. Bordeaux	−1.280	18. Vigo	−1.218	18. Verona	−1.340
19. Lille	−1.959	19. Valencia	−1.269	19. Mannheim	−1.215	19. Rotterdam	−1.303
20. Stuttgart	−1.900	20. La Coruña	−1.141	20. Brescia	−1.207	20. Bordeaux	−1.229
21. Cardiff	−1.871	21. Murcia	−1.047	21. Derby	−1.197	21. Padova	−1.131
22. Rotterdam	−1.842	22. Glasgow	−1.021	22. Edinburgh	−1.186	22. Clermont-Ferrand	−1.115
23. Birmingham	−1.818	23. Lyon	−0.998	23. Madrid	−1.163	23. Augsburg	−1.097
24. Vigo	−1.770	24. Duisburg	−0.990	24. Paris	−1.136	24. München	−1.097
25. Wuppertal	−1.751	25. Hull	−0.873	25. Wuppertal	−1.104	25. Bruxelles/Brussels	−1.080
26. Avilés/Gijón	−1.750	26. Catania	−0.864	26. Frankfurt	−1.044	26. Berlin	−1.077
27. Coventry	−1.684	27. Bochum	−0.848	27. Lyon	−0.964	27. Sunderland	−1.060
28. Zaragoza	−1.579	28. Birmingham	−0.828	28. Düsseldorf	−0.962	28. Nice	−1.044

No.	City	Value	No.	City	Value	No.	City	Value	No.	City	Value
29.	Amsterdam	−1.564	29.	Toulon	−0.822	29.	Liège	−0.954	29.	Edinburgh	−0.903
30.	Hull	−1.541	30.	Wiesbaden	−0.820	30.	Toulouse	−0.949	30.	Bologna	−0.865
31.	Venezia	−1.446	31.	Valladolid	−0.803	31.	Newcastle	−0.929	31.	Palma De Mallorca	−0.839
32.	Hannover	−1.438	32.	Teesside	−0.791	32.	Plymouth	−0.899	32.	Bari	−0.836
33.	Augsburg	−1.266	33.	Leicester	−0.688	33.	Belfast	−0.867	33.	Liverpool	−0.772
34.	Bristol	−1.226	34.	Essen	−0.653	34.	Wiesbaden	−0.861	34.	Köln	−0.753
35.	Valencia	−0.995	35.	Rennes	−0.600	35.	Karlsruhe	−0.842	35.	Karlsruhe	−0.753
36.	Strasbourg	−0.947	36.	Nice	−0.593	36.	Bordeaux	−0.801	36.	Taranto	−0.716
37.	Bari	−0.926	37.	Montpellier	−0.591	37.	Rotterdam	−0.708	37.	Glasgow	−0.651
38.	Saarbrücken	−0.864	38.	Bristol	−0.548	38.	Nürnberg	−0.648	38.	Hull	−0.649
39.	St. Etienne	−0.726	39.	Cardiff	−0.476	39.	Napoli	−0.613	39.	Zaragoza	−0.633
40.	Duisburg	−0.661	40.	Dijon	−0.458	40.	Bonn	−0.609	40.	Nantes	−0.591
41.	Catania	−0.649	41.	Aachen	−0.429	41.	Nice	−0.606	41.	Madrid	−0.530
42.	Palermo	−0.593	42.	Mönchengladbach	−0.390	42.	Augsburg	−0.579	42.	Münster	−0.495
43.	Belfast	−0.555	43.	Saarbrücken	−0.385	43.	Liverpool	−0.451	43.	Newcastle	−0.479
44.	Karlsruhe	−0.552	44.	Leeds	−0.341	44.	Milano	−0.420	44.	's-Gravenhage	−0.457
45.	Rennes	−0.503	45.	Roma	−0.323	45.	München	−0.371	45.	Lyon	−0.446
46.	Norwich	−0.484	46.	Rouen	−0.306	46.	Valenciennes	−0.333	46.	Amsterdam	−0.433
47.	Leeds	−0.425	47.	Manchester	−0.298	47.	Hannover	−0.316	47.	Granada	−0.426
48.	Toulouse	−0.376	48.	Málaga	−0.263	48.	Córdoba	−0.271	48.	Bremen	−0.398
49.	Nottingham	−0.361	49.	St. Etienne	−0.246	49.	Hull	−0.205	49.	Bielefeld	−0.356
50.	Rouen	−0.330	50.	Avilés/Gijón	−0.235	50.	Venezia	−0.196	50.	Mannheim	−0.321
51.	Genova	−0.318	51.	Cosenza	−0.220	51.	Köln	−0.180	51.	Rouen	−0.284
52.	Manchester	−0.278	52.	Dortmund	−0.218	52.	Saarbrücken	−0.156	52.	Murcia	−0.277
53.	Roma	−0.273	53.	Sheffield	−0.199	53.	Nottingham	−0.149	53.	Braunschweig	−0.265
54.	Köln	−0.242	54.	Nancy	−0.177	54.	Braunschweig	−0.144	54.	Stuttgart	−0.210
55.	Liverpool	−0.139	55.	Barcelona	−0.176	55.	Cardiff	−0.135	55.	Paris	−0.188
56.	Palma de Mallorca	−0.137	56.	Kassel	−0.087	56.	Palma de Mallorca	−0.115	56.	Leeds	−0.187
57.	's-Gravenhage	−0.131	57.	Belfast	−0.084	57.	La Coruña	−0.112	57.	Strasbourg	−0.181
58.	Münster	−0.074	58.	Granada	−0.069	58.	Rennes	−0.084	58.	Bochum	−0.148
59.	Le Havre	−0.053	59.	Taranto	0.015	59.	Grenoble	−0.069	59.	Krefeld	−0.144
60.	Edinburgh	−0.049	60.	Orléans	0.048	60.	Münster	−0.048	60.	Kassel	−0.134
61.	Mannheim	−0.010	61.	Madrid	0.098	61.	Le Havre	−0.027	61.	Rennes	−0.121

(continued)

Table 5.5 RESIDUALS FROM REGRESSION EQUATIONS: UNEXPLAINED VARIATION IN CHANGING INCIDENCE OF URBAN PROBLEMS FOR 117 EUROPEAN FURs, 1971–88, AND FOR THREE COMPONENT SUBPERIODS *(continued)*

Whole Period Equation, 1971–88		Subperiod 1		Subperiod 2		Subperiod 3	
Rank, FUR	Residual	Rank, FUR	Residual	Rank, FUR	Residual	Rank, FUR	Residual
62. Krefeld	0.009	62. 's-Gravenhage	0.118	62. Rouen	0.032	62. Aachen	−0.109
63. Clermont-Ferrand	0.032	63. Le Havre	0.135	63. Valladolid	0.055	63. St. Etienne	−0.064
64. Aachen	0.067	64. Berlin	0.182	64. Mönchengladbach	0.132	64. Valencia	−0.027
65. Toulon	0.071	65. Utrecht	0.197	65. Bruxelles/Brussels	0.150	65. Belfast	−0.015
66. Grenoble	0.336	66. Southampton	0.260	66. Cosenza	0.166	66. Le Havre	0.027
67. Stoke	0.359	67. Clermont-Ferrand	0.267	67. Sunderland	0.241	67. Palermo	0.040
68. Nancy	0.381	68. Coventry	0.267	68. Leeds	0.243	68. Mulhouse	0.097
69. Berlin	0.401	69. Mulhouse	0.277	69. Leicester	0.250	69. Firenze	0.138
70. Leicester	0.489	70. Nantes	0.292	70. Valencia	0.281	70. Bristol	0.151
71. Braunschweig	0.515	71. Stuttgart	0.301	71. Portsmouth	0.292	71. Derby	0.163
72. Southampton	0.540	72. Palermo	0.376	72. Norwich	0.381	72. Saarbrücken	0.221
73. Brescia	0.551	73. Augsburg	0.443	73. Firenze	0.402	73. Plymouth	0.230
74. Utrecht	0.581	74. Padova	0.464	74. Torino	0.431	74. Dortmund	0.282
75. Bochum	0.597	75. Karlsruhe	0.479	75. Duisburg	0.436	75. Grenoble	0.294
76. Kassel	0.645	76. Grenoble	0.491	76. Nancy	0.445	76. Hannover	0.304
77. Paris	0.800	77. Rotterdam	0.517	77. Dublin	0.495	77. Montpellier	0.406
78. Bremen	0.803	78. Münster	0.565	78. Clermont-Ferrand	0.497	78. London	0.424
79. Firenze	0.823	79. Portsmouth	0.570	79. Hamburg	0.516	79. Frankfurt	0.455
80. Mulhouse	0.862	80. Napoli	0.581	80. Bilbao	0.562	80. Toulon	0.456
81. Padova	0.962	81. Liverpool	0.588	81. 's-Gravenhage	0.562	81. Duisburg	0.462
82. Marseille	0.966	82. Hamburg	0.599	82. Essen	0.577	82. Marseille	0.465
83. Barcelona	0.985	83. Genova	0.640	83. London	0.581	83. Sevilla	0.468
84. Essen	1.049	84. Wuppertal	0.674	84. Stoke	0.597	84. Dijon	0.491
85. Nantes	1.300	85. Brescia	0.684	85. St. Etienne	0.654	85. Lille	0.520
86. Montpellier	1.433	86. Bremen	0.691	86. Bremen	0.655	86. Nancy	0.621
87. München	1.481	87. Bilbao	0.692	87. Toulon	0.682	87. Sheffield	0.690
88. Brighton	1.491	88. Córdoba	0.696	88. Mulhouse	0.722	88. Cagliari	0.782
89. Dortmund	1.558	89. Vigo	0.727	89. Aachen	0.735	89. Genova	0.906

Rank	City	Score	City	Score	City	Score	City	Score
90	Charleroi	1.641	Lille	0.746	Kassel	0.754	Hamburg	0.927
91	Napoli	1.667	Milano	0.770	Berlin	0.755	Essen	1.068
92	Sunderland	1.676	Köln	0.800	Coventry	0.875	Alicante	1.085
93	Messina	1.710	Firenze	0.853	Orléans	0.889	Orléans	1.138
94	Plymouth	1.820	Alicante	0.861	Cagliari	0.932	Dublin	1.175
95	Sevilla	1.850	Cagliari	0.953	Bielefeld	0.986	Nottingham	1.220
96	Dijon	1.926	Valenciennes	0.971	Manchester	0.989	Teesside	1.221
97	Málaga	2.093	Braunschweig	0.973	Nantes	1.187	Brescia	1.250
98	Bielefeld	2.110	Nürnberg	0.984	Brighton	1.191	Avilés/Gijón	1.256
99	Orléans	2.124	Zaragoza	1.042	Montpellier	1.262	Portsmouth	1.321
100	Milano	2.163	Bonn	1.103	Alicante	1.342	Leicester	1.372
101	Cagliari	2.178	Bielefeld	1.137	Strasbourg	1.351	Norwich	1.372
102	Düsseldorf	2.221	Mannheim	1.202	Birmingham	1.555	Liège	1.495
103	Granada	2.252	Messina	1.295	Antwerpen	1.572	Torino	1.536
104	Portsmouth	2.275	Krefeld	1.331	Bari	1.590	Stoke	1.537
105	Wiesbaden	2.302	Paris	1.424	Dortmund	1.628	Milano	1.550
106	Alicante	2.331	Edinburgh	1.551	Amsterdam	1.660	Charleroi	1.579
107	Valenciennes	2.337	Marseille	1.710	Catania	1.755	Napoli	1.660
108	Bonn	2.337	Charleroi	1.717	Bologna	1.766	Roma	2.056
109	Hamburg	2.370	Torino	1.740	Sheffield	1.790	Bilbao	2.104
110	Dublin	2.447	Toulouse	1.904	Granada	1.799	Southampton	2.173
111	Sheffield	2.600	Plymouth	2.020	Dijon	1.818	Bonn	2.228
112	Bilbao	2.722	Palma de Mallorca	2.040	Messina	1.988	Venezia	2.504
113	Teesside	3.124	London	2.074	Bochum	2.060	Valenciennes	2.611
114	Liège	3.474	Sunderland	2.350	Padova	2.098	Wiesbaden	3.391
115	London	4.137	Brighton	2.650	Teesside	2.293	Málaga	3.745
116	Torino	4.241	München	2.885	Sevilla	2.647	Düsseldorf	4.225
117	Córdoba	5.462	Liège	3.109	Utrecht	2.754	Córdoba	4.709
118			Dublin	3.155	Barcelona	2.979		

Notes: See text for details. Because the problem score for the subperiods is calculated as a form of moving average, the subperiods do not correspond precisely to particular dates. Broadly, however, they represent the change in conditions between 1971 and 1980 (subperiod 1), 1977 and 1984 (subperiod 2), and 1981 and 1988 (subperiod 3).

Overall, these four variables tend, then, to confirm that problems of urban decline have been associated with forms of deindustrialization, but they highlight the problems of deindustrialization for urban regions whose industrial growth might be called resource based (coalfields, natural harbors) rather than skill based; and they challenge the too-ready acceptance of the simple deindustrialization thesis. They also provide support for the view that agricultural transformation is a source of serious urban deterioration. Specialization in agriculture in the wider region in which the FUR is situated was associated with worsening urban problems up to the point at which 15 percent of employment was in agriculture in 1975. A further increase beyond that point was associated with a reduction of problems. This seems to be consistent with the interpretation that in the very poorest and least-developed rural regions of Europe (notably Galicia), problems are concentrated in the countryside, but in the slightly more prosperous regions deterioration is increasingly concentrated in the urban areas. The way in which this pattern has changed over the period 1971–88 is commented on below.

These findings are also consistent with the underlying conceptualization of urban problems suggested earlier, that they represent essentially adjustment problems. The need for change in an urban region is determined by the changing spatial and industrial patterns of demand and comparative advantage, interacting with what can be thought of as the adaptive capacity of the urban economy and society. The important implication of this is that skill-based urban industrial economies, of which Stuttgart is perhaps the supreme example, have greater adaptive capacity than resource-based urban industrial economies such as Liverpool or Valenciennes.

The factors so far discussed all relate to the demand side of the local economy, or to its adaptive capacity. Supply-side factors are relevant, however, especially since the change in unemployment is one of the elements determining the value of the dependent variable. Since migration and commuting flows respond to changes in excess demand, the ideal measure of exogenous supply-induced pressure in the urban labor market would be the change in labor force participation determined by natural change alone. Unfortunately, data for this measure are not available for all FURs, so an alternative, the natural rate of increase of population 1971–81, was entered instead. This measure proved significant at the 1.2 percent level and had the expected sign. This result appears to confirm the hypothesis that an exogenous increase in labor supply, once other factors have been allowed for, is an adjustment problem that tends to make urban problems worse and to lower per capita welfare.

The final set of explanatory variables (table 5.2) represents dummies for particular countries. The fact that after allowing for other factors, Spanish cities did worse than those elsewhere in the EU during the period under analysis comes as no surprise. The observation that French and Italian cities did better over the same period is equally unsurprising. It appears initially more startling to find that, once other factors have been allowed for, British cities did better than average. To a significant extent, however, these country dummies can be interpreted as reflecting the noncoincidence of the economic cycle across the countries of the EU. Cities exist within their national economic and social contexts. A major influence on the per capita welfare levels of their inhabitants is the state of the national economy (just as considerable stability is observed in the relative incidence of regional unemployment). The near-catastrophic problems that afflicted the Spanish economy after 1974 are well documented (see, for example, Cuadrado Roura 1991). Its rapid recovery beginning in mid-1985 occurred too late in the period analyzed to have much impact on the measure of urban problems used here. Britain, in particular, entered the severe recession of the late 1970s and early 1980s somewhat earlier than other countries in the EU and also started its recovery earlier. The negative dummy for British FURs is probably mainly determined by this fact. The evidence is, then, that up to 80 percent of the variation in the performance of the major urban regions of the EU over the period 1971–88 can be explained by the characteristics of those urban regions, including as a characteristic, the country in which they are located.

EXPLAINING THE UNEXPLAINED

What can be said about the pattern of residuals observed (see column 1, table 5.5)? In principle, if the model were fully specified and all variables correctly and accurately measured, the residuals would be random. The results in table 5.5 and other evidence, however, suggest that they are not. Experimentation with different functional forms and specifications generated very robust rankings of the residuals. The pattern of residuals appears to be systematic and suggests, therefore, that significant variables affecting urban performance have been omitted. The technical implication is that the estimates of the coefficients may be biased. The fact that there is a pattern also has a positive implication, however, that seems considerably more interesting: it suggests that the residuals themselves can be interpreted and are related to facts about the individual cities concerned. If 80 percent of the variance in performance over the period 1971–88 can be explained by systematic factors, then the implication is that 20 percent of the variance is explained by other factors (including random error).

The most obvious of these other factors is the variation in local urban policy. Certain European cities stand out on the basis of qualitative evidence as having pursued distinctive and relatively consistent urban policies and as having coordinated a range of policy instruments to achieve strategic goals. These cities were identified and their policies discussed in Cheshire and Hay (1989), before the results presented here became available. Prominent among these cities have been Bologna and Lyon—long-standing urban policies not formulated as a response to serious problems; Glasgow—urban policies formulated as a comparatively early response to perceived problems; Birmingham and Rotterdam—urban policies formulated more recently in response to problems.

For the period being analyzed, recent evidence suggests that Barcelona might be added to the Birmingham and Rotterdam group. (The really important efforts of policy-induced improvements were associated with the period running up to the 1992 Olympics held in Barcelona.) There may also be a contrast between Paris and London, as well as a point of similarity between London and Dublin. Paris pursued a coherent strategic development plan, aided by a consistent administrative system and a regional tier of policy coordination, and modernized its transport infrastructure from the late 1960s. London, however, exhibited both an absence of coordinated strategic planning and a lack of investment significantly caused by planning delays and indecision. It was further hampered by the abolition of its city-wide tier of government in 1984, and the disputes that preceded it. In this respect, London and Dublin had something in common. The abolition of local taxation in Ireland meant that urban governments became wholly dependent on national administrations for finance and, in the difficult economic climate of Ireland during the late 1970s and 1980s, this meant that local authorities became increasingly short of funds. It also separated financial from administrative decisions. Dublin Corporation made proposals for transport investment and new urban highways, but had no resources with which to implement them. Tracts of land became subject to planning blight, leading to a loss of private investment in infrastructure. Thus, in Dublin and in London, planning increased uncertainty rather than reduced it, and strategic coordination of decision making became worse rather than better during the period analyzed here.

This qualitative information can be related to the evidence of the residuals. Allowing for other factors influencing the changing incidence of urban problems since 1971, Glasgow emerges as the fourth most successful city in the EU. It is closely followed by Bologna (the eighth) and by Lyon (the thirteenth). A smaller but still significant relative improvement was exhibited by Rotterdam and Birmingham. Furthermore, as discussed below, the timing of these improvements relative to their characteristics exactly matches the known application of urban policy. Bologna and Lyon outperformed their characteristics most in subperiod 1 (see table 5.5); Glasgow in subperiod 2; and Barcelona, Birmingham, and Rotterdam in the final subperiod, 3.

The case of Rotterdam perhaps provides some predictive test of these results. In that city, there was a conscious change of policy in 1983. New political leadership emerged and swept away a long-standing policy focus on social housing provision and support for traditional port-related, blue-collar activity. The new policy attempted to diversify the local economy, particularly to encourage business services and communications, and gave priority to improving transport and communications within, and to, the city, and to making land available for private housing. A more conservation-minded approach was also developed with respect to older housing and historic districts. In addition, starting in 1986, substantial funds were made available by the central government to support the new policies. The general pattern of the policy changes in Rotterdam was broadly similar to that observed earlier in Glasgow and, more recently, in Birmingham. If the interpretation of events offered here is correct, because the policy changes were comparatively late, one should expect a growing negative residual over the years to about 1993, with any improvement to be concentrated in the final subperiod and to continue beyond 1988. It is interesting that the analysis of urban economic growth between 1979 and 1990 (Cheshire 1997) shows that Rotterdam continued to have a large positive growth residual for the decade as a whole— ranking eighteenth, one place above Barcelona.

Finally, in policy terms, the contrast between Paris and London and the comparison between Dublin and London are interesting. Paris has performed much in line with predictions, based on its characteristics: London over the period 1971–88 deteriorated, relative to that predicted by its characteristics, more than all but two other urban regions in the EU, and Dublin was ranked 110th out of 117; like London, Dublin underperformed its characteristics very seriously. If this analysis provides statistical support for the claim that Glasgow is truly "miles better" (at least given its characteristics), it also provides statistical support for the belief that London and Dublin, given their characteristics, are miles worse. London had the most favorable characteristics and should have been the city that improved most in the United Kingdom; in fact, only six British cities performed worse.

Some other patterns can be seen in the residuals. First, there seem to be some regional effects. Cities in southwestern France, such as Bordeaux and Toulouse, improved compared to their predicted performance; so, too, did some cities in the southern and southeastern parts of the Federal Republic of Germany, the striking exception being München. An interesting phenomenon in Germany is that although cities in the north and center, close to the Ruhr, lost ground in absolute terms, once other factors were allowed for, it was not the old industrial centers that did the worst but the service centers, Bonn and Düsseldorf. The transfer of capital functions to Berlin should reinforce this relative loss. There was also a deterioration of the cities in Andalusia, especially in Córdoba, Málaga and Sevilla. Finally, as expected, there was a strong regional effect in Belgium, with the cities of Wallonia performing below expectations and those in Flanders performing above expectations. There are really two Belgiums, but there were not enough observations to have even one country dummy.

A second pattern that seems to emerge from the residuals is the superior performance of larger service-oriented regional centers, especially when compared to smaller local cities. Thus, there was a contrast between Frankfurt and Wiesbaden; Lille and Valenciennes; Newcastle and Sunderland; Palermo and Messina; and even between Sevilla and Córdoba.

In terms of characteristics, rather than geographic regions, FURs previously diagnosed as having severe problems of growth, such as those of Andalusia, Napoli, or Cagliari in southern Italy, were the other group to exhibit severe deterioration relative to expectations over the period as a whole. This reinforces the suspicion that the problems of poor and backward regions of Southern Europe may have been concentrating in the urban, rather than the rural, areas, as low-skilled, rural residents continued to move to the cities, where no significant economic improvement was apparent, leaving behind an increasingly better capitalized and less-impoverished peasantry. This may be thought of as a reverse Kaldor effect (Kaldor 1970), where transfer of labor out of low-productivity activity was not into higher productivity activity, leading to regional growth, but into unemployment or under-employment, leading to spatially concentrated urban impoverishment.

<hr>

SUBPERIODS

Table 5.5 also shows the residuals from three subperiods during the period 1971–88.[9] The equations generating these are shown in table 5.6. The implications of these results for local policy have already been discussed, but they also throw light on the way in which the effects of different factors had changed through time and had wider implications for explaining and anticipating patterns of urban development.

The dependent variable is the change in the score of each of the three subperiods in table 5.1. Because of the moving average character of these scores, they do not relate to exact years; however, subperiod 1 corresponds broadly to the 1970s, subperiod 2 from the late 1970s to the mid-1980s, and subperiod 3 from the early to late 1980s. In each model the value of the welfare index score at the start of the period is included as an additional variable. This makes it possible to trace the extent to which a lower level of per capita welfare (higher level of problems) was associated with improvement or deterioration through time.[10] Although in subperiod 1 there was a closing of the gap between the worse and better-off cities once their structural characteristics had been allowed for, over the period as a whole there was a tendency for net polarization or divergence. Conditions in cities that started off in a worse position deteriorated further in relation to conditions in cities that started off in a stronger position. Otherwise the model is essentially that used for the aggregate score change reported in table 5.2. As anticipated, there appears to be more random variation in the subperiod score changes, because of the lower reliability of the data, and this is reflected in generally lower R^2s.

The general pattern of results is similar to that previously reported for the period as a whole, and the model is generally stable. Apart from the interpretation of the residuals and the implications of these for the scope and effectiveness of urban policy already discussed, there are some additional points of interest. The change in economic potential always has the anticipated sign and is significant in each subperiod. FURs that gained more tended to improve relative to those that gained less from the process of integration. There is some indication, however, that the form of this influence was changing, with

Table 5.6 CHANGING INCIDENCE OF URBAN PROBLEMS FOR 117 EUROPEAN FURs, SUBPERIODS 1971–88: EXPLANATORY FACTORS

Independent Variables[a]	Dependent Variable: Change in Problem Score Subperiod 1[b] (1970s)	Dependent Variable: Change in Problem Score Subperiod 2[c] (late 1970s–early 1980s)	Dependent Variable: Change in Problem Score Subperiod 3[d] (early–late 1980s)
Intercept	6.6760* (2.37)	0.9569 (1.22)	1.6921** (2.88)
Log total population, 1981	−0.5021* (−2.47)		
Change in economic potential	−1.0780* (−2.46)		−5.6145** (−4.15)
Change in economic potential squared		−0.7380* (−2.49)	2.6290** (3.31)
Percentage of labor force in agriculture: wider region	0.1287** (2.66)		0.0643* (3.21)
Percentage of labor force in agriculture squared: wider region	−0.0055** (−4.04)		
Percentage of labor force in industry: wider region		0.0709** (4.45)	
Dependence of local economy on coal	0.7611** (3.05)		
Dependence of local economy on port	0.3121** (2.92)	0.2573* (2.59)	

Natural rate of population change, 1971–81	0.0817** (2.57)		
Value of score 1 at start of period	−0.1204** (−4.19)	0.0702** (2.84)	0.1049** (3.67)
Country dummies: Federal Republic of Germany			1.5016** (3.76)
France		−2.9569** (−7.76)	2.3493** (5.46)
Italy		−2.1557** (−5.05)	
Spain		6.8251** (12.52)	
United Kingdom		−1.1721* (−2.60)	
Adjusted R^2	0.31	0.84	0.48

Notes: T values are in parentheses: Two asterisks (**) = significant at 1 percent; one asterisk (*) = significant at 5 percent; other variables, except constant, are mainly significant at 10 percent.
[a]Defined as in table 5.2.
[b]Score 2 − score 1.
[c]Score 3 − score 2.
[d]Score 4 − score 3.

some "spread effect" emerging in the most recent subperiod. In this last period there is a strong indication of a quadratic form, with the peak effect being not at the maximum value (confined to a small area of Belgium around Brussels and the Netherlands) but at a value of about 1.25 to 1.35 (compared to a range of 0 to 1.80): these values are in parts of the Federal Republic of Germany, the Netherlands, and Northern France. This is consistent with a process of decentralization and rising land and congestion costs in the immediate core of the EU, and is analyzed in more detail and with supporting evidence for more recent time periods in Cheshire and Carbonaro (1996). The main finding from the analysis of aggregate change, however—that the process of economic integration tended systematically to reinforce the advantages of the more central regions and to penalize regions that lost relatively (those on the southern and northwestern extremities of Europe)—is reinforced by the separate results for the subperiods.

FURs in more agricultural regions deteriorated in the first subperiod; there was no significant effect in the second subperiod; but again a higher dependence on agriculture was associated with deterioration over the most recent subperiod 3. There is, however, an interesting difference: in subperiod 1 the influence was quadratic, with a peak at about 13 percent of the labor force of the wider region engaged in agriculture, whereas in the most recent subperiod the effect was linear. This is consistent with the argument that it is the urban areas of southern Europe that are increasingly becoming the nodes of disadvantage. Agricultural employment has everywhere declined but, in the earliest period, cities in the most agricultural regions (in this sample, all of these were in Spain or in southern Italy) were still nodes of advantage. With continuing rural-urban migration and falling agricultural employment, by the second half of the 1980s even these cities were deteriorating, and the more agricultural their surrounding regions, the more they tended to deteriorate.

There was an association between specialization in industry in the wider region and FUR deterioration only in subperiod 2. Then it was strong and highly significant. The change in measured urban performance over subperiod 2 was determined mainly by the increase in mean unemployment between 1977–81 and 1983–84. What we are observing, therefore, is that the severe recession of 1980 was associated with a particularly rapid loss of industrial jobs. It may be remembered that this was when observers began to talk of a problem of "urban decline in large industrial cities" and also when discussions of the problems of deindustrialization were most intense. Perhaps what they were observing were the effects of a severe recession that bit particularly hard on industry and caused serious, but relatively short-lived, adjustment problems for local economies that specialized in industry.

A dependence on specific, older, resource-based industries—coal mining and port activity—seems, on the basis of these results, to have been a more enduring factor in urban problems. FURs dependent on port activities deteriorated in both the first and second subperiods. By the third subperiod, adjustment to containerization had, perhaps, largely taken place. Those with a dependence on coal deteriorated sharply in the first subperiod, but more questionably in the third subperiod—the variable is only just nonsignificant at 5 percent. There was no significant, or near-significant, relationship in subperiod 2, when the general collapse of industrial employment dominated. The coal variable is measured physically, and it is plausible to argue that the environmental effects of the coal industry (coupled perhaps with the inheritance of skills and industrial relations attitudes) had a longer-lasting adverse effect on local economic adjustment. Overall, therefore, these industrial structure variables reinforce the suggestion of a worse problem of adjustment for urban economies specializing in old resource-based industries than for those specializing more generally in industry—for which the skills may have been more adaptable and the environment (including land availability) more attractive.

CONCLUSIONS

The analysis reported here seems to confirm the conclusion that there were essentially two classic types of problem urban regions in the EU over the 1970–88 period. The first group consisted of those suffering from problems of urban decline. These were strongly concentrated in FURs with local economies specialized in the declining industries— especially the resource-based industries—of the nineteenth century. These FURs were located chiefly in a band running from Genoa and Turin in northeast Italy, through eastern France, the Ruhr, southern Belgium, and northwest through the British Isles to Glasgow and Belfast. Two urban regions of northeastern Spain, Bilbao, and Avilés/ Gijón, seem to have been in the process of joining this group. Within this group port cities in particular have deteriorated.

The other classic type of urban problem was that of the growing cities in southern Europe. These are largely in impoverished and backward rural economies with rural-urban migration, but frequently with outward migration from the wider region as a whole. The incidence of this type of problem FUR was increased considerably by the accession of Spain and Portugal, and the mean intensity of the problem measure of growing, compared to declining, FURs also increased. Over the whole period, the cities with the worst problems tended to deteriorate in relation to the strongest urban regions.

An analysis of the patterns of change in urban problems over the 1971–88 period for the 117 FURs for which there are data shows that up to 80 percent of the variations can be explained in terms of the measurable characteristics of those FURs. Notable among those characteristics was the extent to which they benefited from or were hurt by the impact of European economic integration. That process was continuous from about 1960, and the statistical evidence for its powerful influence is overwhelming. Since barriers to trade in industrial products all but disappeared with the creation of the nine-nation EEC in the early 1970s, the most powerful influence of the Single European Market starting from the end of 1992 must be expected to be in service industries and factor mobility. It is the service industries that grew most rapidly in all the countries analyzed in this chapter and that must be expected to exhibit the most growth in the countries of the EU to the end of the century and beyond. Furthermore, service employment is relatively more concentrated in cities. Together, those two trends suggest that we may expect further sharp improvements in service-oriented cities in the parts of Europe gaining from European economic integration. Analysis of more recent changes in patterns of urban population development in chapter 19 supports this suggestion. But this gain in service-oriented cities, which benefit from European integration and proximity to major metropolitan regions, may be matched by losses in other service cities, particularly those on the European periphery. The increasing polarization between the more successful and the less successful FURs, also noted in terms of economic growth during the 1980s (Magrini 1997), may be significant in this context. The negative impact of industrial specialization—except in the more peripheral Spanish cities—may fall. This is because the impact of integration may already have significantly worked itself through as a locational influence on industry and because, given the extent of job losses in industry over the recent past, the continuing absolute contribution of industrial job losses is likely to fall.

The extent to which the varying performance of the EU's major cities could be explained by systematic factors provides support for the belief that the index of urban problems does reflect some real aspect of the experience of cities. The residuals that remain, however, suggest that urban policy can have some effect—both positive and negative—and provide some quantitative measure of the efficacy (or particularly in the case of London and Dublin, the inefficacy) of local urban policy during the period. Although most of urban performance seems to be determined by factors over which policy can have no influence, there still remains a small but substantial differential element in comparative urban performance that can be closely related to qualitative information on urban policy.

Notes

1. These terms have different nuances of meaning, not fully explored here.

2. Functional urban regions are defined in terms of employment concentrations and commuting patterns. Urban cores are identified on the basis of a minimum threshold number of jobs within one administrative area. Contiguous local administrative areas are then added, so long as job densities exceed a specified threshold. The "hinterland" is then defined by aggregating all those local administrative areas from which more people commute to that core compared to any other. FURs thus broadly correspond to the U.S. concept of the metropolitan statistical area, although their hinterlands tend to be rather more extensive, particularly in more rural areas.

3. The term European Union (EU) is used throughout this chapter, although the name was first adopted in the Maastricht treaty in 1992.

4. This abstracts from the measurement problem: the smaller the area, the more inaccurate measures of GDP become, especially when measured per capita output is measured at workplaces, while people are counted where they live. Net commuting thus seriously distorts measures of per capita GDP. There is also considerable variation over the EU as a whole in the proportionate contribution to local economic activity of the subsistence and underground economies. These difficulties generate strong pragmatic reasons for caution in relying on local GDP as a unique measure of even local economic activity.

5. The considerable help given by that team of advisers is gratefully acknowledged.

6. This data set was put together before the consolidated data for GDP for the Level 3 (in some cases Level 2) regions of the EU were made available by Eurostat in the REG10 data base, published in 1992. The new data formed the basis of the analysis of urban economic growth presented in Cheshire and Carbonaro (1996).

7. It is worth repeating the caution that because this index was originally formulated as a problem index, the more negative the value, the higher the welfare level (the more problem-free the city); and the more positive the value, the lower the welfare level.

8. Level 2 of the nesting set of official EU regions. The largest of these are the *Länder* of the Federal Republic of Germany or the Standard Regions of the United Kingdom; the smallest in common use are the Level 3 regions such as the counties of Great Britain or the *départements* of France.

9. I am grateful to Leo Klaassen for suggesting this analysis and for overcoming my initial doubts.

10. And this could be construed as measuring, in the terminology of Barro and Sala-i-Martin (1992), conditional convergence or divergence.

APPENDIX

The methods used to derive the "problem score" from which the "welfare index" analyzed in this paper was derived were outlined in Cheshire et al. (1986), Cheshire et al. (1988), and Cheshire and Hay (1989). The selection of variables from among available and appropriate candidate variables, and the weights to be attached to each, was resolved by using discriminant analysis. This is a multivariate statistical technique that has been used in a variety of biological, medical, and social science applications (see Hand 1981). If groups can be identified a priori (for example, specimens of particular species or varieties; recovering or nonrecovering patients; or defaulters and non-defaulters on debt) and continuous variables relating to their characteristics identified, discriminant analysis can be used to estimate the weights to be attached to variables and which characteristics differ significantly between groups. Given the data on the characteristics, coefficients can be estimated (the discriminant function) that minimize within-group variance and maximize between-group variance. These coefficients can then be applied to the measured characteristics of all members of the population, including new observations not allocated a priori to any of the original groups, to estimate a discriminant score for each observation.

This discriminant score was used initially as the "problem score," but subsequent analysis and reflection suggested it could be, with reversed sign, interpreted equally well and more intelligibly as a per capita welfare score, given the way the analysis had been set up.

A problem in using discriminant analysis in the present application was that no natural a priori groups existed.[1] These groups—or training sets—were selected by asking the expert advisers to the original study to nominate, blind of the data (which were only then, in 1984, being collected for the first time), the cities in their countries that had the worst urban problems or that were most healthy. The definition of the Organization for Economic Cooperation and Development (OECD 1983) was used: "the spatial concentration . . . of social, economic and environmental problems such as high levels of unemployment and poverty, housing deterioration and decay of urban infrastructure." The national experts—all academics—were:

Belgium	Professor H. Van der Haegen	Economic Geography
	University of Leuven	
Denmark	Mr. B. Grönlund	Urban Planning
	Danish Technology Institute	
France	Professor P. Aydalot	Urban and Regional
	University of Paris	Economics
Germany	Professor K. Kunzmann	Urban and Regional
	University of Dortmund	Planning
Greece	Professor G. Chiotis	Urban and Regional
	The Athens Graduate School	Economics
	of Economics and Business	
	Science	
Italy	Professor P. Costa	Urban and Regional
	University of Venice	Economics
The Netherlands	Dr. L. van den Berg	Urban and Regional
	Erasmus University, Rotterdam	Economics
Portugal	Professor S. Lopes	Urban and Regional
	Technical University, Lisbon	Economics
Spain	Professor B. Ynzenga	Urban Planning
	University of Madrid	
United Kingdom	Professor H.W.E. Davies	Urban Planning
	Professor A.W. Evans	Urban Economics
	Professor P.G. Hall	Geography
	University of Reading	

There was thus a range of disciplines represented, but a weighting toward economics. The OECD definition just quoted was agreed upon by the experts as a working definition of urban problems. It places most weight on economic criteria but included social and environmental conditions.

The distribution of conditions across cities is likely to be continuous rather than dichotomous. It was anticipated that there would be a range of conditions represented in each of the training sets and, indeed, an attempt was made, judgmentally, to include within each training set a range of types of city in different countries. Apart from nominating cities in their own countries for one or other of the training sets, the advisers were also asked to nominate the three or four cities that they judged to be among the best and worst in the European Union as a whole. No city was included in a training set that had not been nominated, but there was some experimentation undertaken, both with respect to the range of city sizes and the balance between countries and types of problem/advantage represented. The cities finally chosen were:

High incidence of problems/ low per capita welfare:		Low level of problems/high per capita welfare:	
Belfast	Liverpool	Antwerp	Munich
Cagliari	Málaga	Augsburg	Madrid
Charleroi	Naples	Bologna	Nice
Duisburg	Saärbrücken	Brussels	Norwich
Genoa	Sunderland	Dijon	Palma de Mallorca
Glasgow	Taranto	Düsseldorf	Strasbourg
Gijón/Aviles	Valenciennes	Florence	Stuttgart
Liège		Grenoble	Venice
		Milan	Wiesbaden

Cities from Greece and Portugal could not be included in the training sets for lack of data, although, wherever possible, scores were calculated for them. Thus, a total of 33 cities out of an effective population of 119 were nominated to the training sets.[2] Two further points should be noted. First, the nomination of a city to one group or another did not necessarily predetermine its classification and score. The analysis could reclassify it as belonging, in a statistical sense, to the other group. In the experimentation with group nominations, this did occasionally happen but, even when it did, the overall pattern of results was not greatly affected. In the training sets ultimately used, there were no such misclassifications. The calculated posterior probability of a city belonging to the training set to which it had been nominated exceeded 0.99 in twenty-seven out of the thirty-three; the lowest posterior probability was for Madrid, which had a probability of only 0.77 of belonging to the "problem-free" group. The second point is that since the discriminant function estimated from the training sets could be used to calculate a score for all cities, conditions in cities not in the training sets could, and frequently were, rated as better or worse than those in the training sets.

The routine used was the STEPDISC procedure available in SAS. The choice of candidate variables was severely constrained by data availability and quality. No official data relating to consistently defined cities existed, so all variables had either to be estimated from official data published by Eurostat or collected ab initio. A system was devised that proved highly effective for estimating FUR data from official data published for the smallest Eurostat regions (NUTS Level 3) and using locally available data to weight Level 3 data for the eight cases where two FURs were wholly or mainly within the same Level 3 region. All candidate variables were judged to be indicators of the "output" rather than the "inputs" into urban welfare. They were:

Per capita GDP in Purchasing Power Standard, estimated where possible from Eurostat Level 3 data. Separate but widely used data from the Bank of Bilbao were used for earlier years for Spanish Level 3 regions. Until 1985, data were only available for some countries for the larger Level 2 or Level 1 regions.[3]

Unemployment rates, estimated from Level 3 Labour Force Survey data, in all cases using standardized Eurostat or almost identical Spanish national definitions.

Net inmigration, collected, or estimated as a residual of actual less natural FUR population change from national Censuses of Population. This indicator was judged to be an appropriate candidate variable on the basis of the extensive literature on interregional migration (for surveys see, for example, Richardson 1973, Greenwood 1975) suggesting that net migration flows respond both to differential labor market conditions as reflected in variations in wage and unemployment and to variation in environmental conditions.

Travel demand index, measured as quality-weighted hotel bedrooms per unit population (source: *Michelin Guides*, various dates) of the core city. It was concluded this was closely correlated with total expenditure by travelers to each city. Such expenditures mainly reflected business travel, but also urban tourism, and so reflected both business conditions and certain urban environment amenities.

Very large numbers of experiments were conducted (excluding candidate variables, using randomized training sets) but the results proved extremely robust (Cheshire and Hay 1989; Cheshire et al. 1986). Particular attention was paid to the consistent selection of unemployment rather than to GDP variables in the stepwise procedures. There was evidence to support the view that data for years close to and immediately preceding the year in which training sets were selected (1984) performed best in estimating the discriminant functions. One problem was that, at the time the work was being done, FUR per capita GDP estimates for 1981 were less reliable than for years after 1984 because in a number of cases (for example, for all British FURs) only Level 1 regional data—areas far larger than all but the very largest urban regions such as London or Paris—were available. Although in principle it might be thought that standardized GDP per capita data would be the best single indicators of local economic welfare, in practice the quality of the data was such that this could not really be tested. In the event, there was in any case colinearity between the local unemployment rate and estimates of GDP per capita, but the stepwise procedures always selected the unemployment variables, with GDP being correctly signed but seldom significant at more than the 25 percent level. Rank orders derived from discriminant functions that were estimated excluding unemployment but including GDP data, were, however, highly correlated with rank orders derived from the best-fit functions.

Appendix Notes

1. This is a less distinctive problem than might appear at first sight. Defining patients who recover, or do not, or debtors who pay up or default is also, to an extent, arbitrary. Have cancer patients who survive five years recovered? Why not four years or six years? Debtors who in one legal system default might not be so classified in another system; some who repay only just do so; some defaulters may equally only fail to pay because of wholly exceptional circumstances.

2. There were 122 FURs of more than one-third of a million inhabitants and with core cities of more than 200,000. In addition, two smaller FURs, Norwich and Cosenza, were included but the four major FURs of Greece and Portugal, and also Aarhus, were excluded.

3. GDP per capita estimates for NUTS Level 3 regions from 1979 became available with the production of Eurostat's REGIO database in 1993. FUR estimates have been derived from this and have been analyzed (see, for example, Cheshire and Carbonaro 1996).

References

Anas, A., and L. Moses. 1978. "Transportation and Land Use in the Mature Metropolis." In *The Mature Metropolis*, edited by C. L. Leven. Lexington, Mass.: D. C. Heath.

Barro, R., and X. Sala-i-Martin. 1992. "Convergence across States and Regions." In *Brookings Papers on Economic Activity* I: 107–82.

Blomquist, G. C., M. C. Berger, and J. P. Hoehn. 1988. "New Estimates of the Quality of Life in Urban Areas." *American Economic Review* 78: 89–107.

Boyer, R., and D. Savageau. 1985. *Places Rated Almanac*. Skokie, Ill.: Rand McNally.

Cheshire, P. C. 1990. "Explaining the Recent Performance of the European Community's Major Urban Regions." *Urban Studies* 27(3): 307–29.

———. 1997. "Moderating the Spatial Impact of European Integration: The Role of Territorial Competition." In *Research Papers in Environmental and Spatial Analysis*, No. 47. London: Dept. of Geography, London School of Economics.

Cheshire, P. C., and G. Carbonaro. 1996. "Urban Economic Growth in Europe: Testing Theory and Policy Prescriptions." *Urban Studies* 33(7): 1111–28.

Cheshire, P. C., and D. G. Hay. 1989. *Urban Problems in Western Europe: An Economic Analysis*. London: Unwin Hyman.

Cheshire, P. C., G. Carbonaro, and D. G. Hay. 1986. "Problems of Urban Decline and Growth in EEC Countries: Or Measuring Degrees of Elephantness." *Urban Studies* 23(2): 131–49.

Cheshire, P. C., R. P. Camagni, J-P. de Gaudemar, and J. R. Cuadrado Roura. 1991. "1957 to 1992: Moving Towards a Europe of Regions and Regional Policy." In *Industrial Change and Regional Economic Transformation: The Experience of Western Europe*, edited by L. Rodwin and H. Sazanami. London: Harper Collins Academic.

Cheshire, P. C., D. G. Hay, G. Carbonaro, and N. Bevan. 1988. *Urban Problems and Regional Policy in the European Community*. Luxembourg: Commission of the European Communities.

Clark, C., F. Wilson, and J. Bradley. 1969. "Industrial Location and Economic Potential in Western Europe." *Regional Studies* 3: 197–202.

Cuadrado Roura, J. R. 1991. "Structural Changes in the Spanish Economy: Their Regional Impacts." In *Industrial Change and Regional Economic Transformation: The Experience of Western Europe*, edited by L. Rodwin and H. Sazanami. London: Harper Collins Academic.

Department of the Environment. 1983. *Urban Deprivation*. Information Note 2, Inner Cities Directorate. London: Her Majesty's Stationery Office.

Evans, A. W., and G. Crampton. 1989. "Myth, Reality, and Employment in London." *Journal of Transport Economics and Policy* 23(1): 89–108.

Fothergill, S., and G. Gudgin. 1982. *Unequal Growth: Urban and Regional Employment Change in the United Kingdom*. London: Heinemann Educational.

Greenwood, M. J. 1975. "Research on Internal Migration in the United States." *The Journal of Economic Literature* 13: 397–433.

Hall, P., and D. Hay. 1980. *Growth Centres in the European Urban System*. London: Heinemann Educational.

Hand, D. J. 1981. *Discrimination and Classification*. New York: John Wiley and Sons.

Kaldor, N. 1970. "The Case for Regional Policies." *Scottish Journal of Political Economy* 17: 337–47.

Keeble, D., J. Offord, and S. Walker. 1988. *Peripheral Regions in a Community of Twelve Member States*. Luxembourg: Office of Official Publications of the European Communities.

Leven, C. L., and M. Stover. 1989. "Some Further Improvements in Rating the Quality of Life in Urban Areas." Paper presented to 33rd European Congress of Regional Science, Cambridge, England.

Magrini, S. 1997. "The Evolution of Income Disparities among the Regions of the European Union." *Research Papers in Environmental and Spatial Analysis*, No. 46. London: Dept. of Geography, London School of Economics.

Organization for Economic Cooperation and Development [OECD]. 1983. *Managing Urban Change*. Paris: Author.

Oxford Regional Economic Atlas: Western Europe. 1971. Oxford, England: Oxford University Press.

Richardson, H. W. 1973. *Regional Growth Theory*. London: Macmillan.

Roback, J. 1982. "Wages, Rents, and the Quality of Life." *Journal of Political Economy* 90: 1257–58.

Rosen, S. 1979. "Wage-Based Indexes of Urban Quality of Life." In *Current Issues in Urban Economics*, edited by P. Mieszkowski and M. Straszheim. Baltimore: Johns Hopkins University Press.

van den Berg, L., R. Drewett, L. H. Klaassen, A. Rossi, and C. H. T. Vijverberg. 1982. *Urban Europe: A Study of Growth and Decline*. Oxford, England: Pergamon.

Part Two

THE DYNAMICS OF METROPOLITAN AREA CHANGE: THEORY AND EVIDENCE

Chapter Six

WHAT MAKES METROPOLITAN AREAS GROW?

Edwin S. Mills

This chapter addresses the determinants of sizes and growth of metropolitan statistical areas (MSAs) in the United States. Anthony Downs, in chapter 2 in this volume, has discussed the differences between the contexts of post–World War II metropolitan development in Europe and the United States. The effects of the differences he discusses on metropolitan structure and development are unknown. Although the current chapter is written in a U.S. context, I believe that the model developed here is nearly as relevant to metropolitan areas worldwide as it is to U.S. circumstances.

The subject of MSA growth determinants is extremely difficult, and little theoretical or statistical research has been devoted to it. There are studies of growth determinants at the county, municipal, state, and regional levels, but only a few at the MSA level. By far the best empirical analysis of MSA growth determinants is that of Bradbury, Downs, and Small (1982), but little has been offered in terms of basic neoclassical analysis. See Mills and Lubuele (1995) for an econometric study. Basic spatial analysis reveals why MSAs and other urban areas exist and the sufficient conditions for their existence. These conditions are substantial scale economies in a variety of manufacturing and service sectors, coupled with transportation costs that reward proximate locations of producers to their vendors (most importantly, their employees) and to their customers; an input-output network that is dense with nonzero entries; and production functions that permit substitution of nonland inputs (capital and labor) for land in urban sectors. Scale economies result in large production facilities in single locations; input substitution permits high population and production densities; high transportation costs motivate proximate locations of related activities; and a dense input-output matrix implies large numbers of related activities that can benefit from proximate locations. The result is large and dense concentrations of households and a variety of production sectors. If one adds international or interregional comparative advantage, one gets mutual trade among the resulting MSAs and the locating of MSAs at natural transportation nodes. (It is remarkable that in a country such as the United States, in which the international sector is small, almost all large MSAs are located on navigable waterways with good ocean access. This includes not only the ports on the two coasts but also those on the Gulf of Mexico, the Great Lakes, those on the Mississippi up to about Saint Louis, and tributary ports such as Pittsburgh. Furthermore, those MSAs have prospered relative to others during much of the postwar period.)

However, the preceding simple neoclassical considerations give only the broadest hints as to the size distribution of MSAs. Virtually the only neoclassical models of MSA size distributions have been done at Brown University—by Beckmann (1958), and Beckmann and McPherson (1970)—and by Henderson (1988). Neoclassical considerations tell us even less about growth, which is presumably movement from one equilibrium size distribution to another. Bradbury et al. (1982) provide interesting conceptual analysis aimed at empirical estimation.

DEFINITIONS

Intuitively, people tend to define generic urban areas as more or less independent of state and local government boundaries and, to some extent, of national boundaries (e.g., Detroit, Mich., and Windsor, Canada, are logically the same MSA). Undoubtedly, the Census Urbanized Area is the best U.S. approximation to large generic urban areas, but data are scarce. Practically speaking, MSAs are the only ball game in town, yet clearly they are much larger than generic urban areas, since more than half their land is rural.

Furthermore, in some cases, MSAs may not correspond at all to the intuitive notion of generic urban areas. The Chicago Consolidated MSA (CMSA) consists of six Primary MSAs (PMSA), and the New York CMSA consists of no fewer than twelve PMSAs. Many MSAs are contiguous because, although largely separate generic urban areas, they have grown together. In many cases, it is unclear whether the PMSA or the CMSA best approximates the generic urban area. Almost the entire East Coast from New Hampshire to Richmond is a set of contiguous MSAs. Yet if you fly over it, much of it appears rural. At the other extreme, some MSAs in the South and West are extremely low density. One, for example, Casper, Wyoming, even has a population density less than that of the average of the forty-eight contiguous states.

Socially speaking, MSA growth is less important than central city (CC) growth (Mills and Lubuele 1997). Most MSA poverty, alienation, unemployment, and economic decline have been in the CCs for forty years. Data are plentiful for CCs; that is not the issue. The issue is that CCs are not generic urban areas and become less so every decade. Mills (1990) has shown that population growth in CCs and suburbs is related, but only weakly so.

Practically, scholars must use MSA data. In several cases, however, it is a matter of judgment whether the unit of observation should be separate PMSAs or the CMSA of which PMSAs are components.

BACKGROUND

MSAs are part of a system. Again, although theoretical treatments are lacking, many studies present empirical analyses of MSA size distributions within and among countries (for example, see Rosen and Resnick 1980). No theory says that the nation-state is the appropriate set of MSAs for empirical estimation. Western Europe, East Africa, the United States west of the Rocky Mountains, or the (former) Soviet Union west of Siberia might be more natural MSA sets for analyses of size distributions. In fact, the Pareto and lognormal provide excellent, and approximately equally good, fits to MSA size distributions. Indeed, a few studies suggest that the fit is almost as good in regions of large countries, such as the United States, India, and Brazil, as in the entire country. That fact may suggest that something is phony about the analysis, since the sum of Pareto or lognormal variables is not Pareto or lognormal.

The Pareto can be written

$$n = AP_n^{-a}, \tag{6.1}$$

where P_n is the population of the nth largest MSA. A and a are parameters to be estimated. The a parameter determines the relative sizes of MSAs; $a = 1$ implies that the nth largest MSA has a $1/n$ times the population of the largest; $a > 1$ implies that the nth largest MSA has more than $1/n$ times the population of the largest MSA. If $a = 1$, A is P_1, the population of the largest MSA.

The point of this is that, for the United States, a has hardly changed for two hundred years, making it perhaps the most durable constant in the social sciences. If, indeed, a is immune to extraordinary changes in income, industrialization, urbanization, and government size and policy, it is probably immune to state and local government MSA growth policies. MSAs do change ranks: for instance, the ranks of Chicago and Los Angeles have risen during the last century or so, whereas those of Philadelphia and Baltimore have fallen. Generally speaking, a varies greatly among countries, but changes only slowly through time.

A first rule of thumb: influences affecting MSA growth probably work in the context of an approximately fixed distribution of relative MSA sizes. If government policies make Gopher Prairie grow to the size of Chicago, some other MSAs will almost certainly shrink. This rule does not say that not all MSAs can grow; only that the relative sizes of MSAs that occupy particular ranks change only slowly. It must also be said that statistical studies of national MSA size distributions are blunt tools of analysis. If the average annual MSA population growth rate is 2 percent, then one MSA can grow at twice the average, at 4 percent, while five others can grow at 80 percent of the average growth rate, at 1.6 percent, without affecting a, at least not for several decades.

REGIONAL ISSUES

Regional influences have clearly always had major effects on MSA growth. Several examples illustrate this point. First, the Los Angeles MSA has grown relative to most other MSAs for 150 years because the West Coast has grown and Los Angeles is peculiarly well situated to benefit from that regional growth. As a second example, from 1974 to 1980 almost all Sunbelt MSAs grew relative to other MSAs because of the high energy prices. (Energy was expensive everywhere, and fuels were not cheaper in the Sunbelt; it was the presence of fuels that promoted growth—basically a balance-of-payments effect.) Third, in the mid-1980s, every Rustbelt MSA shrank relative to others because the dollar was expensive relative to foreign currencies; as a result, U.S.-manufactured exports fell and imports rose, and manufacturing decline was concentrated in the upper Midwest. As a final example, in the late 1980s, East Coast and West Coast MSAs grew relatively. Nobody knows exactly why, but one reason is growth of international trade and finance, resulting in part from the cheap dollar and the fact that these MSAs are best situated for trade with high-income trading partners in Western Europe and East Asia. *A second rule of thumb:* among the important influences on MSA growth are regional phenomena that are outside the control of people or of any set of governments in particular MSAs. Indeed, the last two examples have been of international influences more or less beyond the control of any set of governments in the United States.

Regional issues must be treated with care. During the 1970s, numerous analyses were published showing that amenities (warm weather, etc.) were causing growth of Sunbelt MSAs. Scholars forgot that energy prices, not weather, had changed since the 1960s. However, gradual improvements in transportation and in air conditioning also may have boosted the Sunbelt's growth during this time.

ECONOMIC BASE THEORY

The basic idea of economic base theory is that a certain amount of export production (i.e., to be sold outside the MSA) locates in an MSA, and that the amount of export production affects the MSA size, but not vice versa. For example, if Pittsburgh has a comparative advantage in steel production, then a certain amount of steel production locates there, determined by non-Pittsburgh demands for steel. The export activity is the economic base and generates additional activity in Pittsburgh to service the local population. The sum of the export and local service activities is total activity in the MSA and determines the MSA size. Variants of the theory are applied to regions, as well as to MSAs.

If Ex is exogenous employment in the export sector and E_L is endogenous employment in the local sector, if $E = E_L + Ex$, and if $E_L = bE$, then

$$E = \frac{Ex}{1 - b} \; ; \qquad (6.2)$$

$1/(1 - b)$ is the "multiplier" effect of export employment (or production). This has the same magical appeal to policymakers as does the analogous and completely discredited textbook Keynesian multiplier. It is used to justify any project (such as a new Chicago Bears' stadium) that will bring in "outside" money, because of its multiplier effect, even though privately capturable benefits are far less than costs. It is also used to justify tax "subsidies" for new office buildings, for manufacturing plants, and so forth. The economic base model has been generalized in many ways, but the simple model illustrates the key concept.

The size of an MSA is determined by simultaneous demand and supply equations for an enormous range of inputs and outputs. Manufacturing or other export activities may be affected by what else happens in the MSA, such as the size, quality, and wages of the labor force, and supplies of produced inputs, not to mention local demands for products of local manufacturing activity. Also, as we now know, many nonmanufacturing sectors export large amounts of their output. The services produced by Chicago financial exchanges are largely exported outside the Chicago MSA.

In addition, export base theory suffers all the defects of the analogous textbook Keynesian employment theory. Wages equilibrate labor supply and demand, especially within an MSA. Unemployment among Chicago's poor has to do with their productivity, work habits, human capital, minimum wages, the underground economy, and so on, not with effective demand deficiencies. Likewise, leakages outside an MSA are large, unknown, and probably of unstable magnitude. Finally, when government projects are at issue, the negative multiplier effects of taxes needed to pay for the project are ignored.

General equilibrium analysis is the right approach to understanding MSA sizes, not export base theory.

AGGLOMERATION ECONOMIES

Interestingly, agglomeration economies is among the few topics in economics in which econometrics is ahead of theory. Since the early 1970s, many studies have estimated agglomeration economies. Henderson's study (1988) is the most thorough of these and cites the earlier work. A consensus result is that a doubling of MSA size leads to a 4 to 6 percent increase in MSA total factor productivity. Given the variety of data, specifications, and econometric techniques, the statistical estimates are remarkably robust.

Recent writers (e.g., Henderson 1988) distinguish between urbanization and localization economies. Urbanization economies depend on the total MSA size, whereas localization economies depend on the size of a particular sector in the MSA. A general formulation is

$$Y = A(x)F(K, L, N), \tag{6.3}$$

where Y = MSA output and F is a constant returns production function in capital K, land L and labor N. $A(x)$ represents agglomeration economies, which depend on a vector x of MSA characteristics.

The key question is: What mechanism(s) generate(s) agglomeration economies? One answer, provided by Hoover (1948), is statistical. If a given kind of labor can be used by sectors whose labor demands are not highly correlated, then a given labor force spends a smaller fraction of its time idle if the MSA contains several such sectors. This is an urbanization economy.

A commonly mentioned factor in this regard is that large MSAs have a greater variety of input suppliers than do small MSAs. The claim is correct, but it simply reflects scale economies in input-supplying sectors and was therefore included among the conditions listed early in the chapter as giving rise to urban areas.

Transportation and communication costs must be part of the story. A large MSA produces more intermediate inputs, and buys more outputs, of a given sector than does a small MSA. If transportation and communication costs are lower between MSA businesses, local suppliers, and customers than between MSA businesses and similar people outside the MSA, then output per unit of input rises with MSA size. This, too, is an urbanization economy. A large part of transportation cost is time costs of workers. For example, time costs are about half of workers' commuting costs. Likewise, much of communication cost is the time cost of finding customers and suppliers. These time costs show up in product and service costs, but are not entered directly in national income and product accounts. If large MSAs economize on time costs, this shows up in the MSA accounts as greater total factor productivity. I believe this is the key explanation of agglomeration economies.

The Jacobs (1969) incubator notion is that technology progresses and spreads more quickly if people with similar problems and human capital can interact economically. They could be employees in similar firms, customers, vendors, or people with similar problems or using similar technology but producing unrelated products. This could be a localization or an urbanization economy. Everybody thinks that such an economy is helped along if people embody lots of human capital. The Jacobs (1969) theory implies that technical progress is faster in large MSAs than in small ones, but not that total factor productivity is greater in large MSAs at a given time. Its dimensionality is thus quite different from that of agglomeration economies as defined here.

Most statistical studies (see Henderson 1988 and references therein) conclude that localization economies are more important than urbanization economies. Common sense says that agglomeration economies must become exhausted at some sufficiently large MSA size. That is implied by all the preceding interpretations, but apparently there is no evidence.

The statistical studies suggest that something is hiding in the woods, but no one has explained what. Carlino (1985) contends that agglomeration economies have become less important in manufacturing since the 1950s, perhaps because the interstate highway system and improved communication lowered inter-MSA (and MSA/non-MSA) transportation-communication costs relative to intra-MSA costs. The result, in any case, has been migration of manufacturing to suburbs and to non-MSA counties.

The basic fact recognized by several studies (see Ó hUallacháin and Satterthwaite 1992) is that, if sectors grow, they tend to grow in MSAs where they were already substantial. This fact is usually interpreted as evidence of localization economies, and it may be. However, the observation is consistent with almost any plausible theory. Suppose that a sector's location is influenced by geographical comparative advantage (natural resources, interurban transportation facilities, amenities, enlightened local government, and so on) and that such advantages persist through time. Then growth tends to occur in the same places during the sample period as it did before then. Agglomeration theory says the cause is the substantial initial size of the sectors in the MSA, but the cause may be some condition(s) that produced both the initial size and the subsequent growth.

This is not a counsel of despair. Careful research about mechanisms of agglomeration economies and other causes of growth can reject some hypotheses and support others. In any such research, it is important to distinguish carefully between endogenous and exogenous factors. For example, most educators believe that large quantities of human capital promote growth and prosperity. In the broadest sense, there can be no doubt about it. Among the two or three most important reasons that the United States has higher income per capita than India is that the United States has crammed much more human capital into the heads of its citizens than has India. But human capital accumulation is also an effect. If education contributed nothing to productivity, a rich country would nevertheless provide lots of it for its children because people believe it contributes to the quality of life. Likewise, in an MSA, rich people spend lots of money educating their children, for both productivity and quality-of-life reasons. Thus, whatever the source of the prosperity, lots of human capital is a result. Undoubtedly, the truth is that education is both a cause and an effect of prosperity.

As a second example, take crime. Although total crime rates may not vary much by income level, street crimes (mugging, robbery, drugs, breaking and entering, etc.) certainly have greater incidence among low-income people. It is also true that high crime rates drive out businesses and residents who can afford to go. Thus, crime is probably both a cause and an effect of low incomes in a central city or neighborhood.

Simultaneity, of course, does not mean that estimation is impossible, only that we ignore it at our peril.

GOVERNMENT

State and local governments set most policies that affect growth at the subnational level. However, with few exceptions, no government has an MSA entirely within its jurisdiction. There are more than one thousand governments in the Chicago MSA. That institutional arrangement may be good or bad. But it is a mistake to talk about MSA growth policies, because almost no government has jurisdiction over an MSA.

Nevertheless, some general statements can be made about jurisdictional growth policies. First, however, it should be said that central-city governments are distinctly schizophrenic. While begging firms to locate, stay, or expand there, central cities may also place large obstacles in developers' way. At the same time, many suburban governments want little or no growth and are fighting off developers. That may be good or bad.

I believe two things can be said with confidence about growth policies. First, central-city governments overregulate businesses. (Some suburbs do, too, but most of those that do are not keen on employment growth.) Much of this regulation serves no legitimate social purpose and harms growth. Excessive licensing of businesses and occupations, building codes, and so forth, are important factors inhibiting growth; however, land-use controls are the big offenders. It may take five years to obtain all the needed permissions for a large project in a central city. For example, there is a large site on Chicago's South Side where several developers have wanted to build a shopping center. There are no modern shopping centers in that area. Yet "politics" has stymied the project, and one developer after another has given up.

Second, taxes are higher and government services are of poorer quality in central cities than in suburbs. So long as taxes are not extortionate, the important issue is not tax levels but whether local government services are commensurate with tax levels. CC governments come off badly in comparison with suburbs. Employees, especially in education, are more highly paid and agencies are overstaffed, yet local government service qualities, especially education, are much worse in CCs. Some developers estimate that taxes and costs of obtaining approvals may consume large percentages of the rents on a new project. That situation is vastly more important than all the development incentives that planning agencies can imagine. No study has ever shown that development incentives (tax-exempt bonds, real estate tax abatements, and so forth) have resulted in stimulation of employment. Effects may have been missed, but lack of evidence persists after many attempts.

Suburban governments routinely exclude businesses and low-income residents by land-use and other controls. Tiebout (1956) showed that this may be socially efficient. My view is that it is unconstitutional because it employs the police power to exclude a constitutionally sensitive group—the poor. Only in New Jersey has the state Supreme Court issued such a ruling. If one includes the effects on employment, it is not clear that the status quo has the social efficiency characteristics of the Tiebout hypothesis. If there are many suburban jurisdictions, and the worker-residents of each jurisdiction tend to work outside the jurisdiction, then all jurisdictions may try to exclude businesses, and all may suffer.

Suppose localization economies are important. Then competitive markets generate too little spatial concentration of relevant sectors, since individual firms do not receive the full social returns to spatial concentration. The implied government policy is to encourage spatial concentration, although the best way to do this is not certain (among possibilities are capital subsidies, labor subsidies, tax abatements, and eminent domain for land assembly). The implied burden on city governments is to decide what sectors have potential to grow in that city if a sufficiently large group of firms in the sectors can be assembled. Clearly, not all sectors have the potential to grow in all MSAs. Comparative advantage matters. In addition, demands are limited. For example, there cannot be enough high-tech firms to fill all the high-tech parks that governments have created. Thus, local governments must be able to predict which sectors have the potential to grow in which MSAs. I submit that that is the most difficult economic decision anyone makes; it is better rewarded than almost any other economic activity, as a consequence. It is risking disaster to suggest that big-city governments can pick winners; scholars can do no better.

A fallback position is to ask whether local governments could take any actions that would facilitate growth, especially of small and innovative firms, without having to choose among narrowly defined sectors. All the general improvements in local government actions suggested in the foregoing would help. It is difficult to imagine a program that could selectively stimulate small businesses. The history of U.S. federal, state, and local government small business assistance programs provides no encouragement.

A THEORETICAL MODEL

This section presents a formal model of the determinants of the sizes of MSAs. The key idea motivating the model is that MSAs permit firms to economize on transactions costs involving transportation, communication, and search among businesses, between businesses and employees, and between businesses and consumers.

Models of intra-MSA spatial arrangements simply assume that all goods and services produced in an MSA must be shipped to a predetermined point for sale inside or outside the MSA (see Mills and Hamilton 1994). The point could be an export node (port or railhead) or simply a market. The point then becomes the center of the MSAs central business district (CBD).

The assumption is dramatically false. Most goods produced in MSAs are exported from the MSA directly from suburban production locations, or are shipped directly to local customers from production sites. The approximation is, surprisingly, somewhat better for services. Wall Street financial services are mostly exported from the New York MSA directly from the Wall Street CBD. But most services are not produced in CBDs at all, and they are sold to local or nonlocal customers from production sites. In the model presented here, MSAs are assumed to possess centrality—that is, land values, rents, and densities are highest in CBDs and fall off smoothly with distance from the CBD. As an approximation, the characteristic is well documented. But I make no more specific assumption as to where in the MSA production takes place. Indeed, I pay only minimal attention to the internal structure of the MSA, although this might be helpful when MSA growth is analyzed.

My idea is that what justifies an MSA and generates its centrality is the attempt to economize on transactions costs. Suppose that production and sale of each product or service require a certain number of transactions outside the producing firm. Transactions may be with labor and material input suppliers, with customers, or with others. Lawyers must transact with courts and opposing lawyers, even though they are neither input suppliers nor customers. If transactions entail physical movement of commodities or people, they may be more economical if they are with local parties than if they are with parties outside the MSA. In this example, the transaction cost is transportation cost. Even if transactions do not require physical movement of goods or people (e.g., if they can be consummated by telephone) they are likely to be more economical if they can be local. It is costly to search for the best party with whom to carry on particular transactions. Search costs are generally smaller if search is restricted to the MSA, but search costs per local transaction increase with the size of the MSA.

The model presented here is kept extremely simple to make the basic ideas transparent. Functional forms are elementary and could be generalized and made more realistic in obvious ways. Likewise, I suppress sectoral detail. A multisectoral model is hiding in the background and could be made explicit, but, I suspect, at the cost of considerable complexity.

THE MATHEMATICAL MODEL

Profit-maximizing firms produce goods and services in the MSA. Costs consist of production costs, transactions costs, and rents. Production could be represented in both general and a complex form, as has been done in many urban models. However, my goal is to represent a way of incorporating transaction costs, so production is kept simple.

Each firm produces x units of output. Labor input is proportionate to output. The only other input is land, and it is assumed that each firm uses a fixed amount of land, regardless of its output. This is an obviously unrealistic production function. What is needed is increasing returns at small output levels, as seen later here. The preceding is a crude way of getting the needed result, and could easily be improved upon. With these strong assumptions, the production function can be written

$$x = n, \qquad (6.4)$$

where n is labor input per firm, with appropriate choice of units. In the following equations, n is written for both output and employment per firm.

It is assumed that production requires φ transactions outside the firm per unit of the firm's production. Thus, a firm producing n units of output must make φn transactions. I assume that φ is a constant. Presumably, a more realistic assumption would be φ = φ (n) with φ' > 0 > φ". By appropriate choice of units, φ = 1.

Transactions can be local or nonlocal. Local transactions are normally cheaper than nonlocal transactions, but the cost per local transaction rises with MSA size. Cost per local transaction is t(N), t' > 0. N is total MSA employment, equal to n times the number of firms in the MSA. Cost per nonlocal transaction is t̄, and does not depend on MSA size. Presumably, t(N) looks like figure 6.1. If N is sufficiently large, the MSA is the entire country (or world), so local and nonlocal transactions are the same things. For smaller N, it is assumed that t(N) < t̄, as shown in the figure. If N is very small, the costs of local

Figure 6.1 COST PER LOCAL TRANSACTION, t(N)

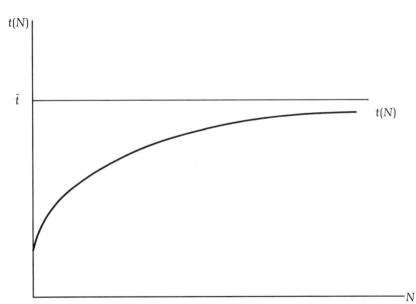

Note: See text for explanation.

transaction costs are small. (If there is only one accountant in town, it is not costly to find the best one.)

The disadvantage of a small MSA is that few transactions can be made locally. I assume that each firm can make a fraction $\theta(N)$ of its transactions locally. Clearly, $\theta(0) = 0$. Likewise, for sufficiently large MSA size, nearly all transactions can be local. Thus, $\theta(\infty) = 1$ and $\theta' > 0$. Figure 6.2 shows a likely form for θ.

Production cost is total wage cost $W(N)n$, plus rent (introduced later here). It is well documented that $W' > 0$, because land rents and values, hence living costs, rise with MSA size. If living costs rise with MSA size, then the wage required to equate utility levels in the MSA with levels obtainable elsewhere increases with MSA size. $W(N)$ is the wage that equates utility in the MSA with that available elsewhere, and presumably looks like figure 6.3. $W(N)$ depends on exogenous MSA amenities, so that $W(N)$ is smaller for each N the better the local amenities. Some amenities may depend on MSA size. For example, a characteristic of large MSAs that is not captured by MSA price indices is that a greater variety of goods and services is available than in small

Figure 6.2 PLAUSIBLE FORM FOR θ

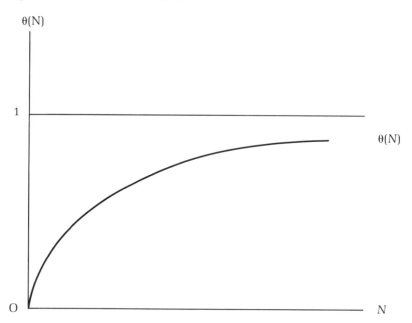

Note: See text for explanation.

Figure 6.3 PLAUSIBLE FORM FOR W(N)

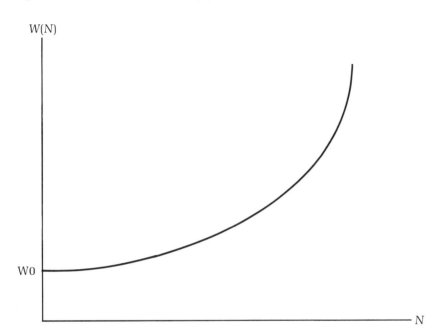

Note: See text for explanation.

MSAs, permitting higher utility levels to be achieved in large MSAs for given wages and price vectors. That simply means that W rises less rapidly with N than it would otherwise.

Total production cost (excluding rent) plus transaction cost is

$$TC = nW(N) + n[t(N)\theta(N) + \bar{t}(1 - \theta(N))] = n\lambda(N). \quad (6.5)$$

The point of equation (6.5) is that TC depends on both firm and MSA sizes. W increases monotonically in N, but the term in square brackets first decreases then increases as N increases, because $t(N) <$ $\bar{t}$, so the weight of $t(N)$ increases and that of $\bar{t}$ decreases as N increases. For sufficiently large N, TC is about equal to $nW(N) + n\,\bar{t}$. Figure 6.4 shows the likely form of $\lambda(N)$.

As in classical location theory, each firm can undercut its rivals' delivered prices for customers sufficiently close to it. Thus, each firm has some small and local monopoly power, which rivals cannot bid away. (This is where an assumption of increasing returns at small n is needed.) Thus, it is assumed that the firm's demand equation is

Figure 6.4 PLAUSIBLE FORM FOR λ(N)

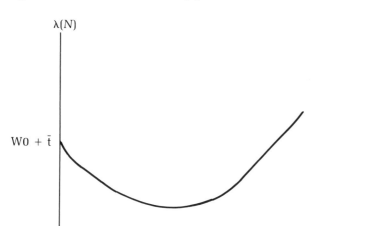

Note: See text for explanation.

$$p = p(n, N), \tag{6.6}$$

where $p_n < 0$ represents the element of local monopoly. The dependence of p on N represents the fact that the firm's demand, at given p, is greater in a large MSA than in a small one. The reason is that there are more customers within the distance from production where the firm has at least some market power, the bigger the MSA. Thus, it is assumed $p_N > 0$. The value of p_N could equal zero if the higher density of customers in a large MSA were completely offset by a higher density of competitors. Scale economies can prevent that, and evidence indicates that firms are bigger in large than in small MSAs. In addition, the part of product demand that is local should logically depend also on the local wage rate.

Now, rents are explicitly added. The firm's rent is $R(N)$, where $R' > 0$. (R could be made to depend on n.) In the simplest intraurban model with no substitutability of capital or labor for land, the land-rent function is as shown in figure 6.5. There, u is distance from the CBD and r_A is the rent on surrounding agricultural land; $r'(u)$ is a constant equal to minus transportation cost per unit mile if all production must be shipped to the center for sale. More realistically, $r' < 0 < r''$, representing incomplete central orientation and substitution of non-land for land inputs as the MSA center is approached and land becomes expensive. A more complex representation is not needed, so it

Figure 6.5 LAND-RENT FUNCTION IS SIMPLEST INTRAURBAN MODEL

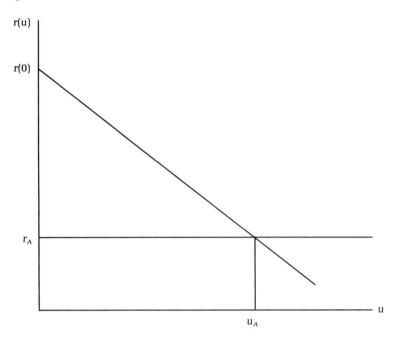

Note: See text for explanation.

is possible to stick to the linear form. u_A is the radius of the MSA, and $u > u_A$ is agricultural land. With the usual assumption that the MSA is circular, or semicircular, total land area, and hence total employment, is proportional to u_A.

Competition among land users within the MSA generates an $r(u)$ such that profit and/or utility levels are the same at each u. Rent in the MSA can be characterized by $r(0)$. Indeed, $r(0) = r_A + (tr)u_A$, where (tr) is transportation cost per unit mile within the MSA. If the $r(u)$ function were too close to the origin, profit would be greater in the MSA than elsewhere. That would induce growth in the MSA, moving $r(u)$ outward parallel to itself. The MSA is of equilibrium size when r (hence MSA size) is such that maximum profit in the MSA is zero. Hence $R(N)$ in the model is an index of MSA rent when MSA size is N. In the intra-MSA characterization just presented, $R(N)$ equals $r(0)$; $r(0)$ equals the rent plus transportation cost paid by firms wherever they are located in the MSA.

Each firm's total profit is

$$\pi = np(n, N) - n \lambda (N) - R(N). \qquad (6.7)$$

Each firm maximizes equation (6.7) with respect to n, assuming N is unaffected by its choice of n:

$$\partial\pi/\partial n = np_n + p - \lambda(N) = 0. \qquad (6.8)$$

Then, free migration of firms among MSAs ensures that the maximized profit is just zero:

$$R(N) = np(n, N) - n \lambda (N). \qquad (6.9)$$

Equations 6.8 and 6.9 must be solved simultaneously for n and N, equilibrium firm and MSA sizes. Then, if N^* and n^* are solution values, N^*/n^* is the equilibrium number of firms in the MSA. In the most interesting cases, most things that increase N^* also increase n^* if N^* is small. (That means that firm size increases with MSA size in small MSAs.)

Of course, there are people and a housing sector in the MSA, but nothing would be gained by an explicit representation of a consumer demand side of the model.

The firm is in Chamberlin equilibrium in this model, as shown in figure 6.6. Unit cost falls as n increases because rent is a fixed cost and is spread over more output as n increases. (Scale economies in a model with an explicit land input would result in the same form for the ATC function.) Marginal cost is constant (equal to $\lambda[N]$). The open-city assumption implies that $R(N)$ makes unit cost tangent to the demand curve.

INTERPRETATION

Clearly, households, as well as housing and other consumer goods and services, could be introduced, as well as a better production side, with a fancier production function. That would avoid the need for the artificial way I computed decreasing unit costs, with a rent function in which rent per firm does not depend on firm size. These changes would, however, add realism without additional important insights.

Introducing several production sectors is another matter. The transactions costs I have analyzed are certainly costs of transacting with other sectors, at least if sectors are defined narrowly. Explicit representation of such transactions could make the model quite complex.

Figure 6.6 FIRM COSTS

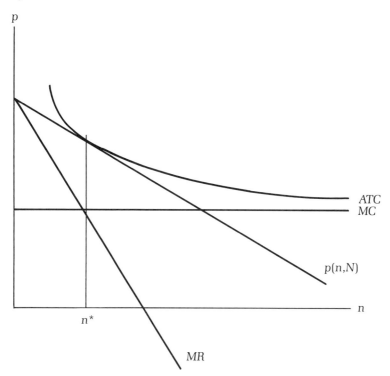

Note: See text for explanation.

The interpretation of the model merits discussion here. The model generates an equlibrium size of the MSA. I suppose that a classical welfare economics analysis would conclude that the equilibrium MSA is suboptimally small, since each firm is producing where marginal cost is less than price and average cost is falling. At least, that is true if the MSA size puts it on the falling part of the $\lambda(N)$ function, for which it is sufficient that marginal production cost is constant and p_n is negative.

This model has been about a single MSA and, of course, says nothing about the size distribution of MSAs. If all MSAs had the same functional forms and parameters, the model says they would all be the same size. Within the model, MSAs can differ for the following kinds of reasons:

1. $p(n, N)$ differs among MSAs. Some MSAs have high export demand for their products because they are favorably located vis-à-vis

other markets or transportation facilities, or because they have comparative advantages in products that have strong demands.

2. The $W(N)$ function is lower, the greater the amenities of an MSA. Workers work in Sunbelt MSAs at lower real wages because the weather is advantageous.

3. $t(N)$ may vary among MSAs for given values of N. It is cheaper to search for efficient transactions in New York if you are in Philadelphia than if you are in San Diego.

4. Presumably, local government service quality affects several parameters in the model. If services are high quality relative to taxes, $W(N)$ is lower. Local government can affect $t(N)$ by affecting the quality of the local transportation-communication system.

How does the model fit with the recent work on localization economies? Localization economies are most naturally interpreted in a multisectoral framework, so this discussion must be set in the context of a nonexistent multisectoral generalization of the model.

One important part of the localization story is certainly captured by the model. The transactions cost function depends on total employment, not on firm employment. In a multisectoral model, that employment could be in the sector or in a set of related sectors (in which case it would be a localization economy), or it could be total MSA employment (in which case it would be an urbanization economy). In any case, it is Hicks-neutral in the model (since it is additive and independent of a firm's input usage), as applied studies have concluded (see Henderson 1988). The transactions cost function is

$$T(N) = t(N)\ \theta(N) + \bar{t}[1 - \theta(N)]. \qquad (6.10)$$

From the foregoing, $T(0) = T(\infty) = \bar{t}$, so $T(N)$ looks like figure 6.7. Appropriate regressions would show increasing total factor productivity with respect to sector (or MSA) total employment up to $N = \bar{N}$.

A second aspect of localization economies is also captured by the model. Earlier, it was suggested that one source of localization (or urbanization) economies is the ability of a large MSA to even out fluctuations in labor demand that exist in certain firms or sectors. The result is to make $W(N)$ rise less with N than it would otherwise. There is, however, no evidence that this or any other reason makes $W(N)$ fall as N increases.

The most difficult interpretation of localization economies is that technical change is promoted by scale and other things, in specific sectors. We know how to measure technical change pretty well, so we can test whether it is promoted by sectoral scale within an MSA. An easy generalization of the model would permit a test of the theory, if

Figure 6.7 FIRM EQUILIBRIUM SIZE

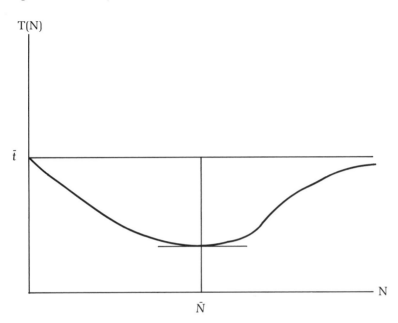

Note: See text for explanation.

we could find data on transactions costs. Even if we could not, the hypothesis that the relevant technical change multiplies the production function, whereas transactions cost are additive, would permit a test. As to a test of the dependence of technical change on the "other things" mentioned earlier, we would need hypotheses about what the "other things" are. An educated labor force? Nearby research institutions? Such effects could be tested.

Finally, a comment about the size distribution of MSAs. In Lösch's (1954) model, MSAs of various sizes are generated by a variety of sectors that have L-shaped unit-cost curves. An MSA has a particular sector if its local demand exceeds the minimum production of the sector dictated by the location of the corner of the L. The difficulty with the model is that there are no transaction costs, and therefore no reasons for MSA demands to be supplied locally. Likewise, there is no internal structure to the MSA, so there is no limit to the size of the MSA in the form of rents that make local production costs greater than the cost of producing elsewhere and shipping the product to the MSA. Both transactions costs that fall as MSA size rises, up to a limit, and land rents that limit the size of the MSA are included in the model presented here. Presumably an MSA size distribution could be generated based on transactions cost function, wage rate equations, and demand equations that varied among sectors. To be realistic, such a model would need to incorporate spatial relations among MSA wage equations, but little is known about transactions cost functions and sectoral demand equations at the MSA level.

CONCLUSIONS

This chapter has endeavored to demonstrate that economizing on transportation and communication costs is the essential motivation and justification for MSAs. At the most fundamental level, the notion is obvious. Anything done in MSAs can, from a technical standpoint, be done in small towns or rural areas. The advantage of dense concentrations of people and businesses in MSAs is that they can interact with each other economically.

The notion of economizing on transactions cost was incorporated here into a simplistic model of MSA size. The most important simplification in the model was the assumption of a single sector in the MSA and a notional concept of transactions in production and sale. Thus, the primary need in formulating a realistic model is to introduce a variety of sectors that are, or might be, in the MSA. Then, explicit transactions among them and between them and a household sector can be introduced. Also needed are an explicit household sector and a more realistic production technology. Economists know how to do all these things in a spatial context. Once they have been incorporated in a model in which sectors transact with each other and/or with the world outside the MSA, the model can be used to gain insight into MSA sizes and growth.

An important insight that such a model could provide concerns which sectors should be expected to locate in particular MSAs, because they interact with each other directly or indirectly through an input-output matrix. The sectoral mix will depend not only on the technology of production and transacting but also on product demands from both MSA sources and sources elsewhere. Another important factor will be transactions costs both within the MSA and between the MSA and other places. For instance, Chicago has a better internal transportation and communication system than Bombay, although they have about the same populations. Similarly, San Francisco and Los Angeles are economically closer together than Boston and Washington, D.C., even though each pair of MSAs is separated by about the same geographical distance. Inter-MSA transactions costs depend on infrastructure and congestion as well as on distance. The most important issue is what makes an MSA grow and what governments can or should do to promote growth. Production technology affects actual and optimum MSA sizes, but state and local governments neither can nor should try to do much about it. In an integrated country such as the United States, knowledge of production technology is approximately uniform throughout the country. However, the technology and costs of transactions within an MSA and between the MSA and other places are very much affected by state and local government actions. The mix, costs, and qualities of intra-MSA transportation facilities are state and local government choices. Such choices may have important effects on MSA size and structure. Rational choices can be made only with knowledge of the kind provided by a realistic model of the MSA.

References

Beckmann, Martin. 1958. "City Hierarchies and Distribution of City Size." *Economic Development and Cultural Change* 6: 243–48.

Beckmann, Martin, and John McPherson. 1970. "City Size Distributions in a Central Place Hierarchy: An Alternative Approach." *Journal of Regional Science* 10: 25–33.

Bradbury, Katharine, Anthony Downs, and Kenneth Small. 1982. *Urban Decline and the Future of American Cities*. Washington, D.C.: Brookings Institution.

Carlino, Gerald. 1985. "Declining City Productivity and the Growth of Rural Regions." *Journal of Urban Economics* 18(1): 11–27.

Henderson, J. Vernon. 1988. *Urban Development*. New York: Oxford University Press.

Hoover, Edgar. 1948. *The Location of Economic Activity*. New York: McGraw-Hill.

Jacobs, Jane. 1969. *The Economy of Cities*. New York: Random House.

Lösch, August. 1954. *The Economics of Location*. New Haven: Yale University Press.

Mills, Edwin. 1990. "Do Metropolitan Areas Mean Anything? A Research Note." *Journal of Regional Science* 30(3): 415–19.

Mills, Edwin, and Bruce Hamilton. 1994. *Urban Economics*, 5th ed. New York, N.Y.: Harper Collins.

Mills, Edwin, and Ivan S. Lubuele. 1995. "Projecting Growth of Metropolitan Areas." *Journal of Urban Economics* 37(3): 344–60.

————. 1997. "Inner Cities." *Journal of Economic Literature* 35(2): 727–56.

Ó hUallacháin, B., and M. Satterthwaite. 1992. "Sectoral Growth Patterns at the Metropolitan Level." *Journal of Urban Economics* 31(1): 25–58.

Rosen, Kenneth, and Mitchell Resnick. 1980. "The Size Distribution of Cities: An Examination of the Pareto Law and Privacy." *Journal of Urban Economics* 8(2): 165–86.

Tiebout, Charles. 1956. "A Pure Theory of Local Public Expenditures." *Journal of Political Economy* 64: 416.

Chapter Seven

THE METROPOLITAN AREA IN ITS WIDER SETTING

John B. Parr

Within the United States and the nations of Western Europe, the larger metropolitan areas continue to dominate the spatial organization of their respective economies and societies. Although such urban concentrations often represent focal points of economic and social stress, they have maintained their position as loci of decision making, innovation, and information processing, and remain centers of political movement and social change, as well as of intellectual, artistic, and other creative endeavors. In the post–World War II era virtually all metropolitan areas of the Atlantic Community have undergone substantial transformation of their economies, reflecting the structural changes that have occurred within the nations concerned. Often, however, the metropolitan areas, because of their previous specializations and emphases, have experienced such changes to a greater extent than the nation as a whole. A case in point is the phenomenon of deindustrialization, the incidence of which has fallen disproportionately heavily on the larger metropolitan areas. Despite this loss of manufacturing activity, metropolitan areas have tended to maintain much of their traditional importance, although the position that they occupy within the space economy of a nation is continuing to change.

An important development, which seems to be present in most economically advanced nations, is the changing size distribution of metropolitan areas. The general trend appears to be that the populations of the very largest metropolitan areas are growing at below-average rates, while the populations of the remaining ones are growing at above-average rates. The overall size distribution may still conform to a pattern approximated by the rank-size function, but the scale and concentration parameters of this function are changing significantly. This was discussed by Mills (chapter 6 of this volume) in terms of the Pareto form of the rank-size function. Particularly noteworthy in this connection is that certain of these larger metropolitan areas are experiencing population and employment decline. The examples in table 7.1 illustrate this point, although it should be stressed that whereas in the United Kingdom, for example, metropolitan decline appears to be a nationwide tendency (Congdon and Champion 1989), it has more of sectional incidence in the United States (Leven, chapter 9 of this volume). In any event, such a development seems to have taken us unawares. To have argued in the 1950s that certain major

Table 7.1 POPULATION DECLINE IN SELECTED METROPOLITAN AREAS

Nation (Period)	Average Annual Percentage Population Change
France (1975–82)	
Lille	−0.01
Lyon	−0.01
Paris	−0.07
Italy (1981–85)	
Milan	−0.35
Turin	−0.79
United Kingdom (1977–81)	
Birmingham	−0.51
Leeds	−0.14
Liverpool	−0.79
London	−0.75
Manchester	−0.47
Newcastle	−0.57
Sheffield	−0.06
United States (1970–80)	
Akron PMSA	−0.28
Boston PMSA	−0.28
Buffalo PMSA	−0.88
Chicago PMSA	−0.05
Cleveland PMSA	−0.80
Dayton MSA	−0.34
Detroit PMSA	−0.15
Milwaukee PMSA	−0.05
New York CMSA	−0.36
Philadelphia PMSA	−0.22
Pittsburgh PMSA	−0.55
St. Louis MSA	−0.21
Springfield MSA	−0.25
Youngstown MSA	−0.11

Sources: France—*Unité Urbaine* (Winchester and Ogden 1989); Italy—metropolitan area (Dematteis and Petsimeris 1989); United Kingdom—metropolitan county, based on the city indicated (Congdon and Champion 1989); United States—metropolitan statistical area, primary metropolitan statistical area, or consolidated metropolitan statistical area, as indicated (U.S. Bureau of the Census 1989).

metropolitan areas would be experiencing population decline well before the end of the twentieth century would have had an unconvincing ring to it. We had become used to the decline of the city proper or the central city, but this was explained away in terms of the growth of the suburbs, which more than offset the decline. The slow growth or decline of the entire metropolitan area is a wholly different matter—or is it?

A tendency exists among urban analysts to regard the metropolitan area as an entity in its own right. This is reasonable enough by virtue of the fact that the metropolitan area has its own economy, its own structure with respect to housing and labor markets, and its own set of policy concerns. Metropolitan areas are also looked at cross-sectionally, usually on a national basis, so that a given metropolitan area is considered in relation to particular economic and social characteristics that it shares with other metropolitan areas of the same category or size class. In both cases it is realized, of course, that the metropolitan area has numerous linkages with the rest of the urban system in terms of trade flows, capital movements, transfers of government funds, flows of factor payments, and so on. As late as the 1930s in the United States, and probably even later in the nations of Western Europe, it was possible to draw a boundary around a metropolitan area and regard this as its overall extent. There was no implication that the metropolitan area was a closed system, but in terms of service provision, the housing market, labor supply, as well as the outward movement of households and employment, this delineation captured the overwhelming bulk of the interaction.

Today such a boundary has considerably less significance: So many of the interactions that relate to the economic functioning of the larger metropolitan area occur across the boundary referred to earlier. In the case of the labor market, for example, long-distance commuting has emerged as an established feature, interestingly enough in an era of energy conservation or at least energy consciousness. Similarly, the reach of the downtown and suburban shopping centers has become considerably enlarged, even for items that were traditionally purchased from smaller nonmetropolitan centers. And in the case of recreation, the metropolitan dweller now ranges well beyond the municipal park or local entertainment center. Furthermore, there appears to have emerged a wider field of disengagement from the larger metropolitan area, involving the movement of households and firms. The phenomenon of disengagement is certainly not new, but whereas it used to relate to the suburbs or to extraregional destinations (and this is still the case), it has now become increasingly regional in character, involving movement well beyond the suburbs of the metropolitan area. This is not only true for households but also for economic activity. Nowadays, for example, it is not uncommon for a firm to relocate in a small city 50 miles (80 km) from a metropolitan area (or even at a larger distance in the United States) to gain access to suitable labor and land and to incur a lower tax liability, whereas fifty years ago or less, advantages of this type were generally possible by relocating toward the edge of the metropolitan area.

Accompanying such trends is the tendency in many nations for the zone beyond the large metropolitan area to grow more rapidly in terms of population and employment than the metropolitan area itself, which may be experiencing stagnation or decline, as already mentioned. In Italy, for example, the population of the five largest metropolitan areas (Rome, Milan, Naples, Turin, and Genoa) grew collectively at an average annual percentage rate of 0.40 during the period 1971–81 and at a rate of zero during the period 1981–85, while the corresponding rates for their surrounding regions were 0.46 and 0.36 (Dematteis and Petsimeris 1989). In the United Kingdom, the London metropolitan area declined in population terms at an average annual percentage rate of 0.09 during the period 1981–86, but the remainder of the London-based region (the Southeast Standard Region) grew at a rate of 0.56, while the Birmingham metropolitan area declined at a rate of 0.31 and the remainder of the Birmingham-based region (the West Midland Standard Region) grew at a rate of 0.29 (Congdon and Champion 1989). A study by Leven (1986) on population change within and beyond the major metropolitan areas of the United States indicated similar trends. With the national population change for the period 1970–80 set at 100, the corresponding figure for the central cities of large SMSAs was −49, for their suburbs 131, for their exurbs (their rings of adjacent counties) 197, and for small-town-based nonadjacent counties 149. In all these nations it seems highly unlikely that this growth in the nonmetropolitan zones was unrelated to the poor growth performance of the corresponding metropolitan areas.

The foregoing discussion suggests that whatever its continuing functional importance, the overall position of the larger metropolitan areas is becoming modified. The intention of this chapter is to explore such changes in terms of developments in the United States and Western Europe over the last forty years or so. I use a framework that places the metropolitan area within a wider economic and spatial setting, but one that is relevant to the contemporary national urban system. Attention is confined, for reasons that will soon be apparent, to the larger metropolitan areas: those in excess of, say, 500,000 population that also have a pronounced regional significance. It is, of course, difficult enough to generalize even across the major geographical sections of the United States or across the nations of Western Europe. To attempt to generalize across both the United States *and* Western Europe may therefore appear ambitious, if not reckless. Nevertheless, there does seem enough preliminary evidence of similarities in spatial-structure change to suggest that such an attempt is worth embarking upon.

THE METROPOLITAN AREA AND ITS REGION

On the basis of the preceding discussion, it may be claimed that the metropolitan area, as currently defined, is coming to represent an inappropriate scale of analysis, simply because it fails to encompass too many of the relevant interactions that affect its existence (Leven 1976). Although it is unreasonable to deny the continuing validity of the metropolitan-area scale for certain types of questions, it certainly appears that the larger metropolitan area is coming to be replaced by a broader entity, which is termed here the metropolitan-area-based region (MBR). Just as fifty years ago it had become obvious that the city proper or central city was an inappropriate scale for examining the metropolitan area, we may now be approaching a situation in which the metropolitan area can only be examined with reference to the MBR. The concept of the MBR resembles in a number of respects the "city region" of Dickinson (1947) and the "polarized region" proposed by Boudeville (1966). The MBR consists of two broad elements: a metropolitan zone, comprising the metropolitan area; and a surrounding nonmetropolitan zone, which, in terms of the pattern of economic and social linkages, is dominated by the metropolitan area. The metropolitan area is typically a major focus of administration (public and private), ownership, decision making, and control, as well as a center from which innovations are diffused, whether or not these originate there. Furthermore, it is a center of transportation and communication, and provides a range of goods and services for household and intermediate consumption to market areas consisting of the entire MBR or simply parts thereof. It may also be a center for processing or assembly industries that draw their inputs (raw materials or manufactured goods) from a supply area comprising all or part of the nonmetropolitan zone.

By contrast, the nonmetropolitan zone of the MBR contains a rural population and generally a much larger urban population distributed in centers (some of them even metropolitan in character) that usually exist within a hierarchical structure, the highest level of which is the metropolitan area itself. A significant portion of the output of the nonmetropolitan zone of the MBR is exported to the metropolitan zone. Conversely, a substantial element of the goods and services that are consumed or used as inputs to production is imported from the metropolitan zone. There is, in general, a high degree of complementarity between the two parts of the MBR, although the MBR itself is an open system. Both parts of the MBR interact with other regions in terms of trade flows and other types of economic linkage. Indeed, the metropolitan zone may interact more with comparable zones in other MBRs than with the nonmetropolitan zone that it dominates. Furthermore, within each zone of the MBR there is considerable internal interaction, and in the nonmetropolitan zone a good deal of this tends to be of an interhierarchical nature.

The MBR, as outlined previously, can be readily identified in the United States and Western Europe. In any system of definition of MBRs within a particular nation, it is imperative to establish precise criteria regarding what constitutes a metropolitan area and what rules govern the delineation of the MBR centered on this. Roughly speaking, anything up to fifty such MBRs are present in the United States, and in France, the reconstituted Federal Republic of Germany, Italy, Spain, and the United Kingdom the number for each nation is from ten to fifteen, while in Austria, Belgium, the Netherlands, Portugal, Switzerland, and the nations of Scandinavia the number is from two to four in each case, although in certain nations of this latter group the size of the metropolitan area is somewhat below the 500,000 limit referred to earlier. The MBR is to be seen as something quite distinct from the functional urban region (FUR), which has been defined for the United States by Berry (1967) and for the nations of Western Europe by Cheshire and Hay (1989). FURs are generally smaller than MBRs, and many of the FURs are based on urban areas that cannot be considered truly metropolitan in nature. Although for a particular nation the core of a larger FUR may be equivalent to the metropolitan zone of the corresponding MBR, the extent of the FUR would usually be considerably smaller than that of the MBR. The concept of the FUR differs fundamentally from that of the MBR, and it was designed with wholly different purposes in mind (Cheshire, chapter 5 of this volume).

The MBR cannot be regarded as a new organizational form, and it is possible to recognize the outlines of the MBR in the United States as early as the Civil War and possibly at an earlier date in Western Europe. What is interesting, however, is the manner in which the MBR has come to represent a dominant feature of the national space economy of developed nations, in much the same way as did the metropolitan area in the latter half of the nineteenth century. Part of the growing prominence of the MBR is the increasing strength of the metropolitan area itself. And yet, as already pointed out, in population and employment terms the larger metropolitan area is often growing slowly or even declining. There is an apparent paradox here, or at least something of an irony: The larger metropolitan area has strengthened its economic linkages with the nonmetropolitan zone (thus contributing to the ascendancy of the MBR), but at the same time its relative position within the MBR has weakened. What appears to be happening in many instances is that the metropolitan area is consolidating and extending its geographic reach as a result of changes in business organization and new systems of communication, but this is not necessarily occurring in a manner that generates population and employment, a phenomenon considered in a later section.

SPATIAL STRUCTURE OF THE MBR

It is necessary here to come to terms with the spatial structure of the MBR in order to appreciate how the constituent parts are related to each other and to grapple with the changes that are occurring within each of these. There are a number of frameworks for approaching this question. Analysis in terms of the size distribution of urban centers within the region offers one possibility, as does urban-system analysis by which various economic flows among the different levels of the hierarchy are examined. The approach considered here, however, involves the concept of the population density function. This has proven extremely useful in the analysis of urban or metropolitan spatial structure, both longitudinally and cross-sectionally. And since it has been argued that the MBR represents in many ways an extension of the metropolitan area, it seems appropriate to attempt to apply the concept of the density function on this wider scale.

Take as a starting point the nature of the density function within the metropolitan area. Over this zone of the MBR the distribution of residential population density in relation to the center of the metropolitan area can be approximated by the negative exponential function proposed by Clark (1951), which has the form

$$\ln D(x) = \ln D(0) + bx \qquad (b < 0; 0 \le x \le x'), \qquad (7.1)$$

where $D(x)$ is the population density at distance x from the metropolitan center, $D(0)$ is the density at the center, b is the density gradient, and x' is the distance from the center to the boundary of the metropolitan area. Such a form is merely an approximation of conditions within the metropolitan area. The fitted value of $D(0)$ is usually far too high and exaggerates the density at or near the center. Clark himself was at pains to point out that $D(0)$ indicates the level to which densities are tending as the center is approached. The negative-exponential form thus fails to take account of densities rising from the center before declining. To incorporate such a density crest, Newling (1969) suggested the quadratic exponential function, which has the form

$$\ln D(x) = \ln D(0) + bx + cx^2$$
$$(b > 0; c < 0; 0 \le x \le x'). \qquad (7.2)$$

Such a function represents an obvious improvement. Not only does it reflect the density crest near the center, but it largely preserves the negative exponential characteristic away from the crest. Unfortunately, the fitted form of the quadratic exponential function often carries the wrong sign on one or both of the parameters of equation (7.2), so that no crest is present. In the case of the gamma function, proposed by Angel and Hyman (1972), this problem is less common.

But what of conditions within the nonmetropolitan zone of the MBR? In an apparently little-known part of *The Structure of the Metropolitan Community* by Bogue (1950), an attempt was made to demonstrate how population densities decline from the edge of the metropolitan area to the boundary of the "metropolitan community" (corresponding approximately to the MBR). Although the form of this decline was not specified, Bogue's various graphical displays indicated that densities tend to decline according to the Pareto function:

$$\ln D(x) = \ln D(1) + d(\ln x) \qquad (d < 0; x' \le x \le R), \qquad (7.3)$$

where the constant $D(1)$ represents the level of density at one unit of distance from the center, d represents the density gradient, and R is the boundary of the region. This pattern of density decay has been observed in a number of cases, although it was usually not characterized in terms of the Pareto function. Thus Ajo (1965) and Mogridge (1985) identified such a pattern for the nonmetropolitan part of the London MBR, whereas Berry and Horton (1970), Blumenfeld (1954), and Hoover and Vernon (1959) presented evidence for a similar pattern for the inner nonmetropolitan zones of the Chicago, Philadelphia, and New York City MBRs, respectively.

In terms of the problem at hand, what is required here is a functional form that splices together functions (7.2), (7.1), and (7.3), or more generally a form that reflects three distinct density characteristics of the various parts of the MBR: the density crest near the center at a distance x^* (equation 7.2); the tendency within the metropolitan area away from the crest for the logarithm of density to decrease with distance at a constant rate (equation 7.1); and the tendency throughout the nonmetropolitan zone of the MBR for the logarithm of density to decrease with the logarithm of distance at a constant rate (equation 7.3). A number of functions present themselves as candidates, but the lognormal form appears to be as robust as any of the functions considered. This has the form

$$\ln D(x) = \ln D(1) + d(\ln x) + g(\ln x)^2$$
$$(d \gtreqless 0; \, g < 0; \, 0 \le x \le R). \quad (7.4)$$

The lognormal function has been shown to have a very good degree of fit, and it accurately predicts, via the parameters $D(1)$, d, and g, the location of the density crest and the density at the crest, as well as other features of the spatial structure such as the total population of the MBR (Parr 1985; Parr and O'Neill 1989). Two versions of the graph of function (7.4) are presented in figure 7.1, where the density crest is apparent. In figure 7.1a the approximate linearity of the lognormal function over the range x^* to x' indicates adherence to the negative exponential form, while in figure 7.1b the tendency toward linearity of the function over the range x' to R represents an approximation of the Pareto form.

A number of statistical and conceptual issues are associated with the use of the density function to characterize patterns of spatial structure. The approach necessarily explains density in terms of a single independent variable, namely distance, which must be regarded as a weakness. Also, no account is taken of direction, so that differences in the sector pattern of the MBR are simply averaged out for each distance. Furthermore, there exists the problem of how the various density observations are to be weighted: Should each density observation be weighted by the population within the unit or by the area of that unit, or should such weighting be dispensed with? An additional question is whether the unit of analysis should represent a concentric (annular) ring or an area such as a census tract or local-government district. Without dismissing these technical considerations, it may be claimed that the density-function approach represents

Figure 7.1 TWO REPRESENTATIONS (a AND b) OF THE LOGNORMAL FUNCTION

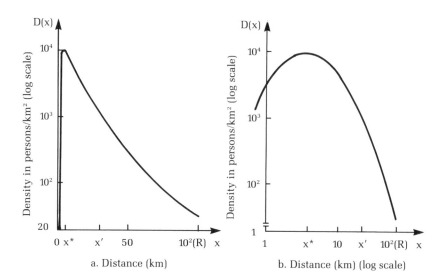

a. Distance (km)   b. Distance (km) (log scale)

a convenient means of dealing with the spatial structure of the MBR. Lest the approach degenerate into an exercise in curve fitting, however, the functional form selected should have a rationale or underlying theoretical basis. At present, no such rationale is available for the lognormal function. The lognormal form is broadly consistent with the existence (beyond the crest) of the negative exponential function, for which various bases have been proposed (Bussière and Snickars 1970; Mills 1972; Muth 1969). It is also possible to explain fairly satisfactorily the density crater and the accompanying density crest, and the study by Fisch (1987) represents one of the more rigorous explanations to date. However, it has not been possible to derive a rationale for the entire function, and more particularly for the manner in which the pattern of density decline throughout the nonmetropolitan zone of the MBR differs significantly from the pattern existing within the metropolitan zone.

Although residential or nighttime population is often used to describe the spatial structure of the MBR, it is also possible (subject to data availability) to use such measures as daytime population, labor force, employment, and so on, and alternative functional forms may be more appropriate than the lognormal in this connection. Indeed, this is a useful supplementary approach, since comparisons between density functions based on different variables may cast additional light on the structure of the MBR. For example, the differences between a density function based on residential or nighttime population and one based on daytime population would offer some indication of the extent to which daily personal movement of all types occurs within the MBR, and would reflect the importance of transportation in different zones. And related to this, a comparison between a function based on labor force and one based on employment would provide an overall indication of the extent of commuting within the MBR.

CONTEMPORARY TRENDS IN SPATIAL STRUCTURE OF MBR

The foregoing clearly represents a static view of the spatial structure of the MBR. Consideration now needs to be given to the changes currently occurring within the MBR, as well as the reasons for these. If it is accepted that the density function represents a reasonable, if imperfect, characterization of the spatial structure of the MBR, then the approach offers one means of dealing with these changes. For the sake of argument, it suffices to consider the density function for two points in time (e.g., 1950 and 1990), as indicated in figure 7.2. This refers to a hypothetical MBR of an extent perhaps more in keeping

Figure 7.2 SPATIAL-STRUCTURE CHANGES WITHIN THE MBR

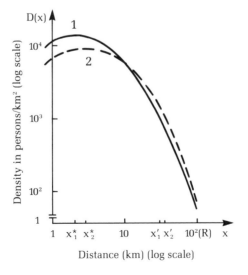

Distance (km) (log scale)

with Western Europe than the United States. Curve 1 in the figure represents the density function (of lognormal form) for 1950 and curve 2 a similar function for 1990. The density crest for 1950 is indicated by the distance x_1^* and that for 1990 by the distance x_2^*, whereas the boundary of the metropolitan area is given for 1950 by the distance x_1' and for 1990 by the distance x_2'.

A number of features can be observed in figure 7.2. First, and perhaps most striking, is the decline of population density (and thus population itself) in the central districts of the metropolitan zone (the distance interval 0–3 km [0–1.8 miles]), such districts having the highest rate of population decline throughout the entire MBR. This characterization, while typical of many metropolitan areas, needs to be tempered by the fact that, for certain U.S. metropolitan areas, the inner area (coinciding approximately with the CBD) is gaining slightly in population. In this connection, inner-area residential revitalization, though often exaggerated in its population-enhancing effect, cannot be neglected. Second, throughout the inner parts of the metropolitan zone, population is in decline, whereas over the outer parts it is still increasing. In metropolitan areas experiencing overall decline in population, the growth rate in the outer areas may also be negative, though not as pronounced as in the inner parts. In any event, there is a tendency toward more evenly distributed densities, and this may be regarded as a tendency toward "decentralization" irrespective of the overall growth or decline of the entire metropolitan population. Third, the nonmetropolitan zone is experiencing population growth throughout, and at a rate greater than that of the metropolitan zone. At the scale of the MBR, therefore, we may speak of "deconcentration" of the spatial structure (i.e., densities over the entire MBR becoming more evenly distributed). Fourth, and implicit in the previous three points, the population growth rate varies considerably throughout the MBR. It is generally at a negative level within the inner part of the metropolitan area and sometimes even in the outer parts, and attains its maximum level at a distance beyond the metropolitan area but before the boundary of the region is reached (Leven 1986; Mogridge 1985).

Decentralization and Deconcentration

The question naturally arises as to the causes of these major trends, which show every sign of continuing, even if at a reduced rate. Obviously, no single force, but rather a complex of forces, is causing the spatial structure of the MBR to develop broadly along the lines just described. In essence, these forces are causing households and employment to become located according to a different spatial pattern within the MBR. Earlier, such change was characterized as decentralization in the case of the metropolitan area and deconcentration in the case of the entire MBR. This nomenclature is maintained in the analysis, but further discussion of these terms is warranted here. The term *decentralization*, for example, carries the connotation of net movement of households or employment from the inner to the outer part of the metropolitan area. This may be an important element in decentralization, of course, but it is by no means the whole story. Net movement from other regions of households or employment into the suburbs (rather than into the inner parts of the metropolitan area) might also be a cause of decentralization, as might high rates of natural increase of population or of indigenous employment growth, relative to those of the inner parts. Similar considerations apply in the case of deconcentration, which does not result solely from net household or employment movement from the metropolitan zone to the nonmetropolitan zone of the MBR. Perhaps better terms in this connection are *statistical redistribution* or *statistical shift*, although apart from being cumbersome, these terms still fail to convey adequately the nature of the changing spatial structure. Decentralization (or deconcentration) is perhaps best viewed in terms of differences in the growth rates in different parts of the metropolitan region (the MBR), the growth rates tending to be inversely related to distance from the center.

A word is also in order regarding the measurement of decentralization (reduced levels of centralization) and deconcentration (reduced levels of concentration). It is typical in this connection to use one or more of the parameters of the function employed. For example, if attention is being focused on the metropolitan area, the parameter b in the negative exponential function of equation (7.1) represents an unambiguous measure of centralization, and a reduction in the absolute value of b over a given time period is indicative of decentralization. Similarly, a decrease in the absolute value of d in the Pareto function of equation (7.3) would indicate deconcentration. The argument here, however, has been that the spatial structure of the entire MBR is capable of being described in terms of a single function. If, therefore, reliance is placed solely on the use of the parameters of the lognormal function of equation (7.4), the measures for the levels of centralization and concentration for a given year will be identical. This problem is avoided if centralization and concentration are each measured in terms of an index which includes a specific distance limit: x' or R (Parr and O'Neill 1989). Consequently, for a given year, the level of centralization within the metropolitan area and the level of concentration over the entire MBR are necessarily different.

Decentralization within the Metropolitan Area

In the case of households, the process of decentralization or suburbanization began on a major scale in the 1920s in the United States, though at a later date in Western Europe. Historically, increasing disposable per capita incomes and improvements in surface transportation to workplaces in the CBD enabled housing and other urban-amenity preferences to be fulfilled (Evans 1973). In the United States, the improvement in transportation was based on increasing car ownership and the development of radial highways, with mass-transit improvements only important in particular cities (Schneider 1980). By contrast, in Western Europe the improvement was in public transportation, and only recently has car transportation (particularly in relation to nonradial journey-to-work movements) assumed a major importance. On both continents, government policies have exerted an influence. Various forms of subsidy to homeownership, which have disproportionately involved the new housing stock (typically associated with outer areas), have contributed to decentralization, as has the existence of residential-density and zoning regulations. The tendency toward decentralization in private housing has been accompanied in certain nations of Western Europe, particularly the Netherlands and the United Kingdom, by the outward shift of public housing. In a deliberate attempt to avoid overcrowding and because of the advantages of land acquisition, much of the investment in public housing has been directed to the suburbs or the metropolitan fringe (Hall et al. 1973).

The trend toward the decentralization of housing has been a powerful stimulus to the decentralization of employment (Stanback and Knight 1976). This was especially true of population-sensitive employment, such as service activity, and was closely related to the fact that the average distance of the consuming population from the center of the metropolitan area was increasing. Suburban locations have come to be locationally attractive in terms of access to a pool of suitable labor—particularly, though not exclusively, female part-time labor, again a reflection of the decentralization of households. A further factor, largely independent of household decentralization, that has favored the decentralization of employment has been the growing unsuitability of the inner areas as manufacturing locations, especially with respect to land availability and the problem of congestion at or near the center. Although employment decentralization has been commonplace for many years, it has more recently received an additional stimulus from such "pull factors" as the development of industrial and office parks and the emergence of circumferential highways, as well as the construction of major airports, which are necessarily located at suburban or exurban sites.

The onset of deindustrialization during the last twenty to thirty years (i.e., the large-scale decline of older industries in the manufacturing sector) has also influenced the decentralization of employment. To the extent that the older industries have been replaced by newer industries and more frequently by service-sector activities, both of which display a preference for suburban locations, the process of decentralization has been strengthened. Even where this industrial decline is not fully compensated by the emergence of new economic activity (e.g., the cases of Cleveland and Pittsburgh in the United States or Glasgow and Newcastle in the United Kingdom), the effect of deindustrialization still causes decentralization. This results from the decline in employment in older industries in the inner districts of the metropolitan area and the absence of a comparable decline in employment (or even the existence of mild employment growth) in the suburban districts.

In the process of changing the spatial structure within the metropolitan area, it is evident that household decentralization and employment decentralization are related, though not straightforwardly. Initially, household decentralization tended to occur independently. This provided the impetus for employment decentralization, particularly with respect to consumer-oriented service-sector activity. An era then followed when manufacturing employment began to decentralize, and although this was often based on reasons of operational efficiency (Anas and Moses 1978), the decentralization of households subsequently began to exert an influence in terms of access to labor. In recent years, however, the decentralization of employment may even be having an effect on the decentralization of households in terms of access to employment. It is probably more accurate, however, to conclude that at present the two types of decentralization are occurring in a mutually reinforcing manner (Linneman and Summers, chapter 4 of this volume).

Deconcentration over the MBR

The process of decentralization within the metropolitan area is accompanied by (and may be considered part of) the broader tendency toward deconcentration at the scale of the MBR, as recently demon-

strated for London (Mogridge and Parr 1997). Deconcentration involves growth in the nonmetropolitan zone at a greater rate than in
the metropolitan area. In the case of households, one element of the
deconcentration process is based on an increase in long-distance commuting, from the nonmetropolitan zone to the CBD of the metropolitan area as well as to suburban employment centers of more recent
origin. Although improved public and private transportation are usually suggested as influences, these are merely facilitating factors. As
in the case of metropolitan-area decentralization, higher incomes have
enabled the preferences to be realized. These refer not simply to type
of dwelling or level of density but also to such considerations as
efficient public services, acceptable levels of taxation, and the sense
of control over one's local environment. Other factors may have contributed to deconcentration of households. The considerably improved
scope for working from home and perhaps only visiting the office or
plant once or twice per week has permitted certain employees, as well
as the self-employed, to reside in the nonmetropolitan zone of the
MBR. Also, the growing tendency of migration to the nonmetropolitan
zone on or before retirement has undoubtedly contributed to the deconcentration of households (Hall 1989). A further important influence here has been the rapid growth of employment opportunities in
the nonmetropolitan zone of the MBR, including those areas beyond
the range of commuting. This influence is considered later in the
chapter.

As with the process of decentralization, the influence of government
policy cannot be neglected. The construction of major highways focusing on metropolitan areas and the maintenance and improvement
of long-distance commuter railways, often involving substantial subsidies, represent some of the more dramatic examples. Mention should
also be made of the impact of land-use controls. Although not rigor-
ously enforced at a regional level in most nations, such controls appear to have had a substantial effect in the Netherlands and the United
Kingdom (Hall 1977). In the latter nation, fairly strong greenbelt policies around each major metropolitan area have had a significant effect
on land values and the supply of housing within the greenbelt, as
well as in the metropolitan area, and have also been responsible for
the "leapfrogging" of urban development into the nonmetropolitan
zone of the MBR (Hall 1989; Parr 1986). Such a process of leapfrogging
has been reinforced by the government-sponsored development of
New Towns and Expanded Towns, located beyond the greenbelt. Although the primary motivation for this policy was based on improving
the quality of housing and reducing congestion within the major met-

ropolitan areas, it inevitably strengthened the trend toward regional deconcentration.

There has also been a marked deconcentration of employment within the MBR. This has been influenced in part by the deconcentration of households, which makes the nonmetropolitan zone of the MBR attractive in terms of markets (particularly for consumer-oriented service activities) as well as labor supply. Also important in this connection is the joint-supply aspect of female, and possibly male, labor (Gillespie and Green 1987). Furthermore, the growing unsuitability of the metropolitan area, especially in terms of the cost of land and labor, must be regarded as a major motivation for selecting a nonmetropolitan location for many types of economic activity (Hansen 1988). In the case of manufacturing, this is most pronounced in those sectors where the output consists of standardized products, where the production runs are long, and where the primary labor requirements involve semiskilled, unskilled, or easily trained workers (Stevens and Brackett 1970). The trend is related to the working through of the product cycle, and involves the firm utilizing a production function that is consistent with the relative factor prices prevailing in the nonmetropolitan zone of the MBR. It should be emphasized that deconcentration may also result from indigenous growth within the nonmetropolitan zone. In parts of Italy, for example, industrial development based on elaborate patterns of subcontracting and linkage among small-scale manufacturing firms located in different urban centers is contributing significantly to the process of regional deconcentration (Senn and Gorla, chapter 8 of this volume).

The Changing Position of the Metropolitan Area

Important in the process of employment deconcentration is the changed locational significance of the metropolitan zone of the MBR. For a widening range of economic activity, the entire metropolitan area, not simply its inner part, represents a location of net negative externalities, where congestion, pollution, and crime have an unfavorable effect on operating costs, frequently via wage bills and levels of local taxes. Related to this is the changing nature of externalities, both positive and negative. Whereas the metropolitan area used to represent a location that could retain a wide range of economic activity through the availability of specialized services and more generally because of the existence of net positive external economies (Hoover and Vernon 1959), this state of affairs is far less common nowadays. Many larger firms have been successful in internalizing certain of the positive externalities. This, in turn, has permitted them to relocate at a nonmetropolitan location, thereby avoiding the negative externalities as well as the high factor costs prevailing in the metropolitan area. Such a changed locational pattern typically involves the production process, with certain headquarters functions (which frequently require contact with government, financial institutions, universities, and research establishments) being retained in the metropolitan area. The selection of nonmetropolitan locations not only applies to plant relocation within the MBR but also to plants with headquarters based in other MBRs. In both cases, the distance of the nonmetropolitan location to the metropolitan area, though crucial, defies generalization and depends upon such considerations as the particular activity, the size of plant, the nature of linkages with the metropolitan area, and the quality of communications systems within the MBR.

But it is not simply a question of firms turning their backs on metropolitan locations because it has been possible to internalize particular erstwhile externalities based largely on agglomeration economies. Certain of these externalities are still sought after, if only because they cannot be satisfactorily internalized within the process of production. Access to specialized business services, major airports, and port facilities are obvious examples. The important point is that the agglomeration economies of the metropolitan area can now be taken advantage of at a considerable distance from it, although this may sound like a semantic contradiction. A location in the nonmetropolitan zone of the MBR increasingly offers the best of both worlds: the possibility of avoiding the high factor costs and negative externalities of the metropolitan area, and the ability to maintain easy access to the positive ones. Thus, whereas agglomeration economies have traditionally been regarded in the Weber (1929) sense as an advantage that was only available at a specific location such as the metropolitan area and that would be foregone by a firm if it did not locate there, these are now more appropriately viewed in the manner of Lösch (1954) as central-place goods that are still supplied from a specific location but are accessible from a market area that may be of considerable territorial extent. The reason for this change and, indeed, for the general trend toward deconcentration, is closely related to the quickening pace of improvements in transportation and telecommunications that has occurred since World War II. To a large extent the deconcentration trend in manufacturing and certain other types of employment can be viewed in terms of the Isard (1956) substitution framework derived from the theory of production. In selecting a nonmetropolitan location for its plant, the firm is substituting transport inputs (broadly defined) for nontransport inputs, that is, it is incurring additional transport outlays that are more than offset by the lower outlays on other inputs to production, particularly land and labor.

Commuting and Migration in the Process of Deconcentration

It is apparent from this discussion that employment deconcentration and household deconcentration represent closely interrelated processes. Certainly household deconcentration is likely to encourage deconcentration of employment, while deconcentration of employment may well foster the deconcentration of households. The role of commuting has an important bearing here, since it connects the two processes, at least over some distance range. Several situations may be considered in this connection. A household may move to the non-metropolitan zone for reasons already discussed, and one or more of its members may commute to the metropolitan area. If the labor market is tight, firms may end up paying for the high commuting costs, so that they have the incentive to relocate in the nonmetropolitan zone of the MBR to reduce labor costs. Alternatively, long-distance commuters may find journey times and travel costs burdensome, and may attempt to gain access to a local labor market in the nonmetropolitan zone of the MBR, thus improving labor-supply conditions at such locations (Hall 1989). A further possibility is that firms may relocate in the nonmetropolitan zone for the reasons described. Their employees may for a while engage in reverse commuting from the metropolitan area but then decide to relocate closer to the workplace. These examples suggest that commuting patterns are subject to change, but also draw attention to the fact that commuting and migration are substitutes as well as complements in the evolution of the MBR's spatial structure (Termote 1978).

IMPLICATIONS OF THE CHANGING SPATIAL STRUCTURE OF THE MBR

The process of decentralization is continuing apace, but it is accompanied to a growing extent by the more general process of deconcentration. The two processes tend to be based on broadly similar underlying factors, although the forces that formerly led to metropolitan decentralization now operate increasingly on a wider scale, thus giving rise to regional deconcentration. These trends provide the back-ground for the future development of the MBR and its constituent parts, and in this setting a number of issues can be expected to assume a growing importance.

Emerging Issues

It is reasonable, for example, to expect a continued drift toward private transportation as a result of the more complex patterns of commuting and freight flows that accompany the increasingly dispersed spatial structure. Many existing highways will be used beyond design capac-ity, and the attendant deterioration and congestion will elicit calls for additional investment. The changing spatial structure is also likely to involve the expansion of urban centers and the invasion of land hith-erto devoted to agricultural and recreational uses, thus heightening the debate on rural-urban land conversion. The concern over environ-mental quality, already well established as an issue, is unlikely to diminish, but it is difficult to predict future attitudes and responses to this problem. Although levels of environmental pollution will in-crease over many parts of the MBR, the trend toward a more even pattern of pollution may be regarded as acceptable, insofar as such a pattern may make it easier to maintain minimum levels of environ-mental quality. A rather different issue relates to the likelihood of growing inter-area inequality or polarization in levels of welfare throughout the MBR. This is closely related to the tendency for levels of segregation to increase, whether this involves ethnic groups, social classes, or both.

A prominent question in this discussion and one that is worth exploring briefly concerns the future of the metropolitan area (i.e., the metropolitan zone of the MBR). Does what has been described earlier suggest the passing of the metropolitan area? The answer is probably not, although it is more than likely that certain metropolitan areas will tend to remain stationary or decline in terms of population and employment. Particular types of manufacturing activity will no longer be associated with the metropolitan area, although many of the nodal functions involving banking and finance, transportation, communi-cations, public administration, higher education, research, and so forth, can be expected to be retained. Also retained by the metropol-itan area will be those sectors of activity that require face-to-face or "back-to-back" contact (Meier 1962). Even in the case of manufactur-ing activity, the situation is not entirely bleak. The metropolitan area is likely to attract those types of manufacturing that are oriented to it by virtue of access to markets or inputs and also often because of their small scale. Furthermore, the traditional role of the large metropolitan area as an incubator for new firms, together with the tendency for there to be a procession of industries passing through it over the long run (Blumenfeld 1955), will both probably continue. To the extent that household location may affect the nature and scope of economic activity within the metropolitan area, the fact that certain groups of the population will still favor an inner-metropolitan environment, which gives them immediate access to specialized entertainment and cultural facilities as well as the satisfaction of high-density urban living, may well foster a certain vitality and capacity for adjustment within the metropolitan economy. The degree to which the presence of such groups leads to the generation of employment and additional population remains to be seen.

Not all parts of the metropolitan area will necessarily flourish, however, and the prospect for the inner areas, for example, is not especially bright. Related to this is the fact that not all income groups are likely to share in whatever gains the metropolitan area is able to make. The existing spatial mismatch between low-skill labor within the inner areas and employment opportunities at suburban locations is likely to be exacerbated as the process of employment decentralization proceeds (Kain 1968; Kasarda and Friedrichs 1986). The problem is rendered more serious by virtue of the fact that it will exist against a backdrop of regional deconcentration, by which employment in the metropolitan area will grow (if it grows at all) at a slower rate than the rest of the MBR. As a consequence, residents of the metropolitan area located in "impacted ghettos" (Hughes 1990) or in public housing schemes on its periphery are in considerable danger of being left behind, as the changing spatial structure of employment reduces still further their access to job opportunities, particularly if there is no improvement in their chronically low levels of mobility (Hughes and Loizillon, chapter 13 of this volume).

Problems of Policy Formulation

There can be little doubt that government will be an important actor in the future development of the MBR, as it has been with past development. Indeed, it would be quite wrong to view the changes outlined in the previous section as representing a market outcome that resulted from the private decisions of households and firms, with government merely having played a passive or reactive role. As already noted, certain government policies have contributed (sometimes unintentionally) to the processes of decentralization and deconcentration, the policies having typically been responses to particular functional concerns such as housing provision, land-use zoning and control, or the securing of adequate levels of transportation. There can, of course, be no satisfactory disentanglement of the public influence from the private. Inevitably, therefore, future policies will have to be implemented not only within the environment of a changing spatial structure but within one in which past policies have exerted, and perhaps continue to exert, a significant influence.

Mention has already been made of some of the policy issues that can be expected to confront government, and although it is impossible to examine any of these in depth here, certain underlying considerations deserve to be mentioned. Perhaps the most obvious is the interrelatedness of the various parts of the MBR, each of which has a high degree of openness. The possibility of leakage may therefore be substantial, so that a government program involving a particular area can be expected to have indirect impacts, both positive and negative, on other parts of the MBR and even beyond. Related to this is the fact that within the MBR the pattern of spatial externalities and spillover effects is becoming increasingly complex, a factor that can only serve to render more difficult the formulation of policy and the gaining of its acceptance. A further point concerns the fact that, as the MBR continues to develop along the lines described, it is likely to require considerable public investment in the infrastructure. If the beneficiaries (households, firms, developers, municipalities) are not charged the full marginal cost of this investment, the processes of decentralization and deconcentration are likely to be enhanced, almost inevitably to the detriment of particular parts of the MBR. In light of this and given the political and even legal difficulties associated with marginal-cost pricing, policymakers may decide that it is futile to resist the apparently inexorable forces that are creating a more complex and more dispersed spatial structure. Instead they may adopt the pragmatic (and enlightened) approach of compensating, by means of carefully targeted expenditures, those groups within the MBR or those parts of it that have been placed at a disadvantage as a result of current trends and the various government policies that support these.

Nature of Government Involvement

Within the modern state, governments of various levels are called upon to make expenditures, particularly with respect to the provision of goods and services that are acknowledged to be beyond the scope of the market. Such expenditures may be seen as having an impact on development of the MBR and its constituent elements, but may also be regarded as means for guiding or channeling this development. These two views of public expenditure are linked to some extent to the distinction drawn by Downs (chapter 2 of this volume) between different types of government involvement. In the United States, Downs argues, governments have not concerned themselves with overall development strategies, the programs of the Appalachian Regional Commission being an obvious exception. By contrast, in Western Europe, governments have tended to adopt explicit strategies at the national and metropolitan area levels. It is as well to remember that there exists a considerable diversity of approaches in the nations of Western Europe, and that in the United States, regional and metropolitan development interests have been served, often very effectively, by federal government expenditures in such areas as defense procurement, river basin development, and the Interstate Highway Program. This contrast in approaches is due to different emphases and traditions of government involvement that are themselves underpinned by considerable differences in political culture. It may also stem from differences in the structure of government. In the United States, the government of the metropolitan area tends to be fragmented or balkanized. Metropolitan government has generally not emerged, the responsibility for the relevant functions often having been shifted to the level of state government. Elements of such a jurisdictional form nevertheless can be identified in the cases of county government and the special district, both of which are concerned with such functions as emergency services, water supply, sewerage, port administration, airport development, public transportation, and so forth (Lynch 1977; Self 1987). At the level of the MBR, however, there is a virtual absence of regional government. Moreover, the system of states, by virtue of its geographic structure, does not provide a satisfactory framework for the government of the various MBRs, although there may be some potential for this in larger states such as California and Texas.

The situation in Western Europe may be compared to that prevailing in the United States. As in the United States, metropolitan government in Western Europe is not the norm. The metropolitan *Länder* of Berlin, Bremen, and Hamburg in the Federal Republic of Germany represent something of an exception, and the comprehensive system of metropolitan government created in the United Kingdom during the 1970s has now been dismantled. In the case of regional government, however, conditions in Western Europe not only stand in contrast to those in the United States but also vary markedly from nation to nation. In the Federal Republic of Germany, for example, the pattern of *Länder* accords reasonably well with the structure of the MBRs. Similarly, in Italy and Spain, which have unitary, rather than federal, systems of government, the pattern of semiautonomous regions established within each nation over the last two decades corresponds fairly closely to the structure of MBRs. In these nations, therefore, a reasonably coherent governmental framework for responding to the planning and development problems of the MBR (and therefore its metropolitan zone) seems to be present. This will also be the case in certain parts of the United Kingdom (Scotland, Wales, and Northern Ireland) that are soon to have subnational governments. In the other nations of Western Europe, regional government is absent, reflecting the more centralized political systems and the usually smaller extent of the nations concerned. Even in these cases, however, a noncentral response to the problems of the MBR may be possible, so long as the relevant parts of central government administration are organized on a regional basis.

The presence of a rational framework for government decision making at the metropolitan and regional levels is no guarantee of efficiency, any more than the stated existence of a strategy will necessarily produce the desired objectives. Nevertheless, the absence of such a framework places a definite barrier in the way of effective public investment and frequently leads to the direct involvement of higher levels of government (the central or federal levels). This is probably not an undesirable development per se, although it is often alleged that the detached and distant nature of such involvement militates against local or regional choice and may result in unwarranted uniformity of policy.

CONCLUSION

The central theme of this chapter has been that the larger metropolitan area in the United States and Western Europe is changing in such a way that it can only be understood in terms of the MBR. Related to this is the fact that the metropolitan area is becoming overtaken by the MBR as the major building block of national spatial structure. This is not to suggest that the metropolitan area has outlived its usefulness as a unit of analysis for approaching certain kinds of problems. Rather, the argument is that an increasing range of developments and policy issues relating to the metropolitan area cannot be understood, let alone analyzed, without reference to the wider MBR, whether one is considering economic performance, the nature of labor markets and housing markets, or patterns of transportation. It is in this sense that the MBR (within a system of MBRs) can be said to be displacing the metropolitan area as an appropriate scale of analysis. Although considerable stress has been placed on the structural interrelations between the metropolitan and nonmetropolitan zones of the MBR, this should not divert attention from the intermetropolitan and interregional (i.e., inter-MBR) connections that are most certainly present. For the concept of the MBR to be of assistance in our understanding of urban economic development, it must pay adequate attention to the fact that the economic position of the metropolitan area and its MBR is subject as much to national and extraregional influences as it is to intraregional ones.

References

Ajo, R. 1965. "On the Structure of Population in London's Field." *Acta Geographica* 18: 1–17.
Anas, A., and L. N. Moses. 1978. "Transportation and Land Use in the Mature Metropolis." In *The Mature Metropolis*, edited by C. L. Leven. Lexington, Ky.: Lexington Books.
Angel, S., and G. M. Hyman. 1972. "Urban Spatial Interaction." *Environment and Planning* 4: 99–118.
Berry, B. J. L. 1967. *Functional Economic Areas and Consolidated Urban Regions of the United States.* Final Report of the Study of Metropolitan Area Classification. New York: Social Science Research Council.
Berry, B. J. L., and F. E. Horton. 1970. *Geographic Perspectives on Urban Systems.* Englewood Cliffs, N.J.: Prentice Hall.
Blumenfeld, H. 1954. "The Tidal Wave of Metropolitan Expansion." *Journal of the American Institute of Planners* 20: 3–14.
————. 1955. "The Economic Base of the Metropolis." *Journal of the American Institute of Planners* 21: 114–32.
Bogue, D. J. 1950. *The Structure of the Metropolitan Community.* Ann Arbor, Mich.: Horace H. Rackham School of Graduate Studies, University of Michigan.
Boudeville, J. R. 1966. *Problems in Regional Economic Planning.* Edinburgh: Edinburgh University Press.

Bussière, R., and F. Snickars. 1970. "Derivation of the Negative Exponential Model by an Entropy Maximising Function." *Environment and Planning* 2: 295–301.

Cheshire, P., and D. G. Hay. 1989. *Urban Problems in Western Europe: An Economic Analysis*. London: Unwin Hyman.

Clark, C. 1951. "Urban Population Densities." *Journal of the Royal Statistical Society* 114 (series A): 490–96.

Congdon, P., and A. Champion. 1989. "Recent Population Shifts in South East England and Their Relevance to the Counterurbanization Debate." In *Growth and Change in a Core Region.* Vol. 20 in London Papers in Regional Science, edited by M. Breheny and P. Congdon. London: Pion.

Dematteis, G., and P. Petsimeris. 1989. "Italy: Counterurbanization as a Transitional Phase in Settlement Reorganization." In *Counterurbanization: The Changing Pace and Nature of Population Deconcentration*, edited by A. G. Champion. London: Edward Arnold.

Dickinson, R. E. 1947. *City, Region, and Regionalism*. London: Routledge and Kegan Paul.

Evans, A. W. 1973. *The Economics of Residential Location*: London: Macmillan.

Fisch, O. 1987. "A Structural Approach to the Form of Population Density Functions." Paper presented at the Nineteenth Annual Conference of the British Section of the Regional Science Association, Stirling, Scotland, September.

Gillespie, A. E., and A. E. Green. 1987. "The Changing Geography of Producer Services Employment in Britain." *Regional Studies* 21: 397–411.

Hall, P. G. 1977. *The World Cities*, 2nd ed. London: Weidenfeld and Nicholson.

———. 1989. "London 2001." In *Growth and Change in a Core Region.* Vol. 20 in London Papers in Regional Science, edited by M. Breheny and P. Congdon. London: Pion.

Hall, P. G., H. Gracey, R. Drewett, and R. Thomas. 1973. *The Containment of Urban England*. London: Allen and Unwin.

Hansen, N. 1988. "Small and Medium-Sized Cities in Development." In *Regional Economic Development*, edited by B. Higgins and D. J. Savoie. Boston: Unwin Hyman.

Hoover, E. M., and R. Vernon. 1959. *Anatomy of a Metropolis: The Changing Distribution of People and Jobs within the New York Metropolitan Region*. Cambridge, Mass.: Harvard University Press.

Hughes, M. A. 1990. "The Formation of the Impacted Ghetto." *Urban Geography* 11: 265–84.

Isard, W. 1956. *Location and Space-Economy*. New York: Technology Press of MIT and John Wiley and Sons.

Kain, J. F. 1968. "Housing Segregation, Negro Employment, and Metropolitan Decentralization." *Quarterly Journal of Economics* 82: 175–97.

Kasarda, J., and J. Friedrichs. 1986. "Comparative Demographic-Employment Mismatches in U.S. and West German Cities." In *The Future of the Metropolis: Economic Aspects*, edited by J. J. Ewers, H. Matzerath, and J. B. Goddard. Berlin: De Gruyter.

Leven, C. 1976. "Economic Maturity and the Metropolis's Evolving Physical Form." In *The Changing Structure of the City: What Happened to the Urban Crisis?* Vol. 16 of Urban Affairs Annual Reviews, edited by G. Tobin. Beverly Hills, Calif.: Sage Publications.

————. 1986. "The Distribution of Its Urban Population as an Issue for the European Community." In *Western Europe in Transition: West Germany's Role in the European Community*, edited by P. M. Lutzeler. Baden-Baden: Nomos Verlagsgesellschaft.

Lösch, A. [1944] 1954. *Die räumliche Ordnung der Wirtschaft*, 2nd ed. Translated by W. H. Woglom and W. F. Stolper as *The Economics of Location*. New Haven, Conn.: Yale University Press.

Lynch, N. F. 1977. "The Politics of Suburban Development." In *The Suburban Economic Network: Economic Activity, Resource Use, and the Great Sprawl*, edited by J. E. Ullmann. New York: Praeger.

Meier, R. L. 1962. *A Communication Theory of Urban Growth*. Cambridge, Mass.: MIT Press.

Mills, E. S. 1972. *Urban Economics*. Glenview, Ill.: Scott, Foresman and Co.

Mogridge, M. 1985. "Strategic Population Forecasting for a Conurbation Using the Negative Exponential Density Model." *Transportation Research* 19 (series A): 189–206.

Mogridge, M., and J. B. Parr. 1997. "Metropolis or Region: On the Development and Structure of London." *Regional Studies* 31: 97–115.

Muth, R. F. 1969. *Cities and Housing: The Spatial Pattern of Urban Residential Land Use*. Chicago: University of Chicago Press.

Newling, B. E. 1969. "The Spatial Variation of Urban Population Densities." *Geographical Review* 59: 242–52.

Parr, J. B. 1985. "The Form of the Regional Density Function." *Regional Studies* 19: 535–46.

————. 1986. "The Regional Density Function: An Application of the Concept in Planning." *Town Planning Review* 57: 319–30.

Parr, J. B., and G. J. O'Neill. 1989. "Aspects of the Lognormal Function in the Analysis of Regional Population Distribution." *Environment and Planning* 21 (series A): 961–73.

Schneider, M. 1980. *Suburban Growth: Policy and Process*. Brunswick, Ohio: King's Court Communications.

Self, P. 1987. "The Role and Limitations of Metro Government in Positive Urban Planning." Occasional Paper 42, Centre for Human Settlements, University of British Columbia. Vancouver: Centre for Human Settlements, University of British Columbia.

Stanback, T. M., and R. Knight. 1976. *Suburbanization and the City.* Montclair, N.J.: Allanheld, Osmun and Co.

Stevens, B. H., and C. A. Brackett. 1970. *Industrial Location: An Annotated Bibliography of Theoretical, Empirical, and Case Studies.* Philadelphia: Regional Science Research Institute.

Termote, M. 1978. "Migration and Commuting in Lösch's Central Place System." In *The Analysis of Regional Structure: Essays in Honour of August Lösch.* Vol. 2 in Karlsruhe Papers in Regional Science, edited by R. Funck and J. B. Parr. London: Pion.

U.S. Bureau of the Census. 1989. *Statistical Abstract of the United States, 1989,* 109th ed. Washington, D.C.: U.S. Government Printing Office.

Weber, A. [1909] 1929. *Über den Standort der Industrien.* Translated and edited by C. J. Friedrich as *Alfred Weber's Theory of Location of Industries.* Chicago: University of Chicago Press.

Winchester, H. P. M., and P. E. Ogden. 1989. "France: Decentralization and Deconcentration in the Wake of Late Urbanization." In *Counterurbanization: The Changing Pace and Nature of Population Deconcentration,* edited by A. G. Champion. London: Edward Arnold.

Chapter Eight

NETWORKING STRATEGIES AS A FACTOR IN URBAN DECENTRALIZATION

Lanfranco Senn and Gianluigi Gorla

One justification for an economic approach to analyzing cities, and changes within and between them, is that individual cities—and the urban system as a whole—are an essential form of social interaction and organization in the creation and distribution of wealth. Indeed, a city may be conceived of as one of the main organizational mechanisms through which efficiency in production and trade is attained and distribution effected.

This economic view is partial, since it ignores other factors that contribute to the organization of social life. However, the economic approach has, and still reveals, powerful insights into our understanding of urban phenomena. It also generates important suggestions for policy. The way in which economic analysis and the methodology of economics have extended into fields of activity—such as planning—that have traditionally been the province of other disciplines is further evidence of the growing awareness of the contribution economics can make to urban analysis. More particularly, urban economic analysis has traditionally been used to answer questions related to the efficient organization of production and trade, such as: Why do cities exist? Why do they differ in size? How and why do they grow or decline? How are they distributed in geographic space?

This chapter analyzes spatial decentralization within the conceptual framework of efficiency. The aim is to show, from a theoretical viewpoint, how the pursuit of efficiency by individual economic actors may lead to locational patterns and mechanisms of growth transmission that are characterized by spatial decentralization, because external economies of scale are not necessarily fully exploited through spatial agglomeration. Activities are spun off larger urban areas to more diffused urban centers of varying size, with consequent implications for the form of the urban system as a whole. The discussion here combines traditional principles of spatial economic analysis with a relatively new concept drawn from the theory of organization—

the concept of the network. This approach, it is argued, helps to explain patterns and tendencies that are difficult to explain with traditional models.

THE HIERARCHICAL PARADIGM

Until now, the framework for analyzing the process of decentralization has essentially been derived from central place theory as originally conceived by Christaller (1933). As its name implies, central place theory

> is based on the idea of the urban area as a trading center: . . . the smallest urban places sell commonplace goods (i.e. they are of lower rank) to the population of larger market areas. . . . In turn there are still larger urban places selling even less purchased goods (i.e., they are of higher rank) to still larger market areas. . . . (Evans 1985: 66)

Within such a framework, decentralization is the outcome of distinct, nonmutually exclusive determinants. This section next reviews the hierarchical patterns.

Destructuring of the hierarchical pattern can be addressed by relaxing the assumption of the presence of all lower-rank functions in the largest centers, and by moving toward a Löschian approach (Lösch 1954) that admits a large number of rank-size distributions, less concentrated than the one associated with Christaller's theory (Beckman and MacPherson 1970). Lower-rank functions are actually more and more underrepresented in the largest centers and overrepresented in the smallest ones. However, the explanation of such a decentralization tendency is not possible within the hierarchical paradigm, because it does not contain any principle capable of explaining the shift from Christaller's determinism to the Löschian latent probabilism.

Restructuring of the hierarchical pattern implies changes within the hierarchy of urban centers. This approach safeguards the hierarchical principle, even though it renders that principle less relevant in comparison with other principles of spatial organization in determining city function and size distributions. Empirical evidence shows that these changes may be ascribed to three different factors.

First, the size of individual firms and plants tended to decline in a number of manufacturing sectors during the 1970s—across the world, and in Italy particularly (Barbetta and Silva 1989). The smaller efficient size could have allowed each plant to supply a market of smaller size. In turn, this could have translated into a spatial diffusion of plants, leading to their location in lower-rank centers of the urban hierarchy. However, since manufacturing does not really locate in a way consistent with central place theory, this explanation applies to only a minority of manufacturing activities. It is more appropriate for service activities.

Second, changes in intraurban hierarchical structures also stem from rising incomes and market growth. When goods and services, previously considered as luxuries or unusual commodities, are demanded in growing quantities and at all levels of the urban hierarchy, the same minimum production levels required to get minimum efficient scale of plant can be achieved at ever-smaller market areas. Again, this entails a spatial diffusion of production units and their location in lower-rank centers of the urban hierarchy. Such a trend appears to be a particularly important explanation of why services that were previously scarce and available only in the largest centers are now demanded and supplied more diffusely and cheaply.

A third factor often invoked as a cause of decentralization is falling transport costs. Using Christaller's (1933) model, the search for economies of scale produces a push toward polarization. The reduction of transport costs, however, is a major explanation of the spatial economic landscape, since the hierarchical paradigm is based on spatial behavior of consumers, which, in turn, relies heavily on transport costs. This tends to make the Christaller approach less relevant.

Finally, the strengthening of spatial market competition favors decentralizing tendencies. New firms that compete with the already existing ones emerge, and a reorganization of the market in smaller areas occurs. Some evidence of this is provided, for instance, by the recent Italian experience, when deregulation in the banking sector led to the setting up of a large number of new branches. According to the Christaller terminology, the "range" approaches the "threshold" as the extra profits of firms disappear. Moreover, the number of market areas increases, and production units tend to locate in centers of lower rank within the urban hierarchy.

The factors considered thus far explain, at least partially, some of the tendencies toward decentralization. They relate exclusively, however, to those activities for which it is possible to define area-type markets on a regional or subregional scale. There are two conditions for a market to exhibit this feature. Transport costs—or any costs of interaction between buyers and sellers—must be significantly affected by the distance between the two; and these costs must have a significant effect on final prices. These conditions indeed apply to most nontradable services, and to the subcontracting activities of manufacturers, when local forward linkages absorb the greatest part of output. But they also apply to those products with low value-added and high transport costs (for example, building materials and bottled beverages). In contrast, they do not apply to most manufacturing activities that supply national or international markets, and to those that supply markets with a considerable volume of horizontal trade: This would be inconsistent with the hierarchical principle.

TOWARD AN INTEGRATED MODEL: HIERARCHY, AGGLOMERATION ECONOMIES, AND ACCESSIBILITY

The hierarchical paradigm is a powerful, but not exhaustive, principle of spatial organization. For instance, it is unable to provide an explanation of visible "anomalies." Camagni (1990), among others, has proposed to integrate the paradigm with two other principles of spatial organization, to obtain a more realistic theory of urban systems and, therefore, a more realistic theory of changes within them.

In addition to the hierarchical principle, if a "synergy" principle is admitted—accounting for the advantages achievable by different activities as a consequence of their spatial agglomeration, apart from transportation costs—it is possible to explain the existence of spatial "units," such as "industrial districts," that are incompatible with central place theory. The term *synergy* implies highly horizontally integrated and specialized areas, where functions characterizing the respective hierarchical level are not all present. There may also be what can be called "system areas"—highly vertically integrated areas where some functions, typical of the higher order in the hierarchy, are actually present. More generally, external economies of scale may provide the rationale for "corridors," "routes," and "valleys," and, of course, for large metropolitan regions outside the scope of central place theory. Furthermore, if the principles of urban accessibility and spatial competition for urban land are also introduced, it becomes possible to explain why lower-order activities are underrepresented in the largest urban centers and industrial districts; these activities are less able to afford the urban rent.

The distinctive feature of this approach, compared to Christaller's, lies in the fact that "the territoriality of economic space is no longer connected with the organization of final demand markets but with the organization of production" (Camagni 1990: 63). In other words, agglomeration advantages should be analyzed on the input side. Location strategies focused on inputs rather than outputs, however, do not in principle imply tendencies toward decentralization, despite the fact that they account for the existence of some dispersal patterns of production and specialization. On the contrary, the opposite should prevail, since the concepts of synergy and of economies of agglomeration stress the comparative advantages achievable through spatial clustering and polarization. Of course, because these advantages may vary for each activity, and even for firms belonging to the same sector, it follows that an urban system has centers of agglomeration of different size, with consequently different levels of land rent.

Given this, other factors must be sought if tendencies toward decentralization are to be satisfactorily explained. These factors may be grouped into two broad categories: The first concerns prices of the less mobile inputs, and the second relates to economies of agglomeration. In fact, a decentralization process may be enhanced by changes either on the demand side—such as the lowering of externality thresholds required for many locations—or on the supply side—through the relative reduction of agglomerative advantages, or the increase of diseconomies of agglomeration, that are found in larger urban places.

For the decentralization process to actually occur, outward push effects must emanate from the largest centers. These effects may result from price differentials of factors that are less mobile in space—most obvious of all, land prices. Such an explanation has been widely discussed in the literature focusing on the potential advantages derived either from lower land prices and the specific features of urban estate markets (Fothergill and Gudgin 1982; Fothergill, Monk, and Perry 1987), or from lower labor costs (Massey and Meegan 1978, 1982). Push effects are particularly relevant when the economy slows down and productive restructuring occurs, but they are also consistent with the more general process of capital intensification (Scott 1982).

The reduction of the locational advantages of larger centers may be ascribed to several diffusing tendencies. Indeed, the influence of several factors generating economies of urbanization—both static (connected to indivisibilities) and dynamic—has spread through space. Dynamic economies of urbanization are associated with the advantages due to the interactions among the actors that allow for the control of information, access to technological innovations, and the reduction of uncertainty. This tendency toward dynamic economies is reinforced by the contrast between the increased accessibility of smaller centers, made possible by improvements and innovation in transport and telecommunications, and the greater difficulties of larger centers caused by growing congestion problems. Though it has been argued in the past that periods of high uncertainty had an agglomerative effect because risk-averse firms imitated the locational choices of those who located centrally to ensure their market share, there are now new factors. Uncertainty is still very high—due to technological changes, increased competition, and globalization—but it is permanent. Firms, therefore, internalize the effects of uncertainty in their strategic behavior, reducng uncertainty to a spatially indifferent factor. This is particularly true for business services (Esparza and Krmenec 1994).

Less evident is the argument that firms demand a lower level of externalities from their locations. This may actually occur when firms grow and internalize several functions previously purchased from the market. The limit to this process lies in firms' ability to achieve a size that allows the internalization of functions, subject to existing indivisibilities, and in their ability to manage those functions efficiently. Empirical evidence of the decreasing demand for agglomeration economies is not unambiguous, however. On the one hand, there is the increased importance of internal economies of scale and of multiplant diversified firms and corporations; on the other hand, there is the decrease in the average size of firms and the parallel increase in the number of firms, leading to the opposite conclusion.

It should be noted, however, that any decline in the significance of externalities is not only the result of the efforts of firms but is also the outcome of change in the technological, market, and organizational environment in which firms operate. This is consistent with the "filtering-down" theory. This theory links spatial relocation of activities to product life cycle, according to a hierarchical "top-down" diffusion process determined by the propensity to develop and exploit technological innovation, rather than by the search for economies of scale. In this sense, decentralization is explained by the "upgrading" (or the approaching maturity) of the production system as a whole, and by the simultaneous inability of the largest centers to develop new activities to substitute for traditional ones. The expulsion of old activities, even when they are not displaced by new emerging activities, would be warranted by the price rigidities of the less-mobile urban factors of production.

In addition to product life, spatial patterns are also affected by life-cycle characteristics. If more advanced areas and larger cities do not maintain the same growth rate as emerging areas and smaller cities—due to the impact of congestion and/or changes in their production mix—there is a filtering down of less competitive activities and a filtering up of more competitive ones (Cheshire and Gordon 1995).

SPATIAL DECENTRALIZATION AND NETWORK STRUCTURES

The lowering of the externality thresholds demanded by firms for their location partly explains patterns of decentralization on the interregional as well as intraregional scales. In contrast, the increasing availability of external economies in smaller centers is mainly relevant to the explanation of patterns of decentralization on the intraregional scale (Fik and Mulligan 1990). In fact, the greater availability of externalities that can be found in smaller centers is not uniquely generated within each of them. It is also the result of increased interaction between centers as a result of improved accessibility among the cities in an intraregional system, connected by improved transportation and communication networks (Esparza and Krmenec 1996). This produces externalities, both among the smaller centers and between smaller centers and the major ones. The outcome is a situation in which, within a regional context, conditions exist that allow some urban functions to be accomplished in a more decentralized way. Localities that have already reached minimum thresholds of urbanization are, of course, at an advantage.

According to Dematteis (1990), the "enlargement" of the field of externalities previously concentrated within the more urbanized areas gives rise to "equipotential networks," defined as spatial networks whose nodes present a locational indifference. The spatial extent of this kind of network, typical of a regional scale, has two constraints. It is limited by the area of locational indifference for the higher central function and by the areas within which agglomeration economies arise from each urban node of the network. The main advantage to belonging to an equipotential network, compared to being a freestanding city or town, is that the network makes it possible to participate in agglomeration economies without bearing the costs of diseconomies that arise within polarized metropolitan regions.

It follows that equipotential networks are formed by several urban centers, where neither the number of nodes nor the size or location of each node is predetermined—as in the Christallerian geometry—by the "level of activity" of the network. In the limiting case, any already existing activity can be undertaken in any node of the network, regardless of its specific size, and the spatial distribution of functions between the nodes would turn out to be "casual over time, without giving rise to a stable local mix, able to produce stabilizing and cumulative synergic effects" (Dematteis 1990: 32). Examples of equipotential networks can be identified in the systems of intermediate cities around Turin in Piedmont, Milan in Lombardy, in several German *Länder*, and in other European countries like the Netherlands and Belgium. The high level of accessibility within each of these regional systems means that there is no net cost difference between locating in one node or another, including the core cities. This does not necessarily hold for all types of activities—only for those that demand externalities and can have access to them in any node of the system through a restructuring of distribution policies and logistic strategies. Other activities supply externalities and need the highest level of centrality for their location. Among these are rare services, most firm headquarters, most locations performing the strategic functions of firms, and some hierarchically superior administrative activities.

The locational indifference associated with an equipotential network allows for the existence of a larger number of centers, in comparison with those that would be expected on the basis of the central place or polarization theories. This is the key original contribution of equipotential networks in explaining decentralization tendencies. However, decentralization patterns may not be reduced exclusively to the intraregional distribution of activities as described here. In fact, decentralization also gives rise to other forms of interregional distribution, such as system areas and industrial districts, and new corridors and routes of development. These spatial structures are often characterized by internal synergies and cumulative mechanisms that make the exploitation of local advantages more favorable and push toward specialization. Specialized areas, however, need functional complementarities present in other nodes: The outcomes of these complementarities are *multipolar networks,* defined as systems of nodes with different specializations and functions.

Network economies arise as a consequence of interaction among highly specialized nodes and with diversified larger centers belonging to the same network. The agglomeration diseconomies of polarized areas are avoided by spatial dispersion, and transaction costs are kept low so far as interactions become stable. Additional economies derive from external economies. The multipolar network, for example, generates and makes available information, just as in equipotential networks, but without requiring spatial proximity. This allows members of multipolar networks to enjoy a greater degree of locational freedom than the equipotential networks, as well as a locational advantage compared to nodes not belonging to the same network.

In the case of equipotential networks, the implicit model of growth transmission is the exogenous type, since the dynamics of each node depends essentially on the dynamics of sectors. In the case of multipolar networks, each node preserves its own identity within the network and develops according to an endogenous model, but interacts with the other nodes of the network. The nodes of a polarized and multipolar network are, in fact, able to compete and catch growth opportunities autonomously and to transmit them to the other complementary nodes. Decentralization trends are speeded up by the formation and strengthening of multipolar networks, since they permit the disaggregation of the production chain on an interregional scale. This gives rise to geographically dispersed units in order to exploit local advantages. Furthermore, these units are the locations of firms, not just plants.

The mechanisms of competition and growth transmission benefit local areas more than was foreseen by Pred (1977), who analyzed the context of an economy dominated by multiplant corporations. In fact, there are now fewer opportunities for both spatial separation of functions internal to the firm and for spatial concentration of headquarters within the major urban centers. In addition, highly specialized service activities can be found within the network both in larger centers and in other lower-rank ones, making the latter more likely to benefit from interfirm linkages than before.

Decentralization is, therefore, an outcome of new organizational patterns and strategies and of new spatial patterns of production. Even smaller-size centers may represent satisfactory locations for many types of firms, their clusters, and their networks. In this framework, interactions and the mechanisms of growth transmission are the core of the analysis. It is necessary, therefore, to look more closely at networks of firms to understand what impact their interactions may have on the polarization or decentralization of urban growth.

CITIES AND DECISION MAKERS: FIRM STRATEGIES

In most aggregate theories of urban growth it is implicitly assumed that decisions concerning the location of firms and residents, inside and outside the urban area, are made as though all actors behaved in exactly the same way and with the same motivations. It is as if the "city" itself were an institutional decision maker. This simplification, however, does not correspond to reality. A city contains many different actors who pursue different objectives—some private, some collective—and whose behavior is often in conflict. Only in three limiting cases does a clear-cut trend emerge in the pattern of urban growth. The first of these limiting cases occurs when an overwhelming majority of actors converge toward similar individual objectives and find no constraints imposed by the behavior of the others. The second occurs when a large proportion of actors explicitly decides to interact to achieve most of their economic objectives and they therefore adopt some strategy of cooperation. The third case occurs when municipal administrations are ruled by an effective city management that is able to drive private and public decisionmakers toward relevant urban development projects (Bramezza 1996).

Concentrating this analysis on the behavior of just one set of these actors—firms—it may be argued that the combined effects of their strategies are important in explaining patterns of urban growth or decline, spatial concentration or decentralization, and the structure and ranking of urban hierarchies. In fact, the growth strategies of firms—initially formulated on an individual basis and then geared either toward cooperation or competition with other firms—imply different locational outcomes.

Three growth strategies may be pursued by a firm. First, a firm may decide to grow on the site which is its sole location. In this uniplant case, it will seek to attain plant scale economies, which, of course, coincide with the overall scale economies of the firm. The firm will not be likely to adopt any strategy of cooperation with other firms. This case is not a focus of interest for this chapter. Alternatively, the firm may decide to grow by spatially organizing its activity on a multiplant basis. The relevant consideration for the firm is to attain overall scale economies, but in most cases there is no guarantee that each plant will minimize its average costs and reach its long-run equilibrium position. As in the first case, the firm will pursue a noncooperative strategy with other firms, because the costs of organizing and coordinating its plants are lower than the transaction costs needed to interact with other firms. This case gives rise to an intrafirm network, the spatial effects of which have already been analyzed by Pred (1977). The analysis is relevant mostly to large multiplant firms, whose strategy is to capture external economies on a multiplicity of "local" input and output markets.[1] The third growth strategy is for the firm to decide to grow on a multiplant basis, but, aware of the increasing costs of internal organization and coordination, to seek to reduce these costs by externalizing some functions. To reduce the uncertainty of transaction costs and dependence on other decision makers, it will look for partners in the market with whom it will establish sufficiently stable relations. With the adoption of such cooperative strategies, the firm will try to interact in such a way as to minimize the sum of internal organization costs and transaction costs with other firms (Cappellin 1988; Johanson and Mattson 1987; Williamson 1990). The inevitable adjustment process is dynamic and evolves by means of successive steps. Figures 8.1, 8.2, and 8.3 show how these adjustments occur.

Figure 8.1 illustrates that a firm may always choose to carry on its activity either by internalizing all functions or by cooperating with other firms. If a firm chooses to act on its own, without cooperating with other firms, both with a uniplant and a multiplant structure, its internal organization and coordination costs will be maximized. These costs decrease as the firm develops cooperative strategies. At the same time, however, transaction costs—which are very low in the

Figure 8.1 OPTIMAL INTERNAL/EXTERNAL MIX OF ACTIVITIES

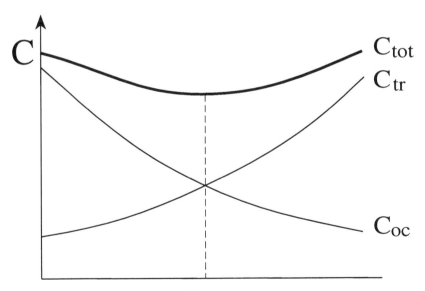

C_{tr} - TRANSACTION COSTS
C_{oc} - INTERNAL ORGANIZATION COSTS
C_{tot} - TOTAL TRANSACTION AND INTERNAL ORGANIZATION COSTS

Figure 8.2 OPTIMAL INTERNAL/EXTERNAL MIX OF ACTIVITIES AS RESULT OF "LEARNING BY INTERACTING"

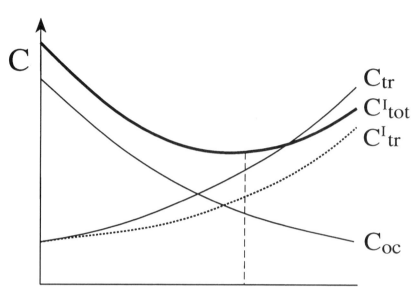

C_{tr} - TRANSACTION COSTS
C_{oc} - INTERNAL ORGANIZATION COSTS
C_{tot} - TOTAL TRANSACTION AND INTERNAL ORGANIZATION COSTS

absence of cooperation among firms—will increase toward a maximum, when the firm externalizes most of its activity. Even in the limiting case, however, in which a firm decides to be "self-sufficient," it will have to meet some transaction costs—for example, to buy some producer services from external supplies via market transactions. Similarly, in the other extreme case, in which a firm adopts a full cooperative strategy, it will always have to face some internal organization and coordination costs to interact with its partners. Generally speaking, all firms combine some internalization and externalization of their activities. At each combination they will have to face the sum of the relative costs. Rational behavior suggests that a firm will choose that mix of internalization and externalization of activity that minimizes the sum of relative costs.

Figure 8.2 shows a situation in which the firm has learned how to manage the relationships with other partners and has achieved the

Figure 8.3 OPTIMAL INTERNAL/EXTERNAL MIX OF ACTIVITIES: DIFFERENT
PATHS OF ADJUSTMENT

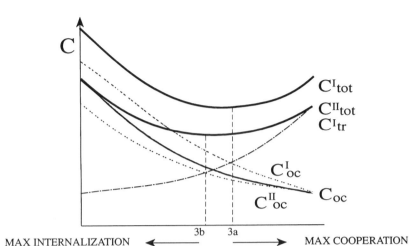

C^I_{tot}
C^{II}_{tot}
C^I_{tr}

C^I_{oc}

C^{II}_{oc} C_{oc}

3b   3a

MAX INTERNALIZATION $\longleftarrow$ $\longrightarrow$ MAX COOPERATION

C_{tr} - TRANSACTION COSTS
C_{oc} - INTERNAL ORGANIZATION COSTS
C_{tot} - TOTAL TRANSACTION AND INTERNAL ORGANIZATION COSTS

ability to select the most reliable ones. The curve of transaction costs
will be lower. The "optimal" mix of internalization and externalization will move toward the latter and produce a reduction of the sum
of average transaction and organization costs. However (see figure
8.3), the new situation may still be unstable. The externalization process may be pushed further, giving rise to costs of internal organization and coordination to control for the uncertainty caused by a higher
number of relationships with other partners. This leads to an increase
in the sum of average transaction and organization costs (figure 8.3,
situation *a*). Alternatively, the reaction to this situation may imply a
move by the firm toward greater internal control of its activity, to be
accomplished via a rationalization of its organization. This will lower
the relative curve (figure 8.3, situation *b*).

THE CONCEPT OF NETWORKING

The dynamic process driving firms to seek an appropriate mix of
internalization and externalization of their activity is unlikely to re-

sult in an optimal solution but, rather, in a limited set of "satisficing" solutions. To reduce the uncertainty linked to these solutions, firms try to stabilize relationships with the partners to whom they have decentralized some productive or service functions. The cyclical alternation of internalization and externalization patterns is of local sectoral specialization. Wherever this is high (in industrial districts, for example) there is a tendency towards the stabilization of "production networks" (Beyers and Lindahl 1996).

In fact, in this process, the usual flexible or "one-off" market relations change their nature into more stable contractual relations that are widely defined as "networks." The notion of networking now belongs to the common language, and a number of authors have stressed its analytical interest (Miles and Snow 1986). However, scientific contributions in this field are still fragmentary and somehow contradictory in the sense that the same term is used to refer to quite different phenomena. The concept of networking used in this chapter represents a choice more suited to locational strategies (Jarrillo 1988). The greater the awareness of the advantage for the firm, the more strategic is networking as a form of organizing and developing the firm's activity. Networking, then, can be defined as a way for a number of firms to organize their market relationships to develop their activities and, at the same time, stabilize their interaction with other counterparts. For example, the partners of a network may be motivated by a desire to benefit from the reciprocal capturing of external economies (estimated to be larger than the economies of scale of the individual firms); they may want to establish supplier-customer relations; they may want to develop technical cooperation, integrate production and distribution of goods and services, and exploit common financial resources to increase productivity, technical efficiency, or organizational flexibility (Krumme 1981); they may want to serve as an information channel (Lambooy 1986), to enter new markets, or to increase control and power (Håkansson 1987); or they may want to reduce uncertainty and risks (Giarini 1989) to allow for adjustments of strategies with lower time constraints. From the viewpoint of each partner in the network, these relationships are established to serve specific functions (Håkansson 1987).

NETWORKING STRATEGIES AND URBAN DECENTRALIZATION

The discussion of networks thus far has been entirely aspatial. But every firm experiences spatial implications as a result of any networking strategy it decides to pursue. Whether the outcome of these strategies is to produce urban centralization or decentralization is clearly the sum of a myriad of everyday decisions.

A correct evaluation of the spatial effects of networking strategies, however, requires the clarification of a few spatial concepts, delineated as follows. First, any decentralization process may be motivated alternatively by disagglomerative economic forces (push effect), or by the attractiveness of other locations (pull effect). Second, urban decentralization may be viewed as a loss of activities by one specific city, or as a trend to move, in general, from urban locations to non-urban (or rural) locations. In the first case, depending on the geographical scale of analysis, decentralization may either be a relocation toward other more distant cities (of the same or of a lower hierarchical level)—or a relocation toward nearby rural areas. In the second case, only the latter process is relevant. Decentralization of service activities usually falls in the first case; decentralization of factories in search of lower costs better exemplifies the second case. Third, the degree of decentralization induced by networking strategies is also a function of distance, where the concept of distance includes both geographical and cultural aspects. Transport and communication technologies now mean that mere geographical distance represents only a minor obstacle. Distance increasingly plays a frictional role with respect to networking strategies in terms of cultural (social and economic) affinity rather than physical affinity. Fourth, from the spatial point of view, the implementation of "networking" takes different forms. The simplest form is the opening of totally new plants. However, more frequently, it is a question of spatial restructuring of the firm, which, according to the firm's strategies, decentralizes some functions and keeps others highly centralized. Another way to establish a network is by linking units, formerly belonging to other firms, that become integrated into the sphere of action of the firm through acquisition or fusions. The most likely form of spatial network, however, is achieved by a variety of mechanisms, such as agreements, alliances, and joint ventures. Fifth, decentralization through networking strategies is a process that is differentiated by the nature of activity and the content of locational decision. Higher value-added functions (such as strategic management, marketing, and research and development) are less likely to be decentralized, whereas routine activities are more easily relocated.

Table 8.1 outlines firms' networking strategies and their expected effects on urban decentralization. Only one cell is filled in the first column of the table, relating to push effects. This reflects the fact that,

Table 8.1 NETWORKING STRATEGIES AND THEIR EFFECTS ON URBAN DECENTRALIZATION

Aims of networking strategies	Urban decentralization effects			
		Attractiveness effects (pull)		
	Deglomerative effects (push)	exerted by cities of higher hierarchical level (filtering up)	exerted by rural areas or by cities of lower hierarchical level (filtering down)	Nonforeseeable urban decentralization effects
Passive (defensive or adaptive) networking strategies	(1) Networks aimed at: reducing diseconomies of scale and/or external diseconomies			(4) Networks aimed at: • reducing uncertainty • searching for greater flexibilities • diversifying activity • tying up competitors to the firm
Active (growth oriented) networking strategies		(2) Networks aimed at: • developing or integrating service activities • management decentralization • conquering new product markets • "learning by interacting" • search for new external economies	(3) Networks aimed at: • subcontracting and franchising • inputs costs reduction • distribution and transport costs reduction • search for amenities • "environmental" scale economies	

consistent with the definition, there are no active networking strategies that generate disagglomeration; disagglomeration could only be caused by strategies aimed at reducing the emerging diseconomies of scale and/or external diseconomies due to congestion and strong local competition. In column 2, decentralization effects are seen as a consequence of the attraction exerted on the firm by the opportunity to have a presence—through other units of the network—in other cities or in lower levels of the spatial hierarchy (either in smaller cities or rural areas). In cell (2), urban decentralization takes the form of relocating or shifting of activities toward other urban places, even of a higher hierarchical order, giving rise to a sort of "filtering-up" process. For example, a metropolitan area may lose activities, in terms of both economic units and employment, as a consequence of establishing networks the control and coordination of which are set in other cities (say, from Milan to London or from Paris to New York). The rationale for this form of local decentralization may, for example, be due to the need to develop or integrate service activities in the sphere of action of the firm; or it may result from the decision to relocate some strategic management functions; or from the decision to introduce new products in highly concentrated markets; or from a search for new external economies, including those activities that produce "learning by interacting" (Lanlajainen and Stafford 1995).

Strictly speaking, urban decentralization occurs on a large scale only when activities move toward lower levels in the spatial hierarchy. Networking strategies, in this sense, are directed toward locating their main decision making in smaller cities or even in scarcely urbanized areas. This is shown in cell (3) of table 8.1. The aims of the network, in this case, appear to be the reorganization of activities through subcontracting and franchising. From this point of view, members of the network are more easily found where the social and family structure are characterized by "rural" origins, or traditional handicraft, or small-scale activities. In terms of Christallerian theory, this case is also described as a shift to lower-order centers.

Other networks likely to be attracted to these areas are those that aim at reducing input, distribution, or transport costs, and those that look for amenities offered by semirural areas. A good example of this pattern is provided by the phenomenon of Italian industrial districts that did not emerge in larger cities, but have found "environmental" scale economies in small towns, despite their orientation to international markets. The third column of table 8.1, cell (4), encompasses both active and passive networking strategies. This combination does not unambiguously predict decentralization patterns. Networks—the formation of which is designed to reduce uncertainty, gain greater flexibility, diversify activities, or "tie in" competitors to the firm— may be established equally well in the original urban location and in the decentralized areas.

CONCLUSIONS

Networking does play a role in urban decentralization, either when firms restructure part of their activities on a multiplant basis (intra-firm networking) or when independent firms establish permanent relationships, with the aim of benefiting from additional external economies without paying proportionally higher agglomeration costs (interfirm networking). The extent and intensity of this role depend on many factors and on the push-pull effects implicit in the complex strategies of the network members. But the contribution of the increasing use of networks to spatial redistribution is not limited to the shift of preexisting activities. The possibility of being connected through networks with the "rest of the world" allows for the birth and growth of new entrepreneurship in decentralized and peripheral areas. The alleged success of local endogenous growth models is but a small aspect of the growing evidence suggesting that networks deserve further attention in the future.

Note

1. A small firm may choose to grow without ever adopting a multiplant strategy, but, instead, may establish cooperative interrelationships with other firms that are engaged in the same function or phase of production (horizontal networks) or other functions or phases (vertical networks). In this case its development path will jump directly from the first growth strategy mentioned in the text to the third strategy.

References

Barbetta, G. P., and F. Silva. 1989. *Trasformazioni strutturali delle imprese italiane*. Bologna: Il Mulino.

Beckmann, M. J., and J. C. McPherson. 1970. "City Size Distribution in a Central Place Hierarchy: An Affirmative Approach." *Journal of Regional Science* 10(1): 25–33.

Beyers, W. B., and D. P. Lindahl. 1996. "Explaining the Demand for Producer Services: Is Cost-Driven Externalization the Major Factor?" *Papers in Regional Science* 75: 351–74.

Bramezza, I. 1996. "The Competitiveness of the European City and the Role of Urban Management in Improving the City's Performance." Tinbergen Institute Research Series 109.

Camagni, R. 1990. "Strutture urbane gerarchiche e reticolari: Verso una teorizzazione." In *Gerarchie e reti di città: tendenze e politiche*, edited by F. Curti and L. Diappi (49–70). Milan: Angeli.

Cappellin, R. 1988. "Transaction Costs and Urban Agglomeration." *Revue d'Economie Régionale et Urbaine*, no. 2.

Cheshire, P., and I. Gordon, eds. 1995. *Territorial Competition in an Integrating Europe*. Aldershot, England: Avebury.

Christaller, W. 1933. *Die zentralen Orte in Süddeutschland*. Darmstadt: Wissenschaftliche Buchgesellschaft. Translated as *Central Places in Southern Germany*. Englewood Cliffs, N.J.: Prentice-Hall, 1966.

Dematteis, G. 1990. "Modelli urbani e rete: considerazioni preliminari." In *Gerarchie e reti di città: tendenze e politiche*, edited by F. Curti and L. Diappi (27–48). Milan: Angeli.

Esparza, A., and A. J. Krmenec. 1994. "Business Services in the Space Economy: A Model of Spatial Interaction." *Papers in Regional Science* 73: 55–72.

————. 1996. "The Spatial Extent of Producer Service Markets: Hierarchical Models of Interaction Revisited." *Papers in Regional Science* 75: 375–96.

Evans, A. W. 1985. *Urban Economies*. Oxford, England: Basil Blackwell.

Fik, T. J., and G. F. Mulligan. 1990. "Spatial Flows and Competing Central Places: Towards a General Theory of Hierarchical Interaction." *Environment and Planning A* 22: 527–49.

Fothergill, S., and G. Gudgin. 1982. *Unequal Growth: Urban and Regional Unemployment Change in the UK*. London: Heinemann.

Fothergill, S., S. Monk, and M. Perry. 1987. *Property and Industrial Development*. London: Hutchinson.

Giarini, O. 1989. "The Service Economy and the Management of Risks." In *Strategic Trends in Service*, edited by A. Bressand and K. Nicolaidis. London: Harper and Row.

Håkansson, H. 1987. *Industrial Technological Development: A Network Approach*. London: Croom Helm.

Jarrillo, J. C. 1988. "On Strategic Networks." *Strategic Management Review*, no. 9.

Johanson, S., and L. G. Mattson. 1987. "Interorganizational Relations in Industrial Systems: A Network Approach Compared with the

Transaction-Costs Approach." *International Studies of Management and Organization*, no. 1.

Krumme, G. 1981. "Flexibility Views in Industrial Location and Location Decision Theory." In *Industrial Location and Regional Systems*, edited by G. Hewings and H. Stafford. New York: Bergin.

Lambooy, J. G. 1986. "Information and Internationalization: Dynamics of the Relations of Small and Medium Sized Enterprises in a Network Environment." *Revue d'Economie Régionale et Urbaine*, no. 5: 719–31.

Lanlajainen, R., and H. A. Stafford. 1995. *Corporate Geography: Business Location Principles and Cases*. Kluwer Academic Publishers.

Lösch, August. 1954. *The Economics of Location*. New Haven, Conn.: Yale University Press.

Massey, D. B., and R. A. Meegan. 1978. "Industrial Restructuring versus the City." *Urban Studies* 15: 273–86.

———. 1982. *The Anatomy of Job Loss: The How, Why, and Where of Employment Decline*. London: Methuen.

Miles, R. H., and C. C. Snow. 1986. "Organizations: New Concepts for the New Forms." *California Management Review* 28(3, Spring).

Pred, A. 1977. *City-Systems in Advanced Economies*. London: Hutchinson.

Scott, A. J. 1982. "Locational Patterns and Dynamics of Industrial Activities in the Modern Metropolis." *Urban Studies* 19.

Senn, L. 1993. "Service Activities, Urban Hierarchy, and Cumulative Growth." *The Service Industries Journal* 13: 11–22.

Williamson, O. E. 1990. "The Firm as a Nexus of Treaties: An Introduction." In *The Firm as a Nexus of Treaties*, edited by M. Aoki, B. Gustafsson, and O. E. Williamson (1–21). London: Sage Publications.

Chapter Nine

REGIONAL CHANGES IN URBAN AND METROPOLITAN POPULATION IN THE UNITED STATES

Charles L. Leven

In any discussion of strategy for metropolitan area economic development, it is important to note that although substantial demographic change in an individual metropolitan area can occur in a fairly short time frame, say within a single decade, changes in the metropolitan or urban distribution of an entire nation must be seen as evolving over a much broader sweep of time. Accordingly, policies affecting a single area may have fairly quick impacts, whereas those targeted to the metropolitan or urban environment in general will be felt over a longer term. Although this volume focuses on change since 1950, it is vital, at least for the United States, to view those changes in historical perspective. Establishing that perspective is the main purpose of this chapter.

Urban activity can be defined by high density of settlement, that is, people living closely together for the purpose of overcoming distance friction in socioeconomic interaction. This concept is more elusive than it may seem, depending on how one draws the boundaries (Leven 1991). I prefer to use the U.S. Census definition of *urban*: population in all incorporated areas—villages, towns, and cities; population in unincorporated communities of 2,500 or more inhabitants; and population in identifiable dense areas contiguous with incorporated areas. This has been the basis for formally defining "urban" population since the 1950 Census; figures for earlier periods also substantially conform to this definition.

Alternatively, one could characterize "urbanness" more functionally than geographically, according to the population scale at which interaction occurs. This definition corresponds more or less in the United States with the Bureau of the Census definition of *metropolitan*. Since 1950, standard metropolitan areas (SMAs) have included any county with an urban community of 50,000 or more (since 1980, the criteria have been somewhat looser), with surrounding counties meeting various criteria of interaction with the central county (U.S. Department of Commerce 1990). For periods before 1950, estimates by Leven and Sheppard (1982) are used, based on the 1950 conception.

These two concepts are neither consistent nor complementary. "Urban" excludes meaningfully interacting population on the fringes of settlement and, more important, it provides no basis for identifying the scale at which urban activity proceeds, since there is no operational rule for aggregating even abutting, much less proximate, separate incorporations. "Metropolitan," on the other hand, includes rural interstices. Of greater concern here, however, is that there is no basis for unambiguously defining the density at which a metropolitan area as a whole is settled, as opposed to some geographically arbitrary constituent part.

Various attempts have been made to describe the extent of urbanness by a joint scale-density distribution (e.g., Barr and Leven 1972), but they have failed to identify a monotonic or even nonambiguous metric. As we delimit urban areas more narrowly, we approach a uniform high-density distribution with a ceiling defined by household size and/or personal spatial occupancy; as we delimit more broadly, differentiation in density can be determined, but not scale. As we impose higher standards on including adjoining territory within metropolitan areas, observed scale will fall and calculated area density will rise; as we are more inclusive of what we regard as above-threshold interaction, observed scale will rise and density will fall.

Accordingly, this chapter separately examines changes in, and the regional distribution of, urban population from both an "urban" and a "metropolitan" standpoint. Currently in the United States the urban and metropolitan populations are about equal (see table 9.1), but historically this has not been so. Metropolitan population initially was much smaller than urban population, and did not exceed it until 1980. The apparent continuation of these trends suggests that metropolitan population may become increasingly greater than urban population as the entire population coalesces into a national metropolitan-regional system (see Leven 1979 for a discussion of the emergence of such a system). The analysis here looks at the regional distribution of urban and metropolitan population in terms of comparisons among the forty-nine states (including the District of Columbia) of the continental U.S. and among the nine multistate Census regions. I also examine the changing degree of concentration in the overall distributions by state. Finally, I identify and briefly comment on a variety of hypotheses that have been proposed to explain recent and earlier historical change.

Table 9.1 URBAN AND METROPOLITAN POPULATIONS IN THE UNITED STATES: 1790–1988

	Total Population		Urban Population			Metropolitan Population		
	Number (thousands)	Percentage Change[a]	Number (thousands)	Percentage Change[a]	Percentage of Total	Number (thousands)	Percentage Change[a]	Percentage of Total
1790	3,931	—	201	—	5.1	168	—	4.3
1800	5,310	35.1	322	60.2	6.1	214	27.4	4.0
1810	7,242	36.4	526	63.4	7.3	311	45.3	4.3
1820	9,636	33.1	693	31.7	7.2	402	29.3	4.2
1830	12,861	33.5	1,127	62.6	8.8	642	59.7	5.0
1840	17,063	32.7	1,846	63.8	10.8	1,033	60.9	6.1
1850	23,193	35.9	3,543	91.9	15.3	2,154	108.5	9.3
1860	31,443	35.6	6,219	75.5	19.8	4,382	103.4	13.9
1870	38,559	22.6	9,902	59.2	25.7	6,615	51.0	17.2
1880	50,158	30.1	14,132	42.7	28.2	9,496	43.6	18.9
1890	62,946	25.5	22,105	56.4	35.1	15,479	63.0	24.6
1900	75,997	20.7	30,158	36.4	39.7	22,780	47.2	30.0
1910	91,972	21.0	41,998	39.3	45.7	32,755	43.8	35.6
1920	105,408	14.6	54,157	29.0	51.4	43,760	33.6	41.5
1930	122,777	16.5	68,958	27.3	56.2	59,161	35.2	48.2
1940	131,669	7.2	74,422	7.9	56.5	67,123	13.5	51.0
1950	150,701	14.5	96,477	29.6	64.0	84,836	26.4	56.3
1960	178,463	18.4	124,700	29.3	69.9	112,386	32.5	63.0
1970	202,143	13.3	148,538	19.1	73.5	138,789	23.5	68.7
1980	225,185	11.4	165,958	11.7	73.7	168,490	21.4	74.8
1988	241,791	7.4	N.A.	N.A.	N.A.	184,339	9.4	76.2

[a]Rate of change per decade.
N.A. = data not available.

URBAN POPULATION

Perhaps the most obvious demographic fact concerning U.S. population is the enormous increase in its urban proportion over time, from about 5 percent of the total population in 1790 to about 74 percent in 1980, as shown in table 9.1 (1988 data for the metropolitan population are analyzed here, but post-1980 data for "urban" population were not available on a comprehensive basis until the detailed 1990 Census results—after this analysis was completed). On the other hand, the rate of urban expansion has been far from uniform. Urban agglomeration proceeded rapidly during the nation-building phase until the Civil War, with the exception of the troubled times of 1810–20. After the Civil War, there was a general fall in the growth rate until 1910, but for the next half-century the rate was remarkably close to 30 percent per decade, except for the 1930s with the sharp, depression-related drop in rural-urban migration (Alonso 1978).

Since 1970, however, there has been a marked alteration in historical trends not readily associated with megafactors like war or depression. The rate of increase of the urban population dropped by a third from the 1960s to the 1970s and by half again in the 1980s. Three-quarters of the U.S. population is now urban; however, it appears that the nation's urbanization is slowing down—note in table 9.1 that the overall percentage of urban population barely changed between 1970 and 1980, though there was a modest increase from 1980 to 1990.

Among individual states, trends in urbanization are much less clear; in many cases the urban proportion of the population has fallen from decade to decade, and it is hard to generalize as to overall trends. Nonetheless, certain aspects of the data in table 9.2 stand out. Note, for example, the slow pace of urbanization in the preindustrial decades; in 1790 only nine of the eighteen states whose territory was then in the Union had any urban population, and by 1820 no state was even one-fourth urban.

After 1820 the rate of urbanization picked up substantially, though almost entirely in northern as opposed to southern states. The one significantly urbanized southern state, Louisiana, showed periods of deurbanization as well as urbanization pre–Civil War, as southern ports lost out relative to the North. This is reflected in declines in the proportion of urban population in South Carolina (the port of Charleston) as early as the 1830s and again in the 1850s. The period of the Civil War and early postwar years—the 1860s—however, was generally one of urbanization nationwide.

The 1870s witnessed a drop in urban population in several western states (as early as the 1860s in Colorado and as late as the 1880s in Arizona and North Dakota and the 1890s in Nevada)—but as a consequence of a nonurban boom in cattle and sheep ranching and other farming rather than any deceleration in urban growth. The first three decades of the twentieth century were a period of increasing urbanization in all states in each decade (minor exceptions were mainly in a few Rocky Mountain states and in Delaware and Maryland in the 1920s).

The 1930s was a period of widespread deurbanization. The United States as a whole experienced the lowest growth rate in urban population of any decade in its history, with the proportion of urban population rising only from 56.2 percent to 56.5 percent over the ten years. Moreover, in seventeen states, all in the Northeast quadrant except Alabama, California, and Washington, there was an actual fall in the urban proportion of total population. In sharp contrast, the period from 1940 to 1970 saw urban growth that was as widespread as in the first thirty years of the century, with an overall urban growth rate almost as great and from a much larger base; only in New England was there any deurbanization pre-1970, mainly as a consequence of the post–World War II collapse of the textile industry and its relocation to the South.

In light of this record of urbanization in the twentieth century, the extensive deurbanization of the 1970s stands in sharp contrast. During that decade, seventeen states—as many as during the 1930s—saw a decline in the urban proportion of their populations, and the overall growth in U.S. urban population, at 11.7 percent, was lower than in any decade in history except the 7.9 percent growth during the Great Depression. Selected data for large cities for 1990 suggest that urban deintensification continued into the 1980s, though the still unresolved issue of undercounting of minorities in central cities mars careful comparisons of 1980 and 1990.

With some time lag, there are indications that similar deintensification has occurred in European Community countries (ben Abdallah and Leven 1989). Of course, many others have earlier noted the occurrence of sharp demographic change beginning around 1970 (e.g., Alonso 1978; Macrae 1978; Sternlieb and Hughes 1975), but how drastic the change was seems that much clearer when viewed in even longer term historical perspective.

These changes are also manifest at the level of the nine broad Census regions, as indicated in table 9.3. In general, all of the regions showed increasing urbanization, with three important exceptions.

Table 9.2 PERCENTAGE POPULATION IN U.S. URBAN AREAS, BY STATE: 1790–1980

	1790	1800	1810	1820	1830	1840	1850	1860	1870	1880	1890	1900	1910	1920	1930	1940	1950	1960	1970	1980
Alabama	0.0	0.0	0.0	0.0	1.0	2.2	4.5	5.1	6.3	5.5	10.0	11.9	17.3	21.7	28.1	30.2	43.8	54.9	58.4	60.1
Arizona	0.0	0.0	0.0	0.0	0.0	0.0	0.0	0.0	30.0	17.5	9.1	15.4	30.9	36.2	34.4	34.9	55.5	74.6	79.6	83.8
Arkansas	0.0	0.0	0.0	0.0	0.0	0.0	0.0	0.9	2.5	4.0	6.5	8.5	12.9	16.6	20.7	22.2	33.0	42.8	50.0	51.6
California	0.0	0.0	0.0	0.0	0.0	0.0	7.5	20.8	37.1	42.9	48.6	52.3	61.7	67.9	73.3	71.0	80.7	86.4	90.9	91.3
Colorado	0.0	0.0	0.0	0.0	0.0	0.0	0.0	14.7	12.5	31.4	45.0	48.3	50.3	48.2	50.2	52.6	62.7	73.7	78.5	80.6
Connecticut	2.9	5.2	6.1	7.6	9.4	12.6	15.9	26.5	33.0	41.9	50.9	59.9	65.7	67.8	70.4	67.8	77.7	78.3	77.3	78.8
Washington, D.C.	0.0	75.0	86.7	91.3	90.0	91.2	92.3	93.3	91.7	89.9	100.0	100.0	100.0	100.0	100.0	100.0	100.0	100.0	100.0	100.0
Delaware	0.0	0.0	0.0	0.0	0.0	10.3	15.2	18.8	24.8	33.3	42.3	46.5	48.0	54.3	51.7	52.1	62.6	65.7	72.3	70.5
Florida	0.0	0.0	0.0	0.0	0.0	0.0	0.0	4.3	8.0	10.0	19.7	20.2	29.1	36.6	51.8	55.1	65.5	73.9	80.5	84.3
Georgia	0.0	3.1	2.0	2.3	2.7	3.6	4.3	7.1	8.4	9.4	14.0	15.6	20.7	25.1	30.8	34.4	45.3	55.3	60.3	62.4
Idaho	0.0	0.0	0.0	0.0	0.0	0.0	0.0	0.0	0.0	0.0	0.0	6.2	21.5	27.5	29.2	33.7	43.0	47.5	54.0	54.0
Illinois	0.0	0.0	0.0	0.0	0.0	2.1	7.5	14.4	23.5	30.6	44.9	54.3	61.7	67.9	73.9	73.6	77.6	80.7	83.0	83.3
Indiana	0.0	0.0	0.0	0.0	0.0	1.6	4.6	8.6	14.8	19.5	26.9	34.3	42.4	50.6	55.4	55.1	59.9	62.4	64.9	64.2
Iowa	0.0	0.0	0.0	0.0	0.0	0.0	5.2	8.9	13.1	15.2	21.2	25.6	30.6	36.4	39.6	42.7	47.7	53.0	57.2	58.6
Kansas	0.0	0.0	0.0	0.0	0.0	0.0	0.0	9.3	14.3	10.5	18.9	22.4	29.1	34.8	38.8	41.9	52.1	61.0	66.1	66.7
Kentucky	0.0	0.0	1.0	1.6	2.3	4.0	7.5	10.5	14.8	15.2	19.2	21.8	24.2	26.2	30.6	29.8	37.1	44.5	52.3	50.9
Louisiana	0.0	0.0	22.1	17.6	21.3	29.8	25.9	26.1	27.9	25.4	25.4	26.5	30.0	34.9	39.7	41.5	54.8	63.3	66.1	68.6
Maine	0.0	2.6	3.1	3.0	3.3	7.8	13.6	16.6	21.1	22.7	28.1	33.6	35.3	39.1	40.4	40.5	51.6	51.3	50.8	47.5
Maryland	4.4	7.9	12.3	16.2	20.4	24.3	32.2	33.9	37.8	40.2	47.6	49.7	50.8	59.9	59.7	59.3	69.0	72.7	76.6	80.3
Massachusetts	13.5	15.4	21.4	22.8	31.1	37.8	50.7	59.5	66.7	74.7	82.0	86.0	89.0	90.1	90.1	89.4	84.4	83.6	84.5	83.8
Michigan	0.0	0.0	0.0	0.0	0.0	0.0	7.3	13.4	20.1	24.7	34.9	39.3	47.2	61.1	68.2	65.7	70.7	73.4	73.8	70.7
Minnesota	0.0	0.0	0.0	0.0	0.0	0.0	0.0	9.3	16.1	19.1	33.8	34.2	40.9	44.1	49.1	49.8	54.5	62.2	66.4	66.9
Mississippi	0.0	0.0	0.0	0.0	2.2	1.1	1.8	2.7	4.0	3.1	5.4	7.7	11.5	13.4	16.9	19.8	27.9	37.7	44.5	47.3

Missouri	0.0	0.0	0.0	3.6	4.2	11.9	17.2	25.0	25.2	32.0	36.3	42.3	46.6	51.2	51.8	61.5	66.6	70.1	68.1
Montana	0.0	0.0	0.0	0.0	0.0	0.0	0.0	14.3	17.9	27.3	35.0	35.4	31.3	33.6	37.9	43.7	50.1	53.5	52.9
New Hampshire	3.5	2.7	3.3	4.8	10.2	17.0	22.1	26.1	30.0	39.3	46.6	51.7	56.4	58.7	57.5	57.6	58.3	56.4	52.1
New Jersey	0.0	0.0	2.9	5.6	10.7	17.6	32.7	43.7	54.4	62.6	70.5	76.4	79.9	82.6	81.6	86.6	88.6	88.9	89.0
New Mexico	0.0	0.0	0.0	0.0	0.0	8.1	5.3	5.4	5.8	6.3	13.8	14.4	18.1	25.3	33.1	50.2	65.8	69.8	72.0
New York	11.5	12.7	12.6	15.0	19.4	28.2	39.3	49.9	56.4	65.1	72.9	78.9	82.7	83.6	82.8	85.5	85.4	85.6	84.6
Nebraska	0.0	0.0	0.0	0.0	0.0	0.0	0.0	17.9	13.5	27.5	23.7	26.1	31.3	35.3	39.1	46.9	54.3	61.6	62.9
Nevada	0.0	0.0	0.0	0.0	0.0	0.0	0.0	16.7	30.6	34.0	16.7	15.9	19.5	37.4	39.1	57.5	70.5	80.8	85.4
North Carolina	0.0	0.0	2.0	1.4	1.7	2.4	2.5	3.4	3.9	7.2	9.9	14.4	21.7	25.6	27.3	33.7	39.6	45.0	48.0
North Dakota	0.0	0.0	0.0	0.0	0.0	0.0	0.0	0.0	8.1	5.8	7.2	9.9	13.6	16.6	20.6	26.6	35.3	44.2	48.7
Ohio	0.0	0.0	1.3	3.9	5.5	12.2	17.1	25.6	32.2	41.1	48.1	55.9	63.8	67.8	66.8	70.2	73.4	75.3	73.3
Oklahoma	0.0	0.0	0.0	0.0	0.0	0.0	0.0	0.0	0.0	3.5	7.3	19.3	26.5	34.3	37.7	51.0	62.9	68.0	67.3
Oregon	0.0	0.0	0.0	0.0	0.0	0.0	5.8	8.8	14.9	27.7	32.1	45.6	49.8	51.4	48.8	53.8	62.2	67.1	67.9
Pennsylvania	10.1	11.3	12.8	15.3	17.9	23.6	30.8	37.3	41.6	48.6	54.7	60.4	65.0	67.8	66.5	70.5	71.6	71.5	69.3
Rhode Island	18.8	20.3	22.9	30.9	44.0	55.4	63.4	74.7	81.9	85.3	88.1	91.2	91.9	92.4	91.6	84.2	86.5	87.1	87.0
South Carolina	6.4	5.5	6.0	5.9	5.7	7.3	7.0	8.6	7.5	10.1	12.8	14.9	17.5	21.3	24.5	36.8	41.2	47.5	54.1
South Dakota	0.0	0.0	0.0	0.0	0.0	0.0	0.0	0.0	7.1	8.3	10.2	13.0	16.0	18.9	24.6	33.2	39.2	44.6	46.5
Tennessee	0.0	0.0	0.0	0.9	0.8	2.2	4.2	7.5	7.5	13.5	16.2	20.2	26.1	34.3	35.2	44.1	52.3	58.7	60.4
Texas	0.0	0.0	0.0	0.0	0.0	3.8	4.5	6.7	9.2	15.7	17.1	24.1	32.4	41.0	45.4	62.7	75.0	79.7	79.6
Utah	0.0	0.0	0.0	0.0	0.0	0.0	20.0	18.4	23.6	35.5	37.9	46.4	48.1	52.4	55.5	65.3	74.9	80.4	84.4
Vermont	0.0	0.0	0.0	0.0	0.0	1.9	1.9	6.9	9.9	15.4	22.1	23.1	31.3	33.1	34.3	36.5	38.5	32.2	33.9
Virginia	1.7	2.6	3.6	4.8	6.9	8.0	9.5	11.9	12.5	15.4	22.1	23.1	29.2	32.5	35.3	47.0	55.6	63.1	66.0
Washington	0.0	0.0	0.0	0.0	0.0	0.0	0.0	0.0	9.3	35.6	40.7	53.1	54.8	56.6	53.1	63.2	68.1	72.6	73.5
West Virginia	0.0	0.0	0.0	0.0	0.0	3.6	5.3	8.1	8.7	10.6	13.0	18.7	25.2	28.5	28.1	34.6	38.2	38.9	36.2
Wisconsin	0.0	0.0	0.0	0.0	0.0	9.5	14.4	19.6	24.1	33.2	38.2	43.0	47.3	52.9	53.5	57.9	63.8	65.9	64.2
Wyoming	0.0	0.0	0.0	0.0	0.0	0.0	0.0	0.0	28.6	33.3	29.0	29.5	29.4	31.0	37.5	49.8	57.0	60.5	62.8

Table 9.3 PERCENTAGE POPULATION IN U.S. URBAN AREAS, BY REGION: 1790–1980

	1790	1800	1810	1820	1830	1840	1850	1860	1870	1880	1890	1900	1910	1920	1930	1940	1950	1960	1970	1980
New England	7.5	8.2	10.1	10.5	14.0	19.4	28.7	36.6	44.4	52.5	61.6	68.6	73.4	75.9	77.3	76.1	76.2	76.4	76.4	75.1
Middle Atlantic	8.7	10.2	11.5	11.3	14.2	18.1	25.5	35.4	44.2	50.2	58.0	65.2	71.2	75.4	77.7	76.8	80.5	81.4	81.7	80.6
East North Central	0.0	0.0	1.1	1.3	2.5	3.9	9.0	14.1	21.6	27.5	37.9	45.2	52.7	60.8	66.4	65.5	69.7	73.0	74.8	73.3
West North Central	0.0	0.0	0.0	0.0	3.6	3.7	10.3	13.3	19.0	18.2	25.8	28.5	33.2	37.7	41.8	44.3	52.0	58.8	63.7	63.9
South Atlantic	2.3	3.4	4.6	5.5	6.2	7.7	9.8	11.5	14.4	14.9	19.5	21.4	25.4	31.7	36.1	38.8	49.0	57.2	63.7	67.1
East South Central	0.0	0.0	0.6	0.8	1.5	2.1	4.2	5.9	8.8	8.4	12.7	15.0	18.7	22.4	28.1	29.4	39.2	48.4	54.6	55.7
West South Central	0.0	0.0	21.8	16.2	19.9	26.2	18.8	14.9	15.8	13.6	16.8	17.8	24.2	31.1	39.3	43.1	60.5	73.8	78.0	78.3
Mountain	0.0	0.0	0.0	0.0	0.0	0.0	6.8	10.3	12.3	21.6	29.2	32.3	35.9	36.5	39.4	42.7	54.9	67.1	73.1	76.4
Pacific	0.0	0.0	0.0	0.0	0.0	0.0	6.6	18.5	32.0	36.2	42.6	46.4	56.8	62.2	67.6	65.3	75.0	81.7	86.5	86.9

First, the West South Central region showed erratic trends in urbanization during several decades of the nineteenth century. Some of this shifting may have been associated with territorial expansion—for example, the annexation of Texas during the 1840s—but the shifting continued after the region's boundaries had stabilized. Second, deurbanization occurred in four of the nine Census regions during the 1930s, but these regions include only those in the Northeast (New England, Middle Atlantic, and East North Central combined) and the Pacific Coast. Third, deurbanization emerges again only in the 1970s. Although several individual states outside the Northeast had declining urban proportions during the 1970s—Delaware, Kentucky, Missouri, Montana, Oklahoma, and Texas—on a regional basis there was a falling urban proportion only in the Northeast, though in all three of its component regions.

METROPOLITAN POPULATION

The figures for urban population in tables 9.2 and 9.3 are compiled directly from data on urban population by state from the U.S. Census for the appropriate years, but the sources of the corresponding estimates for metropolitan population in tables 9.4 and 9.5 need explaining.

The data for 1950 through 1988 are from the Census, though it should be noted that a conceptual change in definition did occur during that period. At the beginning of Census use of the SMA concept in 1950, an SMA had to have at least one central city of 50,000 or greater. Beginning in 1960, SMAs were allowed for "twin cities" totaling 50,000, even though neither legal entity alone had that many—Champaign-Urbana, Illinois, was the first example. Beginning in 1980, SMAs were allowed without respect to any particular central-city size, so long as the central county had a core of sufficient population meeting scale, density, and interaction criteria—Nassau-Suffolk Counties, New York (Long Island outside New York City) was the first example of a Census-designated SMA with no central city.

For 1890 through 1940 the metropolitan population figures are those estimated in an earlier study (Leven and Sheppard 1982). The estimating procedure used there was, briefly, as follows. Any of the Census-designated areas for 1950 which in 1940 did not have a central city of 50,000 or more were eliminated from the list for 1940. Of the remaining areas, those that were single-county SMAs in 1950 were designated as the same counties in 1940. For multicounty areas,

Table 9.4 PERCENTAGE POPULATION IN U.S. METROPOLITAN AREAS, BY STATE: 1790–1988

	1790	1800	1810	1820	1830	1840	1850	1860	1870	1880	1890	1900	1910	1920	1930	1940	1950	1960	1970	1980	1988
Alabama	0.0	0.0	0.0	0.0	0.0	0.0	0.0	0.0	0.0	0.0	0.0	0.0	14.4	17.5	24.5	26.5	34.7	45.5	52.3	62.0	63.8
Arizona	0.0	0.0	0.0	0.0	0.0	0.0	0.0	0.0	0.0	0.0	0.0	0.0	0.0	0.0	0.0	39.3	44.3	71.4	74.5	75.1	76.2
Arkansas	0.0	0.0	0.0	0.0	0.0	0.0	0.0	0.0	0.0	0.0	0.0	0.0	0.0	6.2	7.4	8.0	10.3	19.1	30.9	39.2	40.1
California	0.0	0.0	0.0	0.0	0.0	0.0	0.0	15.0	26.6	27.1	34.1	36.6	51.6	61.0	75.3	77.1	80.2	86.5	92.7	94.9	95.6
Colorado	0.0	0.0	0.0	0.0	0.0	0.0	0.0	0.0	0.0	0.0	32.0	28.3	26.7	27.2	30.0	40.5	48.7	68.0	71.7	80.9	77.3
Connecticut	0.0	0.0	0.0	0.0	0.0	0.0	0.0	21.1	22.7	25.2	25.3	31.1	33.5	36.0	53.1	60.3	69.5	77.6	82.6	88.3	92.5
Washington, D.C.	0.0	0.0	0.0	0.0	0.0	0.0	76.9	81.3	82.6	82.6	100.0	100.0	100.0	100.0	100.0	100.0	100.0	100.0	100.0	100.0	100.0
Delaware	0.0	0.0	0.0	0.0	0.0	0.0	0.0	0.0	0.0	0.0	57.7	59.5	60.9	66.4	67.6	67.4	68.9	68.8	70.4	67.0	66.5
Florida	0.0	0.0	0.0	0.0	0.0	0.0	0.0	0.0	0.0	0.0	0.0	0.0	10.0	20.9	35.1	39.5	47.7	65.6	68.6	87.9	90.1
Georgia	0.0	0.0	0.0	0.0	0.0	0.0	0.0	0.0	0.0	0.0	4.6	8.5	9.9	17.0	23.0	27.8	35.8	46.0	49.7	60.0	64.7
Idaho	0.0	0.0	0.0	0.0	0.0	0.0	0.0	0.0	0.0	0.0	0.0	0.0	0.0	0.0	0.0	0.0	0.0	0.0	15.7	18.3	19.2
Illinois	0.0	0.0	0.0	0.0	0.0	0.0	0.0	8.5	13.8	19.7	35.7	45.1	53.4	59.2	67.7	68.4	72.1	76.9	80.1	81.0	82.5
Indiana	0.0	0.0	0.0	0.0	0.0	0.0	0.0	0.0	4.3	5.2	10.5	12.0	23.5	32.3	38.1	39.9	44.6	48.1	61.9	69.8	68.5
Iowa	0.0	0.0	0.0	0.0	0.0	0.0	0.0	0.0	0.0	0.0	5.9	6.1	7.5	15.9	20.4	24.5	26.9	33.2	35.6	40.1	43.8
Kansas	0.0	0.0	0.0	0.0	0.0	0.0	0.0	0.0	0.0	0.0	3.8	5.0	10.2	10.3	19.2	22.9	29.1	37.4	42.2	46.8	51.2
Kentucky	0.0	0.0	0.0	0.0	0.0	0.0	6.1	7.7	9.0	8.9	10.2	13.8	14.5	14.9	20.0	20.9	27.7	34.1	40.0	44.5	45.6
Louisiana	0.0	0.0	22.1	17.6	13.9	29.0	22.4	23.9	26.3	23.0	22.8	21.9	21.6	22.7	29.7	29.4	38.0	50.0	54.8	63.4	69.2
Maine	0.0	0.0	0.0	0.0	0.0	0.0	0.0	0.0	0.0	0.0	0.0	9.4	10.4	11.8	12.5	12.6	13.1	19.7	21.6	33.0	35.4
Maryland	4.4	7.9	12.3	15.5	18.1	21.7	29.0	30.9	34.2	35.5	48.7	50.5	52.5	55.8	60.7	69.3	76.5	78.2	84.3	88.8	91.1
Massachusetts	11.9	6.6	7.2	8.4	10.2	13.0	14.6	29.2	45.6	73.7	45.6	72.6	77.3	79.8	80.4	80.6	81.7	85.2	84.7	85.3	89.5
Michigan	0.0	0.0	0.0	0.0	0.0	0.0	0.0	10.1	10.1	10.1	19.5	21.6	30.7	49.0	63.0	62.9	67.9	73.1	76.7	82.7	80.1
Minnesota	0.0	0.0	0.0	0.0	0.0	0.0	0.0	0.0	0.0	14.5	24.8	27.5	34.7	36.3	39.4	40.3	44.4	51.3	56.9	64.6	66.3
Mississippi	0.0	0.0	0.0	0.0	0.0	0.0	0.0	0.0	0.0	0.0	0.0	0.0	0.0	0.0	0.0	4.9	6.5	8.6	17.7	27.1	29.9
Missouri	0.0	0.0	0.0	0.0	0.0	0.0	11.4	13.6	18.1	19.9	27.7	31.1	35.6	39.9	47.1	46.3	52.6	57.9	64.1	65.3	65.2

State																			
Montana	0.0	0.0	0.0	0.0	0.0	0.0	0.0	0.0	0.0	0.0	0.0	0.0	0.0	0.0	0.0	22.5	24.4	24.0	24.8
New Hampshire	0.0	0.0	0.0	0.0	0.0	0.0	0.0	0.0	0.0	14.6	16.9	18.1	17.4	16.7	16.5	17.8	27.4	50.7	44.9
New Jersey	0.0	0.0	0.0	0.0	15.1	14.7	30.1	39.4	71.3	77.5	79.5	83.5	83.5	91.2	89.9	78.9	76.9	91.4	95.6
New Mexico	0.0	0.0	0.0	0.0	0.0	0.0	0.0	0.0	0.0	0.0	0.0	0.0	0.0	0.0	21.4	27.5	31.1	42.2	47.1
New York	9.7	10.0	13.1	17.2	28.9	39.1	44.9	49.7	55.5	67.9	71.9	75.7	82.2	83.8	84.0	85.5	86.5	90.1	90.5
Nebraska	0.0	0.0	0.0	0.0	0.0	0.0	0.0	0.0	14.9	13.2	14.2	22.5	24.2	26.5	31.4	37.6	42.8	44.1	46.7
Nevada	0.0	0.0	0.0	0.0	0.0	0.0	0.0	0.0	0.0	0.0	0.0	0.0	0.0	0.0	0.0	74.4	80.6	82.1	81.4
North Carolina	0.0	0.0	0.0	0.0	0.0	0.0	0.0	0.0	0.0	0.0	0.0	0.0	20.0	20.5	22.1	24.6	37.3	52.7	55.1
North Dakota	0.0	0.0	0.0	0.0	0.0	0.0	0.0	0.0	0.0	0.0	0.0	0.0	0.0	0.0	0.0	10.6	12.0	35.8	37.4
Ohio	0.0	0.0	5.5	5.3	7.9	12.6	14.7	20.8	28.9	32.5	42.2	56.0	61.9	63.5	69.0	69.5	77.7	80.3	78.8
Oklahoma	0.0	0.0	0.0	0.0	0.0	0.0	0.0	0.0	0.0	0.0	5.1	11.1	17.1	18.7	25.8	43.9	50.1	58.5	55.8
Oregon	0.0	0.0	0.0	0.0	0.0	0.0	0.0	0.0	0.0	29.7	38.0	39.6	40.3	37.8	40.8	50.4	61.3	64.9	57.7
Pennsylvania	6.7	6.8	5.9	5.5	11.2	25.6	29.4	30.2	49.8	57.0	65.6	71.1	66.8	74.9	78.0	77.9	79.4	81.9	84.1
Rhode Island	0.0	0.0	0.0	53.2	59.5	61.7	68.7	71.5	75.7	81.8	83.2	83.4	86.5	87.4	85.1	86.3	84.7	92.2	90.8
South Carolina	18.9	15.2	14.8	14.0	10.9	9.9	12.6	10.3	9.9	8.8	8.0	9.1	13.6	14.5	25.0	32.2	39.3	59.7	60.0
South Dakota	0.0	0.0	0.0	0.0	0.0	0.0	0.0	0.0	0.0	0.0	0.0	0.0	0.0	0.0	10.9	12.8	14.3	15.8	27.9
Tennessee	0.0	0.0	0.0	0.0	0.0	0.0	0.0	0.0	12.5	13.7	15.6	23.0	33.0	34.3	41.0	45.8	48.9	62.8	65.5
Texas	0.0	0.0	0.0	0.0	0.0	0.0	0.0	0.0	0.0	2.3	12.3	18.3	28.9	35.5	47.2	63.4	73.5	80.0	80.8
Utah	0.0	0.0	0.0	0.0	0.0	0.0	0.0	0.0	0.0	28.2	35.1	35.4	38.2	38.5	52.0	67.5	77.6	79.0	77.1
Vermont	0.0	0.0	0.0	0.0	0.0	0.0	0.0	0.0	0.0	0.0	0.0	0.0	0.0	0.0	0.0	0.0	0.0	22.3	22.3
Virginia	0.0	0.0	0.0	0.0	0.0	5.0	5.4	5.5	5.3	12.4	14.7	21.3	24.7	27.6	36.5	50.9	61.2	69.6	70.4
Washington	0.0	0.0	0.0	0.0	0.0	0.0	0.0	0.0	0.0	21.2	47.7	49.7	49.8	52.0	55.3	63.1	66.0	80.4	80.7
West Virginia	0.0	0.0	0.0	0.0	0.0	0.0	0.0	0.0	0.0	0.0	0.0	8.8	18.6	25.6	31.9	30.9	31.3	37.1	36.8
Wisconsin	0.0	0.0	0.0	0.0	0.0	8.0	8.5	10.5	13.9	17.7	20.6	25.4	35.3	35.1	39.9	46.3	57.6	66.8	60.2
Wyoming	0.0	0.0	0.0	0.0	0.0	0.0	0.0	0.0	0.0	0.0	0.0	0.0	0.0	0.0	0.0	0.0	0.0	15.3	29.8

Sources: See text for explanation.

Table 9.5 PERCENTAGE POPULATION IN U.S. METROPOLITAN AREAS, BY REGION: 1790–1988

	1790	1800	1810	1820	1830	1840	1850	1860	1870	1880	1890	1900	1910	1920	1930	1940	1950	1960	1970	1980	1988
New England	4.5	2.3	2.3	2.7	3.2	6.9	8.5	18.0	26.8	41.6	31.3	50.0	54.6	57.4	61.8	63.1	65.6	70.3	72.1	76.6	78.8
Middle Atlantic	6.5	7.3	7.4	7.0	9.2	11.3	20.8	31.6	37.2	40.6	55.0	64.7	70.4	75.0	76.7	81.7	82.9	81.8	82.4	87.7	90.6
East North Central	0.0	0.0	0.0	0.0	3.5	2.7	3.5	8.3	11.2	15.0	24.5	29.5	38.4	48.8	57.7	58.4	63.2	67.1	73.9	78.1	76.6
West North Central	0.0	0.0	0.0	0.0	0.0	0.0	8.9	7.4	8.1	8.9	15.6	17.4	20.6	24.6	29.5	31.5	36.6	43.3	48.5	53.3	55.8
South Atlantic	3.3	3.7	4.1	4.7	4.6	4.7	6.0	7.5	9.1	8.8	12.6	14.6	15.5	20.9	29.2	36.7	44.1	50.2	57.7	70.4	73.1
East South Central	0.0	0.0	0.0	0.0	0.0	0.0	1.8	2.2	4.4	4.0	6.4	7.6	11.7	14.7	20.6	22.8	29.4	36.0	42.2	51.9	54.1
West South Central	0.0	0.0	21.8	16.2	12.2	22.7	12.3	9.7	9.4	6.5	5.4	5.7	10.5	15.6	23.4	27.3	37.4	53.5	62.7	70.4	72.2
Mountain	0.0	0.0	0.0	0.0	0.0	0.0	0.0	0.0	0.0	0.0	10.9	13.8	13.1	12.4	13.6	20.8	29.2	48.8	56.9	63.1	64.5
Pacific	0.0	0.0	0.0	0.0	0.0	0.0	0.0	12.8	22.1	21.0	21.9	32.1	48.4	55.3	66.4	68.2	72.0	80.1	86.6	90.4	90.7

Sources: See text for explanation.

certain counties designated as outlying counties within SMAs in 1950 were dropped from the designated area in 1940 in cases where their rate of population growth between 1940 and 1950 was sufficiently great, or the absolute level of their 1940 population was sufficiently small, to suggest that a critical level of interdependence with the central county had emerged post-1940. The critical size and growth parameters were estimated from a probit regression relating the probability of addition of an outlying county to its lagged size and growth, based on actual observations of counties added over the 1950–80 period. The definitions for 1930 were derived from those for 1940 in the same way, and so on back to 1890. Compared with over 300 SMAs in 1980 and 121 in 1950, there were only 39 in 1890.

For 1880 and earlier, an even simpler procedure was followed. First, in recognition that the development of intrametropolitan transport systems did not really begin until after 1880 (Holt 1975), no SMA (except New York City) could consist of more than the single central county, including its central city. Second, at progressively earlier periods, lower cutoffs for allowable central-city size were employed: 45,000 for 1880; falling by 5,000 each decade to 20,000 in 1830 and 1820; 15,000 in 1810 and 1800; and 10,000 in 1790. The consideration for choosing this sequence of cutoffs was that it had to be sufficiently large in 1790 to include the major port cities—Philadelphia, New York, Boston, Baltimore, and Charleston—and to grow at first slowly, then after 1830, when urbanization began to take hold, by a constant amount per decade to converge on 50,000 in 1890.

The main conclusion to be drawn from table 9.4 is that metropolitanization (the building of large-scale transactor communities) came later than urbanization (living at high residential densities) but developed more rapidly. Outside of the vacillating metropolitan fortunes of Louisiana and South Carolina before and after the Civil War and of Pennsylvania early in the 19th century, there are not many exceptions to the general trend of increasing metropolitanization until the very recent post-1980 period.

It should be emphasized that in 1860, on the eve of the Civil War (when all of the present states' territories were within the country), only eighteen states had any metropolitan population at all—only three of these states were in the South—and only a handful were more than a quarter metropolitanized. The Civil War period showed increased metropolitanization in all eighteen states by the end of the decade, and the rest of the century showed increasingly widespread metropolitanizing in general (note that the series for Massachusetts is not comparable for 1880 and 1890 because of a shift from county to town definitions of SMAs). By 1900, thirty-three states had some SMA population, and in sixteen states the SMA population was more than a quarter of total state population (see table 9.4). As was true earlier in the century, Louisiana and South Carolina were the only major exceptions to the trend.

The trend toward metropolitan life intensified even further in the early decades of the twentieth century. Only Louisiana, South Carolina, and Colorado continued to lose relatively through 1910 (Colorado, likely owing to the exhaustion of silver mining), and by the 1920s every state experienced an increase in metropolitan intensity. By the end of the 1920s, thirty-nine states had some SMA population. Although the rate of population growth in the 1930s did slow up considerably, SMAs nationwide were still growing much faster than either total or urban population, and only four states showed a drop in their SMA percentage during the decade (see table 9.4).

After the Great Depression the rate of SMA population growth picked up, but has never regained levels as high as those in the preceding one hundred years. Through 1970, however, this somewhat slower rate of growth was widespread. Except for some blips in Delaware (with only three counties in the state, it is very sensitive to change) and what looks like a single quirk in Montana, all other drops in SMA percentage were in New England (see table 9.4). It should be noted that during the 1970s in particular, although total SMA growth had eased off to 21 percent, it was still about twice the growth rate of the total population; for the first time, every state had some SMA population (Vermont and Wyoming were the last holdouts), and all states except Delaware and Montana had an increasing proportion of metropolitan residents.

Again, it is against this background that the 1980s present such a distinct contrast. Metropolitan population growth dropped nationally from 21 percent per decade in the 1970s to only 12 percent for the 1980s, whereas total population growth fell only from 11 percent to 7 percent between the two decades. The metropolitan growth rate exceeded the growth rate for total population by a smaller margin than at any time since the 1810s. In no decade preceding the 1980s had more than four states showed an interdecadal drop in the SMA percentage of population. Through the mid-1980s, twelve states—Colorado, Indiana, Michigan, New Hampshire, Nevada, Ohio, Oklahoma, Oregon, Rhode Island, Utah, West Virginia, and Wisconsin (table 9.4), showed a drop and they were spread over many regions, but by 1990 only two states—Montana and Utah—had lower metropolitan percentages than in 1980.

The widespread nature of the slow-up in metropolitanization is reflected in only one of the nine Census regions—East North Central, which showed a drop in SMA percentage overall during the 1980s, as indicated in table 9.5. Nevertheless, in the other eight regions the increase in SMA proportion was quite small by historic standards. None showed an increase of *more than* 3 percentage points; yet as recently as the 1970s, none of these eight regions had showed an increase of *less than* almost 5 percentage points. It seems likely that this means that the relative slowdown in urbanization that began in the 1970s may have intensified during the 1980s, but not necessarily, since it is a metric of density while SMA proportion is a measure of scale.

CHANGING GEOGRAPHIC DISTRIBUTION

Until 1850 the regional distribution shifted considerably, owing to changing national boundaries, though by 1860, 76 percent of the nation's urban population could still be found in the Northeast, whereas only about 18 percent was in the South (see table 9.6). By 1900 the Northeast's share had dropped to 63 percent, but the South's share had dropped to 15 percent; all of the shift went to the West. From 1900 to 1980, on the other hand, while the Northeast's share continued to drop to 42 percent, the South's share rose to 31 percent, even though the West was gaining in urban share as well. With two very small exceptions during the 1920s, all four of the Northeast and North Central regions had declining shares of the national urban population, and all five of the southern and western regions had increasing shares.

Trends in the regional distribution of metropolitan population are quite similar to those for urban population, though even more accentuated (see table 9.7). In 1860 the Northeast and South had 80 percent and 15 percent of the metropolitan population, respectively, compared to 76 percent and 18 percent of the urban population. By 1900 the Northeast's share had dropped only to 77 percent, while the South's went down to 10 percent. By 1980 the shares of metropolitan population in the Northeast had decreased to 44 percent and had increased to 30 percent in the South, very close to their urban population shares of 42 percent and 31 percent, respectively, for the same year. By 1988 metropolitan shares had shifted still further, down to 41 percent in the Northeast and up to 32 percent in the South. In the early decades of this century, trends in metropolitan shares were not as consistent

Table 9.6 DISTRIBUTION OF U.S. URBAN POPULATION, BY REGION: 1790–1980

	1790	1800	1810	1820	1830	1840	1850	1860	1870	1880	1890	1900	1910	1920	1930	1940	1950	1960	1970	1980
New England	37.8	31.4	28.3	25.3	24.2	23.3	21.9	18.3	15.6	14.8	13.0	12.7	11.4	10.3	9.1	8.6	7.3	6.4	6.0	5.5
Middle Atlantic	41.3	44.4	43.9	43.9	45.2	44.1	42.0	42.1	39.2	37.2	33.2	33.3	32.6	30.9	29.4	28.3	25.0	22.1	20.3	17.7
East North Central	0.0	0.0	0.6	1.4	3.3	6.1	11.4	15.5	19.8	21.7	23.0	23.9	22.8	24.0	24.2	23.3	21.8	21.0	20.1	18.3
West North Central	0.0	0.0	0.0	0.0	0.4	0.9	2.5	4.6	7.3	7.9	10.4	9.7	9.2	8.7	8.0	8.0	7.5	7.2	6.9	6.6
South Atlantic	20.9	24.2	23.2	24.2	20.0	16.4	12.8	9.8	8.4	8.0	7.8	7.4	7.3	8.0	8.2	9.2	10.7	11.8	13.1	14.8
East South Central	0.0	0.0	0.8	1.3	2.5	3.0	4.0	3.8	3.9	3.3	3.7	3.7	3.7	3.7	4.0	4.2	4.6	4.6	4.7	4.9
West South Central	0.0	0.0	3.2	3.9	4.3	6.3	4.9	4.2	3.2	3.2	3.6	3.8	5.0	5.9	6.9	7.5	9.0	9.9	10.1	11.1
Mountain	0.0	0.0	0.0	0.0	0.0	0.0	0.1	0.3	0.4	1.0	1.6	1.8	2.2	2.2	2.1	2.4	2.9	3.7	4.0	5.2
Pacific	0.0	0.0	0.0	0.0	0.0	0.0	0.2	1.3	2.2	2.9	3.6	3.7	5.6	6.4	8.0	8.5	11.2	13.2	14.7	15.8

as those for urban shares, but from 1930 through 1988, with one small exception (East South Central in the 1960s), all of the first four regions in table 9.7 lost metropolitan shares every decade and all of the remaining five regions gained shares.

The percentage distributions of urban and metropolitan populations by state were calculated and are shown in the chapter appendix, tables 9.A-1 and 9.A-2. For a relatively small number of states there are very consistent trends. For example, Arizona, Florida, Idaho, Oregon, Tennessee, Texas, and Utah had consistently rising shares of national urban population and Massachusetts, Pennsylvania, and Rhode Island had consistently falling shares. Consistently rising shares of metropolitan population can be seen in nine states, all in the South or Mountain region, and Delaware and Rhode Island show consistently falling shares. For the great majority of states, however, individual trends are quite mixed, reflecting changing national boundaries, differences in the timing of response to the Civil War, Reconstruction, and the westward movement, and differing adjustments to technological change.

A convenient synthesis of this complex of changes is shown in the Lorenz distributions by state for total, urban, and metropolitan population for selected years (see figures 9.1 to 9.3). The complete set of Lorenz distributions was plotted for each Census year from 1790 to 1988; a few representative illustrations are shown in figure 9.4.

The Gini coefficients for each of the distributions for each Census year are shown in the top half of table 9.8; coefficients of concentration (one minus the Gini coefficient) are shown in the bottom half of the table. Conveniently for this discussion, a higher coefficient of concentration (CC) represents greater concentration rather than greater equality. Although in general the historical tendency is for less geographic concentration of population over time, this is not consistently the case for total population, even since 1850, the beginning date for population data for all of the present continental United States.

The CC for total population showed an alternating pattern up to what still remains the peak of concentration in 1870. Thereafter, concentration became steadily less with the great westward expansion, but after the closing of the frontier around 1910, the CC rose steadily up to 1970. During the 1970s the CC fell, only to increase again in the 1980s. To be sure, fluctuations in the CC have been much smaller ever since 1880 than before, but the observed recent changes do make sense in terms of what we know about the major events in the demographic history of the United States. Although the shift from 1970 to 1988

Table 9.7 DISTRIBUTION OF U.S. METROPOLITAN POPULATION, BY REGION: 1790–1988

	1790	1800	1810	1820	1830	1840	1850	1860	1870	1880	1890	1900	1910	1920	1930	1940	1950	1960	1970	1980	1988
New England	26.8	13.1	10.9	10.9	9.7	14.9	10.8	12.9	14.1	17.6	9.5	12.3	10.9	9.7	8.5	7.9	7.1	6.6	6.2	5.6	5.5
Middle Atlantic	36.9	47.7	48.2	46.8	51.6	49.6	57.0	53.9	49.6	44.9	45.1	43.9	41.5	38.2	34.1	33.2	29.2	24.9	22.1	19.2	18.4
East North Central	0.0	0.0	0.0	0.0	8.1	7.7	7.3	13.2	15.5	17.7	21.3	20.7	21.4	23.9	24.7	23.0	22.5	21.6	21.4	19.3	17.4
West North Central	0.0	0.0	0.0	0.0	0.0	0.0	3.6	3.7	4.7	5.7	9.0	7.9	7.3	7.0	6.6	6.3	6.0	5.9	5.7	5.4	5.3
South Atlantic	36.3	39.3	35.4	35.6	26.0	17.9	13.1	9.2	8.0	7.0	7.2	6.7	5.8	6.5	7.8	9.7	10.9	11.6	12.7	15.5	16.5
East South Central	0.0	0.0	0.0	0.0	0.0	0.0	2.8	2.0	2.9	2.4	2.7	2.5	3.0	3.0	3.4	3.6	3.9	3.9	3.9	4.5	4.5
West South Central	0.0	0.0	5.5	6.7	4.7	9.9	5.4	3.9	2.9	2.3	1.6	1.6	2.8	3.7	4.8	5.3	6.4	8.1	8.7	9.9	10.5
Mountain	0.0	0.0	0.0	0.0	0.0	0.0	0.0	0.0	0.0	0.0	0.9	1.0	1.1	0.9	0.9	1.3	1.7	3.0	3.4	4.3	4.6
Pacific	0.0	0.0	0.0	0.0	0.0	0.0	0.0	1.3	2.3	2.5	2.7	3.4	6.2	7.0	9.2	9.8	12.2	14.5	15.9	16.3	17.2

Figure 9.1 TOTAL U.S. POPULATION

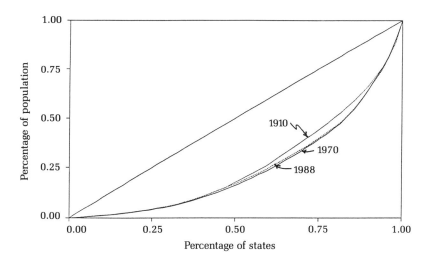

Figure 9.2 U.S. URBAN POPULATION

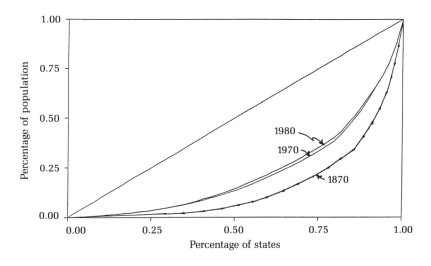

Figure 9.3 U.S. METROPOLITAN POPULATION

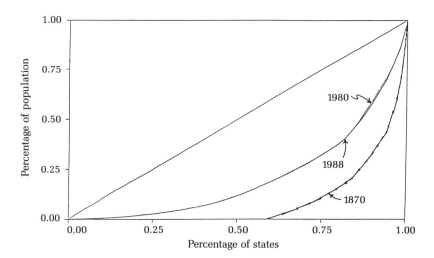

shown in figure 9.1 looks small, it is net of some reversal since 1980, and contrasts with steadily increasing concentration since 1910.

Trends in CC for urban population show much sharper change than those for total population, as indicated by the shifts in figure 9.2. After mixed trends in the early years of the Republic, the CC for urban population reached a local peak in 1870 corresponding to the peak for total population, but CC for urban population has fallen steadily ever since, through 1980. The relative deurbanization of the 1970s, as already discussed, did not affect the direction or rate of dispersal of the urban population among the states.

With amazing consistency, the CC for metropolitan population reached a local (almost a historic) peak also in 1870; then, as with urban population, it fell continuously up through 1970, but it reversed during the 1980s. The reversal is numerically small by historical standards, as shown in table 9.8 (it is hardly visible in figure 9.3), but any reversal at all of a more than one-hundred-year trend ought to attract some attention.

MOTIVATING FORCES

Even though the main task of this chapter has been simply to describe the changes that have occurred in urban and metropolitan population

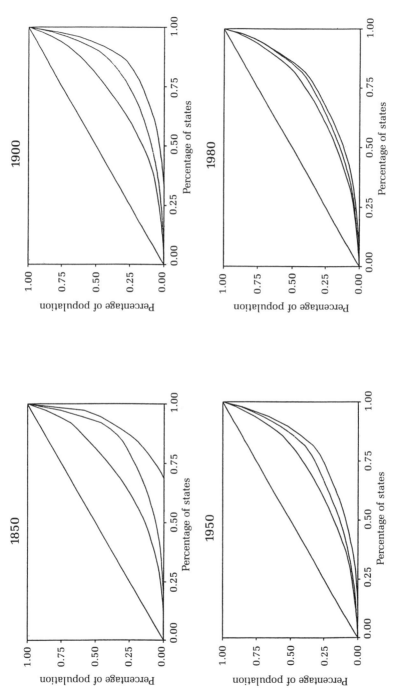

Figure 9.4 LORENZ DISTRIBUTIONS OF U.S. POPULATION FOR SELECTED YEARS

Note: In each of these years, total population is least, urban population more, and metropolitan population most concentrated.

Table 9.8 GINI COEFFICIENTS AND COEFFICIENTS OF CONCENTRATION

	Total Population	Urban Population	Metropolitan Population
a. Gini Coefficients			
1790	0.6877	0.4165	0.4471
1800	0.5840	0.3519	0.1780
1810	0.5341	0.3186	0.2296
1820	0.5739	0.3418	0.2329
1830	0.5812	0.3439	0.2298
1840	0.5933	0.3670	0.2386
1850	0.5337	0.3439	0.2156
1860	0.4980	0.3409	0.2319
1870	0.4822	0.3309	0.1898
1880	0.5202	0.3531	0.1944
1890	0.5244	0.3713	0.2319
1900	0.5310	0.3745	0.2448
1910	0.5509	0.4020	0.2734
1920	0.5488	0.4124	0.2956
1930	0.5359	0.4168	0.3215
1940	0.5391	0.4316	0.3368
1950	0.5350	0.4532	0.3589
1960	0.5235	0.4598	0.3811
1970	0.5176	0.4630	0.3927
1980	0.5295	0.4779	0.4232
1988	0.5247	N.A.	0.4199
b. Coefficients of Concentration			
1790	0.3123	0.5835	0.5529
1800	0.4160	0.6481	0.8220
1810	0.4659	0.6814	0.7704
1820	0.4261	0.6582	0.7671
1830	0.4188	0.6561	0.7702
1840	0.4067	0.6330	0.7614
1850	0.4663	0.6561	0.7844
1860	0.5020	0.6591	0.7681
1870	0.5178	0.6691	0.8102
1880	0.4798	0.6469	0.8056
1890	0.4756	0.6287	0.7681
1900	0.4690	0.6255	0.7552
1910	0.4491	0.5980	0.7266
1920	0.4512	0.5876	0.7044
1930	0.4641	0.5832	0.6785
1940	0.4609	0.5684	0.6632
1950	0.4650	0.5468	0.6411
1960	0.4765	0.5402	0.6189
1970	0.4824	0.5370	0.6073
1980	0.4705	0.5221	0.5768
1988	0.4753	N.A.	0.5801

N.A. = data not available.

in the United States, it seems appropriate to discuss, if only briefly, how the record compares with some of the hypotheses that have been proposed to explain the changing distributions.

Certainly the oldest and perhaps most enduring hypothesis is that of Manifest Destiny (Commager 1977), the idea of the will of a Divine Providence intending that Europeans settle the continent from "sea to shining sea," motivated by Horace Greeley's plea to "Go West, young man, go West!" The idea of Manifest Destiny referred to population in general, not urban population in particular, but as figure 9.5 shows, the center of gravity of the U.S. urban population more or less followed the center of gravity for total population, though with some exceptions. First, it moved west a bit slower than the center of gravity for total population, and until fairly recently remained further north. The center of gravity for metropolitan population retained a bit more of an eastern and northern bias than did that for urban population, though with the country becoming about three-quarters urban and metropolitan, it is not surprising that the centers of gravity for the three distributions have converged. In any event, they certainly have "Gone West" and in the twentieth century a little South too.

The second hypothesis might be called "urbanization as an aspect of industrialization" (Proudfoot 1956). Based on the idea of the urban hierarchy emerging not only from scale but also agglomeration economies (Isard and Smith 1969), this hypothesis suggests that urban areas arise both out of resource availability relative to transport access to markets (Lösch 1954), as well as urban activity begetting more urban activity. But it is the *scale* of urban activity much more than its *density* that is the force of agglomeration. Accordingly, urban activity should more or less follow population (depending on idiosyncrasies of resource location), but with some lag, and metropolitan areas that are defined on scale should show even more inertia relative to dispersal. This is more or less consistent with the Manifest Destiny argument. (Note that in table 9.8 the CCs for metropolitan population since 1800 were consistently above those for urban areas, with the difference rising to a peak in 1880 and thereafter steadily declining through 1980. Note also that the CC for urban population is always above that for total population.)

An urban demographic phenomenon that has attracted somewhat more attention in Europe than in the United States is the supposed differential gravitational pull of the core of the continent versus that of the periphery (Cheshire and Hay 1989). In a European context, it is the core that is supposed to have the stronger pull, whereas in the United States the periphery is considered the stronger force (Leven

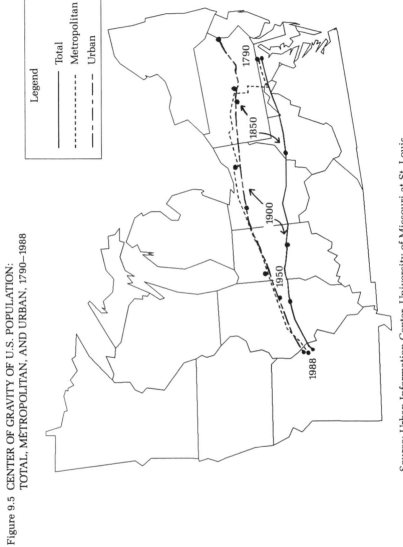

Figure 9.5 CENTER OF GRAVITY OF U.S. POPULATION: TOTAL, METROPOLITAN, AND URBAN, 1790–1988

Legend

Total
Metropolitan
Urban

1790
1850
1900
1950
1988

Source: Urban Information Center, University of Missouri at St. Louis.

1988). It has been shown that during the 1970s specifically, the set of counties within fifty miles of the ocean had substantial net in-migration from the rest of the United States (Alonso 1978), but it is hard to find corresponding confirmation for urban or metropolitan population on a broad regional basis. Except for a small blip in 1910, the proportion of U.S. urban population in the New England, Middle Atlantic, South Atlantic, and Pacific regions combined has consistently fallen from 1790 through 1980. The proportion of U.S. metropolitan population has also fallen, except for two even smaller blips in 1900 and 1940.

An American cousin of the core-periphery idea is the concept of "bicoastal" as an emerging life-style of increasing importance (Toffler 1970). A rough idea of its impact should be reflected in trends in the share of population in the Middle Atlantic and Pacific regions above, areas heavily dominated by New York and California. It may be that "bicoastals" are increasingly identifiable in the jet set, but they are not observable in urban or metropolitan population distributions in general. The share of both of these populations in the two bicoastal regions has decreased fairly steadily since 1790 and without exception since 1910. So much for "bicoastalism" as a force guiding normal folks.

A more strictly American notion is that of "rural renaissance," referring to the observed net in-migration during the 1960s in large numbers of rural counties, mostly remote from SMAs (Beale 1975). This notion was seen as especially noteworthy in that many of these counties had not seen net in-migration in a hundred years. It is also reflected in the data here; note in table 9.3 that the three regions with the least urban population in 1960 had the biggest growth in their urban population percentage during the following decade. But this difference had disappeared by the 1970s. There may indeed have been a rural renaissance in the 1960s, but it was one of the shortest renaissances in history.

Finally, there is the idea of "postindustrial" change involving a shift in demand from goods to services; a shift in production functions involving increased elasticity of substitution of intangible for tangible or on-site labor inputs; an increased transportability of information; and lowered bulk-value ratios for goods (Sternlieb and Hughes 1975). The hypothesized consequences of these changes are an evening-out of the size and spatial distributions of urban and/or metropolitan populations as location becomes more of a demand for scale per se as a determinant for public goods and living amenities (Greenwood, Chalmers, and Graves 1989). This implies that urban and metropolitan populations should be distributed more evenly among those regions that have residential or production attractiveness and more unevenly between such regions and the less attractive regions in total. This is hardly confirmed by the data developed here, but a close look at tables 9.2, 9.4, 9.6, and 9.7 suggests at least a shadow of this image. So does the rapid fall of the average rate of metropolitan growth post-1980. On the other hand, the increasing CC for metropolitan population in the 1980s is not reassuring, even though the amount of shift as shown in figure 9.3 is very small by historical standards. It may be that postindustrial dispersion will be a continuing strong force; or, like rural renaissance, from a historical perspective it may prove to have been a transitory aspect of the 1970s, especially as a boom in corporate mergers on a broad geographic scale become even more significant.

CONCLUSIONS

To summarize the preceding section, it appears that the more traditional explanations of Manifest Destiny and urbanization as a consequence of industrialization hold up fairly well in light of the database generated for this study. On the other hand, core-periphery or bicoastal explanations do badly. Rural renaissance seems clearly to have been a transitory phenomenon, and the jury is still out on the durability of postindustrialism as a motivating factor.

Another aspect of the data should also be stressed—the conceptual difference indicated at the beginning of this chapter between "urban" and "metropolitan" as organizing principles for observing population and economic behavior. In the United States these concepts are converging on each other empirically, but this may represent either an enduring congruence or a way station to a world where metropolitan scale may become the central organizing principle of "urban" life, with the older distinction of urban versus rural losing much of its significance.

Resolving the future of postindustrial transformation will require the unraveling of a number of mysteries. First, the turnaround in large metropolitan areas is based on renewed vitality of service employment there. But what are the agglomeration advantages for these services? Can they be explained by the lower transaction costs for job search in the large metropolis for the two-worker family?

Second, why has metropolis business-service-related new construction been occurring simultaneously both in or near the central business district and in the suburban ring? Is this explained by differences in segments of the labor supply? Are these differences related to differences in transport access? Or are there differences in service markets we are just not seeing (maybe because of data classification)?

Finally, what kind of productivity differences exist between big cities and small cities, between similar cities in different regions, and between core and suburb of SMAs? How much of the apparent fall in U.S. productivity, for example, is an artifact of a shift in employment to sectors where output is measured by inputs (i.e., most services), and how much is real? To determine this, we need employment data classified by the tangibility of inputs, not outputs.

The research agenda for understanding urban and metropolitan change thus contains many unanswered questions for the United States alone. Beyond that is the question to which this volume is addressed, namely, whether such changes in the United States and Europe are simply different stages in the same dynamic or quite different processes entirely.

Appendix Table 9.A-1 DISTRIBUTION OF U.S. URBAN POPULATION BY STATE: 1790–1980

	1790	1800	1810	1820	1830	1840	1850	1860	1870	1880	1890	1900	1910	1920	1930	1940	1950	1960	1970	1980
Alabama	0.0	0.0	0.0	0.0	0.3	0.7	1.0	0.8	0.6	0.5	0.7	0.7	0.9	0.9	1.1	1.2	1.4	1.4	1.4	1.4
Arizona	0.0	0.0	0.0	0.0	0.0	0.0	0.0	0.0	0.0	0.0	0.0	0.1	0.2	0.2	0.2	0.2	0.4	0.8	0.9	1.4
Arkansas	0.0	0.0	0.0	0.0	0.0	0.0	0.0	0.1	0.1	0.2	0.3	0.4	0.5	0.5	0.6	0.6	0.7	0.6	0.6	0.7
California	0.0	0.0	0.0	0.0	0.0	0.0	0.2	1.3	2.1	2.6	2.7	2.6	3.5	4.3	6.0	6.6	8.9	10.9	12.2	13.0
Colorado	0.0	0.0	0.0	0.0	0.0	0.0	0.0	0.1	0.1	0.4	0.8	0.9	1.0	0.8	0.8	0.8	0.9	1.0	1.2	1.4
Connecticut	3.5	4.0	3.0	3.0	2.5	2.1	1.7	2.0	1.8	1.8	1.7	1.8	1.7	1.7	1.6	1.6	1.6	1.6	1.6	1.5
Washington, D.C.	0.0	1.9	2.5	3.0	2.4	1.7	1.4	1.1	1.2	1.1	1.0	0.9	0.8	0.8	0.7	0.9	0.8	0.6	0.5	0.4
Delaware	0.0	0.0	0.0	0.0	0.0	0.4	0.4	0.3	0.3	0.3	0.3	0.3	0.2	0.2	0.2	0.2	0.2	0.2	0.3	0.3
Florida	0.0	0.0	0.0	0.0	0.0	0.0	0.0	0.1	0.2	0.2	0.3	0.4	0.5	0.7	1.1	1.4	1.9	2.9	3.7	4.9
Georgia	0.0	1.6	1.0	1.2	1.2	1.4	1.1	1.2	1.0	1.0	1.2	1.1	1.3	1.3	1.3	1.4	1.6	1.7	1.9	2.1
Idaho	0.0	0.0	0.0	0.0	0.0	0.0	0.0	0.0	0.0	0.0	0.0	0.0	0.2	0.2	0.2	0.2	0.3	0.3	0.3	0.3
Illinois	0.0	0.0	0.0	0.0	0.0	0.5	1.8	4.0	6.0	6.7	7.8	8.7	8.3	8.1	8.2	7.8	7.0	6.5	6.2	5.7
Indiana	0.0	0.0	0.0	0.0	0.0	0.6	1.3	1.9	2.5	2.7	2.7	2.9	2.7	2.7	2.6	2.5	2.4	2.3	2.3	2.1
Iowa	0.0	0.0	0.0	0.0	0.0	0.0	0.3	1.0	1.6	1.7	1.8	1.9	1.6	1.6	1.4	1.5	1.3	1.2	1.1	1.0
Kansas	0.0	0.0	0.0	0.0	0.0	0.0	0.0	0.2	0.5	0.7	1.2	1.1	1.2	1.1	1.1	1.0	1.0	1.1	1.1	0.9
Kentucky	0.0	0.0	0.8	1.3	1.4	1.7	2.1	1.9	2.0	1.8	1.6	1.6	1.3	1.2	1.2	1.1	1.1	1.1	1.1	1.1
Louisiana	0.0	0.0	3.2	3.9	4.1	5.7	3.8	3.0	2.1	1.7	1.3	1.2	1.2	1.2	1.2	1.3	1.5	1.7	1.6	1.7
Maine	0.0	1.2	1.3	1.3	1.2	2.1	2.2	1.7	1.3	1.0	0.8	0.8	0.6	0.6	0.5	0.5	0.5	0.4	0.3	0.3
Maryland	7.0	8.4	8.9	9.5	8.1	6.2	5.3	3.7	3.0	2.7	2.2	2.0	1.6	1.6	1.4	1.5	1.7	1.8	2.0	2.0
Massachusetts	25.4	20.2	19.2	17.2	16.9	15.1	14.2	11.8	9.8	9.4	8.3	8.0	7.1	6.4	5.6	5.2	4.1	3.5	3.2	2.9
Michigan	0.0	0.0	0.0	0.0	0.0	0.5	0.8	1.6	2.4	2.9	3.3	3.2	3.2	4.1	4.8	4.6	4.7	4.6	4.4	3.9
Minnesota	0.0	0.0	0.0	0.0	0.0	0.0	0.0	0.3	0.7	1.1	2.0	2.0	2.0	1.9	1.8	1.9	1.7	1.7	1.7	1.6
Mississippi	0.0	0.0	0.0	0.0	0.3	0.2	0.3	0.3	0.3	0.2	0.3	0.4	0.5	0.4	0.5	0.6	0.6	0.7	0.7	0.7

State																				
Missouri	2.0	2.2	2.3	2.5	2.6	2.7	2.9	3.3	3.7	3.9	3.9	4.3	3.3	2.3	0.9	0.4	0.0	0.0	0.0	0.0
Montana	0.3	0.2	0.3	0.3	0.3	0.3	0.3	0.3	0.3	0.2	0.0	0.0	0.0	0.0	0.0	0.0	0.0	0.0	0.0	0.0
New Hampshire	0.3	0.3	0.3	0.3	0.4	0.4	0.5	0.5	0.6	0.7	0.7	0.8	1.2	1.5	1.6	1.2	1.0	1.3	1.6	2.5
New Jersey	4.0	4.3	4.3	4.3	4.6	4.8	4.7	4.6	4.4	4.1	4.4	4.0	3.5	2.4	2.2	1.6	1.0	1.1	0.0	0.0
New Mexico	0.6	0.5	0.5	0.4	0.2	0.2	0.1	0.1	0.1	0.0	0.0	0.1	0.1	0.1	0.0	0.0	0.0	0.0	0.0	0.0
New York	9.0	10.5	11.5	13.1	15.0	15.3	15.9	17.1	17.6	17.7	20.3	22.1	24.5	24.6	25.5	25.5	23.2	23.0	23.3	19.4
Nebraska	0.6	0.6	0.6	0.6	0.7	0.7	0.7	0.7	0.8	1.3	0.4	0.2	0.0	0.0	0.0	0.0	0.0	0.0	0.0	0.0
Nevada	0.4	0.3	0.2	0.1	0.1	0.0	0.0	0.0	0.0	0.1	0.1	0.1	0.0	0.0	0.0	0.0	0.0	0.0	0.0	0.0
North Carolina	1.7	1.5	1.4	1.4	1.3	1.2	0.9	0.8	0.6	0.5	0.4	0.4	0.4	0.6	0.7	0.9	1.9	0.0	0.0	0.0
North Dakota	0.2	0.2	0.2	0.2	0.2	0.2	0.2	0.2	0.1	0.0	0.0	0.0	0.0	0.0	0.0	0.0	0.0	0.0	0.0	0.0
Ohio	4.8	5.4	5.7	5.8	6.2	6.5	6.8	6.3	6.6	6.8	7.3	6.9	6.4	6.8	4.5	3.3	1.4	0.6	0.0	0.0
Oklahoma	1.2	1.2	1.2	1.2	1.2	1.2	1.0	0.8	0.2	0.0	0.0	0.0	0.0	0.0	0.0	0.0	0.0	0.0	0.0	0.0
Oregon	1.1	0.9	0.9	0.8	0.7	0.7	0.7	0.7	0.4	0.4	0.2	0.1	0.0	0.0	0.0	0.0	0.0	0.0	0.0	0.0
Pennsylvania	5.0	5.7	6.5	7.7	8.9	9.5	10.5	11.0	11.4	11.6	12.6	13.3	14.4	15.4	16.7	18.3	19.6	19.8	21.1	21.9
Rhode Island	0.5	0.6	0.6	0.7	0.9	0.9	1.0	1.2	1.3	1.3	1.6	1.6	1.8	2.3	2.6	2.7	2.7	3.4	4.3	6.5
South Carolina	1.0	0.8	0.8	0.8	0.6	0.5	0.5	0.5	0.6	0.5	0.5	0.6	0.8	1.4	1.8	3.0	3.6	4.8	5.9	8.0
South Dakota	0.2	0.2	0.2	0.2	0.2	0.2	0.2	0.2	0.1	0.1	0.0	0.0	0.0	0.0	0.0	0.0	0.0	0.0	0.0	0.0
Tennessee	1.7	1.6	1.5	1.5	1.4	1.3	1.1	1.1	1.1	1.1	0.8	0.9	0.8	0.6	0.4	0.5	0.0	0.0	0.0	0.0
Texas	6.8	6.0	5.8	5.0	3.9	3.5	2.8	2.2	1.7	1.6	1.0	0.6	0.4	0.2	0.0	0.0	0.0	0.0	0.0	0.0
Utah	0.7	0.6	0.5	0.5	0.4	0.4	0.4	0.4	0.3	0.3	0.2	0.2	0.1	0.0	0.0	0.0	0.0	0.0	0.0	0.0
Vermont	0.1	0.1	0.1	0.1	0.2	0.2	0.2	0.2	0.3	0.2	0.2	0.2	0.1	0.2	0.0	0.0	0.0	0.0	0.0	0.0
Virginia	2.1	2.0	1.8	1.6	1.3	1.1	1.2	1.1	1.1	1.3	1.3	1.5	1.9	2.5	3.8	4.4	5.1	6.1	6.5	6.0
Washington	1.8	1.7	1.6	1.6	1.2	1.3	1.4	1.4	0.7	0.6	0.0	0.0	0.0	0.0	0.0	0.0	0.0	0.0	0.0	0.0
West Virginia	0.4	0.5	0.6	0.7	0.7	0.7	0.7	0.5	0.4	0.4	0.4	0.4	0.3	0.3	0.4	0.0	0.0	0.0	0.0	0.0
Wisconsin	1.8	2.0	2.0	2.1	2.3	2.3	2.3	2.4	2.6	2.5	2.2	2.1	1.8	0.8	0.0	0.0	0.0	0.0	0.0	0.0
Wyoming	0.2	0.1	0.2	0.2	0.1	0.1	0.1	0.1	0.1	0.1	0.0	0.0	0.0	0.0	0.0	0.0	0.0	0.0	0.0	0.0
Total	100.0	100.0	100.0	100.0	100.0	100.0	100.0	100.0	100.0	100.0	100.0	100.0	100.0	100.0	100.0	100.0	100.0	100.0	100.0	100.0

Appendix Table 9.A-2 DISTRIBUTION OF U.S. METROPOLITAN POPULATION BY STATE: 1790–1988

	1790	1800	1810	1820	1830	1840	1850	1860	1870	1880	1890	1900	1910	1920	1930	1940	1950	1960	1970	1980	1988
Alabama	0.0	0.0	0.0	0.0	0.0	0.0	0.0	0.0	0.0	0.0	0.0	0.0	0.9	0.9	1.1	1.1	1.2	1.3	1.3	1.4	1.4
Arizona	0.0	0.0	0.0	0.0	0.0	0.0	0.0	0.0	0.0	0.0	0.0	0.0	0.0	0.0	0.0	0.3	0.4	0.8	1.0	1.2	1.4
Arkansas	0.0	0.0	0.0	0.0	0.0	0.0	0.0	0.0	0.0	0.0	0.0	0.0	0.0	0.2	0.2	0.2	0.2	0.3	0.4	0.5	0.5
California	0.0	0.0	0.0	0.0	0.0	0.0	0.0	1.3	2.3	2.5	2.7	2.4	3.7	4.8	7.2	7.9	9.9	12.1	13.3	13.3	14.4
Colorado	0.0	0.0	0.0	0.0	0.0	0.0	0.0	0.0	0.0	0.0	0.0	0.7	0.7	0.6	0.5	0.7	0.8	1.1	1.1	1.4	1.4
Connecticut	0.0	0.0	0.0	0.0	0.0	0.0	0.0	2.2	1.8	1.7	1.2	1.2	1.1	1.1	1.4	1.5	1.6	1.7	1.8	1.6	1.6
Washington, D.C.	0.0	0.0	0.0	0.0	0.0	0.0	1.9	1.4	1.6	1.5	1.5	1.2	1.0	1.0	0.8	1.0	0.9	0.7	0.5	0.4	0.3
Delaware	0.0	0.0	0.0	0.0	0.0	0.0	0.0	0.0	0.0	0.0	0.6	0.5	0.4	0.3	0.3	0.3	0.3	0.3	0.3	0.2	0.2
Florida	0.0	0.0	0.0	0.0	0.0	0.0	0.0	0.0	0.0	0.0	0.0	0.0	0.2	0.5	0.9	1.1	1.5	2.9	3.4	5.1	5.9
Georgia	0.0	0.0	0.0	0.0	0.0	0.0	0.0	0.0	0.0	0.0	0.5	0.8	0.8	1.1	1.1	1.3	1.4	1.6	1.6	1.9	2.2
Idaho	0.0	0.0	0.0	0.0	0.0	0.0	0.0	0.0	0.0	0.0	0.0	0.0	0.0	0.0	0.0	0.0	0.0	0.0	0.1	0.1	0.1
Illinois	0.0	0.0	0.0	0.0	0.0	0.0	0.0	3.3	5.3	6.4	8.8	9.5	9.2	8.8	8.7	8.0	7.3	6.9	6.4	5.5	5.2
Indiana	0.0	0.0	0.0	0.0	0.0	0.0	0.0	0.0	1.1	1.1	1.5	1.3	1.9	2.2	2.1	2.0	2.1	2.0	2.3	2.3	2.1
Iowa	0.0	0.0	0.0	0.0	0.0	0.0	0.0	0.0	0.0	0.0	0.7	0.6	0.5	0.9	0.9	0.9	0.8	0.8	0.7	0.7	0.7
Kansas	0.0	0.0	0.0	0.0	0.0	0.0	0.0	0.0	0.0	0.0	0.3	0.3	0.5	0.4	0.6	0.6	0.6	0.7	0.7	0.7	0.7
Kentucky	0.0	0.0	0.0	0.0	0.0	0.0	2.8	2.0	1.8	1.5	1.2	1.3	1.0	0.8	0.9	0.9	1.0	0.9	0.9	1.0	0.9
Louisiana	0.0	0.0	5.5	6.7	4.7	9.9	5.4	3.9	2.9	2.3	1.6	1.3	1.1	0.9	1.1	1.0	1.2	1.4	1.4	1.6	1.7
Maine	0.0	0.0	0.0	0.0	0.0	0.0	0.0	0.0	0.0	0.0	0.0	0.3	0.2	0.2	0.2	0.2	0.1	0.2	0.2	0.2	0.2
Maryland	8.3	12.6	15.1	15.7	12.6	9.9	7.8	4.8	4.0	3.5	3.3	2.6	2.1	1.8	1.7	2.7	2.9	2.2	2.4	2.2	2.2
Massachusetts	26.8	13.1	10.9	10.9	9.7	9.3	6.7	8.2	10.1	13.8	6.6	8.9	7.9	7.0	5.8	5.1	4.5	3.9	3.5	2.9	2.8
Michigan	0.0	0.0	0.0	0.0	0.0	0.0	0.0	1.7	1.8	1.7	2.6	2.3	2.6	4.1	5.2	4.9	5.1	5.1	4.9	4.5	4.0
Minnesota	0.0	0.0	0.0	0.0	0.0	0.0	0.0	0.0	0.0	0.0	2.1	2.1	2.2	2.0	1.7	1.7	1.5	1.6	1.6	1.6	1.5
Mississippi	0.0	0.0	0.0	0.0	0.0	0.0	0.0	0.0	0.0	0.0	0.0	0.0	0.0	0.0	0.0	0.2	0.2	0.2	0.3	0.4	0.4
Missouri	0.0	0.0	0.0	0.0	0.0	0.0	3.6	3.7	4.7	4.5	4.8	4.2	3.6	3.1	2.9	2.6	2.4	2.2	2.2	1.9	1.8

State																					
Montana	0.0	0.0	0.0	0.0	0.0	0.0	0.0	0.0	0.0	0.0	0.0	0.0	0.0	0.0	0.0	0.0	0.0	0.1	0.1	0.1	0.1
New Hampshire	0.0	0.0	0.0	0.0	0.0	0.0	0.0	0.0	0.0	0.0	0.0	0.3	0.2	0.2	0.1	0.1	0.1	0.1	0.1	0.3	0.3
New Jersey	0.0	0.0	0.0	0.0	0.0	0.0	3.4	2.3	4.1	4.7	6.7	6.4	6.2	6.0	5.7	5.6	5.1	4.3	4.0	4.0	4.2
New Mexico	0.0	0.0	0.0	0.0	0.0	0.0	0.0	0.0	0.0	0.0	0.0	0.0	0.0	0.0	0.0	0.0	0.2	0.2	0.2	0.3	0.4
New York	19.6	28.5	30.9	30.8	39.1	40.5	41.6	34.6	29.8	26.6	21.5	21.7	20.0	18.0	17.5	16.7	14.6	12.8	11.4	9.4	8.8
Nebraska	0.0	0.0	0.0	0.0	0.0	0.0	0.0	0.0	0.0	0.0	1.0	0.6	0.5	0.7	0.6	0.5	0.5	0.5	0.5	0.4	0.4
Nevada	0.0	0.0	0.0	0.0	0.0	0.0	0.0	0.0	0.0	0.0	0.0	0.0	0.0	0.0	0.0	0.0	0.0	0.2	0.3	0.4	0.4
North Carolina	0.0	0.0	0.0	0.0	0.0	0.0	0.0	0.0	0.0	0.0	0.0	0.0	0.0	0.0	1.1	1.1	1.0	1.0	1.4	1.8	1.9
North Dakota	0.0	0.0	0.0	0.0	0.0	0.0	0.0	0.0	0.0	0.0	0.0	0.0	0.0	0.0	0.0	0.0	0.0	0.1	0.1	0.1	0.1
Ohio	0.0	0.0	0.0	0.0	8.1	7.7	7.3	6.7	5.9	7.0	6.8	5.9	6.1	7.4	7.0	6.5	6.4	6.0	6.0	5.1	4.6
Oklahoma	0.0	0.0	0.0	0.0	0.0	0.0	0.0	0.0	0.0	0.0	0.0	0.0	0.3	0.5	0.7	0.6	0.7	0.9	0.9	1.1	1.0
Oregon	0.0	0.0	0.0	0.0	0.0	0.0	0.0	0.0	0.0	0.0	0.0	0.5	0.8	0.7	0.6	0.6	0.7	0.8	0.9	1.0	0.9
Pennsylvania	17.3	19.2	17.4	15.9	12.5	9.1	12.0	17.0	15.7	13.6	16.9	15.8	15.4	14.2	10.9	11.0	9.6	7.8	6.7	5.8	5.4
Rhode Island	0.0	0.0	0.0	0.0	0.0	5.6	4.1	2.5	2.3	2.1	1.7	1.5	1.4	1.2	1.0	0.9	0.8	0.7	0.6	0.5	0.5
South Carolina	28.0	22.6	20.3	19.9	13.4	8.0	3.4	1.6	1.3	1.1	0.7	0.5	0.4	0.4	0.4	0.4	0.6	0.7	0.7	1.1	1.1
South Dakota	0.0	0.0	0.0	0.0	0.0	0.0	0.0	0.0	0.0	0.0	0.0	0.0	0.0	0.0	0.0	0.0	0.1	0.1	0.1	0.1	0.1
Tennessee	0.0	0.0	0.0	0.0	0.0	0.0	0.0	0.0	1.1	0.8	1.4	1.2	1.0	1.2	1.5	1.5	1.6	1.5	1.4	1.7	1.7
Texas	0.0	0.0	0.0	0.0	0.0	0.0	0.0	0.0	0.0	0.0	0.0	0.3	1.5	2.0	2.8	3.4	4.3	5.4	5.9	6.8	7.4
Utah	0.0	0.0	0.0	0.0	0.0	0.0	0.0	0.0	0.0	0.0	0.0	0.3	0.4	0.4	0.3	0.3	0.4	0.5	0.6	0.7	0.7
Vermont	0.0	0.0	0.0	0.0	0.0	0.0	0.0	0.0	0.0	0.0	0.0	0.0	0.0	0.0	0.0	0.0	0.0	0.0	0.0	0.1	0.1
Virginia	0.0	0.0	0.0	0.0	0.0	0.0	0.0	1.4	1.0	0.9	0.6	1.0	0.9	1.1	1.0	1.1	1.4	1.8	2.1	2.2	2.3
Washington	0.0	0.0	0.0	0.0	0.0	0.0	0.0	0.0	0.0	0.0	0.0	0.5	1.7	1.5	1.3	1.3	1.5	1.6	1.6	2.0	2.0
West Virginia	0.0	0.0	0.0	0.0	0.0	0.0	0.0	0.0	0.0	0.0	0.0	0.0	0.0	0.3	0.5	0.7	0.7	0.5	0.4	0.4	0.4
Wisconsin	0.0	0.0	0.0	0.0	0.0	0.0	0.0	1.4	1.4	1.5	1.5	1.6	1.5	1.5	1.8	1.6	1.6	1.6	1.8	1.9	1.6
Wyoming	0.0	0.0	0.0	0.0	0.0	0.0	0.0	0.0	0.0	0.0	0.0	0.0	0.0	0.0	0.0	0.0	0.0	0.0	0.0	0.0	0.1
Total	100.0	100.0	100.0	100.0	100.0	100.0	100.0	100.0	100.0	100.0	100.0	100.0	100.0	100.0	100.0	100.0	100.0	100.0	100.0	100.0	100.0

References

Abdallah, A. ben, and C. L. Leven. 1989. "Growth Trends in Intermediate-Size Metropolitan Regions." *Review of Urban and Regional Development Studies* (July).

Alonso, W. 1978. "The Current Halt in the Metropolitan Phenomena." In *The Mature Metropolis*, edited by C. L. Leven. Lexington, Mass.: D. C. Heath.

Barr, J. L., and C. L. Leven. 1972. "The Spatial Dimension of the Economy as a Social Outcome: Some Theoretical and Empirical Issues." In *Spatial, Regional, and Population Economics*, edited by M. Perlman, C. L. Leven, and B. Chintz. New York and London: Gordon and Breach.

Beale, C. 1975. "The Revival of Population Growth in Nonmetropolitan America." Economic Research Service, Paper ERS-605. Washington, D.C.: U.S. Department of Agriculture.

Cheshire, P. C., and D. G. Hay. 1989. *Urban Problems in Western Europe: An Economic Analysis*. London: Unwin Hyman.

Commager, H. S. 1977. *The Empire of Reason*. Garden City, N.Y.: Doubleday.

Greenwood, M. J., J. A. Chalmers, and P. E. Graves. 1989. "Regional Location Patterns in the United States: Recent Changes and Future Prospects." In *Migration and Labor Market Adjustment*, edited by J. Van Dijk, H. Folmer, H. W. Herzog, Jr., and A. M. Schlottman. Dordrecht, The Netherlands: Kluwer.

Holt, G. E. 1975. "The Shaping of St. Louis." Ph.D. dissertation, University of Chicago.

Isard, W., and T. Smith. 1969. *General Theory; Social, Political, Economic, and Regional*. Cambridge, Mass.: MIT Press.

Leven, C. L., 1979. "Growth and Nongrowth in Metropolitan Areas and the Emergence of Polycentric Metropolitan Form." In *Papers of the Regional Science Association*, vol. 41.

————. 1988. "Post-Industrialism, Regional Change, and the New Urban Geography." In *America's New Market Geography*, edited by G. Sternlieb and J.W. Hughes. New Brunswick, N.J.: Rutgers University, Center for Urban Policy Research.

————. 1991. "Distance, Space, and the Organization of Urban Life." *Urban Studies* (June).

Leven, C. L., and S. Sheppard. 1982. "Regional Shifts in Population and Changes in Metro-Nonmetro Boundaries in the U.S." Institute for Urban and Regional Studies, Working Paper RPS 1. Saint Louis: Washington University, Institute for Urban and Regional Studies. July.

Lösch, A. 1954. *The Economics of Location*. Translated by W. Stolper. New Haven, Conn.: Yale University Press.

Macrae, N. 1978. "Tomorrow's Agglomeration Economics." In *The Mature Metropolis*, edited by C. L. Leven. Lexington, Mass.: D. C. Heath.

Proudfoot, M. J. 1956. *European Refugees*. Evanston, Ill.: Northwestern University Press.

Sternlieb, G., and J. Hughes, eds. 1975. *Post-Industrial America: Metropolitan Decline and Inter-Regional Job Shifts*. New Brunswick, N.J.: Rutgers University, Center for Urban Policy Research.

Toffler, A. 1970. *Future Shock*. New York: Random House.

U.S. Department of Commerce. 1975. *Historical Statistics of the U.S.*, Part 1 (6–72). Washington, D.C.: U.S. Government Printing Office.

_____. 1990. *Statistical Abstract of the U.S., 1990* (908–09). Washington, D.C.: U.S. Government Printing Office.

Chapter Ten

URBAN DECENTRALIZATION PROCESSES IN WESTERN EUROPE

Rainer Mackensen

This chapter addresses the historical conditions and governmental policies affecting urbanization in Western Europe and the United States, as well as current economic, political, and demographic trends in this regard in Europe, focusing particularly on Germany.

URBANIZATION IN WESTERN EUROPE AND THE UNITED STATES: HISTORICAL CONDITIONS AND GOVERNMENT POLICIES

Historical Conditions

It is important to understand that the current patterns of urbanization and urban development in Western Europe are composed of several layers of historical patterns, each bearing the mark of past political regimes. These regimes, which were numerous and diversified, contributed to the relative predominance of specific cities and regions in the urban landscape.

In Italy, the city of Rome, in particular, has historically enjoyed a long-established high rank; in more recent history, this role has been reduced by the power and economic strength of northern Italian families, industries, and cities. In France and Great Britain—and also in the Northern European countries—where national states were formed relatively early in history, the capital cities have also maintained a dominant position. By contrast, in Germany, for example, a national state was formed only relatively recently, for a limited time, and in a particular fashion. There, as in the Netherlands, Belgium, and northern Italy, a parallel development occurred in the strong power of numerous regional princes and cities. The resultant economic development pattern was a relatively even distribution of cities of similar comparable rank. In Eastern and Southeastern Europe, the longlasting competition between national and imperial powers did not permit other cities to develop into the predominant positions of Vienna and Byzantium/Constantinople/Istanbul. And in Eastern Europe, over the centuries, different imperial powers influenced national formation and regional development in a way that did not allow single cities to develop into regional importance for more than limited periods of time.

Western Europe (Great Britain, France, the Netherlands, Belgium, Switzerland, Austria, northern Italy, and Germany) has high overall population densities and a large numbers of cities, given the square mileage of the countries. Urbanization in these countries is highly developed, although their population densities are not comparable to that of the northeastern United States. Other regions have a more agrarian economic structure and a more centralized urbanization pattern. The picture for Europe as a whole is that Northern, Eastern, and Southern Europe have less dense areas with smaller numbers of cities, and that Western Europe has denser areas with larger numbers of cities.

Urbanization patterns formed differently during periods of mainly agrarian production, compared with periods dominated by medieval long-distance trade; in periods of feudalism compared with those of absolute monarchies; and in times of growing wealth of the urban bourgeoisie compared with those of imperialism and industrialization. Since these economic and political characteristics applied to different areas of Europe at different times, urbanization developed sporadically across the continent. For the last one hundred years, particularly, industrialization in Great Britain, France, Belgium, the Netherlands, Germany, and northern Italy has promoted the development of large agglomerations and metropolitan areas—forming a "banana" (Illeris 1991) from central Britain south to northern Italy, whereas, in other parts of the continent, comparatively few metropolitan areas serve larger regions or larger parts of their country.

Compared to the pattern of urbanization in the United States, the pattern in Western Europe is more dense and more centrally oriented, whereas it is more evenly distributed in Central Europe. Strong differences between Western European and North American urbanization processes stem from the different overall density patterns, which, in turn, are derived from their different political histories.

Another important difference between America and Western Europe that affects urbanization patterns relates to the regional mobility of people, which is much higher in America than in Europe. Americans seem less bound to their home, as well as to their city and region, than Europeans. Most Europeans, in contrast, have a strong relationship toward both their home and city, and are more likely to submit to the inconveniences of long-distance commuting, if this allows them to stay in their home and city. The same commuting distance in a densely settled area in Western Europe covers a broader variety of occupational opportunities than in much larger regions in the United States, where greater numbers of people are inclined to change residence and move to a city a long distance away, if the occupational opportunities are attractive. The result is that the economic situation deteriorates in the original city of residence while it improves in the city with the attractive job opportunity. These movements seem to function like the stock market—if some people make a move, more people will regard it as reasonable to move in the same direction. Consequently, in a relatively short time period, a certain city may become relatively depopulated, at least by a particular sector of the resident population, and another city will become crowded by the same process. This phenomenon is one of the elements of "deurbanization" in certain parts of the United States, but is almost unknown in Western Europe and almost impossible to imagine there. To the contrary, firms in Western Europe increasingly tend to choose locations on the basis of the resident population and their occupational characteristics; in the United States, locations are chosen on the basis of a wide range of cost factors and management preferences, on the assumption that the labor components are ready to move. Development of a similar tendency in Western Europe will be constrained by the fact that a much smaller part of the population would be mobile.

Owing to Western Europe's high density, the relatively small area size of its nations—resulting in small distances between agglomerations—and the area's economic and political history, real estate markets there are not as rich, vivid, and powerful as they are in North America. Less land is available, and the market is heavily regulated by zoning, housing policies, and other legal restrictions. These factors have all strongly influenced recent processes of urbanization in Western Europe.

Government Policies

The shape of urban development in Western Europe is due not only to market forces but also to official government policies. The importance of these policies is a major factor contributing to the different characteristics of North American and European urbanization. However, these differences are not simple to identify and describe, because the interplay of market and government forces in Western Europe urbanization is complex. In contrast to the United States, not only are there highly developed administrative authorities and procedures in Western Europe for urban and regional development, but they differ from nation to nation, and, over time, governmental strategies here changed considerably with the party in power.

In Western Germany, for example, a set of laws and institutions was developed after World War II that has been admired by regional planners in other countries. But what is often overlooked is that legally prescribed procedures may not turn out to be as effective in practice as they were intended, and may not materialize at all. Further, neither state and regional development programs nor local spatial planning have any legal power. They are implemented only through other instruments, such as administrative actions or specific local building plans—which are frequently not accessible, or are decided a posteriori, after certain political actions, such as decisions about roads or locations of firms, have been taken. The strongest political power rests with the local governments, which can only act together through bilateral or multilateral bargaining processes. The results are not always consistent with rational planning, nor are they in any scientific way systematic.

Although the organizational setup of regional and urban development differs among Western European nations, and is far more extensive than in the United States, this does not mean that urban development in the former is fully determined by public planning. Many policies there run counter to urban and regional planning, such as those on overall economic development, and fiscal and social policies. Also, efforts to develop coherent regional planning are hampered by the tendency of local government bodies to act, to a large degree, in ways contradictory with each other; they tend to be more competitive than cooperative. Frequently, European urban and regional planning—particularly during the last two or three decades—has had to follow, rather than lead, other political, economic, and technical policies in regional development, because the power of urban and regional planning forces in local, regional, state, and national government is comparatively small. Therefore, the urbanization process in Western Europe cannot be regarded as a result mainly of rational or systematic planning; rather, it is the product of divergent interests and powers.

The political values and goals of the Western European nations place significant limitations on the free rein of economic forces, and hence on urbanization processes. The constitutional history of European states has resulted in relatively more intervention by national, regional, and local government institutions into private economic interests than in the United States. Their land is almost totally allocated to local and regional political and administrative units, which have more power, rights, and obligations than their analogs—local governments and states—in the United States. There is variation, of course, across Western Europe. In France and Great Britain the national governments have considerable responsibility for regional development, though they are yielding increasing power and financial resources to their subnational units. In Germany, local communities are constitutionally totally responsible for their jurisdictions, but can be influenced by state and national governments, by financial subsidies, and some general rules. These higher levels of government have virtually absolute power over taxation and the distribution of financial resources among regional authorities. Constitutionally, the responsibility for urban development and planning rests totally with the local communities. In principle, state and federal governments have very limited responsibilities regarding locational decisions, such as for health service institutions, education, highways, waterways, and the larger railroads. In reality, however, the influence is much greater, because local communities are highly dependent on financial aid through state and federal programs—which gives these bodies considerable regulatory power over regional and urban development decisions.

If one examines urbanization processes that have already occurred, the processes are rationalized a posteriori, and one can never be sure that the causal connections being searched for are identical with the forces that have been responsible for the development. It is, therefore, crucial to describe the process of urbanization before analyzing the forces behind it, and to clearly define which characteristics of the process need explaining. The process itself is necessarily the result of many, and often diverging, conditions. Though the contemporary urban scenery may, on the surface, appear similar in both continents, it may well be the result of very divergent influences.

THE GERMAN EXAMPLE IN
THE WESTERN EUROPEAN CONTEXT

The German experience, although naturally exhibiting certain unique characteristics, serves to demonstrate the existing fundamental differences between recent Western European and North American urbanization patterns.

After World War II, and also during the 1980s, the population of metropolitan areas in Germany continued to grow relative to total national population. In more recent decades, the cores did not grow, but population growth occurred in their fringe areas. As in the United States, the fringe areas around cities built up higher densities and expanded into the open landscape, while social distances between the agglomerations of the central cores and their peripheral regions grew. In general, suburbanization continues to be the major trend in Western European urbanization patterns. The concentration of larger parts of the population in metropolitan areas of the country, the territorial expansion of these agglomerations into the wider landscape, and the decentralization of populations within the agglomerations are predominant features. (These features are discussed in more detail later in this chapter.)

The period 1950–96 was not a homogeneous one in terms of urban centralization and decentralization in Western Europe. The first decade after World War II was a time of reconstruction, during which settlement patterns and population distributions generally returned to their prewar character, only with higher levels of density.

One strong influence in this immediate postwar period was the spatial political reorganization in Central, Eastern, and Southeastern Europe, resulting in population distributions similar to those before the war, but with a more or less total exchange of populations. In Western Europe, reconstruction was primarily directed toward reorganizing the producing economies from war to peace demands. Somewhat induced by these efforts, immigration from former colonies and from socialist countries added to the urban populations. Most Western European nations experienced immigration during this immediate postwar period. Growth agglomerations during this time reflected not only increased concentrations of existing national populations but, to a greater extent, the incorporation of additional populations into existing urban settlements. Very few "new towns" have been established in this period.

The next period, up to around 1970, was characterized by stronger economic development, accompanied by increasing immigration from countries around the Mediterranean and from previously dependent areas overseas into Northern, Western, and Central European countries. For West Germany, this period is divided into two phases. The first phase, up to 1961, was influenced mainly by German immigration from East Germany. The second phase was characterized by labor immigration from Southern Europe, somewhat like the development in other Western European countries. In the next major period, after the series of oil crises around 1970, this influx diminished, and many immigrants moved back to their home countries, where economic conditions had improved and social security nets were in place (Mackensen 1979, 1989).

It was mainly during this last period—since the early 1970s—that urban deconcentration and decentralization became an issue of political and scientific discussion. The tendency toward decentralization was reinforced by the population decreases of the indigenous populations, starting in both German states in the mid-1960s and spreading into Northern and Western European countries. With national population decreases and large portions of national populations living in urban agglomerations, the numbers of urban inhabitants declined beyond the national averages. This occurred because urban agglomerations usually kept and increased their number of inhabitants only by migration, and migration became a scarce source since the national populations were no longer growing, except for immigration from foreign countries. At the same time, and associated with general economic and population developments, technological change also became a prominent feature of urbanization.

Since around 1990 urban development throughout Europe has been influenced by dramatic political and economic changes. Revolutionary developments in Eastern and Southeastern Europe swept away socialist governments and economies. This resulted in some economic breakdown in most of those nations, and in the development of the beginnings of democratic governments and the establishment of the fundamentals of market economies. The Gulf War of 1991 changed the relationships with the Near East countries, and the civil war in the former Yugoslavia since 1992 has created economic turbulence and disrupted important transport routes. The result has been an increase in migration streams of a different character into Central and Western Europe, which have influenced urban economic development patterns.

CURRENT FORCES BEHIND WESTERN EUROPEAN URBANIZATION

Present economic, political, and demographic trends tend to further accentuate the concentration tendency in Western Europe, and to increase the decentralization within the agglomerations by expanding their area. Major forces in this process are technological change, trends toward economic harmonization and political convergence, international and internal migration patterns, and housing and planning policies. The urban agglomeration patterns of the 1980s were as distinct from former periods in Western Europe as they are different from those in the United States—and have become even more so in the 1990s.

Technological Change

Recent technological change influenced urbanization processes in Western Europe, though somewhat later than in North America. Because the divergent history and government policies of individual countries caused these processes to vary, the technological changes had different effects in different countries. Technological change strengthened the development of metropolitan agglomerations in southern France, Great Britain, and West Germany relative to northern metropolitan areas, and strengthened northern metropolitan areas relative to agglomerations in southern Italy. But, in France, metropolitan expansion was due more to policies of "regionalization," whereby improved infrastructure nationwide, and governmental encouragement of economic development in many parts of the country, stimulated areas other than the traditional ones. Many of the new, technologically advanced industries might have chosen Paris as a location if regional policy had not encouraged development in other agglomerations. This policy has now become a major force in France. For instance, the construction of rapid trains (TGV, *Train à Grande Vitesse*) is one of the strong signals of the decisive political decentralization occurring in France.

In Great Britain, the primacy of the metropolis has never really been challenged, and urban and industrial developments in England have, in addition, strengthened the London agglomeration. Industrial and urban developments in the middle northern part of the country never achieved a similar ranking. These regions of original industrialization suffered from the technological developments of the 1970s and 1980s, and received little governmental support for structural modernization. Recent urban development in Great Britain, therefore, still tends to follow the traditional settlement pattern. Regional initiatives have been encouraged there only recently. These have combined with national economic strength to produce a recovery in the urban economies around the older industrial centers.

TECHNOLOGY AND THE LOCATION OF GROWTH

In West Germany, a prominent topic in urbanization discussions during the last decade has become the "south-north-differential" of agglomeration developments (Friedrichs et al. 1986). Traditional growth poles—like the Ruhr district and the Aachen and Saar regions—have been declining in population as a consequence of their concentration in heavy industry. Agglomerations situated in the south—like Frankfurt, Stuttgart, and Munich—have become the new growth poles. But, in Germany, this migration of growth poles was due, at least to a high degree, to political conditions—perhaps more so than to industrial location decisions based on efficiency. The migration of growth poles is not only the result of technological developments, regionally differentiated labor supply, climate, and landscape preferences, all of which certainly contribute to economic development decisions. The changed locus of economic growth is also associated with traditionally differentiated patterns of labor qualification, overlapping periods of industrial strategies, and political conditions (postwar occupation force zoning) and initiatives (Bavaria). The top management of most of the large firms left Berlin during the Cold War years, and since the north German industrial districts still flourished then, with conditions of full employment, they sought surplus labor in southern centers. There they also expected (and received) more subvention, first because these areas were an American Zone and later because of German state politics. Frankfurt profited from its earlier development as a financial center, as well as by the fact that it was also the center of the American administration in Germany. Only the Stuttgart region had a population highly qualified for modern industrial work for historical reasons. And in Bavaria, state politics pushed a new wave of industrialization.

Technological change has an impact not only on location but also—and primarily—on the internal and external organizational features of a firm, including the organization of production, among many other factors. These effects exert definite influences on the urban scenery by changing the industrial composition of many urban areas, as well as their social stratification and patterns of segregation. Developments in industrial strategies during the 1980s and technological possibilities also strengthened the traditional agglomeration effects. The concept of broader responsibility for productive employees meant that firms invested more in the qualifications and satisfaction of their employees. Personnel strategies and the culture of enterprises strove to reduce fluctuations in the number of employees and to strengthen the qualifications of those already employed. These attitudes reinforced the case for agglomeration. But, they also—and, in recent years increasingly—reduced the number of people employed in large firms. Unemployment rates have increased in all European countries. Social and fiscal problems of cities are one of the consequences.

Beyond these internal pressures to enlarge and reinforce the local agglomeration tendencies of industrial complexes, there are external pressures. More parts are being purchased for the mother firms that were once produced internally, and more delivery firms, therefore, are required to deliver inputs promptly—thus forcing the delivery firms to add to the agglomeration by organizing production and transport close to the purchasing firm. These technological concentrations seem to be combined with a relative increase in consumption-oriented services. These services, of course, cluster close to the resident population, comprised in part of the qualified personnel of the technology-oriented industries.

Since 1990, though, even more profound changes have occurred because of mass automation and job reduction. Many firms have moved to urban fringes to establish new production lines and automated depots. Many are using the cheaper labor of East European and East Asian countries. A sharp reduction in industrial employment has resulted, particularly in East Germany. In addition, cheaper foreign labor has entered the job markets—particularly in the building industries. And, public investment—restricted because of the large subvention demands in the new states of the former German Democratic Republic—has been reduced, with particularly negative effects on the production of heavy goods and infrastructure.

TECHNOLOGY AND THE URBAN SCENE

Agglomerations tend to be defined as industrial and service locations. It is important to observe, however, that, depending upon their particular business structure, agglomerations are characterized by a related social structure of their inhabitants. Young and mobility-minded workers will look for the broader educational and employment opportunities found in larger agglomerations—particularly in the most modern ones. Technology, therefore, changes not only the numbers but also the qualitative characteristics of the resident population— beyond the mere labor qualifications of the producing industries.

An examination of the inner-urban housing scenery reveals that the gentrification of these centers has become a fashionable feature in Western Europe (Dangschat and Friedrichs 1989; Nelson 1988; Smith and Williams 1985). In comparison to the gentrification tendencies in the United States, though, the scope is relatively limited in Europe.

The concurrent interest of younger management and technological and commercial employees, on the one hand, and of city management and planning, including real estate management, on the other hand, has improved housing conditions in inner cities. Prices of housing have increased considerably as a result of these pressures—and also as a result of immigration, particularly in inner-urban districts and especially in technologically advanced agglomerations. People with lower incomes leave these centers and look for cheaper housing in the fringes. This exchange of housing population in urban centers has been unbalanced. More inhabitants have left centers than have moved in, and emigrants and immigrants have been of remarkably different social structures. This change in social structure is the second phase of gentrification, begun in Western Europe during the 1980s and currently spreading over the agglomerations.

Space and buildings devoted to housing are scarce in zones attractive to the clientele of the first phase of gentrification, even though this clientele is not large. In addition, the demand for space for business, traffic, and greenery has increased in the inner urban zones— and a public aversion to high-rise buildings (at least in Germany) is shared by many architects, planners, and politicians. As a consequence, demand for housing space in city centers cannot be solved by high-rise buildings. The first phase of gentrification does not, therefore, seem to have had a strong continuous impact on further urban concentration. It has improved housing quality in the center, but it has also strengthened urban spatial expansion by increasing land and rent prices in the cores, thus forcing the broader population out of town.

The second phase of the gentrification process encompasses not only young urban professionals but a broader stratum of the urban population. This is now observable in the core zones of most agglomerations. In larger agglomerations, improvement in the quality of buildings and urban infrastructure has not been able to reach all the mass of older buildings in transitional zones adjacent to the center, though there was considerable improvement in many West German cities in the 1980s. Only during the late 1980s, when public awareness of the housing shortage increased and public support for housing modernization and construction was regained, have these zones been visibly upgraded. With that start, further changes in the local social composition of core zones in large urban areas had been expected, as a result of further increases in household incomes for a larger part of urban populations. But the expectations have changed as a consequence of (1) increased social costs for the unemployed, low-income population and immigrants; (2) the reduction in public monies; and (3) the reduction in private consumption and investment in antici- pation of economic changes and the introduction of a common Eu- ropean currency.

Technological developments have influenced urbanization patterns during the last two decades in Great Britain, France, Benelux, the northern states, northern Italy, and western Germany more than in other European countries. Comparable trends are expected in the East- ern European countries over the next two decades, as the economic and political integration of the European Community, and Europe, in general, increases. But current observations suggest these changes may occur more slowly in Eastern Europe.

Economic Harmonization and Political Convergence

During the last decade, the configuration of Europe has been changed more than that of any other continent. Political conditions, more than economic or technological conditions, are at the heart of these changes. These conditions have changed the urban pattern fundamen- tally and will continue to do so during the next several decades. Two processes, independent from each other in the beginning but converg- ing more and more, are decisive in this development: first, the increas- ing harmonization within the European community and, second, the remodeling of Eastern Europe from socialistic into market economies.

Both of these processes originated in the increasing cooperation among Western European countries, leading to the development of the European Community and to more definite steps toward a political union. Another force was added by the liberalization processes in Eastern Europe beginning in the 1980s. Major changes in the urban landscape had been expected to follow the full realization of the Western European open common market in 1993, but there have been few visible effects. Gradually, the effects of migration, capital concen- tration, and larger markets are becoming apparent—but have not yet been translated into increased employment. The effects on urban- ization have also been less spectacular than expected. Inspection of previous migration patterns shows that migration has tended to de- cline with increasing integration of countries into the European Com- munity (Mackensen 1992). Development of social security schemes and improved economic prospects in Southern European nations, brought about by political stabilization in Spain, Portugal, Greece, and Yugoslavia during the 1970s, increased the willingness of people to stay in their homelands, and of labor migrants to return there, a trend that has reversed in parts of war-torn Yugoslavia. The European Community plans to invest heavily in regional development (allocated funds for 1992 were double those of 1988), and individual nations are trying to compensate for the decreasing interest in the labor they supply to other countries by supporting economic development in their own country.

The attraction of agglomerations for immigrants, however, depends mainly on labor demand, and there is scarcely enough of such demand in the European Community, even for its own population. Thirteen million people are currently unemployed in the Community (excluding unemployment, still rising, in the area that was formerly East Germany), and there is strong pressure to increase productivity. It is important to note that there is a large potential supply of female labor (at least in Great Britain and in Central and Southern Europe), which could meet any expanded demand for labor.

Future immigration is one of the most uncertain factors in further urbanization. Most of the prospective immigrants will ultimately locate in metropolitan areas. The magnitude of potential immigration of resident population relative to the magnitude of available space is much larger in Western Europe than in North America and is one of the important differentiating factors between the two continents. In Europe, the pressure of immigration on the labor and housing markets will ultimately decide the future of urban development. Additional demand for building space could still increase the areas of settlement around cities, and uncertain or absent opportunities for labor could give rise to the possibility of slum developments that, thus far, have been kept within narrow limits in most European cities.

International and Internal Migration

The political and economic changes discussed in the preceding subsection have resulted in population movements within Europe, and from beyond the continent, that have altered the background of the urbanization process. Recent political developments in Eastern Europe initiated heavy migration flows into Western Europe and accentuated the centralization pattern of urbanization, at least in Germany. Although indigenous populations (particularly urban populations) shrank, foreign migration provided surplus labor and exerted additional demand on housing. The tendencies toward contraction inherent in the established urban economic systems were counteracted by the need of metropolitan areas to integrate these immigrants, and they began to grow again—with the resultant substantial housing short-ages, growing rents, and changed regional priorities (Frey 1988).

The particular characteristics of these immigrants affect both hous-ing and labor markets. In Germany, there have been growing numbers of migrants of German origin, but also of other origins, particularly from the former Soviet Union, Romania, and Poland. They will need considerable time to become integrated into the housing and labor markets. In addition, there has been an influx from previously social-ist countries and from different parts of Asia and Africa. These im-migrants ask for political asylum, which has been guaranteed by the German constitution to anyone needing it; but only a small number of these migrants has been granted this status. In spite of their illegal status, for humanitarian reasons, only small parts of this group are being returned to their countries of origin and they form a growing crowd of people demanding housing, as well as a growing pool of unskilled labor demanding work. These two migration streams, to-gether with a large group of refugees from the former Yugoslavia who can be returned only when there has been reconstruction of institu-tions and of buildings in their home countries, create a potential problem in terms of social segregation in metropolitan areas, although there are still minor chances of integrating these individuals into the smaller and rural areas. In addition, there has been the large stream of immigrants from the former German Democratic Republic, which started in late 1989 and continued through 1991.

On the one hand, these developments have burdened the housing and labor markets. On the other hand, they reduced unemployment for a period of a few years, by opening up new consumer markets of considerable size and potential in Eastern Europe for Western Eu-rope's suppliers—particularly for those in West Germany. The impact on production, employment, and housing was spectacular for a while. So long as these developments continue, and if economic conditions improve in Eastern Europe, urbanization in Western Europe will ex-perience another massive expansion period, which will gradually, and increasingly, diffuse into Eastern Europe.

At present, the strongest impact of German unification, and of lib-eralization processes in other European countries, is on the economy of western Germany, although other West European countries are ex-periencing effects. Though unemployment is seriously high in eastern Germany, and wages there have only reached little more than 60 per-cent of the western German wage level, demand from eastern German and East European markets has expanded western German production and, for a while, the accompanying demand for skilled labor. At the same time, strong pressures to achieve higher productivity and to send production abroad have weakened the labor market. Migration from East to West Germany was subsidized in late 1989, but since the middle of 1990 migration has become possible only with documented labor and housing contracts in place—so this migration, which may have amounted to another 150,000 to 200,000 persons in 1991, is increasing housing production and employment, not unemployment, in western German urban areas.

A new experience is the recent increase in immigration within Eastern Europe. Only very recently have migrants from regions in Southeast and Far Eastern Europe begun to enter the Eastern European countries that have started market economies. The targets of immigration are always the larger cities. In Eastern European states the history of centralized political regimes created a difficult legacy on which to build strong regional and urban structures. Decentralization by the development of federalist structures will become an important target, but one that will be difficult to reach. Improved economic conditions will mean that the rural and heavily industrial districts will have lower incomes—agrarian overproduction can be envisaged as the result of increased productivity and competition. Age structures in the regions of outmigration have become unbalanced so that the manpower to develop alternative economic activities is diminished. Much is being expected from the current regionalization measures, with anticipated strengthening of political and administrative infrastructure in rural and old industrial regions. But the process of establishing this infrastructure in East European countries demands large quantities of human and financial capital, which will not be available in the near future. The regionalization process, therefore, will take a considerable length of time to become effective.

Clearly, the pattern of international migration in Europe changed drastically during the 1980s and left its impact on urban regions. The patterns of internal migration changed as well. International migration does not add much to internal migration, since immigrants tend to move mostly from their home countries and then stay in the agglomerations where they first settled. The influence of international migration on urban concentration is a relative one, adding to the total population mostly by adding to the numbers of inhabitants of large agglomerations. In contrast, the process of internal migration is one of regional distribution. It adds to both the process of concentration in large agglomerations and the process of decentralization, by enlarging the physical area included in these large agglomerations.

Internal migration occurs mainly over short distances. About two-thirds of all internal migrants move not farther than 30 miles; only 20 percent move beyond 80 km (about 50 miles). Long-distance moves are made mostly by specialized, skilled labor and, increasingly, by people about to retire. Short-distance moves, on the other hand, consist mostly of changes of housing within either metropolitan areas (among core and fringe and larger areas of influence and commuting), rural communities or their metropolitan areas (among rural towns and minor central places), or from rural to urban housing.

The result is increased pressure for growth on the rings around central cities and on the wider metropolitan region. Urban communities of more than 10,000 inhabitants and neighborhoods close to them continue to decrease everywhere in Western Germany, but smaller communities gain inhabitants. The growing, relatively wealthy family is no longer seeking spacious living on the outskirts of cities, as it formerly did. The poorer family, which cannot afford the rising land values and rents of inner cities, must look for housing farther from the center. A different development pattern has started in East Germany, where private housing was almost impossible before. People with some resources move out from the deteriorated housing areas and industrially built complexes to the outskirts of cities, and start to establish there what has long been known in Western nations as the "suburban fringe." There is increased settlement in the "open landscape," at least in the less densely settled areas around cities within the zone of influence of the agglomerations—and this zone continues to expand. This pattern also characterizes rural areas in West Germany, where zones of housing and commuting are building up even around smaller cities. Peasants have to add to their rural income by taking up additional "urban" jobs, or they change to urban occupations. The result is that villages change into bedroom communities of accessible cities. In addition, in rural areas, secondary housing expands. Urban residents buy or rent houses in rural settlements for recreational purposes. As farming, under the current global and European conditions, becomes less profitable for smaller farms, many peasants sell land and houses. Communities expect additional economic activity from this recreational demand, and build recreational settlements in considerable numbers. But the economic effects for the resident population seem small, and the burden on the local infrastructure seems large. In East Germany, though, rural and heavily industrialized areas struggle to attract economically viable businesses—many hope for tourism.

These processes change the spatial social structure of metropolitan areas. Recreationally attractive communities are being left by peasants and settled by urban people. The areas immediately around central cities are being filled more and more by urban dwellers. The structure of more inner-urban residential areas has also changed. Immigration and housing developments have increased the social segregation within central cores. In some agglomerations, like Frankfurt, parts of the core area are being occupied by a majority of immigrants already; in others, like Berlin, specialized living quarters have developed; and in some cities, like Cologne, urban planning has begun to focus on locational characteristics of neighborhoods and quarters. East German agglomerations are trying to restore center cities, but shopping centers in the fringes draw most of consumer spending; private investment is going to the building of new structures, not the restoration of old ones; and the office space built during the last few years is likely to suffice for decades. This development resembles much of the experience of North American urban areas. The segregation patterns of the American experience, where ethnic separations have been characteristic, can increasingly be applied to European cities, where the ethnic factor is just one element of segregation.

Housing and Planning Policies

Housing and planning policies differentiate European from North American urbanization processes. For the last decade in Western Europe these policies have been comparatively weak. The increasing housing shortages and the magnitude of the economic disparities, however, will necessitate more vigorous political action in the years ahead.

Urban policies differ strongly in European countries. In Eastern Europe, private housing and urban sprawl have expanded visibly in the last ten years, particularly in metropolitan and industrial regions, and can be expected to increase further as a consequence of political and economic change. In Western Germany, after a period in which social housing has been neglected, social changes have forced a renewal of housing programs. The real estate market is regarded as inadequate to react to demand by itself. Housing shortages have increased during the last decade because of immigration and a variety of social changes. Household structure has changed considerably, and average household size has declined as the numbers of consensual unions and singles have increased. The demand for more spacious living quarters has also risen during the last fifteen years, owing to the building of larger flats and homes and the purchasing of spacious, formerly peasant-owned houses. Other tendencies add to the growing demand. Shrinking families have a tendency not to move into smaller flats or houses. There is less readiness to sublet rooms to students and apprentices, and young people leaving the homes of their parents increasingly expect to find opportunities to live in flats of their own. To add to Germany's housing shortage, there is an inadequate supply of cheap and publicly supported housing for lower-income groups. Even when income rises, many people continue to occupy flats originally provided them when they had lower incomes. With higher old-age pensions, single pensioners tend to keep larger flats at older ages, and the eldest cohort of the population increases in number and proportionally. Up to about ten years ago, the building of private houses with additional flats to be rented (or reserved for the older generation of the family) was publicly supported. However, changes in this public program led to a change in the actual number of available flats; about a half a million smaller flats have simply been incorporated into single-family flats and homes. It is now against the law to rent flats for limited periods—occupants are not required to leave after the intended period. The result is that flats are not offered for rental at all if they are available for limited periods only. The poor condition of housing, old and recent, in the former Eastern Germany, and in other Eastern and Southeastern European countries (and also in Western Germany), adds to the housing shortage.

In Germany, during the last decade, increasing shortages of public funds have reduced not only housing but other social security measures (health, education, old age plans) as well. During the 1980s the shortage of public funding was due mainly to increasing demand for unemployment security and to increased prices of services. In the 1990s the shortage was aggravated by the costs of reunification and by economic and social change in Eastern Europe. Public and private investment in housing is now being expanded but has not yet resolved the shortages. Together with the developments in the housing market, this implies that the factors encouraging segregation remain. The result is a growing importance of informal social networks in neighborhoods and organizations, particularly in certain regions and center cores, where public support became less satisfactory and employment opportunities more specialized.

RESULTS: THE GERMAN EXAMPLE

Three tendencies have characterized the West German urbanization process: the differentiation between agglomerations according to their economic structure; the continued relative attractiveness of agglomerations (concentration); and the expanding influence of agglomerations into the "wider setting" (as referred to by Parr in chapter 7 of this volume) of the settlement landscape (decentralization). East German urbanization was managed by central government policy, which concentrated on new structures, though older stocks deteriorated.

Data for metropolitan area agglomerations in Germany are shown in table 10.1. (See figure 10.1 in conjunction with the tables in this chapter.) It is evident from the table that not all agglomerations lost population during the 1980–92 period. Among the metropolitan areas, only Nuremberg gained inhabitants in all three of the four-year periods. All the rest lost during 1980–84, though some only slightly (e.g., Rhine-Neckar). It is only between 1984 and 1988 that the large southern agglomerations gained, while the northern ones lost. Medium-sized agglomerations lost during 1980–84, but all gained during 1988–92, as did all metropolitan areas. It is not so much then, that the southern areas proved successful—typical medium-sized areas like Osnabrück, Münster, Karlsruhe, and Augsburg are among the winners. This observation makes it clear that two factors accounted for agglomeration growth during the periods observed: immigration (low during 1980–84 and high during 1988–92) and being a service (rather than industrial) agglomeration (Mackensen 1994, 1995). In West Germany, large agglomerations did not shrink, as many seem to think. Only in the Ruhr area, Rhine-Mark, Rhine-Neckar, Aachen, and the Saar—the old industrialized agglomerations—and in Stuttgart and Bielefeld did the areas around the central cores decline during 1980–84, but all—except the Saar—recovered during 1984–88 and 1988–92. (See table 10.2.) All other fringe areas in West Germany grew, even during 1980–84.

As table 10.2 indicates, with the exception of Münster and Freiburg, all central cores lost populations. Some agglomerations are still in the suburbanization phase (as defined by Klaasen and Burns 1987)— Hannover, Cologne-Bonn, Rhine-Neckar (Mannheim-Heidelberg), Nuremberg, and even Munich. But in Hamburg, Ruhr, Rhine-Main (Frankfurt), and Stuttgart, this did not apply during the 1980–84 period. For both the later periods the cores lost few people, and all cores finally gained residents. The expansion of the agglomerated areas continues in West Germany—but only as a consequence of surplus immigration.

In East Germany, the story is entirely different. With the exception of Erfurt and East Berlin, all agglomerations lost inhabitants in all the periods. The strong preferences for the capital of the GDR for the supply of consumer goods, for housing development, and for investment in

Table 10.1 POPULATION AGGLOMERATIONS IN GERMANY, 1980–92

Agglomeration	Population (thousands)				Density[3] 1992 (No. per sq. km.)	% Change in Population			Relative % Change in Population, 1980–92
	1980	1984	1988	1992		1980–84 (1980 = 100)	1984–88 (1980 = 100)	1988–92 (1980 = 100)	
METROPOLITAN AREAS[1] (without Berlin)	34,865	34,485	34,568	35,938	434	98.9	100.2	104.0	100.4
West Germany	31,573	31,225	31,364	32,966	456	98.9	100.4	105.1	101.8
Hamburg	2,935	2,913	2,906	3,058	366	99.3	99.7	105.2	101.5
Bremen	1,814	1,798	1,780	1,856	185	99.1	99.0	104.3	99.7
Hannover	1,831	1,814	1,802	1,872	287	99.0	99.3	103.9	99.6
Ruhr[a]	4,899	4,779	4,736	4,885	1,158	97.5	99.1	103.1	97.1
Rhine-Mark[b]	4,371	4,287	4,281	4,471	807	98.1	99.9	104.4	99.6
Cologne-Bonn	3,160	3,132	3,151	3,318	550	99.1	100.6	105.3	102.3
Rhine-Main[c]	3,899	3,867	3,909	4,137	459	99.2	101.1	105.8	103.5
Rhine-Neckar[d]	1,869	1,866	1,886	2,004	402	99.9	101.1	106.3	104.6
Stuttgart	3,247	3,232	3,318	3,567	491	99.5	102.2	107.5	107.2
Munich	2,216	2,203	2,243	2,361	429	99.4	101.8	105.2	103.9
Nuremberg	1,331	1,323	1,351	1,436	296	100.1	101.4	106.3	105.2
East Germany									
Leipzig	2,004	1,985	1,946	1,806	282	99.1	98.0	92.8	87.5
Dresden	1,287	1,274	1,258	1,167	290	99.0	98.7	92.8	88.0
MEDIUM AGGLOMERATIONS[2]									
West Germany	10,282	10,243	10,891	10,867	286	99.6	100.4	105.7	103.0
Kiel	684	682	677	702	203	99.7	99.3	103.7	100.0
Lübeck	449	441	436	449	197	98.3	98.8	102.9	97.3
Brunswick	470	958	951	994	242	98.7	99.2	104.5	99.8
Osnabrück	442	444	446	484	216	100.4	100.4	108.6	106.8
Bielefeld	1,451	1,428	1,431	1,528	375	98.5	100.2	106.8	102.7

Münster	1,348	1,358	1,362	1,447	244	100.8	100.3	106.7	104.7
Aachen	524	519	519	543	767	99.0	100.0	104.6	100.9
Kassel	417	410	411	433	309	98.4	100.1	105.5	101.2
Saar[e]	1,112	1,098	1,086	1,107	419	98.7	99.0	101.9	96.9
Karlsruhe	1,134	1,135	1,152	1,229	438	100.1	101.5	106.8	105.8
Freiburg[f]	826	838	860	926	223	101.4	102.6	107.7	109.5
Ulm	403	401	408	439	220	99.6	101.8	107.5	106.3
Augsburg	523	531	542	586	293	101.5	102.1	108.2	109.4
East Germany	2,917	2,884	2,871	2,693	294	98.9	99.5	93.8	89.7
Chemnitz	1,825	1,792	1,762	1,644	311	98.2	98.3	93.3	87.4
Erfurt	327	329	332	312	273	100.6	100.8	93.9	92.6
Magdeburg	493	484	485	457	245	98.3	100.1	94.2	90.1
Rostock	273	279	292	281	323	102.2	104.6	96.3	100.3
ALL AGGLOMERATIONS (including Berlin)	52,076	51,638	51,919	53,798	393	99.2	100.5	103.6	100.7
Berlin	4,013	4,028	4,200	4,299	586	100.3	104.3	102.4	104.5
West Germany	41,855	41,468	41,645	43,833	398	99.1	100.4	105.3	102.1
East Germany	6,209	6,144	6,074	5,666	289	99.0	98.9	93.3	88.6
REST OF GERMANY	26,169	26,146	26,644	26,523	120	99.9	101.9	99.5	98.7
ALL GERMANY	78,245	77,784	78,562	80,321	225	99.4	101.0	102.2	100.0

Source: Calculated from official census data. Data for West Germany corrected to 1987 census definitions; data for East Germany prior to 1990 reported in DDR statistics.

Notes: (1) Metropolitan areas are defined as areas that have central cities with more than 500,000 people in the core central city and in other city counties within the fringe area, counties in the fringe area with more than 300 inhabitants per square kilometer, and counties in the outer parts of metropolitan areas (field) that have most of their territory within 100 km of the central city. (2) Medium agglomerations are defined as areas that have central cities with more than 150,000, but less than 500,000, people in the core central city and in other city counties within the fringe area, counties in the fringe area with more than 300 inhabitants per square kilometer, and counties in the outer parts of the areas that have most of their territory within 50 km of the central city. (3) Density = Population ÷ square kilometers. (4) Percentage change in population, 1980–92 ÷ mean All Germany percent change in population (= 102.6) multiplied by 100.
Central cities: (a) Essen; (b) Düsseldorf; (c) Frankfurt/Main; (d) Mannheim; (e) Saarbrücken; (f) Breisgau.

Table 10.2 ZONAL STRUCTURE AND CHANGE IN AGGLOMERATIONS OF POPULATION IN GERMANY, 1980–92

Agglomeration	Core			Fringe			Field		
	1980–84 (1980 = 100)	1984–88 (1984 = 100)	1988–92 (1988 = 100)	1980–84 (1980 = 100)	1984–88 (1984 = 100)	1988–92 (1988 = 100)	1980–84 (1980 = 100)	1984–88 (1984 = 100)	1988–92 (1988 = 100)
METROPOLITAN AREAS[1] (without Berlin)	97.2	99.1	102.8	99.9	101.3	104.9	100.8	100.9	104.8
West Germany	97.0	99.1	103.9	100.0	101.6	105.6	101.1	101.4	106.6
Hamburg	97.5	98.5	104.9	99.6	101.8	104.7	102.1	101.2	106.0
Bremen	97.1	97.8	103.8	—	—	—	100.7	99.8	104.6
Hannover	96.4	97.6	104.8	100.6	100.3	104.5	99.8	99.8	102.8
Ruhr[a]	96.7	98.1	102.5	98.9	100.8	104.2	—	—	—
Rhine-Mark[b]	96.6	98.6	103.6	99.5	101.3	105.2	101.2	101.0	105.8
Cologne-Bonn	96.7	99.5	103.5	101.6	101.8	106.4	100.3	100.9	107.1
Rhine-Main[c]	97.4	100.2	104.6	99.9	101.7	105.8	100.4	101.3	107.4
Rhine-Neckar[d]	98.3	100.9	106.2	100.4	101.5	105.9	100.9	100.9	106.5
Stuttgart	96.2	101.5	106.6	99.6	102.7	106.6	101.5	103.4	109.8
Munich	96.5	100.3	102.9	103.7	103.3	106.8	102.9	103.8	108.7
Nuremberg	98.2	100.5	104.9	103.1	102.2	106.4	102.2	102.4	108.1
East Germany	100.0	99.3	92.0	97.4	96.2	93.3	98.8	98.0	93.4
Leipzig	100.1	99.0	91.4	97.0	95.6	94.0	98.8	98.0	94.0
Dresden	99.7	100.0	93.1	97.9	97.2	92.4	98.8	98.0	92.7
MEDIUM AGGLOMERATION[2]	98.9	99.9	101.8	99.2	99.7	101.7	100.0	100.6	104.8
West Germany	98.3	99.5	104.9	99.6	100.4	105.3	100.5	100.9	106.4
Kiel	98.0	99.0	103.7	—	—	—	100.6	99.5	103.7
Lübeck	96.6	97.7	102.9	—	—	—	100.0	99.8	103.0

Brunswick	97.5	98.5	102.8	—	—	—	100.1	100.1	106.4
Osnabrück	97.6	99.3	109.4	—	—	—	101.9	101.0	108.1
Bielefeld	97.5	100.2	104.6	99.1	100.3	107.0	98.4	100.1	107.7
Münster	100.1	96.3	107.7	—	—	—	100.9	101.3	105.9
Aachen	98.2	99.6	105.4	99.6	100.3	103.9	—	—	—
Kassel	95.7	100.2	105.2	—	—	—	100.9	100.0	105.7
Saar[e]	98.4	97.9	101.6	98.7	99.3	102.7	99.5	99.7	100.0
Karlsruhe	98.9	100.4	106.1	100.9	101.7	106.5	100.0	102.2	108.1
Freiburg[f]	103.1	104.1	107.0	—	—	—	101.0	102.2	107.9
Ulm	98.6	104.9	107.2	100.0	100.7	107.3	99.8	100.9	107.9
Augsburg	99.3	100.9	106.6	—	—	—	103.3	103.2	109.5
East Germany	100.6	101.2	93.4	98.4	98.1	93.2	97.0	98.6	95.1
Chemnitz	99.5	99.4	91.2	98.2	97.8	93.1	97.2	98.2	95.3
Erfurt	101.2	102.1	92.7	—	—	—	99.6	98.5	96.2
Magdeburg	100.5	100.5	94.4	—	—	—	95.2	99.6	93.9
Rostock	102.2	104.7	96.3	102.2	104.3	95.9	—	—	—
ALL AGGLOMERATIONS (including Berlin)	98.0	100.2	102.8	99.7	101.0	104.2	100.4	100.7	104.4
Berlin	100.4	105.4	103.8	—	—	—	100.2	99.4	95.6
West Germany	97.2	99.2	104.1	100.0	101.4	105.5	100.9	101.2	106.5
East Germany	100.3	100.2	92.6	98.0	97.3	93.3	98.1	98.2	94.1

Sources: See Table 10.1.
Notes: See Table 10.1. Agglomerations that have no fringe or field area are marked —.

Figure 10.1 METROPOLITAN AREAS AND AGGLOMERATIONS IN GERMANY

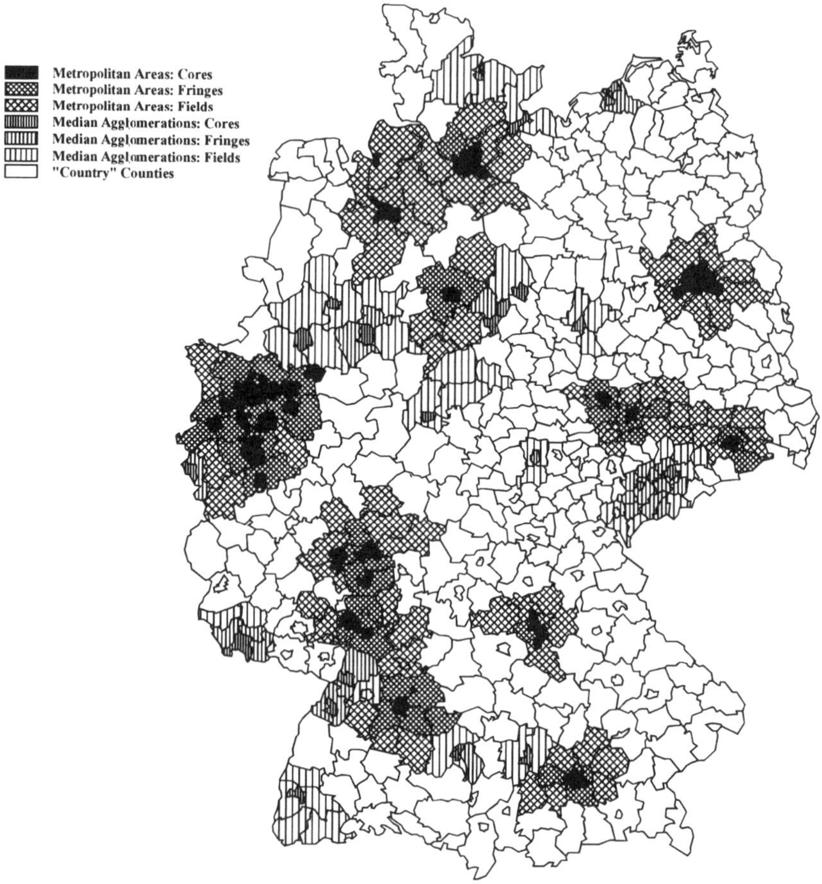

Metropolitan Areas: Cores
Metropolitan Areas: Fringes
Metropolitan Areas: Fields
Median Agglomerations: Cores
Median Agglomerations: Fringes
Median Agglomerations: Fields
"Country" Counties

industry resulted in large migration flows to East Berlin. Building policies in the GDR favored large housing projects close to urban concentrations—not the suburbanization experienced in Western nations. Rostock was the exception. Shipyards and recreational developments along the Baltic coast produced a special trend. But since unification, all agglomerations have continued to lose inhabitants.

Urban development does not, of course, only differ between agglomerations and rural areas; it also differs within each. Urban areas within rural counties have participated in patterns of urban decline similar to those experienced by the agglomerations. Rural counties are sometimes part of agglomerations, forming their fringes and cores in wide fields of agglomeration influence; and sometimes rural areas form apart from agglomeration. Some rural areas (with low densities) are strongly industrialized; others are economically strong agrarian areas, with intensive agricultural production. Some rural regions have increasing tourism; but only a few are economically viable from tourism alone. (West Germany in the vicinity of the Alps is an example.) Table 10.3 provides data on these rural areas.

Urban development is comparatively weak in dense industrial metropolitan areas, as well as in rural areas, except for tourist regions. But, in the nearby fringes and the wider geographic areas around the central cores, urban areas continue to grow—whether characterized by service or industrial agglomerations. These latter agglomerations

Table 10.3 URBAN AND RURAL INDUSTRIAL DEVELOPMENT AND POPULATION CHANGE IN WEST GERMANY, 1980–87

	Percentage Population Change in Urban and Rural Communities in Rural Counties, 1980–87			
	Fringes		Fields	
Types of Rural Counties in Agglomerations	Urban[a]	Rural[a]	Urban[a]	Rural[a]
Large service agglomerations	1.007	1.076	0.999	1.017
Large industrial agglomerations	0.997	1.023	1.016	1.029
Medium service agglomerations	1.011	1.025	1.009	1.018
Medium industrial agglomerations	0.977	1.025	1.008	1.027
	Urban Communities		Rural Communities	
Counties in rural areas[b]	0.995		1.020	
Rural industrial areas[c]	0.997		1.012	
Rural agrarian areas[d]	0.983		1.006	
Rural tourist areas[e]	1.010		1.033	
Rural peripheral areas[f]	0.985		1.015	

Notes: For definitions of large and medium agglomerations, see notes to table 10.1.
a. Urban places are communities in rural counties with more than 10,000 inhabitants in 1987; smaller communities are labeled "rural."
b. Rural areas are counties not included in agglomeration fields or fringes.
c. Industrial areas have a higher percentage of industrial employment than agrarian.
d. Agrarian areas have a higher percentage of agrarian employment than industrial.
e. Tourist areas are the counties in the Northern Alps.
f. Peripheral areas are counties far from agglomerations with severe structural imbalances.

may be due to an industrial tendency to choose smaller cities for locations. Here, too, the expanding population is being housed in smaller communities. Population growth in the vicinity of industrial agglomerations is greater in the more remote areas than in the fringes. This is not true for service agglomerations, which still adhere more to the traditional suburbanization format—fringes grow more than fields. The most striking result of this analysis is that small communities are expanding everywhere, near large and medium-sized metropolitan areas and in rural areas. In the context of rural areas, this expansion can be described as "desuburbanization," whereas in the context of the large population concentrations—the metropolitan areas—it can be described as "decentralization."

SUMMARY

Technological, political, and demographic changes in Western Europe suggest continued increased concentration of population in the large metropolitan regions. In spite of some gentrification, core central cities are increasingly business-based, despite the outmigration of many production units. New concentrations of population are growing continuously to fill the landscape between former small cities and rural settlements. These changes in the population density map have been influenced by population decline, immigration, and national policies. Decentralization—in Western Europe—does not mean decreasing attractiveness of the largest metropolitan centers. It means that higher population densities and higher land use exist in all portions of the urban areas.

References

Dangschat, J. S., and J. Friedrichs. 1989. *Gentrification in der Inneren Stadt von Hamburg*. Hamburg: Gesellschaft für Sozialwissenschaftliche Stadtforschung.
Fassmann, H., and R. Muenz, eds. 1996. "Historische Entwicklung und gesellschaftliche Folgen" in *Migration in Europa, 1945–2000*. Frankfurt am Main: Campus.

Frey, W. H. 1988. "The Reemergence of Core Region Growth: A Return to the Metropolis." *International Regional Science Review* 11.

Friedrichs, J., et al. 1986. *Nord-Südgefälle in der Bundesrepublik?* Opladen: Wesdt. Verlag.

Illeris, S. 1991. "Urban and Regional Development in Western Europe in the 1990s—Will Everything Happen in the London-Brussels-Frankfurt-Milan 'Banana'?" Paper presented at the meeting of the IGU Commission on Urban Systems and Urban Development, Budapest. June.

Klaasen, L., and L. Burns. 1987. *Spatial Cycles.* Edited by Leo van den Berg. Aldershot, England: Gower.

Mackensen, R. 1979. *Regionale Mobiltätsprozesse in der Bundesrepublik Deutschland.* Berlin: TUB Arbeitshefte ISR 12.

————. 1992. "Aussenwanderungen der Bundesrepublik Deutschland-Geschichte und Perspektiven." *Klagenfurter Geographische Schriften* 10. Klagenfurt: Institut für Geographie der Universität für Bildungswissenschaften.

————. 1994. "Urbanization under Federalist and Centralist Government: The Case of Two German States, 1980–1988." *Acta Demographica.* Heidelberg: Physika.

————. 1995. "Die deutschen Agglomerationen, 1980–2010: Regionale Entwicklungen und Verflechtungen aus der Sicht der Bevölkerungsentwicklung." *Jahresbericht 1995, Verband Deutscher Städtestatistiker.* Leipzig: Amt für Statistik und Wahlen.

Nelson, K. P. 1988. *Gentrification and Distressed Cities.* Madison: University of Wisconsin Press.

Nijkamp, P. 1993. *Europe on the Move.* Aldershot, England: Avebury.

Smith, N., and P. Williams. *Gentrification of the City.* Winchester, England: Allen and Unwin.

Part Three

IMPLICATIONS OF
METROPOLITAN CHANGE

Chapter Eleven

FISCAL CONSEQUENCES FOR U.S. CENTRAL CITIES OF THE CHANGING URBAN FORM

Helen F. Ladd

Changes in the economic structure of urban areas in the United States have potentially powerful effects on the fiscal condition of the nation's central cities. In contrast to Europe, many American cities have significant responsibility for providing redistributive services. Movement of middle- and upper-income households and jobs out of the central city to the suburbs reduces the taxable base of the city and may raise the cost of providing adequate public services to the remaining relatively poorer city residents. In addition, because cities rely heavily on property taxes, shifts in the composition of city employment away from property-intensive manufacturing activity toward labor-intensive services could possibly weaken the fiscal condition of cities.

Three strategies are available for examining how changes in the economic structure of urban areas affect the fiscal condition of central cities. One strategy is to undertake a detailed case study of a single metropolitan area.[1] With this approach, full account can be taken of the economic and fiscal variation among suburban communities within the metropolitan area and of the institutional environment in which fiscal decisions are made. However, conclusions from a detailed investigation of one area are often hard to generalize to other areas. A second strategy is to undertake a cross-sectional analysis of changes within many metropolitan areas. In this type of study, one might look at such questions as how changes in city relative to suburban employment vary across metropolitan areas with changes in city relative to suburban tax burdens. By focusing on changes in each city relative to those in the suburbs, this approach highlights the effects of changes within metropolitan areas, but is subject to the criticisms that suburban communities within each metropolitan area are not homogeneous and that any conclusions about fiscal changes in cities are relative to what is happening in the suburbs.

A third strategy, focusing on central cities alone, is pursued here. This strategy involves analyzing how economic and social forces affect the fiscal condition of central cities, not relative to their suburbs, but relative to those same cities in some baseline year. If done carefully, this approach indicates how the underlying, or structural, fiscal condition of one city compares to that of another at one point in time and how the fiscal condition of each city has changed over time. Incorporated into the measure of fiscal condition would be the effects not only of changes in urban form but also of a broader set of economic and social forces. Hence, a possible disadvantage of this approach for the present purpose is that the effects on city fiscal condition of economic changes within urban areas cannot be separated from those of the broader set of forces. However, one can gain insight into the effects of changes in urban form by examining how the measured changes in city fiscal condition vary across cities grouped by changes in various characteristics of the city economy.

The first section of this chapter contains background information on U.S. central cities. Section two develops the main themes of the chapter: first, that economic and social forces have led to a significant deterioration over time in the ability of many U.S. central cities to provide adequate services to city residents at reasonable tax burdens; and, second, that this deterioration has been most severe in the largest cities and in those experiencing the slowest rates of growth in city economic activity and income of city residents. Section three discusses the important role of intergovernmental assistance to cities, documenting the rapid growth in assistance during the 1970s and the dramatic decline during the 1980s. Whereas sections two and three focus on the underlying or structural condition of city finances reflecting patterns of economic development and the sharing of fiscal responsibilities with higher levels of government, the following section four turns to the manifestations of this condition, namely, higher city tax burdens and lower service levels. The chapter ends with a brief concluding section emphasizing the great fiscal difficulty many American cities are likely to confront in the absence of more participation by state and federal governments.

BRIEF CHARACTERIZATION OF U.S. CENTRAL CITIES

The U.S. Census defines a central city as the principal city that serves as the center of a larger unit such as a metropolitan statistical area.

In some metropolitan areas, two or three cities (each with a minimum population of 50,000) are designated as central cities; these multiple central cities together form the core of the metropolitan area.

Two samples of central cities are used throughout this chapter. The larger sample of eighty-six cities includes all cities that fall into one or both of the following categories: cities with populations over 300,000 in 1970 or 1980 and central cities in one of the nation's fifty largest metropolitan areas in either 1970 or 1980. This is not a random sample of central cities; instead, it is the universe of major central cities in the nation. These eighty-six cities range from the giants of New York, Chicago, and Los Angeles—with 1980 populations over 2.9 million—to Troy, N.Y., and Passaic, N.J., with 1980 populations below 60,000. The absence of complete data for some of these cities limits this sample to seventy-one (or seventy when Washington, D.C., is excluded) for much of the analysis. The second sample (the big-city sample) is a subset of the first and includes thirty-three of the nation's most populous cities.

Table 11.1 provides basic descriptive data for the sample of thirty-three big cities. In 1980 the city share of metropolitan population averaged about 40 percent, but varied significantly across areas, ranging from 20 percent or less in Boston, Pittsburgh, and Saint Louis to highs of 73 percent in Jacksonville and San Antonio. This share changes over time at different rates across cities, both because of differing rates of growth of metropolitan areas and because some central cities, especially newer cities in the Southwest, are empowered to annex surrounding territory. Phoenix, Arizona, and the three Texas cities of Dallas, Houston, and San Antonio all increased their land area between 1970 and 1980 by 25 percent or more. Such annexations both helped these cities to capture some of the growth of their metropolitan areas and to maintain income levels of city residents close to those of their metropolitan areas. In contrast, the older cities in the Northeast, such as Philadelphia, Boston, and New York, have limited powers of annexation and, consequently, over time have accounted for smaller portions of their metropolitan areas and have increasingly become the home of the disadvantaged and minorities who do not have access to the wealthier suburbs. Clearly, some of the fiscal challenges facing many U.S. central cities today relate to rigid boundaries in many areas that prevent city fiscal bases from expanding along with the metropolitan area that they help sustain.[2]

Historically, central cities were the center of manufacturing and retail activity, but this characterization no longer coincides with the facts (see table 11.2). Moreover, the average economic structure,

Table 11.1 POPULATION, PER CAPITA INCOME, AND LAND AREA FOR 33 BIG U.S. CITIES

	City Population		City Population/Metropolitan Area Population		City Per Capita Income/Metropolitan Per Capita Income		Land Area of City (square miles)	
	1980	% Change, 1970–80	1980 (%)	% Change, 1970–80	1979 (%)	% Change, 1969–79	1982	% Change, 1972–82
Atlanta	425,022	−14.5	21.0	−32.8	83.8	−7.3	131.5	0.0
Baltimore	786,775	−13.1	36.2	−17.3	76.5	−11.3	78.3	0.0
Boston	562,994	−12.2	20.4	−7.9	80.1	−3.9	46.0	0.0
Buffalo	357,870	−22.7	28.8	−16.0	83.8	−2.2	41.3	0.0
Chicago	3,005,072	−10.7	42.3	−12.4	81.0	−9.0	222.8	0.0
Cincinnati	385,457	−14.8	27.5	−15.7	91.5	−6.3	78.1	−0.0
Cleveland	573,822	−23.6	30.2	−16.9	71.0	−7.8	75.9	0.0
Columbus	564,871	4.7	51.7	−2.6	91.1	0.2	180.1	22.5
Dallas	904,078	7.1	30.4	−14.4	104.1	0.3	351.5	31.7
Denver	492,365	−4.3	30.4	−26.8	96.1	−4.9	110.1	13.2
Detroit	1,203,339	−20.4	27.6	−18.9	73.3	−14.6	138.0	0.0
Houston	1,595,138	29.5	54.9	−10.9	98.8	−0.8	519.3	28.3
Indianapolis	700,807	−5.7	60.1	−10.2	97.8	−2.9	366.0	−3.5
Jacksonville	540,920	4.4	73.3	−12.0	100.3	0.5	765.7	−0.0
Kansas City	448,159	−11.7	33.8	−15.2	91.6	−4.5	316.3	0.0
Los Angeles	2,966,850	5.4	39.7	−0.8	101.3	−0.1	464.6	0.2
Memphis	646,356	3.7	70.8	−5.3	99.4	−3.1	280.8	19.1

Miami	346,865	3.6	21.3	−19.2	78.8	−3.5	34.3	0.0
Milwaukee	636,212	−11.3	45.5	−10.9	85.0	−6.3	95.0	−0.0
Minneapolis	370,951	−14.6	17.6	−20.6	92.0	−4.2	53.4	0.0
New Orleans	557,515	−5.7	47.0	−16.9	92.0	−4.3	197.1	0.0
New York	7,071,639	−10.4	77.5	−2.0	92.0	−9.1	299.7	0.0
Philadelphia	1,688,210	−13.4	35.8	−11.4	81.2	−8.0	128.5	0.0
Phoenix	789,704	35.8	52.3	−12.6	97.9	−4.0	322.1	25.3
Pittsburgh	423,938	−18.5	18.7	−13.5	88.9	−7.5	52.2	0.0
Portland, Ore.	366,383	−4.2	29.5	−22.4	97.1	−3.6	106.8	15.6
Saint Louis	453,085	−27.2	19.2	−25.5	76.7	−6.3	61.2	0.0
San Antonio	785,880	20.1	73.3	−0.5	92.0	−2.7	263.6	33.1
San Diego	875,538	26.2	47.0	−8.0	100.7	−1.3	323.5	0.2
San Francisco	678,974	−5.1	20.9	−9.3	96.6	−5.9	45.4	0.0
San Jose	629,442	41.8	48.6	16.6	88.0	−0.1	157.3	10.5
Seattle	493,846	−7.0	30.7	−17.6	99.9	−5.4	83.6	0.0
Washington, D.C.	638,333	−15.6	20.9	−19.8	87.4	−2.8	61.4	0.0
Average (33)	998,982	−3.2	38.9	−13.0	89.9	−4.6	195.6	5.9
Average (no annex)	1,091,341	−9.9	35.1	−14.6	87.6	−5.6	173.5	−0.1
Average (annex >0)	752,691	14.9	49.1	−8.8	96.1	−2.1	254.6	22.2

Sources: U.S. Bureau of the Census, 1983, Current Population Reports, series P-25 and P-26 (Washington, D.C.: U.S. Government Printing Office); U.S. Bureau of the Census, 1983, County and City Data Book, 1983 (Washington, D.C.: U.S. Government Printing Office); and U.S. Bureau of the Census, 1987, 1988 Statistical Abstract (Washington, D.C.: U.S. Government Printing Office), table 34.

Table 11.2 PRIVATE-SECTOR EMPLOYMENT AND PAYROLLS IN THE UNITED
STATES, 1982 (AVERAGE, 86 CITIES)

	Private-Sector Employment		Private-Sector Payrolls	
	Cities (%)	U.S. (%)	Cities (%)	U.S. (%)
Manufacturing	20.7	26.5	24.3	32.1
Retail	17.0	20.7	9.6	11.8
Services	29.6	25.2	25.6	21.3
Wholesale	8.0	7.1	9.8	8.7
TCPU[a]	8.0	7.1	9.8	8.7
FIRE[b]	11.1	7.4	12.5	8.0
Construction	4.8	5.3	5.9	6.6
Minerals	0.8	1.6	1.3	2.4
Total	100.0	100.0	100.0	100.0

Source: Ladd and Yinger (1991: table 2.3); original table based on data from U.S. Bureau
of the Census, 1984, County Business Patterns, 1982 (Washington, D.C.: U.S. Government Printing Office).
[a]Transportation, communications, and public utilities.
[b]Finance, insurance, and real estate.

defined in terms of the mix of jobs and payrolls, of the eighty-six
major central cities differs substantially from that of the nation as a
whole. In 1982, only about 21 percent of private-sector city employment was in manufacturing, in contrast to almost 27 percent for the
nation. Similarly, retail trade accounted for only 17 percent of employment (and even less for payroll) in cities, compared to about 21
percent in the nation.[3] Services accounted for the largest proportion
of city employment, almost 30 percent in 1982. Other information-
and communication-based sectors (transportation, communications,
and public utilities [TCPU] and finance, insurance, and real estate
[FIRE]), as well as wholesale trade, are also disproportionately represented in cities.

These city averages mask wide variation in the mix of jobs across
cities. Cities characterized as manufacturing centers, such as Detroit,
Akron, and Pittsburgh, developed initially as major manufacturing
centers specializing in particular products such as automobiles or
steel. In the twenty-two cities of this type, nearly one in three private-
sector jobs is in manufacturing. Only in these cities does the share of
manufacturing jobs on average exceed the share of service jobs. Other
cities can be characterized as diversified service centers catering to
national, regional, or subregional markets. Such cities typically have
large employment shares in services. Other cities can be characterized

as centers of government and education—such as Washington, D.C., and state capitals—with large employment shares in public-sector jobs; as industrial, mining, and military centers that typically include major military installations and have many public-sector jobs; and as residential, resort, and retirement centers that have strong consumer-oriented economies based on both retailing and consumer services (Ladd and Yinger 1991: 30–33).

Although the U.S. Constitution assigns various fiscal roles to the federal and state governments, it says nothing about the role of cities. Cities are creatures of their states. Consequently, the fiscal responsibilities and powers of cities vary across states, depending on state laws and constitutional provisions, and sometimes across cities within states, depending on the home-rule powers of individual cities. Most cities have responsibility for providing a standard package of municipal services that includes, for example, public safety, sanitation, and local parks. Some cities, however, also are responsible for providing services such as health and welfare programs that are provided by overlying counties in other areas or for providing elementary and secondary education, which are often provided by separate school districts. Similarly, cities differ in the broad-based taxes they are empowered to use. Although all cities rely on property taxes, only half of the major cities use general sales taxes, and less than a quarter use income or payroll taxes. For example, San Francisco, Washington, D.C., and Saint Louis are each empowered to use a general sales tax and an earnings or payroll tax along with the property tax, whereas cities like Boston are limited to the property tax. Differing service responsibilities plus other factors also lead to large variations across cities in the share of revenue from intergovernmental grants. As elaborated upon in the next section, this variation in fiscal structure complicates the task of developing measures of city fiscal health that are comparable across cities and over time.

ECONOMIC AND SOCIAL TRENDS AND THE FISCAL HEALTH OF U.S. CITIES

In recent years, powerful national trends have affected the strength and structure of city economies and the income and social characteristics of city residents.[4] These trends include the movement to the suburbs of middle-income households and jobs, the shift in employment from manufacturing to services, population migration from the

Northeast to the Southwest, the associated interregional movement of jobs and investment, the urbanization of poverty, and rising social problems such as teenage pregnancy, drug-related crime, AIDS, and homelessness.

Although common to all cities, these trends are likely to have different effects on city economies and the income of city residents across cities, depending on the city's demographic and economic characteristics and also, in part, on the location of city boundaries. If the city covers most of its metropolitan area, decentralization may not move jobs and people out of the city. In contrast, if the city is small relative to its metropolitan area, decentralization could be associated with significant changes in the economic and social characteristics of the city.

The analytical question is: How have these social and economic trends affected the fiscal health of U.S. central cities? Following Ladd and Yinger (1991), the term *fiscal health* refers to the ability of a city to provide adequate public services to its residents at reasonable tax rates. More specifically, fiscal health measures the balance between a city's revenue-raising capacity and its expenditure need. The concept of revenue-raising capacity is based on a standard tax burden on city residents that is uniform across cities and over time. The concept of expenditure need recognizes that, through no fault of their own, some cities face higher costs of providing a given package of public services than other cities. These higher costs arise because of city characteristics that are outside the control of city officials, such as above-average population density or poverty rates. A city with poor fiscal health has to impose above-average tax burdens to provide a standard package of services or must accept low service levels if it chooses to impose average tax rates. A city with strong fiscal health, in contrast, has substantial capacity to raise revenues relative to its expenditure needs and can achieve standard service levels at below-average tax rates.

Determining the net effect of the economic and social trends on the fiscal health of U.S. cities is complicated by the variation across cities in fiscal structures and powers. For example, when people move out of the city to the suburbs, a city that is empowered to tax the earnings of nonresidents working in the city need not experience a fall in its revenue-raising capacity. Conversely, without such taxing power, the city's ability to raise revenue would fall. Similarly, the impact of homelessness and of other social problems on the costs of providing city services will vary depending on the degree to which the city is responsible for providing social services.

Ladd and Yinger (1991) dealt with this analytical problem by developing a measure of the fiscal health of cities that is standardized to a uniform set of fiscal institutions. They define *standardized fiscal health* (SFH) as the difference between a city's revenue-raising capacity and its expenditure need expressed as a percentage of capacity, where capacity and need are calculated as though all cities operated within the same set of fiscal institutions. This measure reveals the net effect of a city's economic, social, and demographic characteristics, but not of its specific fiscal arrangements, on the city's ability to deliver a standard level of public services at a standard tax burden on its residents.

Cities differ from one another first in terms of their *revenue-raising capacity*, that is, the per capita amount of revenue a city can raise from three standard tax bases—property, general sales, and earnings—while imposing a standard tax burden on its residents.[5] With the standard tax burden set at a fixed percentage of resident per capita income, revenue-raising capacity varies across cities for two reasons: differences in the average per capita income of residents and differences in the ability of cities to shift the burden of taxes to nonresidents. For example, at the standard tax burden, a city with richer residents can raise more revenue per resident than can a city with poorer residents. And a city with a large proportion of its property tax base in the form of business property, with a large proportion of its retail sales to nonresident commuters or tourists, or with a large proportion of earnings generated in the city accruing to nonresident commuters, can substantially increase its revenues by exporting tax burdens to nonresidents (see Bradbury and Ladd 1985; Ladd and Yinger 1991).

Just as cities differ in their revenue-raising capacity, they also differ in the amount of money they must spend to achieve a standardized package of public services, that is, in their *expenditure need*. The cost to a city of providing a standard package of services that people value, such as protection from crime, a clean city, or adequate education, varies with the social and demographic characteristics of the city. For example, a city with the social and economic conditions that breed crime will have to pay more per capita to obtain a given level of crime protection than will a city facing more favorable conditions; a city with densely packed, wooden housing will have to pay more per resident to obtain a given level of fire protection than one with newer housing; or a city with a large proportion of its public school pupils from disadvantaged households will have to pay more per pupil to obtain a given quality of education. Hence, the harshness of a city's environment is a major determinant of public service cost and thereby of a city's expenditure need (see Bradford, Malt, and Oates 1969). To calculate each city's expenditure need, Ladd and Yinger (1991) used regression analysis to isolate the effects of these environmental cost factors that are outside the control of city officials.[6]

Several environmental characteristics turn out to be powerful determinants of the cost per city resident of providing various types of city services (Ladd and Yinger 1991: chap. 4). Poverty, for example, has a big impact on the costs of providing public safety. A city with a poverty rate 1 percentage point higher than another city's will have police costs that are 5.5 percent higher, on average. Furthermore, a city with a poverty rate one standard deviation above the 1982 mean must pay 36.4 percent more for police services than a city with average poverty. The size of a city, as measured by its population, and the amount of its economic activity, as measured by private employment per capita, also increase the costs of public services. In addition, the larger the population in the city's surrounding metropolitan area relative to the city's population, the higher the city's costs of providing general and police services. And, finally, the composition of city property affects police and fire costs. Rental property, for example, is more expensive to protect from crime and fire than is owner-occupied property. Property used for wholesale and retail trade is also relatively costly, whereas property used for services or manufacturing is relatively cheap to protect from fire.

Deterioration in the Standardized Fiscal Health of Big Cities, 1972–82

Table 11.3 presents indexes of standardized fiscal health in 1982 as well as its components for six illustrative big cities and averages for seventy major central cities grouped by size of city.[7] The indexes are constructed using a 1972 baseline service level, that is, the quality of services that the average city could provide at the standard tax burden in 1972.[8] A positive fiscal health index, such as that for Denver or Washington, D.C., implies that the city's revenue-raising capacity was greater than its expenditure need and indicates that the city's fiscal health in 1982 exceeded that of the average major central city in 1972. The specific value (5 percent for Denver and 14 percent for Washington, D.C.) indicates the percentage of a city's revenue that would have been left over for increases in service quality, or tax cuts, in 1982 after the city had provided the 1972 average service quality at the standard tax burden.

Table 11.3 STANDARDIZED U.S. FISCAL HEALTH IN 1982 (ILLUSTRATIVE CITIES AND AVERAGES, 70 CENTRAL CITIES)

	Number of Cities (1)	Revenue-Raising Capacity ($) (2)	Standardized Expenditure Need ($) (3)	Capacity Minus Need ($) (4)	Fiscal Health Index (%) (5)
Illustrative Cities:					
Atlanta	1	505	640	(136)	−26.9
Baltimore	1	331	483	(152)	−45.7
Boston	1	501	561	(59)	−11.9
Detroit	1	341	654	(313)	−91.9
Denver	1	532	505	27	5.0
Washington, D.C.	1	624	535	89	14.3
All Cities in Sample:					
Average	70	425	458	(33)	−10.9
Standard deviation	70	80	109	128	32.2
Maximum	70	649	737	290	47.2
Minimum	70	286	243	(386)	−109.7
Cities Grouped by Population (in thousands):					
Less than 100	6	457	384	74	16.4
100–250	19	473	421	52	9.1
250–500	26	420	473	(53)	−13.5
500–1000	14	385	466	(80)	−22.9
Greater than 1,000	5	341	586	(245)	−72.8

Source: Ladd and Yinger (1991: tables 5.1, 5.2).
Note: Sample excludes Washington, D.C.

A negative fiscal health index, such as those for Atlanta, Baltimore, Boston, and Detroit, implies that a city's 1982 capacity was less than its expenditure need and indicates that the city's fiscal health was weaker in 1982 than that of the average major central city in 1972. For example, Detroit's fiscal health index of − 92 indicates that it had a standardized expenditure need that was almost twice as high as its standardized revenue-raising capacity. Detroit would have had to receive a 92 percent boost in its revenue-raising capacity from outside sources to be able to provide services of the quality that the average city could provide out of its own broad-based revenue sources in 1972.

The average standardized fiscal health of the seventy central cities in the Ladd and Yinger (1991) study was about − 11 percent in 1982. This figure implies that the typical central city would have needed a boost in revenues of 11 percent from outside sources in 1982 to provide the 1972 baseline service level at the standard tax burden. In other words, economic and social forces weakened the fiscal health of the typical city during the period. The results for cities grouped by population size indicate that the standardized fiscal health of America's big cities in 1982 was significantly poorer than that of smaller central cites. In contrast to the − 11 percent index for all seventy cities, cities in the largest three size categories had average indexes of − 14 percent, − 23 percent, and − 73 percent, respectively.

As shown in table 11.3, the weaker fiscal health in the larger cities relative to the smaller cities reflects both their lower revenue-raising capacity and their higher expenditure needs. Particularly high police costs, but also above-average costs for fire and general services, create their high expenditure needs. These costs are high both because population itself, holding all other factors constant, increases costs and because city population is positively correlated with other characteristics such as the city's poverty rate or private-sector wage rates that also increase the costs of providing services to city residents.

The larger cities had relatively poor fiscal health in 1982, both because they had poor fiscal health in 1972 and because they experienced above-average declines in fiscal health between 1972 and 1982. (The declines are shown in table 11.4. Because the 1982 index is constructed relative to the 1972 average, the average decline over all seventy cities is the same as the average SFH index in 1982.) Revenue-raising capacity diminished only in the cities with population over one million. Nonetheless, large increases in expenditure need led to declines in fiscal health in each size category of city. Interestingly, expenditure need grew fastest not in the largest central cities, but, rather, in the cities with populations between 100,000 and

Table 11.4 CHANGES IN STANDARDIZED U.S. FISCAL HEALTH, 1972–82
(AVERAGES, 70 CITIES BY CATEGORY)

		Percentage		Percentage Points
	Number of Cities	Potential Revenue-Raising Capacity	Standardized Expenditure Need	Standardized Fiscal Health Index
City Size in Thousands:				
Less than 100	6	10.3	12.6	−1.6
100–250	19	10.9	23.2	−9.3
250–500	26	9.5	20.4	−11.4
500–1,000	14	8.2	17.0	−10.3
Greater than 1,000	5	−5.6	12.3	−27.2

Source: Ladd and Yinger (1991: table 5.3).
Note: Sample excludes Washington, D.C.

250,000. Nonetheless, the net effects of social and economic forces on the revenue and the expenditure sides of the fiscal picture produced the greatest declines in the standardized fiscal health of the cities with population over one million.

In sum, America's big cities experienced significant deterioration in their standardized fiscal health over the 1972–82 period. This finding implies that economic and social trends, such as the decline in real income of residents in many cities and the rising rate of poverty among city residents, worsened the balance between revenue-raising capacity and expenditure need in the typical big city during this period. As a consequence of this deterioration, cities would have had to impose higher tax burdens on their residents to provide the same level of services in 1982 as the average city in 1972 or would have had to make do with lower service levels if they chose to maintain 1972 tax burdens. This tightening of the fiscal constraints on cities contrasts with a 5.4 percent increase in the real disposable income of consumers in the nation as whole. During this period, therefore, the constraints on consumption in general were loosening, while the economic constraints on city finances were becoming more restrictive.

Role of Changes in City Economic Activity, Job Mix, and Resident Income

By construction, these measures of city fiscal health reflect a broad set of economic and social forces, included among which are the decentralization of households and firms within metropolitan areas.

The effects on fiscal health of these intrametropolitan shifts are difficult to isolate. Nonetheless, one can learn something about them by examining the extent to which changes in standardized fiscal health are systematically related to three manifestations of the changing form of urban areas: changes in the amount of economic activity in the city, in the mix of city jobs, and in the income of city residents.

CHANGES IN CITY ECONOMIC ACTIVITY

City economic activity is measured here by the number of private-sector jobs located in the city relative to the size of the city population.[9] This per resident approach makes city economic activity directly comparable to the concept of standardized fiscal health, which is also measured on a per capita basis, but it also implies that a city experiencing identical percentage decreases (or increases) in jobs and population is deemed to experience no change in economic activity. As measured here, an increase in city economic activity is typically associated with an increase in the proportion of city jobs occupied by nonresident commuters into the city.

In the first panel of table 11.5, major central cities are grouped into categories based on changes in their economic activity between 1972 and 1982. The eighty-six major cities were first divided into those with below-average and above-average private-sector employment per capita in 1972. Within each grouping, cities were further divided into three groups characterized by low, medium, and high growth. Cities in the low-growth category experienced changes in private employment per capita ranging from − 22 percent to + 14 percent. Thirteen of these cities experienced a decline in jobs relative to the size of their populations during the period, and five cities—Detroit, Chicago, Baltimore, Philadelphia, and Newark, New Jersey—suffered absolute declines in employment. Medium-growth cities experienced growth in jobs per resident of between 14 percent and 30 percent; and high-growth cities experienced growth of between 30 percent and 120 percent. Most of the cities in this last group are in the South and West. Heading the list are Boulder, Fort Lauderdale, and Garden Grove, California.

An increase in a city's level of economic activity is predicted to have both positive and negative effects on the fiscal health of the city. On the one hand, an increase in the number of jobs per resident is predicted to increase the ability of the city to raise revenue either because the jobs augment the income of city residents or because the jobs enable the city to shift a larger share of its tax burden to nonresidents. The latter occurs whenever the jobs are filled by nonresident

Table 11.5 CHANGES IN STANDARDIZED U.S. FISCAL HEALTH, 1972–82
(AVERAGES, 70 CITIES BY CATEGORY)

		Percentage		Percentage Points
	Number of Cities	Revenue-Raising Capacity	Standardized Expenditure Need	Standardized Fiscal Health Index
Economic Activity[a]				
Below-average economic activity				
Low growth	11	2.8	13.9	− 15.8
Medium growth	9	5.8	17.9	− 12.2
High growth	15	16.0	25.4	− 5.8
Above-average economic activity				
Low growth	15	3.9	17.3	− 15.9
Medium growth	13	6.6	18.2	− 10.9
High growth	7	19.5	22.5	− 1.5
Economic Structure[b]				
Low employment growth				
Low structural change	5	5.4	17.1	− 10.6
Medium structural change	6	1.6	20.1	− 27.1
High structural change	15	3.5	13.7	− 13.2
Medium employment growth				
Low structural change	9	6.5	19.6	− 12.6
Medium structural change	7	10.3	16.6	− 5.7
High structural change	6	1.1	17.6	− 16.6
High employment growth				
Low structural change	8	16.6	25.6	− 5.3
Medium structural change	11	17.1	21.7	− 3.1
High structural change	3	18.8	31.7	− 7.1
Resident Income				
Below-average income				
Low growth	18	2.1	19.8	− 21.2
Medium growth	10	6.4	18.7	− 12.4
High growth	6	19.5	16.7	1.6
Above-average income				
Low growth	7	− 1.3	14.3	− 17.4
Medium growth	17	9.9	19.1	− 6.7
High growth	12	18.9	23.3	− 2.6

Source: Ladd and Yinger (1991: table 5.3).

[a]Measured as private-sector jobs in city divided by city residents. Growth can be negative.

[b]Structural change measures are discussed in the text.

commuters who are subject to an earnings tax or when a portion of the property tax burden on the employers is ultimately borne by non-resident owners. Working in the other direction, however, is the fact that the additional jobs may increase the costs of providing a standard level of public services to city residents; for example, a larger daytime population relative to the resident nighttime population increases the cost per resident of providing public services by increasing congestion and creating more trash. How these two forces balance out is an empirical question.

The results in table 11.5 for the seventy cities for which complete data are available are consistent with the predictions of the two opposing forces: cities with the highest growth in jobs per capita experienced the highest average growth both in revenue-raising capacity and in expenditure need. The latter increases are somewhat larger on average. Thus, even cities with private economies that are growing relative to city population are not immune to declines in fiscal health. Nevertheless, standardized fiscal health fell 10 to 15 percentage points, on average, in cities with limited growth in the number of private jobs per resident, whereas it fell by only 1 to 6 percentage points, on average, in cities experiencing rapid growth. Although growth in the private economy does not ensure improvements in fiscal health, the evidence suggests that a growing private economy is more conducive to fiscal stability than a declining one.

STRUCTURAL CHANGE IN CITY ECONOMIES

A second economic manifestation of the changing urban arena is a shift in the composition of city jobs away from manufacturing and toward services. Between 1972 and 1982, manufacturing's share of employment in the average major central city declined by 9 percentage points. This structural change in city economies partially reflects differing rates of suburbanization within metropolitan areas for different types of jobs. In addition, however, structural change in city economies reflects two other trends. The first is the well-publicized national industrial trend of declining employment in manufacturing and increasing employment in services. Nationally, between 1972 and 1982, manufacturing's share of total private employment decreased by 6 percentage points, while the share in the service sector increased by the same amount. The second trend is the continuing interregional disparity in the rates of business investment, with more investment in the Sunbelt states than in the Frostbelt states. Because the relative attractiveness of regions varies by industry, the variation by region in the rates of business investment changes the mix of employment in the various regions and in the cities within those regions.

An index was created to measure the amount of structural change experienced by each city, with *structural change* defined as the shift away from jobs in the manufacturing sector to jobs in the services and finance, insurance, and real estate (FIRE) sectors. Specifically, the extent of structural changes is measured as the absolute value of the change in manufacturing's share of total private employment plus the absolute value of the change in service and FIRE's share of total private employment between 1972 and 1982. For example, if manufacturing's share falls from 18 percent to 12 percent of total private employment and the share of services and FIRE employment increases from 25 percent to 34 percent, the city's structural change index would be 15 percent.[10]

To determine whether the resulting structural changes in city economies have affected the ability of U.S. cities to provide public services, cities have been grouped into categories defined by the degree of their structural change, controlling for changes in city economic health (see second panel of table 11.5). Because most cities rely heavily on property taxes (a fact reflected in the standard tax system on which the standardized fiscal health measures are based), a common concern is that a shift away from capital-intensive manufacturing activity toward labor-intensive services might reduce the revenue-raising capacity of cities. Similarly, the shift to services might put additional upward pressure on the costs of providing public services.

Somewhat surprisingly, no systematic patterns emerge by the structural change categories. The absence of a systematic relationship with respect to revenue-raising capacity reflects the fact that many of the service industries are able to export tax burdens to nonresidents equally as well as the manufacturing industries.[11] On the expenditure-need side, the absence of a relationship reflects the finding that changes in economic structure have essentially no effect on the costs of providing general or police services. Although individual components of economic structure apparently affect the cost of providing fire services, the fact that both manufacturing and services activity are relatively inexpensive to protect from fire (compared to owner-occupied housing and retail activity) means that a shift from one to the other has virtually no effect on the cost of fire protection. Because structural change is systematically related neither to changes in revenue-raising capacity nor to changes in standardized expenditure need, it bears no systematic relationship to changes in city fiscal health.

CHANGES IN THE INCOME OF CITY RESIDENTS

In contrast, a strong systematic pattern of changes in fiscal health emerges across cities grouped by a third manifestation of changes in urban form, the rate of growth of income of city residents. Such income changes reflect a complex set of forces, including the extent to which city residents share or do not share in the income growth of the metropolitan area. The third panel of table 11.5 groups cities by growth in the real per capita income of city residents, controlling for 1971 per capita income level. The growth categories of low, medium, and high refer to thirds of the eighty-six-city distribution of growth rates in real per capita income.[12] Ten-year growth rates ranged from − 15.8 percent to + 3.0 percent in the low-growth category, with fourteen cities (eleven in the seventy-one-city subsample of cities with complete data) experiencing falling real income during the period. Growth rates ranged from 3.8 percent to 8.5 percent in the medium-growth category, and from 8.7 percent to 27.5 percent in the high-growth category. At one extreme are the cities with low initial resident income and slow growth, such as Cleveland, Boston, and Philadelphia. In each of these cities, the per capita income of city residents declined relative to metropolitanwide resident income during the 1970s (table 11.1). At the other extreme are cities for which income was above average in 1971 and grew rapidly during the decade. Included in this category are many southwestern cities such as Houston, Denver, and San Diego, all of which were able to maintain the income of city residents close to that of the metropolitan area during the 1970s.

Increases in the revenue-raising capacity of cities are strongly correlated with the growth of resident income. For cities experiencing low growth (or decline) in income during the period, revenue-raising capacity on average either declined slightly (in cities with above-average income at the beginning of the period) or rose only slightly (in cities with below-average initial income). In contrast, cities experiencing growth in the income of city residents experienced average increases in revenue-raising capacity of about 19 percent. This positive correlation is not surprising, given the key role of resident income in the measure of capacity; at the standard tax burden (specified as a fixed percentage of resident income), an increase in the income of city residents produces proportionately more revenue. Significantly, however, part of the variation in growth rates of capacity is associated with the more rapidly rising proportions of the tax burden that are exported to nonresidents in cities with rapidly rising income than in those with slowly growing income.

On the expenditure-need side, the patterns are less clear and consistent. For cities with below-average income in 1971, the highest average increase in expenditure needs is in the cities with low growth. For cities with above-average income in 1971, the highest average increase is in the cities with the fastest growth. The bottom line is that the patterns on the revenue side dominate those on the expenditure side in determining the relationship between income growth and changes in fiscal capacity. Cities that experienced low or negative growth in real resident income during the period experienced much larger declines in their ability to provide public services at standard tax burdens than cities experiencing high growth in resident income.

SUMMARY

Between 1972 and 1982, social and economic trends led to a significant deterioration in the ability of many central cities to provide adequate services at reasonable tax rates. This deterioration was most severe in the largest cities and in those experiencing the least growth in jobs per resident and in the income of city residents. Thus, to the extent that changes in urban form are responsible for limited growth in city jobs or in the income of city residents, such changes weaken the fiscal health of U.S. central cities.

Recent Trends

Because 1982 was a recession year, one might wonder whether cities' poor fiscal health in that year reflects a short-term cyclical downturn rather than the effects of longer-term trends. Recent trends in two key contributors to a city's fiscal health, the income of city residents and central-city poverty rates, plus some updated estimates by Ladd and Yinger, shed light on this issue.

PER CAPITA INCOME

Table 11.6 reports changes in the per capita income of city residents for thirty-three big cities during the periods 1977–81, 1981–85, and 1985–89.[13] The table shows that the 1981–85 period was somewhat *worse* for big cities than the 1977–81 period. During the four years ending in 1981, real resident income declined in ten big cities, whereas the average city experienced a 1.8 percent increase. During the following four-year period, resident income declined in fifteen cities and the average city experienced only a 0.5 percent increase in real income. Because changes in city fiscal health tend to vary in line with changes in the per capita income of city residents, these figures suggest that

Table 11.6 CHANGES IN PER CAPITA RESIDENT INCOME IN THE UNITED
STATES, 1977–89 (33 BIG CITIES)

	City Income, 1989 ($)	Percentage Change in Real Income		
		1977–81	1981–85	1985–89
Atlanta	15,279	−1.4	7.6	29.6
Baltimore	11,994	−4.4	−0.9	21.7
Boston	15,581	8.3	12.3	26.9
Buffalo	10,445	2.3	0.4	3.6
Chicago	12,899	1.8	−6.2	17.4
Cincinnati	12,547	−0.5	2.7	7.4
Cleveland	9,258	−2.0	−4.4	1.3
Columbus	13,151	3.1	1.4	16.4
Dallas	16,300	6.8	0.6	11.6
Denver	15,590	3.0	−1.8	9.5
Detroit	9,443	−11.8	1.2	−6.4
Houston	14,261	10.9	−8.4	3.3
Indianapolis	14,605	0.6	−1.2	18.2
Jacksonville	13,857	5.5	3.3	16.2
Kansas City	13,799	0.4	2.7	8.6
Los Angeles	16,188	4.3	−0.2	17.6
Memphis	11,682	−1.6	0.7	9.4
Miami	9,799	−2.1	−0.3	−3.5
Milwaukee	11,106	0.7	−4.4	−0.2
Minneapolis	14,830	2.2	5.2	5.8
New Orleans	11,372	9.9	−9.2	11.2
New York City	16,281	6.9	3.8	27.6
Philadelphia	12,091	−5.7	0.5	20.5
Phoenix	12,752	3.5	3.3	−1.6
Pittsburgh	12,580	1.2	−2.0	10.4
Portland, Ore.	14,478	−15.4	9.5	17.9
Saint Louis	10,798	−1.1	1.2	7.7
San Antonio	10,884	4.9	−0.6	12.4
San Diego	16,401	7.6	−0.4	22.3
San Francisco	19,695	1.7	−0.2	27.3
San Jose	16,905	9.9	1.7	17.9
Seattle	18,308	1.8	−4.8	24.3
Washington, D.C.	18,881	6.8	3.0	22.4
Average	13,759	1.8	0.5	13.2
Minimum	9,258	−15.4	−9.2	−6.4
Maximum	19,695	10.9	12.3	29.6

Sources: U.S. Bureau of the Census, *Current Population Reports*, various years, series
P-26.

Note: Data are deflated by implicit price deflator for state and local governments.

many big cities probably continued to experience declining fiscal health through 1985.

However, the income picture brightened significantly during the subsequent four-year period, 1985–89. As shown in the third column of table 11.6, real income fell in only three cities and increased by 13.2 percent in the typical big city during these four years. Cities experiencing impressive income growth during the 1980s include Atlanta, Boston, New York City, and Portland, Oregon. In 1989 the national economy was booming and was seven years into the expansion phase of the economic cycle. Thus sustained national economic growth during the mid-1980s clearly helped many big cities. Despite this growth, however, poverty rates continued to rise.

INCIDENCE OF POVERTY

In the absence of city-specific data on poverty rates for the recent period, one must turn instead to the more aggregate poverty data summarized in table 11.7. The table shows that the 1994 poverty rate of 21.1 percent in all central cities (not just the eighty-six major cities) was substantially higher than in 1970, at 14.2 percent. These figures provide little reason for optimism. The poverty rate in U.S. central cities has exceeded the U.S. average by about 40 percent for each of the past several years, and the disparity in the 1980s and early 1990s was larger than in the 1970s. These figures suggest that the poverty situation in central cities has not improved enough in recent years to offset the decline in fiscal health reported in tables 11.3 and 11.4 for the nation's major central cities, and that the relative worsening of their poverty rates places continuous pressure on their budgets.

MORE RECENT ESTIMATES OF STANDARDIZED FISCAL HEALTH

Furthermore, Ladd and Yinger's updated estimates of standardized fiscal health for 1990 indicate only limited improvement in the average fiscal health of the seventy major central cities between 1982 and 1990. In the absence of complete data for 1990, Ladd and Yinger used the statistical relationship between 1982 standardized fiscal health and four variables for which data were available both for 1982 and for either 1989 or 1990—the per capita income of city residents, city population, the per capita income of city residents relative to per capita income in the metropolitan area, and the ratio of city to metropolitan population—to predict the standardized fiscal health of each of the major central cities for 1990. Their results indicate that the standardized fiscal health of most big cities improved during the 1980s. The only exceptions are New York, Detroit, Milwaukee, and

Table 11.7 POVERTY RATES IN THE UNITED STATES, 1970 AND 1975–94

	Inside Central Cities	Total United States
1994	21.1	14.5
1993	21.5	15.1
1992	20.9	14.8
1991	20.2	14.2
1990	19.0	13.5
1989	18.1	12.8
1988	18.1	13.0
1987	18.4	13.4
1986	18.0	13.6
1985	19.0	14.0
1984	N.A.	14.4
1983	19.8	15.2
1982	19.9	15.0
1981	18.0	14.0
1980	17.2	13.0
1979	15.7	11.6
1978	15.4	11.4
1977	15.4	11.6
1976	15.8	11.8
1975	15.0	12.3
1970	14.2	12.6

Sources: 1991–94: U.S. Department of Commerce, Bureau of the Census, Poverty in the United States: 1995. 1988–91: U.S. Department of Commerce, Bureau of the Census, Measuring the Effect of Benefits and Taxes on Income and Poverty, 1989 (issued Sept. 1990) and 1987–88 (issued Nov. 1990), Current Population Reports, Series p. 60, Table 2. 1987: U.S. Department of Commerce, Bureau of the Census, Money Income and Poverty Status in the U.S. 1988, Current Population Reports, Series p. 60, No. 166, (Washington, D.C.: GPO, October 1989), Table 17 (issued Oct. 1989). 1984–86: U.S. Department of Commerce, Bureau of the Census, Poverty in the United States, 1986, pp. 19–23 (issued June 1988); 1985 (issued Oct. 1987); 1987, table 6 (issued Feb. 1989). 1970, 1975–1983: U.S. Department of Commerce, Bureau of the Census, Characteristics of the Population Below the Poverty Level, 1983 (issued Feb. 1985); 1980, (issued July 1982); 1979 (issued Dec. 1981); 1976, (issued July 1978).

N.A. = Data unavailable.

Miami. Nonetheless, despite this improvement, the typical big city still was worse off in 1990 than the average major central city in 1972. In addition, many cities still had very poor standardized fiscal health in 1990. According to Ladd and Yinger's estimates, national economic growth during the 1980s was beneficial, but not sufficiently powerful to offset the other social and economic forces that adversely affected the ability of cities to provide adequate services.

ROLE OF INTERGOVERNMENTAL ASSISTANCE

In addition to being affected by changing economic and social conditions, the fiscal condition of U.S. central cities is also affected by changes in the intergovernmental fiscal environment in which they operate. Between 1972 and 1982, U.S. central cities benefited from additional assistance from the federal and state governments that partially offset the adverse fiscal effects of the economic and social changes. However, more recent years have witnessed a dramatic reduction in federal assistance to U.S. cities, and the future does not bode well for significant new injections of state assistance for cities.

Beneficial Effects of State and Federal Assistance, 1972–82

Cities receive assistance from both their state government and the federal government. Assistance from the federal government comes primarily in the form of intergovernmental grants. In contrast, state assistance to cities should be viewed not narrowly, in terms of monetary aid alone, but, rather, as a package that includes both monetary aid and assistance through the design of the fiscal institutions under which the cities operate. The subsections below focus on the effects on city fiscal health of changes first in state assistance and then in federal assistance.

STATE ASSISTANCE TO CENTRAL CITIES, 1972–82

State governments assist their cities in several interrelated ways. The first and most obvious way is by providing monetary grants-in-aid. A second method is by assuming responsibility for certain spending responsibilities previously assigned to cities. Consider, for example, social service programs. State governments can assist their cities in meeting their responsibilities by providing more monetary aid. Alternatively, states can assist cities by assuming responsibility for all or part of such services. When the latter route is chosen, state aid to cities would decline; hence, exclusive attention to changes in grants-in-aid would provide a misleading and incomplete picture of the change in assistance provided by a state government to its central cities. In addition, the package of state assistance includes empowering cities to use broad-based taxes that permit the city to capture revenue from nonresident commuters and tourists. Hence, state assistance to cities should be defined broadly to include assistance through the design of the fiscal rules under which the city operates as well as assistance through grants-in-aid.[14]

Measuring the amount of this broadly defined state assistance presents a formidable challenge, but Ladd and Yinger (1991) provided estimates of such assistance relative to a 1972 baseline for each of the major central cities. Specifically, they estimated state assistance as the difference between a city's *actual fiscal health* and its standardized fiscal health. In contrast to standardized fiscal health, which is based on a uniform set of state fiscal institutions, each city's actual fiscal health is calculated based on the specific state fiscal institutions under which the city operates. (The effects of variation in federal aid are not included in the concept of actual fiscal health.) Hence, the difference between the two represents the effect of state fiscal institutions and grants on a city's fiscal health.

Table 11.8 reports the Ladd-Yinger (1991) estimates of standard and actual fiscal health and the implied amounts of state assistance for each of the thirty-three big cities, listed in ascending order of standardized fiscal health.[15] Cities falling into the lowest quartile of standardized fiscal health include New York, Detroit, New Orleans, Philadelphia, Cleveland, Chicago, and Buffalo. A comparison of the standardized and actual fiscal health of these cities shows that in all except New Orleans, state governments partially offset the adverse fiscal effects of the economic and social trends. In New York, Detroit, and Buffalo, the state assistance comes primarily in the form of grants. In Philadelphia, Cleveland, and Chicago, the assistance comes primarily through the favorable design of fiscal institutions; Philadelphia and Cleveland, for example, benefit from access to an earnings tax that applies to commuters as well as to residents, and Chicago benefits from relatively low service responsibilities.[16]

Table 11.8 indicates that state assistance in 1982 was reasonably well targeted to the big cities that needed it the most, namely those with the lowest standardized fiscal health. However, such aid was not perfectly targeted to all needy cities. The fact that standardized fiscal health exceeds actual fiscal health in cities such as Los Angeles, Memphis, Atlanta, and Pittsburgh implies that state policies toward these cities exacerbated the adverse fiscal effects of economic and social trends.

Table 11.9 shifts the focus to *changes* in state assistance between 1972 and 1982 and sheds additional light on the degree to which state assistance was targeted to the cities that needed it the most. For this table, the seventy major central cities are grouped into quintiles based on changes in their standardized fiscal health. Quintile I includes the

Table 11.8 STATE ASSISTANCE IN THE UNITED STATES, 1982 (33 BIG CITIES)

Cities by SFH Quartile (low to high)	SFH Index, 1982 (1)	Actual Fiscal Health Index, 1982 (2)	State Assistance, 1982 (2) − (1)
Quartile I			
New York	− 104.6	− 63.2	41.4
Detroit	− 91.9	− 30.8	61.1
New Orleans	− 72.7	− 72.8	− 0.1
Philadelphia	− 59.9	− 23.1	36.8
Cleveland	− 58.7	− 29.3	29.4
Chicago	− 58.5	− 43.8	14.7
Buffalo	− 52.6	− 26.2	26.4
Quartile II			
Los Angeles	− 48.9	− 79.7	− 30.8
Baltimore	− 45.7	6.8	52.5
Saint Louis	− 37.7	− 31.3	6.4
Columbus	− 36.9	− 10.4	26.5
Kansas City	− 33.6	8.6	42.2
Cincinnati	− 33.1	5.9	39.0
Milwaukee	− 33.1	12.3	45.4
Quartile III			
Memphis	− 30.1	− 56.1	− 26.0
Atlanta	− 26.9	− 65.9	− 39.0
Indianapolis	− 25.0	26.5	51.5
Minneapolis	− 14.8	− 1.5	13.3
San Diego	− 13.0	− 16.0	− 3.0
Jacksonville	− 12.8	28.3	41.6
Boston	− 11.9	2.3	14.2
Quartile IV			
Phoenix	− 11.2	11.4	22.6
Portland, Ore.	− 9.8	− 10.2	− 0.4
Pittsburgh	− 7.8	− 34.7	− 26.9
Denver	5.0	− 4.9	− 9.9
San Francisco	7.7	8.0	0.3
Miami	17.5	5.6	− 11.9
San Jose	18.4	16.7	− 1.7
Washington, D.C.	14.3	10.0	− 4.3
Dallas	N.A.	N.A.	N.A.
Houston	N.A.	N.A.	N.A.
San Antonio	N.A.	N.A.	N.A.
Seattle	N.A.	N.A.	N.A.
Average (29)	− 29.8	− 15.8	14.2

Source: Ladd and Yinger (1991: tables A5.1, A9.1, A11.1).

SFH = Standardized fiscal health.
N.A. = Not available; applies to all N.A.s in table.

Table 11.9 CHANGES IN STATE AND FEDERAL ASSISTANCE TO U.S. CENTRAL
CITIES, 1972–82 (AVERAGE, 70 CITIES BY SFH CHANGE CATEGORIES)

	Number of Cities	SFH[a]	Average Percentage Point Change	
			State Assistance (as percentage of revenue-raising capacity)	Federal Aid (as percentage of revenue-raising capacity)
All cities	70	−10.9	6.0	7.0
Cities grouped by quintiles of changes in SFH (low to high)				
I	14	−32.1	13.4	11.2
II	14	−16.2	7.0[b]	7.3
III	14	−8.5	0.1	6.2
IV	14	−2.7	1.6	5.6
V	14	5.5	2.0	5.0

Sources: Calculated from Ladd and Yinger (1991: table A11.1) and unpublished data on federal aid from Ladd and Yinger.

Note: Sample excludes Washington, D.C.

[a]SFH = Standardized fiscal health; see text for explanation.

[b]Excludes Cincinnati because of potential data problem relating to 1972 level of state assistance.

cities with the greatest declines in SFH and quintile V the cities with the greatest increases. The table shows that state assistance increased as a percentage of revenue-raising capacity by 6 percentage points in the typical city during the period. Moreover, changes in such assistance were well targeted; cities in quintile I received additional state assistance equaling, on average, 13.4 percent of their revenue-raising capacity, almost double the average amount received by cities in the second quintile. Cities in the bottom three quintiles received, on average, only about 1 percentage point more than the 1972 baseline level. On average, a 1 percentage point decrease in a city's standardized fiscal health leads to a 0.51 percent increase in state assistance, and this relationship is statistically significant. In other words, about one-half of the decline in standardized fiscal health is offset by state actions.[17]

Overall, the picture is relatively clear. State assistance, broadly defined to include assistance in the form of institutions as well as aid, partially offset the negative effects of economic and social trends on the fiscal health of the typical U.S. central city. This assistance was targeted reasonably well to the cities that, because of economic and social trends outside their control, needed it the most.

ASSISTANCE FROM THE FEDERAL GOVERNMENT, 1972-82

Federal aid first became an important source of revenue for cities in the late 1960s, when Great Society initiatives provided cities with grants to support manpower training, elementary and secondary education, and community development. Many of these programs continued to grow during the 1970s. They were supplemented in 1974 by general revenue sharing, which provided unrestricted funds to all general-purpose local governments, and later by several counter-cyclical grant programs passed in response to the 1974–75 recession.

Direct federal grants to cities peaked in 1978, at which time they accounted for over 25 percent of cities' own-source revenues, with the contribution of federal aid exceeding 50 percent of own-source revenue in a few cities, including Buffalo and Detroit. The period of growth in federal aid to cities ended in 1978 with the elimination of the countercyclical programs and the leveling off of other programs. The 1980 election of President Ronald Reagan accelerated this turnaround. By 1982, federal aid to cities had declined to 18.4 percent of own-source revenues—the level it had attained in the early 1970s— and equaled about $116 per capita in the average major central city. On average, federal aid to major cities grew about 4 percent per year over the 1972–82 decade, measured in constant dollars.

Table 11.9 summarizes Ladd and Yinger's estimates of the 1972–82 changes in the impact of federal assistance on the fiscal health of major cities. Like state assistance, federal aid, as measured here, is not an absolute concept. Instead, it measures federal aid as a percentage of each city's revenue-raising capacity relative to a 1972 baseline.[18]

During the 1972–82 decade, increased federal aid significantly contributed to the fiscal health of the U.S. central cities; overall, federal aid improved the fiscal health of the typical U.S. central city by 7 percentage points. Federal aid (as a percentage of revenue-raising capacity) increased the most (11.2 percentage points on average) in the cities experiencing the greatest declines in fiscal health, and the increases declined monotonically across groups ranked in ascending order of changes in standardized fiscal health. However, compared to changes in state assistance, changes in federal aid were more evenly spread among cities; even the cities with the strongest fiscal health received substantial additional federal aid during the period.[19]

TOTAL INTERGOVERNMENTAL ASSISTANCE

Table 11.9 clearly demonstrates the importance to cities of increases in state and federal assistance during the 1972–82 decade. Even accounting for such assistance, however, many cities, especially those experiencing the largest declines in their standardized fiscal health, found it increasingly difficult to provide public services at reasonable tax rates. Because some of the assistance, especially that from the federal government, was not well targeted to needy cities, some central cities benefited not only from increases in their standardized fiscal health but also from increases in intergovernmental assistance.

Recent Changes in Intergovernmental Assistance

DEMISE OF THE FEDERAL-LOCAL PARTNERSHIP

Recent years have witnessed the virtual end of the federal-local partnership that had emerged during the 1970s. Committed to reducing the size of government and decreasing federal involvement in state and local affairs, President Ronald Reagan proposed major cutbacks in aid to state and local governments. Congress resisted some of the cutbacks, but nonetheless federal grants bore a disproportionate share of the spending cutbacks. In the 1981 Omnibus Budget Act, for example, grant programs absorbed 29 percent of all reductions in budget authority, despite representing less than 10 percent of spending on all programs that were cut.[20]

Moreover, grant programs directed toward cities tended to be harder hit than those to states. This outcome occurred in part because the programs most vulnerable to cuts were the new programs of direct aid to localities introduced under Presidents Lyndon B. Johnson and Richard M. Nixon. Another factor was that many narrowly defined categorical programs were consolidated into block grants. By designating state governments as the recipients of the new block grants, the Reagan administration expressed its philosophy that state governments are often in a better position than the federal government to deal with the fiscal problems of cities and other local governments. Of the seventy-seven grants that were consolidated into block grants in 1981, forty-seven formerly delivered federal funds directly to localities (Ladd 1984: 190). Although the U.S. Congress mitigated to some extent the short-run effects of this reorientation by pass-through requirements and earmarking of funds to previous recipients, the effect was generally to redistribute aid away from larger cities to rural areas and smaller communities.

In addition, three programs of special importance to urban governments—urban development action grants (UDAGs), housing subsidies, and training and employment programs—suffered cuts over 45 percent between 1980 and 1987, while other programs such as wastewater treatment construction, transportation assistance, and community development block grants (CDBGs) were cut by more than 20 percent. Finally, general revenue sharing, which by this time provided aid only to local governments, was eliminated in 1986. The fall from grace of the cities during the Reagan years is demonstrated by the fact that aid programs for urban areas declined by 47 percent between 1980 and 1987 at the same time that all other federal grant programs (including Aid to Families with Dependent Children and Medicaid) experienced a 47 percent increase.[21]

The magnitude of these changes is portrayed in figure 11.1. As stated earlier, by 1982, federal aid to cities (all cities, not just the major central cities) had dipped to 18.4 percent of own-source revenue, its level in the early 1970s; and by 1989 it had declined further, to 7.1 percent.[22] Moreover, the huge federal budget deficits—combined with

Figure 11.1 DIRECT FEDERAL AID TO U.S. CITIES, 1965–89 (AS PERCENTAGE OF OWN-SOURCE REVENUES)

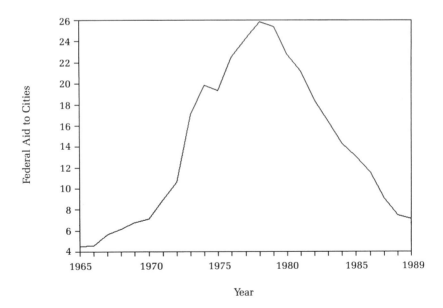

Source: U.S. Bureau of the Census, various years, *City Government Finances* (Washington, D.C.: U.S. Government Printing Office).

the 1985 Gramm-Rudman-Hollings mechanism to reduce them—portend, if not a continuation of the downward trend, certainly no turnaround. Thus, during this period, the federal government made it clear that it would no longer serve as the funding source for increased city spending or alleviate the fiscal stress of cities during recessions. Instead, the cities were left to fend with some combination of their own resources and assistance from their states.

SUPPORT FROM STATE GOVERNMENTS

Unfortunately, state governments have not been in a strong position to provide additional support to their cities in recent years. Facing both significant voter opposition to raising taxes as well as tremendous pressures to spend more in the areas of Medicaid and corrections, states have few funds left over for new programs of state assistance to cities. By at least one measure of state financial condition—year-end balances expressed as a percentage of general fund spending—state governments were just as pinched in 1986 and 1987 as in 1982, and substantially more so than in the late 1970s. Their improved position in 1984 and 1985 partially reflects large state tax increases in 1983, but many of these increases were temporary, and others were reversed. Thus, there is little reason to believe that states have been able to do more to offset the adverse effects of social and economic trends on the fiscal health of their cities during recent years than they did between 1972 and 1982.

How much the states have actually done to help their major cities since 1982 is difficult to determine because, as already discussed, state assistance encompasses more than just the provision of state aid; it also includes state assumption of city expenditure responsibilities and authorization to use additional broad-based taxes. Focusing just on state aid, however—the one component of the assistance package for which recent data are available—we find no evidence of increased state support for big central cities in recent years. Indeed, between 1982 and 1986, on average state aid to the thirty-two big cities (excluding Washington, D.C.) remained constant at 19 percent of city general expenditures; aid as a percentage of spending went down in seventeen cities and up in fifteen cities. Moreover, no clear pattern emerges across cities grouped by their 1982 fiscal health. This trend since 1982 contrasts with the trend before 1982 when state aid increased on average from under 16 percent to 19 percent of city spending.

The outlook for substantial new state assistance to central cities is not promising. The states will continue to be pressured by cutbacks in federal aid, by the devolution of responsibilities to the state level, by and rising spending pressures. In the face of such pressures, aid to local governments is not likely to be a high priority.[23]

Conclusion

As delineated in this section, many central cities, through no fault of their own, are finding it increasingly difficult to finance adequate public services at reasonable tax burdens out of their own resources. During the 1970s, assistance from higher levels of government helped cities cope with the adverse fiscal effects of the social and economic forces affecting them. In recent years, however, intergovernmental assistance, especially that from the federal government, has declined markedly. Like the decentralization of economic activity, this trend does not bode well for the future fiscal health of many U.S. central cities.

FISCAL PERFORMANCE

By definition, a city in poor fiscal health faces a less favorable trade-off between taxes and public services than a city in strong fiscal health. In other words, the tax effort of the less healthy city must be higher, or the services it provides to its residents must be lower than those of a healthier city. Over time, a city with declining fiscal health can choose to increase tax burdens and maintain service levels or to hold tax burdens constant and decrease the quality of services it provides to its residents. This section describes the choices cities have made about taxes and service levels and how these choices vary with the fiscal health of the city.

Tax Effort

The concept of tax burden and tax effort are essentially the same; a city that imposes a higher tax burden on its residents is also making more of a tax effort. Regardless of the term one uses, however, measuring tax burdens on city residents can be tricky, for two reasons. First, a portion of the burden of city taxes is not borne by city residents. For a city that shifts a large portion of its tax burden to nonresident taxpayers in the form of higher prices paid by tourists or commuters or lower prices of factor inputs owned by nonresidents, total taxes collected significantly overstate the tax burden that falls on city residents. Hence, in such a city total taxes expressed per city resident or per dollar of resident income would yield misleadingly high measures of tax burdens on residents, and consequently of tax effort. An accurate measure of tax burdens requires some adjustment for tax exporting.

Second, as noted earlier, cities differ in the range of public services for which they are responsible, and hence in the taxes required to meet their responsibilities. Unless city tax burdens are adjusted for differing responsibilities, one could easily draw the wrong conclusion from high or low city taxes expressed either on a per capita basis or in relation to resident income. For example, the residents of a city that has an overlying county that provides a variety of social services might face a low *city* tax burden, but at the same time an average or high city-plus-county tax burden.[24]

Hence, in measuring city tax burdens, one should adjust both for tax exporting and for differing roles of overlying governments. One way to achieve this end is to express city taxes as a fraction of a city's revenue-raising capacity, with capacity measured in terms of the taxes the city is empowered to use after adjusting for the capacity "used up" by overlying governments.[25] Because the choice of the initial tax burden is somewhat arbitrary, one should pay more attention to how the measures change over time or how they vary across groups of cities than to the absolute levels.[26]

By this definition, tax burdens in the thirty-three big cities declined between 1977 and 1982, but then increased sufficiently after 1982 to produce a higher tax burden on city residents in 1986 than in 1977 (see table 11.10). This conclusion holds both for the three broad-based taxes and also for all city taxes.[27] The decline in tax burdens in the early period largely reflects the effects of the nationwide tax revolt: between 1977 and 1982, taxpayers nationally became much less willing to bear the burden of state and local taxes. Even though few big cities experienced the property tax rollbacks faced by California and Massachusetts cities, fear of taxpayer revolts apparently made city councils less willing to raise taxes than they might have been in a different tax environment.

After 1982, city officials became more willing to increase taxes. This increased willingness was partially a response to large cutbacks in federal aid under the Reagan administration, but may also reflect rising costs of providing public services and a desire to maintain the quality of public services. Between 1982 and 1986, tax burdens on city residents rose by 19 percent for three broad-based taxes and by

Table 11.10 U.S. TAX BURDENS, 1977, 1982, 1986 (AVERAGES, 33 CITIES BY SFH
        CATEGORIES)

	Number of Cities	1977	1982	1986
Three taxes	33	0.926	0.887	1.058
All taxes	33	1.153	1.142	1.376
Three taxes by SFH quartiles				
I (low)	7	1.29	1.22	1.38
II	7	0.79	0.78	0.95
III	7	0.82	0.87	0.87
IV (high)	7	0.92	0.79	1.13

Note: All entries are city taxes divided by a city's restricted revenue-raising capacity as described in the text. Three taxes include property, sales, and earnings taxes. See table 11.8 for cities by SFH quartiles.

SFH = Standardized fiscal health.

21 percent for all city taxes.[28] Unless these tax increases were offset by comparable increases in local public services, these changes imply that city residents were worse off on average in 1986 than in 1982 or 1977.

The bottom panel of table 11.10 summarizes average tax burdens by cities grouped by their standardized fiscal health. One would expect that cities with poor fiscal health would tax their residents more heavily than would their healthier counterparts. Only if such cities chose to respond to their poor fiscal health by providing much lower services than other cities would this outcome not occur. The table shows that the cities with the lowest fiscal health did in fact impose the highest tax burdens on their residents in all three years. In each year, tax burdens in these fiscally unhealthy cities exceeded the average by about a third. Within this category, the highest 1986 tax burdens were in Philadelphia, Detroit, New York City, and Chicago.

Expenditures and Services

A standard approach for determining what has happened to the quantity and quality of public services over time is to examine per capita spending adjusted for inflation. Moreover, because different cities have differing expenditure responsibilities, one typically looks at several categories of spending: current spending on all functions, which ignores the variation across cities in responsibilities; spending on a set of functions that are common to most cities; and public safety, which is the primary municipal service provided by all cities (see, for example, Peterson 1976). As shown in table 11.11, per capita spending (deflated by the national deflator for state and local government purchases) declined during the 1977–82 period and then rebounded sharply after 1982. Over the entire period, real per capita spending increased by about 6 percent.

It would be a mistake, however, to conclude that the quality or quantity of services increased by 6 percent during this period. The main reason is that the state and local deflator does not include the effects on the cost of providing public services of changes in the environmental characteristics of the city. As discussed earlier, a city that has a harsher environment for providing public services, perhaps because a greater number of its residents are poor or because it has more commuters to serve, will have higher costs of providing services than a city with a less harsh environment. Consequently, deterioration in the conditions under which cities provide services, caused, for example, by an increase in the incidence of poverty, will boost the costs of providing a given quality of public services. In addition, the use of a national deflator does not capture the fairly significant salary and benefits differences across the country.

Although measures of service costs for big cities are not available for 1986, the cost increases estimated by Ladd and Yinger (1991) for the periods 1972–77 and 1977–82 are suggestive. As noted earlier, these measures are designed to capture the effects on costs of trends that are outside the control of local officials. They reflect changes in variables such as the poverty rate, per resident private employment in the city, and the composition of economic activity in the city. As shown in table 11.12, the costs of general services and police services

Table 11.11 PER CAPITA U.S. EXPENDITURES, 1977–86 (AVERAGES, 32 BIG CITIES)

	1986 ($)	Percentage Change		
		1977–82	1982–86	1977–86
All functions (current account)	735	−1.8	9.7	5.6
Common functions	446	−2.9	9.6	6.3
Public safety	222	−5.0	12.7	6.6

Source: U.S. Bureau of the Census, various years, *City Government Finances* (Washington, D.C.: U.S. Government Printing Office).

Notes: Washington, D.C., is excluded. Expenditures were deflated by the implicit price deflator for state and local government purchases. Common functions include highways, public safety, sanitation, parks and recreation, and administration.

Table 11.12 GROWTH IN PUBLIC SERVICE COSTS IN THE UNITED STATES, 1972–
82 (AVERAGES, 33 BIG CITIES)

	1982 ($ per capita)	Percentage Change		
		1972–77	1977–82	1972–82
Police	206	7.0	44.8	54.9
Fire	141	– 3.8	34.8	29.5
General	122	4.3	5.7	10.3

Sources: Cost estimates for 1972 and 1982 are from Ladd and Yinger (1991: table A4.1); cost estimates for 1977 are from unpublished data from Ladd and Yinger.

Note: See text for definition of public service costs.

rose on average by 4 percent and 7 percent, respectively, in the 1972–77 period, while the costs of providing fire services apparently declined somewhat. In contrast, the following period, 1977–82, witnessed dramatic increases in costs, especially those for police and fire services. Presumably, the 45 percent increase in police costs largely reflects the rapid growth in many cities' poverty rates during this period. These 1977–82 cost estimates imply that per capita spending on general services would have had to grow by about 6 percent, per capita spending on police by about 45 percent, and per capita spending on fire by about 35 percent, on average, simply to maintain service levels during this period. Because deflated spending did not increase at all during that period, the clear implication is that city service levels were substantially lower in 1982 than in 1977.

The absence of information on cost increases for the more recent 1982–86 period makes it difficult to determine how the 9 to 13 percent growth in spending during that period translates into service changes. The apparent decline observed here in central city poverty rates from their 1982 peak suggests that cost increases in the post-1982 period are likely to have been much more moderate than those of the 1977–82 period. But even assuming no cost increases in the recent period, the spending rebound in the recent period falls far short of what would be needed to offset the service declines of the previous five years. Hence, the data suggest that service levels in big cities were lower in 1986 than in the mid-1970s.[29]

Output Measures of Services

Another way to gauge changes in service quality over time is to focus on specific program areas. Although measuring outcomes is difficult, some insight can be gleaned from looking at changes in crime rates and the problems faced by urban schools.

CRIME

From the perspective of city residents, a rising crime rate represents a decline in the quality of life. If correctly measured, higher crime rates indicate a higher probability that any resident will be victimized by crime. Although crime rates based on police records (and reported yearly in the Federal Bureau of Investigation's *Uniform Crime Reports*) may not accurately reflect these probabilities at any one point in time or may not be fully comparable across cities, nonetheless changes in such crime rates over time in the same city undoubtedly provide useful information about changes in a city's safety.[30] Table 11.13 shows changes in the crime rate (defined as all crimes other than arson, per 1,000 people) over the 1977–94 period for each of the big cities. Consistent with the previous inference that service levels declined substantially between 1977 and 1982, the crime rate in the thirty-three big cities increased by 18 percent on average during that period, with huge increases in Detroit, Miami, Philadelphia, Seattle, and Washington, D.C. During this period, only four of the thirty-three big cities experienced declines in the reported crime rate. After 1982, the situation apparently improved, with sixteen of the cities experiencing declining crime rates between 1982 and 1986, and fourteen cities between 1986 and 1994. Nonetheless, even in this more recent period, the crime rate increased on average, yielding an average increase over the whole period of over 20 percent. This overall increase provides support for the view that residents of big cities experienced a lower level of public safety in the mid-1980s than in the mid-1970s.

Many factors are associated with rising crime rates. Nonetheless, as shown in table 11.14, the changes in crime rates in the big cities are loosely correlated with 1982 levels of standardized fiscal health. Between 1977 and 1982, cities in the lowest two quartiles of standardized fiscal health experienced average increases in crime rates that exceeded the average increases in quartiles III and IV. Although no pattern emerges between 1982 and 1986, over the following period, 1986–1994, crime rates increased in the bottom two quartiles and decreased in the top two quartiles.[31]

URBAN SCHOOLS

A recent comprehensive study of the problems of urban education begins: "It is no secret that the quality of education in urban areas of this country has suffered during the past twenty years" (Newman,

Table 11.13 CHANGES IN CRIME RATES IN THE UNITED STATES, 1977–94
(33 BIG CITIES)

	Percentage Change		
	1977–82	1982–86	1986–94
Atlanta	21.6	12.3	8.1
Baltimore	12.6	−6.5	43.2
Boston	21.9	−8.9	−20.8
Buffalo	0.8	−6.8	24.7
Chicago	−8.8	59.7	3.1
Cincinnati	19.7	−16.0	6.7
Cleveland	8.9	−16.0	9.6
Columbus	6.4	−4.8	6.1
Dallas	20.8	24.9	−37.9
Denver	2.7	−5.5	−37.3
Detroit	40.0	−3.7	−7.8
Houston	27.6	1.1	−24.7
Indianapolis	0.9	−15.9	12.2
Jacksonville	19.0	20.0	−1.0
Kansas City	20.3	20.6	2.4
Los Angeles	34.4	−5.1	−22.8
Memphis	28.7	15.6	−2.0
Miami	40.5	13.9	9.6
Milwaukee	37.3	8.5	2.5
Minneapolis	13.6	15.7	−4.3
New Orleans	23.3	16.1	−1.0
New York	16.2	−8.8	−19.1
Philadelphia	40.7	−7.8	23.1
Phoenix	−8.0	8.9	0.0
Pittsburgh	19.0	14.7	−14.5
Portland, Ore.	20.6	29.1	−30.2
Saint Louis	28.4	−12.6	36.7
San Antonio	16.5	35.2	−20.0
San Diego	−12.5	9.8	−16.5
San Francisco	−9.0	−23.8	9.2
San Jose	16.9	−30.3	−18.2
Seattle	38.8	27.9	−23.0
Washington, D.C.	40.3	−20.0	33.7
Average	18.2	4.3	−2.7

Source: U.S. Federal Bureau of Investigation, *Uniform Crime Reports*, various years.

Note: Crime rate is annual number of offenses for all categories other than arson known to the police divided by city population in thousands.

Table 11.14 CHANGES IN CRIME RATES IN THE UNITED STATES (AVERAGES, 28 CITIES BY 1982 SFH CATEGORY)

SFH Quartiles	Number of Cities	Percentage of Change in Crime Rate		
		1977–82	1982–86	1986–94
I	7	17.3	4.7	1.9
II	7	22.7	− 2.3	10.7
III	7	13.2	6.9	− 3.5
IV	7	11.8	1.0	− 11.6

Sources: Federal Bureau of Investigation, Uniform Crime Reports, various years, and table 11.13, this chapter; see table 11.8 for listing of cities by SFH quartile.

SFH = Standardized fiscal health.

Palaich, and Wilensky 1990: 61). A major explanation for this declining quality is the expanding proportion of city public school students from disadvantaged households and neighborhoods. Cities are the home for increasingly large numbers of minority households, who experience poverty at much higher rates than white households, and for large numbers of families headed by single parents with children under 18 who also are disproportionately poor. In addition, cities are increasingly bearing the burden of concentrations of extreme poverty. Thus, urban school systems must cope not only with the learning handicaps associated with poverty in individual households but also with problems such as drug use, teenage parenting, violence, and unemployment associated with concentrations of extreme poverty.

Moreover, even after fifteen years of busing and other court-ordered remedies, black students remain isolated, and Hispanic students have become increasingly isolated. In New York State, for example, in 1984, 85 percent of the Hispanic students attended predominantly minority schools, and 59 percent were in intensely segregated schools that were 90–100 percent minority. Achievement levels are low and dropout rates are high throughout urban school districts, but especially so in predominantly minority schools. For example, the dropout rate in Chicago public schools in the class of 1982 was 43 percent overall, but 54 percent for Hispanic males and 53 for black males, many of whom were in predominantly minority schools (Newman et al. 1990: 68).

The magnitude of the educational problems facing urban school districts in association with the increasing isolation of the poor and minorities varies across cities. For example, New York, Chicago, and Los Angeles face much more serious problems in this regard than do Denver and Minneapolis. Nonetheless, to some extent all big cities are experiencing a trend of isolation of the poor and minorities in certain urban neighborhoods, and therefore face increasingly formidable educational challenges.

Conclusion

In summary, the evidence on city tax burdens and service levels is consistent with this chapter's conclusions about city fiscal health, namely, that the fiscal condition of many big cities is deteriorating. The data suggest that big cities apparently have responded to their declining fiscal health by both raising tax rates and reducing service levels.

CONCLUSION

Two major sets of factors influence the fiscal condition of U.S. central cities. The first and most basic includes economic and social forces that affect the revenue-raising capacity of cities and the costs of providing public services. Among these forces are economic changes in the structure of urban areas. Based on the work of Ladd and Yinger, this chapter argues that the economic and social trends have significantly reduced the fiscal health of many big U.S. cities during the past two decades. The deterioration in fiscal health across cities is correlated with two manifestations of changes in urban form: slow growth in city jobs relative to the population and slow growth in the income of city residents. Somewhat surprisingly, the deterioration in city fiscal health is not closely linked to a third manifestation of the changing urban form, that of changes in the structure of the local economy as measured by the shift away from manufacturing toward service jobs.

The second set of factors involves changes in the intergovernmental environment in which cities operate. During the 1970s, changes in intergovernmental relations proved highly beneficial to cities and helped offset the adverse effects on their fiscal health of the economic and social trends. However, the situation changed dramatically in the 1980s, with large cutbacks in federal assistance to cities and increasing fiscal pressure on state governments.

Not all cities face declining fiscal health. Some cities should be able to manage adequately without additional intergovernmental assistance. However, many others, including the largest cities and those with slow growth in city jobs and in income of city residents, will continue to struggle; facing powerful economic and social forces outside their control, they will find it increasingly difficult to provide adequate levels of public services at reasonable tax burdens on city residents. For such cities, additional intergovernmental assistance would be both desirable and appropriate, given the fiscal pressures associated with concentrations of high-need populations.

Notes

This chapter draws heavily on Helen F. Ladd and John Yinger, 1991, *America's Ailing Cities: Fiscal Health and the Design of Urban Policy* (Baltimore: Johns Hopkins Press, updated edition); and on Helen F. Ladd, "Big City Finances," in George E. Peterson, editor, *Big-City Politics, Governance, and Fiscal Constraints* (Urban Institute Press, 1994). The chapter was written while I was on leave from Duke University as a Senior Fellow at the Lincoln Institute of Land Policy. I am grateful for the support of the Lincoln Institute and for the research assistance of K. Russell LaMotte.

1. See, for example, the excellent study of the Philadelphia region by Luce and Summers (1987).

2. For a more complete discussion of this issue, see George Peterson (1976), especially pp. 72–84. Although Peterson argued in favor of reuniting the city with its economic base, he concluded that "the political prospects for more vigorous annexation by central cities or widespread tax-base sharing between cities and suburbs must be judged to be somewhere between negligible and nil—and probably closer to the latter" (117–18). The fiscal problems for central cities that do not share in the growth of the metropolitan area are graphically illustrated for the city of Philadelphia in Luce and Summers (1987).

3. The smaller contribution of retail, and also services, in both cities and the nation to total payroll reflects the disproportionately high reliance on part-time workers and the relatively low wage rates in these sectors.

4. This section draws extensively from chapters 3–5 of Ladd and Yinger (1991).

5. The uniform property tax base is defined broadly and includes no exemptions other than those such as church property, which is exempt everywhere. The sales tax base includes food, but, consistent with normal practice, excludes services. The earnings tax base includes earnings both of city residents and of nonresidents working in the city.

6. Ladd and Yinger (1991) were careful not to include cost differences over which city officials have some control. For example, because city officials have some control over the wage rates paid to city workers, Ladd and Yinger measured differences in input prices across cities by private- rather than public-sector wage rates; cities in high-wage regions have higher expenditure needs, all else constant, because they must pay more than other cities to entice private workers into city jobs.

7. The seventy central cities represent the subset of the sample of eighty-six major central cities for which complete data are available, minus Washington, D.C., because of its special characteristics as the nation's capital.

8. Because the indexes in 1982 are defined relative to a 1972 baseline, they reflect both cross-sectional and time-series variation in fiscal health.

9. Measuring city economic activity in terms of jobs is easy to comprehend and has the additional advantage of being part of the language of local public officials. Local economic development, for example, typically is discussed in terms of jobs. Although employment is a less complete measure than value added in the city (a concept that is comparable to gross national product at the national level), such a measure is not available for cities.

10. This approach is similar to that used by Noyelle and Stanback (1983) to analyze patterns of structural change across metropolitan areas. Their measure differs from this one in that it is based on changes in employment shares for all categories of employment, rather than just manufacturing and services (plus FIRE). Although the Stanback-Noyelle measure indicates overall economic disruption, the index used here focuses on structural changes that are likely to have the clearest impacts on city fiscal health.

Like all summary measures, this index must be interpreted carefully. Various combinations can produce the same value of the index. For example, an index value of 15 could reflect a 5 percentage point decline in manufacturing's share combined with a 10 percentage point increase in service's share; or a 2 percent increase in manufacturing's share combined with a 13 percent increase in service's share; or any other combination that adds up to 15. Strictly speaking, therefore, the measure represents changes in sector shares without necessarily implying a shift away from manufacturing and toward services and FIRE. However, the data show that most cities experienced declines in the manufacturing share and increases in the service share during the 1972–82 period. In general, the growth in the services share exceeds the decline in the manufacturing share.

11. For a more complete look at the effects of structural change on revenue-raising capacity, see Ladd and Yinger (1991: chap. 3) and Bradbury and Ladd (1985).

12. The income figures are deflated by the national implicit price deflator for state and local public-sector purchases.

13. The intermediate year used in table 11.6 is 1981, because the Ladd-Yinger fiscal capacity measures for 1982 in fact are based on 1981 income (city income is not available for even years).

14. Yinger and Ladd (1991) developed a model of the state aid decision and showed that assistance through the design of institutions and assistance through grants are substitutes.

15. This measure of state assistance is a relative, rather than an absolute, concept. First, it is relative to the specific set of fiscal institutions built into the definition of standardized fiscal health; a different definition, for example, of the standard or uniform tax system would alter each city's standardized fiscal health and also the calculated amount of state assistance. Second, the measure is relative to a 1972 baseline. In other words, the 1982 amounts of state assistance are all relative to the level of state assistance in the average city in 1972. Because state assistance is a relative measure, it can be negative.

16. The breakdown between assistance through grants and through other fiscal institutions is not shown in table 11.8, but can be found in table A11.1 in Ladd and Yinger (1991).

17. This statement is based on a descriptive regression of the change in state assistance on the change in standardized fiscal health. The coefficient on the latter is -0.51 and its t-statistic is -2.8.

18. Because federal aid is calculated relative to a 1972 baseline, it can be negative. For details of how it was constructed, see Ladd and Yinger (1991): 269.

19. A regression of changes in federal aid on changes in standardized fiscal health indicates no linear relationship between the two variables.

20. See Ellwood (1982: table 11.1). For more information on federal grant policy under Reagan, see Ladd (1984).

21. The federal programs of importance to urban local governments and the percentage change in their budget authority between 1980 and 1987 include Wastewater Treatment Construction (− 32.2), Urban Mass Transportation (− 27.4), Urban and Secondary Roads (− 22.5), Community Development Block Grants (− 20.0), Urban Development Action Grants (− 66.7), Housing Subsidy Programs (− 56.7), Training and Employment (− 46.0), Compensatory Education (− 10.3), and General Revenue Sharing (− 100). Together the budget authority for these programs declined from $45.3 billion in 1980 to $24.1 billion in 1987. During this same period, budget authority for all other grants increased from $59.7 billion to $87.6 billion. Excluding Aid to Families with Dependent Children (AFDC) and Medicaid, budget authority for all other grants increased from $37.6 billion to $49.5 billion, or by 31.8 percent. See Cuciti (1990: table 13.3).

22. See Reischauer (1990) for a discussion of the forces that led to the rise and fall of federal aid to urban areas. During the 1990–91 recession, federal aid declined even further to 6.7 percent of own-source revenue in 1990, and to 6.5 percent in 1991.

23. Estimates of elasticities of changes in state aid to local governments with respect to increases in state budgetary resources indicate that aid does not increase in proportion to changes in state resources (see Ladd 1990, 1991). Useful discussions of the outlook for state aid are found in Yinger (1990) and Gold (1990).

24. Bradbury (1982) dealt with this complexity by looking at aggregate state and local taxes in each city, rather than city taxes alone.

25. The expression for restricted revenue-raising capacity is

$$KC * Y (1 + e'), \tag{11.1}$$

where KC is the city-specific standardized tax burden, Y is the per capita income of city residents, e' is a weighted average of the export ratios (defined as dollars from nonresidents per dollar from residents) from each of the three broad-based taxes that the city is authorized to use, and the weights are the proportions of revenue from each source. For further explanation, see Ladd and Yinger (1991: chaps. 6 and 7).

26. Technically, a ratio less than one implies that the city is not using its full available capacity; that is, it is imposing a lower tax burden on its residents than the standard burden used to construct the measure of revenue-raising capacity.

27. Conceptually, the measure for the three taxes (property, sales, and earnings) is preferred to the measure for all taxes (which includes selected sales and other miscellaneous taxes), but both are presented to give a more complete picture of the burden of all city taxes. The measure for three taxes is preferred, since the denominator of the ratio for both measures is based on export ratios for the three taxes alone; to the extent that the potential for exporting the burdens of other taxes is higher than the average for the three broad-based taxes (as it might well be for selected sales taxes), revenue-raising capacity would be understated and tax burdens for all taxes would be slightly overstated.

28. The 1986 tax burdens are based on estimates of revenue-raising capacity that reflect actual changes between 1982 and 1986 in the income of city residents and the composition of tax revenues (used for weighting the individual export ratios), but assume no change in the individual export ratios or in the city-specific standard tax burden.

29. For completeness, it should be noted that changes in total current account spending over time may also reflect changes in the services for which cities are responsible. On

average, these responsibilities did not change significantly during the 1977–82 period, and the change in the 1982–86 period is not known.

30. Criticisms of the *Uniform Crime Reports* include the fact that the crime index includes only those crimes known to the police, that guidelines for reporting crimes may vary from one police department to another, that police officers have some discretion in what they report, that the index weights different crimes equally, and that rates are not expressed relative to the populations that could be exposed to that crime (see, for example, Reiss 1970). Although the National Crime Survey victimization studies solve some of these problems, they face their own reliability and validity problems, and, because they are costly to administer, victimization surveys are not available for specific cities. For a discussion of these measurement problems, see Skogan (1975).

31. Because each quartile contains only seven big cities, a few cities can have a big impact on the quartile average. For example, eliminating Miami and Portland, Ore., both of which have large increases in crime rates, from quartile IV would lower the average increase in the crime rate between 1977 and 1986 in that quartile to 7.5 percent. This smaller entry for quartile IV would strengthen the argument that fiscal health and service levels are positively correlated.

References

Bradbury, Katharine L. 1982. "Fiscal Distress in Large U.S. Cities." *New England Economic Review* (Jan./Feb.): 32–43.

Bradbury, Katharine L., and Helen F. Ladd. 1985. "Changes in the Revenue-Raising Capacity of U.S. Cities: 1970–82." *New England Economic Review* (Mar./Apr.): 20–37.

————. 1987. "City Property Taxes: The Effects of Economic Change and Competitive Pressures." *New England Economic Review* (July/Aug.): 22–36.

Bradford, David F., R. A. Malt, and Wallace E. Oates. 1969. "The Rising Cost of Local Public Services: Some Evidence and Reflections." *National Tax Journal* 22 (June): 185–202.

Cuciti, Peggy L. 1990. "A Nonurban Policy: Recent Public Policy Shifts Affecting Cities." In *The Future of National Urban Policy*, edited by Marshall Kaplan and Franklin James (235–50). Durham, N.C.: Duke University Press.

Ellwood, John William. 1982. *Reductions in U.S. Domestic Spending*. New Brunswick, N.Y.: Transaction Books.

Gold, Steven. 1990. "State Finances in the New Era of Fiscal Federalism." In *The Changing Face of Fiscal Federalism*, edited by Thomas Swartz (88–126). Armonk, N.Y.: M. E. Sharpe.

Ladd, Helen F. 1984. "Federal Aid to State and Local Governments." In *Federal Budget Policy in the 1980s*, edited by J. Palmer and G. Mills. Washington, D.C.: Urban Institute Press.

————. 1990. "State Assistance to Local Governments: Changes during the 1980s." *American Economic Review* 80 (2, May): 171–75.

————. 1991. "The State Aid Decision: Changes in State Aid to Local Governments, 1982–1987." *National Tax Journal* 44 (4, Part 2, Dec.): 477–96.

————. 1994. "Big City Finances." In *Big-City Politics, Governance, and Fiscal Constraints,* edited by George E. Peterson (201–69). Washington, D.C.: Urban Institute Press.

Ladd, Helen F., and John Yinger. 1991. *America's Ailing Cities: Fiscal Health and the Design of Urban Policy,* updated edition. Baltimore, Md.: Johns Hopkins University Press.

Luce, Thomas F., and Anita A. Summers. 1987. *Local Fiscal Issues in the Philadelphia Metropolitan Area.* Philadelphia: University of Pennsylvania Press.

Newman, Frank, Robert Palaich, and Rona Wilensky. 1990. "Reengaging State and Federal Policymakers in the Problems of Urban Education." In *The Future of National Urban Policy,* edited by Marshall Kaplan and Franklin James (61–88). Durham, N.C.: Duke University Press.

Noyelle, Thierry J., and Thomas M. Stanback, Jr. 1983. *Economic Transformation of American Cities.* Totowa, N.J.: Rowman and Allanheld.

Peterson, George E. 1976. "Finance." In *The Urban Predicament,* edited by W. Gorham and N. Glazer (35–118). Washington, D.C.: Urban Institute Press.

Reischauer, Robert D. 1990. "The Rise and Fall of National Urban Policy: The Fiscal Dimension." In *The Future of National Urban Policy,* edited by Marshall Kaplan and Franklin James (225–34). Durham, N.C.: Duke University Press.

Reiss, Albert J., Jr. 1970. "Assessing the Current Crime Wave." In *Crime in Urban Society,* edited by Barbara McLennan (23–44). New York: Dunellen.

Skogan, Wallace G. 1975. "Measurement Problems in Official and Survey Crime Rates." *Journal of Criminal Justice* 3: 17–32.

Yinger, John. 1990. "States to the Rescue? Aid to Central Cities under the New Federalism." *Public Budgeting and Finance* 10 (Summer): 27–44.

Yinger, John, and Helen F. Ladd. 1989. "The Determinants of State Assistance to Central Cities." *National Tax Journal* 42 (4, Dec.): 413–28.

Chapter Twelve

THE STRUCTURE OF LOCAL PUBLIC FINANCE AND THE QUALITY OF LIFE IN THE UNITED STATES

Joseph Gyourko and Joseph Tracy

The consequences of the absence of a common urban development strategy across cities in the United States and Western Europe have been discussed earlier in this volume by Downs, in chapter 2. Ladd, in chapter 11, furthermore documents that there is substantial heterogeneity in local fiscal climates and that these conditions change through time. This chapter provides a measure of how much people value various parts of the differing fiscal packages that U.S. cities provide. The results indicate that city residents value the fiscal climate commensurately with a standard set of local amenities including location, weather, and pollution conditions. Finally, these findings are used to construct quality-of-life rankings for a set of 130 U.S. cities.

Urban quality-of-life rankings date back to work by Liu (1976). Rosen (1979) and Roback (1980, 1982) provided a theoretical foundation for these rankings by identifying market prices for amenities that can serve as weights in constructing quality-of-life measures. These prices are implicitly generated by the capitalization of interurban amenity differences into local land rentals and wage rates. There was renewed interest in this topic with Blomquist, Berger, and Hoehn (1988), who extended the Rosen/Roback framework to include agglomeration economies. Other recent efforts at estimating compensating differentials arising from city attributes include Berger and Blomquist (1988), Hoehn, Berger, and Blomquist (1987), Gyourko and Tracy (1989a, b), Leven and Stover (1989), Roback (1988), and Voith (1990).

This chapter relaxes three important assumptions traditionally made in this literature. The first is that all city characteristics used to construct the quality-of-life measure are pure amenities. A pure amenity is a nonproduced public good such as weather quality that has no explicit price. In practice, previous empirical studies included some government services, such as education or public safety, with their marginal valuations measured using implicit prices. However, government services are not pure amenities, in that they are produced and have explicit tax prices. If a service is fully priced via local taxes, then independent of the actual marginal valuation of the service, no implicit price in terms of wage or land rent capitalization will exist for the service. Estimating the full price for services necessitates adding state and local taxes to the land rental and wage specifications. It is found that intercity fiscal differentials have nearly as much influence on the quality-of-life index values and rankings as do intercity amenity differentials.

The second assumption that is relaxed is that all locational rents are capitalized into land rentals and/or private-sector wages. This assumption has been employed to ensure that the implicit prices fully reflect marginal valuations of the amenities. However, Ehrenberg and Schwarz's (1986) and Freeman's (1986) reviews of the increasing unionization of the local public sector over the last thirty years cast doubt on the validity of this assumption. Collective bargaining by local public unions may lead to sharing of locational rents between residents and local public workers. This can give rise to explicit tax prices even for pure amenities. Consider an extreme case in which all of the locational rents derived from an amenity are captured by the local public union in the form of wage premia. There would be no capitalization of the amenity in either the land or (private-sector) labor markets. The value of the amenity would be reflected in the differential tax burdens the residents must pay to finance the union wage premia. This provides a second rationale for including controls for local taxes in quality-of-life measures. Consistent with our earlier work (Gyourko and Tracy 1989b), we find that land prices are lower in cities with more highly organized public sector work forces. However, holding taxes and service measures constant, the independent impact of local public unionization is very small on average.

The third assumption that is relaxed is that there are no uncontrolled-for city-specific group effects present in the housing and wage expenditure hedonics. Our data strongly indicate that the error terms in these equations contain both city-specific and individual-specific components. The city-specific components reflect systematic influences of omitted attributes on land rentals and wages. An important question is whether these city-specific effects should be included in the calculation of the quality-of-life rankings. If they reflect unmeasured housing structure quality or worker human capital, then they should not be included in the rankings. However, if they reflect omitted amenity and/or fiscal variables that would have been included in the specifications had the data been available, then they should be priced out and included in the rankings. Because it is not possible to clearly identify the source of these city-specific group effects, quality-of-life rankings with and without the group effects are reported. The fact that including the group effects materially alters the rankings highlights the need for better worker, housing, and city data to pin down more precisely the true urban quality of life.

The following section briefly outlines an expanded Rosen/Roback model, incorporating locally provided services and taxes as well as a rent-seeking local public sector. The third section describes the data used in the empirical analysis. The fourth section details the econometrics and reports results on trait prices and quality-of-life rankings. The chapter ends with a short conclusion and a data appendix.

AN EXPANDED ROSEN/ROBACK MODEL

Government services and taxes can easily be included in the Rosen/Roback model, as Gyourko and Tracy (1989a, b) show. Because the underlying Rosen/Roback model is now well known, this section reproduces only the essential equations from previous works.

Workers and firms compete for scarce sites across jurisdictions. Assume that a representative worker-resident is consuming a composite traded good Y, land services N, and a package of locally provided services and amenities (G_j, A_j) for each city j. The service/amenity package is taken as exogenous by all potential residents and firms. The service package (G) is financed using one or more of the following taxes: a sales tax of rate s on the composite good whose price is the numeraire, an income tax of rate z on gross wages W^g, and a property tax of rate t per local land rental n. There is endowment income of I. Firms use land services, labor, and intermediate goods in production. The latter are assumed to be subject to the sales tax.

Via the standard utility and profit maximizations, worker and firm evaluations of communities are given by an indirect utility function (V) and an indirect profit function (π). With perfect mobility in the long run, both worker utility and firm profitability must be equalized across jurisdictions, as shown in equations (12.1) and (12.2).

$$V = V[(1 - z_j)W^g_j, (1 + t_j)n_j, (1 + s_j), I; A_j, G_j] \text{ for all } j \quad (12.1)$$

$$\pi = \pi[(W^g_j, (1 + t_j)n_j, (1 + s_j); A_j, G_j] \text{ for all } j \quad (12.2)$$

Worker utility in jurisdiction j is determined by the net wage received

[(1 − z_j)W_j^g], gross-of-tax land rentals [(1 + t_j)n_j], what is essentially the nonland cost-of-living (1 + s_j), and the amenity and public service package (A_j, G_j). Firm profits are determined by similar factors, although firms care about the gross wage paid (W_j^g). We assume that the amenity-service package enters the firm's indirect profit function through its underlying effect on the firm's production function.

These equilibrium conditions can be solved implicitly for the reduced-form wage and land rental equations (with R_j defined as the gross-of-tax land rent) in equations (12.3) and (12.4).

$$W_j^g = W[(1 + s_j), z_j, I, G_j, A_j] \qquad (12.3)$$

$$R_j = (1 + t_j)n_j = N[(1 + s_j), z_j, I, G_j, A_j] \qquad (12.4)$$

The equilibrium wage and land rental price are given by the intersection of the level sets of equations (12.1) and (12.2), as illustrated in figure 12.1. The comparative statics for the reduced-form equations are straightforward and are derived from Gyourko and Tracy (1989a, b).

As Linneman (1978) implied, if equations (12.3) and (12.4) could be estimated with exact measures of all fiscal variables, then the full

Figure 12.1 EQUILIBRIUM WAGE AND RENT DETERMINATION

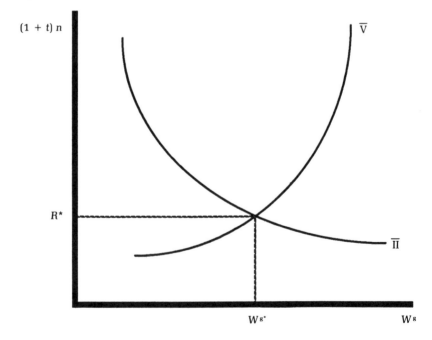

prices for amenities and services could be recovered even when rent sharing occurs between residents and local public unions. (However, the marginal impact of local public employee rent-seeking could not be directly observed.) Because of the inevitably inexact natures of our tax and service variables, it is helpful to augment the land rent and wage equations with a direct measure of local public union rent-seeking (U). That measure should reflect potential residents' perceptions of the union's ability to extract current and future rents. This requires some estimate of the union's long-run institutional strength, and motivates the use of the extent of local public-sector union coverage in the empirical work described in the next section. Note that to the extent the fiscal proxies already incorporate some impacts of rent-seeking activity, the measured influence of U on wages and land prices will not fully capture the costs (or benefits) to worker-residents of local public unionization.

DESCRIPTION OF THE DATA

Data were collected for 130 cities throughout the United States. A house value measure is used to proxy for land prices (n_j), because there is no consistent land price series for our sample. Both the housing value and wage data (W^g) are from a 1 percent random subsample of the 1/1,000 "Public-Use: A Sample of the 1980 Census of Population and Housing," and are for the year 1979. There are 5,263 observations on housing units and 38,870 observations on individual workers.

The wage variable used is the worker's average weekly wage for 1979. To be included in the sample, the resident had to be a full-time labor market participant in the private sector. Public-sector workers are excluded because tax rates and service levels cannot be considered exogenous determinants of their wages, as shown by Inman (1981, 1982).

The housing expenditure variable is based on a reported interval of housing values in the U.S. Census data. A two-step procedure is used to impute a specific housing value to each interval. First, an estimate is made of the continuous distribution of housing values that best accords with the observed frequencies for each interval. This estimated distribution is then used to calculate expected housing values conditional upon being in each interval.[1] The imputed housing expenditure is the conditional expected housing value converted into an annual rent using the 7.85 percent discount rate from Peiser and Smith's (1985) user cost analysis.

A variety of other selection criteria was also employed in generating the sample. First, the wage sample is restricted to individuals who live and work in the central city, whereas the housing sample is restricted to homes located in the central city. This is necessary for matching with city-specific fiscal data collected for central cities of major standard metropolitan statistical areas (SMSAs). Given the heterogeneity in fiscal conditions across any given urban area, it is important that the dependent variables pertain to the same jurisdiction as the right-hand-side fiscal measures. The housing sample is further restricted to units on lots of one acre or less in order to narrow the quality range of houses analyzed.

The model in the second section of this chapter assumes a given quality worker and housing unit. To help control further for quality differences in housing structures, the housing expenditure specification includes a variety of structural traits reported in the Census. The wage specification includes the standard set of human capital proxies, which are also interacted with the worker's sex. Finally, a series of twenty-two major industry and occupation classifications are controlled for.

A host of city characteristics is merged with the Census data. Appendix table 12.A-1 describes these variables and their sources in more detail. The set of amenities includes the following weather and pollution variables: average annual precipitation, relative humidity, average wind speed, the percentage of days with sunshine, heating and cooling degree days, and an air pollution variable measuring mean total suspended particulates.[2] A dichotomous variable was also created indicating whether the city borders an ocean, the Gulf of Mexico, or one of the Great Lakes. Metropolitan area size, measured by the population of the standard metropolitan statistical area (SMSA), is included as another amenity proxy. U.S. Bureau of Labor Statistics (BLS) intermediate family metropolitan budget data, adjusted to remove housing costs, are used to approximate the nonland cost of living. Owing to missing observations, this variable had to be imputed for many of the cities in the sample. All standard errors have been adjusted to reflect the imputation (see notes to appendix table 12.A-1 for details). A final locational amenity controlled for is the percentage of workers in a city who work in another SMSA. This variable is intended to control for access to alternative labor markets. City size held constant, a Connecticut city near New York City is different from a similarly sized city in, say, Iowa, because location near a large labor market makes the opportunity set of the Connecticut residents larger than that of the Iowa residents.

Data were collected on seven fiscal variables. Each of these measures is for the central city only and is not a metropolitan area average. The income tax variable is the sum of state and local income tax rates. Data on state corporate tax rates are also included. The effective local property tax rate variable used is identical to that in Gyourko and Tracy (1989a) and is the product of the nominal rate times the assessment-sales ratio. Four government services are controlled for: police, fire, health, and education. An attempt has been made to construct output measures for each service, as expenditures probably are very poor service proxies for many of the central cities in our sample. For police services, the per capita incidence of violent crimes is used. However, health services are proxied for by an input measure that is the number of hospital beds per thousand capita.[3] The measure used for fire services is a rating scheme developed by insurance companies for setting premiums in a city. The ratings range from 1 to 10, with 1 being best. The last service controlled for is education. Data problems prevent employing standardized test scores as an output measure. Consequently, the student-to-teacher ratio is used.[4]

The measure of the institutional strength of public-sector unions used to proxy for the perceived union rent-seeking potential (U) is the percentage of local public workers in the central city who are organized. By the late 1970s, public-sector unionization had leveled off. Differences in public-sector organization strength across cities in 1979 reasonably could be perceived by residents as reflecting long-run differences in union bargaining power.

ECONOMETRIC SPECIFICATION AND RESULTS

To estimate the reduced-form wage equation given in (12.3), the wage for individual i in city j is assumed to be represented as

$$\ln W_{ij} = \beta_0 + X_i\beta_1 + Y_i\beta_2 + Z_j\beta_3 + u_{ij}, \quad u_{ij} = \alpha_j + \epsilon_i, \quad (12.5)$$

where X_i = vector of individual worker traits,

$\quad\quad\quad Y_i$ = vector of industry and occupation controls, and

$\quad\quad\quad Z_j$ = vector of community amenity and fiscal attributes,

$\quad\quad\quad\quad \alpha_j \tilde{\ } N(0, \sigma_\alpha^2), \epsilon_i \tilde{\ } N(0, \sigma_\epsilon^2).$

To estimate the reduced-form housing expenditure equation in (12.4), it is assumed that the housing expenditures for individual i in city j are represented as

$$\ln n_{ij} = \gamma_0 + H_i\gamma_1 + Z_j\gamma_2 + v_{ij}, \quad v_{ij} = \delta_j + \eta_i, \qquad (12.6)$$

where H_i = vector of housing unit structural traits, and
$\quad\quad Z_j$ = vector of community amenity and fiscal attributes,[5]
$\quad\quad \delta_j \tilde{} \ N(0, \sigma_\delta^2), \ \eta_i \ N(0, \sigma_\eta^2)$.

In estimating equations (12.5) and (12.6), the error terms can contain both an individual and a city component. The city component in each equation is common to all workers or housing units in a given city and is assumed uncorrelated across observations from different cities.

To test for the appropriateness of ordinary least squares (OLS) versus random effects in each specification, we calculated the one-sided Lagrange Multiplier statistic for the null hypothesis that (either) $\sigma_\alpha^2 = 0$ or $\sigma_\delta^2 = 0$. In each case, the data strongly reject the null hypothesis of a zero group variance. A possible correlation between the city-specific error component and the included variables was also tested for using the procedure described in Hausman and Taylor (1981). The data did not reject the null of zero correlation in either specification.

The results from the underlying wage and housing expenditure hedonics are presented in the first two columns of table 12.1. Findings are reported only for the city-specific traits, since the results on the individual worker and housing unit traits yielded no surprises and are similar to other estimates in the literature. As Roback (1980, 1982) showed, the compensating differentials estimated from equations (12.5) and (12.6) can be used to compute implicit prices of the amenities and fiscal conditions. The full implicit price of a given city trait is the sum of the land price differential and the negative of the wage differential.[6] Columns 3–5 of table 12.1 present the full implicit prices as well as the component prices in terms of housing expenditures and wages. Except for the dichotomous Coast variable, the calculations are based upon an assumed 1 percent change about the mean of each variable. All prices are stated in terms of annual housing expenditures or annual earnings (assuming 1.5 earners per household).

Although there are anomalies, the full implicit prices generally have the expected signs, in that beneficial traits have positive prices, with the converse being true for traits that are "bads." Consistent with Gyourko and Tracy (1989a) and Blomquist et al. (1988), for many city traits, the full price largely reflects capitalization in the labor, rather than the land, market.

As a group, the eleven amenities are highly statistically significant (at better than the 1 percent level) in both the wage and housing hedonics. The same is true for the fiscal variables as a group (seven in the housing hedonic and six in the wage hedonic). Many of the amenity variables have been used in other hedonic estimations, and given this chapter's interest in the influence of the fiscal climate, attention is focused on the taxes and services in the following discussion.[7]

The full implicit price for each service proxy has the anticipated sign, with public safety and health services having the largest prices (in absolute value). Most of the impact of these two variables occurs via wage differentials. The property tax coefficient of -0.1037 in table 12.1 implies that property taxes are virtually fully capitalized into land prices. Holding services constant, higher income taxes are viewed as a "bad," with most of the compensation coming through the land market. The effect on wages is small and positive, indicating that gross wages do not rise nearly enough to keep net wages constant. Entrants to high corporate tax rate cities pay higher land rents and accept lower wages. This would be expected if the tax burden is being shifted to nonresidents. This seems unlikely, given that many firms in the corporate sector produce for regional or national markets, making forward-shifting to consumers difficult. It may be that this variable is picking up beneficial aspects of agglomeration that are being appropriated by the government through the tax. It is also possible that the variable might be proxying for the state's overall economic condition. Finally, cities with higher public-sector unionization rates do have somewhat lower land prices, but the partial correlation is not statistically significant.[8]

The underlying quality-of-life index value (QOL) is created as in the following equation:

$$QOL_j = \Sigma_k FP_k * T_{kj} \tag{12.7}$$

where FP_k is the full implicit price of city trait k and T_{kj} is the quantity of that trait in city j. Quality-of-life values are relative to a standardized (and hypothetical) city having the average values of all city traits. The index is measured in 1979 dollars and reflects the premium that individuals are willing to pay to live in city j relative to the hypothetical city with the sample average amenity, fiscal, and public-sector union conditions.

Information on the relative contributions of the amenity, fiscal, and public-sector union conditions to the quality of life is presented in columns 1 and 2 of table 12.2. The full range of quality-of-life values

Table 12.1 REGRESSION RESULTS AND TRAIT PRICES: RANDOM-EFFECTS SPECIFICATION: 130 U.S. CITIES, 1979

City Trait	Annual Housing Expenditure Hedonic[a]	Weekly Wage Hedonic[b]	Annualized Trait Prices[c,d]		
			Housing ($)	Wage ($)	Full ($)
PRECIPITATION	-0.0139 (0.0030)	-0.0027 (0.0009)	-22.82 (4.98)	-21.59 (6.83)	-1.22 (8.45)
COOLING DEGREE DAYS (thousands)	-0.1344 (0.0562)	0.0031 (0.0157)	-7.97 (3.33)	0.89 (4.49)	-8.86 (5.59)
HEATING DEGREE DAYS (thousands)	-0.0277 (0.0248)	0.0172 (0.0069)	-5.65 (5.06)	16.93 (6.82)	-22.58 (8.49)
RELATIVE HUMIDITY	0.0145 (0.0053)	0.0033 (0.0015)	36.53 (13.36)	40.14 (18.67)	-3.61 (22.95)
SUNSHINE (percentage possible)	0.0079 (0.0056)	-0.0005 (0.0016)	21.84 (15.38)	-6.03 (21.97)	27.87 (26.82)
WIND SPEED (mph)	-0.0427 (0.0179)	-0.0192 (0.0055)	-18.18 (7.62)	-39.57 (11.31)	21.39 (13.64)
PARTICULATE MATTER	-0.0019 (0.0013)	-0.0003 (0.0004)	-6.36 (4.20)	-4.34 (-5.79)	-2.01 (7.15)
COAST	0.1345 (0.0694)	-0.0201 (0.0199)	654.15 (360.15)	-435.70 (429.20)	1089.86 (560.28)
COST OF LIVING	0.6496 (1.6197)	0.2633 (0.4208)	28.89 (71.94)	56.58 (90.42)	-27.70 (115.55)
VIOLENT CRIME	0.0574 (0.0425)	0.0705 (0.0109)	2.51 (1.86)	14.91 (2.31)	-12.40 (2.97)
STUDENT/TEACHER	-0.0107 (0.0096)	-0.0010 (0.0027)	-6.84 (6.14)	-3.09 (8.31)	-3.76 (10.33)
FIRE RATING	0.0498 (0.0255)	0.0156 (0.0078)	6.93 (3.55)	10.48 (5.28)	-3.55 (6.36)
HOSPITAL BEDS	0.0031 (0.0037)	-0.0036 (0.0010)	1.82 (2.12)	-10.03 (2.82)	11.85 (3.53)
PROPERTY TAX RATE	-0.1037 (0.0399)	— —	-6.14 (2.37)	— —	-6.14 (2.37)

STATE + LOCAL INCOME TAX RATE	-0.0287 (0.0101)	0.0020 (0.0029)	-3.99 (1.41)	1.37 (1.95)	-5.36 (2.41)
STATE CORPORATE TAX RATE	0.0208 (0.0100)	-0.0067 (0.0029)	5.97 (2.88)	-9.33 (3.98)	15.30 (4.91)
% PUBLIC UNION ORGANIZATION	-0.1646 (0.1302)	-0.0041 (0.0385)	-3.29 (2.60)	-0.39 (3.72)	-2.89 (4.54)
SMSA POPULATION (millions)	0.0376 (0.0223)	0.0096 (0.0057)	1.27 (0.76)	1.57 (0.93)	-0.30 (1.20)
% WORKING IN OTHER SMSA	1.4693 (0.6325)	0.1052 (0.1969)	5.34 (2.30)	1.85 (3.46)	3.49 (4.15)

Summary Statistics

σ^2_α	0.0434	
σ^2_ϵ	0.1801	
σ^2_α	—	0.2905
σ^2_η	—	0.0023
N	5,263	38,870

Note: Dashes (—) signify that the entry is not relevant.
[a] Housing hedonic contains 20 structural trait controls. All results are available upon request to the authors. Estimated standard errors are in parentheses.
[b] Wage hedonic contains 11 worker quality variables and controls for 22 major industry and occupation groups. All results are available upon request. Estimated standard errors are in parentheses.
[c] Calculations in columns 3–5 are based upon a 1 percent change about the variables, except for the dichotomous COAST variable, whose prices are based on a discrete change from non-coast to coastal status. All figures in these three columns are annualized. We assume 1.5 wage earners per household and that each earner works 49 weeks. These are the sample averages.
[d] Standard errors of the implicit prices are in parentheses. They are calculated via the "delta" method.

Table 12.2   AMENITY, FISCAL, AND PUBLIC-SECTOR UNION IMPACTS ON QUALITY OF LIFE AND INTERCITY HOUSING AND WAGE DIFFERENTIALS: 130 U.S. CITIES, 1979

Variable Set	Quality-of-Life Range ($)	Quality-of-Life Interquartile Range ($)	Housing		Wage	
			Maximum Partial R^{2} [a]	Minimum Partial R^{2} [b]	Maximum Partial R^{2} [a]	Minimum Partial R^{2} [b]
All city traits	8,227	1,484	0.55	—	0.44	—
Amenity component	3,979	1,372	0.43	0.39	0.23	0.20
Tax/service component	6,582	1,188	0.16	0.12	0.21	0.20
Public union component	571	193	0.00	0.00	0.06	0.00

Note: Dashes (—) signify that the entry is not relevant.

[a] The maximum partial R^{2} for the vector of traits in each row is defined as the second-stage R^{2} from the regression containing only the city traits listed in each row.

[b] The minimum partial R^{2} for the vector of traits in each row is defined as the difference between the R^{2} obtained when including all city-specific variables (row 1) and the R^{2} from the regression omitting the city traits listed in the relevant row.

based on all city traits is $8,227. This band is wide owing to a few extreme cities. The interquartile range is only $1,484. The separate impact of the eleven amenity variables (which include the weather and pollution variables, coastal status, cost-of-living, access to other labor markets, and size variables) can be seen in the second row of columns 1 and 2, table 12.2. All else constant, one would pay $3,979 more to live in the top amenity city than in the city with the worst amenity set. Note that there is a particularly wide range for the impact of the seven tax-service variables ($6,582, row 3). However, restricting attention to the middle of the distribution shows that the fiscal vector makes approximately the same contribution as the amenity vector to the dispersion of quality-of-life index values ($1,188 versus $1,372, respectively). For the typical city, the public-sector union coverage variable does not have an economically important independent impact on the overall quality-of-life index (row 4).

Columns 3–6 of table 12.2 summarize the relative importance of the amenity, fiscal, and public-sector union variables in explaining the variation in quality-adjusted housing prices and wages across cities. The minimum and maximum partial R^2s presented are calculated using a two-step procedure. In the first step, city fixed effects are estimated using OLS, controlling for housing or worker quality. The second step involves a generalized least squares (GLS) regression of the fixed effects coefficients on the city-specific variables.[9] The city-specific variables explain 55 percent of the variation in quality-adjusted house prices and 44 percent of the variation in quality-adjusted wages across our 130 cities. The remaining rows in columns 3–6 document the relative importance of the amenity, fiscal, and union variables. Fiscal differentials clearly are empirically important, in that they account for at least 21 percent of the explained variation in housing prices (0.12/0.55) and at least 45 percent of the explained variation in wages (0.21/0.44) across cities. However, variation in the degree of public-sector unionization has no ability to explain intercity wage or housing price differentials.

The rankings and quality-of-life index values based on the prices in table 12.1 are presented in the first two columns of table 12.3. Recall that the reason for estimating a random-effects specification is to control for the influence of omitted traits common to a city-specific group of workers or housing units. If the group effects reflect omitted amenities and/or fiscal variables that would be included if observable, they should be priced and included in the quality-of-life computation. In contrast, if these traits reflect unmeasured heterogeneity in housing structure quality and worker human capital, then they should not be

Table 12.3 QUALITY-OF-LIFE INDEX VALUES AND RANKINGS: 130 U.S. CITIES, 1979

City	Random Effects		Random Effects (group effects included)		OLS: All Fiscal Variables		OLS: No Taxes/No Union	
	Ranking	Index Value	Ranking	Index Value	Ranking	Index Value	Ranking	Index Value
Norwalk, Conn.	1 (4.1)[a]	3986 (1135)[b]	23 (20.9)[a]	2132 (2226)[b]	1 (0.4)[a]	5192 (705)[b]	1 (0.8)[a]	4335 (685)[b]
Pensacola, Fla.	2 (4.0)	2963 (714)	6 (3.8)	3812 (1601)	4 (1.5)	3145 (401)	5 (2.9)	2588 (347)
Gainesville, Fla.	3 (7.3)	2819 (890)	46 (23.5)	1019 (2408)	5 (2.2)	3115 (533)	3 (2.6)	3026 (512)
San Diego, Calif.	4 (8.4)	2574 (860)	4 (3.2)	4474 (999)	2 (1.1)	3586 (299)	4 (1.8)	2971 (277)
Stamford, Conn.	5 (9.4)	2497 (875)	38 (20.6)	1339 (1808)	17 (7.4)	1668 (462)	58 (15.3)	137 (354)
Columbia, S.C.	6 (14.7)	2459 (1137)	7 (9.0)	3792 (1693)	3 (2.8)	3556 (677)	2 (0.9)	4135 (653)
Santa Rosa, Calif.	7 (11.4)	1955 (744)	45 (18.8)	1024 (1462)	6 (2.7)	2443 (324)	10 (2.6)	2309 (284)
Bridgeport, Conn.	8 (9.3)	1944 (630)	3 (2.4)	4532 (1580)	10 (3.3)	2245 (335)	50 (9.4)	305 (209)
Tucson, Ariz.	9 (13.5)	1822 (780)	17 (12.6)	2325 (1182)	9 (4.3)	2259 (415)	22 (8.7)	929 (330)
Shreveport, La.	10 (7.3)	1802 (473)	39 (11.5)	1318 (1172)	18 (3.9)	1619 (232)	31 (6.3)	682 (179)
Lancaster, Pa.	11 (9.0)	1784 (547)	16 (8.9)	2327 (1164)	19 (4.7)	1582 (265)	28 (7.1)	762 (198)
Modesto, Calif.	12 (9.4)	1678 (550)	62 (15.6)	517 (1485)	11 (3.2)	2053 (249)	12 (2.5)	2141 (217)
Asheville, N.C.	13 (11.8)	1577 (622)	32 (21.6)	1418 (3036)	20 (6.5)	1464 (346)	7 (2.9)	2364 (301)
New Orleans, La.	14 (10.8)	1565 (570)	42 (14.3)	1170 (879)	13 (4.5)	1818 (304)	40 (10.0)	506 (260)

Fall River, Mass.	15 (16.5)	1549 (795)	85 (22.4)	-327 (2379)	22 (8.3)	1417 (453)	6 (3.0)	2536 (416)
Danbury, Conn.	16 (22.1)	1498 (1009)	1 (1.9)	6662 (3658)	33 (15.9)	826 (587)	9 (4.5)	2329 (540)
Amarillo, Tex.	17 (16.9)	1475 (795)	59 (20.9)	680 (1612)	24 (9.3)	1232 (472)	37 (15.7)	551 (418)
Jacksonville, Fla.	18 (13.1)	1463 (630)	103 (13.1)	-992 (1003)	27 (6.4)	1113 (322)	30 (9.7)	694 (291)
San Francisco, Calif.	19 (16.4)	1416 (796)	29 (16.1)	1578 (884)	8 (2.8)	2296 (291)	13 (3.0)	2046 (279)
San Jose, Calif.	20 (16.2)	1403 (740)	75 (19.1)	208 (898)	15 (5.0)	1744 (299)	15 (3.0)	1849 (281)
New Britain, Conn.	21 (23.1)	1389 (1003)	35 (22.8)	1395 (1931)	7 (6.2)	2335 (592)	8 (4.9)	2345 (569)
Lake Charles, La.	22 (15.9)	1388 (725)	113 (11.4)	-1636 (1800)	25 (7.6)	1177 (365)	36 (9.7)	588 (252)
New Bedford, Mass.	23 (17.9)	1316 (765)	51 (20.2)	791 (1692)	54 (14.2)	179 (387)	34 (12.1)	652 (344)
Tyler, Tex.	24 (14.6)	1175 (605)	11 (8.3)	2773 (2030)	35 (7.8)	776 (326)	18 (2.4)	1411 (228)
Odessa, Tex.	25 (17.1)	1118 (671)	61 (19.4)	577 (2953)	30 (8.9)	960 (393)	42 (14.3)	478 (366)
Erie, Pa.	26 (18.4)	1103 (706)	18 (11.8)	2299 (1390)	23 (7.2)	1250 (347)	64 (12.7)	-30 (291)
Phoenix, Ariz.	27 (26.5)	1097 (1038)	78 (24.8)	59 (1158)	31 (10.4)	932 (424)	20 (10.4)	993 (408)
Knoxville, Tenn.	28 (10.7)	1071 (412)	83 (11.1)	-143 (1024)	28 (4.5)	1100 (208)	26 (5.9)	811 (165)
Lafayette, La.	29 (15.2)	930 (548)	13 (7.6)	2615 (1709)	26 (5.8)	1164 (284)	78 (9.8)	-290 (229)
Monroe, La.	30 (11.1)	905 (404)	19 (7.3)	2287 (1740)	42 (5.9)	524 (194)	60 (6.9)	82 (169)
Wilmington, Del.	31 (19.2)	898 (666)	72 (17.9)	363 (1141)	16 (5.4)	1675 (309)	19 (4.4)	1146 (244)

(continued)

Table 12.3 QUALITY-OF-LIFE INDEX VALUES AND RANKINGS: 130 U.S. CITIES, 1979 (continued)

City	Random Effects		Random Effects (group effects included)		OLS: All Fiscal Variables		OLS: No Taxes/No Union	
	Ranking	Index Value	Ranking	Index Value	Ranking	Index Value	Ranking	Index Value
Waco, Tex.	32 (21.4)	880 (745)	21 (13.1)	2162 (1560)	32 (10.7)	870 (430)	24 (10.9)	859 (379)
Springfield, Mo.	33 (11.8)	753 (386)	22 (7.2)	2154 (1443)	57 (6.7)	151 (184)	32 (5.8)	659 (158)
Sacramento, Calif.	34 (18.0)	703 (564)	24 (11.3)	1832 (956)	29 (6.7)	991 (267)	29 (8.5)	753 (235)
Lubbock, Tex.	35 (20.3)	690 (650)	106 (12.7)	−1107 (1400)	34 (9.5)	796 (378)	46 (13.5)	410 (330)
Los Angeles, Calif.	36 (15.1)	605 (930)	10 (4.6)	2941 (960)	14 (2.7)	1804 (254)	17 (1.6)	1604 (244)
Birmingham, Ala.	37 (25.8)	590 (823)	41 (19.6)	1201 (1120)	43 (12.0)	507 (391)	14 (3.1)	1962 (308)
Jersey City, N.J.	38 (29.7)	573 (984)	95 (20.7)	−831 (1407)	12 (8.6)	1883 (587)	11 (4.8)	2231 (544)
Fresno, Calif.	39 (24.6)	542 (773)	60 (20.3)	604 (1265)	21 (7.0)	1446 (365)	16 (3.9)	1668 (344)
Roanoke, Va.	40 (16.7)	518 (490)	87 (13.4)	−378 (1415)	44 (7.7)	434 (238)	68 (7.0)	−79 (158)
Columbia, Mo.	41 (22.5)	464 (667)	5 (3.7)	4155 (2299)	63 (12.4)	−108 (292)	25 (8.5)	844 (261)
El Paso, Tex.	42 (25.8)	438 (787)	8 (8.0)	3165 (1271)	36 (11.4)	737 (424)	27 (11.5)	810 (375)
Savannah, Ga.	43 (20.8)	428 (600)	52 (16.6)	787 (1477)	51 (9.8)	294 (288)	23 (6.8)	899 (249)
Richmond, Va.	44 (20.4)	398 (575)	110 (9.9)	−1366 (1022)	40 (8.8)	548 (288)	35 (8.4)	604 (213)
Topeka, Kans.	45 (14.4)	383 (392)	64 (12.1)	478 (1508)	41 (6.2)	532 (200)	44 (7.3)	450 (164)

City															
Baton Rouge, La.	46	(18.9)	376	(540)	93	(12.2)	−676	(1176)	39	(8.1)	562	(268)	99	(8.1)	−756	(237)
Albuquerque, N.M.	47	(23.4)	365	(673)	20	(11.9)	2166	(1197)	53	(14.4)	183	(381)	79	(15.5)	−290	(351)
Memphis, Tenn.	48	(20.2)	325	(576)	47	(14.8)	1014	(945)	50	(10.0)	316	(296)	71	(9.8)	−156	(225)
Orlando, Fla.	49	(20.0)	308	(545)	67	(15.3)	420	(1021)	47	(9.6)	344	(286)	57	(11.7)	139	(264)
Fort Wayne, Ind.	50	(16.1)	303	(437)	76	(12.3)	199	(1073)	49	(7.8)	331	(215)	73	(7.7)	−216	(164)
Evansville, Ind.	51	(16.5)	286	(455)	49	(14.0)	891	(1709)	46	(8.4)	359	(239)	47	(7.6)	348	(161)
Pittsburgh, Pa.	52	(27.4)	275	(846)	90	(18.2)	−647	(976)	38	(10.7)	589	(351)	85	(13.7)	−474	(330)
Fayetteville, N.C.	53	(19.8)	274	(543)	37	(14.2)	1357	(1727)	37	(7.5)	675	(264)	55	(6.7)	206	(147)
Mobile, Ala.	54	(24.7)	250	(712)	15	(11.3)	2346	(1345)	62	(14.8)	−91	(363)	51	(13.1)	299	(31.4)
Wichita, Kans.	55	(17.7)	246	(474)	54	(12.8)	785	(996)	72	(11.4)	−286	(250)	74	(10.9)	−225	(232)
Lynchburg, Va.	56	(16.3)	241	(439)	30	(10.6)	1548	(1505)	69	(10.5)	−211	(234)	65	(8.8)	−30	(201)
Worcester, Mass.	57	(21.6)	216	(599)	14	(8.4)	2599	(1386)	77	(14.2)	−379	(315)	21	(7.6)	969	(278)
Austin, Tex.	58	(23.7)	180	(666)	33	(15.6)	1415	(1124)	60	(14.2)	−24	(357)	41	(12.7)	479	(321)
Lawton, Okla.	59	(21.0)	178	(578)	57	(22.5)	750	(2940)	59	(12.2)	−20	(308)	49	(12.7)	308	(290)
San Antonio, Tex.	60	(25.7)	110	(740)	9	(7.7)	3069	(1025)	56	(14.1)	173	(389)	45	(15.0)	444	(372)
Waterbury, Conn.	61	(24.1)	107	(684)	73	(20.9)	311	(1868)	107	(11.3)	−995	(353)	104	(8.1)	−914	(303)
Springfield, Ohio	62	(14.1)	101	(363)	27	(9.0)	1688	(1484)	66	(8.1)	−184	(192)	101	(3.1)	−832	(132)

(continued)

Table 12.3 QUALITY-OF-LIFE INDEX VALUES AND RANKINGS: 130 U.S. CITIES, 1979 (continued)

City	Random Effects		Random Effects (group effects included)		OLS: All Fiscal Variables		OLS: No Taxes/No Union	
	Ranking	Index Value	Ranking	Index Value	Ranking	Index Value	Ranking	Index Value
Jackson, Miss.	63 (18.7)	18 (504)	40 (12.8)	1237 (1349)	61 (10.9)	−79 (267)	43 (8.0)	477 (192)
Chattanooga, Tenn.	64 (18.9)	−41 (496)	66 (13.8)	430 (1086)	68 (11.5)	−202 (262)	89 (10.1)	−540 (255)
St. Joseph, Mo.	65 (17.9)	−53 (479)	12 (7.3)	2735 (1985)	76 (10.5)	−374 (237)	38 (8.1)	523 (176)
Pueblo, Colo.	66 (21.0)	−89 (564)	96 (13.1)	−861 (1935)	52 (11.3)	185 (303)	39 (11.6)	513 (279)
Manchester, N.H.	67 (26.5)	−100 (765)	53 (20.6)	786 (1758)	64 (17.2)	−135 (418)	61 (16.7)	45 (375)
Terre Haute, Ind.	68 (15.4)	−112 (404)	94 (9.9)	−677 (1659)	80 (8.1)	−444 (187)	88 (6.4)	−491 (176)
Bakersfield, Calif.	69 (27.6)	−120 (807)	112 (13.4)	−1546 (1522)	48 (11.0)	341 (321)	33 (11.3)	654 (300)
Macon, Ga.	70 (16.9)	−140 (453)	65 (14.9)	463 (1954)	86 (11.1)	−562 (236)	52 (6.3)	259 (156)
Charleston, W.Va.	71 (23.5)	−158 (647)	36 (16.1)	1370 (1598)	55 (11.7)	177 (314)	83 (10.8)	−466 (248)
Decatur, Ill.	72 (18.4)	−161 (495)	107 (9.7)	−1161 (1572)	90 (10.3)	−635 (244)	72 (9.7)	−207 (228)
Colorado Springs, Colo.	73 (22.0)	−165 (598)	70 (16.7)	384 (1479)	65 (13.7)	−147 (329)	93 (11.9)	−605 (305)
Lincoln, Neb.	74 (18.1)	−185 (470)	25 (10.3)	1768 (1327)	91 (9.7)	−638 (212)	95 (7.9)	−674 (203)
Altoona, Pa.	75 (27.7)	−187 (820)	34 (19.4)	1396 (1896)	105 (13.5)	−963 (413)	97 (12.6)	−700 (370)
Huntsville, Ala.	76 (19.1)	−199 (519)	26 (11.0)	1732 (1271)	104 (9.5)	−926 (271)	81 (9.6)	−411 (231)

Anderson, Ind.	77 (18.2)	-234 (458)	124 (3.5)	-2951 (1585)	71 (11.3)	-268 (247)	56 (11.5)	170 (238)
Oklahoma City, Okla.	78 (24.4)	-257 (694)	55 (18.2)	769 (1032)	78 (15.3)	-384 (354)	70 (15.0)	-98 (341)
Billings, Mont.	79 (26.7)	-285 (786)	114 (12.9)	-1649 (2137)	113 (9.3)	-1375 (400)	109 (7.7)	-1361 (378)
Syracuse, N.Y.	80 (24.8)	-301 (707)	44 (18.1)	1062 (1168)	67 (14.2)	-188 (337)	87 (11.3)	-478 (272)
Columbus, Ga.	81 (22.4)	-305 (634)	50 (18.1)	808 (1974)	111 (9.3)	-1135 (325)	54 (10.0)	223 (238)
Buffalo, N.Y.	82 (27.1)	-314 (806)	102 (16.3)	-901 (1055)	73 (15.7)	-287 (368)	59 (13.7)	86 (309)
Canton, Ohio	83 (14.8)	-340 (375)	74 (11.2)	274 (1090)	74 (8.9)	-296 (195)	84 (8.4)	-472 (178)
Omaha, Neb.	84 (12.8)	-379 (337)	104 (6.7)	-1051 (994)	94 (7.4)	-700 (173)	77 (7.1)	-283 (150)
Springfield, Ill.	85 (14.0)	-409 (362)	58 (12.1)	747 (1703)	87 (8.1)	-566 (162)	90 (7.1)	-551 (158)
Miami, Fla.	86 (29.1)	-445 (925)	31 (20.7)	1439 (1114)	45 (14.5)	411 (435)	69 (17.8)	-86 (410)
South Bend, Ind.	87 (15.6)	-468 (430)	105 (8.8)	-1079 (1357)	92 (9.5)	-649 (222)	107 (3.2)	-1116 (187)
Salem, Ore.	88 (21.1)	-488 (604)	123 (4.6)	-2898 (1704)	110 (8.6)	-1070 (288)	75 (11.3)	-260 (257)
Tulsa, Okla.	89 (13.7)	-496 (377)	80 (10.1)	-31 (807)	85 (8.9)	-548 (182)	100 (5.4)	-792 (151)
Portland, Maine	90 (26.5)	-498 (812)	28 (17.6)	1659 (1568)	88 (17.0)	-597 (419)	62 (16.4)	15 (381)
Akron, Ohio	91 (15.8)	-520 (438)	77 (12.2)	173 (944)	75 (9.2)	-302 (205)	106 (3.7)	-1036 (164)
Harrisburg, Pa.	92 (24.3)	-537 (724)	111 (12.2)	-1408 (1194)	102 (13.9)	-904 (388)	53 (15.4)	253 (352)
Cincinnati, Ohio	93 (16.8)	-544 (484)	56 (13.2)	759 (798)	58 (9.1)	68 (243)	82 (9.4)	-426 (220)

(continued)

Table 12.3 QUALITY-OF-LIFE INDEX VALUES AND RANKINGS: 130 U.S. CITIES, 1979 (continued)

City	Random Effects		Random Effects (group effects included)		OLS: All Fiscal Variables		OLS: No Taxes/No Union	
	Ranking	Index Value	Ranking	Index Value	Ranking	Index Value	Ranking	Index Value
Cedar Rapids, Iowa	94 (18.1)	-544 (529)	71 (14.9)	363 (1460)	99 (9.4)	-823 (258)	94 (8.8)	-659 (248)
Indianapolis, Ind.	95 (16.3)	-600 (477)	118 (5.1)	-2147 (715)	106 (7.6)	-983 (242)	105 (4.3)	-935 (188)
Reno, Nev.	96 (29.1)	-639 (977)	119 (11.7)	-2186 (1551)	97 (19.2)	-816 (542)	48 (17.0)	-315 (412)
Sioux City, Iowa	97 (17.9)	-675 (553)	92 (14.1)	-653 (2041)	93 (10.8)	-656 (270)	91 (9.7)	-582 (262)
Dayton, Ohio	98 (18.2)	-699 (532)	89 (12.5)	-536 (958)	81 (11.7)	-484 (240)	102 (6.8)	-863 (208)
Des Moines, Iowa	99 (14.0)	-700 (440)	81 (11.5)	-50 (1082)	101 (7.0)	-884 (2148)	98 (6.7)	-707 (200)
Trenton, N.J.	100 (21.7)	-715 (679)	68 (18.4)	415 (1337)	120 (4.8)	-1698 (3089)	67 (12.3)	-68 (266)
Philadelphia, Pa.	101 (20.7)	-736 (813)	117 (8.1)	-1991 (869)	109 (7.3)	-1043 (269)	108 (3.7)	-1343 (248)
Louisville, Ky.	102 (13.3)	-794 (429)	120 (4.4)	-2248 (851)	79 (9.5)	-433 (205)	76 (8.0)	-264 (181)
Columbus, Ohio	103 (11.6)	-811 (384)	101 (7.4)	-899 (722)	83 (8.4)	-514 (185)	115 (2.3)	-1756 (154)
Seattle, Wash.	104 (25.1)	-816 (848)	82 (20.9)	-58 (969)	70 (14.9)	-248 (346)	96 (11.0)	-690 (312)
Rochester, N.Y.	105 (20.8)	-842 (671)	122 (5.9)	-2607 (1018)	82 (13.2)	-495 (299)	80 (11.6)	-298 (262)
Tacoma, Wash.	106 (21.7)	-846 (723)	97 (15.1)	-862 (1256)	89 (15.0)	-599 (347)	66 (13.6)	-50 (289)
Mansfield, Ohio	107 (20.4)	-965 (710)	48 (19.1)	934 (1861)	103 (12.0)	-920 (349)	126 (2.2)	-2443 (312)

City								
Boise, Idaho	108 (13.6)	−972 (486)	2 (1.5)	5117 (1553)	98 (9.8)	−822 (265)	92 (8.1)	−596 (207)
Toledo, Ohio	109 (12.9)	−1013 (479)	91 (10.5)	−647 (847)	95 (9.0)	−761 (237)	121 (2.6)	−1974 (168)
Boston, Mass.	110 (18.3)	−1067 (703)	63 (17.8)	512 (902)	96 (12.4)	−764 (309)	103 (8.8)	−908 (299)
Minneapolis, Minn.	111 (20.8)	−1147 (816)	43 (19.8)	1082 (917)	84 (14.2)	−520 (327)	122 (3.9)	−1987 (241)
Chicago, Ill.	112 (17.3)	−1209 (1031)	109 (12.2)	−1337 (1061)	112 (3.5)	−1334 (249)	111 (2.8)	−1486 (240)
Tuscaloosa, Ala.	113 (13.7)	−1259 (584)	99 (13.8)	−879 (2004)	123 (3.7)	−1981 (299)	86 (9.8)	−475 (235)
Muncie, Ind.	114 (12.9)	−1373 (595)	126 (3.7)	−3290 (2113)	124 (3.0)	−2021 (306)	124 (3.5)	−2122 (281)
Ann Arbor, Mich.	115 (14.9)	−1450 (697)	86 (17.6)	−376 (1497)	126 (3.0)	−2215 (343)	63 (12.7)	7 (270)
Cleveland, Ohio	116 (10.9)	−1492 (560)	108 (9.6)	−1218 (748)	100 (9.8)	−851 (267)	116 (3.8)	−1833 (223)
Rockford, Ill.	117 (7.0)	−1532 (399)	88 (10.0)	−431 (1200)	122 (2.8)	−1955 (211)	117 (3.2)	−1845 (176)
Peoria, Ill.	118 (6.5)	−1634 (411)	125 (2.6)	−3052 (1150)	121 (2.4)	−1937 (203)	110 (2.2)	−1396 (175)
Spokane, Wash.	119 (11.6)	−1815 (728)	84 (18.0)	−273 (1324)	116 (6.0)	−1544 (343)	114 (4.2)	−1623 (255)
Portland, Ore.	120 (8.7)	−1874 (607)	69 (16.3)	388 (807)	119 (3.9)	−1640 (264)	119 (3.9)	−1890 (249)
Kansas City, Mo.	121 (5.4)	−1900 (441)	121 (3.7)	−2523 (682)	118 (3.4)	−1634 (230)	113 (3.1)	−1600 (203)
Atlanta, Ga.	122 (9.7)	−1916 (671)	116 (8.1)	−1980 (841)	114 (5.5)	−1489 (285)	120 (4.2)	−1939 (251)
Hartford, Conn.	123 (13.9)	−1931 (871)	79 (22.4)	0 (1377)	117 (7.5)	−1631 (434)	129 (1.5)	−2839 (347)
Baltimore, Md.	124 (9.4)	−1934 (662)	115 (8.4)	−1843 (806)	115 (5.1)	−1530 (274)	112 (3.8)	−1524 (223)

(continued)

Table 12.3 QUALITY-OF-LIFE INDEX VALUES AND RANKINGS: 130 U.S. CITIES, 1979 (continued)

City	Random Effects		Random Effects (group effects included)		OLS: All Fiscal Variables		OLS: No Taxes/No Union	
	Ranking	Index Value	Ranking	Index Value	Ranking	Index Value	Ranking	Index Value
Newark, N.J.	125 (9.8)	-2477 (914)	100 (26.7)	-884 (1798)	108 (14.0)	-1002 (427)	125 (4.9)	-2176 (395)
Las Vegas, Nev.	126 (9.0)	-2832 (1027)	128 (3.4)	-4198 (1403)	125 (6.1)	-2125 (553)	128 (4.2)	-2637 (523)
Grand Rapids, Mich.	127 (2.6)	-2947 (589)	98 (12.3)	-865 (1009)	127 (0.7)	-3908 (306)	123 (3.6)	-1991 (245)
Saginaw, Mich.	128 (1.4)	-3668 (646)	129 (0.6)	-5273 (1423)	128 (0.7)	-3939 (315)	118 (3.4)	-1881 (225)
Detroit, Mich.	129 (1.1)	-4153 (751)	130 (0.6)	-5273 (1423)	129 (0.6)	-4188 (267)	127 (1.5)	-2544 (288)
Flint, Mich.	130 (1.2)	-4241 (786)	127 (3.5)	-3537 (1251)	130 (0.2)	-4893 (407)	130 (1.1)	-2917 (331)

[a] Numbers in parentheses in columns 1, 3, 5, and 7 are estimated standard errors of the rankings. Standard errors for the rankings were calculated using a sample of 100,000 simulated rankings. Housing and wage coefficient vectors were drawn from the relevant normal distributions implied by the appropriate regression analysis. Full implicit prices and associated quality-of-life rankings were calculated for each set of simulated coefficient vectors. The reported standard error for a city ranking is the standard deviation in the sample of the given city's simulated rankings.

[b] Numbers in parentheses in columns 2, 4, 6, and 8 are estimated standard errors of the index values. They are calculated via the "delta" method.

included in the quality-of-life computation. Unfortunately, it is not readily apparent how to discriminate between these sources.

The correlation between the errors of the two equations might allow some insight into the nature of the city-specific group effects, but only if we know much more about the underlying structure of the model than our reduced-form estimations afford. If both worker and housing quality were systematically underestimated (or overestimated) by city, a positive error correlation would result. However, a negative error correlation would ensue if quality were overestimated in, say, the housing market and underestimated in, say, the labor market. If high-quality workers demand high-quality housing, then we would expect any systematic mismeasurement of quality to produce a positive error correlation. In contrast, if the group effects solely reflect an omitted amenity valued only by the workers, a negative error correlation across equations would be expected. This is because an omitted city trait that is beneficial to workers but not firms implies a negative wage residual and a positive land rent residual. However, if firms also value this trait, they might bid up wages, with the resulting error correlation across equations being of indeterminant sign. It simply is not possible to be certain that the impact from the worker side of the model is dominant, particularly for any omitted fiscal traits.[10] Consequently, the sign of the correlation does not reliably identify the source of the group effects without specific assumptions about the underlying model structure.[11]

Because one cannot be sure about the origin of the group effects, columns 3 and 4 of table 12.3 present the rankings and index values when the group error terms are included. There still is a fairly strong positive correlation between the rank orderings of the indexes with and without the group effects ($\rho = 0.63$). However, the rankings of many cities are materially affected by the inclusion of the group effect. The mean absolute change in rankings is 26.8, and the standard deviation of that change is 20.7. Norwalk, Connecticut drops from being the top-ranked city to being number 23. Lake Charles, Louisiana, suffers the biggest decline, with its ranking falling from 22 to 113. Boise, Idaho, exhibits the biggest rise, increasing in rank from 108 to 2. For the cities exhibiting substantial decreases (increases) in ranks, it is typically the case that observed wages are much higher (lower) than predicted by the right-hand-side variables.[12]

The last four columns of table 12.3 present quality-of-life rankings and index values based on two OLS specifications, one with and the other without the fiscal/union variables. They provide a base for comparison with previous work that has neither controlled for the tax side of local finance nor estimated random-effects specifications. The results indicate that the rankings are materially influenced not only by including the tax and public-sector union variables but also by the econometric method used to estimate the prices. With the full set of amenity and fiscal variables included, the mean absolute change in rankings based on the random-effects estimation (excluding group effects, columns 1–2) versus the OLS-based results (columns 5–6) is 10.2, with an associated standard deviation of 9.56. The mean absolute dollar change in index value is $391, with a standard deviation of $320.

The impact of including the tax and union vector can be seen by comparing the rankings based on the two OLS specifications (columns 5–6 versus columns 7–8). The mean absolute change in rankings when these variables are added is 16.2, with a 15.2 standard deviation. The mean absolute dollar change in these index values is $603, with a standard deviation of $527.[13]

Importantly, the influence of the fiscal variables does not appear to be the result of spurious correlation with broader regional forces. For example, when three region dummies are included in the specifications, the joint significance of the fiscal variables continues to hold at very high confidence levels (the same is true for the amenities). When group effects are controlled for, the only significant region effects are for the West, where housing expenditures are substantially higher (by about 63 percent, on average) and wages are slightly higher (by about 8 percent, on average). Counting the regional effects as amenities does not materially change the relative aggregate effects of the amenity versus fiscal variables (columns 1–2, table 12.2) or the rankings themselves (column 2, table 12.3). In the random-effects specification, the correlation between the sets of rankings with and without the region dummies included in the underlying hedonics is 0.97.

It is also noteworthy that the findings are robust with respect to some nonlinear specifications. A random-effects specification was estimated in which those city traits with the highest coefficients of variation were entered in quadratic form. Trait prices changed only slightly over the range of city trait amounts found in the data, and rankings and index values were essentially unaltered. With only 130 cities, it was decided to include only the linear terms. A Box-Cox analysis of the specification underlying the results in columns 5–6 of table 12.3 was also performed. In addition, the housing hedonic was estimated using *only* the information on the interval of house values to which an observation belonged. Although that analysis did reject the log specification for both hedonics, this estimation procedure yielded results virtually identical to the OLS-based findings. The simple correlation between the Box-Cox and OLS rankings is 0.98. The mean absolute change in rankings was about 0.5 ranks. Estimating a random-effects model in a nonlinear environment involves an order-of-magnitude increase in computing difficulty and cost, and our experimentation with this sample clearly shows modeling group effects to be far more important than incorporating nonlinearities.

Although the pattern of results appears to be robust with respect to specification and functional form, two important notes of caution about the general reliability of quality-of-life rankings should be made. The reliability issue is starkly illustrated by the large standard errors in the quality-of-life rankings based on the random-effects estimates. These errors are significantly higher than those calculated using the OLS estimates. This is not surprising, as Moulton (1986, 1987) has shown that, when group effects exist in the data, the standard errors for the OLS coefficient estimates for variables having no within-group variation are downward biased. In our data, the random-effects estimation typically results in a doubling in the standard error of a city's quality-of-life ranking. The average standard error of the rankings based on random effects (columns 1–2 of table 12.3) is 16.9, versus an average of 8.6 for the rankings based on OLS (columns 5–6 of table 12.3). At standard confidence levels, it becomes difficult to differentiate among many cities unless the comparison is between a very high-ranked city and a very low-ranked city (e.g., top twenty versus bottom twenty).[14] The sharp drop in the precision of the full price estimates and of the accompanying quality-of-life rankings points out the need for better data to reduce the magnitudes of the city-specific error components and to more precisely estimate a city's quality of life.

An added reliability concern arises from the fact that an arbitrary assumption typically is made as to who the marginal entrant is. It was assumed that the marginal entrant was the household with the sample average number of wage earners (1.5) and amount spent on housing per year ($4,524). The first four columns of table 12.4 illustrate how the top- and bottom-ranked cities change as the number of wage earners changes in the assumed marginal entrant household. (Of course, a similar point could be illustrated by varying the amount of housing expenditures.) Note that the rankings and quality-of-life index values do not change because the underlying hedonic coefficients change; those coefficients are unaltered. However, the trait prices do change, because they are based upon some assumed degree of exposure to capitalization in the land and labor markets. The implicit assumption

Table 12.4 RANKINGS FOR HOUSEHOLDS WITH DIFFERENT NUMBERS OF WAGE EARNERS: TOP- AND BOTTOM-RANKED U.S. CITIES, 1979

Rank	Households with 1.5 Earners ($)	Households with 0 Earners ($)	Households with 1 Earner ($)	Households with 2 Earners ($)	Net Subsidy for Retired Household with 0 Earners ($)
1	Norwalk, Conn. (3,986)[a]	San Francisco, Calif. (4,232)[a]	Norwalk, Conn. (3,408)[a]	Norwalk, Conn. (4,564)[a]	Gainesville, Fla. (3,240)[b]
2	Pensacola, Fla. (2,963)	San Diego, Calif. (4,075)	San Diego, Calif. (3,075)	Pensacola, Fla. (4,040)	Pensacola, Fla. (3,230)
3	Gainesville, Fla. (2,819)	Los Angeles, Calif. (3,709)	San Francisco, Calif. (2,355)	Gainesville, Fla. (3,899)	Columbia, S.C. (3,163)
4	San Diego, Calif. (2,574)	San Jose, Calif. (2,997)	Santa Rosa, Calif. (2,156)	Columbia, S.C. (3,513)	Tyler, Tex. (2,339)
5	Stamford, Conn. (2,497)	Santa Rosa, Calif. (2,557)	Stamford, Conn. (1,993)	Stamford, Conn. (3,001)	Lake Charles, La. (2,282)
6	Columbia, S.C. (2,459)	Norwalk, Conn. (2,253)	San Jose, Calif. (1,934)	Tucson, Ariz. (2,445)	New Bedford, Mass. (2,249)
7	Santa Rosa, Calif. (1,955)	Chicago, Ill. (1,762)	Pensacola, Fla. (1,886)	Shreveport, La. (2,300)	Amarillo, Tex. (1,950)
8	Bridgeport, Conn. (1,944)	Sacramento, Calif. (1,741)	Gainesville, Fla. (1,739)	Lancaster, Pa. (2,266)	Tucson, Ariz. (1,869)
123	Hartford, Conn. (−1,931)	Oklahoma City, Okla. (−1,070)	Tuscaloosa, Ala. (−1,448)	Portland, Ore. (−2,590)	Saginaw, Mich. (−2,593)
124	Baltimore, Md. (−1,934)	Saginaw, Mich. (−1,075)	Atlanta, Ga. (−1,452)	Hartford, Conn. (−2,711)	Las Vegas, Nev. (−2,644)
125	Newark, N.J. (−2,477)	Tyler, Tex. (−1,164)	Baltimore, Md. (−1,503)	Grand Rapids, Mich. (−3,659)	San Francisco (−2,816)
126	Las Vegas, Nev. (−2,832)	Louisville, Ky. (−1,181)	Las Vegas, Nev. (−1,951)	Las Vegas, Nev. (−3,714)	Chicago, Ill. (−2,971)
127	Grand Rapids, Mich. (−2,947)	Birmingham, Ala. (−1,221)	Grand Rapids, Mich. (−2,235)	Newark, N.J. (−3,763)	Los Angeles, Calif. (−3,104)
128	Saginaw, Mich. (−3,668)	Mobile, Ala. (−1,399)	Saginaw, Mich. (−2,804)	Saginaw, Mich. (−4,532)	Detroit, Mich. (−3,320)
129	Detroit, Mich. (−4,153)	Altoona, Pa. (−1,478)	Flint, Mich. (−2,929)	Detroit, Mich. (−5,259)	Newark, N.J. (−3,858)
130	Flint, Mich. (−4,241)	Tuscaloosa, Ala. (−1,826)	Detroit, Mich. (−3,406)	Flint, Mich. (−5,554)	Flint, Mich. (−3,939)

[a] Numbers in parentheses in columns 1–4 are quality-of-life index numbers assuming the marginal household is that listed at the top of the column.
[b] Net subsidy number in parentheses in column 5 reflects the difference between the marginal valuation of city's amenity, fiscal, and public-sector union traits and the actual prices faced by a retired household with no wage earners. The marginal valuation calculation assumes identical preferences across household types and that the 1.5 wage-earner family is the true marginal entrant.

made here and in other quality-of-life studies is that the assumed wages and rents reflect the preferred degree of exposure based on the marginal entrant's utility function.

The rankings for households with 1, 1.5, and 2 wage earners are highly correlated ($\rho > 0.87$ in all pairwise comparisons), as suggested by the fact that the top- and bottom-ranked cities tend to have substantial overlap. However, the rankings for the zero-earner household in column 2 are not nearly so strongly correlated with the other sets of rankings. The smallest correlation of -0.02 is between the rankings for the zero-earner household and the two-earner household. The highest correlation of 0.38 is achieved with the rankings of the one-earner household.

Finally, it is worth noting that even assuming identical preferences among households, the equilibrium prices typically will not make all households indifferent as to location. This is a direct consequence of the observed differential capitalization of amenity and fiscal traits in the land and labor markets. As an example, assume that the 1.5 wage-earner household has been correctly identified as the marginal entrant to all cities. In this case, the quality-of-life index values reported in table 12.3 would correctly measure the marginal valuations for all households. At these prices, a 1.5 wage-earner household would be indifferent across cities. However, a retired couple household would be inframarginal because the prices they face are radically different, owing to their lack of exposure to labor market capitalization. Column 5 of table 12.4 lists the cities that provide the largest and smallest implied net subsidies to a retired couple household. The net subsidy is defined as the difference between the 1.5 earner household's marginal valuation of the city's amenity, fiscal, and public-sector union package and the price the retired couple household actually has to pay to consume that package. The highest-subsidy cities tend to be southern and western cities with high-value weather amenities whose full prices tend to contain large wage components (see table 12.1). The lowest-subsidy cities are a more diverse lot, including some northern cities as well as a few western cities with very high land values.[15]

CONCLUSIONS

We have long known that differences in the local fiscal climate generate compensating differentials across local land and labor markets. Thus, they should affect the local quality of life. This chapter has presented new estimates of the quality of life that highlight the importance of local fiscal conditions. Unlike standard locational amenities, the fiscal climate is under the control of local authorities. Thus, the quality of life may be more malleable than has been previously thought.

This possibility has important implications not just for urban scholars but for city officials and potential residents (whether firms or households). The impact of the fiscal climate is so large that quality-of-life rankings almost certainly change through time with the fiscal effectiveness of municipalities. For example, performing this study with 1990 Census data probably would result in lowered rankings for many of the cities in the northeastern part of the United States (Connecticut, in particular) as their tax burdens have risen and their effective service provisions have fallen over the decade of the 1980s.

Finally, accounting for city group effects through a random-effects estimation is found to have a similarly strong impact on the rankings and their associated standard errors. The presence of strong group effects begs the question of whether these should be included in the quality-of-life index. Because the proper procedure to follow is not apparent, rankings with and without the group effects should be presented to give readers some idea of potential problems from omitted variables.

Future research in this area should attempt to control for intercity differences in public wealth. Recent work by Haughwout and Inman (1996) shows that the mean value of local infrastructure per capita across thirty-four large cities was over $13,000 (in 1990 dollars). The mean level of unfunded pensions per capita was over $2,500 (with a standard deviation almost equal to the mean). It is possible that these measures of the stock of public wealth are as influential as current tax rates and service qualities in determining wage and rent differentials across cities.

Appendix Table 12.A-1 VARIABLE DESCRIPTION AND SUMMARY STATISTICS

Variables	Description	Source	Mean[a] (std.)
PRECIPITATION	Annual inches (multiyear average)	U.S. Department of Commerce, Comparative Climatic Data (1983)	36.17 (13.38)
COOLING DEGREE DAYS	Thousands per year (multiyear average)	U.S. Bureau of the Census, County and City Data Book (1983)	1.31 (0.84)
HEATING DEGREE DAYS	Thousands per year (multiyear average)	U.S. Bureau of the Census, County and City Data Book (1983)	4.49 (1.90)
RELATIVE HUMIDITY	Percentage (multiyear average)	U.S. Department of Commerce, Comparative Climate Data (1983)	55.58 (8.74)
SUNSHINE	Percentage of possible (multiyear average)	U.S. Department of Commerce, Comparative Climatic Data (1983)	61.02 (8.31)
WIND SPEED	Miles per hour (multiyear average)	U.S. Department of Commerce, Comparative Climatic Data (1983)	9.36 (1.65)
PARTICULATE MATTER	Micrograms per cubic meter (1979 data)	U.S. Environmental Protection Agency, 1979 Air Quality Data—Annual Statistics (1980)	73.30 (21.71)
COAST	Dichotomous; 1 if on border of ocean, Great Lake, or Gulf of Mexico; 0 otherwise	Created by authors	0.20 (0.41)
NONLAND COST-OF-LIVING	Logged Index number[b]	U.S. Department of Labor, Three Standards of Living for an Urban Family of Four Persons (1977)	0.98 (0.02)
SMSA POPULATION	Millions of persons (1979 data)	U.S. Bureau of the Census, County and City Data Book (1983)	0.744 (1.122)
% WORKING IN OTHER SMSA	Percentage; variable entered as spline; cities with less than 16 percent of their residents working in another SMSA (one standard deviation above the sample mean) have a value of 0; all others are coded as their actual percentages minus 0.16 (16 percent)	U.S. Bureau of the Census, Census of Population and Housing, 1980: Public Use Microdata Samples Technical Documentation (and data tapes) (1983)	(0.013) (0.042)

continued

Appendix Table 12.A-1 VARIABLE DESCRIPTION AND SUMMARY STATISTICS (continued)

Variables	Description	Source	Mean[a] (std.)
VIOLENT CRIME RATE	Per 100 capita	U.S. Bureau of the Census, County and City Data Book (1983)	0.96 (0.64)
STUDENT/TEACHER RATIO	Ratio of students to full-time-equivalent instructional employees[c]	U.S. Bureau of the Census, Census of Governments, vols. 2, 3 (1982)	14.07 (2.46)
FIRE RATING	Insurance company rating of fire department quality: 1 = best; 10 = worst	International City Management Association, The Municipal Year Book, 1976 (1976)	3.07 (0.90)
HOSPITAL BEDS	Public beds per 1,000 capita in the city	U.S. Bureau of the Census County and City Data Book (1983)	12.73
EFFECTIVE PROPERTY TAX RATE	Nominal rate times assessment-sales ratio; 1979 numbers[d]	Assessment/Sales and Assessed Base: U.S. Bureau of the Census, Census of Governments, Taxable Property Value and Assessment-Sales Prices Ratios, vol. 2 (1982)	7.59
		City and Special District Property Tax Revenues: U.S. Bureau of the Census, City Government Finances, 1978–79 and U.S. Bureau of the Census, Survey of Governments (data tapes) (1979)	1.31 (0.79)

(continued)

Variable	Description	Source	Value
STATE + LOCAL INCOME TAX RATE	State rate: average rate in 1979 after deductibility for person with $20,000 adjusted gross income Local rate: flat rate typically; if not, highest rate applicable used	State rate: Feenberg and Rosen, in *Studies in State and Local Public Finance* (1986, table 6.6) Local rate: Tax Foundation, Inc., *Facts and Figures on Government Finances* (1978)	3.61 (2.71)
STATE CORPORATE INCOME TAX RATE	Highest rate applicable as of July 1, 1980; (for most states, highest bracket began at a fairly low profit level)	Advisory Commission on Intergovernmental Relations (ACIR), *Significant Features of Fiscal Federalism 1979–80* (1981, table 89)	6.32 (3.05)
% PUBLIC UNION ORGANIZATION	Percentage of local public workers in the central city who are organized[e]	U.S. Bureau of the Census, *Survey of Governments* (data tapes) (1979)[f]	0.44 (0.21)
HOUSING EXPENDITURES	Annual housing expenditures; converted using 7.85 percent discount rate	U.S. Bureau of the Census, *Census of Population and Housing, 1980: Public Use Microdata Samples Technical Documentation* (and data tapes) (1983)	$4542 (3904)
WAGES	Weekly wages	U.S. Bureau of the Census, *Census of Population and Housing, 1980: Public Use Microdata Samples Technical Documentation* (and data tapes) (1983)	$299 (208)

(continued)

Appendix Table 12.A-1 VARIABLE DESCRIPTION AND SUMMARY STATISTICS (continued)

[a]Summary statistics for all city-specific variables are unweighted (by housing or worker observations) means and standard deviations over the 130 cities in the sample.

[b]In adjusting the cost-of-living data, the shelter component of the Index was deleted except for costs associated with maintenance and furnishings. Property taxes and mortgage payments were also deleted. The nature of the Bureau of Labor Statistics (BLS) data is such that we could not avoid deleting some costs such as utilities that are associated with normal upkeep. The remaining upkeep costs amount to 25 percent of the overall shelter budget on average. Social security as well as all income taxes were also deleted. Intercity variation in federal tax burdens reflects differences in income more than differences in the intrinsic cost of living. State and local taxes are controlled for separately, except for sales taxes, which are reflected in the cost-of-living index. (It was not possible to obtain local sales tax data for many cities in our sample. Further, it is difficult to compute an effective sales tax rate because the base for the tax appears to differ widely across cities.) Finally, the BLS reports direct metropolitan-area budget data for only 38 of the cities in our sample. We imputed a cost-of-living index for the other cities. This was done by regressing the adjusted budget data on regional dummies and SMSA population density, with the resulting coefficients used to impute the missing index values. The R^2 for the regression was 0.51. Those results are available upon request to the authors. All standard errors reported in the tables have been adjusted to account for the imputation of the missing cost-of-living index data. (See Pagan [1984] and Murphy and Topel [1985] for a description of the procedure.)

[c]Data employed pertain to the year 1982. Similar data for many of our cities are also available for the year 1977. There is a strong positive correlation between ratios across the two years.

[d]Nominal rate is calculated by dividing total property tax revenues by the assessed base. It is noteworthy that our property tax revenue includes funds raised by the city municipal government as well as special districts within city boundaries. The nominal rate is then multiplied by the city's median aggregate assessment-sales ratio to obtain the effective rate.

[e]As with the property tax revenue data, these percentages are based upon municipal workers as well as employees of special districts.

[f]The Survey of Governments also provides information on the percentage of workers in bargaining units. That variable is a ratio in which the numerator and denominator come from different surveys conducted by the U.S. Bureau of the Census. Various cities were found to have nonsensical coverage ratios far in excess of 1 when the bargaining unit data were examined. The organization numbers do not suffer from this defect.

Notes

We are grateful to Glenn Blomquist for his help in supplying some of the data. We also benefited from the comments of James Heckman, Kevin M. Murphy, James Poterba, and Harvey Rosen, as well as from participants in workshops at the University of Chicago, the Federal Reserve Bank of Philadelphia, the National Bureau of Economic Research's State and Local Finance Summer Institute, and the conference on "Comparisons of Urban Economic Development in the United States and Western Europe, 1950–87," in Bellagio, Italy. Financial support to Gyourko from the Wharton Real Estate Center is gratefully acknowledged. Robert Stoddard provided excellent research assistance. The usual caveat applies.

1. These results are available upon request to the authors.

2. Glenn Blomquist provided us with added pollution measures used in Blomquist, Berger, and Hoehn (1988). These included the number of effluent discharges, metric tons of landfill waste, and the number of treatment, storage, and disposal sites. Blomquist's data are at the county level, so it is sometimes difficult to match them with individual cities. Including these added pollution measures reduced the sample size to under ninety cities. To have as much variation as possible in fiscal conditions, it was decided to drop the added pollution measures in order to obtain the 130-city sample size, which serves as the base for all results reported in the text. Wage and housing expenditure equations that included the added pollution variables were estimated on the smaller sample. The added pollution variables are not statistically significant (individually or jointly) in the random-effects specification. Further, the estimated group effects are only marginally smaller than those reported in table 12.1.

3. In previous work, both violent and property crime rates were experimented with, but no significant effects of property crime (holding violent crime constant) were found. Alternative input and output health measures, including infant mortality rates, the number of physicians per capita, and the number of medical specialists per capita, were also investigated. These variables can only be measured at the county level. Consequently, the city-specific hospital beds measure is employed.

4. Even test-score data have the potential of confounding the quality of educational services provided with the ability of students attending the schools. For example, the Scholastic Aptitude Test (SAT) is taken only by those students applying to college, the fraction of which varies by state and city. Dynarski (1987) and Hanushek and Taylor (1988) have demonstrated how to adjust statewide SAT scores for the selection bias. We were not successful in collecting district test score data via telephone or letter surveys. Many districts claim not to have collected or saved data for 1979 or adjacent years. This made it impossible to implement the preceding authors' selection correction procedure with the city district as the unit of collection. Although there is little statistical evidence that class size affects student achievement (e.g., Hanushek 1986), Card and Krueger (1990) found a strong correlation between class size and subsequent labor market performance.

5. Note that the effective property tax rate is included in the housing expenditure equation but not in the wage equation. The property tax is solved out of the reduced-form wage equation. The equilibrium model in the second section of the chapter implies full capitalization into land prices. The results presented here do find virtually full capitalization.

6. Roback's (1980, 1982) equation works with actual land prices. In this chapter, housing expenditures are used in which land rents are bundled with structural traits. As Blomquist et al. (1988) noted, the problem is easily handled by putting housing instead of land into the utility function and incorporating a housing production function into the model. The full implicit price equation is essentially unchanged, with the quality

of housing purchased replacing the quantity of land. See Blomquist et al. (1988: equation 6, p. 92).

7. However, two of the individual amenity findings are of unique interest. First, the influence of the size variable (SMSA population) is small. By way of comparison, Roback's (1982) OLS-based findings for the impact of SMSA population are approximately double the magnitude of our OLS and random-effects findings. We also experimented with land area and population density measures at both the SMSA and central city levels. Those variables were not found to be influential or to impact upon other variables' coefficients. Second, there is a particularly strong influence for access to nearby labor markets, as indicated by the coefficient on the percentage of residents working in another SMSA. For cities in the San Francisco Bay area and near New York City, where 30 percent to 40 percent of residents work in another SMSA, the land rent coefficient on this variable implies that land prices are from 15 percent to 30 percent higher, ceteris paribus.

8. A dichotomous union coverage variable was also experimented with. The variable was coded as a 1 if the city had a public-sector coverage rate that was at least one standard deviation above the sample mean (>67 percent). As in Gyourko and Tracy (1989a), the transformed variable generated statistically significant lower land prices of about 10 percent. However, the full implicit price was little changed, as were the resulting quality-of-life rankings.

9. The variance-covariance matrix used in the GLS estimation is the sum of the fixed effects variance-covariance matrix and a diagonal matrix with the estimated group error variance along the diagonal. This particular variance-covariance matrix reproduces the random-effects coefficients and standard errors reported in table 12.1.

10. For example, transportation service quality is not controlled for because such a measure simply is not widely available. It is easy to imagine both the marginal worker and firm highly valuing that attribute.

11. Slight positive correlations are found across the error terms, although neither is significantly different from zero at standard confidence levels. When the group error terms are weighted by the number of housing observations in the relevant cities, $\rho = 0.14$. When the number of wage observations serves as the basis for the weights, $\rho = 0.10$.

12. A reasonable number (well into double figures) of individual worker wage observations typically are available, making it unlikely that the large group effects found for some cities are the result of a few idiosyncratic working observations.

13. It should be noted that there still is a moderately strong positive correlation among the sets of rankings. The rankings based upon random effects with group effects included (ranking #2 in columns 3–4, table 12.3) are the least strongly correlated with the other sets of rankings. Pairwise correlation coefficients between ranking #2 and the others range from 0.54 to 0.63. Pairwise correlations among the other three sets of rankings range from 0.85 to 0.94.

14. It should be emphasized, however, that the random-effects estimates do make some progress toward differentiating among cities. If rankings were randomly assigned to each city, then the implied standard error for a city's rank would be 37.5. This is substantially larger than the average standard error of 16.9 produced from the random-effects specification.

15. There is some evidence that retired worker households are sorting into the highest net subsidy cities. Using the 1980 Census tapes, we calculated for each city the ratio of retired residents to the sum of full-time labor market participants plus retired residents. Retired residents were defined to be people aged 50 or older who do not work and are not looking for work. The correlation between this ratio and the net subsidy figures listed in column 5 of table 12.4 was then computed. When the 130 observations

are unweighted, $\rho = 0.15$ (probability value $= 0.08$ for the null of $\rho = 0$). When the city observations are weighted by the total number of full-time labor market participants plus retired residents, the correlation rises to 0.35 (probability value $= 0.0001$ for the null of $\rho = 0$).

References

Advisory Commission on Intergovernmental Relations. 1981. *Significant Features of Fiscal Federalism, 1979–80*. Washington, D.C.: Author.

Berger, Mark C., and Glenn C. Blomquist. 1988. "Income, Opportunities, and the Quality of Life of Urban Residents." In *Urban Change and Poverty*, edited by Michael McGeary and Lawrence Lynn. Washington, D.C.: National Academy Press.

Blomquist, Glenn C., Mark C. Berger, and John P. Hoehn. 1988. "New Estimates of the Quality of Life in Urban Areas." *American Economic Review* 78(1, Mar.): 89–107.

Card, David, and Alan Krueger. 1990. "Does School Quality Matter? Returns to Education and the Characteristics of Public Schools in the United States." Princeton University, Industrial Relations Working Paper 265. Princeton, N.J.: Princeton University. April.

Dynarski, Mark. 1987. "The Scholastic Aptitude Test: Participation and Performance." *Economics and Education Review* 6(3): 263–73.

Ehrenberg, Ronald, and Joshua Schwarz. 1986. "Public Sector Labor Markets." In *Handbook of Labor Economics*, edited by O. Ashenfelter and R. Layard. Amsterdam: North Holland.

Feenberg, Daniel, and Harvey Rosen. 1986. "State Personal Income and Sales Taxes, 1977–83." In *Studies in State and Local Public Finance*, edited by Harvey Rosen. Chicago: University of Chicago Press.

Freeman, Richard. 1986. "Unionism Comes to the Public Sector." *Journal of Economic Literature* 24(1, Mar.): 41–86.

Gyourko, Joseph, and Joseph Tracy. 1989a. "The Importance of Local Fiscal Conditions in Analyzing Local Labor Markets." *Journal of Political Economy* 97(5, Oct.): 1208–31.

————. 1989b. "Local Public Sector Rent-Seeking and Its Impact on Local Land Values." *Regional Science and Urban Economics* 19(3, Aug.): 493–516.

Hanushek, Eric. 1986. "The Economics of Schooling." *Journal of Economic Literature* 24(3, Sept.): 1141–79.

Hanushek, Eric, and Lori Taylor. 1988. "What Can Be Done with Bad School Performance Data?" University of Rochester Working Paper 126. Rochester, N.Y.: University of Rochester. March.

Haughwout, Andrew, and Robert P. Inman. 1996. "State and Local Assets and Liabilities, 1972–1992." Wharton Real Estate Center, draft working paper. Philadelphia, Pa.: University of Pennsylvania.

Hausman, Jerry A., and William E. Taylor. 1981. "Panel Data and Unobservable Individual Effects." *Econometrica* 49(6, Nov.): 1377–98.

Hoehn, John P., Mark C. Berger, and Glenn C. Blomquist. 1987. "A Hedonic Model of Interregional Wages, Rents, and Amenity Values." *Journal of Regional Science* 27(4, Nov.): 605–20.

Inman, Robert P. 1981. "Wages, Pensions, and Employment in the Local Public Sector." In *Public Sector Labor Markets*, edited by Peter Mieszkowski and George Peterson. Urban Institute Press COUPE Papers on Public Economics. Washington, D.C.: Urban Institute Press.

————. 1982. "Public Employee Pensions and the Local Labor Budget." *Journal of Public Economics* 19: 49–71.

International City Management Association. 1976. *The Municipal Year Book, 1976.* Washington, D.C.: Author.

Leven, Charles, and Robert Stover. 1989. "Advances in Rating the Quality of Life in Urban Areas." Washington University Working Paper. Saint Louis: Washington University. August.

Linneman, Peter. 1978. "The Capitalization of Local Taxes: A Note on Specification." *Journal of Political Economy* 86(3, June): 535–38.

Liu, Ben-Cheih. 1976. *Quality of Life Indicators in U.S. Metropolitan Areas.* New York: Praeger.

Moulton, Brent. 1986. "Random Group Effects and the Precision of Regression Estimates." *Journal of Econometrics* 32: 385–97.

————. 1987. "Diagnostics for Group Effects in Regression Analysis." *Journal of Business and Economics Statistics* 5(2, Apr.): 275–82.

Murphy, Kevin M., and Robert H. Topel. 1985. "Estimation and Inference in Two-Step Econometric Models." *Journal of Business and Economic Statistics* 13(4, Oct.): 370–79.

Pagan, Adrian. 1984. "Econometric Issues in the Analysis of Regressions with Generated Regressors." *International Economic Review* 25(1, Feb.): 221–47.

Peiser, Richard B., and Lawrence B. Smith. 1985. "Homeownership Returns, Tenure Choice, and Inflation." *AREUEA Journal* 13(4, Winter): 343–60.

Roback, Jennifer. 1980. "The Value of Local Urban Amenities: Theory and Measurement." Ph.D. diss., University of Rochester, Rochester, N.Y.

————. 1982. "Wages, Rents, and the Quality of Life." *Journal of Political Economy* 90(6, Dec.): 1257–79.

————. 1988. "Wages, Rents, and Amenities: Differences among Workers and Regions." *Economic Inquiry* 26(1, Jan.): 23–36.

Rosen, Sherwin. 1979. "Wage-Based Indexes of Urban Quality of Life." In *Current Issues in Urban Economics*, edited by Peter Mieszkowski and Mahlon Straszheim. Baltimore: Johns Hopkins University Press.

Tax Foundation, Inc. *Facts and Figures on Government Finances.* New York: Author.

U.S. Bureau of the Census. 1979. *Survey of Governments* (data tapes). Washington, D.C.: U.S. Government Printing Office.

————. 1982. *Census of Governments,* vols. 2–4. Washington, D.C.: U.S. Government Printing Office.

————. 1983. *Census of Population and Housing, 1980: Public Use Microdata Samples Technical Documentation* (and data tapes). Washington, D.C.: U.S. Government Printing Office.

————. 1985. *County and City Data Book, 1983.* Washington, D.C.: U.S. Government Printing Office.

————. Various issues. *City Goverʌ ment Finance.* Washington, D.C.: U.S. Government Printing Office.

U.S. Department of Commerce. 1983. *Comparative Climatic Data.* Asheville, N.C.: National Climatic Data Center.

U.S. Department of Labor. 1977. *Three Standards of Living for an Urban Family of Four Persons.* Washington, D.C.: Bureau of Labor Statistics.

U.S. Environmental Protection Agency. 1980. *1979 Air Quality Data—Annual Statistics.* Washington, D.C.: U.S. Government Printing Office.

Voith, Richard P. 1990. "Capitalization of Local and Regional Attributes into Wages and Rents: Differences across Residential, Commercial, and Mixed Use Communities," Federal Reserve Bank of Philadelphia Working Paper. Philadelphia: Federal Reserve Bank of Philadelphia.

Chapter Thirteen

OVER THE HORIZON: JOBS IN THE SUBURBS OF MAJOR METROPOLITAN AREAS

Mark Alan Hughes and Anaïs Loizillon

Sweeping changes in the *settlement structure* of the United States motivate many strategies designed to reduce inner-city poverty. Settlement structure refers to both the physical landscape of buildings and streets and the social landscape of boundaries and routes. It is so basic that settlement structure is beyond question for most people— as is the other basic structure that organizes our lives: time.

The influence of settlement structure, however, is profound. When someone locks the doors of their car as they enter a certain neighborhood, they are reacting to their understanding of settlement structure. When someone buys a home based on its school district, they are responding to settlement structure. When someone makes a quick exit off the expressway as dozens of brake lights appear, they are referring to settlement structure. Settlement structure is the way all these diverse things—houses and schools, routes and travel times, neighborhoods and personal safety—are related. And our mental map of the settlement structure is our way of navigating, literally, the complex terrain in which we live.

Antipoverty strategists are no less dependent on mental maps. During recent decades, they have recognized settlement structure as an obstacle to their goals.[1] Consequently, most antipoverty strategies are attempts to change the geography of where poor people live or work. Either they propose to move poor people from bad locations to good locations or they propose to transform bad locations into good locations by moving good things around. Consider scattered-site public housing programs that seek to disperse low-income households from slums to good neighborhoods. Or think of enterprise zone programs that seek to rebuild the employment base of once-central cities by attracting firms that would otherwise locate elsewhere. In a fundamental way, these are geographical exercises.

In this chapter, we examine the suburbanization of employment as a key change in settlement structure. High quality, locally produced studies exist for most of the metropolitan areas we examine. However, local studies, based on particular surveys or methods, do not allow meaningful comparisons across metropolitan areas. This limits their usefulness to national policy makers and to local policy makers seeking to learn from other metropolitan areas. On the other hand, national studies conducted by research scholars rarely provide the kind of descriptive detail needed to inform policy. Local variation in that kind of research is typically reduced to one or two variables in a regression equation. This might be sufficient for relatively simple hypothesis testing, but it rarely proves relevant to the concerns of decision makers.

This chapter seeks to occupy that difficult ground between the breadth of a national study and the depth of a local study. After an introductory overview, we present three related arguments. First, we briefly portray the conditions that characterize contemporary urban poverty in the United States. These conditions animate the call to "do something" about the increasingly desperate violence and deprivation found in many larger U.S. cities. The statistics cited will be familiar to most readers, and our main contribution here will be to present current information for the nation's largest metropolitan areas.

Second, we present information on the changing location of employment in a group of nine large metropolitan areas.[2] They were identified in 1993 by Public/Private Ventures as potential sites for a demonstration project by virtue of their extensive suburbanization of employment as documented in earlier studies. Here, we focus on job suburbanization, using the most detailed and current data available. These data provide new insights into the suburbanization of employment in these metropolitan areas.

Our intention in the first and second sections is not to measure impacts and test hypotheses regarding cause and effect. In particular, we will not be in a position to establish the effect of job suburbanization on inner-city poverty. One reason why debates about this effect (and about settlement structure and poverty in general) go round and round is that conventional data and methods have been no match for the complexities at issue. Instead, our intention is simply to establish a reasonable case for experimenting with an antipoverty strategy that would mitigate the effects of job suburbanization. Those effects may turn out to be irrelevant to, or only a very small part of, poverty and employment in the inner city. But only a well-conceived demonstration will ever answer this question adequately.

In the third section, we discuss the implications for antipoverty strategy of poverty concentration and job suburbanization. We place particular emphasis on a strategy that is a small but growing part of the Clinton administration's Empowerment Zone program. This strategy is designed to connect inner-city residents to suburban employment through a combination of training, placement, and support services, delivered through a partnership that would build bridges across metropolitan areas and across areas of programmatic responsibility. In a series of reports and conferences, we have proposed such a mobility strategy.[3] We stress here and throughout this chapter, however, that there are many open questions regarding the mobility strategy; the prudent course of action remains a demonstration approach exemplified by the Bridges to Work demonstration.[4]

In one of the most important statements of antipoverty strategy during the 1960s, Anthony Downs wrote of the need to "envision alternative futures for the American ghetto" as a prerequisite to formulating strategies to combat inner-city poverty.[5] With such a vision in place, Downs argues, the policy strategist can then identify actors needed to realize the alternative future, enumerate incentives needed to motivate those actors, and name or invent mechanisms needed to allow key actors to pursue those incentives. This chapter is presented in the spirit of Downs's policy strategizing. We attempt to portray recent conditions, draw working conclusions about the policy implications of those conditions, and propose strategies that might improve those conditions. The chapter does not present original research, nor even research at all, in the conventional social science sense. Rather, we make informed judgments about the current state of labor markets in the inner cities of several major metropolitan areas and present a case for employing demonstration research to help sort out policy options.

Geography is certainly history but it need not be destiny. By examining metropolitan settlement structure, we may come to understand how inner cities have been assaulted by change in recent decades, and how the residents of our inner cities can be helped to avoid the grim destiny these changes portend.

AN OVERVIEW OF METROPOLITAN SETTLEMENT STRUCTURE

In this section, we introduce a series of definitions and measurements that are important to understanding the issues discussed later. Although some of this material might seem better placed in an appendix, we suggest that an understanding of metropolitan settlement structure and how it is defined and measured is crucial to understanding the problems of inner-city poverty in the 1990s.

Since the end of World War II, the United States has built enormous metropolitan settlements that now organize the daily lives of most Americans. A majority of the U.S. population resides in metropolitan areas containing one million or more persons, and one out of four Americans now reside in the eight largest consolidated metropolitan statistical areas (CMSAs),[6] the best unit for observing the full growth of our metropolitan settlements. Adjacent MSAs are consolidated if total commuting between them exceeds 15 percent of the workers in the smaller MSA, and if the combined population of the CMSA exceeds one million. This is important since it is these commuting relationships that help explain the focus of this study on CMSAs rather than their component MSAs.[7]

Here is how the definitions work with regard to metropolitan Chicago. Figure 13.1 displays a map of the consolidated metropolitan statistical area of Chicago. The heavy lines indicate county boundaries and the thin lines represent the boundaries of minor civil divisions (MCD), which is the Census term for cities and townships. For refer-

Figure 13.1 HIGHLIGHTING THE CHICAGO PMSA WITHIN THE MORE BROADLY DEFINED CHICAGO CMSA

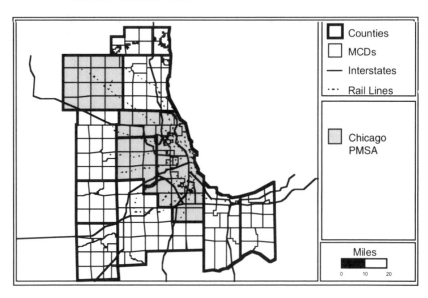

ence, the figure also shows the interstate highways and commuter railroad lines. Shaded in grey is the Chicago Primary Metropolitan Statistical Area, or PMSA, which consists of only three counties: Cook, DuPage, and McHenry. It is conventional in urban research to use the PMSA (in earlier censuses, these were typically labeled as SMSAs) as the unit of analysis. However, if one is interested in the suburbanization of population and employment away from the historically dominant city, then looking only at the Chicago PMSA would cause one to miss changes quite near the city but outside the PMSA boundaries.

Figure 13.2 displays all six of the component PMSAs of the Chicago–Gary–Lake County CMSA. These PMSAs are linked by economy as well as by geography. The map shows that the six PMSAs are contiguous. But the Census definition of a CMSA also requires that component PMSAs have a significant degree of commuting across PMSA boundaries. And so, importantly for our purposes, these are not just many metropolitan areas that happen to be next to one another. Rather, these PMSAs are an integrated metropolitan system defined precisely by the fact that thousands of commuters cross PMSA boundaries every day. In many ways, the edges of the PMSAs, and not their formerly central cities, are the most important locations in the metropolitan area. This is the landscape with which antipoverty strat-

Figure 13.2 THE SIX COMPONENT PMSAs OF THE CHICAGO CMSA

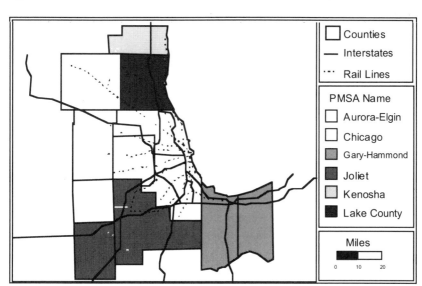

egists must come to grips when they make assumptions about the location of households and workplaces and then imagine policies to change those locations.

Figure 13.3 presents one last bit of explanation before moving on to the findings of the next section, which focuses on differences between central cities and suburbs.

A central city may be thought of as the historical core of a metropolitan area. Every PMSA has a designated central city, and therefore CMSAs always have more than one central city. Also, individual PMSAs often have more than one central city within their own boundaries (reflecting an earlier consolidation of once-distinct urbanized areas). The Chicago PMSA, for example, has three central cities— Chicago, Evanston, and Chicago Heights, all in Cook County—while the Chicago CMSA has twelve central cities (figure 13.3).

In the next section, we compare a variety of conditions in the cities and suburbs of the metropolitan areas in our study. By any measure, disadvantage is concentrated in the central cities of these metropolitan areas, and antipoverty strategists must recognize this concentration as an essential feature of the problems they face.

Figure 13.3 THE TWELVE CENTRAL CITIES AND OTHER EMPLOYMENT
LOCATIONS IN THE CHICAGO CMSA

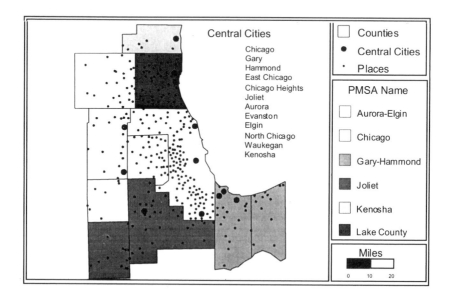

THE GEOGRAPHY OF ISOLATION

In the 1990s, metropolitan areas are no longer dominated by their so-called "central cities." Instead, most residences and, often, most work-places are now located beyond big-city boundaries in a new kind of suburbia that we are still struggling to understand.[8] At the same time, poverty and disadvantage are concentrated in the former central cities. In this section, we compare conditions in cities and suburbs in the eight largest metropolitan areas and four additional metropolitan areas.

Figure 13.4 presents the change in population from 1980 to 1990. Of these dozen metropolitan areas, all but metropolitan Detroit gained in total population during the 1980s. The metropolitan areas are arranged in the figure from left to right in order of total population size in 1990. BDC refers to the Baltimore–Washington CMSA and DFW refers to the Dallas–Fort Worth CMSA. So although metropolitan New York–Newark is still the largest settlement, by far the largest increase in population occurred in metropolitan Los Angeles (3 million versus

Figure 13.4 TWELVE U.S. METROPOLITAN AREAS: CHANGE IN POPULATION FOR THE ENTIRE METROPOLITAN AREA, CENTRAL CITIES, AND SUBURBS, 1980–1990

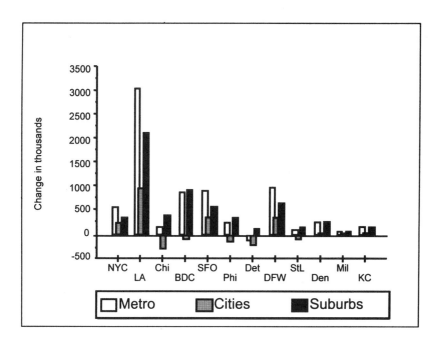

one-half million). In fact, the four largest gains in population occurred in Sunbelt metropolitan areas: Los Angeles, Dallas–Fort Worth, San Francisco–Oakland, and the "border" area of Washington–Baltimore. However, consider where this population growth was located *within* the metropolitan areas. In seven areas, the central cities lost population during the 1980s. Perhaps the most dramatic shift was in metropolitan Washington–Baltimore where the central cities lost population even though the CMSA gained nearly a million new residents—all of them in the suburbs. Metropolitan Chicago had the largest decline in central city population, losing over one-quarter million persons during the 1980s. Even in the three areas with the largest population growth during the 1980s (Los Angeles, San Francisco–Oakland, and Dallas–Fort Worth), the central cities captured only about one-third of metropolitan growth. The older regions of the Northeast and Midwest have declining central cities and growing suburbs (the exception, again, is New York–Newark). The newer metropolitan areas of the West and South have growing cities and (faster) growing suburbs (the exception is Denver).

In order to control for the relative size of the city and suburban populations,[9] we now compare the percentage change in city and suburban populations. Figure 13.5 presents these percentages for the cities and suburbs of each metropolitan area. In none of these metropolitan areas is city population growth (if any) keeping pace with suburban population growth.

By 1990, this process of population suburbanization had gone so far that suburban residents outnumbered city residents in all twelve of the metropolitan areas. Figure 13.6 displays the 1990 population for cities, suburbs, and the metropolitan area as a whole. This figure also shows the differences in the degree of suburbanization across metropolitan areas. Baltimore–Washington, Detroit, Saint Louis, and Philadelphia are less than half the size of their surrounding suburbs, while Dallas–Fort Worth, New York–Newark, and Chicago–Gary are about the same size as their surrounding suburbs. Because of these differences, it is more revealing to use percentages in comparing metropolitan areas, as in the percentage of persons in poverty or unemployed. We follow this method in the remainder of this section.

It is important to note that this process of suburbanization has not been uniform. The most extreme example is the continuing concentration of African Americans in central cities. In general, African Americans are more segregated than any other ethnic group, and this segregation has not declined as black incomes and education have

Figure 13.5 TWELVE U.S. METROPOLITAN AREAS: PERCENTAGE CHANGE IN
POPULATION FOR ENTIRE METROPOLITAN AREA, CENTRAL
CITIES, AND SUBURBS, 1980–1990

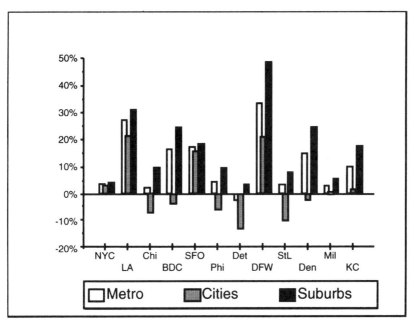

risen.[10] In figure 13.7, we consider this segregation at the very gross
scale of city and suburbs. The figure shows the percentage of the
population in 1990 in central cities and suburbs that was African
American. In metropolitan Chicago, for example, the central cities
were 36.3 percent black and the suburbs were 5.6 percent black. That
is, the percentage of the city that was black in metropolitan Chicago
was about six-and-a-half times that of the suburbs (36.3/5.6). Note
that, with no racial segregation, the percentage in the cities and suburbs would be the same. Since metropolitan Chicago as a whole was
19.2 percent black in 1990, the cities in the region had about twice,
and the suburbs had about one-quarter, as many African Americans
as they would have had with no racial segregation.

   In every one of these metropolitan areas, the percentage of the city
population that was African American was at least twice as high as
that of the suburbs, and in half of them it was at least four times as
high. Note that the cities have been reordered in figure 13.7 to give us
additional information: Metropolitan areas are presented in order of

Figure 13.6 TWELVE U.S. METROPOLITAN AREAS: POPULATION FOR CMSAs,
CENTRAL CITIES, AND SUBURBS, 1990

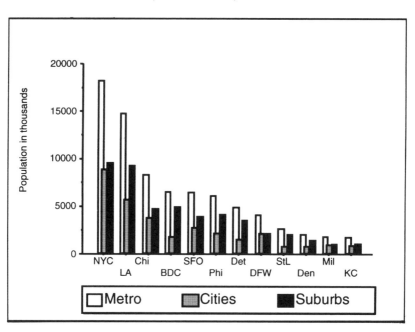

their ratio of city and suburban percent black, from most divergent on the left to least divergent on the right. In Milwaukee, the most divergent metropolitan area, the central cities were 26.9 percent black and the suburbs were a mere 0.8 percent black. Even in metropolitan areas with large suburban African American populations, the pattern of black city/white suburbs remains very strong.[11] For example, the Baltimore–Washington CMSA has the nation's largest suburban black population, 788,000 in 1990. This is over three times the size of Chicago's suburban black population. But still suburban Washington–Baltimore had only about two-thirds as many suburban blacks as it would if there were no racial concentration. (And of course, this level of analysis neglects the fact that a majority of the CMSA's suburban blacks reside in a single county of the region, Prince George's, Maryland. As this shows, suburbanization alone is a poor indicator of integration.)

So cities remain disproportionately black, and, in every one of our study areas, most metropolitan African Americans reside in central cities. Obviously, this discussion is far from exhaustive, nor is it in-

Figure 13.7 TWELVE U.S. METROPOLITAN AREAS: PERCENTAGE AFRICAN
AMERICAN IN CITIES AND SUBURBS, 1990

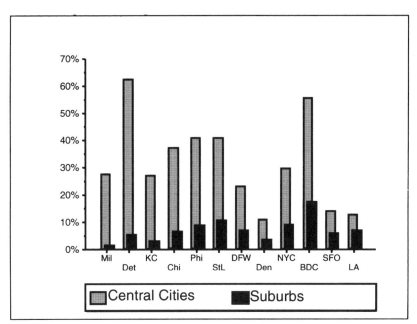

tended to substitute for an examination of racial segregation at the
level of neighborhoods within cities and suburbs (which is the scale
to which most people refer when they speak of segregation). Instead,
we intend simply to demonstrate the degree to which African Americans are concentrated in central cities.[12] The following graphs present
some of the economic conditions (poverty, unemployment, and job
growth) in these central cities compared to those in their surrounding
suburbs. The fact that these problems are borne disproportionately by
African Americans has implications for policy strategy.

Figure 13.8 compares the poverty rates in cities and suburbs. Again,
the metropolitan areas are arrayed from left to right in descending
order of the city/suburban ratio of poverty rates. Cities are much
poorer than suburbs: In metropolitan Milwaukee, Chicago, Detroit,
and Philadelphia, central cities are four times poorer; in metropolitan
Baltimore–Washington, New York, Saint Louis, and Denver, cities are
three times poorer; and in metropolitan Kansas City, Dallas–Fort
Worth, San Francisco–Oakland, and Los Angeles, cities are about
twice as poor as their suburbs.

Figure 13.8 TWELVE U.S. METROPOLITAN AREAS: POVERTY RATES IN CITIES
AND SUBURBS, 1990

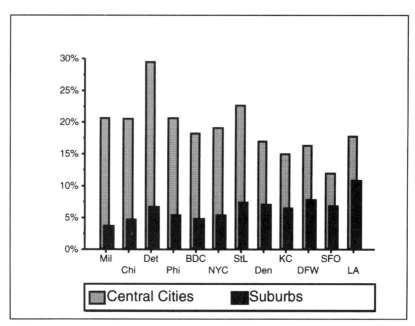

In this graph, and in all the later graphs, we see the presence of a
strong regional pattern. The metropolitan areas fall into perfect Frost-
belt/Sunbelt categories. Metropolitan Milwaukee, Chicago, Detroit,
Philadelphia, Baltimore–Washington (something of a border area),
New York, and Saint Louis have the greatest city/suburb disparities.
Metropolitan Denver, Kansas City, Dallas–Fort Worth, San Francisco–
Oakland, and Los Angeles have the smallest disparities.

As used here, Frostbelt and Sunbelt are abbreviations for the many
dimensions along which these metropolitan areas differ. Climate is
one; history is another. The Frostbelt metropolitan areas expanded to
metropolitan scale earlier than the Sunbelt metropolitan areas. This
history holds implications for the demography of these areas, for the
age of their housing stock and infrastructure, for the types of industries located there, and so on. They also differ in terms of what we
might call the technology of their settlement structure. For example,
the commuter transportation system of Chicago is not simply older
than that of Dallas–Fort Worth; it is also based on a different technology. Chicago depends on both fixed-rail train systems and auto-

mobiles using road systems. Dallas–Fort Worth remains almost wholly dependent on the latter.

Figure 13.9 displays the unemployment rates in cities and suburbs. We array the metropolitan areas from the largest city/suburban difference in rates on the left to smallest difference on the right. The differences range from 11 percentage points in metropolitan Detroit to less than 2 points in Los Angeles. The unemployment differences between cities and suburbs are smaller than the differences in poverty rates. This is not surprising. Persons can be poor for many reasons: because they are elderly, disabled, children in poor households, and/ or because they are unemployed or employed but paid low wages. The unemployment rate, however, is a very different kind of indicator. It is focused on a specific group of people: those adults of working age who are actively looking for work and cannot find it. It does not include people who might be so discouraged by their prospects that they have given up looking, nor does it include people who might be working part-time but would rather work full-time, nor does it include people who, some might say, are too lazy to look for work. It is a much

Figure 13.9 TWELVE U.S. METROPOLITAN AREAS: UNEMPLOYMENT RATES IN CITIES AND SUBURBS, 1990

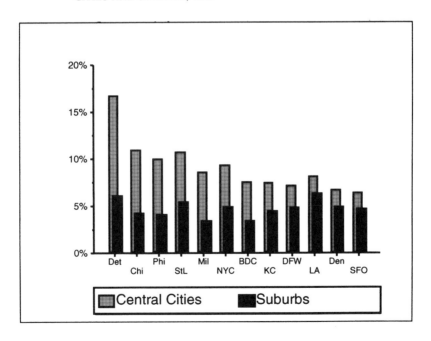

more powerful indicator of the disadvantage of city residence than poverty rates.

In every metropolitan area, the city unemployment rate is higher than the suburban unemployment rate. In every Rustbelt metropolitan area (in the graph, from Detroit to Baltimore–Washington), the city rate is at least 4 percentage points higher than the suburban; it is also at least *twice* the suburban rate. Once again, the Sunbelt metropolitan areas display less city/suburban disparity: 2- to 3-point differences in each case.

Much has been written about the link between inner-city poverty and unemployment (also, lower earnings and even social deviance) on the one hand, and the suburbanization of unemployment on the other. This link is known to social scientists as the spatial mismatch hypothesis, and the debate over its veracity is now over thirty years old.[13] Although this chapter is clearly sympathetic to the mismatch hypothesis, it will not contribute to the complex scientific debate on the question. Rather, we simply seek to suggest why the mismatch seems like such a compelling partial explanation for inner-city poverty.

Many statements of spatial mismatch use very simple categories, such as cities and suburbs, to document job suburbanization. Many conventional data sources report only this broad level of geographical detail. In fact, it is difficult to get data on employment of city residents by job location for census decades. Most studies must rely on county-level data to track changes in employment at the location of the job (such as the County Business Patterns).

Figure 13.10 shows the change in employment location between 1980 and 1990 for central counties and suburban counties in each metropolitan area (see note 7 for the definition of central county). The reliance on county data has three important consequences. First, it means the employment numbers are not comparable to the preceding population, race, poverty, and unemployment numbers, which have been based on central cities, not central counties. Second, the relationship between cities and counties varies widely across metropolitan areas. For example, Philadelphia City and County share the same boundary, while Los Angeles City and *all* of its PMSA suburbs are contained within Los Angeles County. Thus in Philadelphia central county equals central city, whereas in Los Angeles central county equals primary metropolitan statistical area. Third, since central counties are usually much larger than the central cities they contain, the figure understates the degree to which new jobs are located outside central cities. That is, new jobs located outside Los Angeles City but

Figure 13.10   TWELVE U.S. METROPOLITAN AREAS: CHANGE IN EMPLOYMENT
LOCATED IN CENTRAL AND SUBURBAN COUNTIES, 1980–1990

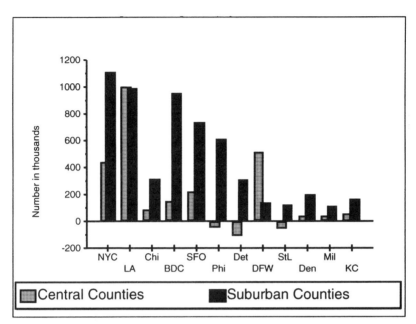

inside Los Angeles County are placed in the central, not the suburban, column of figure 13.10.

In spite of this last bias, the figure shows an enormous degree of employment suburbanization during the 1980s. In every metropolitan area, employment growth was disproportionately located in the suburban counties (even in Los Angeles and Dallas–Fort Worth). In six of the eight largest metropolitan areas, most if not all job growth during the 1980s was located in the suburbs. In the nine areas visited by Public/Private Ventures staff in 1993, which were chosen by virtue of their extreme job suburbanization, more than 90 percent of job growth was located outside the central county in every CMSA but San Francisco–Oakland.[14] The suburbs appear to be the engines of employment growth in all twelve metropolitan areas.

In sum, there is an extreme pattern in these metropolitan areas: Poverty and joblessness are concentrated in formerly central cities while prosperity and job growth are deconcentrating toward the metropolitan periphery.[15]

But these data raise more questions than they settle. First of all, we must understand employment changes in the actual central cities of these metropolitan patterns. This consistency is important for making comparisons with the earlier data on central city poverty and unemployment. But it is even more important for policy studies. Cities are jurisdictions within which decisions are made and services delivered. City boundaries often mark stark differences in race, taxation, school quality, and presumably in employment change. Central counties are a poor marker for central cities, especially when we focus on the real world of policy-making and implementation.

Second, most previous studies of employment location within metropolitan areas have reported only county-level data. However, because counties are so large, this technique represents only a small improvement over the simple city/suburban distinction. The latter is not helpful when it comes to employment location because it creates the impression that jobs are scattered across the suburban countryside. In order to clarify our understanding of employment suburbanization, we need information on what is occurring at the local level within suburbia, where patterns of job location probably have more to do with interstate highways than with county boundaries. Only at this level of detail can we usefully consider the accessibility of suburban jobs to central city residents.

THE GEOGRAPHY OF OPPORTUNITY

In this section, we examine job suburbanization in nine large metropolitan areas chosen for study by Public/Private Ventures during the course of the development of their Bridges to Work demonstration. We focus on the Chicago CMSA and provide a summary of findings for eight other metropolitan areas: Baltimore–Washington, San Francisco–Oakland, Philadelphia, Detroit, Saint Louis, Denver, Milwaukee, and the Kansas Cities. We return to the Chicago example of the first section to introduce the data used in this section.

In Figure 13.3, the smaller circles mark the center of each census place in the Chicago CMSA (census places are essentially all incorporated places and special census-designated places of 1,000 persons or more, that are identifiable as a single place but are not legally incorporated). The Economic Censuses (the Census of Manufacturing, the Census of Retail Trade, etc.) provide detailed information on firms every five years. The Economic Censuses are conducted on an establishment basis, with an establishment defined as a single location where work is performed. Most importantly for this chapter, the Economic Censuses present how many employees in each industry actually work *at* all census places at which there are at least 350 employees (450 for manufacturing). The downside of this detailed data source is that the most recent Economic Census available during our research for this chapter was that from 1987. So we must sacrifice some timeliness for detail.

We use this information to measure the change in employment between 1977 and 1987 for three major industries—manufacturing, retail trade, and services—at locations throughout this study's nine metropolitan areas. Together these three industries represented 72 percent of the national labor market in 1987.[16]

We present six maps detailing the Chicago CMSA, two maps for each of the three industries. For each industry, the first map shows the change in the number of paid employees in the industry who work at each census place in the metropolitan area. The filled circles at the center of each place are proportional in size to the change in the number of workers at that place: the larger the circle, the larger the change. The grey circles indicate a decrease in workers and the black circles represent an increase in workers. Figure 13.11 shows the

Figure 13.11 CHICAGO CMSA: CHANGE IN MANUFACTURING PRODUCTION
JOBS, 1977–87

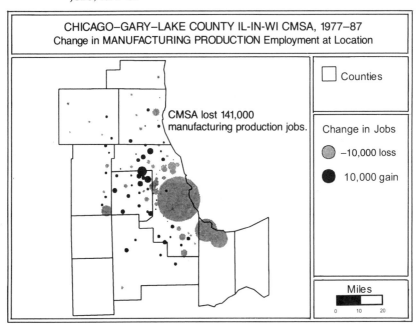

CHICAGO–GARY–LAKE COUNTY IL-IN-WI CMSA, 1977–87
Change in MANUFACTURING PRODUCTION Employment at Location

Counties

CMSA lost 141,000
manufacturing production jobs.

Change in Jobs

-10,000 loss

10,000 gain

Miles
0   10   20

change between 1977 and 1987 in the number of *manufacturing production* workers at locations throughout the Chicago CMSA. The city of Chicago lost about 105,000 manufacturing production workers during the period, and Gary and Hammond lost proportionally large numbers. All of the region's central cities (Evanston, Kenosha, Joliet, Aurora, Elgin, and so forth—see figure 13.3) and most of the inner suburbs of Cook County lost manufacturing jobs. As a whole, the region lost 141,000 manufacturing production jobs.

But notice that this gloomy overall picture contains some selective bright spots which would be hidden in regional or city/suburb-level statistics. In particular, the suburbs west of O'Hare Airport in DuPage and northwestern Cook Counties (e.g., Schaumburg) show considerable increases in manufacturing production employment. This kind of clustering, and airport-centered clustering in particular, is seen in many of the other metropolitan areas studied.

These maps are useful for identifying emerging employment growth locations in a metropolitan area, and for comparing the relative employment growth of central cities and suburbs. However, when we focus our attention on local labor market prospects, we need to examine shifts in the locations of both employment *and* population. Losing 10,000 jobs in a county probably would not strain the local labor market if the county lost 30,000 residents at the same time. So we need to have a sense of the changing ratio of jobs to people. Furthermore, the mismatch argument requires evidence about the spatial distribution of labor demand and supply. In simple terms, spatial mismatch means that some parts of a metropolitan area have more jobs than workers while other places have more workers than jobs. So we need to know how the changing ratio of jobs to people varies across different parts of the metropolitan area.

In the second map for each industry, we attempt to identify possible mismatches. These maps display the change in the ratio of jobs to population in each county as well as in the largest central cities of the Chicago metropolitan area. We return to the county scale for these maps since this ratio, and the mismatch to which it points, only make sense over a distance and area greater than individual places. We can think of the jobs-to-population ratio as a measure of the changing employment density or employment opportunities of a county. The ideal measure of employment opportunities and excess labor demand, of course, would be job openings in places across the Chicago CMSA, not data on filled jobs. But there are no data on job openings by industry for local places within regions nationwide. So we proxy employment opportunities and labor demand with changes in employment density, or jobs per capita. Surely employment prospects are brighter in places with an increasing number of jobs per person than in places with decreasing jobs per person.

In Figure 13.12, we present the changing number of manufacturing production jobs in the Chicago CMSA per 100 residents in each county and in the city of Chicago of the Chicago CMSA. We divide the counties into three broad categories of change. In figure 13.12, the dark grey areas lost three to six production jobs per hundred residents between 1977 and 1987.[17] These are large losses, and the map shows graphically the collapse of manufacturing during the 1980s in metropolitan Chicago. The light grey areas lost one to two production jobs per hundred residents during the period. Most of the region falls into this category. Overall, the region lost two jobs per hundred residents, falling from about eleven per hundred in 1977 to about nine per hundred in 1987.

Once again, however, we see that parts of the region survived the manufacturing crash. DuPage and Kendall counties had the same number of manufacturing production jobs *per capita* in 1987 as in 1977. This occurred despite the facts that the region as a whole lost

Figure 13.12 CHICAGO CMSA: CHANGE IN MANUFACTURING JOBS/POPULATION
RATIO FOR COUNTIES, 1977–87

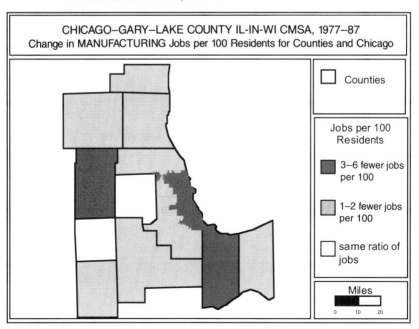

141,000 such jobs and that both counties gained population during the period—DuPage's population growing nearly 20 percent between 1977 and 1987.

We provide these two maps of changing local employment and changing county jobs/resident ratios for each of the three major industries. Figure 13.13 displays the changing *retail trade* employment at places throughout the Chicago CMSA, and figure 13.14 displays the changing ratio of retail jobs to resident population in the counties and the city of Chicago. Figures 13.15 and 13.16 show the same changes for *service* employment.

In metropolitan Chicago, each industry presents a distinct locational pattern. Manufacturing declined regionally, with enormous losses in the region's central cities, proportional losses in most places throughout the region, and occasional gains in some places, especially in DuPage County. Retail trade employment increased regionally by about 67,000 jobs. However, the city of Chicago *lost* about 24,000 retail jobs during the period, and there were fewer retail jobs per capita in 1987 than in 1977. Here we see an example of absolute suburbanization, with job loss in the city (indeed, in all the central cities of the

Figure 13.13 CHICAGO CMSA: CHANGE IN RETAIL TRADE EMPLOYMENT, 1977–87

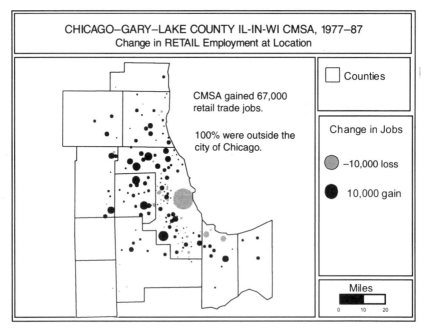

Figure 13.14 CHICAGO CMSA: CHANGE IN RETAIL JOBS/POPULATION RATIO FOR COUNTIES, 1977–87

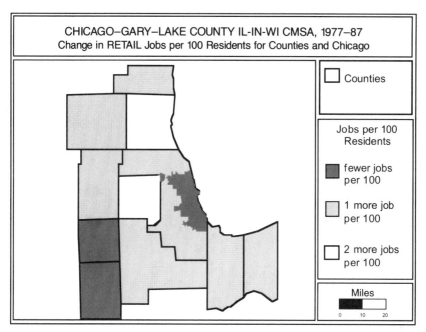

CMSA) and job gain in the suburbs, especially those along the region's I-290/I-294 beltway.

Service industry employment presents a different pattern—relative suburbanization—with growth in both cities and suburbs but at a higher rate in the suburbs. As a whole, the CMSA gained about 311,000 service jobs, of which the city of Chicago gained about 83,000. But note two things. First, fewer jobs per hundred residents were gained in services than were lost in manufacturing and retail: There were about three more service jobs per hundred Chicago residents in 1987 than in 1977 compared to three fewer jobs per hundred in manufacturng and less than one fewer in retail. Second, 73 percent of new service jobs were located outside the city (only 45 percent of service jobs were located outside Chicago in 1977). So, although service employment is often considered the great comparative advantage of central cities, and although this was a growth area for Chicago during the period, even service jobs were shifting rapidly to the suburbs.

Rather than presenting the reader with a detailed exegesis of each metropolitan area's change in local employment and its ratios of county jobs to resident population, we will simply summarize the

Figure 13.15 CHICAGO CMSA: CHANGE IN SERVICE EMPLOYMENT, 1977–87

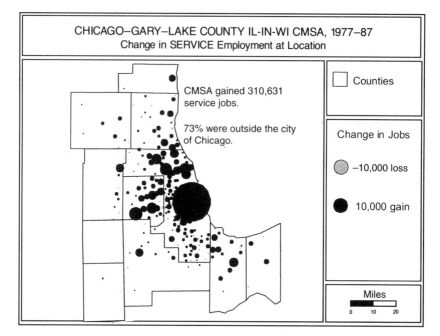

CHICAGO–GARY–LAKE COUNTY IL-IN-WI CMSA, 1977–87
Change in SERVICE Employment at Location

CMSA gained 310,631 service jobs.

73% were outside the city of Chicago.

☐ Counties

Change in Jobs

⊘ –10,000 loss

● 10,000 gain

Miles
0   10   20

patterns (and exceptions) across the nine metropolitan areas stud-ied.[18] The descriptors *weakest, average,* and *strongest* designate the city or county change in the jobs/population ratio, relative to the overall metropolitan change in the jobs/population ratio. Therefore, weakest may be read as a change in employment opportunities that lags behind that of the metropolitan area as a whole.

The total number of manufacturing production jobs declined in all the metropolitan areas, except San Francisco–Oakland and Denver–Boulder. All of the twelve large cities except San Francisco and Wash-ington, D.C., were in the weakest category of manufacturing job loss per capita. In the cities of Chicago, Philadelphia, Detroit, and Mil-waukee, there were three fewer manufacturing jobs per hundred res-idents in 1987 than in 1977 and therefore about six fewer jobs per hundred persons in the labor force. Yet during the same period, at least one suburban county in every metropolitan area—and typically two or three—retained the same ratio of manufacturing jobs per res-ident, even while their resident populations grew.

Given the overall decline of manufacturing in these metropolitan areas, the retail and service sectors are perhaps the better sources for employment prospects. All nine regions gained retail and service jobs

Figure 13.16 CHICAGO CMSA: CHANGE IN SERVICE JOBS/POPULATION RATIO
FOR COUNTIES, 1977–87

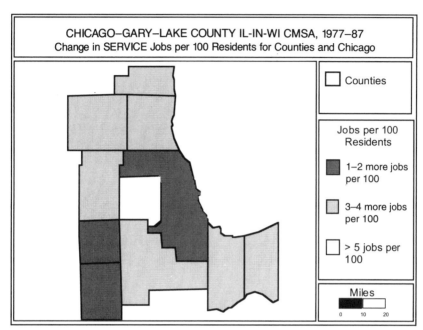

between 1977 and 1987. The Chicago pattern of city retail decline occurred in only two other large cities: Detroit and Kansas City, Kansas. Only the city of Chicago actually had fewer retail jobs per resident (Detroit and Kansas City, Kansas, had the same ratio). However, even the cities with gains in retail employment captured only small shares of their region's overall retail growth. In six of the nine metropolitan areas (Chicago, Baltimore–Washington, Detroit, Saint Louis, Milwaukee, and the Kansas Cities), more than 95 percent of new retail jobs were located outside the large cities. At least 85 percent were outside the large cities in every metropolitan area. Seven of the twelve large cities (Chicago, Baltimore, Oakland, Philadelphia, Detroit, Milwaukee, and Kansas City, Kansas) were in the weakest category of retail change per capita and only one (San Francisco) was in the strongest category.

Large cities fared better with service employment, which increased in every city and region during the period. However, even in this sector, no large city captured more than a third of the regional growth in service jobs and, in most regions, including the Chicago CMSA, more than 70 percent of new service jobs were located outside large cities (disproportionately high growth in every region). Service jobs are not a reliable foundation for a continuing central city role in metropolitan economies. In Chicago, as well as in Philadelphia, Detroit, Saint Louis, and Milwaukee, the increase in service jobs did not offset the decrease in manufacturing jobs. Furthermore, Chicago, Philadelphia, Detroit, Baltimore, Oakland, Milwaukee, and the two Kansas Cities were *not* in their region's strongest area of changing service employment opportunity. These cities were being outpaced by their suburban counties even in service employment growth.

The suburbs were the engines of metropolitan employment growth during this period. DuPage County in the Chicago CMSA is a spectacular example. This centrally located county in the Chicago CMSA was in the strongest category of employment opportunity in all three industrial sectors, exemplifying the industrial diversity that once characterized only central cities. Waukesha County in the Milwaukee CMSA faced a similar growth pattern. Eight other suburban counties were in the strongest category in both of the growing sectors, retail and services. These were Montgomery and Howard Counties in the Baltimore–Washington CMSA, Marin and San Mateo Counties in the San Francisco–Oakland CMSA, Montgomery and New Castle Counties in the Philadelphia CMSA, and Oakland and Washtenaw Counties in the Detroit CMSA. *All but one of these increasingly job-rich counties are adjacent to the central county(ies) of their metropolitan areas.* Thus metropolitan employment growth occurred outside central cities but tended to concentrate in suburban counties adjacent to them.

In addition to these general patterns, there are several specific regional conditions worth noting. Usually the fortunes of the central city and the central county of a metropolitan area are closely tied, and the divergence occurs in comparing central with outlying counties. However, Milwaukee and Oakland both show an unusually strong divergence from their own county. The city of Milwaukee had no change in the ratio of retail jobs per capita between 1977 and 1987, while Milwaukee County had one more retail job per 100 residents. The city gained three service-industry jobs per hundred residents, while the county gained five. The divergence in local retail employment opportunities was even greater between Oakland and Alameda County. The city of Oakland had no change in the ratio of retail jobs per capita between 1977 and 1987, while surrounding Alameda County gained three retail jobs per hundred residents.

Metropolitan Kansas City best illustrates the economic development effects of major airports. A new international airport opened in Platte County in the decade before our 1977–87 data period. The county's population grew by about 25 percent during the period, yet it retained the same ratio of manufacturing jobs per capita and gained four retail jobs per hundred residents. Metropolitan Philadelphia illustrates the high-technology corridor effects familiar in many metropolitan areas. All of the counties with the strongest increases in service jobs per capita are crossed by the region's booming Route 202 corridor, arcing around the western side of the city of Philadelphia.

The evidence presented in this section suggests the virtual necessity of including the suburban labor market in any sustainable inner-city employment strategy. Our argument here is *not* that a ride to a suburban job is all that is needed to solve inner-city unemployment, although for some potentially large fraction of the urban unemployed in these metropolitan areas, that may well be enough to find a job or a better-paying job. Nor is our argument even necessarily predicated on the position that employment alone is sufficient to solve the web of problems called inner-city poverty, although, again, we are sympathetic with the position that a good job would in fact solve a multitude of problems.

Rather, our argument is much narrower. Regardless of which activities antipoverty strategists propose to combat urban poverty (boot camps, role models, drug rehab, job training), if *work*, and especially work in the private sector, plays any part in that strategy, then the dominance of the suburban employment market must be considered. In these nine metropolitan areas at least, which together accounted for nearly one-fifth of the urban poor in 1990, jobs are no longer around the corner. Jobs are over the horizon. Whether policy strategists seek to bring jobs to the poor or bring the poor to jobs, making this connection appears to be an unavoidable component of antipoverty strategy. That strategy can only be improved if policy strategists think more explicitly in locational terms. In the next section, we expand on the policy implications of this new, unavoidable metropolitan reality confronting inner-city policy makers.

ANTIPOVERTY STRATEGY AS A GEOGRAPHICAL EXERCISE

In the face of this powerful metropolitan pattern—poverty at the center, opportunity on the edge—the search for an antipoverty strategy takes on a profoundly geographic character. For a quarter-century, policy analysts and advocates have been talking, often implicitly, about reconfiguring geography. The goals have been to decentralize problems and/or recentralize solutions. The means have been to change the "where" of housing, employment, racial and income groups, public services, and so on. Any strategy that attempts to reduce inner-city poverty, especially through work, must engage in this geographical exercise.

We have noted elsewhere the three basic strategies that have emerged and been labeled dispersal, development, and mobility.[19] Briefly, the dispersal strategy seeks to decentralize the housing of the poor from the city to the suburbs. The development strategy seeks to recentralize employment from the suburbs to the city. The mobility strategy seeks to connect the ghetto poor to suburban opportunities as a tool for pursuing both the increased choices of a dispersal strategy and the community-building of a development strategy. In the remainder of this chapter, we describe each strategy and discuss the particular strengths and weaknesses of each. The three strategies play off each other in complex ways, and we conclude the chapter with a discussion of these interactions.

The **dispersal strategy** is the most straightforward and constitutionally compelling of the three strategic approaches. It is straightforward because it takes seriously the observation of few jobs and bad schools in the city, many jobs and good schools in the suburbs, and focuses on unlocking the suburban gates that exclude the poor and the black. It is constitutionally compelling because surely U.S. citizens have a right to live anywhere they can afford. The strategic goal is to provide the ghetto poor with the opportunities that come with a suburban residence: newer, lower density housing in safer, cleaner neighborhoods with better funded schools and a growing labor market. There are three broad mechanisms in the dispersal strategy. First, there are civil-rights-based efforts to ensure that people are not excluded from affordable housing because of race (or religion or, in some states, family size or type). Second, there are land-use-based efforts to reform local zoning laws that restrict the construction of housing types (multifamily units, rental units with several bedrooms, and so on) that make housing more affordable to low-income households. Third, there are public-housing-based efforts to disperse the construction of new public housing units and subsidize rental throughout the metropolitan housing market through the use of vouchers.

Perhaps the most famous early example of a comprehensive dispersal strategy is New Jersey's Mount Laurel policy. In 1975, the New Jersey Supreme Court ruled in a suit brought by the local chapter of the NAACP that Mount Laurel Township, located ten miles from Philadelphia and then at the edge of the metropolitan area, unconstitutionally excluded low-income housing within its borders through its zoning laws, which in effect allowed only industrial uses and construction of single-family homes.[20] Not only did the courts rule that there are severe limits on the right of suburban communities to restrict the entry of lower-income households (itself something that few other state courts have done, and certainly the U.S. Supreme Court does not consider income a suspect category), but the New Jersey Supreme Court also insisted that the state's municipalities have an affirmative obligation to redistribute low- and moderate-income households more evenly across the state. It thus set in motion probably the most fundamental redistribution of property rights ever attempted by a state government.

After several years of stiff noncompliance, the court in 1983 prescribed a set of specific remedies that required each municipality to plan and zone for its fair share of the statewide need for lower-income housing. Furthermore, the court required each municipality to, in effect, spend a part of any wealth created by its zoning powers, which can restrict development and thus raise the value of land, to induce developers to build housing affordable to low-income households. Finally, in 1986 the court recognized its limited administrative capacity to continue the dispersal strategy.[21] In a third ruling, the court effectively sanctioned a legislative proposal to create a new agency to monitor the implementation of the Mount Laurel policy. Significantly, this legislative solution included a provision for Regional Contribution Agreements, or RCAs, under which a municipality, typically one that is wealthy and suburban, may satisfy one-half of its low-income housing obligation by paying another municipality, typically one that is poor and urban, to assume that obligation as its own.

In general, the Mount Laurel controversy represents a fascinating shift from old- to new-style dispersal policies. It is a shift from a period when state and federal governments could significantly influence dispersal via the construction of new public housing and the subsidy of housing expenditures by low-income households, to a period when the key actors in the housing market, such as developers and current homeowners, are relied on to provide the housing. It is a shift from a period when removing explicit racial barriers from the suburbs was a major agenda item, to a period when finding affordable housing anywhere is the basic problem. The rallying cry of today's dispersal strategy for reducing poverty is "affordable housing."

But the nearly two-decade evolution of Mount Laurel policy reveals the internal tensions in the dispersal strategy. One acute tension arises between its goals for housing provision and its goals for access to suburban employment and public services. In some ways, the genius of the RCAs provision in current Mount Laurel policy is that it taxes exclusion as a source of low-income housing revenues. Indeed, RCAs create a market for exclusion that could extract the full willingness to pay to exclude if the agreements between cities and suburbs were properly arranged.[22] At any rate, the point is that by attempting to reconfigure the geography of low-income residence, dispersal strategies are inevitably related to housing policy. And in the current low-income housing climate, in which construction and subsidy budgets are highly constrained and existing, highly centralized, public housing stock is too valuable to be abandoned, dispersal policy and housing policy often conflict.

Furthermore, the political obstacles to fully implementing a dispersal strategy are enormous. People born in the year of the first Mount Laurel rulings are now old enough to vote for legislators who subvert those rulings. That is a telling illustration of the dispersal strategy's basic weakness—not a conceptual weakness, and certainly not a moral one, but an operational weakness. Many actors have incentives to thwart the dispersal strategy and these actors have many mechanisms at their disposal. Our fragmented, parochial systems of metropolitan government could hardly be better designed to prevent dispersal. It is difficult to see what local effective political interest is served by dispersal. Even big-city politicians would, under a successful dispersal campaign, only lose or decrease the minority constituencies that have helped elect minority mayors and congressional representatives. And finally, the dispersal outcome is inherently unstable. The strategy could enforce mechanisms that ensure the right of poor blacks to enter a particular neighborhood or jurisdiction, but no conceivable mechanisms could prevent affluent whites from leaving thereafter.

Today's most prominent dispersal strategy is the Gautreaux Assisted Housing Program of the Chicago Housing Authority. This program has helped about 5,000 African-American families to leave virtually all-black Chicago public housing for predominantly white city neighborhoods and suburbs. Careful research has shown that the moves have had significant positive impacts on the lives of both the adults and children in the households.[23]

Conducting more small-scale experiments in more cities and suburbs will be a useful exercise. But the real question looming before Gautreaux, and all dispersal strategies, is the scale question. How large could a Gautreaux program become before it faced challenges similar to the Mount Laurel program? Even longtime advocates of

Gautreaux in Chicago recognize the political limits to implementing the strategy beyond the few thousand who now participate.[24] In 1994, the U.S. Department of Housing and Urban Development was unable to sustain its plans for a $240 million expansion of its Gautreaux-like program named Moving to Opportunities. Political opposition to the program led to the termination of its budget by Congress.

Simply consider that for African Americans to be represented in the Chicago CMSA suburbs in proportion to their presence in the metropolitan area (which is 27 percent black as a whole), the 1990 suburban black population would have to have been quadruple its actual level: 1,076,000 rather than 254,000. Likewise, for poor people to be represented in the Chicago CMSA suburbs in proportion to their presence in the metropolitan area (which is 11 percent poor as a whole), there would need to have been more than 300,000 more poor suburban residents in 1990: 503,000 rather than 193,000.

The **development strategy** takes a different approach. It moves from the same observation: Poverty is concentrated at the center of the metropolitan area, opportunity is dispersing toward its periphery. However, cognizant of the considerable political obstacles to dispersal, development strategists attempt to recentralize some of the opportunities associated with suburban residence. Chief among these are employment opportunities. The development strategy is also quite straightforward in that it seeks to return the system to an earlier state: jobs have left the central city, so policy should intervene to induce their return.

There are two related arguments that often accompany the development strategy. These were probably best articulated by Bennett Harrison in the early 1970s.[25] One of the great risks of the dispersal strategy is that it would dissipate the political strength of minority groups, particularly blacks. Much of this political strength comes from the leverage commanded by black pluralities or majorities in central cities. In effect, residential segregation has created the possibility of black representation in mayoral and congressional elections. The dispersal strategy inherently breaks up poor, minority residential concentrations in the central city, and thus it would also diminish the electoral base founded on these residential concentrations.

These electoral demographics aside, there is a simpler electoral dynamic that undermines the dispersal strategy. The chief beneficiaries of a dispersal strategy are precisely those persons who leave the central city jurisdiction and suburbanize. Thus they change their voting address, and make it difficult for central city politicians to capture the electoral benefits of the strategy. There would seem to be little incentive for elected officials to expend much effort to work for a constituency that would soon be unable to vote for them.

The second and somewhat related argument made by development strategists is that geographical distance is a trivial barrier between blacks and suburban jobs. The far more important barrier, development strategists argue, is racial discrimination. Dispersing the residences of inner-city blacks would do nothing to alter this discrimination in the labor market. Blacks would face the same practices if they suddenly lived in the suburbs. Better to enrich the opportunities of the ghetto, say the development strategists, since discrimination would be presumably lower in the city than in the suburbs.

The major contemporary federal program consonant with the development strategy is, of course, urban enterprise zones. Enterprise zones have received a substantial amount of criticism as ineffective and costly.[26] Although such zones are perhaps politically important for the retention of firms in some central cities, it would be very costly to actually attract sufficient employment to address the needs of the impacted ghetto in this way. Perhaps most importantly, critics have long argued that development strategies do nothing to overcome patterns of metropolitan segregation and even encourage "separate but equal" communities—the point being that such communities would be anything but equal in reality.[27] John F. Kain and Joseph J. Persky considered ghetto development policies to be a "morally objectionable" acquiescence to racism.[28]

Both the dispersal and development strategies' proponents make compelling arguments in their favor. Unfortunately, they also offer powerful critiques of the other strategy. Each strategy works against a set of entrenched local interests. In essence, dispersal strategists underestimate the politics of our metropolitan settlements, which provide numerous mechanisms to prevent dispersal. On the other hand, development strategists underestimate the economics of employment suburbanization, which has relocated jobs to the metropolitan periphery for reasons that would be costly to reverse, if they could be reversed at all.

The goal of a **mobility strategy** is to reconnect the ghetto to opportunity in ways that leverage a variety of local interests. That connection has been disrupted by metropolitan decentralization and other factors. The ghetto was once the place of low-cost housing adjacent to entry-level employment. The components of the mobility strategy are designed to restore that connection by exploiting the very incentives created by decentralization itself. City residents get access to economic opportunity without sacrificing community networks such as extended family and institutional affiliations. Suburban employers get access to the entry-level workers who are increasingly absent from suburban labor markets. City governments retain voters who have received the benefits of the strategy. Suburban governments can ease housing development pressures being driven by the excess labor demand of decentralizing employment within the region. A well-designed program strategy would create mechanisms that allow these actors to respond to these incentives.

The mobility strategy builds on earlier efforts. None of its components is new. Indeed, the central transportation components were the subject of a series of program demonstrations during the late 1960s and early 1970s, reviewed in 1992 by the Drachman Institute.[29] The mobility strategy has been the subject of sufficient interest during the last few years that it has attracted some criticism, including research by the Drachman Institute and a speech by the Federal Transit Administrator.[30] These criticisms posit a straw man called *reverse commuting* and then declare its inadequacy to confront inner-city poverty. This chapter would not disagree that ad hoc transportation to suburban employers has had, and surely would have, a minimal effect on ghetto unemployment. Furthermore, it is true that small companies cannot make a profit transporting public housing residents to suburban office parks. It is true that America is moving toward two societies, one white and one black. It is true that it is unjust to invest billions in light rail systems to provide comfortable suburb-to-suburb commutes for white-collar workers, while providing only second-hand vans to help the poor travel two hours to reach a fast-food job in the suburbs.

But this kind of comment commits the common and, in this case, sadly destructive, error of allowing the best to be the enemy of the good. When an inbound commuter train is filled with trench-coat-wearing, *Wall-Street-Journal*-reading investment bankers, we think of the transportation as enviable, even elitist. But when that same train, on its reverse run, carries workers, say poor African-Americans and Latinos, to suburban jobs, we think of apartheid. Such criticism confuses the transportation mode with the underlying differences in social class. It expresses the critic's feelings toward *poverty,* not toward so-called reverse commuting. And this criticism not only obstructs the development of programs that might enhance the accessibility of jobs for poor people. It also, in a tragic irony, undercuts the dignity of a worker's journey to work, simply because he or she is poor. Should someone not travel to suburban workplaces in the utter absence of closer opportunities simply because they must rely on assistance to get there? Such a criticism is easy for an affluent professional to make, but not for an inner-city resident who may be a bit tired of waiting for an enterprise zone or for an affordable house in the professional's suburb.

Another criticism of the mobility strategy is that it maintains historic patterns of residential segregation. The mobility strategy appears to be the kind of "separate but equal" approach that is so effectively damned by dispersal strategists. But caricatures of the mobility strategy as American apartheid, with transit passes drawn as "day permits" for black workers to enter white enclaves, are irresponsible. The mobility strategy is formulated within formidable political constraints and, as the Mount Laurel legacy in New Jersey clearly shows, the process of opening up the suburbs will be long and difficult.

There are at least three related counterarguments to criticisms of the mobility strategy. First, although probably not a sufficient condition, greater socioeconomic parity between whites and blacks is almost certainly a necessary condition for sustainable residential integration. The mobility strategy attempts to achieve that parity by enhancing African-American employment opportunities. Thus, the mobility strategy, by integrating the workplace first, might be an instrumental, though admittedly an incremental, step toward eventual neighborhood integration.

Second, there are many arenas in which we may work out our racist attitudes and actions. Explicitly geographic arenas include residential neighborhoods, places of work, and, to a lesser extent, schools. There are more and less volatile arenas in which to intervene against racism, and the workplace is a considerably less volatile arena than either neighborhoods or schools. Perhaps it is better to reshape people's racial and ethnic attitudes through actual daily contact at work than to expend enormous energies over potential contact in neighborhoods. Furthermore, there is the problem of exit. Policy may be able to ensure and realize the right of poor blacks to move into a neighborhood, but how can it require more affluent whites to remain? Although coworker and customer discrimination will almost certainly prevent workplace integration from being easy, surely these will be less virulent than the "neighbor discrimination" that lies behind white flight from integrating neighborhoods.

Third, there is a certain hypocrisy to calls for residential integration. There are rather severe limits to governmental capacity to intervene in housing markets. There are only so many public housing units that can be built and maintained, and there are only so many public dollars that can be used to subsidize the entry of low-income households into the private housing market. This means that the burden of genuine, everyday racial integration at the neighborhood level almost always falls on poor and working-class blacks and whites. Most affluent families have abandoned racially integrating neighborhoods, and the rest always could. Less mobile households must stay to work within an integrated society. This is not to say that working-class racism is somehow excusable. However, we might find middle-class calls for residential integration more compelling if they could demonstrate how middle-class neighborhoods would participate in the vision.

Rather than rearranging the geography of housing or the geography of firm location, the mobility strategy represents a more direct approach: Make available the opportunities of the region to the residents of the inner city by confronting the training, information, and transportation barriers that a decentralized region creates. The mobility strategy does not hold hostage the fortunes of impacted ghetto residents to our political and economic capacity to rebuild downtown blue-collar economies or open up the suburbs to affordable housing.

An important qualification to this emphasis on the mobility strategy is that the three strategies are not necessarily alternatives or substitutes. Clearly, no commitment to connecting inner-city residents to suburban jobs relieves city or suburban governments from protecting the civil rights of people to reside anywhere they can afford. And clearly, a commitment to connecting inner-city residents to suburban jobs does not mean that city governments should or would abandon their local economic development agenda. Indeed, the three strategies could be very effective complements. Connecting lower-skill city residents to the suburban labor market allows city economic development officials to focus on sectors in which the central city often retains a powerful comparative advantage, such as tourism, upscale retail, and business services. Also, the economic gains afforded by the mobility strategy can lead to community resources sufficient to support neighborhood businesses. Suburban Job Link, a Chicago program that helps inner-city residents gain access to suburban work, claims to return over $4 million in annual wages to its inner-city neighborhood by connecting residents to suburban jobs. This must improve the prospects for developing sustainable local enterprises to serve this potential consumption base.

Clearly, the pieces of this puzzle will not simply fall into place and remain fixed. Metropolitan areas are complex and dynamic. Some ghetto residents will get jobs and incomes and buy a car, no longer relying on the transportation programs of the mobility strategy. Some people will get jobs and higher incomes and move to the suburbs,

perhaps no longer relying on or contributing to the community institutions strengthened by the mobility strategy. The broadest goal of the
mobility strategy is to transform the impacted ghetto into a viable
place with access to the same resources that make any neighborhood
viable: safety in the streets, education and human services in the
community, and access to employment opportunities throughout the
region. People may want to move when given the option, or people
may choose to rebuild and remain in their neighborhoods rather than
leave them. But whatever their choice, the mobility strategy would be
successful precisely because the poor would have a real choice: between safe, productive, accessible neighborhoods in the inner city or
the attractions of the suburbs.

That choice is, ultimately, the ingredient mobility strategists seek
to emphasize in the antipoverty strategy mix. We will never know the
strategy's capacity to increase choice without demonstration results.

Notes

The authors are, respectively, Vice President for Policy Development, and Program and
Policy Analyst, at Public/Private Ventures. They gratefully acknowledge support from
The John D. and Catherine T. MacArthur Foundation for this study, and from The Ford
Foundation and the Lincoln Institute of Land Policy for earlier research on which this
study is based. The authors thank the harried government documents librarians at the
Free Library of Philadelphia, one of the nation's great public libraries and civic insti-
tutions. Errors are ours alone.

1. Although this chapter is not intended to serve as a literature review, we note throughout the chapter scholarship that has been particularly important to policy formation.
The most influential research recognizing settlement structure's role in inner-city poverty is that of Wilson 1987. Wilson's discussion of the social isolation of the inner city
has framed the last ten years of poverty research and policy.

2. These nine are the metropolitan statistical areas of Chicago–Gary–Lake County (Ill.,
Ind., Wisc.), Washington, D.C. (D.C., Md., Va.) and Baltimore (Md.) (we use the new
combined CMSA for these two areas), San Francisco–Oakland–San Jose (Calif.),
Philadelphia–Wilmington–Trenton (Penn., N.J., Del., Md.), Detroit–Ann Arbor (Mich.),
Saint Louis (Mo., Ill.), Denver–Boulder (Colo.), Milwaukee–Racine (Wisc.), and Kansas
City (Mo., Kans.).

3. Hughes 1989, 1992a, 1992b, 1993.

4. For a detailed description of the Bridges to Work demonstration (which Public/
Private Ventures is managing for the U.S. Department of Housing and Urban Development and the Ford, MacArthur, and Rockefeller foundations), see Palubinsky and Watson 1997.

5. Downs 1968.

6. These are the consolidated metropolitan statistical areas of: New York–Northern New Jersey–Long Island (N.Y., N.J., Conn.), Los Angeles–Anaheim–Riverside (Calif.), Chicago–Gary–Lake County (Ill., Ind., Wisc.), Washington–Baltimore (D.C., Md., Va.), San Francisco–Oakland–San Jose (Calif.), Philadelphia–Wilmington–Trenton (Penn., N.J., Del., Md.), Detroit–Ann Arbor (Mich.), Dallas–Fort Worth (Tex.) (defined as of April 1, 1990, with the exception of the newly consolidated Washington–Baltimore region, which we have adopted to conform with current practice).

7. A Metropolitan Statistical Area, or MSA, begins with a city that, with contiguous densely settled territory, constitutes an urbanized area (Census definition) of at least 50,000 population. Any county with at least 50 percent of its population residing within this central urbanized area is designated the (or a) central county of the MSA. Outlying counties are added to the MSA if their resident population exceeds certain thresholds regarding (1) commuting to the central county and (2) population density. The component MSAs of a CMSA are designated as Primary Metropolitan Statistical Areas, or PMSAs. Also important for reading this chapter is the definition of the central cities of metropolitan area. Central cities include the largest city in an MSA, all other cities with a population over 250,000 or employment over 100,000, and all other cities with a population exceeding 25,000 *and* an employment/residence ratio exceeding 0.75. The preceding is a heavily abbreviated version of confusing Census Bureau definitions. For more detail, see Appendix 1, U.S. Bureau of the Census 1991.

8. For a thoughtful discussion of the issues, see Downs 1989. For an introduction to the research debates, see Frey and Speare 1991. For a more popular introduction, see Garreau 1991.

9. That is, if the central city population is, say, one-half the size of the suburban population, then we might expect the city column to be one-half the height of the suburban column in figure 13.4. But if the city population was, say, twice as large as the suburban population, then extensive suburbanization would be indicated if the city gained only one-half as many persons as the suburbs. We can make these controlled comparisons by comparing the percentage change in city and suburban populations.

10. This phenomenon has been well documented in an influential series of papers by Douglas S. Massey and his coauthors. These include Massey and Denton 1987 and Massey 1990.

11. Non-Hispanic whites are a majority in the suburbs of all twelve metropolitan areas. In fact, the suburbs are more than 80 percent white in nine of the metropolitan areas (all except Los Angeles, San Francisco–Oakland, and Washington–Baltimore).

12. The general pattern holds for all minorities. We focus here on African Americans in order to facilitate the exposition. Those interested in more detail on residential patterns should see the definitive study by White 1987.

13. For an excellent introduction to this now large literature, see Silver et al. 1993. This study also demonstrates the difficulties in sorting out definitive effects from these complex processes.

14. The San Francisco–Oakland CMSA includes all of Alameda County, which contains Oakland, as "central."

15. Readers of the scholarly literature on spatial mismatch will note, with Harry Holzer, that mismatch can be said to exist only if labor supply does not adjust to changing labor demand—in our terms, spatial mismatch would exist if a change in employment location (labor demand) was *not* followed by a change in residential location and/or commuting patterns (both labor supply). For policy purposes it is more important, in our judgment, to document where the jobless are now, so we omit a discussion of how local joblessness has changed over time. But the dynamic effect is the proper measure for the mismatch issue itself. Though not our agenda here, we can confirm for those interested that city and suburban unemployment ratios diverged during the 1980s.

Though we have not correlated the divergence of these ratios with the suburbanization of employment across our small (and biased) sample of metropolitan areas, the Rustbelt areas had the greatest divergence. For a discussion of the salient research issues, see Holzer 1991.

16. Manufacturing is defined as the mechanical or chemical transformation of substances or materials into new products. The assembly of component parts of products also is considered to be manufacturing if the resulting product is neither a structure nor other fixed improvement. (Construction is covered by a separate Economic Census.) Throughout this chapter, we refer only to production workers in manufacturing. Production workers include workers up through the line-supervisor level. Retail Trade is defined as the selling of merchandise for personal or household consumption and of services incidental to the sale of merchandise. Examples include department stores, food stores, auto dealers and gas stations, drug stores, and restaurants and bars. Service Industries are defined as establishments that render a wide variety of services to individuals, businesses, and other organizations. Examples include hotels, auto repair and parking, amusements (e.g., movie theaters and museums), business services (e.g., advertising, security, maintenance, and secretarial), health services (e.g., hospitals, HMOs, and hospices), and legal services (e.g., law firms and legal aid societies). Paraphrased from "Source Notes and Explanations" (pp. 315–20) in U.S. Bureau of the Census 1991.

17. Data availability forces us to compare job change to total resident persons rather than to the labor force or to the number of households. As an estimate, the dark grey areas in figure 13.12 translate into about eight to sixteen fewer jobs per hundred households and six to twelve fewer jobs per hundred persons in the labor force.

18. These include the following twelve large cities: Chicago; Baltimore; Washington, D.C.; San Francisco; Oakland; Philadelphia; Detroit; Saint Louis; Denver; Milwaukee; Kansas City, Mo.; and Kansas City, Kans.

19. Hughes 1991.

20. This discussion is drawn from Hughes and VanDoren 1990.

21. For a fascinating recent study of judicial capacity, see DiIulio 1990.

22. Perhaps not surprisingly, they are not now structured in this way. Suburban areas are being allowed to pay too little for release from their housing obligations because the arrangements now lead central cities, somewhat desperate for housing revenues, to bid down the RCA offers from suburbs. But the bargaining arrangements could be changed so that suburbs would bid up their offers to get cities to accept the obligations. See Hughes and McGuire 1991.

23. Rosenbaum and Popkin 1991 and Rosenbaum 1992.

24. Davis 1993.

25. Harrison 1974.

26. Jacobs and Wasylenko, 1981; Massey 1982; Glickman 1984; Rubin and Zorn 1985; Boarnet and Bogart 1993.

27. Downs 1968.

28. Kain and Persky 1969.

29. The Drachman report (1992) is the best single review of the earlier round of so-called "reverse-commute" demonstrations and provides a good presentation of the evidence from the early demonstrations. Unfortunately, the report presents its own survey of contemporary programs as somehow evidence comparable to that provided by the older demonstrations. However, in fact, we have had no adequate demonstrations of contemporary programs that seek to address the broad mobility needs of the poor.

Although the Drachman report provides thoughtful discussions of many operations, it also exhibits a limited capacity to identify existing programs in the field. Several times the report simply states its inability to find programs (pp. 30, 51). In fact, a major survey by the American Public Transit Association (1993) identified programs in every one of the places in which the Drachman report found nothing.

30. Linton 1993.

References

American Public Transit Association. 1993. *Access to Opportunity: A Study of Reverse Commuting Programs.* Washington, D.C.: Author. September.

Boarnet, Marlon G., and William T. Bogart. 1993. *Economic Development Policy and Municipal Growth: Evidence from the New Jersey Urban Enterprise Zone Program.* Working paper, Department of Urban and Regional Planning, University of California, Irvine. October.

Davis, Mary. 1993. "The Gautreaux Assisted Housing Program." In *Housing Markets and Residential Mobility,* edited by G. Thomas Kingsley and Margery Austin Turner. Washington, D.C.: Urban Institute Press.

DiIulio, John J. Jr., ed. 1990. *Courts, Corrections, and the Constitution.* New York: Oxford University Press.

Downs, Anthony. 1968. "Alternative Futures for the American Ghetto." *Daedalus* 97: 1331–79.

————. 1989. "The Need for a New Vision of U.S. Metropolitan Areas. Goldman Sachs Real Estate discussion paper. New York: Goldman Sachs.

Drachman Institute, University of Arizona. 1992. *Reverse Commute Transportation: Emerging Provider Roles.* Report FTA-TX-11-0021-92-1, prepared for U.S. Federal Transit Administration. March.

Frey, William, and Alden Speare. 1991. *U.S. Metropolitan Area Population Growth: 1960–1990.* Research Report No. 91-212. Cambridge, Mass.: The Lincoln Institute of Land Policy. May.

Garreau, Joel. 1991. *Edge City: Life on the New Frontier.* New York: Doubleday.

Glickman, Norman J. 1984. "Economic Policy and the Cities: In Search of Reagan's Real Urban Policy." *Journal of the American Planning Association* 50: 471–78.

Harrison, Bennett. 1974. *Urban Economic Development.* Washington, D.C.: Urban Institute Press.

Holzer, Harry J. 1991. "The Spatial Mismatch Hypothesis: What Has the Evidence Shown?" *Urban Studies* 28: 105–22.

Hughes, Mark Alan. 1989. *Fighting Poverty in Cities.* Report to the National League of Cities. Washington, D.C.: National League of Cities.

————. 1991. "Decentralization and Accessibility: A Strategy for Stimulating Regional Mobility." *Journal of the American Planning Association* 57: 288–89.

————. 1992a. *The New Metropolitan Reality.* Report to the Urban Institute. Washington, D.C.: Urban Institute Press.

————. 1992b. Speech presented at Mobility Strategy Policy Conference, Washington, D.C. December.

————. 1993. Speech presented at National Reverse Commute Seminar, American Public Transit Association Annual Meeting, New Orleans, La. October.

Hughes, Mark Alan, and Therese J. McGuire. 1991. "A Market for Exclusion: Trading Low-Income Housing Obligations under Mount Laurel III." *Journal of Urban Economics* 29: 207–17.

Hughes, Mark Alan, and Peter M. VanDoren. 1990. "Social Policy through Land Reform: The Mount Laurel Controversy." *Political Science Quarterly* 105: 97–111.

Jacobs, Stephen, and Michael Wasylenko. 1981. "Government Policy to Stimulate Economic Development." In *Financing State and Local Government in the 1980s: Issues and Trends,* edited by Norman Walzer and David L. Chicoine. Cambridge, Mass.: Oelgeschlager, Gunn, and Hain.

Kain, John F., and Joseph J. Persky. 1969. "Alternatives to the 'Gilded Ghetto.'" *The Public Interest,* Winter: 77–91.

Linton, Gordon J. 1993. Keynote address, Reverse Commuting Workshop, American Public Transit Association Annual Meeting, New Orleans, La. October.

Massey, Doreen S. 1982. "Enterprise Zones: A Political Issue." *International Journal of Urban and Regional Research* 6: 429–34.

Massey, Douglas. 1990. "American Apartheid: Segregation and the Making of the Underclass." *American Journal of Sociology* 96: 329–57.

Massey, Douglas, and Nancy A. Denton. 1987. "Trends in the Residential Segregation of Blacks, Hispanics, and Asians." *American Sociological Review* 52: 802–25.

Palubinsky, Beth, and Bernadine Watson. 1997. *Getting from Here to There: The Bridges to Work Demonstration: First Report to the Field.* Philadelphia: Public/Private Ventures.

Rosenbaum, James E. 1992. "Black Pioneers—Do Their Moves to the Suburbs Increase Economic Opportunity for Mothers and Children?" *Housing Policy Debate* 4: 1179–1213.

Rosenbaum, James E., and Susan J. Popkin. 1991. *The Gautreaux Program: An Experiment in Racial and Economic Integration.* Evanston, Ill.: Northwestern University, Center for Urban Affairs and Policy Research.

Rubin, Barry M., and C. K. Zorn. 1985. "Sensible State and Local Economic Development." *Public Administration Review* 45: 333–39.

Silver, Hilary, Michael White, and John Iceland. 1993. "Job Suburbanization and Black Disadvantage: A Dynamic County-Level Test of the Mismatch Hypothesis." Working paper, Department of Sociology, Brown University. August.

U.S. Bureau of the Census. 1991. *State and Metropolitan Data Book*. Washington, D.C.: U.S. Government Printing Office.

White, Michael. 1987. *American Neighborhoods and Residential Differentiation*. New York: Russell Sage.

Wilson, William Julius. 1987. *The Truly Disadvantaged: The Inner City, the Underclass, and Public Policy*. Chicago: University of Chicago Press.

Part Four

THE ROLE OF GOVERNMENT

Chapter Fourteen

NATIONAL ASSISTANCE TO URBAN AREAS IN THE UNITED STATES

Dick Netzer

The case for central government action directly to assist households and firms located in central cities and to provide financial aid to the subnational governmental entities that serve central cities is a familiar one to public finance economists, rooted in the conceptual framework developed by Richard Musgrave (1959) forty years ago.[1] According to this framework, the central government ought to be (and is, in most countries of the Organization for Economic Cooperation and Development [OECD]) responsible for the alleviation of poverty and related economic distress (Musgrave's redistribution branch); the central government has primary responsibility for stabilization of the economy and therefore should intervene to offset the localized effects of regionally differentiated recessions, as well as dealing with the cycle on a geographically macro basis; and, in Musgrave's allocation branch, the central government ought to be active in the provision of those few public goods whose spatial reach is national, whether the public services in question are produced by the central government itself or by the subnational units. This chapter adheres to that conventional approach. In the next two sections, the actual extent of U.S. federal government assistance to cities and recent trends in that assistance are described. Subsequent sections discuss the appropriateness of present arrangements, in the conventional Musgrave scheme. At the end of this chapter, however, the possible irrelevance of this analysis in the context of American politics in the 1990s is noted.

FEDERAL ASSISTANCE TO U.S. CITIES: WHERE WE ARE NOW

National assistance to cities takes three forms. The first is assistance to households and firms and the direct provision of federal services in cities, rather than assistance to the governmental entities that provide public services within cities. The second type of assistance is federal financial aid to the state governments, some of which is expended directly by state government agencies for programs within cities and some of which is paid to local authorities that serve cities.[2] The third type of assistance is direct aid to the urban local authorities themselves: the municipal governments that are normally referred to as city governments, the autonomous special-purpose authorities (most notably, school districts) that exist in nearly all large urban areas, and, often, county governments that overlay the central cities but include suburban territory as well.

The U.S. federal government has never been important, relatively, as a direct provider of public services. In 1994, state and local government purchases of goods and services were more than five times as great as federal government nondefense purchases of goods and services.[3] Prior to the Great Depression, the federal government was unimportant in other respects as well, but since then has assumed a major role in making transfer payments to persons—primarily for income support and social security programs—and in making grants to state and local governments.

Table 14.1 describes the character of federal spending in calendar 1994, in terms of both the economic classification of the expenditures and whether or not the expenditures are especially relevant to cities. Because more than 60 percent of federal spending (defense and interest payments aside) is for transfers for income support, social security, and welfare—and such transfers clearly are important components of the incomes of central city residents (many of whom are elderly)—most federal spending does appear to be city-related. But all other federal expenditures for transfers to persons, subsidies, and purchases of goods and services that have much relevance to the populations of central cities as such are less than 0.5 percent of the gross domestic product (GDP).[4]

Thus, social security aside, the first form of federal assistance to cities—direct provision of services and subsidies to city-resident households and firms—is not, and never has been, important. As table 14.1 suggests, most federal grants-in-aid to state and local governments are for purposes that are highly relevant to cities; in some cases, the specific program definition leads to a concentration of the spending of the grant funds in cities, because the program focus is on the low-income population. However, in 1991–92, only 11 percent of all federal grants to subnational governments went to local authorities. So, the predominant form of federal assistance to cities is the second one, grants to state governments that either provide services in cities directly or that pass-through the federal funds to local authorities.

Unlike the federal government, the state governments *are* major direct service providers in the American governmental system, and also are much more important than the federal government as providers of fiscal assistance to local authorities. The state governments are the most important level of government—in terms of direct expenditure—with regard to higher education, courts, prisons, mental health institutional care, highways, medical care for the indigent (Medicaid), and cash public assistance payments (generally known as "welfare" in political and journalistic usage).[5] There is relatively little federal aid to the states for the first four of the seven functions on this list; federal aid amounts to about one-third of state expenditure for highways and about one-half of state expenditure for the last two items on the list, Medicaid and "welfare."

The state governments pass through some of the federal aid they receive in the form of direct services to city residents, notably for explicitly redistributive programs and (to a lesser extent) for highways. In some of the states, where local governments participate in the administration of Medicaid and "welfare," the state passes on to local authorities federal aid received for this purpose. In nearly all of the states, the state governments also pass on to local authorities the relatively small amounts of federal aid they receive for elementary and secondary education and some parts of the federal highway aid they receive.[6]

The modest direct federal fiscal assistance to local authorities— only about 5 percent of their own-source revenue in 1991–92— consists mainly of grants for housing purposes, for urban mass transportation capital and operating subsidies, as well as a small amount of school aid. Both the housing grants and the school aid are, in the main, explicitly redistributive (a substantial portion of the housing grants are for continuing subsidies to low-income public housing built mostly between 1955 and 1975; much of the rest of the housing grants are for housing voucher programs of the 1980s). Moreover, unlike most past and present federal programs, the surviving direct federal grants to local authorities have a high degree of targeting on the central cities—where the public housing and urban mass transportation are.

The term *surviving* is used advisedly here. Direct federal aid to city governments (including cities of all sizes and functional description, but excluding aid to special districts and counties that overlie the

Table 14.1 CHARACTER OF FEDERAL GOVERNMENT EXPENDITURES, CALENDAR YEAR 1994 (IN MILLIONS OF CURRENT DOLLARS)

	National Totals	Expenditures of Relevance to Cities[a]	Other[b]
Total Federal Expenditure	1,632,612		
Less: national defense, space, and international affairs	388,899		
Less: net interest paid	201,434		
Equals: civilian expenditure for transfers to persons, subsidies, purchases of goods and services, and grants to state and local governments	1,042,279	854,747	187,532
Transfers payments	666,917		
Income support, social security, and welfare		632,367	
Housing and community services		55	
Recreational and cultural activities		426	
Labor training and services		552	
Other (mainly veterans' benefits and higher education grants and loans)			33,517
Subsidies	36,868		
Housing		19,679	
Urban mass transportation		767	
Other (mainly to agriculture and postal service)			16,422
Purchases of goods and services	145,902		
Administration of city-relevant programs listed above		16,039	

Water transportation ("rivers and harbors")		6,776
Air transportation (mainly air navigation aids)		11,163
Other (mainly central administration, federal policing and corrections, and veterans' services)		111,924
Grants to state and local governments	192,592	
Elementary and secondary education		11,351
Health and hospitals		7,932
Income support and welfare		132,372
Housing and community services		6,675
Recreational and cultural activities		129
Airports		1,632
Urban mass transportation		2,630
Economic development assistance		521
Labor training and services		3,681
Other (mainly highway grants)		25,669

Source: U.S. Department of Commerce. 1996. *Survey of Current Business*, table 3.15. (Washington, D.C.: U.S. Government Printing Office.) The definitions and concepts are those of the National Income and Product Accounts, which differ in some respects from the U.S. Bureau of the Census reporting on governmental finances, which is the basis for other data in this chapter.

[a]Attributions of relevance are by the author. Some entries shown here are programs or activities for which central cities account for major shares of the expenditure, like urban mass transportation, cultural programs, air transportation and, most important, federal grants for income support and welfare programs. Other entries are listed here even though most of the expenditure is made outside central cities, because of the great importance of the programs or activities to cities as places—notably, social security payments and federal expenditures for housing programs.

[b]There are expenditures that benefit cities within these categories, but the main focus and rationales for the expenditure are not urban.

cities) was the most spectacular fiscal manifestation of the era of federal government social activism from the mid-1960s to the late 1970s. In the mid-1960s, federal direct aid to city governments was trivial, mainly for schools in cities like Norfolk, Va., where there was a major federal presence, as well as for airports, and amounted to only about 3 percent of cities' own-source revenues. Thereafter, the amounts, and the percentage, climbed steeply, reaching a peak of just under 19 percent in 1977–78. After fiscal year (FY) 1978, the absolute amount of federal aid remained almost constant for seven years; it has fallen considerably since then, and in FY 1992 was far below the 1978 level in real terms. As figure 14.1 shows, the percentage of own-source revenue has fallen back to the levels of the late 1960s. The reduction includes major cutbacks in some programs that continue to exist (some housing programs), complete elimination of some manpower and social service programs, termination of the so-called Anti-Recession Fiscal Package, adopted in 1977 as a belated response to the 1974–75 recession, and elimination of general revenue sharing.

Figure 14.1 DIRECT FEDERAL AID TO CITIES AS PERCENTAGE OF CITY OWN-SOURCE REVENUE

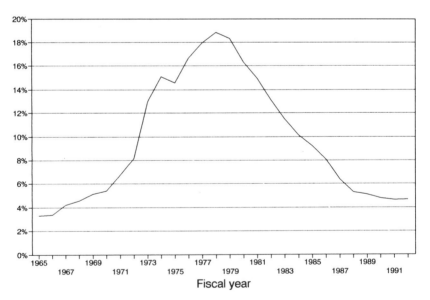

Source: U.S. Bureau of the Census. *City Government Finances*, various years, 1964–1992. (Washington, D.C.: U.S. Government Printing Office.)

DIFFERENCES AMONG CITIES IN THE EXTENT OF
FEDERAL AID

Ladd and Yinger, in chapter 11 of their painstaking 1989 analysis of the fiscal health of the universe of American central cities, provided a thorough treatment of the differential incidence of federal aid to central city governments in 1982, and of the changes between 1972 and 1982. They found a wide range in the ratio of federal aid to the cities' revenue-raising capacity for the 71 cities in this part of their analysis: federal grants in 1982 did more for the fiscal health of the largest cities than the small ones; they made a large difference in the fiscal health of the cities with the poorest residents; and they were inversely, but weakly, related to the strength of the city's economy.[7] Federal grants were strongly related to their overall measure of fiscal health, a standardized gap between expenditure need and fiscal capacity.

However, it is not self-evident that this generally encouraging set of relationships continues to apply, since federal aid to cities, relative to their own-source revenues, has declined so sharply since 1982, as figure 14.1 shows. To reproduce the Ladd-Yinger (1989) analysis for a more recent fiscal year would be a massive undertaking. Instead, an admittedly simplistic effort to explain differences in federal aid as a percentage of own-source revenue in 1991–92 is made here, using obvious independent variables. The cities are the sixty-three central cities in the Frostbelt states (that is, those in the Northwest and Midwest) with populations of more than 100,000. Although fifty-one of the sixty-three had smaller populations in 1990 than in 1970, they differ considerably in their characteristics, including rate of population decline.

Federal aid for the sixty-three cities amounted to 6.7 percent of own-source revenues in 1991–92, as both the numerator and denominator are defined here.[8] The percentage is somewhat higher if New York City, which has a disproportionate influence on aggregate city finance data, is excluded—9.9 percent.[9] The range was from zero to 36.4 percent, with a standard deviation of 6.3 percent. Unlike the Ladd-Yinger (1989) findings, there seems to be no relationship between federal aid and city size (but that may be because the Ladd-Yinger denominator is a sophisticated measure of fiscal health), but there is a strong relationship between federal aid and the percentage of the population below the poverty line (in 1989): a 1 percentage point increase in the incidence of poverty is associated with an increase in the federal aid ratio of 0.5–0.6 percentage points, in the different models. Thus, the surviving federal assistance programs do seem, appropriately, redistributive. The only other independent variable with any explanatory power (among numerous ones that were tested) is own-source revenue per capita, where the relationship is, weakly, inverse. Own-source revenue per capita appears to be a measure that mainly reflects differences in the extent of governmental responsibilities assigned to central-city municipal governments (rather than to state governments or overlying local authorities), so the inverse relationship between revenue per capita and the federal aid percentage is not easy to explain. One would anticipate that a wider range of responsibilities—for example, for housing programs and transit system operations—would attract more federal aid.

FEDERAL ASSISTANCE TO CITIES AS REDISTRIBUTION

To the extent that federal fiscal aid to city governments is designed to be a form of income redistribution, it is, of course, redistribution in kind, rather than in money, so far as low-income residents of cities are concerned. There are worthy and venerable arguments in favor of helping the poor by giving money to people rather than places, even if a "places aid" policy can be designed to make it truly redistributive.[10] First, aid to people facilitates geographic mobility, whereas aid to places does the opposite; geographic mobility is a good thing in general and can be especially important for economically active people who have been displaced by economic change. However, the economic incentives for migration, apart from the federal grant system, are now so strong that it seems likely that many of the poor in central cities are in effect stranded there by assorted disabilities, with the grant system of little consequence.

A more persuasive argument for national government assistance to people rather than places is that assistance in the form of public services rather than money is clearly not preferred by the poor.[11] Most of the goods and services that the nonpoor majority would like to see increased for the poor appear to have very low income elasticities among the poor and may even be good examples of the economists' artifact, the inferior good, at least in the bottom quintile or quartile of the income distribution.

Very low income elasticity is certainly true of housing, as shown in both the large-scale social experiments and in careful analyses of housing microdata sets. It seems true of health care—there is virtually zero private spending among nonaged near-poor for health care. It may be true of education: the low take-up rates for the lowest-tuition sectors of public higher education are suggestive. From the standpoint of the overwhelming majority of the nonpoor, the ultimate merit good that we think the poor should consume more of is surely labor force participation. The income maintenance experiments afford good evidence that labor force participation declines with higher cash assistance payments.

So, perhaps, this is true of local government services in general. However, there are two arguments on the other side, in favor of transfers in kind, that are apposite in this discussion. First, the superiority of cash transfers is lessened when the markets for the services proposed to be provided in kind work poorly, because of highly imperfect information on the part of poor consumers, noncompetitive aspects, discontinuities, and economies of scale. Those properties describe the major services provided by city governments. Second, there is the question of the preferences of the donors with respect to income redistribution: it is entirely reasonable for taxpayers to specify in-kind aid in the form of ordinary local government services as an additional element of the income redistribution that they, the taxpayers, prefer. Both donors and recipients are likely to feel themselves better off when a considerable amount is spent for redistribution but some of it is noncash, than when a much lower amount is provided, but entirely in cash.

Oakland (1979) proposed that ordinary local government services, like public safety and the provision of infrastructure, should be seen as elements of the standard of living of the immobile urban poor.[12] That formulation fits well with the Ladd-Yinger scheme mentioned earlier, in which federal aid is allocated to the cities on the basis of their measured fiscal health. Relatively healthy cities—because of a strong local economy, the ability to export city tax burdens, and/or limited fiscal responsibilities for some costly services—can finance a decent package or ordinary city services even if they have many poor residents. Less healthy cities cannot. In the absence of federal assistance, this means that the overall fiscal system treats equally poor people unequally, the treatment depending upon the city in which the poor live (see Buchanan 1950, for the classic discussion of this).

The appropriate form of federal aid would seem to be unconditional grants tied to measures of fiscal health. If that makes no sense in

American politics (which may be the case—see the next section), then the appropriate form is the matching categorical grant, for those city services deemed most important to the poor, with the matching percentage tied to a measure of fiscal health.

NATIONAL ASSISTANCE TO FOSTER LOCAL ECONOMIC DEVELOPMENT

Federal aid to local governments to foster local economic development can be viewed as income redistribution—bringing jobs to relatively immobile poor, or less directly, increasing the fiscal health of the city so that local authorities can afford to provide better public services to the poor. This is not a wholly unreasonable idea, in light of the large adverse economic changes many central cities have suffered, originating in broad technological, economic, and social trends far beyond the capacity of local governments to affect. In concept, federal aid to promote local economic development could take two forms: the financing of explicit subsidies to private investors undertaking specific economic development projects, or aid to improve the scope and quality of local public services in the expectation that such improvements would attract private business investment and increase the residential attractiveness of communities.

Although federal expenditure to promote local and regional economic development through both direct subsidies and infrastructure has a long history, making such expenditure via local authorities is of more recent vintage. It dates back to the 1960s and the Appalachia and Economic Development Administration legislation.

First, consider federal aid to improve the quality of public services. This strategy differs from the one discussed in the previous section, in that the services to be improved are not likely to be those of special value to the poor, but, rather, the services that are intermediate business inputs (transport services, water supply, etc.) and amenities that are attractive to both businesses and affluent potential residents. The poor benefit by the economic improvement that is fostered by the service improvements (and, at least marginally, from the service improvements themselves). The real issue is the efficacy of such service improvements in developing the local economy.

In the past few years, a considerable amount of literature has been published relevant to this issue. It began at the national level, with the observation that the post-1973 reduction in productivity gains coincided with a large reduction in investment in public capital in real terms, and an actual decline in the net stock of reproducible public capital (overwhelmingly owned by state and local governments). Subsequent econometric investigation suggested that the trends were in fact linked, and that reductions in the public capital stock do restrain increases in total factor productivity (see Munnell 1990 and Morrison and Schwartz 1996 for summaries). The inquiry continued in the subnational sphere, with comparisons of public capital stock levels and changes and economic growth rates of U.S. metropolitan areas and states. The most recent work suggests that local public investment and private capital are complementary, that the relationship is stronger in distressed cities than in growth cities, and that in older cities public investment tends to be an initiating, rather than a passive, factor in the development process (Eberts 1990). The elasticity coefficients look small, but can be interpreted in ways that make the elasticities seem impressive.

Nonetheless, it is not clear that federal fiscal assistance in conceivable amounts can result in service improvements sufficient to stimulate economic development that, in turn, will lead to better lives for some of the urban poor. This is not to say that the recent literature is wrong, but only that the many links in the chain make this type of income redistribution policy very roundabout—and therefore uncertain.

In contrast, there is some certainty regarding the other form of federal fiscal aid designed to promote local economic development— federal assistance to local governments explicitly tied to specific economic development projects. By and large, these programs have had little or no net multiplier effect: in most cases, the private economic activity induced by the subsidy soon vanished, or there was no real inducement but a superfluous subsidy paid for a location decision that would have occurred in any case.[13] Nor is it obvious that low-income people gain much from successful subsidized economic development efforts. Indeed, it may be that most such efforts have distributional effects much like municipal promotion of commercial sports: enriching the impresarios and the owners of adjacent sites, period.

There is an efficiency argument, in addition to the equity one, for federal intervention to foster local economic development, and therefore for federal grants to local authorities to this end. The argument is that the declining cities contain spatially immobile resources with substantial remaining useful lives that are essential to location decision makers, notably, the public and quasi-public infrastructure. The infrastructure cannot be moved, but would have to be replaced in new areas (suburbs or other regions) to accommodate relocators. Since the location decisions do not confront explicit prices for the services of the infrastructure that are based on the marginal costs of the services they consume, they ignore resource cost considerations that should be factors in determining optimality in location of economic activity.[14]

This, then, is obvious market failure. One difficulty with the argument is that the remaining value of the existing infrastructure in the worst-off cities may be trivial, because the quality of the services the capital produces is so poor. But, in any case, intervention with economic development subsidies seems the wrong way to deal with the obvious problem, the absence of appropriate price signals. Federal policy might contribute efficiently by encouraging, rather than discouraging, marginal cost pricing of local utility and public infrastructure services, by example and by precept.[15]

INCREASING REGIONAL ECONOMIC DIFFERENTIATION AND THE FEDERAL ROLE

The income-redistribution case for federal aid that is founded on the obligation to help people stranded in cities that have been afflicted by major economic transformations has been strengthened in recent years by what appears to be increasing regional economic differentiation in the United States—local and regional cycles that are quite large in amplitude but vary considerably in timing. This is not just a redistribution argument; in the Musgrave (1959) scheme it also has a stabilization aspect. The more decentralized the public finance system, and the greater the regional economic differentiation, the greater the chances that retrenchment by subnational governments in severe regional recessions will increase the severity and perhaps widen the geographic scope of those recessions.[16]

It seems obvious that a relatively modest fiscal role for the central government will be more efficient and equitable, the less the regional variations in the local fiscal resource base. For decades in the United States, regional disparities were declining, but in the past twenty years or so, the movement has seemed to reverse itself. As the OECD 1989 *Economic Outlook* makes clear,[17] this was the usual case in OECD countries during the 1980s, when the measure of regional differentiation was the rate of unemployment. In 1987, the regional variation in unemployment rates in the United States was less than that in any OECD country except Japan,[18] but the *increase* in variation since 1975 was one of the sharpest of any country.

This is true of other measures of the level of economic activity.[19] A measure that is highly relevant to the question of fiscal federalism is the size of a standardized tax base, that is, what has been called "taxable capacity." There is evidence that the interstate disparities in taxable capacity have been widening, not narrowing, in part because of the uneven distribution of taxable mineral production. The Advisory Commission on Intergovernmental Relations measures relative taxable capacity by the per capita yield of a "representative tax system," that is, the revenue generated in each state if it imposed all the major state and local taxes at the national average rate for each tax. The standard deviation, for the fifty states and the District of Columbia, from the U.S. average in 1986 was 21.1 percent of that average, compared to 15.7 percent in 1980 and 10.4 percent in 1975 (see Lucke 1982 and Advisory Commission on Intergovernmental Relations 1989).

Although, in theory, fiscal decentralization is inconsistent with large regional economic differentials, whether fiscal decentralization actually makes things worse at a given time is an empirical question. In the United States, federal grants to state and local governments historically have not been at all equalizing. For example, in 1980, the standard deviation of state-local tax capacity plus all federal grants was 14.2 percent, compared to 15.7 percent for tax capacity exclusive of federal grants. Indeed, if all existing federal grants in 1980 had been distributed on a per capita basis, the equalizing effect would be substantially greater: the standard deviation would have been 11.1 percent. This suggests that the substantial reduction in federal grants that occurred during the Reagan years must have been a good thing, from the standpoint of equalization. However, this was not the case. In 1986, the standard deviation of state-local tax capacity plus all federal grants was 24.8 percent, compared to 21.1 percent for tax capacity exclusive of federal grants, so the federal grants programs that had survived the Reagan retrenchment increased inequality. In 1986, if all existing federal grants had been distributed on a per capita basis, there would have been a significant equalizing effect: the standard deviation would have been 16.2 percent.

There is another aspect to American regional economic differentiation that may be even more important for policy with regard to fiscal federalism. Unlike other OECD countries, in which the regions tend to maintain their relative positions over time, in the United States over the past twenty years there have been sharp shifts in relative economic status. That is, regions have experienced cycles that are *not* coincident with national cycles, as well as divergent secular trends. For example, the OECD study showed that there was a fairly high positive correlation between the regional pattern of unemployment in 1975 and in 1987—0.4 to 0.9—in all the larger OECD countries, but a negative correlation in the United States.

The data in table 14.2, on growth rates in gross regional product in real terms for ten U.S. regions, show these discontinuities.[20] New England, New York State, the rest of the Mideast, and even California were relatively depressed in the 1967–73 period, but all showed strong growth in the 1982–92 period; the Southwest, the Mountain states, and the Plains states showed the opposite time path. Except for the Southeast region, which had above-average growth rates in all the periods, each region moved from one to another side of the national average at least once during this twenty-nine-year period.[21] The standard deviation in regional growth trends for these periods was much larger in the 1970s and 1980s than it had been in the 1960s.[22]

This form of regional differentiation has been in evidence for individual urban economies. A number of the largest ones have experienced sharp, relatively short-term economic cycles that are related to events in the world and national economies, but are magnified in those cities and different in timing from the national and international economic cycles. There are obvious examples in the economic histories, over the past three decades, of Boston, New York, Chicago, and the oil- and natural-resource-dependent cities of the West. During the 1950s and early 1960s, while the national economy was growing— with only minor cyclical downturns—and most urban economies were also doing well, the Boston economy was doing quite badly, in both secondary and tertiary industries. From the late 1960s until the late 1980s, however, the Boston economy did extremely well in its service-producing sectors (especially financial services, education, and health) and in high-technology manufacturing, even in periods of national recession. But, in the late 1980s, the area's economy suffered severely from the national recession that focused on defense industries, financial services, and real estate. Similarly, the New York economy declined sharply from 1969 to 1977, in periods of national economic strength like 1972 and 1973 as well as in periods of national recession like 1969–70 and 1974–75. However, between 1977 and 1989, the New York economy had strong growth and was barely affected by the recessions of the early 1980s. Like the Boston economy, New York's did very badly in the 1989–91 recession. Indeed, by 1996, there had been almost no recovery in New York, unlike other places

Table 14.2 REGIONAL DIFFERENCES IN GROWTH IN GROSS PRODUCT IN THE UNITED STATES, SELECTED YEARS, 1963–92
(PERCENTAGE CHANGE IN GROSS STATE PRODUCT FROM PREVIOUS PERIOD, IN CONSTANT DOLLARS)

	1963–67	1967–73	1973–75	1975–79	1979–82	1982–89	1989–92
U.S. average[a]	24.7	32.3	0.7	22.7	−0.5	29.4	3.4
New England	26.4	24.1	−4.0	19.2	2.4	43.7	−3.2
New York State	22.0	20.9	−4.3	7.6	1.2	26.2	−0.2
Mideast region, excluding New York[b]	25.2	27.3	−1.4	13.8	−2.0	34.1	1.3
Great Lakes	23.1	23.6	−4.1	19.3	−11.4	25.7	2.7
Plains	22.3	37.2	−1.7	21.7	−4.6	21.3	5.5
Southeast	29.4	44.9	1.8	26.3	2.8	33.7	5.7
Southwest	24.9	47.9	11.6	37.7	13.1	13.9	6.8
Mountain	15.7	51.0	7.8	34.4	5.5	12.0	10.3
California[c]	24.9	31.0	5.5	28.0	−0.0	41.8	0.4
Far West region, excluding California[c]	24.0	35.2	5.1	37.1	−7.8	31.5	12.1
Standard deviation	3.4	10.2	5.3	9.5	6.6	10.1	4.6

Sources: Renshaw, Vernon, Edward A. Trott, Jr., and Howard L. Friedenberg. "Gross State Product by Industry, 1963–86." *Survey of Current Business* 68(5): 30–46 (May 1988); Beemiller, Richard M., and Ann E. Dunbar. "Gross State Product, 1977–91." *Survey of Current Business* 74(8): 80–97 (August 1994); Beemiller, Richard M. "Gross State Product, 1991–92." *Survey of Current Business* 75(5): 47–56 (May 1995).

Notes: Data on gross state product in current dollars were published in *Survey of Current Business*, May 1988, and were converted to constant 1982 dollars using the price index for the entire gross national product. Gross state product data are on an annual basis only in the years beginning in 1972; the only earlier data are for the years 1963 and 1967. The years 1963 and 1967 are not cyclical turning points, but the subsequent years were peaks and troughs for GNP.

a. Includes Alaska and Hawaii, not included in the rest of the table's data.

b. New York is part of the Mideast region, and accounted (in 1992) for about 43 percent of total regional product.

c. California is part of the Far West region, and accounted (in 1992) for about 73 percent of total regional product.

that had been hard-hit by the national recession. In contrast, the Chicago economy was prosperous almost continuously from the end of World War II until the late 1970s, and was highly resistant to national recessions during that thirty-year period, but had serious economic difficulties in the first half of the 1980s. Chicago was only moderately affected by the 1989–91 recession, and recovered relatively quickly, unlike cities in the Northeast and in California.

IMPLICATIONS FOR FISCAL FEDERALISM

Despite the failure of the U.S. grant system to be geographically equalizing in effect, it is not difficult to design measures of fiscal federalism that address the two traditional problems of regional economic weakness: long-term economic decline because the main industries of a region are in decline, and the differential vulnerability of regional economies to national economic recessions. It is considerably more difficult to design grant programs that address the more erratic type of regional economic differentiation that has occurred in recent years. The sharp local economic recessions can produce fiscal crises, and have done so on a number of occasions since 1969, not only in the well-known case of New York City. If the local recessions do not coincide with national ones, it is not plausible that a central government would intervene systematically to prevent fiscal crises in individual states or cities.

That is exactly what happened: When most states and cities were in difficulty because of the 1974–75 recession, Congress enacted an Anti-Recession Fiscal Package to help all local governments, but New York was the only city with an individual fiscal crisis to receive federal government aid, and then only because of the fear that if New York City defaulted on its debt obligations, the nation's banking system would be threatened, given the size of the city's debt and the distribution of the holdings of that debt among banks. The Anti-Recession Fiscal Package ended with national economic recovery, and the cities with subsequent fiscal crises, like Cleveland and Chicago, did not receive any federal help.

One reason why the emergence of a pattern of divergent regional and local cycles *should* lead to more, rather than less, central government intervention is that, in the absence of such intervention, there will be stabilization-branch actions at the regional and local levels. State and local governments will engage in policies to counter the local effects of the cycles, because they must do so. Economic theory tells us that subnational stabilization policies will be at best ineffectual, because of the "leakages" to other regions. More likely, they will be inefficient in a microeconomic sense, increasing locational distortions. At worst, they will add up to a national macroeconomic policy that is cyclically perverse, as state and local governments in combination increase taxes and reduce spending in recession and do the opposite in periods of inflationary expansion.[23]

Data for the period since 1982 show that subnational governments, as expected, do not respond coherently to variations in their economic fortunes. Differences in regional economic growth rates (measured by gross product) explain less than half the variation in revenue growth rates; there is no relationship between economic growth rates and the change in the ratio of revenue to gross product; there is little relationship between differences in the tax burden at the beginning of the period and changes in the tax burden during the period. Some, but not all, states responded to slow growth with increases in the average effective rate of taxation. Some states with relatively fast growth rates in the 1980s actually increased effective tax rates (like New York), while others used their prosperity to reduce tax burdens. Subnational stabilization policy was even more incoherent in years when the regional economic differentials were larger, like the mid-1970s, the 1979–82 period, and the 1989–91 recession.

No doubt, few people other than economists are concerned about whether regional fiscal actions add up to a coherent macroeconomic policy. Decision makers, as well as the general public, *are* concerned with the effects of sharply different regional economic trends—in a fiscal regime with a small federal government role—on the provision of public services. From the political perspective, the issue is this: if relatively short, but very sharp, economic cycles are to be the normal experience for regions and even more for individual large cities, especially cycles that are not coincident with the national cycles, then we need new financing institutions and methods for providing services continuously and as a basis for making rational, long-term plans.

It is both inefficient and inequitable for publicly financed services to undergo sharp contractions and expansions along with the local economy, which is what happened in the large-city fiscal crises of the 1970s and early 1980s in the United States, and when fiscal crises affected state governments in the Midwest and Southwest in the 1980s. Moreover, such fluctuations discourage serious long-term planning. It is noteworthy that few large American cities have been doing long-term planning since the mid-1970s. One reason for the decline in interest in long-term planning is the fact that many such plans had serious technical problems, in the design of the forecasting models and in the form of gross overestimates of population and related growth rates. But the sharp cyclical fluctuations are an equally important reason: long-term planning seems futile, if the policies and projects in the plan must be discarded almost as soon as the plan is published.

CONCLUSION: POLICY CHOICES

As noted earlier, Oakland more than a decade ago and Ladd and Yinger recently have advanced ideas for a new type of federal aid to city governments, one whose major objective may be characterized as ensuring "adequate levels of important public services, including education and police and fire protection, for poor and disadvantaged city residents" (Ladd and Yinger 1989: 306). The logic would extend, presumably, to other local public services that can be construed as elements of a decent minimum standard of living. The longer the list of services provided by city governments that are deemed deserving of federal grants, the more the resulting package will look like unconditional grants and, to some extent, will work like unconditional grants, as the recipient local authorities adjust their use of own-source revenue to the availability of grants for the different functions.[24]

However, I am not advocating reviving unconditional grants to local governments, replacing the old general revenue-sharing program. First, the literature documents that, in theory and practice, unconditional grants have far less effect in stimulating expenditure than matching categorical grants.[25] The Ladd and Yinger (1989) findings show this for large cities in the 1972–82 period, which is consistent with the earlier literature. If the main objective is to improve the standard of living of the poor in cities, it makes little sense to adopt a federal grant program whose main effects are to facilitate reductions in local taxes not paid by the poor or to encourage local authority capital spending for facilities that are only remotely related to the needs of the poor, both of which general revenue sharing did.

Second, although most federal grant programs are designed to diffuse the funds widely in a geographic sense, the experience with general revenue sharing was perhaps worse in this respect than was the case in any other federal aid program. The complex distribution formulas assured that even the least active and most affluent local authority received nontrivial amounts of money. The politics of state government school aid in some states suggest that categorical grants can be vulnerable to the same antitargeting pressures, but there does seem to be a large difference in degree at the federal level, with the categorical grants likely to have at least some element of targeting.[26]

Assume, then, that these grants should be categorical matching grants, rather than a variant of general revenue sharing for cities with poor fiscal health. It is fairly easy, technically if not politically, to target unconditional grants, by making both eligibility for the grants and the amount distributed to each city functions of the city's fiscal health. But the amount of a matching categorical grant received by any given city should be based on its own decision, confronted by an open-ended grant with a specified matching percentage. One device for targeting such grants to poor cities would be a binary eligibility rule: the grant is fully open-ended but available only to cities in poor fiscal health (using appropriate measures to avoid creating perverse incentives with regard to state government assistance), with zero aid to all other cities. That is unlikely in American politics. Perhaps the best device is a variable matching percentage, with a very low federal share for healthy cities and up to more than 50 percent for the poorest cities.

This bears a resemblance to a proposal by Gramlich (1985c: 58) for "categorical-equity grants to poorer communities for merit public services such as education, health, and housing." However, certain aspects of the American experience with federal categorical grants during the 1965–80 period make one hesitant about this genre of proposals. A large number of new federal categorical grants were advocated, and sold, as programs to help poor people in inner cities via their local and, sometimes, state governments. Many such programs failed two crucial tests. First, the expenditure was often for services that are not conspicuously directed at the poor—if at all. Massive capital grants to build new rail metro systems provided the most spectacular example of this type of dissembling. Second, the local public services that were aided often were ones whose benefits are entirely internal to the local jurisdiction—for example, federal grants to acquire land for small local parks. American federal-level decision makers—and the media, with the avid assistance of academic "pop" writers—tend to interpret the fact that many cities confront similar demands for public services as proof that the "problems" are nationwide in incidence.

Therefore, there is the hazard that a new federal interest in "categorical-equity" grants to cities would replicate the earlier experience of highly inefficient and not especially equitable grants made in the name of equity. Presumably, the inefficiency could be minimized if, as a general rule, the federal matching percentages for most categorical grants were low, rather than high, as they have been in the recent past: by 1980, the federal matching percentage for most categorical grants was 80.[27] One element of Gramlich's program for reforming fiscal federalism in the United States is to lower the federal matching share on all existing categorical grant programs to 20 percent, and make them truly open-ended, so that the grant appropriately lowers the tax-price of marginal dollars of spending by local authorities. Criticism of the implicit exaggeration of the external benefits of many of the spending programs of state and local governments, in the form of excessive federal shares and federal aid for expenditure with virtually no external benefits, dates back to at least 1967 (Break 1967); Gramlich has been one of the most persistent critics, and by now there is wide agreement among American public finance economists on this proposition.

Another major element of Gramlich's plan for reform of American fiscal federalism is nationalization of the present federal/state income support system, that is, replacing federal grants to the states that result in highly nonuniform benefits by direct federal income-support programs with minimal supplementation by the states. This enjoyed widespread support among academic policy analysts in the 1960s and 1970s, but that support has diminished with the rise of the revisionist (revision of Musgrave, that is) view that income redistribution is a legitimate function of subnational governments. Many analysts, myself included, have not been persuaded by the revisionists and, with Gramlich, favor nationalization of public assistance. Few cities spend much, if any, of their own funds for public assistance (New York State is the main exception to the rule that the nonfederal share of the funds must come from the state government), but the cities have two interests in nationalization. First, more uniformity in assistance payments levels would be good for cities. Increases in the level of assistance payments in the states where payments are now relatively low, which would occur with nationalization, would directly aid poor people in cities in those states, and more uniformity would decrease the incentives for poor people to concentrate in the cities of the states with relatively high assistance payments levels. Second, the budgetary relief to state governments that nationalization would provide, especially in states with poor fiscal health themselves, should make it feasible for them to do more for their ailing cities.

Gramlich's plan pays for the "equity-categorical" grants and the nationalization of public assistance, first, by the reduced federal matching share for categorical grants and, second—this is also in concert with most public finance economists—by eliminating the federal income tax deduction for state and local tax payments.[28] The argument is that, like all other tax preferences, deductibility is distorting and generates horizontal inequity in order to provide a highly inefficient subsidy to state and local governments. The inefficiency is in lowering the tax price of expenditure with little, if any, relevant geographic externalities. Indeed, the critics generally take the position that a large share of all expenditure by American state and local governments comprises local private goods, including local public goods converted into "club" goods by exclusionary land-use controls exercised by small suburban local authorities.[29] Thus, no federal aid in support of this expenditure, of any kind, is warranted, even aid in the efficient form of optimizing categorical matching grants.

I and a few other academics have dissented from this dominant position on federal deductibility (e.g., Chernick and Reschovsky 1987; Musgrave 1985; Netzer 1985; Oakland 1986). The dissenters have explicitly noted that much public expenditure in large central cities is for public goods, in that the expenditure is occasioned by the presence of poor people combined with a weak revenue base.[30] Deductibility may be a very inept form of federal aid to cities, but it is better than nothing, if other forms of federal assistance are unavailable.

The final element of the Gramlich plan reflects a view not widely shared: activist stabilization policies by state governments. I argue the opposite, as the preceding discussion of increasing regional economic differentiation should suggest. Under conditions of increased regional economic differentiation, state government action is less appropriate than ever. The leakages are at least as great as they always have been, and the vulnerability to adverse locational shifts in response to increased state government tax burdens is greater than ever.

A conceivable case for a role for subnational governments in the stabilization branch might be based on the hypothesis that the critical factor driving long-term regional economic growth is the supply side, the relative quality of local inputs. To the extent that this is true, it is an argument for discretionary action by regional and local authorities to improve the quality of inputs, making strategic choices that central governments do not make wisely (at least in a large country like the United States, where the design, if not the actual effect, of federal policy tends to be as uniform as possible over the regions). But regional and local authorities will not be able to implement sustained policies to improve the quality of inputs if they experience sharp, even violent, fluctuations in their fiscal conditions.

Even if the federal budget deficit were small or nonexistent, it would be difficult to design politically acceptable, and durable, grant mechanisms to ensure against serious impairment of services in particular regions and cities, when those regions and cities suffer from sharp cyclical fluctuations with severe effects on their revenues, and when the cycles do not coincide with national cycles. The Anti-Recession Fiscal Package of the late 1970s was momentarily acceptable because of the national recession of mid-decade, but it was not durable, in large part because it had one highly desirable feature: a high degree of targeting. There were two "triggers," national economic conditions and local economic conditions. The worse were the national economic conditions, the larger was aggregate size of the national program, but how much (if anything) of the national total any city received was a function of its own circumstances.

That program affords a precedent for a new countercyclical federal assistance program, although the design of the earlier program was not ideal. If the goal is to counter the effect of local and regional cycles on the finances of cities (and states), whether or not those cycles coincide in timing with the national cycles, then the only "trigger" that is appropriate is a measure of local conditions. The measure used as the trigger in the earlier program was the unemployment rate, which is not an accurate mirror of variations in local fiscal circumstances. However, the unemployment rate may be the only rapidly available measure of short-term changes in local economic circumstances. Also, the federal countercyclical grants should be explicitly unconditional, rather than nominally conditional, as in the earlier program; the purpose of the grants is not necessarily to stimulate more local spending by lowering the tax prices of merit goods, but to offset declines in the own-source revenue of local authorities, to permit them to maintain total spending at pre-recession levels.[31] With a high degree of targeting, the federal countercyclical grant program would cost little in the aggregate in years in which the national economy was in good shape, while providing substantial assistance to the few cities that were at the bottom of their own cycles.

In an era of national government budgetary stringency, what about priorities among the three forms of federal assistance to cities proposed earlier? Nationalization of public assistance is third on my list, because its effects on the cities would be so indirect in most cases (and because it is surely the least attractive in the context of American

politics). An expanded and well-designed program of "equity-categorical" grants is strongly grounded in the theory of fiscal federalism
and in the empirical work of Ladd and Yinger, but I place countercyclical grants highest on my list, principally because of the experience of the 1980s. The sharp decline in federal assistance to cities
was *not* a serious problem in the booming regions, but was in the
ailing ones. If the divergence in regional economic conditions that
has characterized the 1970s, 1980s, and 1990s continues, the local
cycles will have much worse effects on the afflicted cities and on the
poor people within those cities than will a declining level of federal
categorical grants.

In 1997, these policy prescriptions may seem in the realm of fantasy.
Doing good for large cities has not been important in national government policy throughout the 1990s, and much of the serious federal
expenditure reduction has been focused on urban programs. More
important (because those programs were quite small by the late
1980s), far from nationalizing public assistance, the national Congress
has replaced the sixty-year-old public assistance grants to the states—
one of the very few open-ended federal matching-grant programs,
with the efficiency advantages of such grant programs—with a fixed-
sum "block grant" to the states, the fixed amounts being rougly equal
to the 1996 grants under the old program. The passage of time will
quickly convert this into a lump-sum grant without effective matching
requirements. The ostensible objective was to increase the role of the
state governments in redistribution policy, by giving them wide discretion over program content. However, the actual legislation includes
specific federal rules that preclude benefit payments to whole classes
of previously eligible low-income recipients and other rules that
should dramatically reduce the income redistribution which the program has done over its history. Most of those now excluded from the
program, like immigrants (legal as well as illegal), live in large central
cities. Similar changes have been promised for other federal programs
that focus on poor people in cities, notably medical assistance for the
poor and the surviving housing programs. Meanwhile, the surviving
federal categorical grants—most of which have little to do with income redistribution—continue to have absurdly high matching percentages. It has not been a success story for the conventional wisdom
among American public finance economists.

Notes

1. In the Musgrave (1959) formulation, government activity is divided into three "budget
branches": the stabilization branch, concerned with affecting the overall level of

economic activity; the redistribution branch, concerned with altering the distribution of real incomes among households; and the allocation branch, concerned with altering the composition of the output of goods and services. The roles of the different levels of government in the Musgrave scheme are determined by their capacities to achieve the respective goals.

2. Of course, much of the federal aid to state governments is spent, directly or in grants, outside central cities of metropolitan areas.

3. "Nondefense" also excludes federal spending for international affairs and for space programs (data from Survey of Current Business, June 1996, tables 3.15 and 3.16, pp. 40–41).

4. In 1994, direct federal nondefense expenditure other than social security that actually took place within central cities (other than Washington, D.C.) probably amounted to no more than $20 billion.

5. The functions listed accounted for 65 percent of state government direct expenditure (excluding interest and employee retirement payments) in 1991–92.

6. In Hawaii, the schools are operated by the state government, and in Alaska schools in remote areas are state-operated. Otherwise, schools are operated by local authorities, with (on average) just over half the funds provided by state governments.

7. Because of commuting to and from work across municipal boundaries, the relative strength of the city's economy and the relative incidence of poverty in its resident population do not necessarily coincide.

8. To reduce the extent of noncomparability attributable to the wide variation in the roles of the municipal governments (specifically, the extent to which the data reflect assignment of major functions to other governmental entities), own-source revenues of independent school districts are added to those of the municipal governments, and federal aid for schools (includes aid that passed through the state governments) is added to the numerator.

9. New York City's influence is disproportionate because the role of local governments vis-à-vis the state government is unusually large in New York State. Also, New York City does assume responsibility for functions not done generally by local governments anywhere else in the United States, and the role of separate, overlying local authorities is trivial in New York City.

10. The usual obstacles to a truly redistributive aid program in the United States are: (a) it is politically difficult to keep the allocation formula targeted on places with poor residents, so the aid is often spread widely and thinly, as was the case with general revenue sharing in its fifteen-year history; (b) the rhetoric notwithstanding, some categorical grant programs support services that are not especially oriented toward the poor, such as grants for mass transportation; and (c) federal grants programs frequently require state and local governments to devote a substantial portion of the grant funds to administration, rather than service provision, which means that the program is income-redistributive only if it is staffed by people who otherwise would have been unemployed and poor.

11. Any transfer in kind must be worth somewhat less to the recipient than a transfer in money. The issue here is whether these transfers in kind are worth a great deal less than the same amounts provided in cash.

12. Oakland (1979: 351) justified this proposal primarily on efficiency grounds: it would deal with the locational distortions caused by the excessive tax burden on central-city nonpoor residents and firms to finance the local public service consumption of the poor. But, as Oakland also stated, such a grant program would put the "responsibility for providing the public needs of the poor" on the same footing as "is currently the

case for the private needs of the poor," that is, the federal/state income-maintenance program.

13. See Netzer (1991) for a summary account.

14. Much of the governmentally provided infrastructure is financed from general taxes. Where there are user charges, they are, at best, based on average rather than marginal costs; at worst, they are wholly unrelated to unit costs of any kind. In most cases, utility services provided by "investor-owned" firms are priced *above* marginal costs to business users in old cities and *below* marginal costs in newer places.

15. The federal government has explicit prices for few of its services, even in cases where state and local governments often have explicit pricing (for example, none of the federal museums—even the heavily congested Air and Space Museum—charge admission fees), and marginal-cost-based pricing in no cases. Moreover, federal law forbids explicit marginal-cost-based pricing by state and local governments in several important cases—for airport use and on most of the Interstate Highway System. Local authorities widely believe that federal approval is required for any major innovation in pricing of facilities built with federal aid or of services subject to federal nonprice regulation (notably, waste management).

16. Most of this section is adapted from Netzer (1990). That paper addresses the somewhat different question of the appropriateness of the fiscal decentralization that occurred in the United States during the 1980s, in light of what I have called increasing regional economic differentiation. The extent of fiscal decentralization has been very large, for so short a period. In 1965, the federal government financed one-third of all civilian public expenditure other than health and retirement benefits for the elderly. In 1980, the federal share had risen to 44 percent. By 1987, the federal share was back at the 1965 level, and declining.

17. This account is based on the summary of the OECD study that appeared in *The Economist* of July 29, 1989, p. 55.

18. Even so, the unemployment rate for the regions that contain the quartile of the labor force with the highest rate was twice that of the regions with the quartile of the labor force with the lowest unemployment.

19. The change from economic convergence among regions to economic divergence extends even to wage rates (see Eberts 1989).

20. There are eight regions in the standard statistical series; I have broken out California and New York from their respective regions because they are large and have had trends that occasionally diverge from the rest of their regions. Texas is also very large relative to its region, but the trends for Texas and the rest of the Southwest region have coincided.

21. Although some states diverge from the trends in their regions, most do not: the picture for the individual states in much like that in table 14.2.

22. As the gross product data imply, for eighteen of the states, the relative positions of states and regions changed considerably between 1975 and 1986 with regard to the "representative tax system" measure of tax capacity. Five of these states were high in the distribution in 1975, but low in 1980 and 1986; eight were relatively low in 1975, but high thereafter; four were low in 1975 and 1986, but high in 1980; and one was low only in 1980.

23. Older readers will recognize this as the "fiscal perversity" hypothesis first proposed by Hansen and Perloff in 1944 to characterize the behavior of American state and local governments during the Great Depression. Subsequent writers have challenged the empirical validity of the proposition in those years. The controversy is reviewed and the evidence for the 1945–64 period examined in Rafuse (1965).

24. This will not be true if the categorical grants are efficiently designed "optimizing grants"—that is, open-ended matching grants with matching percentages that, for each function, closely correspond with the ratio of benefits realized outside the local jurisdiction to the benefits realized internally. This is discussed later in the text.

25. It is true that unconditional grants in practice seem more stimulative than theory would predict—that is, theory predicts minimal effects—because of the celebrated "flypaper effect": the tendency, at least in the United States, for the recipient subnational governments to spend a substantial portion of unconditional grants, rather than reduce local taxes to an extent consistent with our estimates of the elasticity of voters' demand for local public goods. But the stimulative effects of unconditional grants are relatively small, nonetheless.

26. State school aid often takes the form of lump-sum, rather than matching, grants. If the local tax price for the grant is zero, legislators should be expected to insist on their bits of pork.

27. A number of the supposedly categorical grant programs required no local matching of the federal funds. The local authorities in such cases were acting as administering agents of the federal government, rather than as autonomous decision makers confronting a set of tax prices. Usually, that real relationship was not explicit, leading to substantial and recurring misunderstandings.

28. See Gramlich (1985a, b) and Kenyon (1986) for statements of this position.

29. The extreme case for this has been advanced by Sparrow (1986). The implication is that the deductibility of the local property tax should be eliminated even if that of state income taxes is continued.

30. Gramlich (1985a), in a paper that uses empirical evidence for Michigan, did recognize this point. He concluded that deductibility is of little use in lowering the tax price of local public expenditure in the city of Detroit, because incomes are so low that the median voter is almost certainly not affected by deductibility. However, he conceded that the elimination of deductibility is likely to speed the emigration of the relatively few remaining well-off residents of the city.

31. Two of the three components of the 1970s "package" nominally had restrictions on the use to which the grants could be put, they appeared to require some forms of matching, and they had "maintenance of effort" requirements designed to ensure that the grants were stimulative, rather than substitutes for spending from local funds. All these provisions were easily overcome, so that the conditions amounted to no more than a minor increase in the local administrative costs of complying with the federal rules.

References

Advisory Commission on Intergovernmental Relations. 1989. *1986 State Fiscal Capacity and Effort*, Information Report M-165. Washington, D.C.: Author.

Break, George F. 1967. *Intergovernmental Fiscal Relations in the United States.* Washington, D.C.: Brookings Institution.

Buchanan, James M. 1950. "Federalism and Fiscal Equity." *American Economic Review* 40: 583–99.

Chernick, Howard, and Andrew Reschovsky. 1987. "The Deductibility of State and Local Taxes." *National Tax Journal* 40: 95–102.

Eberts, Randall W. 1989. "Accounting for the Recent Divergence in Regional Wage Differentials." *Economic Review* (Federal Reserve Bank of Cleveland) 25(3): 14–26.

————. 1990. "Public Infrastructure and Regional Economic Development." *Economic Review* (Federal Reserve Bank of Cleveland) 26(1): 15–27.

Economist, The. July 29, 1989: 55.

Gramlich, Edward N. 1985a. "The Deductibility of State and Local Taxes." *National Tax Journal* 38: 447–66.

————. 1985b. *Economic Consequences of Tax Simplification.* (Discussion of Netzer paper.) Proceedings of a conference sponsored by the Federal Reserve Bank of Boston.

————. 1985c. "Reforming U.S. Federal Fiscal Arrangements." In *American Domestic Priorities: An Economic Appraisal,* edited by J.M. Quigley and Daniel L. Rubinfeld. Berkeley and Los Angeles: University of California Press.

Hansen, Alvin H., and Harvey S. Perloff. 1944. *State and Local Governments in the National Economy.* New York: W.W. Norton.

Kenyon, Daphne A. 1986. "Federal Tax Deductibility of State and Local Taxes." *Federal-State-Local Fiscal Relations, Technical Papers.* U.S. Treasury Department, Office of State and Local Finance. Washington, D.C.: U.S. Government Printing Office.

Ladd, Helen F., and John Yinger. 1989. *America's Ailing Cities: Fiscal Health and the Design of Urban Policy.* Baltimore: Johns Hopkins University Press.

Lucke, Robert M. 1982. "Rich States—Poor States: Inequalities in Our Federal Systems." Advisory Commission on Intergovernmental Relations. *Intergovernmental Perspective* 8(2): 22–28.

Morrison, Catherine J., and Amy Ellen Schwartz. 1996. "State Infrastructure and Productive Performance." *American Economic Review* 86: 1095–111.

Munnell, Alicia H. 1990. "Why Has Productivity Growth Declined? Productivity and Public Investment." *New England Economic Review* (Federal Reserve Bank of Boston) (Jan./Feb.): 3–22.

Musgrave, Richard A. 1959. *The Theory of Public Finance.* New York: McGraw-Hill.

————. 1985. "An Overall Assessment—Is It Worth It?" In *Economic Consequences of Tax Simplification.* Proceedings of a conference sponsored by the Federal Reserve Bank of Boston.

Netzer, Dick. 1985. "The Effect of Tax Simplification on State and Local Government." In *Economic Consequences of Tax Simplification.*

Proceedings of a conference sponsored by the Federal Reserve Bank of Boston.

————. 1990. "Fiscal Federalism and Regional Economic Differentiation in the United States." Paper presented at the 19th annual meeting of the Western Regional Science Association, February.

————. 1991. "An Evaluation of Interjurisdictional Competition through Economic Development Incentives." In *Competition among States and Local Governments: Efficiency and Equity in American Federalism,* edited by Daphne A. Kenyon and John Kincaid. Washington, D.C.: Urban Institute Press.

Oakland, William H. 1979. "Central Cities: Fiscal Plight and Prospects for Reform." In *Current Issues in Urban Economics,* edited by Peter Mieszkowski and Mahlon Straszheim. Baltimore: Johns Hopkins University Press.

————. 1986. "Consequences of the Repeal of State and Local Tax Deductibility under the U.S. Personal Income Tax." In *Federal-State-Local Fiscal Relations, Technical Papers.* U.S. Treasury Department, Office of State and Local Finance. Washington, D.C.: U.S. Government Printing Office.

Rafuse, Robert W., Jr. 1965. "Cyclical Behavior of State-Local Finances." In *Essays in Fiscal Federalism,* edited by Richard A. Musgrave. Washington, D.C.: Brookings Institution.

Sparrow, F. T. 1986. "The Subsidy Value and Incidence of Tax Expenditures which Benefit State and Local Government—The Case of the Property Tax." In *Federal-State-Local Fiscal Relations, Technical Papers.* U.S. Treasury Department, Office of State and Local Finance. Washington, D.C.: U.S. Government Printing Office.

U.S. Department of Commerce. 1996. "Comprehensive NIPA Revision: Newly Available Tables." *Survey of Current Business* 76(6): 39–50.

Chapter Fifteen

TECHNOLOGY DEVELOPMENT PROGRAMS, INTERGOVERNMENTAL RELATIONS, AND BALANCED REGIONAL GROWTH

Michael I. Luger

In the United States, as in other industrialized countries, increasing emphasis has been placed on "technology development" as a means to achieve desired economic outcomes. In many countries, regional governments have been playing a particularly important role in that economic development strategy, directly and through their state-supported universities.

Recent literature has excelled more at explaining *why* technology development has become the centerpiece of regional policy than at evaluating technology's likely, or actual, economic consequences. Yet, it is possible that technology policy has affected location patterns and the distribution of wealth among and within regions. Either ex post analyses of technology development programs have not been done, on the grounds that those initiatives are too new to have measurable consequences, or they have been too narrowly focused or anecdotal to allow generalizable policy lessons to be drawn. Ex ante analyses typically have not been done, according to some observers, because technology programs have independent "symbolic" value, indicating to voters that the policy makers who support them are "progressive" (e.g., see Edelman 1964, 1971).[1] Similarly, R. A. Joseph (1989) has written: "Political myths about technology exist in western societies, one of which is the Silicon Valley model." In the same article, Joseph argues that public policies based on myth "need not be thought of as solely aiming to solve problems . . . [but, rather, as] means to the creation of public images of society and politics" (364).

Joseph's explanation would seem to account for the multiplication of technology development programs in the absence of knowledge of their consequences. In this vein, Watkins (1985) noted: "Despite the fact that there is little known empirically about the effect of the state policies promoting economic development via science and technology, most states have fully accepted the doctrine that state governments can be a powerful catalyst in the innovation process."

In the United States, for example, estimates of the amount spent by states on science and technology programs range from $143 million to over $1 billion, with the most recent estimate of almost $385 million for fiscal year 1994. When combined with federal spending of $2,717 million for cooperative technology programs in the same year, total spending on cooperative technology programs alone exceeds $3,101 million, an increase of 56.6 percent from fiscal year 1992 (Coburn and Bergland 1995). Funds are expended on a variety of programs, including technology offices, technical/managerial assistance to technology-oriented businesses, research grants, high-tech incubators, technology transfer programs, technical training programs, technology/research centers, seed capital programs, information/networking programs, equity investments, royalty programs, and tax incentives for high-tech businesses (Office of Science and Technology, Minnesota Department of Trade and Economic Development 1988). State-supported universities spend millions of dollars more on licensing and patenting assistance to faculty, technical/managerial assistance to technology-oriented businesses, equity investments in technology start-ups, specialized labs for joint research projects with industry, incubators, and research parks (Goldstein and Luger 1990). Similarly, in Germany, *Länder* are estimated to have spent some 26 million DM on research and development (R&D) programs and millions more on technology transfer, technology centers, and related programs (Henschel 1990). And, in the United States, Germany, and other countries, central governments continue to support technology development in a variety of ways. In the United States, for example, the federal government spent approximately $68 million in 1988 on just four high-tech programs: small business development centers, university centers, industrial applications centers, and trade adjustment assistance centers (Clark and Dobson 1989: 31).[2] This sum does not include the largest type of federal government technology spending—on R&D, for defense and other purposes—which in FY 1996 is estimated at approximately $71 billion (U.S. Office of Management and Budget 1996).[3]

Because these expenditures are sizable—consuming an increasingly large proportion of state governments' discretionary budgets—their net benefits should be considered carefully. It may be possible to achieve both economic development and a "positive state image" in a less costly manner. To that end, this chapter takes a sober look at technology development as regional economic policy. It attempts to draw some generalizable policy lessons about the intergovernmental framework for regional technology policy. It focuses on one type of economic outcome: the "evenness" of growth throughout a national system when policymaking is decentralized in different ways: as substantial financial devolution to regional (state, *Länder*) governments, as in the United States and, as an administrative partnership, as in France and Japan. I tentatively conclude here that the decentralization of technology policy unwittingly can exacerbate spatial disparities, especially when there is little policy coordination by the central government. The conclusion is tentative because this analysis runs into the two problems that most evaluations of this type confront: a relatively short time frame for outcomes to be observed, and a paucity of appropriate data. The views expressed here are based on a combination of logical reasoning, the literature, and circumstantial evidence, mostly from eight U.S. states.

The remainder of this chapter is divided into four sections. Section two documents the growing importance of technology programs in economic development strategies, particularly in American states. Section three develops the conceptual argument that this policy trend aggravates spatial disparities. Section four presents evidence to substantiate the claim. And section five contains a summary and the policy conclusions.

GROWTH AND DEVOLUTION OF TECHNOLOGY POLICY MAKING

Regional (mostly state) governments in the United States long have been involved in technology policy making, especially for internal improvements (Dupree 1957). Early examples of state-sponsored programs that can be construed as "technologically oriented" include the Erie (and other) canals, agricultural extension services, state support of education, and geological surveys (see Schmandt 1988). However, in the perspective of overall technology policy making, the role of regional governments has waxed and waned over the past two centuries. Schmandt (1988) argues that the federal government periodically assumes responsibility for technology policy from the states, either because the states' commitment to it weakens, or compelling national needs in wartime require centralized action, or fundamental economic and demographic changes require investments too large for states to handle by themselves (see also Greenberg 1967).

The latest round of regional technology policy making in the United States can be traced to the 1960s, to the onset of what has been called the "Third Industrial Revolution," in which technologies developed during World War II were put to peacetime use (Schmandt 1988: 17). In the first decades of this period, the federal government maintained dominance in technology policy, partly in the race to put a man on the moon (Schmandt and Wilson 1988) and partly as a result of Cold War and Vietnam-era defense-related R&D.

This period of centralized technology policy making corresponds generally to a period of centralized economic development policy making. Goldstein (1990) has noted that for the first time in the 1960s, Congress recognized the need for federally sponsored programs to help fill pockets of chronic poverty in the United States. In Appalachia and the South, for example, federal dollars were spent to develop organizations, such as the Appalachian Regional Commission, that could serve as focal points for concerted development efforts. In the latter years of the 1960s and early 1970s, the federal government's role in economic development policy continued to grow, with programs to subsidize the private sector's use of capital and labor.

Beginning in the late 1960s, and continuing through the administrations of Richard Nixon, Gerald Ford, and Jimmy Carter, Congress began to devolve responsibility (but not financing) for economic development to the state-local sector, through the introduction of block grants. Allocation formulae for block grant and other programs during that period recognized that some areas of the United States had greater financial needs than others.

The 1960s and 1970s also saw renewed regional activity in technology policy, largely financed by the federal government. For example, the Urban Observatories Program, funded by the U.S. Departments of Housing and Urban Development and Health, Education, and Welfare, was intended to link university research with policy making on urban problems in ten demonstration cities (Szanton 1981). In the 1970s, the National Science Foundation initiated the State and Local Intergovernmental Science Policy Planning Program, expressly designed to strengthen state science and technology capacity (Paget 1988).

Also in the 1970s, states initiated technology programs using their own resources. California, for example, encouraged aerospace companies to bid on contracts with the state, "to study problems in criminal justice, waste management, mass transportation, and information storage and retrieval" (Paget 1988). In 1977, California established the California Policy Seminar as a direct effort "to make the research resources of the University of California better known and more accessible to state government officials" (Paget 1988). In addition, 10 of the approximately 120 technology parks that currently exist in the United States were established in the 1970s, with varying degrees of state involvement (Luger and Goldstein 1991).[4] Fourteen of these parks were established between 1951 and 1970; the rest were built in the 1980s and 1990s.

The decade of the 1980s was a policy watershed in the United States and other industrialized countries. In response to a worldwide recession that had begun in the late 1970s, and for strictly ideological reasons, central governments in the United States and other large industrial countries began to redefine their roles in economic development and technology policy making. In some countries, notably the United States and Germany, regional governments were accorded considerable autonomy in the formulation and implementation of technology policy, and were required to draw substantially on their own financial resources and to forge partnerships with the private sector (see, for example, Henschel 1990 and Neumann 1989). Elsewhere, central governments used regions as outposts for regionally based technology policy. In France and Japan, for example, central ministries maintain planning oversight and major financial responsibility for technology policy (see Neumann 1989; Tatsuno 1989).

In the United States, the redefinition of federal policy making has accelerated regional governments' independence in the domestic policy arena, leading to what some observers have called "the resurgence of the states" (see Barke 1986, 1988; Bowman and Kearney 1986).[5] The resurgence in technology policy making, according to Barke, falls into three categories: the capture of policy fields from the federal government, the seizure of leadership roles in ongoing intergovernmental programs, and policy innovation (1988: 6).

In the United States, the tangible evidence of the states' "resurgence" has been a proliferation of state-sponsored technology programs. The exact number of these programs is somewhat elusive because data on them are decentralized and often difficult to obtain, and there is no consensus about what constitutes a "technology program." The best estimates are provided in the Minnesota study cited earlier (Office of Science and Technology, Minnesota Department of Trade and Economic Development 1988). Defining the set of technology programs as the thirteen that are shown in table 15.1, the count as of 1988 was approximately 250. While this figure is only a "snapshot" of state technology programs at a single point in time, more recent research supports this figure—and, once again, depending

Table 15.1 STATE TECHNOLOGY DEVELOPMENT PROGRAMS, 1988

State	A	B	C	D	E	F	G	H	I	J	K	L	M	Sum	Funding ($)	Dollars Spent per Employee
Alabama	1	1	1	x	1				1					5–6	2,855,205	2.53
Alaska	1	1												2	30,000	0.13
Arizona		1		1			1							3	7,000,000	10.96
Arkansas	1	1		1	1	1		1					1	7	3,150,000	3.03
California			1	1		1								2	5,900,000	0.63
Colorado	1			1			1		1					5	3,700,000	3.10
Connecticut	1		1	1	1				1	1		1		7	12,550,000	9.11
Delaware	1	1	1	x				1	1				1	6–7	1,650,000	6.68
Florida	1			1		1	1	1	1					5	27,958,000	7.49
Georgia	1	1		1		1	1			1				7	11,094,430	5.32
Hawaii	1	1		1	1		1	1						6	2,851,000	8.71
Idaho				1			1							3	0	0.00
Illinois	1	1		1	1	1					1	1		6	13,540,000	53.53
Indiana	1	1	1	1	1	1		1						7	10,637,500	2.60
Iowa	1	1	1	1	1		1					1	1	8	4,895,000	2.71
Kansas	1	1	1	1		1	1	1		1				8	3,550,000	4.55
Kentucky	1	1	1		1	1	1							6	560,000	0.57
Louisiana				x										0–1	0	0.00
Maine	1		1	1		1			1					5	184,280	0.52
Maryland	1	1		1	1		1		1	1				6	7,365,750	4.86
Massachusetts	1						1		1		1			4	14,665,000	5.56
Michigan	1	1	1	1		1	1	1	1	1		1		10	13,063,500	4.42
Minnesota	1	1	1	1		1	1		1				1	8	39,439,200	25.10
Mississippi		1				1								3	9,300,000	14.63
Missouri	1			1	1	1	1		1	1				7	28,566,000	16.12
Montana	1	1	1	1		1		1					1	6	3,550,000	17.43
Nebraska	1	1		1			1							3	858,500	1.32

Key for Programs / column codes: A—Technology offices, B—Technical/managerial assistance, C—Research grants, D—Research parks, E—Incubators, F—Technology Transfer, G—Technology/research centers, H—Seed capital programs, I—Technical training, J—Information/networking, K—Equity investments, L—Royalty programs, M—Tax incentives

State	A	B	C	D	E	F	G	H	I	J	K	L	M	No.	State funding	%
Nevada							x							0	0	0.00
New Hampshire	1	1				1	1							2	200,000	0.51
New Jersey	1	1	1	1	1	1	1							6	76,345,000	26.45
New Mexico	1			1		1	1							5	7,654,000	20.39
New York	1	1	1	1	1	1	1		1					6	22,129,300	3.40
North Carolina	1	1	1	1		1	1	1						8	23,357,000	10.52
North Dakota	1	1												3	207,000	0.82
Ohio	1	1	1	1		1	1		1					7	18,000,000	4.90
Oklahoma	1	1	1	1		1	1		1		1			7	12,046,375	12.81
Oregon	1	1	1	1	1	1	1		1		1			8	2,215,000	2.67
Pennsylvania	1	1	1	1	1	1	1							7	49,050,000	12.06
Rhode Island	1	1	1		1	1								3	2,000,000	4.66
South Carolina	1	1	1				1							3	0	0.00
South Dakota			1											1	3,050,000	12.25
Tennessee	1	1	1	1		1	1					1		5	13,109,400	8.40
Texas	1	1	1	1		1	1	1				1		5	60,690,000	10.79
Utah	1	1	1	1		1	1		1			1		3	5,187,000	10.86
Vermont	1	1	1	1	1	1	1							3	0	0.00
Virginia	1	1	1	x	1	1	1					1		7–8	9,400,000	5.06
Washington	1	1	1	1	1	1	1					1		7	11,000,000	8.23
West Virginia							1	1	1					2	150,000	0.09
Wisconsin		1	1	1		1	1							5	18,978,000	43.20
Wyoming	1													1	0	0.00
United States	36	30	25	32	18	26	29	10	15	2	5	11		249–52	563,681,440	6.95

Sources: A–C, E–M, from Office of Science and Technology (1988); D from Luger and Goldstein (1991).

Notes: An "x" indicates that information about state funding was not available. The states shown to have parks either operate the parks directly, arrange to have them run by a state university, or provide some funds for their operation.

Key for Programs:
A—Technology offices E—Incubators H—Seed capital programs K—Equity investments
B—Technical/managerial assistance F—Technology Transfer I—Technical training L—Royalty programs
C—Research grants G—Technology/research centers J—Information/networking M—Tax incenives
D—Research parks

upon definition, suggests state technology programs numbered 394 in fiscal year 1994 (Coburn and Bergland 1995). Table 15.1 also shows the distribution of the programs, by state, and the absolute and per capita levels of funding. Technology offices, research parks, and technical/managerial assistance programs were most common. Figure 15.1 shows the distribution of programs in a pie chart.

Figures 15.2 and 15.3 attempt to uncover gross patterns in per capita spending by displaying that variable by states' regional classification and percentage of high-tech employment. Figure 15.2 indicates that two groups of states have been particularly aggressive in developing technology programs: those in the old manufacturing belt (the Middle Atlantic and midwestern states), stretching from Chicago to New York City; and those in the energy belt (West South Central—in Texas, Arkansas, Oklahoma, and Louisiana). Both groups of states were hit hard by economic events in the 1980s. Figure 15.3 indicates another pattern: states with above-average high-tech employment have spent relatively more on technology programs than states with below-average high-tech employment. The first pattern (figure 15.2) suggests that technology policy is conducted as a means of revitalizing declining economies. The second pattern (figure 15.3) suggests either that technology policy is conducted as a means of capitalizing on existing

Figure 15.1 TYPE OF TECHNOLOGY PROGRAMS IN THE UNITED STATES

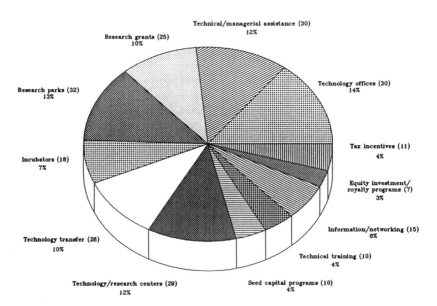

Figure 15.2 DOLLARS SPENT PER WORKER IN THE UNITED STATES

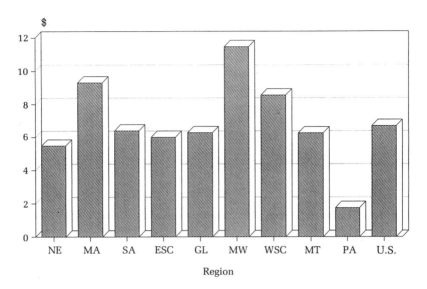

Figure 15.3 DOLLARS SPENT PER WORKER IN THE UNITED STATES

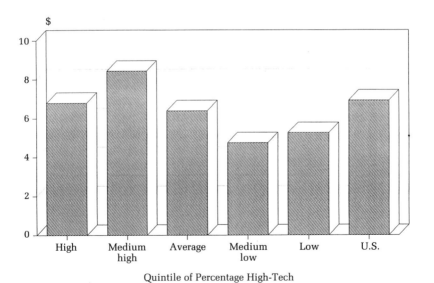

strengths in the region or of rewarding powerful industrial lobby groups. These possibilities are discussed in the professional literature (see Luger, Goldstein, and Atkinson 1990; Malecki 1984, 1987, 1988; Malecki and Nijkamp 1989).

Technology policy also is conveyed by the states through institutions of higher learning, many of which are state-affiliated.[6] A survey of ninety research universities, doctoral-granting institutions, and specialized four-year technical/professional institutions (for example, engineering institutes), indicated that 83 percent of all institutions provide patenting and licensing assistance to faculty, 52 percent provide technical/managerial assistance, 13 percent have small business assistance centers, 10 percent make equity investments in high-tech start-ups, 40 percent sponsor specialized research laboratories in partnership with private industry, 27 percent sponsor incubators, and 83 percent have joint research ventures with the private sector.[7] The state government funds that are used for these initiatives are not generally included in table 15.1.

Henschel (1990) and Neumann (1989) have documented trends for Germany that are similar to those just described. Elaborating on tendencies in economic development policy since 1980, Henschel stated, "The regional level gains importance. The Länders' task is to take up the needs of the regional industrial structures, while the Bund and the EC [European Community] support technological developments of national and European dimensions." As indicated earlier, in Germany, as in the United States, regional government has become increasingly active in the development of technology parks, technology offices, and technology transfer agencies, as well as in the provision of financial programs for technology-oriented businesses. Also, in Germany, Länder provide a large share of the funds for universities. In France, regional governments are expected to establish "regional poles of technology" within the framework of a regional plan, and in conjunction with scientific and research organizations in the region.[8] At the same time, however, the regions are required to participate in an annual research and technology conference to ensure that the regional plans are consistent with national goals (Henschel 1990: 213). And most funds for technology programs come from the central government (Henschel 1990: 215).[9] Similarly, in Japan, "central government ministries (mostly MITI) provide the broad policy framework and national tax incentives for regional innovation programmes, which are developed and implemented at the local level by towns, cities, and prefectural governments" (Tatsanu 1989: 234).

The trends outlined in this section—toward increased regionalization of technology development policy, primarily through states and state-supported universities—are likely to continue into the 1990s, in the United States and other large industrialized countries. It is important, therefore, to ask whether that trend is desirable.

REGIONALLY BASED TECHNOLOGY POLICY AND UNEVEN GROWTH: CONCEPTUAL ISSUES

Institutional changes in policy making, such as those just described, occur for many reasons, and with many objectives.[10] No central government that has devolved responsibility for technology policy making, nor any state (Länder, prefecture, etc.) that has assumed that responsibility, has intended decentralization to exacerbate intra- or interstate economic outcomes. In that regard, to the extent that outcomes have widened and policy has been responsible for that process, what has been observed constitutes an unintended policy consequence.[11]

This section has two parts. The first part documents the widening of economic outcomes just referred to for the United States. The second part discusses how the technology programs presented in the second section of this chapter may help account for those outcomes.

Widening Disparities in the 1980s

Figure 15.4 shows trends in per capita personal income, by Bureau of Economic Analysis region.[12] Note that: (1) New England and mideastern states that are historical "leaders," and that had been declining steadily toward the U.S. average, reversed their decline around 1979 (New England's growth turned down at the end of the 1980s, but has started again to grow); (2) the Far West, also a historical leader, declined steadily toward the mean until the early 1970s, but since then has approached the U.S. mean more slowly, largely on the strength of California's high-tech boom; (3) southwestern states, historical "laggards," but which had been improving toward the mean, declined sharply between 1982 and 1988, then flattened; (4) southeastern states, historically the poorest region, but which also had been approaching the national mean at a rapid pace throughout the 1940s, 1950s, and 1960s, improved their relative position more slowly in the 1980s and

Figure 15.4 TRENDS IN PER CAPITA U.S. PERSONAL INCOME, BEA REGIONS,
1929–1995

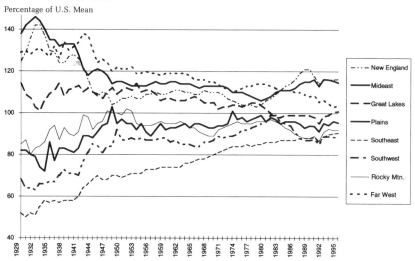

Percentage of U.S. Mean

Legend:
- - - - New England
——— Mideast
— — Great Lakes
——— Plains
- - - Southeast
— - Southwest
——— Rocky Mtn.
• - • Far West

Year

Source: U.S. Bureau of Economic Analysis (BEA), personal communication to author,
Sept. 1991, and *Survey of Current Business*, May 1996.

1990s; and (5) the Mountain states, also historical laggards, after having gained ground toward the national average during the 1970s, declined precipitously between 1982 and 1988, and then have continued
to approach the national average. The overall picture that emerges is
that interregional income differences today are about as wide as they
were in the early 1970s.

To assess changes in regions' relative position, standard deviations
of indices of per capita personal incomes were calculated across regions, for years between 1929 and 1995. This showed that interregional variation declined steadily until 1981, reversed itself during the
1980s, peaked in 1988, and is resuming its downward movement in
the 1990s.[13] This widening of regional disparities is also observable
at the state level. Ranking states by 1988 per capita personal income
shows that the highest-income states improved their position between
1982 and 1988, while the position of the lowest-ranked states deteriorated (U.S. Bureau of the Census 1996). Between 1988 and 1995,
however, the lowest-ranked states have shown the most improvement.
With the exception of the District of Columbia, which showed the
most improvement over this time period, seven of the next eight states
showing the most improvement were ranked in the bottom quintile in

1988. In short, much evidence illustrates the same outcome: a reversal of regional economic convergence in the United States during the decade of the 1980s.

Data on intraregional economic outcomes reveal similar patterns. For example, table 15.2 contains coefficients of variation of per capita personal income by county, for selected years in three sample states (Indiana, New York, and North Carolina). Higher coefficients indicate greater inequality. Indiana and New York exhibit increasing coefficients throughout this period. North Carolina, however, shows a reversal of the trend toward greater inequality since 1988—in line with the interregional data discussed earlier. This divergence was a reversal of a trend in North Carolina and an acceleration of trends in the other two states.

An examination of county data in each of the states indicates that much of the divergence cited earlier here is between metropolitan and nonmetropolitan counties. In North Carolina, for example, the percentage difference in per capita personal income between metropolitan and nonmetropolitan counties was 16 percent in 1972, 18 percent in 1976, 21 percent in 1980, 27 percent in 1984, and 26 percent in 1987 (see figure 15.5). Since around 1990, however, the difference between metropolitan and nonmetropolitan counties has resumed its historical convergence.

The reversal of historical convergence in regional economic well-being that occurred in the 1980s can be attributed to two related phenomena: the process of economic restructuring since the mid-1970s that favored economic centers already well endowed with skilled labor, physical infrastructure, and social infrastructure, such as educational facilities; and the increased use of regionally based technology policy since around 1980, as demonstrated here. The resumption of convergence since 1990 suggests that market forces that favor equilibration have overcome the effects of policy. The unevenness of state-based policy may also have lessened as a result of widespread economic growth.

Table 15.2 INTRASTATE VARIATION IN PER CAPITA PERSONAL INCOMES

State	1970	1980	1984	1988	1994
Indiana	0.099	0.105	0.114	0.134	0.136
New York	0.159	0.160	0.189	0.261	0.304
North Carolina	0.166	0.136	0.149	0.178	0.156

Source: U.S. Bureau of Economics Analysis (1996), data tape.

Figure 15.5 PER CAPITA PERSONAL INCOME, NORTH CAROLINA, SELECTED
YEARS

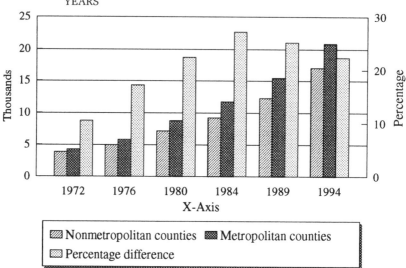

Source: U.S. Bureau of Economic Analysis, *Survey of Current Business*, June 1996.

Technology Development Programs and Economic Development Disparities

This subsection analyzes how regionally based technology policy is likely to exacerbate regional inequality. Five groups of technology programs are discussed, as follows:

1. Efforts to recruit high-tech branch plants that have been hived off from their parent by means of a battery of location incentives (for example, via the "tax incentives" included in table 15.1);
2. Programs to help businesses in traditional industries become technologically more advanced—for example, by encouraging investment in high-tech equipment and processes (such as robots, computerized numerical control machines, automated material handling and packaging systems, flexible manufacturing cells and systems, and computer-aided design) or assisting firms in "upskilling" their labor force (for instance, by using tax incentives, technical/managerial assistance, and technical training, also included in table 15.1);
3. Initiatives to help "new technology" businesses to start up, or to assist existing businesses of this type to expand—for example, by

providing debt or equity capital, technical assistance, and incubator space;

4. Encouragement of closer university-industry ties to strengthen the universities' research capacity, and to facilitate technology transfer; and,

5. Efforts to create a suitable locational environment for technology-oriented firms, by providing the necessary physical, cultural, knowledge, and social infrastructure (for example, the development of technology parks, the construction and operation of state-run technology centers, and the establishment of specialized university programs). (These groups of programs subsume most of the 13 technology programs listed in table 15.1.)[14]

The first of these groups of programs—recruiting high-tech branch plants—is popular within state government because it represents business as usual for departments of commerce and industry. The only thing new about this type of recruitment is the target. Recruiting, however, has been criticized as a means of coping with restructuring (Luger 1984, 1985). The main problem is that there is only a fixed number of target firms to recruit, and competition to land them could be costly (this process has been referred to as "short-stack chasing" as opposed to "smoke-stack chasing"). From a national perspective, industrial recruitment shifts existing jobs from one place to another more than it leads to net new job creation.

The second use of resources—to help declining industries modernize through the use of technology—has only begun to gain adherents among state officials. In part, those officials are realizing that the innovation is more complex than previously conceived, and that upgrading existing technology can be as important as developing and transferring new technology (Atkinson 1989). The northeastern and midwestern states, with large traditional manufacturing sectors, have taken the lead in developing these programs. States such as Michigan (automotive), New York (machinery), and Pennsylvania (steel) have expended considerable effort to assist small and medium-sized manufacturing firms to adopt new technologies. This approach bears some risk, however, since the forces that led to the lack of competitiveness in the first place may be too strong for policy to overcome, at least without an unacceptable expenditure (see Clark 1988).

The third type of expenditure—on programs to help new firms start up or existing firms to expand—is viewed favorably in the economic development literature because of its potential to increase the level of long-term economic activity. The new local economic activity is not considered to be merely a shift from one location to another but a net gain for the national economy (Friedman and Schweke 1981; Harrison and Kanter 1978).

Building closer (public) university-industry ties, the fourth type of investment, takes several different forms, including licensing of inventions developed by university faculty and staff, joint research projects, and university-based research centers that are sponsored by individual businesses (that, in turn, have proprietary rights to research outcomes) (for example, see: Feller 1988; Fowler 1984; Haller 1984; Peters and Fusfeld 1983; Praeger and Omenn 1980). This type of state technology policy is supposed to lead to greater product and/ or process innovation by the collaborating businesses, and hence greater long-term competitiveness in the global marketplace. There is a long history of university-industry collaboration, but only recently has it become widely popular as part of state economic development strategy.

The fifth policy thrust—social, knowledge, and physical infrastructure investment—is also viewed favorably, but can only be effective as a long-term strategy. Because the cost of infrastructure development is normally steep, it would take many years for the investment to pay off, in a cost-benefit sense. Because the payback period is attenuated, there is still some uncertainty about the net benefit of these programs.

At least four of the five types of programs (and possibly the fifth) might be expected to exacerbate the widening disparities problem described earlier in this section, even though many individual programs were conceived as a means to make growth more even. The "widening disparities" issue is addressed for each program in the subsections following.

High Tech Recruitment

The common conclusion among economists is that, in general, tax incentives and other pecuniary inducements play a minor role in businesses' decision to relocate from one region to another (Harrison and Kanter 1978; Vaughan 1980; Wasylenko 1985). This judgment applies to technology-oriented firms as well as to businesses in traditional industries (see Hekman and Greenstein 1985). Other factors— such as prevailing wage and benefit levels, access to markets, and the general business environment—are considered more important.

That is not to say that recruitment does not bear some fruit. Discussions with economic development officials throughout the United States suggest that there are exceptions to the general rule (though it is difficult to ascertain businesses' real reasons for moving and whether expensive state lures in the form of tax abatements and other incentives are really necessary to induce a move) (Atkinson 1989). The issue, however, is not *whether* recruitment induces some relocations, but at what cost.

Recruitment of technology-oriented businesses presents an additional problem for state officials who are concerned with the evenness of economic growth. Namely, those types of businesses, if they are interested in moving to a given state at all, are usually not willing to locate in areas that need new businesses the most (i.e., in nonmetropolitan countries). Technology-oriented businesses normally require a broad pool of labor (including workers with specialized skills) and a variety of business services, neither of which usually exists outside sizable metropolitan markets. Many also require proximity to a major airport, a research university, and an already-existing concentration of technology-related activity, all of which also tend to be located in metropolitan areas (Malecki 1980, 1987; Markusen, Hall, and Glasmeier 1986; Oakey 1981). Finally, because technology-oriented businesses employ a relatively large proportion of well-educated and well-paid professionals, they place a higher premium on urban and cultural amenities than do traditional businesses (Luger and Goldstein 1991; Markusen et al. 1986; Premus 1982). These, too, are more available in metropolitan centers.

The upshot is that if recruitment is successful in inducing technology-oriented businesses to move into the state, it is likely to exacerbate economic disparities, since most of the incoming businesses will locate in the best-endowed and most dynamic metropolitan areas rather than the sluggish areas. As a result, job growth rate and income growth rate differences would be expected to widen between and within states.

POLICIES TO MODERNIZE DECLINING INDUSTRIES

States have been aiding existing industries in mature or declining regions for some time. However, it is only recently that some states have begun to adopt comprehensive approaches to help firms incorporate new process technologies (robotics, computerized numerical control machines, etc.) and to assist them in retraining their labor force. It is too early to assess the success of these efforts. However, several concerns should be raised.

In some instances the forces working against successful restructuring may be too great for public policy to overcome. These forces include considerable differences in labor costs between the United

States (even the most rural areas) and developing countries; the evaporation of markets for some domestically produced goods; increased foreign competition; and the strength of the dollar relative to foreign currencies (at least until 1988) (Schechter 1988).

To the extent that these programs are successful, they may serve to widen the interregional differences in employment growth and per capita income. The expected impacts of these programs on *intra*-regional equality, however, are more uncertain. Data indicate that the largest concentrations of manufacturing firms are in the regions that were identified previously as historical "leaders" (i.e., with above-average employment growth and income) (Luger, Goldstein, and Atkinson 1990). These regions are New England, the Mideast, the Great Lakes, and the Far West. If policies succeed in improving outcomes for traditional manufacturing industries, those regions would improve even more than they have (or are projected to improve), absolutely and relative to other regions.

Because small- and medium-sized manufacturing facilities tend to be more dispersed than large facilities (because there are more of them), efforts to support their modernization may result in more widely dispersed growth. On the other hand, as manufacturing technologies become more complex and workers' skills more technical, some areas, especially those that are rural, may find it difficult to compete. However, policy efforts directed at upgrading technology are not likely to benefit economically healthy regions disproportionately. Thus, of the five types of programs considered, this is the only one in which the direction of the expected effect on intraregional inequality is ambiguous.

ASSISTING FIRMS TO START UP AND EXPAND

Efforts to help firms start up and expand tend to widen disparities among and within regions for the same reasons that recruitment does: viable technology-oriented firms require locations in places with good endowments of skilled labor and physical and social infrastructure, whether those businesses are recruited, newly established, or expanding. It could be argued, in fact, that new and small enterprises are even *more* tied to locations that are vibrant economically, because those firms do not have the means to replace internally the ingredients for success that have been described (business services, worker education, etc.). As a consequence, targeted assistance programs are unlikely to alter the location choices of technology-related firms at the levels they are offered. Indeed, for behavior to be altered, subsidies often have to be so steep that it is not possible to justify them on benefit-cost grounds (Harrison and Kanter 1978; Luger 1987).

Bergman shows that new start-ups and expansions are more likely to occur in counties with the following characteristics, than in other counties: large populations, good air service, a large pool of residents with doctorates, and a concentration of other technology-related activity (Bergman 1989). Moreover, given increased state efforts to stimulate research and development through incentives to universities, the first-round impacts of these efforts are to increase economic activity in counties with research universities. These counties' economies are likely to be well-positioned to take advantage of economic restructuring. Assuming that nonspatially targeted government policies can facilitate start-ups and expansions, it is likely they would contribute to the problem of widening disparities.

BUILDING UNIVERSITY-INDUSTRY COLLABORATION

This type of program targets public universities. The state's investment typically is to increase funds for faculty, staff, and/or equipment and facilities in those university departments or research institutes that have the greatest potential for inventing products and processes with commercial applications. Universities often enter into collaborative arrangements with individual businesses or consortia to increase the likelihood that commercial applications will indeed be realized. The impact of this type of technology transfer on the state's economy thus depends on the extent to which the businesses that collaborate with the universities are based within the state. This can vary widely. Many of the universities that have licensing offices, for instance, market university patents to businesses all over the world, for obvious reasons. Businesses that are most likely to enter into collaborative arrangements with universities tend to be large corporations with their own R&D branch plants. These corporations pool their risk by collaborating with a number of different, nationally prominent universities (Luger and Goldstein 1991). If the corporate branch plant is located within the state, chances are it will be located in the above-average income areas of the state, in order to attract or retain its skilled labor force.

Although the returns both to the university and in-state businesses can be very high in the case of a particular invention, the probability (expected value) of a positive payback is very low (Fowler 1984; Long and Feller 1972). Diversification among a number of different potential technology development areas can increase the expected returns, but it is also quite costly. Also, it is well known that universities and

industry often find it difficult to develop effective collaborative arrangements because of strong interorganizational barriers (Dill 1989;
Klausner 1988).[15]

The target of the last type of technology development programs considered here is the local economy as a whole, rather than individual
businesses. The logic of this approach is impeccable: since technology-
oriented businesses require specific amenities tied to location, those
amenities should be provided as a way to enhance the economic prospects of distressed areas.

This approach is costly to carry out in practice, however. Recent
studies indicate that the individual locational prerequisites are not
separable; rather, they are mutually interdependent (Bergman 1989;
Luger and Goldstein 1991). That is, to make a region viable as a location for technology-oriented businesses, government must build, or
improve, airports, roads, and research universities, for instance.
These broad requirements are quite costly to provide. Moreover, physical and social infrastructure are necessary, but not sufficient, conditions for successful technology-related development; in most
instances there must also be a good business climate, an agglomeration of other technology-oriented businesses, a supply of business
services, and a stock of skilled workers—most of which are difficult
to affect through policy, especially in the short- and medium-terms.
Consequently, investments in infrastructure for the purpose of developing a technology-oriented economic base, where few parts of the
infrastructure already exist, may be ineffective.

The development of research parks provides an illustration. During
the past quarter century several hundred of these parks were opened
in the United States, most with some state and/or local government
involvement, and most with an explicit objective to provide a viable
location for technology-oriented businesses. At least half of these
parks failed completely as real estate ventures (Franco 1985). Approximately one-half of the remainder could not attract a sufficient number
of technology-oriented businesses to remain viable, so they changed
their focus to office functions, less technology-oriented manufacturing, or warehousing functions (Luger and Goldstein 1991). In brief,

> The various attributes of a science/research park's location critically
> affect the success of that park as an economic development policy.
> Those location attributes include not only spatial proximity—for ex-
> ample, of park enterprises to markets and factor inputs—but also, the

regional economic "environment" which has the potential to provide
enormous positive external economies to businesses in the park.

(Luger and Goldstein 1991: 6).

It is not surprising, then, that over 85 percent of all research parks
that are still in existence are located in metropolitan regions, and
more than half of those are in large metropolitan centers (with total
populations of 500,000 or more). Most of the remaining parks (located
in nonmetropolitan areas) are in counties adjacent to metropolitan
areas, and virtually all are near a major research university.

If the surviving parks generate the magnitude of benefits to regional
economies that their developers claim, they would serve to widen
regional disparities further, since most surviving parks are in the best-
endowed and most economically vital areas (which accounts for their
survival in the first place).[16]

SPATIAL DISTRIBUTION OF STATE TECHNOLOGY POLICIES

This section analyzes the data on the spatial distribution of expenditures on state technology policies in eight states in order to test the
preceding arguments. The states are: Illinois, Indiana, Massachusetts,
Michigan, New York, North Carolina, Oregon, and Pennsylvania. Although these do not constitute a random sample of American states,
they do vary both by region of the United States and by economic
structure.

Expenditure data on the following types of programs were obtained
from each state: (1) state seed or venture capital investments in firms,
(2) efforts to help manufacturing firms modernize, (3) grants to university research centers, (4) grants to firms and universities to encourage closer collaboration, and (5) incubators and research parks.
For most programs, data were obtained on the distribution by county
of all grants and awards made between 1978 (or the year in which the
program was initiated) and 1987. Expenditures were summed across
programs, by county, to obtain an aggregate figure. Expenditures by
county, for individual programs and for the total, were then divided
by county employment in 1980 to obtain measures of expenditure
standardized by size of county.[17]

The rank-order correlation (Spearman's) can be examined between
the standardized measures of expenditures by county and two different measures of county-level economic well-being. The first measure

is the level of county per capita personal income in 1979.[18] This indicates how well-to-do the county was, on average, prior to implementation of most state technology programs during the time period covered. The second measure is the percentage of families in poverty in 1979 (U.S. Bureau of the Census 1983). This measure provides an indicator of the incidence of pockets of chronic economic distress among the county's resident population.

In addition to assessing the correlation between the program expenditures and county economic well-being, the degree to which expenditures are spatially concentrated can also be measured. A concentration index measures how evenly expenditures are spread throughout the state, or how concentrated they are in a few areas.

State Technology Policy Expenditures and Economic Well-Being

The hypothesis is that regionally based technology programs exacerbate spatial economic inequality within regions. The evidence from the eight states generally supports this view, but not consistently, and with some qualifiers. The results of the rank-order correlations are summarized in tables 15.3 and 15.4.

These tables provide evidence that in six of the eight states, technology program expenditures, in general, have favored the most affluent counties, either as measured by per capita income or the incidence of poverty. In one state, Massachusetts, there is no statistically significant relationship. In another, Pennsylvania, two types of technology programs have favored the more affluent areas, but one type, manufacturing modernization assistance, has favored the less affluent and more distressed counties.

In terms of total technology program expenditures, there is a statistically significant relationship in the hypothesized direction with at least one of the two measures of county economic well-being in five of the eight states. The correlations are strongest in Oregon and North Carolina. Among the eight states, those two have perhaps the greatest degree of intrastate income inequality, and the largest disparities between metropolitan and nonmetropolitan areas in infrastructure, education, and economic base. In New York, Pennsylvania, and Massachusetts, wide intracounty variation in economic well-being may be one explanation for statistically insignificant relationships. That is, some of the largest cities in these states—for example, New York, Rochester, Pittsburgh, Philadelphia, and Boston—have pockets of both the wealthiest and poorest populations, but also have the greatest concentration of resources with which to support technology-based

Table 15.3 RELATIONSHIP BETWEEN TECHNOLOGY PROGRAM EXPENDITURES AND THE INCIDENCE OF POVERTY, BY COUNTY, SELECTED STATES

State	Total	Type of Program				N
		Venture Capital	Manufacturing Modernization	Support for Research	University/Business Collaboration	
Illinois	−0.18*	−0.20**				102
Indiana	−0.19*	−0.05	−0.18*	−0.18*		92
Massachusetts	0.11	0.03		0.17		14
Michigan	−0.23**	−0.12	−0.17		−0.20*	83
New York	−0.03	−0.20	−0.13	0.08		62
North Carolina	−0.26**	−0.30**		−0.17*		100
Oregon	−0.42**					36
Pennsylvania	0.08	−0.21*	0.35**	−0.26**		67

Notes: (1) Numbers are Spearman rank-correlation estimates; (2) Poverty is measured as percentage of families below the poverty line, 1980 (U.S. Bureau of the Census 1983); (3) Expenditure data are from 1978–87; (4) Two asterisks (**), significant at the 0.05 level; (5) One asterisk (*), significant at the 0.10 level.

Table 15.4 RELATIONSHIP BETWEEN PER CAPITA INCOME AND TECHNOLOGY PROGRAM EXPENDITURES, BY COUNTY, SELECTED STATES

			Type of Program			
State	Total	Venture Capital	Manufacturing Modernization	Support for Research	University/Business Collaboration	N
Illinois	−0.25**	−0.26**				102
Indiana	0.17	0.17	0.14	0.23**		92
Massachusetts	−0.08	0.10		−0.44		14
Michigan	0.15	0.27**	0.12			83
New York	0.10	0.30**	0.23*	0.08	0.19*	62
North Carolina	0.36**	0.34**		0.33**		100
Oregon	0.44**					36
Pennsylvania	−0.09	0.28**	−0.32**	0.31**		67

Notes: (1) Numbers are Spearman rank-correlation estimates; (2) Income data are for 1980 (U.S. Bureau of Economic Analysis tapes); (3) Expenditure data are from 1978–87; (4) Two asterisks (**), significant at the 0.05 level; (5) One asterisk (*), significant at the 0.10 level.

economic development. In the case of Pennsylvania, differences in spatial distribution of expenditures by program type dilute the significance of the relationship for total expenditures.

The relationship between expenditures for the provision of venture capital and other forms of assistance to start up businesses, and at least one measure of economic well-being, are positive and significant in five of the seven states where program expenditure data are available. In the other two states, Massachusetts and Indiana, there is no significant relationship.

Expenditures to support basic or applied research in specific technology areas are positively and significantly correlated with county economic well-being in three of the five states where data are available. Correlations are not significant for Massachusetts, again, and New York, perhaps because of intracounty variation in economic well-being. Also in Massachusetts, Hampshire County, the location of the main state university campus (Amherst), received a disproportionately large expenditure for its small size, and thus represents an outlier in a state where there are only fourteen units of observation. In Michigan, where there are separate data on expenditures to support university-business collaborations, the correlation of expenditures and economic well-being is positive and significant.

Expenditures for modernization of existing manufacturing facilities are positively and significantly correlated in two of the four states for which data are available. The results demonstrate the point I discussed earlier: that *within* states, existing manufacturing establishments in need of modernization tend to be located within areas of higher economic distress, caused in part by the economic restructuring process, and partially explainable by product cycle theory. In the Northeast and North Central states, the areas with the highest concentrations of manufacturing, although often distressed, also have strengths—such as access to skilled labor and agglomeration economies—that provide reasonable expectations of program effectiveness. That is perhaps most clear in Pennsylvania, where there is a significant and negative relationship between manufacturing modernization expenditures and county economic well-being.

Spatial Concentration of State Technology Programs

Although state technology programs generally exacerbate spatial inequality, they also contribute to a spatial concentration of economic activities. This is especially evident at the national level, where half the obligations for federal R&D go to only four states, and 75 percent

Table 15.5 SPATIAL CONCENTRATION OF EXPENDITURES ON STATE
TECHNOLOGY PROGRAMS

Illinois	82
Indiana	95
Massachusetts	80
Michigan	95
New York	97
North Carolina	100
Oregon	100
Pennsylvania	87

of all federal obligations go to states with only 50 percent of the population (Atkinson 1988). A similar, but even more extreme, pattern occurs at the state level. The proportion of all state technology expenditures going to counties that cumulatively account for one-half the state's population ranges from 80 percent to 100 percent among the six states. *All* the expenditures in North Carolina and Oregon go to counties that together comprise 50 percent or less of the state's population (see table 15.5).

SUMMARY AND IMPLICATIONS FOR POLICY

Considerable policy attention has been focused on technology development programs in the United States and other industrialized countries, especially in the past several years. This chapter has sought to assess the effectiveness of those programs as economic development policy, particularly in terms of their ability to reduce regional economic disparities. Few analyses of this type have been performed ex ante, largely because policy makers have placed independent symbolic value on technology programs, and ex post, because of data limitations.

The particular impetus (other than for their symbolic value) for technology development programs varies from country to country, but generally, these programs were intended to help declining regions overcome economic problems associated with the process of restructuring. The "conventional wisdom," according to Malecki (1988: 4), is that "where R&D takes place, production will also take place, generating jobs and economic growth. . . . Since it is basic research from which innovation ultimately flows, basic research is a necessary object of policy."

The argument in the previous section three was that the logic of most types of technology programs works against balanced growth. By their nature, many technology programs help the strongest (core) regions at the expense of the periphery. In short, viable technology-oriented firms require locations in places with good endowments of skilled labor and physical and social infrastructure, whether those businesses are recruited, newly established, or expanding.

Not surprisingly, the data that were reviewed on regional economic outcomes in the United States (section two) indicate that intra- and interregional economic disparities have at least persisted, and in some cases, grown worse over time. Metropolitan (core) areas, especially with high-tech economic bases, generally have fared better than non-metropolitan (peripheral) areas. This was illustrated for the United States with national personal income data, and with county data for three sample states. It is discussed in the literature for other countries. Hilpert (1989: 15–16), for example, has said:

> Economic development in the industrialized countries is very much characterized by differences in the spatial pattern of techno-industrial innovation. . . . In Great Britain there is a strong concentration of the growing industries in the South East, close to London. . . . In West Germany . . . the situation is very similar. . . . In France . . . there is the crisis of the industrial regions in the Lorraine and Nord-Pas-de-Calais [and] the dominating position of the Ile-de-France was reinforced . . . . [And] in Italy . . . the pre-existing dominating position of the North remained unchanged.

The challenge in this chapter has been to relate these persistent disparities to technology policy, when, in fact, they could reflect other forces in the economy and the institutional framework. Because the necessary data to solve this attribution problem are not available, less formal methods were used to build a body of circumstantial evidence. One piece of that evidence came from correlation analysis (section four), which suggested that technology program expenditures have favored the most affluent counties in six of eight sample American states, and that such expenditures contribute to a spatial concentration of economic activity interregionally. Similar conclusions are drawn for European countries by Neumann (1989), Henschel (1990), Hilpert (1989, 1990) and others.

The conclusions here are similar in some respects to those of Downs in chapter 2 of this volume. He likewise argues that governmental fragmentation and the absence of a coherent national development policy in the United States have contributed to economic disparities between and within regions. He contrasts the U.S. approach to economic development (what he calls a "nonstrategy") to the European mode, which generally ascribes a stronger role to a central government. However, it is important to note that central government responsibility for economic development policy making varies among European countries. In some countries, notably Germany, there has been a similar devolution of economic development policy making to that which has occurred in the United States. Downs agrees that in these cases it is increasingly difficult to attain the goal of balanced regional growth.

Assuming the conclusions in this chapter are valid, what do they imply about public policy? Is technology policy an inappropriate means to economic development? The answer to this question is a cautious no. The literature reviewed here suggests that technology programs can be effective in stimulating regional growth, subject to the following caveats:

1. Not all programs are appropriate for all regions. Some technologies can thrive only in the presence of essential social and physical infrastructure, or where there already is a concentration of related activity.
2. Many peripheral regions that are now barren can be fertilized into productive seedbeds via some of the technology development programs discussed here. However, within any national economy, there can only be a limited number of growth poles.

These caveats raise a critical issue regarding the necessity for some central coordination and regulation for technology policy to work. In the United States, this coordination and regulation is absent. States tend to use technology programs as a means to compete for a fixed amount of technology activity. Osborne (1988, 1989) and others argue that this competition is efficient because it serves as a testing ground for ideas, with good ideas surviving and bad ones dying. However, because ex post analysis of programs usually is not done, there is little basis for judging what constitutes "good" compared to "bad" programs. Moreover, in a system in which financial responsibility is devolved to the regions (as in the United States), wealthier regional governments are able to spend more on technology programs. If those programs have any stimulative effect, disparities will be exacerbated. Finally, in a fully decentralized system, no hard choices are made about the number, nature, and location of growth poles. That leads to an oversupply of technology parks, technology corridors, and other spatially based technology policies.

The conclusion that seems to emerge from this is that the intergovernmental framework for the conveyance of technology policy is as important as the programs themselves. The substantial devolution of responsibility that has occurred in the United States, and, to a somewhat lesser degree, in Germany, compounds the tendency for technology programs to exacerbate economic disparities. The models used in France and Japan—where regional governments are administrative arms of the central government and formal frameworks exist for intergovernmental cooperation—seem much more suitable. Indeed, the nascent analytic literature on the French and Japanese experience indicates generally positive outcomes (see Kawashima and Stöhr 1988; Perrin 1988).

This conclusion about the importance of the intergovernmental framework is particularly timely in light of the growing demands for regional autonomy, not only in such places as Spain, Italy, and the United Kingdom, where regionalism has been an issue for some years, but also in Eastern Europe and the former Soviet Union.

APPENDIX: DATA SOURCES

The specific technology programs for which county-level expenditure data were requested are, by state:

Illinois—Equity Investment Fund; Business Innovation Fund; university-based incubators and miscellaneous university research funded by the Governor's Commission on Science and Technology.

Indiana—Corporation for Science and Technology research grants; Corporation for Innovation Development venture capital grants; and firms assisted by the Purdue University Technology Assessment Program.

Massachusetts—Centers of Excellence grants to firms and universities; Technology Development Corporation venture capital investments; Product Development Corporation grants.

Michigan—Research Excellence Fund university research grants; Technology Transfer Network university centers; seed capital investments; research centers; and firms assisted by the Michigan Modernization Service.

New York—SBIR grants to firms; Corporation for Innovation Development venture capital investments; Centers for Advanced Tech-

nology at universities; regional Technology Development Organizations; Industrial Effectiveness Program assistance to firms.

North Carolina—Biotechnology Center research grants; Technology
Development Authority product development grants.

Oregon—Research and Technology Development Corporation seed
capital investments and applied research grants.

Pennsylvania—Ben Franklin Challenge Grant Program research
grants; Ben Franklin seed grants; Engineering Equipment
Grants to universities; Industrial Resource Centers and the
Pennsylvania Technology Assessment Program for manufacturing modernization.

Notes

Much of the research on which this paper is based was done in collaboration with
Harvey A. Goldstein and with the financial support of the Ford Foundation and the
Forum for Higher Education Financing. The author alone is responsible for any errors
of fact or interpretation contained herein.

1. In the United States, it is common for elected officials to "sell" technology programs
to the public and legislators by describing technology as "the goose that lays the golden
egg" (see Luger 1981).

2. Figures from Clark and Dobson's (1989) table were inflated by the ratio of survey
responses to the population.

3. Markusen et al. (1988) is the most recent in a series of published studies tracing the
distinct regional effects of defense spending.

4. More than these ten parks opened during the 1970s, but many failed.

5. These writers attribute the resurgence to a lack of confidence in the federal government (the "post-Watergate" phenomenon), state constitutional and institutional re-
forms, and a strengthening of intergovernmental lobbies, as well as to an effort to fill a
funding void.

6. In some states the line between private and public universities is blurred by large
subsidies paid to the private institutions or their students.

7. The survey was administered by Harvey Goldstein and myself in July 1989.

8. This program is stipulated in the 1982 Research Bill (see Neumann 1989: 212).

9. Neumann (1989) showed that one region, Rhône-Alpes, spent 50 million Fr. on
projects in 1986, compared to 2.5 billion Fr. spent by the central government in that
region (or 0.2 percent).

10. Sections three and four of this chapter draw heavily from an unpublished paper I
wrote jointly with Harvey Goldstein and Robert Atkinson (Luger, Goldstein, and Atkinson 1990).

11. For an international, political-economic perspective, see Ulrich Hilpert (1990).

12. These regions are named differently than those referred to earlier in the chapter. Far West corresponds to the Pacific region, Middle Atlantic is subsumed within the Mideast region, and the Midwest is included within the Plains. The West South Central states in the U.S. Bureau of the Census classification are divided here between Southeast and Southwest.

13. The indices were all relative to the national mean for the relevant year, so that comparisons over time are not misleading. This procedure is similar to calculating the coefficient of variation.

14. The discussion here is limited to programs centered on businesses and regions. For that reason, patenting and licensing and education programs are omitted. Arguments similar to those made here could be advanced for these other types of programs (see Robert Atkinson 1989).

15. Klausner (1988) argued that university-industry research relationships are inappropriate and need to be restructured.

16. Luger and Goldstein (1991) have calculated that counties with research parks (mostly dating from 1982) had an average employment growth rate between 1976 and 1985 that was 85 percent higher than the respective statewide employment growth rate for the same period.

17. Not all eight states had programs in all categories, and in some cases expenditure data were not available on a county, or other substate, basis. As a result, correlations were calculated for four specific types of technology-based economic development programs, in addition to the total. The specific program types included in the analysis are: manufacturing modernization programs; venture capital and other programs to help new business startups; support for basic and applied research in targeted technology areas; and support for university-business collaborations.

18. Personal income data, by place of residence, provided by the U.S. Department of Commerce, Bureau of Economic Analysis, Washington, D.C., on magnetic tape.

References

Atkinson, Robert. 1988. *Science and Technology Trends in the South.* Research Triangle Park, N.C.: Southern Growth Policies Board.
_____. 1989. *Some States Take the Lead: Explaining the Formation of State Technology Policies.* Ph.D. diss., University of North Carolina, Chapel Hill.
Barke, Richard P. 1986. *Science, Technology, and Public Policy.* Washington, D.C.: Congressional Quarterly Press.
_____. 1988. "Technology and Economic Development in the States: Continuing Experiments in Growth Management." In *Growth Policy in an Age of High Technology: The Role of Regions and State Governments,* edited by Jürgen Schmandt and Robert Wilson. Lyndon Baines Johnson School of Public Affairs, University of Texas, Austin. Photocopy.
Bergman, Edward M. 1989. *Industrial Transition Paths.* Final Report to the U.S. Economic Development Administration, Department of Com-

merce. Chapel Hill, N.C.: Department of City and Regional Planning, University of North Carolina.

Bowman, Ann O'M., and Richard C. Kearney. 1986. *The Resurgence of the States.* Englewood Cliffs, N.J.: Prentice-Hall.

Clark, Gordon. 1988. "Corporate Restructuring in the Steel Industry: Adjustment Strategies and Local Labor Relations." In *America's New Market Geography: Nation, Region, and Metropolis,* edited by George Sternlieb and James Hughes. New Brunswick, N.J.: Center for Urban and Regional Policy, Rutgers University.

Clark, Mariann, and Eric Dobson. 1989. *Promoting Technological Excellence: The Role of State and Federal Extension Activities.* Washington, D.C.: National Governors' Association.

Coburn, Christopher, ed., and Dan Bergland. 1995. *Partnerships: A Compendium of State and Federal Cooperative Technology Programs,* Columbus, Ohio: Battelle Press.

Dill, David. 1989. "University/Industry Research Collaboration: An Analysis of Interorganizational Relationships." School of Education, University of North Carolina, Chapel Hill. Photocopy.

Dill, David, Harvey Goldstein, and Michael Luger. 1990. "Universities and Technology Development." Department of City and Regional Planning, University of North Carolina, Chapel Hill, July. Photocopy.

Dupree, A. Hunter. 1957. *Science in the Federal Government: A History of Politics and Activities to 1940.* Cambridge, Mass.: Belknap Press of Harvard University Press.

Edelman, M. 1964. *The Symbolic Uses of Politics.* Chicago: University of Illinois Press.

———. 1971. *Politics as Symbolic Action.* Chicago: Markham Publishing Co.

Feller, Irwin. 1972. "State Support of Research and Development: An Uncertain Path to Economic Growth." *Land Economics* 48: 220–27.

———. 1988. "University-Industry Research and Development Relationships." *Growth Policy in an Age of High Technology: The Role of Regions and State Governments,* edited by Jürgen Schmandt and Robert Wilson (chap. 13). Lyndon Baines Johnson School of Public Affairs, University of Texas. Photocopy.

Fowler, D. 1984. "University-Industry Research Relationships: The Research Agreement." *Journal of College and University Law* 9: 515–31.

Franco, M. R. 1985. *Key Success Factors for University-Related Research Parks.* Ph.D. diss., University of Rochester, Rochester, N.Y.

Goldstein, Harvey A. 1990. "Regional Policies, the State, and the Patterns of Regional Economic Development: The Case of the Postwar United States." *Revue d'Economic Regionale et Urbaine* 5: 655–81.

Greenberg, Daniel C. 1967. *The Politics of Pure Science: An Inquiry into the Relationship between Science and Government in the United States.* New York: Plume Books.

Haller, H. 1984. *Examples of University–Industry (Government) Collaborations.* Ithaca, N.Y.: Cornell University Press.

Harrison, Bennett, and Sandra Kanter. 1978. "The Political Economy of State Job Creation Incentives." *Journal of the American Institute of Planners* (Oct.): 424–35.

Heckman, John S., and Rosalind Greenstein. 1985. "Factors Affecting Manufacturing Location in North Carolina and the South Atlantic." In *High Hopes for High Tech: Planning for the Microelectronics Industry in North Carolina,* edited by Dale Whittington. Chapel Hill: University of North Carolina Press.

Henschel, Carsten. 1990. "State Strategies of Research and Industry Policy in the Federal Republic of Germany." Department of City and Regional Planning, University of North Carolina, Chapel Hill, June. Photocopy.

Hilpert, Ulrich. 1989. "Regional Policy in the Process of Industrial Modernisation: Decentralization of Innovation by Regionalization of High Tech?" In *Regional Innovation and Decentralization,* edited by Ulrich Hilpert. London: Routledge, Chapman and Hall.

————. 1990. "Techno-Industrial Innovation, Social Development, and State Policies." *International Political Science Review* 11(1): 75–86.

Joseph, R. A. 1989. "Silicon Valley Myth and the Origins of Technology Parks in Australia." *Science and Public Policy* 16 (6, Dec.): 353–65.

Kawashima, T., and W. Stöhr. 1988. "Decentralized Technology Policy: The Case of Japan." *Environment and Planning C: Government and Policy* 6: 427–39.

Klausner, Samuel Z. 1988. "Dilemmas of Usefulness: Universities and Contract Research." Paper presented to the American Bar Foundation, April 18.

Luger, Michael I. 1981. "Microelectronics: The Economic Hope—Promises and Policies." *NCInsight* 4(3).

————. 1984. "Does North Carolina's High Tech Development Program Work?" *Journal of the American Planning Association* 50(3): 280–90.

————. 1985. "The States and High Tech Development: The Base of North Carolina." In *High Hopes for High Tech: Planning for the Microelectronics Industry in North Carolina,* edited by Dale Whittington. Chapel Hill: University of North Carolina Press.

————. 1987. "State Subsidies for Industrial Development: Program Mix and Policy Effectiveness." In *Perspectives on Local Public Finance and Public Policy,* edited by John Quigley. Greenwich, Conn.: JAI Press.

Luger, Michael I., and Harvey A. Goldstein. 1991. *Technology in the Garden: Research Parks and Regional Economic Development.* Chapel Hill: University of North Carolina Press.

Luger, Michael I., Harvey A. Goldstein, and Robert D. Atkinson. 1990. "State Technology Policies, Economic Restructuring, and Uneven Growth in the United States." Department of City and Regional Planning, University of North Carolina, Chapel Hill. Photocopy.

Malecki, Edward J. 1980. "Dimensions of R&D Location in the United States." *Research Policy* 9: 2–22.

————. 1984. "High Technology and Local Economic Development." *Journal of the American Planning Association* 50: 262–69.

————. 1987a. "The R&D Location Decision of the Firm and 'Creative' Regions." *Technovation* 6: 205–22.

————. 1987b. "Regional Economic Development and State Science Policy." Paper presented at the National Science Foundation PRA Workshop on State Science Policy Research, Washington, D.C., September.

————. 1988. "Technological Innovation and Paths to Regional Economic Growth." In *Growth Policy in an Age of High Technology: The Role of Regions and State Governments*, edited by Jürgen Schmandt and Robert Wilson (chap. 5). Lyndon Baines Johnson School of Public Affairs, University of Texas, Austin. Photocopy.

Malecki, Edward J., and Peter Nijkamp. 1989. "Technology and Regional Development: Some Thoughts on Policy." *Environment and Planning C: Government and Policy* 6.

Markusen, Ann, Peter Hall, and Amy Glasmeier. 1986. *High Tech America: The What, How, Where, and Why of the Sunrise Industries*. Boston: Allen and Unwin.

Markusen, Ann, Peter Hall, Sabina Dietrich, and Scott Campbell. 1988. *The Rise of the Gunbelt*. Evanston, Ill.: Center for Urban Affairs and Policy Research, Northwestern University.

Neumann, Wolfgang. 1989. "Politics of Decentralization and Industrial Modernisation—France and West Germany in Comparison." In *Regional Innovation and Decentralization*, edited by Ulrich Hilpert. London: Routledge, Chapman and Hall.

Oakey, R. P. 1981. *High Technology Industry and Industrial Location*. Hampshire, England: Gower Publishing Co.

Office of Science and Technology, Minnesota Department of Trade and Economic Development. 1988. *State Technology Programs in the United States, 1988*. St. Paul, Minn.: Author. July.

Osborne, David. 1988. *Laboratories of Democracy*. Boston: Harvard Business School Press.

————. 1989. *State Technology Programs: A Preliminary Analysis of Lessons Learned*. Washington, D.C.: CSPA, November.

Paget, Karen M. 1988. "State Government/University Cooperation" In *Growth Policy in an Age of High Technology: The Role of Regions and State Governments*, edited by Jürgen Schmandt and Robert Wilson (chap. 14). Lyndon Baines Johnson School of Public Affairs, University of Texas, Austin. Photocopy.

Perrin, J. C. 1988. "A Deconcentrated Technology Policy—Lessons from the Sophia-Antipolis Experience." *Environment and Planning C: Government and Policy* 6: 415–25.

Peters, L., and H. Fusfeld. 1983. "Current U.S. University/Industry Research Connections." In National Science Foundation, *University-Industry*

Research Relationships: Selected Studies. Washington, D.C.: National Science Board.

Praeger, D., and G. Omenn. 1980. "Research, Innovation, and University-Industry Linkages." *Science* 207 (Jan.)

Premus, R. 1982. *Location of High Technology Firms and Regional Economic Development.* Washington, D.C.: U.S. Government Printing Office.

Schechter, H. 1988. "Global Imbalances and the Metropolitan Economy." In *America's New Market Geography: Nation, Region and Metropolis,* edited by George Sternlieb and James Hughes. New Brunswick, N.J.: Center for Urban and Regional Policy, Rutgers University.

Schmandt, Jürgen. 1988. "Regional Roles in the Governance of the Scientific State." In *Growth Policy in an Age of High Technology: The Role of Regions and State Governments,* edited by Jürgen Schmandt and Robert Wilson. Lyndon Baines Johnson School of Public Affairs, University of Texas. Photocopy.

Schmandt, Jürgen, and Robert Wilson. 1988. "State Science and Technology Policies: An Assessment." *Economic Development Quarterly* 2(2, May): 124–37.

Szanton, Peter. 1981. *Not Well Advised.* New York: Russell Sage and Ford Foundations.

Tatsuno, Sheridan. 1989. "Building the Japanese Techno-State: The Regionalization of Japanese High Tech Industrial Policies." In *Regional Innovation and Decentralization,* edited by Ulrich Hilpert (231–50). London: Routledge, Chapman and Hall.

U.S. Bureau of the Census. 1983. *County and City Data Book.* Washington, D.C.: U.S. Government Printing Office.

————. 1989a. *Statistical Abstract of the United States, 1989.* Washington, D.C.: U.S. Government Printing Office.

————. 1989b. *Survey of Current Business, 1989.* Washington, D.C.: U.S. Government Printing Office.

————. 1996. *Survey of Current Business, 1996.* Washington, D.C.: U.S. Government Printing Office.

U.S. Office of Management and Budget. 1996. *1997 Budget of the United States, Government Analytical Perspectives.* Washington, D.C.: U.S. Government Printing Office.

Vaughan, Roger. 1980. "State Tax Incentives: How Effective Are They?" *Commentary* 4 (1, Jan.).

Wasylenko, Michael. 1985. "Business Climate, Industry, and Employment Growth: A Review of the Evidence." Metropolitan Studies Program Occasional Paper 90. Syracuse, N.Y.: Maxwell School, Syracuse University.

Watkins, C. B. 1985. *Programs for Innovative Technology Research in State Strategies for Economic Development.* Washington, D.C.: National Governors' Association. February.

Chapter Sixteen

DECENTRALIZATION AND RESIDENTIAL CHOICES IN EUROPEAN CITIES: THE ROLES OF STATE AND MARKET

Duncan Maclennan

Research on the decentralization of employment and population from European and American cities has focused largely on the identification of patterns of spatial change. Such research has had to overcome a paucity of appropriate spatially and temporally referenced data. These efforts have contributed greatly to the understanding of contemporary urbanization.

However, the concentration upon broad outcomes has contributed to at least two important gaps in knowledge. First, the broad subdivision of urban space into inner city, periphery, or whatever, has concealed both opportunities and problems for urban policies. Not all neighborhoods close to city centers are devastated and declining in population, nor are all suburbs or metropolitan edge centers affluent or growing. In essence, at the level at which urban microeconomic models are specified, and indeed housing policy initiatives undertaken, there is a mosaic of residential/neighborhood choices and issues for policies that are often ignored in more aggregative analyses. Second, in the absence of systematic understanding of the microeconomic basis for decentralization decisions, there is room for uncertainty in the academic discussion of both the trigger "causes" of spatial change and the cumulative (or otherwise) dynamic of ensuing developments. In analyzing residential location choices, potentially key influences such as dwelling size, dwelling age, location relative to workplace, racial composition of neighborhoods, and so forth, are often highly colinear (especially when aggregated to zonal levels). It may then be likely that the "causality" of change is either difficult to identify or "preferred" on various theoretical criteria.

The conventional wisdom on decentralization in many European contexts, especially Britain, disregards problems of spatial aggregation and uncertainty of causal mechanisms. Put crudely, it is that deindustrialization and employment decentralization have had an adverse impact upon the incomes and employment probabilities of core city residents, leaving poorer and older populations in the urban core. Residents with jobs and growing incomes decentralize as suburban housing markets offer higher housing and neighborhood quality as well as larger space units at lower prices (standardizing for the mix of housing characteristics), and this price/quality combination offsets the direct and time costs of commuting longer distances to job centers.

In brief, the prevailing "theoretical" view of urban decentralization is essentially the same in Europe and the United States. This conceptual view explains shifts in employment and income by urban economic base theory and the consequential residential location choices by a generalized access-space trade-off model within a central-business-district-dominated, unitary metropolitan housing market. This perception of the world embodies a pessimistic future for many core urban areas and is based on the presumption that market forces lead change. Accordingly, growth in private-sector productivity is, in a very general sense, the key to urban regeneration.

Such an emphasis may well be appropriate in North America. It may also be a predominant explanation for some European cities. But, as I argue here, there are a number of major European cities for which this explanation may be a minor, rather than a major, factor in postwar patterns of spatial change. It ignores the possibility that policy actions, particularly in housing and planning, have led and sustained population loss from core urban areas. By implication, increases in state "productivity," largely by reversing anti-core policies, may halt or even reverse population decentralization.

This chapter examines the impact of housing policies in Western Europe, particularly Great Britain, on urban spatial structure and decentralization. That is, the concern is to illuminate how state action has shaped developments now regarded as problematic.

THE EUROPEAN SWEEP OF HOUSING POLICIES

The European urban context for housing markets and policies varies both across and within countries; it is also manifestly different from that in North America. There are obvious historical differences. On the one hand, many major European cities contain historic prestigious neighborhoods in the urban core that have never "filtered down." On the other hand, the early, rapid industrialization of some cities prior to public transport development created dense, low-quality slums that were infinitely poorer in quality than working-class housing developed in American cities after 1890. This latter historical inheritance created an early European imperative for government housing action. It is, of course, the long-standing scale and form of policy intervention in housing and land markets that most distinguishes European (Mediterranean countries excepted) and American systems and cities. The broad shape of these differences in the postwar period is indicated in table 16.1.

Rent controls, with long periods of rent freeze or prices set below those that would secure economic returns and associated security of tenure rights, were introduced in Britain and Ireland in 1915. German-speaking countries commonly put them in place after 1935. France and the Iberian countries introduced them by 1949 and the Scandi-

Table 16.1 HOUSING TENURES IN ADVANCED ECONOMIES, CIRCA 1980

Country	Overall Split		Date of First Rent Controls if Known	Rental Split	
	Owned[a] (%)	Rented (%)		Private Rented (%)	Social Rented (%)
West Germany	40	60	1935	70	30
Switzerland	30	70	—	80	20
Turkey	81	19	—	96	4
Greece	72	28	1980	95	5
Australia	70	30	—	94	6
Finland	71	29	—	91	9
Belgium	61	39	1939	87	13
Portugal	59	41	1947	89	11
Austria	58	42	1935	81	19
Canada	62	38	1979	80	20
United States	65	35	1919	85	15
New Zealand	71	29	1952	78	22
Spain	77	23	1948	75	25
Norway	75	25	—	74	26
France	55	45	1948	66	34
Italy	60	40	—	63	37
Japan	62	38	—	61	39
Denmark	56	44	1930s	47	53
Ireland	75	25	—	45	55
Sweden	58	42	1930s	33	67
United Kingdom	61	39	1915	30	70
Netherlands	44	56	1930s	25	75

Sources: United Nations/ECE (1985) and BSA (1986).

[a]Includes cooperative ownership.

navian countries by 1950. Given that private rental housing was the major form of urban housing provision in European cities until the 1950s, decades (even half-centuries) of national policies for control have had a major impact upon the quality and status of core-area housing until the present time. This impact has varied in context as the nature of rent controls has differed across countries. In Spain and Portugal, for instance, rents were frozen in nominal terms from 1949 to the 1980s; in Britain the pricing system ("Fair Rents") generated returns below "economic" levels from 1965 to 1988; and over the same two decades, the Federal Republic of Germany, and Denmark raised rent levels to allow investors "economic" rates of return.

Many European countries have attempted not merely to suppress the price mechanism but have also, via the provision of social housing, supplanted them. By the end of the 1970s, Germany, France, Italy, and Denmark had about one-fifth of households in nonmarket housing; for Britain, Sweden, and the Netherlands, the proportion was between 30 percent and 40 percent (see table 16.2).

This point finds reinforcement in that, like the private rental sector, social housing can have marked spatial concentrations. Social housing provision, given its raison d'être, has not been uniformly spread

Table 16.2 EVOLUTION OF OWNER OCCUPATION AS A PERCENTAGE OF TOTAL HOUSING

	1950 (%)	1970 (%)	1980 (%)	More Recent
United States	55	63	65	65 (1983)
Canada	—	60	62	—
Australia	54	69	70	—
Ireland	—	67	73	—
Japan	—	60	60	62 (1983)
Austria	36	41	53	51 (1982)
Belgium	39	55	60	—
Denmark	—	49	52	—
Finland	56	60	64	—
France	36	45	47	52 (1982)
West Germany	—	36	37	50 (1982)
Netherlands	29	35	45	44 (1982)
Norway	—	53	65[a]	67 (1983)
Sweden	—	35	42[a]	—
Switzerland	—	28	30	—
Italy	40	51	58	—
Spain	50	64	77	—

[a]Figures for Norway include cooperative owners, but they are excluded from the Swedish total.

within the national economic space. Rather, it has often been concentrated in the cities and regions where low incomes indicated either an outdated economic base, ripe for deindustrialization, or where employment decentralization had commenced. For instance, in Britain the northern regions commonly had a tenure share (by 1970) of 45–50 percent of households in the social sector. Scotland, which in 1970 was the highest unemployment rate of any region of Great Britain, had 62 percent of its households in public housing, and in Glasgow, then Britain's poorest and fastest declining city, this proportion was 66 percent. As late as 1980, every core city of more than 500,000 population in Britain had half of its residents in council housing. The dominant form of housing production and allocation there was not the market, but municipal monopolies.

This massive-scale social housing investment had major intra-urban impacts upon the quality, type, and spatial pattern of low- and middle-income residential choices in Europe. The development of social housing, especially after 1945, usually implied the clearance of war-damaged sites, the use of greenfield sites nearer the edge of the municipal area, and, with the post-1960 development of high rises, the reutilization of cleared core-area slum sites (previously occupied by low-income private rental units). Such policies in Britain and Europe were aimed at reducing core-area populations, and this process deliberately suburbanized low-income residents.

The spatial and population impacts of social housing have not been restricted to the developmental phase. Housing developments had potentially adverse, enduring labor-market impacts by attracting workers away from "convenient" locations through deep housing subsidies. And subsequent housing allocation and maintenance policies, as discussed later in this chapter, have, in some instances, turned the "innovative" housing developments of the 1950s into the key urban problem areas of the 1980s. Further, as large public sectors often had local political mix effects, then-anti-owner occupation stances by municipalities may have contributed to suburbanization of owner-occupiers as ownership options were restricted in core urban areas.

In the owner-occupied sectors, most European countries until the 1980s had less generous tax breaks for homeowners than in the United States, and there were fewer special low-cost homeownership programs—though in this respect, Britain is a major exception. At least until the 1970s, therefore, policies for the owner-occupied sector in combination with tight land-zoning policies (in many European countries) were less likely to encourage decentralization than in the United States. Indeed, the general trends have been that deconcentration away from metropolitan areas—assumed to be inevitable in the published literature of the 1980s—appears to have widely slowed and reversed in some countries. Further, across a wide range of European city-regions, household numbers in core city areas have stabilized or increased in many cities. A marked increase in central city households has occurred in some cities.

This introductory section has emphasized, in broad terms, the different roles of state and market in European as opposed to American cities. The next section addresses some of these key notions in more depth, based on household survey data for 1988 for six British urban regions delimited by travel-to-work patterns. The patterns reported illustrate how the simple geographies associated with core-periphery and access-space model assumptions form a doubtful basis for understanding British patterns of urban residential choice and change, and, by implication, European urban systems with extensive social housing sectors. The third section explores in more detail how housing policies have influenced housing choices in the city of Glasgow, with particular reference to decentralization impacts. The fourth section indicates how pro-urban housing policies, which have become more commonplace in the 1980s, have reversed some well-established patterns of core-area decline in Glasgow. A brief conclusion ends the chapter.

SPATIAL STRUCTURE OF SIX BRITISH HOUSING SYSTEMS

Housing policy researchers are well familiar with the observations that housing policies can influence residential decentralization decisions and that, in a broad sense, the European policy mix differs from that in North America. However, to advance beyond these generalizations, it is important first to have a clear view of the spatial structure of European housing markets and then to establish the impact of policies on that structure. Appropriate data and analytical studies of residential decentralization do not exist for many European cities. It is now possible, however, to examine the general spatial structure of six British urban housing systems, which is the task of this section. Detailed spatial impacts of policies are examined for Glasgow in the next section.

Six British Housing Systems

As part of a larger study of the incidence and impact of the housing finance and subsidy system in Britain, the Joseph Rowntree Foundation funded detailed local case studies in six British urban areas. The six urban areas (Inner London, Bristol, Birmingham, Sheffield, Newcastle, and Glasgow) were chosen to reflect the variety of British urban housing systems. The areas selected were not defined by the administrative borders of "core" municipalities but were the travel-to-work areas (TTWAs) around each core—broadly covering a distance of 20–25 kilometers (12–15 miles) from the CBD (with, on average, the municipal core occupying the 0–10 km rings) (see table 16.3). Within

Table 16.3 TENURE DISTRIBUTION AND SPATIAL RINGS: PROPORTION OF HOMEOWNERS BY RING (KILOMETERS FROM CENTRAL BUSINESS DISTRICT)

Spatial Ring	Birmingham	Bristol	Glasgow	London	Newcastle	Sheffield
1	0	46	20	23	4	0
2	8	66	3	10	29	44
3	36	56	34	46	38	48
4	63	67	36	38	54	57
5	57	62	42	37	42	55
6	75	70	28	36	48	47
7	66	64	36	31	44	55
8	53	66	41	30	82	61
9	63	91	48	31	40	72
10	63	91	43	64	49	80
11	69	63	45	73	59	54
12	69	86	40	59	77	100
13	76	83	43	53	58	65
14	96	77	37	70	71	66
15	86	94	33	66	71	83
16	100	88	39	95	75	100
17	80	89	31	75	92	—
18	25	100	40	76	47	—
19	38	86	72	90	89	67
20	67	86	50	61	100	56
21	73	—	43	74	40	100
22	60	—	100	87	44	—
23	68	—	—	72	83	—
24	67	90	83	72	—	—
25	100	57	—	71	—	—

Source: Joseph Rowntree Foundation survey, 1988.

each of the areas, which varied by population size, household surveys were completed for about 2,000 households; the samples reflected the housing and neighborhood characteristics within each TTWA.

Tenure Patterns

Tenure patterns in Britain reveal a great deal about the nature and intensity of intra-urban variations in housing policy impacts. The overall tenure shares of the six areas reflect the grand scale of state intervention in British cities. As indicated in table 16.4, the private rental sector, which constituted 90 percent of British urban housing in 1914, comprises only 11 percent of Inner London and is but 3 percent of Glasgow TTWA. In four of the six urban areas, social rental housing provides 30–40 percent of units, with Bristol (at 20 percent) and Glasgow (at 58 percent), respectively, reflecting more "private" and "public" cities. The owner-occupied sector, with the exception of Bristol, houses less than three out of five households. At the least, state action has had a *fundamental* effect upon the residential choice of 40 percent of households.

In the context of decentralization debates it is, of course, the intra-urban (or TTWA) structure of tenures that is more pertinent. In five of the six TTWAs, Bristol excepted, social rental housing dominates housing provision in the inner three kilometer rings; this observation alone calls into question the "conventional wisdom" outlined previously. The social sector also commonly provides the majority tenure in rings 5–9, reflecting a second wave of social investment; and even in the 15–25 kilometer rings, social housing often houses one-fifth of the population. The state has shaped the peripheral suburban areas as well as the heart and fringes of core cities. In the Glasgow TTWA, social housing dominates all of the 25-km rings around the CBD.

The converse is also true. In Bristol, owner occupation is the dominant sector in every ring. In the other areas, owner occupation is the majority tenure in ring 4 and then from rings 10 to 25. Private rental housing is never the majority tenure, usually peaking at 15 percent to 20 percent of stock in rings 2 and 3 before sharply leveling out to less than 5 percent. Naturally, successive kilometer rings house different proportions of a city's population, reflecting city size, land-use mix, and so forth. If proportions of total population in each ring are contrasted with the distribution of population in different tenures by rings, then three broad observations are apparent from table 16.5.

Table 16.4 TENURE OF HOUSING GROUP BY CASE STUDY AREA

	Birmingham (%)	Bristol (%)	Glasgow (%)	Inner London (%)	Newcastle (%)	Sheffield (%)	Total (%)
Owner	59.8	64.0	39.5	57.5	49.6	54.1	54.1
Local authority	25.9	16.1	54.4	25.7	35.2	35.7	32.2
Housing association	5.5	3.7	2.9	4.8	7.0	1.5	4.2
Private rent	8.2	15.4	3.1	11.3	7.2	8.3	8.9
Lodger/board	0.6	0.7	0.1	0.7	0.9	0.4	0.6
Column number	1,528	1,655	1,564	1,459	1,701	1,656	9,563
Total (%) row	16.0	17.3	16.4	15.3	17.8	17.3	100
Total (%) column	100	100	100	100	100	100	100

Table 16.5 DISTANCE RINGS AND PROPORTIONAL SPECIALIZATION OF TENURE SHARE (IN RELATION TO POPULATION SHARE)

	Owner Occupation						Social Renters					
Ring	A	B	C	D	E	F	A	B	C	D	E	F
0–5 km	−	−	−	−	−	−	+	=	+	+	+	+
6–10 km	=	+	−	−	−	=	=	+	+	+	+	+
11–15 km	+	+	=	+	+	+	−	−	−	−	−	−
16–20 km	=	+	+	+	+	=	+	−	−	−	−	−
> 21 km	+	+	+	+	=	=	−	=	−	−	=	=

Notes: (1) The 0–5 km and 6–10 km rings contain shares of social housing for the TWA greater than their total population share; (2) the 11–15 km and 16–20 km rings house shares of owner-occupiers for the TWA greater than their total shares of population; (3) the 21–25 km ring is more mixed.

Housing Costs, Types, Conditions

The "conventional wisdom," based on deductive economic models, implies that at increasing distances from the CBD there will be: (a) a falling share of densely developed dwelling types; (b) an increase in neighborhood quality; (c) an increase in dwelling size; and (d) a falling (hedonically adjusted) price for rooms, gardens, and so forth.

An analysis of the Rowntree data indicates that these relationships are quite weak upon examining the sample as a whole, without standardizing for zonal housing tenure. In a broad sense, state action appears to have "flattened out" the surfaces usually generated from a standard access-space model. Taking all households together, dwelling type and size do shift toward more detached and larger units in rings 4 to 9, but thereafter remain quite flat. Perceived (resident assessed) neighborhood quality is moderate in zones 1 to 3, rises in zones 4 to 6, then falls sharply in zones 7 to 9 (although Inner London does not fit this pattern), before rising and flattening from zones 10 to 25. This is an extremely important observation, given presumptions about inner city decline. Dwelling size, measured by the number of rooms, rises only marginally to ring 9, and thereafter remains constant until the edge of the TTWA, when a sharp increase is observed.

These patterns noted above were reanalyzed by examining the relevant patterns within the owner-occupied and social rental sectors. In the owner-occupied sector, the proportion of flatted dwellings (with the exceptions of Glasgow and London) exceeds 15 percent in the first 4 rings, then falls below 10 percent; but again the relationship is relatively flat until 20–25 km out. House size, after ring 4, remains broadly constant until the urban edge.

Dwelling prices and rents were analyzed separately for each tenure sector. Hedonic equations for all six case studies had a significant, negative relationship with distance from the CBD (at least from 4 km out), although the coefficients were relatively small.

The social sector had a markedly different spatial pattern. Flats dominated provision in rings 1 to 3, but even thereafter flats commonly comprised a quarter of social stock in each locale. House size was not sorted by distance from the CBD. Further, and this result is unsurprising to those familiar with administered pricing schemes, rent hedonics did not contain a significant distance-from-CBD price effect and, moreover, seldom explained more than a quarter of the variation in rents (in contrast to two-thirds in the owned sector).

Although the owner-occupied sector, therefore, did display some weak distance ordering effects, the absence of distance ordering in the social sector in relation to prices and structure types meant that the overall form of spatial relationships with the TTWA was much weaker than would have been anticipated in purely private cities.

Households

Household and head-of-household incomes were examined for each distance ring and housing tenure. For household incomes, the average for owner occupiers was above the city mean in rings 1 to 3; the average then fell, followed by a gradual rise through rings 4 to 20 before rising sharply in rings 21 to 25. For social renters there was a very gradual rise from rings 1 to 9, then a fall, and a general flattening to the edge of the TTWA. Once again, therefore, when aggregates were examined that incorporated all tenures, the overall distance/income relation was flattened with only a minimal gradient, except beyond ring 20, in average household income. The relationship was even flatter for head-of-household income, reflecting the propensity for smaller households to live nearer the CBD. Relevant distance decay functions are presented in table 16.6. Travel-to-work times varied little by distance from the CBD, probably reflecting the wide spread of non-CBD employment locations and reverse commuting. Mean travel-to-work time rose from 22 to 28 minutes from ring 1 to ring 19, and it was only after ring 20 that mean travel-to-work times increased sharply, averaging 38 minutes.

Differences in income and travel time were grouped more by housing tenure than distance from the CBD. If it can be accepted that tenure represents an adequate proxy for the form and intensity of state action, then this brief section has an important implication for under-

Table 16.6 DISTANCE DECAY RELATIONSHIPS FOR KEY VARIABLES IN SIX UNITED KINGDOM CITIES (LOG-LONG ESTIMATES)

		All Households		Council Tenants		All Households	
		Gross Incomes	Head-of-Household Income	Gross Incomes	Head-of-Household Income	Number of Rooms	Travel-to-Work Time
Birmingham	R^2	0.02	0.026	0.026	0.03	0.001	0.006
	Slope	0.021*	0.025*	0.017*	0.20*	0.002	-0.011*
Bristol	R^2	0.03	0.033	0	0.004	0.019	0.0003
	Slope	0.031*	0.035*	0	-0.012*	0.011*	0.003
Glasgow	R^2	0.025	0.023	0.016	0.01	0.045	0.008
	Slope	0.027*	0.028*	0.017*	0.016*	0.017*	0.018*
London	R^2	0.013	0.021	0	0	0.038	0.004
	Slope	0.017*	0.022*	-0.0004	-0.0002	0.013*	-0.002
Newcastle	R^2	0.023	0.027	0.012	0.017	0.022	0.0001
	Slope	0.026*	0.03*	0.014*	0.018*	0.010*	-0.002
Sheffield	R^2	0.018	0.028	0.013	0.023	0.014	0.0008
	Slope	0.03*	0.039*	0.019*	0.027*	0.01*	0.007

Source: Joseph Rowntree Foundation survey, 1988.

*Statistically significant at the .05 level.

standing the structure of urban systems. Unless the state, especially in the social sector, is sensitive to the land economics of development and uses distance coefficients in its own pricing, then it cannot be anticipated that state-intensive metropolitan areas will have the same broad structure as market-oriented cities. And if they do not have the same structure, then it is erroneous to utilize simple spatial structure explanations of residential choice and residential change. Access-space models, even if much modified, will have to operate in a greatly distorted structure, for which it is difficult to make a priori simplifying assumptions.

At best, the conventional wisdom of core-area decline, which has influenced policy perceptions in the 1980s in Britain, is unproven; at worst, it is misleading. The poorest homeowners do not live in the heart of the core, which is dominated by social renting. Perceptions of area quality also suggest that core centers are not always the most problematic locations; social areas on the fringe of core urban areas may be the poorest quality residential zones. Social housing means that the metropolitan fringe contains significant populations of low-income households. Post-1990 Census results and ad hoc studies in Western Europe, especially in the United Kingdom, confirm growing inequalities within cities, and an apparent increasing concentration of the poor into particular neighborhoods, often dominated by social housing. Employment site decentralization has produced flat commuting surfaces within TTWAs.

These cameo descriptions from six British urban systems clearly indicate that in intervention-rich European cities, extensive urban geography must preface convincing urban economics. But if this section confirms that British cities do not conform to the conventional wisdom, then the evidence only indirectly indicates that the state has contributed greatly to decentralization. The contention is difficult to sustain without more detailed analysis. The next section attempts such an analysis for Glasgow.

GLASGOW: THREE DECADES OF ANTICORE POLICIES

This section integrates the results of a series of investigations undertaken in Glasgow from 1976 to 1990. The studies cover a period when Glasgow shifted from being Britain's most rapidly declining core city (in an overall declining metropolitan area) to a position where overall population loss has slowed and the inner core area appears to be expanding in population. This shift has occurred during a time in which the core and regional economic bases have been subject to sustained decline but in which housing policies have switched from an anti-urban to a pro-urban bias. The economics of this switch are examined here.

The following brief descriptions of housing policies and their impacts are presented in the order in which the policies were initiated. Obviously, different sectoral policies, as well as their more general interactions, have changed over time.

Rent Controls and Decentralization

The history of British rent controls and more recent developments is reviewed elsewhere (Maclennan 1982, 1987). Glasgow, as part of national policy development, was rent controlled in 1915, when more than 90 percent of residents lived in private rental units. In general, the bulk of pre-1919 housing stock still remaining in the city (some 20 percent of the total stock, or almost half of private-sector residences) has been subject to long periods of rent control.

The overall private rental sector share fell at roughly 1 percent per annum, largely owing to demolition and tenure switch. The details of this process, which could have highlighted the long-term quality consequences of strict controls, have not been subjected to economic analysis for the critical period 1915–50. However, some retrospective analysis for the period 1947 to 1977 has been undertaken for private-sector tenements that were still standing in 1977 (arguably an upwards-biased sample of quality in the sector).

Housing transactions in Scotland (prices, ownership, and dates of sale) can be traced through the Register of Sasines. For owner-occupied units, the real price of pre-1919 units increased less rapidly than for post-1919 owned units for the period 1947 through to 1965. Real prices of pre-1919 units in central zones, unlike general housing prices in the city and region, then fell marginally from 1965 to 1972. Subsequently (see Maclennan and Munro 1987), the bottom end of the city's owner-occupied market (lowest decile excepted) appreciated significantly in price relative to the city mean.

The price profile for rental units at date of first sale into the home-owner sector shows a very different pattern. Although small nominal increases occurred in the 1950s, the real price level fell consistently from 1947 until the mid-1970s (when units presumably acquired increased "shell" values with the onset of large-scale public and private renovation programs). The real capita values of owner-occupied and rental units diverged at an average rate of 1.7 percent per annum from 1947 to 1972. Since the resold owner-occupier and rental sale price series included transactions of similar dwelling types and sizes and locations, it is likely that the real price divergence observed reflected increasing quality disparities. These quality disparities reflected, in part, the long-run consequences of sustained rent controls.

A detailed technical housing condition survey of the pre-1919 tenement stock, still standing in 1985, indicated that the private rental stock required £9,000 per unit to put it into good repair, compared with £5,000 per unit for all owner-occupied units. These figures represent, respectively, a half and one-eighth of the relevant capital values.

Rent controls, in short, had a pronounced negative effect on property values, internal amenity, dwelling condition, and external unit appearance throughout the period studied. The consequences of subsequent demolition and clearance of deteriorated units are indicated in the section following on social housing development. But where demolition did not occur, there were further negative consequences for the condition of older neighborhoods.

The residual units, by the 1960s, largely housed older, low-income households paying rents that absorbed less than 10 percent of their incomes. They had few incentives or resources to move unless they were rehoused by the social sector. Above-middle-income homeowners, even as late as 1976 (see the next subsection) avoided choosing such locations because they perceived the areas to be run down and unlikely to be improved. Mixed tenures within tenements precluded rehabilitation (this held true into the 1980s) and also discouraged institutional lending for housing purchases (see Maclennan and Jones 1988). It is not an exaggeration, particularly in view of post-1981 developments, to claim that it may well have been the policy that led to poor-quality inner neighborhoods, rather than the desirability of suburban living per se, that encouraged middle-income decentralization in the period 1950 to 1975. Through that period, the core city simply did not offer levels of housing quality and tenure mixes that meshed with the growing income elastic demands for higher housing quality and homeownership. Policy fueled the outward shift of those outside the social sector.

The Social Sector

Social housing has had a sustained growth in scale in Glasgow since 1919. From 1919 until the early 1930s, municipal housing was developed in inner suburban areas, generally in rings 5 to 10. The units were low rise, were built to a high standard, and were provided with extensive garden spaces and public and private facilities (indeed since the 1980 policies to foster the sale of council houses, these units command prices close to the mean value for owned stock in the city). These areas now form the "elite" social housing in the city. The development of these areas, and extensive public land banking in the same period, may well have displaced homeownership from the core city; however, this did not involve extensive clearance and demolition of older areas.

The second major wave of municipal housing provision was initiated to meet the "needs" of welfare state objectives. Large-scale areas of social housing, with not a single piece of private land or property remaining, were developed at the four corners of the city from 1953 until 1975. These estates, which lie in the 8–15 km rings, and have become known as the peripheral estates, largely housed residents cleared from central city neighborhoods.

Peripheral estate development and related inner-city clearance, therefore, suburbanized 180,000 residents in the period 1951–75. Further, the strategy for reducing core population included moving core area residents to New Towns in the metropolitan periphery, and 100,000 Glaswegians were relocated in the process. In addition, nonmetropolitan municipalities throughout Scotland were subsidized to house 80,000 residents from central Glasgow.

Over this period the population of the core city fell from 1,250,000 (1951) to 750,000 (1981). The population of the inner wards decreased from 500,000 to just over 100,000 in the same period. In broad terms, half of inner-city population decline was a direct consequence of public action, and state action led a third of total population loss for the city as a whole.

By the 1960s a supplementary program of social housing construction in cleared areas was introduced. However, this program produced a landscape of modernist, nontraditional houses rising like sea stacks in an ocean of derelict land and residual blocks of low-quality private rental and owner-occupied units.

It is obvious that in meeting emerging housing "needs" and in responding to the bleak inheritance of rent controls, the city (and indeed the majority of surrounding municipalities), further eschewed market mechanisms and solutions. The vast scale of state action clearly displaced owner occupation in the local housing system. Deep subsidies, estimated at 40 percent of rental market values, attracted into social housing not only poor households but middle-income groups that in other British conurbations were housed by the market—entry to social housing was not formally means tested, and effective subsidies were not income related. The 1988 surveys indicate that Glasgow and London have higher proportions of more affluent socio-economic groups within the social sector than the other case study regions. And it was not until the late 1960s, with growing tax expenditure subsidies to homeowners (after 1963), and rising inflation rates in the 1970s, that the tenure incentive pattern shifted markedly. Indeed, with high housing price appreciation, growing tax subsidies, and reductions in council sector subsidies after 1977, the tenure structure of the city was badly designed to capture benefits from the new order (or disorder) in British housing subsidy policy after 1980.

State action also displaced the owner-occupied sector in a spatial sense. The municipality either owned or had planning controls over all developable land in the city. There was not a single year from 1953 to 1980 when the private sector added more than 250 units to the owner-occupied stock. In consequence, average-quality owned units in the city inflated above the long-run United Kingdom average—in spite of the declining economic base. Over the period, rising prices induced a growing number of younger first-time buyers to purchase starter homes in the 15–25 km rings.

A survey of homeowners in Glasgow undertaken in 1976, near the end of this phase, indicated that half of the first-time buyers purchasing in suburban municipalities started their search processes within the city, worked in the city, and would have preferred to locate within Glasgow. Of those locating within Glasgow, only a fifth would have preferred a suburban location. Within the city, only 10 percent of first-time buyers considered a location within the five inner wards, and they largely rejected such locations for well-defined reasons. Low housing prices, low price-rise expectations, the physical appearance of the areas (especially vacant and derelict land), and problems in securing mortgage finance all overcame perceived benefits of accessibility and rich public infrastructure.

It is clear, therefore, that into the 1970s the tenure-structure consequences and physical landscape produced by past state action both discouraged homeowners from the inner wards of the city and encouraged suburbanization to the metropolitan edge. In Glasgow at least, state-induced supply restrictions, rather than income-elastic demands for space, shaped spatial outcomes of housing choices. This period also saw a major growth in British academic interest in inner cities. And Glasgow was held up as the British example par excellence of the consequences of core-area decline induced by economic change. Clearly, the causes of change were not adequately researched.

Support for the argument that much of the city's decentralization was policy-induced must be tempered by the difficulties of analyzing and interpreting modern history. However, during the 1970s, housing policies in the city were altered dramatically, and, during the 1980s, new patterns of economic activity probably played a role. Many commentators have argued that new communication technologies induce decentralization of jobs and homes. But, this argument appears to be too simplistic and aggregative. In spite of new technologies, it is clear that creative and strategic functions within and between firms require recurrent, frequent, and sometimes random contacts to facilitate innovation and growth. They need a core location. In addition, as income and leisure times rise, urban cores are playing a growing role as locations of personal service production. It is pertinent to consider the relative centralizing effects of such changes.

GLASGOW: REHABILITATION AS PRO-CORE POLICY

Rehabilitation and Recentralization

The rationale for the policy shift from new construction of social housing to rehabilitation, as well as the details and agents of policies, have been examined elsewhere (Maclennan 1985; Maclennan and Gibb 1991). Program impacts have also been analyzed (Maclennan 1990). The broadest details of change are recorded in this section.

In the early 1970s the Glasgow City Council recognized that older neighborhoods still contained 90,000 pre-1919 units that had low amenity standards, were in poor condition, and were often located in areas blighted by "Comprehensive Renewal." In contrast to the municipal demolition strategy of 1950 to 1975, the council developed a strategy to rehabilitate these areas. The key thrust of the approach was to agree to the formation of twenty-six locally based (not-for-profit) housing associations operating in neighborhoods with 1,000–2,000 houses. The associations were supervised and funded not by the municipality but by the Housing Corporation (a "quango").

These associations emphasized community participation, and they organized major upgrading of dwellings and surrounding environments. Properties, largely bought from the residual rental sector, were rehabilitated at a cost of £25,000–30,000 (1989 prices). They were let at rents determined in the rent control system, and 90-percent-plus capital subsidies meant that none of the existing population of elderly and low-income tenants was displaced. From 1975 to 1989, some 25,000 units were rehabilitated, absorbing more than £1,000 million of government expenditure (rent controls are expensive for government in the long run).

Until 1980, this program was still largely perceived as fixing up old houses for the poor. However, it was realized ex post that upgrading investment had important spillovers into associated areas. Property prices in zones adjacent to association activity rose by 5 percent per annum more than anticipated in the period, reflecting the capitalization of favorable externalities. Homeowners in these blocks also markedly increased the rate and share of private-sector rehabilitation grants used in older neighborhoods. More than 50,000 units have been upgraded in this way since 1978, with grant aid of £600 million. Financial institutions also displayed a renewed confidence, and the proportion of mortgages funded by building societies rose from 14 percent to 85 percent between 1975 and 1985. Clearly, a decade of purposive prourban housing policy had begun to shift private perceptions of the older areas.

Private developers were acutely aware of the juxtaposition of upgraded housing association blocks, good public infrastructure, and extensive vacant land. From 1980 to 1985 developers, guided by public agencies, began to develop new private housing adjacent to associations. As these sites were successfully marketed (in all but one instance), developers became confident at assembling and developing larger sites, especially in the old warehousing and dockside areas of the city, thus simultaneously removing decay externalities and increasing core area population. There is a key lesson in this experience: If cities such as Glasgow undergo severe erosion of the economic base, resulting in derelict land and buildings policy, action is required if areas are to be recycled quickly to new leisure and residential uses. It was noted earlier that from 1950 to 1980 production of private housing in the city never exceeded 250 units, reflecting the orientation of housing and planning policies. Since 1980 there has not been a single year when private output, chiefly on brownfield sites, has fallen below 1,000 units. Most of these units are small, though larger, up-market units have been produced since 1987. At present these developments house around 15,000 people, and an additional 4,000 units are in the development pipeline to 1995. Planning and land-use policy has place a new emphasis on the reutilization of brownfield sites to minimize the environmental damage arising from growing household numbers.

The 1976 survey of homebuyers in the city and surrounding municipalities was replicated in 1981 and 1987. Three main points have emerged over time. First, an increasing proportion of households who start a housing search in the city are housed in the city. They are not "forced" to decentralize. Second, an increasing share of households originating in the suburban municipalities, or outside the conurbation, search for housing and eventually locate in Glasgow—there is some intergenerational recentralization. Third, more than half of first-time buyers searching in the city now examine housing options in the inner wards, compared with 10 percent in 1976. House type and size, rather than area characteristics, are now the key constraints on inner-area residential choices.

It is not yet clear how far this process will go. Until the late 1980s, recentralization occurred in a context of continuing economic decline and conurbation population loss, and it was largely a re-sorting effect reflecting changes in housing and planning policies. However, the changing image of the city may now be about to sustain a recovery in urban economic activity that will fuel further reutilization of still-extensive vacant land. It is unclear whether Glasgow's recentralization will be at the cost of the communities on the edge of the metropolitan area.

From Solution to Problem

A major limitation upon the image and marketing of Glasgow is that after two decades and £2,000 million of housing policy capital expenditures, the city still has notoriously bad housing and neighborhood conditions. But now, as in numerous other European cities, these problematic areas are not in older, inner-city neighborhoods. They are in peripheral social housing estates—the solutions of the 1980s have now become the key problems for the 1990s. Decline on the edge of core cities is not solely a Glasgow phenomenon; other British and European cities are similarly afflicted (e.g., Botkyra in Stockholm, Biljermeer in Amsterdam, and Les Minguettes in Lyons). However, European housing systems have so distorted urban spatial patterns that similar decay can be encountered in inner cities (e.g., London), in mid-cities, and on the metropolitan edge. The peripheral estates of Glasgow do, however, reflect the causal mechanisms of decline quite acutely. At least three broad processes have been at work.

As estates have aged, the social ownership mechanisms in place, often disregarding citizen participation, have resulted in sharp declines in property quality (with low-rent/low-maintenance regimes) and in the environment. As incomes have grown, initially poor amenity provision has seldom been upgraded. Most of the areas concerned have markedly poorer housing and neighborhood conditions than when they were built two or three decades ago.

RELATIVE INCOME DECLINE

Prospering households and employed youngsters raised in the peripheral schemes have sought homeownership options since the 1970s. As housing purchase was precluded (at least until the 1980s) in the estates, these households have left—often recentralizing to areas from which their families had been "cleared" in the 1960s.

When the peripheral estates were populated, houses were let generally to families with at least one member of the household in the labor force. Of course, most of these employees were unskilled manual workers. The massive contraction of the city's economic base since the 1960s did not primarily impact upon inner-city residents but upon residents in social housing. In 1985 the unemployment rate for male adults in Glasgow was 21 percent. This rate seldom exceeded 5 percent in private housing areas, and it averaged 24 percent for the council sector. The equivalent rate was 35 percent to 38 percent on the four peripheral estates. And even for those who were employed, more than half had encountered unemployment spells of at least three months' duration between 1980 and 1985. Low and insecure incomes have become the hallmark of these estates since the 1970s. Reductions in housing subsidies, the trimming of social security benefits, and the poll tax all had an adverse impact upon these groups from 1988 to 1991.

RESIDUALIZATION

As estates deteriorate, they become unpopular and exhibit high turnover and vacancy rates (now 10–15 percent). New entrants to social housing with temporally urgent needs and minimal market power accept housing offers in poor locations—the state has been as effective as the market in meshing low-income groups with poor neighborhoods. As a result, the peripheral housing estates have disproportionately housed low-income single-parent families, the physically disabled, young unemployed persons, and alcohol- and drug-dependent households. If Britain has created an underclass in the 1980s, it is most surely in contexts similar to the peripheral estates of Glasgow.

Since 1989, government policy in Scotland, having learned its lesson from Glasgow's inner-area experience, has developed new emphases for urban housing policies—to revitalize peripheral estate areas, to promote homeownership, and to diversify the management of social housing. Citizen participation and joint public/private partnerships are the order of the day. However, the implications for further recentralization/decentralization are unclear. In the medium term, homeownership development might slow the shift back to older neighborhoods but could, at the same time, attract lower-income potential owners back from municipal housing on the metropolitan edge. Demolition and thinning out of the estates would encourage recentralization. In the longer term, a widespread successful upgrading could encourage more high-income residents to live in the city, as opposed to distant suburbs. There is no reason to believe that housing and planning policies will encourage decentralization within the metropolitan area.

CONCLUSION

It can be safely predicted that housing and planning policies, rather than free market choices, will determine the broad structure of the Glasgow conurbation by the year 2000. On balance, this prediction applies to most Northern European urban systems over the same period. The increased emphasis on the flexibility of free market arrangements, with cities both competing and cooperating, will mean that policies for the disadvantaged will be a critical factor in the ability of dense cores to attract or hold a range of income groups. A concentrated growing population of the socially excluded generates negative externalities and public policy costs that will reduce opportunities to use space effectively. Dense core living of mixed income groups requires effectively. Dense core living of mixed income groups requires social cohesion, which is still apparent in European cities.

It is essential that researchers understand the plethora of detailed forces that shape residential location choices. Policy, preference, and income effects must be disentangled. Rather than interpreting ex post outcomes as though they were produced by market outcomes driven by income and employment change, we must assess the extent of state influences. And if policy choices run counter to market preferences, as they so clearly did in Glasgow from 1950 to 1975, we must be able to say so at the time and not, as in this chapter, luxuriate in the comfort of informed hindsight.

More active urban policies will strengthen city cores. But active policy requires effective urban planning. The chapter is critical of how professional beliefs within the planning system contributed to core area residential decline in the post-war period, largely by suppressing market mechanisms. However, good quality cities will require planning systems to deal with environmental issues and other market failures, and to give some certainty to investors. But, in so doing, they should aim for an informed enabling of markets, rather than their controlled displacement.

Note

Research support for this chapter was provided by the Economic and Social Research Council and the Joseph Rowntree Memorial Trust.

References

Maclennan, Duncan. 1982. *Housing Economics: An Applied Approach.* Harlow: Longmans.

————. 1985. "Urban Housing Policy: An Encouraging Example." *Policy and Politics* 7.

————. 1987. "Private Rental Housing: A View from Abroad." In *Private Rental Housing in Britain,* edited by P. Kemp. London: Gower Press.

————. 1990. *Evaluating the Impact of Rehabilitation Programmes.* University of Glasgow. Mimeo.

Maclennan, Duncan, and A. Gibb. 1991. "Glasgow—From Mean City to Miles Better." In *Housing Markets and Housing Institutions: An International Comparison,* edited by B. Housman and J. Quigley. New York: Academic Press.

Maclennan, Duncan, and C. A. Jones. 1988. "Building Societies and Credit Rationing." *Urban Studies* 24 (1).

Maclennan, Duncan, and M. Munro. 1987. "Urban Housing Price Change: Glasgow 1974–84." *Housing Studies* 2 (1).

Chapter Seventeen

THE URBAN LIFE CYCLE AND THE ROLE OF A MARKET-ORIENTED REVITALIZATION POLICY IN WESTERN EUROPE

Leo van den Berg

In the past several decades, spatial deconcentration has been the hallmark of urban development in Europe as well as the United States, with a steep decline in population and employment in the major urban regions as principal effects. In this chapter I first examine the general factors responsible for the rise and descent of urban systems. I then attempt to determine whether the trend of spatial deconcentration will continue to govern the future development of the major urban regions in Europe. Finally, I identify the conditions under which a market-oriented urban policy, such as is now being adopted by a growing number of cities, can help to revitalize major urban regions and convert their decline into new growth.

A THEORY OF URBAN DYNAMICS

This section addresses the mechanisms of urban dynamics, by which is generally meant urban growth and decline. To that end, I begin by discussing a theory of urban dynamics I developed some time ago (1987). Urban dynamics, as analyzed here, is predicated on the assumption that urban growth is primarily the result of the way urban actors—families, companies, and public authorities—behave in space. Based on that principle, and on certain assumptions about the spatial behavior of the three groups of actors, an integral, theoretical concept of urban development and planning can be elaborated. One assumption is that families and companies direct their behavior toward certain objectives: increased welfare for families and continuity of profits for firms. Another assumption is that the welfare of the population depends on the agreement between the supply of welfare elements and their needs and preferences; analogously, a company's continuity of profits at a certain location rests on the agreement between the supply of locational factors and the company's needs and preferences. The problem is that the desired and actual supply of welfare and location potentials are nearly always at variance. Both groups will then presumably try to diminish the discrepancies by their spatial behavior. Among the actions open to them are, first, migration and, second, adjustment of their transport behavior. Such actions may lead to changes in the welfare and location potentials of the regions involved, and hence in their relative attraction as residences and locations. These changes may invoke new adjustments in the spatial behavior of families and companies—and thus spatial dynamics is continued.

In this approach, the spatial behavior of families and companies is largely determined by the development of the various welfare and location potentials. By the policies they pursue, public authorities can greatly influence this development, which is why government behavior has been explicitly included in the formation of the theory of urban dynamics. Presumably, governments want to further social welfare, and they behave accordingly. Again, there are discrepancies between the welfare potential they think desirable and the actual potential that exists. These discrepancies are related in part to the objectives set by the government in such policy areas as housing, the level of provisions, transport infrastructure, the environment, and employment. The theory of urban dynamics gives explicit attention to the evolution of these partial objectives, on the assumption that they are based to some extent on the effective demand for urban provisions exerted by the population and private enterprise. In that sense, government policy is led by demand, adjusting regularly to changes in it. A new policy affects welfare and location potentials, therefore stimulating various actions and reactions of families and companies, to which the government responds. In that way a process of actions and responses is triggered, one actor's behavior influencing the other's. Accordingly, the theory of urban dynamics endeavors to account explicitly for the interdependencies in the spatial behavior of people, companies, and authorities. To that end, the partial behavioral models have been integrated in one dynamic system.

The dynamics of the overall urban system is propelled first of all by fundamental changes in technology, social values, demography, and politics, which make varying and continuous impacts on spatial and urban growth from one period of history to another. Since the industrial revolution, the combined workings of these factors have led to such basic changes in society as, in succession,

Stage I: Industrialization (leads to spatial concentration);

Stage II: Rise of the service and transport sectors (spatial deconcentration);

Stage III: Increased appreciation of the living environment (spatial deconcentration); and

Stage IV: Rise of the information sector (further spatial deconcentration).

Some further features of these stages include the following:

Stage I: High priority for economic growth;
            Location of large-scale industries;
            Development of local public transport;

Stage II: Rapid rise of prosperity;
            Rapidly increasing car ownership;
            High priority in government policy for expansion of transport infrastructure;
            Rapid growth of the number of offices;

Stage III: Rapid rise of energy prices;
            Contraction of average family size;
            Public transport, town renovation, and spatial planning are given more weight in government policy;

Stage IV: Strong computerization of society;
            Increasing attention for small-scale industry; and
            Structural increase of leisure time.

The general conclusion of this theoretical exercise is that the industrialization stage leads to spatial concentration, and that stages II and III lead to spatial deconcentration. Spatial concentration is evident, for example, in the rapid growth of employment and population in towns with good access to physical raw materials. Spatial deconcentration is apparent in stage II with the drop in population and employment in the large industrial cores and the growth of population and employment in the surrounding suburban municipalities, the so-called hard ring. In stage III, population growth shifts to the smaller municipalities, outside the large agglomerations or FURs, the so-called soft rings (functional urban regions equal the core plus the hard ring),[1] as well as to medium-size and small FURs with a relatively attractive living environment, a development that leads to population losses in the large FURs and accelerated growth of the soft rings and medium-size and small FURs. At this stage, the hard ring becomes more and more a center of employment and facilities, functioning as a core in its own right, as confirmed by the increasing commuting from the surrounding rural regions to the urbanized hard ring. As a result, numerous small-scale FURs may spring up around the hard ring, as illustrated in figure 17.1.

In the stage of concentration, spatial development is governed by the spatial behavior of companies; in the subsequent deconcentration stages the spatial behavior of families is the dominating factor. The spatial deconcentration of stage II springs, among other things, from the increased need for a better living environment and the extension of the maximum acceptable commuting distance, the demand-following

Figure 17.1 PROLIFERATION OF FUNCTIONAL URBAN REGIONS (FURs)

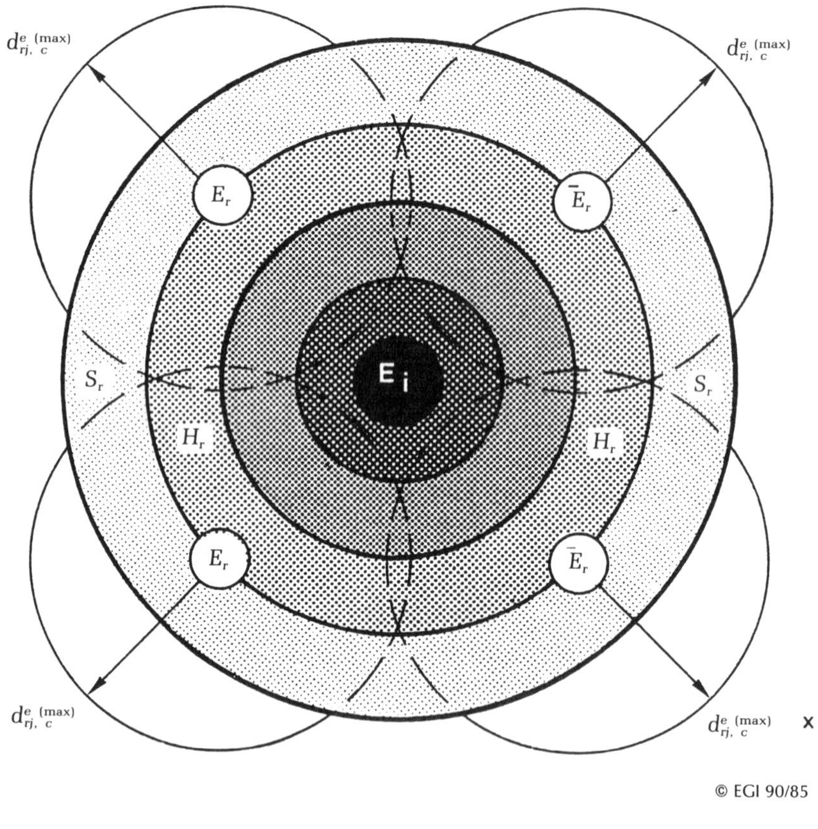

© EGI 90/85

Source: van den Berg (1987).

Note: E_i, employment core; E_r, employment ring; H_r, hard ring; S_r, soft ring; $d_{rj,c}^{e(max)}$, maximum acceptable commuting distance (rj) by car (c).

government policy acting as a catalyst. The structural increased appreciation of the environment in stage III makes people prepared to pay an even higher (transportation) price for living in pleasant surroundings, so that the spatial deconcentration can extend still farther. The improved job opportunities in the hard ring, referred to earlier, open prospects of living at still greater distances from the large town. The relative competitive position of the large declining cores is thus steadily deteriorating, and from the previous theoretical exercise we know that the policy of town renewal pursued at this stage of development has done little to improve it. Far from being reversed, the downward spiral of large industrial cores continues, while towns with attractive living environments continue to grow.

The pattern of urban development just described is largely the result of changes in the relative welfare position of cores, rings, and FURs. The welfare development of the core and ring is visualized in figure 17.2. The first stage is one of swiftly increasing prosperity, resulting in fast demographic growth. The suburbanization of stage II is a result of the relatively favorable evolution of suburban welfare levels coinciding with loss of welfare in the central town. In stage III, the growing

Figure 17.2 DEVELOPMENT PATTERN OF URBAN WELFARE LEVELS

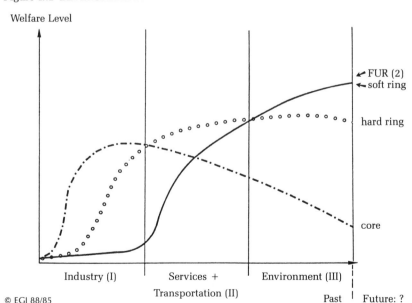

© EGI 88/85

Source: van den Berg (1987).

medium-size and small FURs and the large FURs' soft ring experience higher welfare than the declining large FUR itself. The loss of welfare in the central towns of large FURs results from declines in both the quality of housing and facilities and in the supply of jobs.

The negative development of the employment potential in the core corresponds to the drop in the core's own location potentials and the simultaneous rise of the location potentials in the core's ring and the smaller FURs. Figure 17.3 provides a graphic illustration of this.

As shown in figure 17.3, already in stage I, the core starts to lose its attraction as a location for traditional industrial companies, A_c^{ind}, when industrial sites are becoming scarce, traffic gets more congested, and land prices are escalating. The suburbs, on the contrary, with

Figure 17.3 DEVELOPMENT PATTERN OF LOCATIONAL POTENTIALS IN URBAN AREAS

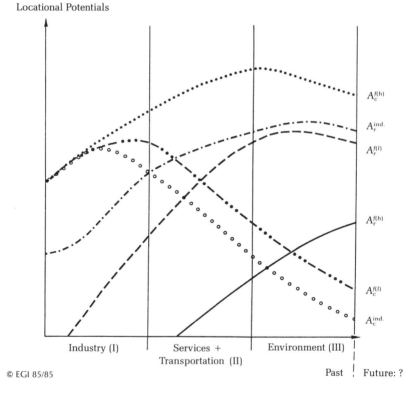

Locational Potentials

$A_c^{f(h)}$

$A_r^{ind.}$

$A_r^{f(l)}$

$A_r^{f(h)}$

$A_c^{f(l)}$

$A_c^{ind.}$

Industry (I) | Services + Transportation (II) | Environment (III)

© EGI 85/85

Past | Future: ?

Source: van den Berg (1987).

their generous package of industrial sites, good accessibility, and relatively low land prices, are becoming more and more attractive to these companies. From stage II onward, suburbs offer to traditional industries a more favorable location climate than the core. During this stage, the core is also losing its attraction as a location for companies providing for the population $A_c^{f(l)}$, because the market potential of the core is declining whereas that of the ring is rising. For the time being, the core remains attractive to those economic activities that appreciate agglomeration advantages, a generous, high-quality labor supply, and the status of the location, $A_c^{f(h)}$. However, congestion and disurbanization are making inroads into the location potential, through the labor-market potential, for example.

Having described the relationship between the progress of population and employment and the development of welfare and location potentials, the next step is to relate the demographic evolution to that of employment in the core and the ring. In stage I, the growth of employment in the core entails demographic growth, the rate of growth being faster for employment than for population. In stage II, demographic and employment growth in the core are both slowing down, and eventually turn into decline, with population leading and employment following at a faster diminishing rate. As shown in figure 17.4, demographic changes in the core are slower than changes in employment, in times of growth as well as decline. With respect to the ring, the assumption is, on the contrary, that employment changes proceed slower than demographic ones. In the course of stage II, both employment and population in the core decline, whereas the ring is achieving its most spectacular growth of population and employment, more than compensating for the decline in the core. On balance, the total FUR composed of the core and the ring keeps growing at this stage. The turning point comes in stage III, when the growth of employment and population in the ring slows down, with no compensating decline in the core. On balance, the total population and total employment of the FUR fall into a decline. Disurbanization sets in with the decline of both the FUR's population and employment.

The urban development patterns described here are the result, among other things, of past technological and social innovations and other exogenous developments. These patterns are documented in several empirical studies (Cheshire and Hay 1989; Hall and Hay 1980; van den Berg 1987; van den Berg et al. 1982). Future urban developments will, in turn, be initiated by new innovations and societal and demographic changes. These are discussed in the next section.

Figure 17.4 DEVELOPMENT OF POPULATION AND EMPLOYMENT IN A
FUNCTIONAL URBAN REGION

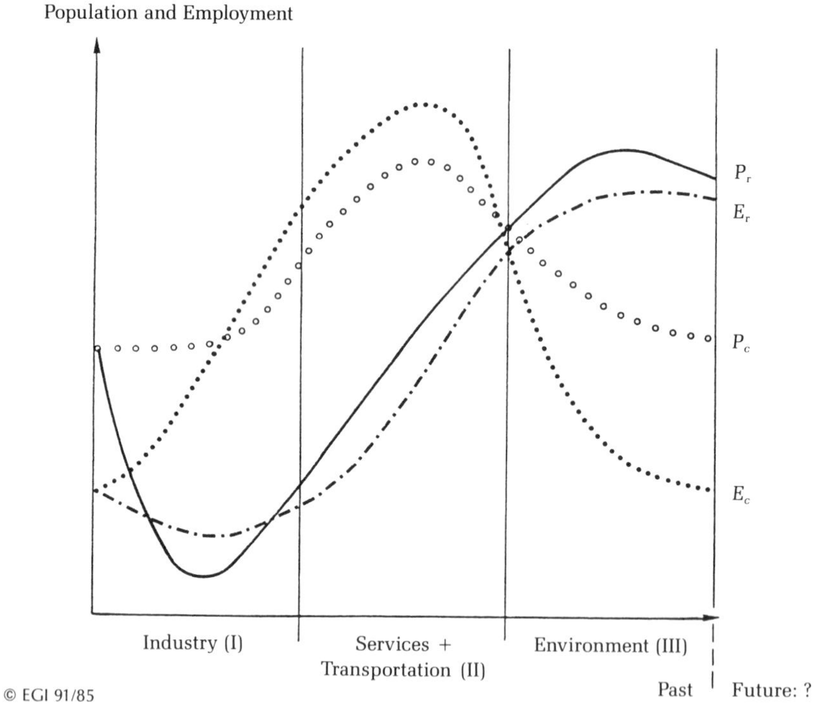

Population and Employment

Industry (I)   Services +   Environment (III)
                      Transportation (II)

© EGI 91/85   Past   Future: ?

P_r
E_r
P_c
E_c

Source: van den Berg (1987).

THE FUTURE OF THE MAJOR EUROPEAN CITIES

Future urban development is largely determined by two fundamental
trends now in evidence, namely, the transition to a knowledge-
intensive society and the European integration (not only within the
European Community but also between Eastern and Western Europe).[2] The evolution to a knowledge-intensive society can be considered the most fundamental trend now confronting Europe's major
cities. It finds its origin notably in technological innovations in microelectronics. Many fundamental changes in the past have also been
initiated by technical innovations; yet, new trends never thrive on
technical progress alone. As previously indicated, three other factors
invariably appear to underlie the dynamics of our society—namely,

demographic evolution, social preferences, and politics. Fundamental changes in these factors inspire new trends that can essentially transform societal and hence urban development. The decision to complete the European integration, and, more recently, societal developments in Eastern Europe, are illustrative of fundamental political changes.

Private enterprise and public authorities in many countries are making every effort to respond adequately to the new European relationships. These efforts alone evoke dynamic forces that may achieve great things for the life of European cities. The future of these urban entities depends significantly on their ability to anticipate and accommodate the changes inherent in the transition to knowledge-intensive society and European integration. Many important changes can be expected in this context, including the following:

1. *The growing importance of the quality of the living and location environment as a determinant of economic growth.* The evolution toward a knowledge-intensive society is in full swing. In such a society the quality of the labor supply appears to be an essential location factor for a growing number of companies. In fact, the demands made by business companies on the educational level of their workers are steadily increasing. High-skilled workers, for their part, set great store by the quality of the living environment. Thus, the future economic growth of a town or region will largely be determined by the quality of its living environment.

2. *Fast-intensifying spatial interaction among European towns with respect to goods transport, as well as business, leisure, and social traffic.* In general, the abolition of political, technical, physical, and fiscal barriers within Europe can be said to improve the accessibility of all European towns and regions. Access to urban services, input markets, sales markets, and urban labor markets alike will become easier. As a consequence, in the short run the prosperity and economic potential of the European towns and regions will increase. In turn, within Europe there will be a growing demand for goods and services, which will encourage expansion of production. More production will entail intensified trade relations on a larger spatial scale among European regions. Thus, European integration is likely to induce more business traffic and goods transport among the European cities. Moreover, the prospering population will have a greater need for all kinds of services, such as shops, cultural institutions, and leisure-time amenities. Enhanced prosperity also enables people to utilize more fast-

transport modes, such as aircraft and high-speed trains, bringing far-flung amenities within their reach. Hence, intensified and longer-distance social travel among Eurocities will occur.

3. *Increasing economic competition among European towns and regions.* The developments described in number 2—in particular, easier access to all regions—make for keener competition between private enterprises located in different European towns and regions. Indeed, better access leads to new market situations, since existing companies will work to penetrate one another's markets. This holds for obtaining inputs and selling products as much as for recruiting personnel. Companies not operating in an optimal mode may lose out and be obliged to close down or move. In general, that implies the relocation of certain economic activities, a process from which some towns will emerge as winners and others as losers.

   In the losing towns the question will likely be raised as to why local enterprise is no longer able to sustain its competitive advantage with companies elsewhere. Are the companies themselves to blame, or is the quality of the town's locational environment unsatisfactory? If the latter, the city government may decide to improve the locational environment by pursuing an active strategy to reinforce the town's competitive position as a location for business enterprise. Naturally, such a strategy may invite reactions from other towns. The upshot, then, is that improved access will elicit greater economic competition among towns, in the wide sense of vying for trading, transport, and distribution companies; leisure-time amenities; shops; government agencies; tourists; and higher-income population.

4. *Diminishing influence of national governments and growing influence of regional and supranational governments.* The transition to an integrated Europe implies that the power of Europe's administrative entities, including the European Parliament, is enhanced, while that of the national governments is reduced. Decisions concerning the large European infrastructure and spatial and regional, as well as economic and financial politics, will progressively be made on the European level. A logical complement of such transfer of sovereignty is to reduce the distance between the governing bodies and the population by establishing direct contact between the regions and Brussels. The question is how to organize such contact to the best effect. An obvious solution would be for each of the major European regions to appoint a representative to Brus-

sels to act as regional ambassador. Several European cities have already taken that step.

What can European cities do, besides appointing regional ambassadors, to anticipate the impending changes? The following suggestions highlight areas of special urgency:

1. *Give higher priority to the promotion of the living environment.* Since the future economic growth of Eurocities will increasingly depend on the quality of their living environment, these cities must give priority to this aspect. Cities need to develop a strategy of supplying better-quality housing, shops, and cultural and leisure-time provisions. The natural environment also needs upgrading; polluted soil, air, and water have no place in a high-grade living environment. Moreover, municipal authorities need to understand how much the quality of the urban environment depends on the accessibility of workplaces and services.

2. *Improve access to cities in general and inner cities in particular.* In view of the serious traffic problems in most large European towns, town governors must make serious policy efforts to render office complexes, shopping centers, leisure complexes, and residential quarters more accessible. The reduction of the colossal traffic congestion in, around, and between many cities is probably the greatest problem facing urban planners in the future.

3. *Give more attention to intercity connections.* The expected rapid increase of business, goods, and social traffic among the European metropolises calls for a proper response. In practice, this means that the towns will have to provide adequate road, rail, and air connections with as many (European) destinations as possible. For the sophisticated interurban transport infrastructure required for such connections, Eurocities will need to cooperate closely with one another and with the responsible regional and national—possibly also supranational—governments. This does not preclude cities taking the initiative, by developing regional airports, for example.

4. *Meet the increasing need for city marketing.* If economic competition among European cities indeed increases according to expectations, businesslike and efficient urban management will be necessary. Far more than before, a city will need to be managed as a business enterprise, pursuing a policy to ensure the continuity of the "urban enterprise." To that end, urban management should develop an integrated strategy that takes account of the interrelat-

edness of planning for housing, offices, industrial complexes, shopping centers, and transport infrastructure. The municipal government should be organized to permit an integrated policy with active participation of urban private enterprise. For many Eurocities this will call for administrative reorganization, not only functionally, but spatially. In practice, the fragmented administrations of large agglomerations obviously have not always succeeded in achieving balanced and efficient management of entire urban entities. Given that in the coming years an energetic urban policy will be essential, the question of how far existing administrative structures will need to be adjusted to achieve that goal is an important one. To replace all municipal structures with one agglomeration government could be a solution, but one apt to provoke political objections. An alternative, now finding more support, is to collaborate in restricted policy areas, or on the level of projects, in the form of so-called public-public partnerships. Such strategic partnerships need not be limited to municipalities of a specific agglomeration. In principle, a city should develop a partnership with all cities that are relevant for its functioning, including cities in other countries. International cities with big seaports will be especially interested in developing partnerships with foreign cities. However, for such forms of cooperation a relationship of trust and confidence between partners is indispensable.

Intensified economic competition among European cities implies that these towns will need to increasingly reorient their development strategies to stimulate activities that enhance their location environment. More than ever, this means that towns will have to be alert to special opportunities, while constantly trying to improve their competitive stance.

What counts is a city's relative appeal not only as a location for business but also as a magnet for investors, visitors, and inhabitants. A city that fails to attract investors and developers will be hard put to carry through the renovation it needs. By the same token, cities that lack appeal to visitors cannot profit from the strong expansion of the tourist sector, which increasingly, and for a growing number of cities, is becoming a pillar of the local economy. Finally, cities that are unpleasant places in which to live lack a foundation for future economic growth. As stated earlier, for a growing number of companies, the availability of high-skilled personnel is becoming a necessary locational condition. Therefore, local administrators must give more and more thought to the assets that can make their town attractive to the populations concerned. In conclusion, then, the future policy of European towns should be to enhance their appeal in the broadest sense: as a residence, in particular for the better educated; as a location for business companies; as an opportunity for investment; and as a point of attraction for business and other tourists. To achieve that objective, market analysis and city marketing are essential instruments. Indeed, city marketing is expected to be practiced increasingly, for more and more aspects of urban society and in a growing number of cities.

The net result of the evolution just described would be a sharpening of competition, between cores and hard and soft rings, and between these areas and other FURs, for high-skilled, high-income people as well as for innovative employment. The improved competitive position of the core is not likely to lead to a population explosion, because today's high demands on housing and environment preclude high population densities. Large cities cannot become as large as they used to be, and therefore core population and employment will only show modest quantitative growth. However, the possible return of higher-income groups to the large cores augurs well for the creation or preservation of high-grade facilities, which will make the core even more attractive to these groups. There will be favorable effects on urban income and thus on the financial position of the core, the latter enabling municipal authorities to upgrade the urban living environment. On balance, the result might be a considerable rise in the standard of urban welfare. Reurbanization, as interpreted here, means primarily the recovery of the large core. Because the growth of population and employment will be limited, the reurbanization of large towns does little to reverse the trend of spatial deconcentration, which will continue in the medium term. How far it will ultimately progress will depend on urban policy and the progress of prosperity. Reurbanization and deconcentration are not necessarily mutually exclusive; they may indeed proceed side by side.

URBAN POLICY AND MARKET ORIENTATION

By adopting a policy of urban revitalization, local governments try to upgrade their city's attraction for the "market parties," that is, for inhabitants, business companies, visitors, and investors. To succeed, such a policy must be developed in close cooperation with those market parties and with an eye to their various preferences. To induce a particular development, a local government may be tempted to comply in full with the wishes of one market party; whether such a policy really furthers municipal welfare, not only in the short run but in the long run, is questionable. The issue of whether or not a local government can enhance the well-being of its citizens without heeding the ambitions of the market parties is easier to answer: since most market parties will be little inclined to cooperate with a local government, such a policy certainly cannot contribute to a maximum growth of municipal welfare. Whether the same answer applies to the situation in which the local government is responding to a private initiative cannot be decided offhand. It depends, among other things, on the concrete proposal the municipality has in mind and on the market parties involved. The following illustration of the need for caution by a local government that is veering toward a more market-oriented policy may be useful. Care is required lest the revitalization policy prove more harmful than beneficial to the local citizenry (van den Berg et al. 1993 and 1997).

Revitalization and the Investor's Strategy

On the whole, real estate investors are free to choose an investment project as well as the country or region to invest in. Investors naturally prefer high-return, low-risk projects. Within a given country, the investment climate of individual cities depends, among other factors, on the diversification of the urban economy; the town's market potential; and the quality of the town's living environment (Liebe 1987; van Lammeren 1989).

A one-sided economy entails more risks to the investor than a more diversified one. On the whole, therefore, the narrower the economic base of an urban region, the less attractive it is to investors. Obviously, the nature and quality of local enterprise are other important aspects of a town's investment climate. A city where the majority of private companies are flourishing will appeal to investors. There should be evidence that local enterprise is well managed, that there are no bottlenecks in the urban economy, and that the so-called growth sectors are well represented. All these aspects are important indicators of the city's investment climate, because they have a positive influence on its market potential, that is, on its annual demand for industrial and office accommodations.

To properly appreciate a town's investment climate for real estate, supply in the estate market must be considered as well as demand. If

there is already an excess supply of offices and industrial accommo-
dation, new office complexes and industrial estates became hard to
realize. The surplus is visible as either excess supply of existing offices or as a generous supply of locations suitable for the development
of offices. Cities with a surplus of offices and office locations have
been found to yield a far lower return on investment in real estate
than cities where the supply is relatively scarce (see, for example, van
Lammeren 1989). Thus, would-be investors will be inclined to prefer
the latter. Indeed, investors want local governments to create land
scarcity through their spatial policy. In particular, they would like
local governments to focus their promotional strategy on a limited
number of locations, in the belief that new office locations are more
likely to be successful if planned for prime locations, especially when
the prime locations already occupied lack opportunity for expansion.

Another determinant of a city's appeal to real estate investors that
is coming more to the fore is the quality of life. This chapter's investigation and others have found that the economic potential of a city
appears to depend increasingly on the quality of the living environment. One reason given is that there is a rising demand in private
enterprise for well-educated, high-skilled staff, the very people who
make ever-higher demands on the living environment. It would seem
that a company has a better chance of recruiting suitable staff by
locating in or near cities with attractive living environments (i.e.,
those with an excellent housing supply and accessible services [edu-
cation, museums, shops, leisure provisions]).

A city's ability to attract office investments depends, then, on the
quality of a multiplicity of aspects. This implies that office developments that reduce the quality of the urban living environment will in
the end also reduce the realty value of the very offices involved. Therefore, investors are well advised, in their own interest, to advocate
office developments that are likely to enhance the urban environment
in the widest sense.

But do investors agree with that advice? Investors appear to value
locations largely by the value of the land, the underlying rationale
being that the risk of investing in real estate is smaller as the share of
the land price in the total investment costs is greater. In the major
Dutch towns, for example, this share is currently only about one-
fourth: the building itself representing three-fourths of the investment
costs (see, for example, van Lammeren 1987). In London, Paris, Frankfurt, New York, and Tokyo, however, the ratio is reversed. At a time in
which offices tend to depreciate rapidly, the investors' preference for

cities with high land prices is understandable. To make Dutch towns competitive, in the eyes of investors, with the foreign cities just mentioned, land prices would have to rise steeply. This is why investors are advising Dutch local governments to proceed to so-called city building, the highly concentrated development of offices at the smallest possible number of prime locations. This conjures up an image of the central business district, the type of city building particularly evident in many American cities. The emphasis thus given, however, to the productive function of a city does nothing to promote a harmonious evolution of the entire urban region; on the contrary, it spells serious traffic congestion and an inhospitable, desolate city center. Nor does such city building in the long run favor optimum welfare development in the urban region (van den Berg et al. 1990).

The conclusion must be that if investors persist in developing urban realty projects in the city-building mode just described, serious negative effects on city welfare will accrue, effects that will rebound on the investors themselves. This is a remarkable outcome, since a high quality of life is one determinant of investors' behavior. Evidently, then, investors tend to judge possible projects primarily by the current quality of life, economic structure, and market potential of a city, that is, by very short-term criteria. The question thus arises, how can the long-term effects of developments supported by investors be incorporated into their development criteria? One answer has already come from the investors themselves. Van Lammeren (1987), for one, has advised local governments to design a so-called masterplan for their city. Because such a masterplan delineates with some precision the long-term outcomes that the local government is trying to achieve, it limits the risk incurred by investors participating in the plan's projects. A masterplan ensures the continuity of local policy, which is also a good thing for investors.

To prepare a masterplan may be useful in another respect. In designing strategy, local governments should try to calculate the indirect effects of several development scenarios, and evaluate the outcomes together with partners from the private and public sectors. The point would be to illustrate the implications of certain policy choices for the suburban municipalities, the city, investors, and private enterprise, with the end purpose being to ensure that the chosen strategy rests solidly on *relevant information*. On the strength of such information, investors may be persuaded to replace their short-term view with one more mindful of the long-term effects, thus also protecting themselves.

Of course, other parties are involved in the development of a strategy. A strategy is useless without sufficient societal support. Indeed, local government must negotiate with, and consider the needs of, the local population, private companies, and tourists. These aspects are considered in the following section.

Urban Revitalization and the Population

It is a well-known fact that many major European cities have been confronted in the past several decades with a massive outflow of population. Initially, local governments responded by adopting a policy of town renovation in the hope of improving the local housing quality sufficiently to stem the exodus (van den Berg 1987). "Building for the neighborhood" was the acknowledged credo, with the central focus being to assist lower-income groups to obtain better dwellings. However, this type of town renovation offered no relief for the economic crisis in which the towns found themselves. It was finally understood that restoring the urban economy was as urgent as improving the housing situation in old town quarters. In the latter half of the 1980s, that insight inspired the so-called policy of urban revitalization, which was directed to the economic recovery of towns. As observed earlier, the economic recovery of towns calls for the availability of well-educated, high-skilled personnel, as well as first-class locations. Unfortunately, however, high-skilled individuals were the very people who had in large numbers first turned their backs on the city, and then on the agglomeration factors. The need to refocus revitalization policy to raise the city's appeal as a residence for the better educated and for those with high incomes was understood, and implied a radical change from the course followed previously with respect to housing and public services.

An important problem for local governments to solve is by what means and to what extent to try to adjust the quality of the labor supply. The decision demands a fair knowledge of the demands that economic revitalization makes upon the quality of the labor supply and the city's economic strength, and of the relation of both to the present demographic situation. Without sufficient clarity on those points, a local government might adopt a revitalization policy with inadvertent and undesirable consequences, such as the displacement of the current urban population, or extreme differences in the welfare of certain groups of citizens. Displacement may occur when measures toward economic revitalization cause the price of land to rise to a point where citizens, and in particular the lowest-paid among them, can no longer afford to live in town, so that the city loses its residential function. That has happened in many major cities with a central business district, not only in the United States but also in Europe (e.g., Frankfurt and Brussels) and Japan (e.g., Tokyo). In their city centers, revitalization has accelerated the growth of employment for well-trained individuals, far outpacing the job opportunities for the unskilled and low-skilled. As a result the latter, the ones that concentrate in the inner cities, hardly profit from the revitalization measures. The erosion of the residential function, and the widening gap between rich and poor, are the results of a policy that is oriented too much to the economy, while neglecting the social implications. Extreme wealth and bitter poverty are often found side by side in those towns. Such a situation breeds serious social tension. In the face of such unfortunate developments, the revitalization policy will first lose societal support and finally be doomed to fail.

The question then arises, In whose interest was the revitalization policy initiated in the first place? In the extreme case just described, evidently the welfare of the town's own population was not the first objective of the revitalization policy. A local government that is serious about the welfare of its own citizens should prefer a policy by which it can achieve economic revival in a socially equitable manner. The upgrading of the labor supply required for revitalization should be managed gradually and by two approaches: by attracting and/or holding onto well-educated population groups, and by raising the social status of the town's citizenship through training courses, employment projects, and other measures to boost their chances in the labor market.

If revitalization policy is to improve the welfare of the entire population, and not fail for lack of social support, then economic revival should go hand in hand with "social innovation." In designing policy, the local government must be conscious of the opportunities and limitations of its own population. Only then can it select the proper spearheads for economic development, and intervene in a timely manner to ensure that citizens profit fully from, and are not victimized by, their city's economic revival.

The preceding arguments underscore that it is easier to claim that the objective of urban policy (city marketing) should be to raise popular welfare than it is to establish exactly which citizens should be the recipients of assistance or how the specific needs of that "market party" can be met. Clarity on this point is a necessary condition for the development of a city-marketing policy.

CONCLUSIONS

The theory of the dynamics of urban regions rests on the assumption that urban systems rise and fall according to the spatial behavior of urban actors, who, for their part, are motivated by successive combinations of changing exogenous variables, such as demographics, politics, social values, and technology. According to this theory, future urban developments will be dominated by a persistent trend toward urban deconcentration and larger functional urban regions. That trend is encouraged by the transition to an information-intensive society and by the European integration, which, in turn, are determined by political movements and the advances in (transport) technology (high-speed trains, for example). Lately, however, forces with an opposite spatial effect have also made themselves felt, forces mainly associated with the ambition of many major cities to end disurbanization by an active revitalization policy. One major weapon wielded by the cities in the struggle toward reurbanization is a new, market-oriented policy. Such a policy is undoubtedly a necessary condition for revitalization, especially in a time of increasing competition and mutual dependency between urban regions. However, this type of policy is not a sufficient condition for economic revitalization: the city itself must also exhibit potential for new growth. The discussion of local policy presented here suggests, moreover, that an unbalanced, market-oriented policy may even sow the seeds of a new and serious urban decline. Such a situation could emerge if municipalities allow their development strategies to be governed entirely by the (mostly short-term) preferences of investors. Only an urban policy with a balanced market orientation can prevent the new prosperity of major towns from being short-lived. Indeed, the future development of the urban life cycle depends largely on the emphasis municipalities are giving to the general concept of market-oriented policy.

Notes

1. Hard ring: if more than 15 percent of the professional population of a ring municipality is working in the core.

2. See also van den Berg and Klaassen (1989).

References

Bade, F. J. 1985. *The De-industrialisation of Industrial Countries and Its Spatial Implications: The Example of the FRG.* Berlin: Deutsches Institut für Wirtschaftsforschung.

Cheshire, P., and D. Hay. 1989. *Urban Problems in Western Europe.* London: Unwin Nyman.

Hall, P., and D. Hay. 1980. *Growth Centres in the European Urban System.* London: Heinemann.

Klaassen, L. H., L. van den Berg, and J. van der Meer. 1989. *City: Engine behind Economic Recovery.* Aldershot, England: Avebury.

Liebe, T. 1987. "Investing in Urban Renewal." In *Public and Private Investments in Urban Renewal* [translation from the Dutch]. The Hague: NIROV.

van den Berg, L. 1987. *Urban Systems in a Dynamic Society.* Aldershot, England: Gower.

van den Berg, L., and L. H. Klaassen. 1989. *The Major European Cities Underway to 1992.* Rotterdam: EURICUR.

van den Berg, L., E. Braun, and J. van der Meer. 1997. *Metropolitan Organising Capacity.* Aldershot, England: Avebury.

van den Berg, L., L. H. Klaassen, and J. van der Meer. 1990. *Marketing Metropolitan Regions.* Rotterdam: EURICUR.

van den Berg, L., M. A. van Klink, and J. van der Meer. 1993. *Governing Metropolitan Regions.* Aldershot, England: Avebury.

van den Berg, L., R. Drewett, L. H. Klaassen, A. Rossi, and C. H. T. Vijverberg. 1982. *Urban Europe: A Study of Growth and Decline.* Oxford: Pergamon.

van Lammeren, C. A. 1987. "Commercial Real Estate Investment Criteria." In *City: Engine behind Economic Recovery,* edited by L. H. Klaassen, L. van den Berg, and J. van der Meer. Aldershot, England: Avebury.

Part Five

SUMMARY AND CONCLUSIONS

DECENTRALIZATION IN THE UNITED STATES AND THE UNITED KINGDOM: COMMONALITIES IN THE EVIDENCE

John M. Quigley

In substance, this volume's chapter 4 (by Linneman and Summers) and chapter 16 (by Maclennan) are highly complementary. Both are rich in "facts" about intraurban location patterns and the centralization or decentralization of economic activity in cities. The vast differences in style, organization, and emphasis between the two chapters may obscure the complementarity of the evidence presented. The following discussion restates, in rather different form, the principal conclusions of the respective authors and provides some comparative interpretation.

Both chapters are essentially descriptive, covering changes in the centralization of economic activity in the post-1960s environment. Linneman and Summers focus on the sixty largest metropolitan areas in the United States, whereas Maclennan (despite the chapter's broad title) presents evidence primarily from six metropolitan areas in the United Kingdom. The Linneman-Summers chapter is statistical and systematic; the Maclennan chapter is anecdotal and provocative. Despite these and other important differences, the two chapters arrive at a quite similar central empirical finding, namely, that differentiation between central and noncentral locations within metropolitan areas has become less pronounced with the passage of time.

DECENTRALIZATION IN THE UNITED STATES

Linneman and Summers provide fascinating and rigorous documentation of trends in population and employment within major U.S. metropolitan areas from 1970 to 1987. The analysis is based upon a unique body of original data painstakingly gathered by the authors and comprising the only consistent time series on intraurban trends available for American cities over the past three decades. Thus, the facts presented by Linneman and Summers are extremely valuable to the policy-making community.[1]

As I interpret the findings, the authors document nine summary facts. Six of these are related to the distribution of economic activity within urban areas and three to the distribution of activity among urban areas. These latter findings about intermetropolitan differences have been documented elsewhere, but nowhere have they been analyzed so systematically.

The crucial facts are:

First, the decentralization of population and employment within metropolitan areas has continued unabated throughout the 1970s and 1980s.

Second, the relative decline in more central places includes the decline of central portions of large cities (the central business district or CBD) relative to the rest of the central city itself and also the decline of the central city as a whole relative to the suburbs.

Third, the relative decline in central places has been somewhat less pronounced in the decade of the 1980s than in the 1970s. In only a few of the sixty largest U.S. urban areas was there an absolute increase in economic activity in the center during the 1980s, but the pattern is clear. The decade of the 1980s was better for the central business districts relative to the rest of the central city, and also better for the central cities relative to their suburban areas, than was the decade of the 1970s.

Fourth, the authors document the existence of some very strong central business districts in large cities during the decade of the 1980s. The systematic comparison provided by the authors is very different from the popular generalization based on the fate of well-known cities in the Rustbelt. Linneman and Summers present convincing evidence that, for a third of the largest U.S. metropolitan areas, absolute growth in employment was not only positive in the 1980s but also larger than in the 1970s.

Fifth, there are important spillover effects between population and employment growth in U.S. central cities and the corresponding growth of the suburbs. Growing central cities have had positive effects upon the growth of suburban areas.

Sixth, this spillover effect was apparently much stronger in the 1970s than in the 1980s. Thus, the economic health of central cities is increasingly independent from that of suburban areas.

The last three findings regarding intermetropolitan economic activity have been documented elsewhere, but without the rich detail provided by Linneman and Summers.

Seventh, the authors find that urban areas that formerly had strong manufacturing bases suffered declines in both employment and population. The timing of these losses is significant. During the 1970s, central cities with historically strong manufacturing bases declined. By the 1980s, those suburban areas that had had strong manufacturing activity also declined. Over the period as a whole, there was a general decline in those urban areas that had specialized in traditional manufacturing activity—central cities first, then suburban rings.

Eighth, there was a general movement of economic activity to the Sunbelt. The shift from the Northeast was more pronounced than from the other parts of the country. Relative decentralization was greatest from the oldest large metropolitan areas to the newest cities of the South and Southwest.

Ninth, the large and the medium-sized metropolitan areas of the United States grew in population relative to the rest of the country. Urbanization continues and is still the engine of growth.

DECENTRALIZATION IN THE UNITED KINGDOM

Similarly, Maclennan's chapter utilizes unique and detailed household surveys for the United Kingdom. The analysis is based, in large part, on responses obtained for six major metropolitan areas in Britain, defined by commuting-to-work patterns. The chapter also utilizes evidence from a variety of studies directed by Maclennan on the economic geography of the Glasgow metropolitan area. As I interpret the evidence, seven central facts emerge. Some are documented within the chapter itself; and others are asserted or summarized on the basis of evidence presented elsewhere. Four of these conclusions arise from analysis of the six U.K. metropolitan areas, and another three from the Glasgow experience.

First, for each of the six urban areas, homeownership levels increase substantially with distance from the urban core. At a distance of only five km (three miles) from the CBD, homeownership rates of 55 percent to 62 percent are estimated for Sheffield, Birmingham, and Bristol, and rates of 42 percent are estimated for Glasgow and Newcastle. Three-eighths of London households living five km from the CBD are owner occupants. At ten km (six miles), the fraction is about two-thirds. Glasgow is a conspicuous exception to the pattern of a sharply increasing incidence of owner occupancy with distance from downtown.

Second, the share of social rental housing is large, ranging from 19.8 percent in Bristol to 57.3 percent in Glasgow, and the social housing sector "commonly provides the majority tenure" within nine km of the CBD in these cities.

Third, the spatial variation in other measures of housing quality is quite modest. Dwelling unit size increases "marginally" up to nine km and then is flat; perceived neighborhood quality does not vary systematically over space.

Fourth, explicit tests for price gradients reveal significant negative relationships between housing prices and distance in the private sector and an insignificant relationship for public-sector housing. Explicit tests for income gradients reveal significant, but small, positive gradients of two or three percent in the six areas.

From Maclennan's detailed studies of Glasgow, clearly an atypical housing market by British standards, he recounts three more important facts.

Fifth, dwelling units in Glasgow that had previously been subject to rent controls and had then been sold into owner occupancy commanded lower prices, reflecting the quality differences arising from landlords' investment responses to sustained rent regulation.

Sixth, the spatial development of population in Glasgow was essentially determined by state action, at least until the 1980s.

Seventh, the extent of socially owned slum housing in Glasgow and its suburban spatial pattern are reflected in the employment conditions of residents. With unemployment rates five times as large among council tenants as among those in private housing (in 1985 at least), and with unemployment rates of 35 percent to 38 percent in peripheral housing estates, the peripheral location of residual housing is clear.

COMMONALITIES IN THE EVIDENCE

In both chapters, the stylized facts noted here are documented and qualified in detail (especially so in Linneman and Summers). Rather than elaborate further here, I offer several points of interpretation.

First, many but not all of the facts and trends reported in these two chapters represent inexorable extensions of the work first undertaken by Edwin Mills in 1972 and extended by his students and colleagues in the two decades following. The gradients of economic activity in urban areas have been declining systematically for as far back in time as we have data. This is true for both population and employment as well as housing prices, and applies to cities in North America and Europe, and even for city-states in ancient Greece. The gradients of income have also been declining (in absolute magnitude, of course), but most of the evidence for this conclusion is based on U.S. cities. In contrast, the intercepts of gradient functions have declined only sporadically. There is less than convincing evidence that the absolute levels of central activity have declined.

Thus, the weight of much empirical evidence suggests that gradients have become flatter over time. Economic theory suggests that this is an efficient market response to differences in relative costs. Technical change in transportation and communications has rendered individual plots of land at different metropolitan locations more substitutable in production or consumption, leading to less spatial differentiation in the sites of more profitable economic activity or of activity yielding higher utility.

These theoretical deductions are consistent with the empirical evidence catalogued by Linneman and Summers and by Maclennan. They are also consistent with the broader historical data presented by Charles Leven in chapter 9 of this volume.

Second, an intertemporal variation in the decline of the center of U.S. metropolitan areas relative to their peripheries is documented by Linneman and Summers.[2] Comparisons between CBDs and suburbs outside the central city (OCCs) in employment and population are consistent with comparisons between central cities and their suburban rings. These comparisons clearly indicate that the decline of the center relative to the periphery was slowed in the 1980s. The decline of central business districts and of the central cities themselves was less pronounced in the 1980–87 period than in the 1970–80 period.

The lesson I draw from this is clear. U.S. metropolitan areas are greatly affected by demographic trends, and their health is closely intertwined with the performance of the macroeconomy. They are much less affected by central government actions that could be termed "urban policies." Consider the effects of the macroeconomy. The period from 1980 to 1985 witnessed the first real income declines in the United States in a generation and the highest real interest rates in recent history. Both of these forces—the Reagan recession and high real interest rates—were powerful forces discouraging decentralization. They reduced the demand for housing, in particular the demand for owner-occupied housing at noncentral locations. These same forces lowered the demand for new capital investment and thus inhibited the dispersion of production sites to the suburbs. In turn, both of these outcomes greatly affected the relative position of central versus noncentral parts of metropolitan areas. Each tended to strengthen the central part of the metropolitan area at the expense of the noncentral parts.

Now contrast these economic market forces with the government's urban policies from 1980 to 1987 relative to the 1970s. The one success of the Reagan revolution, perhaps its only enduring success, was the dismantling of American urban policy, largely by eliminating federal grants-in-aid to state and local governments. The period from 1980 to 1987 witnessed a 70 percent decline in grants-in-aid to state and local governments in real terms. Despite these huge reductions in aid, the position of central areas relative to noncentral areas improved, at least in the two dimensions reported here. This suggests that urban policies per se may be less important in affecting urban outcomes than the general course of the economy.

The importance of general economic conditions in affecting urban outcomes is also evident in Maclennan's tale of Glasgow. With neighborhood unemployment rates hovering at about 40 percent in 1985, and with half of those currently employed experiencing significant spells of unemployment, there can be little doubt that the housing problems of the peripheral estates were severe. Indeed, with metropolitan unemployment rates at the levels indicated by Maclennan, housing is surely one of a long list of social problems directly attributable to the operation of the economy at the macro and regional levels.

The U.S. experience of the 1990s only reinforces the greater importance of demographics and the macroeconomy in affecting urban outcomes, as compared to urban policies per se. The widely observed decreases in urban crime and the encouraging reductions in poverty levels in large cities arose, so it appears, from the aging of central city populations and the tight labor markets associated with strong economic growth in the national economy of the United States. There is little evidence that national or local urban policy had much influence.

Finally, Maclennan is correct in cautioning against interpreting events as though they arose solely from simple textbook models, whether those models are written down in Cambridge, Massachusetts, or Cambridge, England. Nevertheless if, as Maclennan asserts, the state rather than the market will determine the spatial structure of Northern European urban systems, a high payoff would result from diffusing the reasoning behind these models to the individuals making expensive allocation decisions.

Notes

1. The raw data underlying this analysis were recently made available by Linneman and Summers on diskettes.

2. Note, again, that the employment data presented on the CBD and outside the central city (OCC) are the only systematic evidence on employment location within central cities published since Meyer, Kain, and Wohl in 1966.

References

Meyer, John R., John F. Kain, and Martin Wohl. 1966. *The Urban Transportation Problem.* Cambridge, Mass.: Harvard University Press.

Mills, Edwin S. 1972. *Studies in the Structure of the Urban Economy.* Baltimore, Md.: Johns Hopkins University Press.

Chapter Nineteen

A POSTSCRIPT: EXURBIA OR ISLINGTON?

Paul C. Cheshire

BACKGROUND

The conference from which this book derives was held in July 1990. The analysis underlying the contributions to the conference was mainly based on the experience of the 1970s and early 1980s. That experience, in both the United States and in the mature industrialized countries of Europe (see chapters 3, 4, 5, and 9 of this volume by Linneman and Summers, Hall, Cheshire, and Leven), was of a sharp acceleration in the trends established during the 1950s. Suburbanization of jobs and people had given way to decline, and even abandonment, of significant swathes of the centers of large cities. This was commonest in the older industrial cities of the United States, but abandonment and urban decline could be found in European cities such as Liverpool, Glasgow, Duisburg, or Liège. The American experience was summarized by Greenwood and Stock (1990):

> . . . important changes have occurred in the pattern of . . . decline. Until the 1940s both population and employment were growing in most central cities and suburban areas, but the city's share of metropolitan population and employment was falling. During the 1950s, however, absolute population and employment decline began in many cities, and such decay in the nation's major metropolitan areas is now widely recognized. During the 1970s, especially in the Northeast and Midwest, many central cities continued to experience population and employment loss . . . even service employment fell in a number . . .

The 1970s were not only a decade in which suburbanization accelerated, there were tales of the revival of rural areas (starting with Beale 1975). These may have turned out to be oversimplifications. Much of the growth in nonmetro areas in the United States appeared, on close examination (Vining and Strauss 1977), to have been in rural counties contiguous to metro areas, and were therefore more of an extension of suburbanization to exurban, fringe counties. It was not so much a question of a rural revival as of "the cities moving to the countryside" (Leven 1978). Any real rural revival was very short-lived. Nevertheless, there were remote rural areas in the United States which, during the 1970s, experienced growth for the first time in the twentieth century.

Growth of population in all American nonmetro areas combined increased from 2.5 percent in the 1960s to 14.4 percent in the 1970s while growth of population for the country as a whole declined from 13.4 percent to 11.4 percent between the same decades (Bourne 1995). Nor were these trends confined to the United States. In the United Kingdom, for example, the 1981 population census revealed that there was a near perfect positive correlation between an area's degree of rurality and its rate of population growth during the previous decade. It might reasonably be argued that in the United Kingdom, however, there were virtually no rural areas which were not contiguous to metropolitan areas. Consonant with this view, a few of the most isolated rural areas in North Wales and Scotland did continue to lose population. They were, however, numerically and statistically swamped by the exurban rural areas including quite remote areas, such as those parts of the Highlands of Scotland within reach of the North Sea oil boom—which grew much more rapidly than either the traditional suburbs or the large cities.

As early as 1976 the phrase "counterurbanization" was gaining currency (Berry 1976) to describe a process going beyond suburbanization. As suburbanization proceeded, the traditional historic core city, or downtown, still remained the focal point of metropolitan regions. Visions were as influential as hard and detailed analysis. By 1980 these visions of the future of cities ranged from "Can cities survive?" (Pettengill and Uppal 1974), to a system of settlements based on highly dispersed multinodal metro regions ("the mature metropolis" in Leven 1978) with "edge-cities" added later (Garreau 1991), to an idyllic return to rural roots, populated by "telecottagers" or self-sufficient communities.

The details of change during the 1970s were impressive. Within American metropolitan areas there was a substantial dispersion of people to less densely populated counties (Long and Nucci 1995). The central cities compared to the suburbs did markedly worse, not only in terms of population growth but also on economic indicators such as employment, migration, and relative property price changes (Linneman and Summers 1993; Jensen and Leven 1997). There was a sense in which, not just in the United States, the 1970s, in the phrase of Vining and Strauss (1977), represented a "clean break with the past."

It was against this background that the contributions to this book were prepared. Data from the 1990/91 censuses were not yet available. Perceptions were conditioned by apparently remorseless trends of decentralization and the decline of historic city cores. The theoretical analyses explaining these trends were apparently equally linear. The Muth-Mills engine of suburbanization was driven by rising incomes. The Anas and Moses (1978) explanation of employment decentralization in goods-handling activities was driven by the substitution of trucks, highways, and containerization for railways and traditional port technology. Neither of these seemed likely to be reversed. The power of these forces was reinforced by the growth of air travel and air freight. Airports are land-extensive and cause localized environmental problems. They therefore tended to be located on the urban fringe and become decentralized employment nodes in their own right.

In turn, these forces causing decentralization of both industrial jobs and workforces interacted with the process of economic transformation, that is, the decline of employment in industry and the growth of service sector employment in mature economies. This economic transformation (sometimes called "deindustrialization") has been a universal and predictable aspect of such economies (see Rowthorne and Wells 1987). It has been associated with a number of interrelated changes. Industrial production has been transferring to low-labor-cost, newly industrializing countries, while production that remained in mature economies has become more capital intensive, with an associated increase in human capital. There has been rapidly rising labor productivity in manufacturing (the change in composition of output is much less marked in terms of value than of employment). In addition, activities have been progressively reclassified, as large integrated plants (including a range of functions such as transport, marketing, or administration) have given way to outsourcing and more specialized units, each in cost-minimizing locations.

The pattern of decentralization that this produced in Europe's cities from 1951 to 1981 is demonstrated in tables and figures 19.1 and 19.2.[1] The data relate to the percentage distribution of all Functional Urban Regions (FURs) in the European Union of twelve member states (the EU12) between eight phases of centralization/decentralization for each decade from the 1950s to the 1980s. FURs are classified into one of eight categories or stages according to the relative rates of population growth in their cores, in their hinterlands, and in the urban region as a whole. Four of these stages, defined in the footnotes to table 19.1, relate to centralization and four to decentralization. The final two

Table 19.1 SOUTHWARD MOVEMENT OF DECENTRALIZATION: ALL FURs OVER 330,000 (PERCENTAGE DISTRIBUTION), 1951–1991

	Stages of development of urban region[a]								Urban cores	
	1	2	3	4	5	6	7	8	gaining	losing
	Centralization				Decentralization				2+3+4+5	1+6+7+8
1951–61										
N. Europe[b]	1	10	8	**37**	32	11	0	1	87	13
France + N. Italy	0	12	**48**	35	5	0	0	0	100	0
S. Europe[c]	0	**72**	7	22	0	0	0	0	100	0
1961–71										
N. Europe	1	1	3	14	**47**	26	5	1	65	35
France + N. Italy	0	1	18	**63**	17	0	0	0	100	0
S. Europe	0	**67**	13	13	2	0	0	4	96	4
1971–75										
N. Europe	7	9	2	19	26	**42**	12	1	38	62
France + N. Italy	0	1	5	35	**28**	27	3	0	70	30
S. Europe	0	4	11	**46**	33	7	0	0	93	7
1975–81										
N. Europe	15	0	1	3	17	**33**	27	4	22	78
France + N. Italy	3	1	1	7	30	**42**	12	3	40	60
S. Europe	0	2	15	**48**	17	15	0	2	83	17
1981–91										
N. Europe	6	0	3	15	**30**	28	10	10	47	53
France + N. Italy	0	2	0	8	38	**32**	12	8	48	52
S. Europe	2	9	14	14	**19**	33	5	5	56	44

Cell indicated in **bold** and underlined contains the median.
[a] Stage 1 Core, hinterland, and FUR losing; core rate of loss less than hinterland
Stage 2 Core gaining; hinterland and FUR losing
Stage 3 Core and FUR gaining; hinterland losing
Stage 4 All gaining; rate of core growth greater than that of hinterland
Stage 5 All gaining; rate of core growth less than that of hinterland
Stage 6 Core losing; hinterland and FUR gaining
Stage 7 Core and FUR losing; hinterland gaining
Stage 8 Core, hinterland, and FUR losing; core rate of loss greater than hinterland
[b] N. Europe = German Federal Republic, Benelux, Denmark, and United Kingdom
[c] S. Europe = Italy south of Rome, Greece, Portugal, Spain, and Republic of Ireland.

columns of the table show just the proportion of FUR core cities gaining or losing population in each time period. The tables show the variation in patterns of decentralization in broad bands of Western Europe, corresponding to maturity of economic development. Table 19.2 shows the pattern for the larger countries. The figures show the same data but divided into two city-size groups. Figure 19.1 shows the frequency distribution for the largest FURs—those of more than a third of a million population in 1981 and with a core city of more than 200,000 at some date since 1951; figure 19.2 shows the pattern

Table 19.2 STAGES OF DEVELOPMENT OF FURs IN LARGER COUNTRIES: ALL FURs OVER 330,000 (PERCENTAGE DISTRIBUTION), 1971–91

			Stages of Development of Urban Region[a]									Urban Cores	
			Centralization				Decentralization				Total	Gaining	Losing
			1	2	3	4	5	6	7	8			
Benelux NL+B (not GdL)	1971–81	n	0	0	0	0	10	**13**	1	1	25	10	15
		%	0	0	0	0	40	**52**	4	4		40	60
	1981–91	n	1	0	3	4	**8**	8	1	0	25	15	10
		%	4	0	12	16	**32**	32	4	0		60	40
FDR	1971–81	n	2	0	0	5	6	**25**	5	8	51	11	40
		%	3.9	0	0	9.8	11.8	**49.0**	9.8	15.7		22	78
	1981–91	n	2	0	0	7	**26**	14	0	2	51	33	18
		%	3.9	0	0	13.7	**51.0**	27.5	0	3.9		65	35
France	1971–81	n	0	1	1	6	**23**	6	1	0	38	31	7
		%	0	2.6	2.6	15.8	**60.5**	15.8	2.6	0		82	18
	1981–91	n	0	0	0	4	**23**	8	1	2	38	27	11
		%	0	0	0	10.5	**60.5**	21.0	2.6	5.3		71	29
Italy	1971–81	n	0	1	0	4	11	**15**	5	0	36	16	20
		%	0	2.8	0	11.1	30.6	**41.7**	13.9	0		44	56
	1981–91	n	0	1	1	3	1	**21**	6	3	36	6	30
		%	0	2.8	2.8	8.3	2.8	**58.6**	16.7	8.3		83	17
Spain	1971–81	n	0	4	14	**19**	4	0	0	0	41	41	0
		%	0	9.8	34.1	**46.3**	9.8	0	0	0		100	0
	1981–91	n	1	6	8	**6**	7	9	2	2	41	27	14
		%	2.4	14.6	19.5	**14.6**	17.1	22.0	4.9	4.9		66	34
UK	1971–81	n	2	0	0	0	3	**17**	11	3	36	3	33
		%	5.6	0	0	0	8.3	**47.2**	30.6	8.3		8	92
	1981–91	n	4	0	0	3	1	**10**	9	9	36	4	32
		%	11.1	0	0	8.3	2.8	**27.8**	25.0	25.0		11	89

Note: Number in **bold** and underlined indicates cell contains the median.
[a]As defined in table 19.1.

for the medium-sized FURs—those with more than a third of a million inhabitants but with a core city of less than 200,000.

What emerges from this analysis is that from 1951 to 1981 there was a very regular pattern of change. Urban regions moved steadily from stages of centralization to decentralization, with decentralization ap-

Figure 19.1   FREQUENCY DISTRIBUTION FOR LARGEST FURs[a] BY STAGE OF DEVELOPMENT,[b] 1951–1991

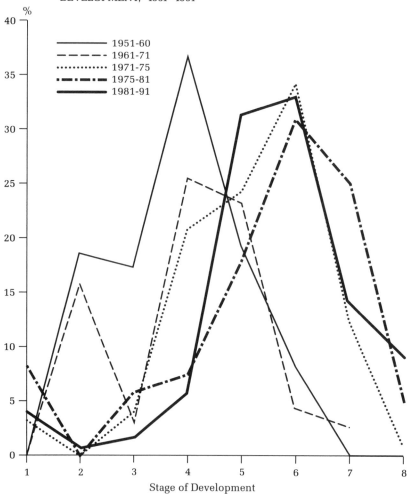

———— 1951-60
– – – – 1961-71
············· 1971-75
▪—▪—▪— 1975-81
━━━━ 1981-91

Stage of Development

[a]More than a third of a million population in 1981, and a core city of more than 200,000 at some date since 1951.
[b]For definition of stages of development see footnotes to table 19.1.

Figure 19.2 FREQUENCY DISTRIBUTION FOR MEDIUM-SIZED FURs[a] BY STAGE
OF DEVELOPMENT,[b] 1951–1991

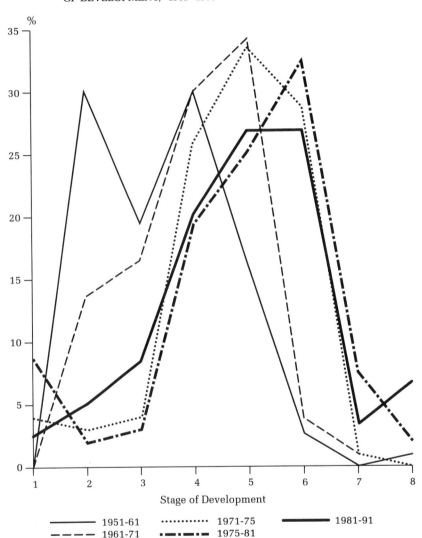

Stage of Development

	1951-61		1971-75		1981-91
	1961-71		1975-81		

[a]More than a third of a million population in 1981, and a core city that was below
200,000 since 1951.
[b]For definition of stages of development see footnotes to table 19.1.

pearing first in the cities of northern Europe and spreading south-wards, and spreading from the largest to the smaller cities. In northern Europe there may have been some acceleration of this trend in the first half of the 1970s; in France and Northern Italy the trend may have accelerated in the second half of the 1970s. The evidence that such a change in trend occurred, however, is not overwhelming. This was the regular and apparently accelerating trend that led commentators in the mid-1980s to start discussing the future pattern of urbanization as one of "disurbanization," and the process of decentralization as if it would inevitably continue for the indefinite future.

CIRCA 1980: A CHANGING BALANCE OF FORCES?

The problem with this projection of events is captured in the old adage, "A trend is a trend is a trend: the question is when will it bend." Without an adequate understanding of the reasons for the trend, predicting bends was impossible. In fact even in the 1970s there was empirical evidence pointing to the possibility of future bends. A close study of net migration flows into major north European capitals showed that the peak of outflow in Copenhagen was actually in the early 1970s and, although still negative, net outward migration had already all but ceased by 1980 (Matthiessen 1983). An analysis of London showed a virtually identical pattern (Cheshire and Hay 1986). By 1987 (Champion and Congdon 1987) the data showed that, not only had net outmigration ceased from Greater London (close in definition to the core city of the London FUR), but total population was growing. Growth was only by some 6,000 a year between 1983 and 1986, but it represented the first gain in Greater London's population since 1939 and compared to annual losses of nearly 90,000 in the early 1970s. In this sense it was a dramatic reversal. Nor was the population gain confined to those areas, such as Docklands, where industrial land had been redeveloped for residential use. There was also a parallel, if temporary, gain noted soon afterwards in London's employment (Evans and Crampton 1989). There were similar signs in other comparable European cities. Dangschat (1993) reports that the population of inner West Berlin, which had declined continuously from 1950, began to increase in 1985 and continued to do so through 1991.

As Thurston and Yezer (1994) demonstrate, the causal interrelations between employment and residential decentralization are complex. Intraurban locational determinants vary between sectors in ways that are not fully understood. Some sectors, mainly retailing and personal services, tend to follow their markets and so follow the decentralization of population. But other sectors of employment may lead decentralization. Anas and Moses (1978) argued that the catalytic role in the decentralization of employment in manufacturing, and other activities handling goods in bulk, was played by the substitution of trucks and highways for railways. This seems particularly persuasive. Manufacturing may be sensitive to labor costs and may have become more sensitive to land costs over the past fifty years as it has become more capital intensive (and more reliant on road transport both for access to its labor force and for shipping its goods), but land and labor have always been cheaper in decentralized locations. Indeed they were considerably cheaper relative to central city locations in the 1950s than in the 1980s. So the search for cheap land and labor seems intrinsically unlikely to have been the initiating factor in industrial decentralization.

A driving force in determining patterns of urban growth and centralization in Europe was the restructuring and capitalization of traditional peasant agriculture. This process started in Britain. Already by the 1950s there was no British region with more than 10 percent of its labor force in agriculture, although in southern Europe there were regions in several countries in which more than 50 percent of the labor force worked in agriculture. In proportionate terms, the rate of outflow of agricultural labor and the associated rural-urban migration flows varied, but varied surprisingly little across the regions of Europe. The absolute numbers, however, varied in proportion to the size of the agricultural labor force. This would seem to be a reason why decentralization moved southwards. At any point in time, as moving southwards in Europe the importance of agriculture in the labor force rose, so the absolute size of the rural-urban stream of migration also rose. As rising incomes and decentralizing industrial employment caused existing urban population and employment to decentralize in northern Europe, there was already little offsetting flow of population to the cities from the countryside by the 1950s. This offsetting flow increased going southwards, however, just as the industrial outflow was relatively smaller, since at that time industrial employment was proportionately less important.

In the same way, as falling absolute numbers in agriculture meant that, even if there were constant rates of job loss, the rural-urban migration flow fell over time, so it was also with industrial employment. Although the rate of loss of industrial jobs in core cities continued throughout the 1970s and 1980s, as the employment base fell, so the absolute number of jobs, and the number of jobs lost per inhabitant, declined. As was noted above, intraregional locational factors vary by sector. The growing service sectors were far less constrained by relative costs than was industry in choosing decentralized locations. Some of the most rapidly growing sectors of employment during the 1970s and early 1980s—such as finance, insurance, and real estate (FIRE), other business services, or the media—exhibited strong agglomeration economies and grew most strongly in central-city locations of the larger metro areas. The location of others, such as retail and personal services, was significantly influenced by the location of population (Thurston and Yezer 1994).

Other growing sectors, such as research and development (R&D), design, or publishing, were relatively less constrained in their intraregional locational choice. In some contexts, they grew in urban cores; in others, in satellite nodes; and in yet others, in low density, high amenity, exurban areas. An important determinant seems to be the availability and supply price of highly skilled labor, and that was influenced by both the local supply of natural environmental amenities and by urban amenities (Gyourko and Tracey, chapter 12 of this volume, or Furtado 1997). Compared to activities that handle goods in bulk, the dependence of these activities on road transport is limited. So, too, is their demand for space. Apart from skilled labor, access to interregional and international communications and to supporting services seem important. Thus, access to factors that conditioned the preferred location of their workforces, whether green amenities, such as mountains, or urban amenities, such as better quality local public goods or cultural facilities, was more influential in determining the location of these new activities than was the traditional pull of cheap land or access to long-distance transport networks. The most significant exception to this is access to airports (Cheshire and Gordon 1995). In a future European context it may, perhaps, include high-speed rail.

At the same time as the net loss of jobs in urban cores was tending to fall and to become potentially more variable, there were parallel changes occurring which influenced residential choice. In the traditional Muth-Mills model rising incomes, interacting with the relative income elasticities of demand for space compared to travel cost (including time), drive residential decentralization. Although space was the specific variable, it signified rather more: private space as a green amenity. By the later 1970s the typical household was changing in ways that gave travel costs relatively greater weight. The number of children per household was falling and the labor force participation rates of married women were rising, as was the proportion of house-holds consisting only of adults or single people. The price of space was becoming relatively less important for such households than access to the labor market. In cities where the most important concentration of jobs still remained downtown and/or where transport routes continued to be primarily radial, thereby giving more central areas greater accessibility, this increased importance of travel costs also helped change the balance of relative advantage between central and decentralized locations. Access to the urban labor market was maximized in more central locations.

In addition, the assumption of homogeneous preferences and a single composite green amenity good is very strong. There is a demonstrable demand for urban amenities, mainly urban cultural goods and services and certain types of urban public goods such as cityscape, as witnessed by the booming export trade Europe does in such items to American tourists. There are households, especially those without young children, which value such amenities, and if the incentive for such households to recentralize for labor market reasons increased, their presence as urban consumers would improve the range and quality of urban amenities. Revealed preference would suggest that those choosing to recentralize for a given change in relative incentives would be those with the highest weights in their preference functions for urban amenities.

CUMULATIVE CAUSATION IN DECENTRALIZATION AND RECENTRALIZATION

These arguments suggest a set of interrelated factors leading to cumulative causation in patterns of urban change. By about 1980 there was an underlying change in the balance of labor market forces. This was generated by the increasing weight of travel costs in household budgets and, to an extent varying between cities, an increasing availability of jobs in central areas because of the slowing absolute loss of industrial jobs and the growth of the FIRE sector as well as some other sectors more oriented to central locations. There would be variation in the extent to which cities were subject to these changing balances of opportunity, however, depending on their initial economic structure and the availability of critical labor skills and infrastructure. In addition, the institutional factors discussed below condition the extent to which the net balance of advantage between central and decentralized locations could change.

Existing patterns of residential segregation and the availability of urban amenities also played a part in determining the potential for job growth. Since there is a positive price paid for neighborhood socioeconomic characteristics reflecting a concentration of higher income groups (Cheshire and Sheppard 1995) and also a positive income elasticity of demand for such neighborhood characteristics, there is a self-reinforcing element in residential segregation. Richer neighborhoods are attractive to richer and more skilled residents simply because they are richer. If such neighborhoods are all in the urban periphery, then growing sectors such as R&D, marketing, or design, which are influenced in their locational choice by the quality of local labor force skills, will be differentially located in the periphery. Other employment, such as retail and personal services, will follow them as population and purchasing power increase. But in cities in which there were established neighborhoods in central areas with higher income and more skilled residents, firms seeking skilled labor might choose central locations with similar self-reinforcing tendencies.

These patterns in turn should be expected to interact with the availability of urban amenities. Superior urban amenities in a city, other things being equal, would mean more households responding to the changing balance of labor market forces and recentralizing. This too would have a cumulative effect. Public policy is also likely to play a role, influencing both the supply of suitable housing for more highly skilled groups (Maclennan, chapter 16 of this volume) and transport networks and transport costs through fuel taxes and subsidy of public transport. In some institutional contexts policy will also determine the proportion of income paid in tax (Linneman and Summers, chapter 4 of this volume).

So far no mention has been made of one special but highly influential factor acting on the relative advantage of central compared to suburban locations in American cities. Recent research has shown that the combined effects of the fiscal system in the United States and the degree of localized responsibility for antipoverty measures create not just a permanent financial disincentive for location in central cities but a disincentive that changes and may grow over time (Pack 1995; Gyourko 1997; Gyourko and Summers 1997; Summers 1997). Although antipoverty programs are explicitly a federal and state responsibility, the reality is that a significant additional burden falls on administrations where the poor are concentrated. In the context of the United States that, of course, means the central city.

Increased concentrations of poor residents impose both direct and indirect costs on city administrations and these increased costs are significantly met out of local revenues (Gyourko and Summers 1997). Direct costs come via increased expenditures on health and problems of homelessness not fully offset by transfers from federal and state governments. While local governments across the United States devote on average 12 percent of their own revenues to public welfare, health, and hospitals, large cities (those with populations exceeding 300,000) spend 30 percent, compared to only 9.1 percent for cities of less than 75,000. Transfers from state and federal governments only partially offset this imbalance. Indirect costs are also imposed by concentrations of poverty. Policing and education spending rise with the incidence of poverty. The poverty rate in large cities was 43 percent higher than in the nation as a whole. In the case of policing, this higher poverty rate was associated with an increase in expenditure of 29 percent (Gyourko 1997). There were similar uncompensated increases in spending on education, estimated to represent a mean of 42 percent of locally derived revenues for the seventy-three largest American cities (Summers and Ritter 1996).

In the United States, where local governments are dependent to a considerable extent on their own fiscal capacity, not only does this fiscal penalty generate an incentive for richer households to locate in the suburbs but it operates as a financial penalty on employment in the central city. The extent of this disincentive to central city locations changes over time as the spatial concentration of the poor changes. The spatial concentration of the poor responds both to the location decisions of the rich[2] and to the overall incidence of poverty in society. Since the distribution of income in the United States became markedly more unequal from the mid-1970s to the early 1990s (Joseph Rowntree Foundation 1995), the spatial concentration of the poor intensified. On the margin this factor therefore changed in a way that increased the incentive to decentralize. But it was an incentive created by the particular fiscal and institutional circumstances of local government in the United States, interacting with more fundamental forces working on the distribution of household incomes.

DIVERGING EXPERIENCES IN THE 1980s

The result was twofold. First the underlying balance of forces was shifting during the 1970s so that by about 1980 there was a potential for some cities to recentralize. The second was that the extent of, or indeed whether there was any, recentralization would vary greatly between cities in a cumulatively reinforcing way.

Table 19.1 illustrates the first point with respect to the cities of the twelve members of the European Union (EU12). During the 1980s in northern Europe, the distribution of cities by stages of development showed a substantial reversion to core growth and centralization. The median of the distribution moved back a stage, having moved forward in each previous time period since 1951, and the proportion of core cities gaining population increased from 22 to 47 percent. In French and northern Italian cities there was also some reversion. Only in southern European cities did the trend towards decentralization continue unchecked.

Evidence has also emerged from other countries which is consistent with these arguments. Some urban population revival was first noted in European cities by Champion and Congdon (1987) and Cheshire (1987). But a similar if more restricted phenomenon was noted at almost the same time in the United States by Long and DeAre (1988), even if a good part of apparent metropolitan area growth turned out to have resulted from annexation and consequent reclassification of rural/nonmetropolitan counties. Changing migration patterns examined by Frey (1993) also showed that metro area decentralization patterns in the 1980s were different from, and far less severe than, they had been in the 1970s. A later and more detailed analysis by Long and Nucci (1995) showed similar patterns. They examined annual data on changes in the concentration of population for three categories of areas in the United States: all counties, Bureau of Economic Analysis (BEA) Economic Areas, and BEA Metropolitan Economic Areas (broadly identifiable with FURs). From 1970, the first year for which the necessary data became available, concentration was falling in all three types of areas. The county-based index was the earliest to show a change of trend. It began to move towards concentration in the second half of the 1970s. Positive concentration began to occur between 1982 and 1983. This was quickly followed by positive concentration appearing in the indexes for the other two types of areas. Concentration in all three, however, peaked in the mid- to late 1980s. By 1990 to 1991 all three were showing that population deconcentration was present again.

Jensen and Leven (1997) show that, on the basis of rather strong assumptions, relative rates of change in the measure of quality of life (QOL) developed by Blomquist et al. (1988) can be calculated from data available for central cities and for metro areas as a whole. They derived a simple model which implied that, if house prices in the central city are rising or wages are falling relative to the metro area as a whole, then the QOL of the central city is rising relatively; and when net migration into, or labor supply in, the central city is rising relative to the metro area as a whole, similarly the QOL of the central city is rising relative to the metro area. It should be noted that all these measures of QOL are relative. An improvement in central city QOL would be perfectly consistent with the absolute value of QOL in the suburbs and exurbs continuing to be far superior.

The advantage of this approach is that, since it rests on revealed preference, it can be applied in the absence of information on amenities contributing directly to quality of life. Not only are there strong assumptions, however, but not all the appropriate data were available. In particular wages for homogeneous labor were missing and were proxied with family incomes, modified with a crude measure of changes in human capital. The values for these changes in relative QOL were calculated for the twenty-five largest SMSAs combined for each decade from 1950 to 1990.

The results are quite strong and consistent. All indicators except the wage proxy pointed in the same direction and showed statistically significant changes in the relative position of central cities compared to their metro areas. Between the 1970s and 1980s, there was a sharp change of trend in central city house prices compared to those of metro areas and rather less sharp changes in trend in the other indicators. The analysis supports the view that there was significant improvement in the relative position of the central cities of the twenty-five largest United States SMSAs during the 1980s. The tests of significance do not apply to individual SMSAs, although the data suggest that there was substantial variation between them in the extent to which they improved.

SYSTEMATIC FACTORS IN THE VARIATION OF DECENTRALIZATION

Figures 19.1 and 19.2 illustrate a second tendency observable in the FURs of the EU12. Although relative and, in some periods, absolute recentralization was apparent in some of the largest cities such as London, Berlin, and Copenhagen, it was statistically more common in medium-sized cities. The data in table 19.3 further illustrate this phenomenon and suggest the reasons for it. The table presents a mea-

Table 19.3. TURNAROUND IN NORTHERN EUROPEAN FURs BETWEEN THE 1970s AND THE 1980s (WITH RATE OF RELATIVE RECENTRALIZATION OF MORE THAN 1% DURING 1980s)

Country/FUR	Index of FUR Turnaround[a]	% Change in Core City Population: 1980s	Size Group[b]
Germany (West)			
Ulm	13.88	13.67	M
Krefeld	14.36	10.34	L
Freiburg	9.12	8.41	M
Benelux			
Maastricht	27.52	16.57	M
Brugge	14.26	−1.10	M
Zwolle	24.88	14.17	M
Groningen	25.32	3.53	M
Devente/Apeldoorn	4.45	4.90	M
UK			
Glasgow	24.17	−4.83	L
Canterbury	6.74	8.24	M
Oxford	23.16	10.64	M
Cambridge	33.19	11.68	M
Denmark			
Odense	10.67	6.09	M
Aarhus	17.10	9.08	M
Alborg	10.36	1.44	M

[a]Turnaround defined as: (% change in $Hinterland_{70s}$ − % change in $Core_{70s}$) − (% change in $Hinterland_{80s}$ − % change in $Core_{80s}$).
[b]L = Largest, M = Medium.

sure which can be thought of as an index of turnaround. The difference in the rates of population growth between the core and the hinterland in a given time period is a measure of relative (de)centralization. The change in this difference between two time periods is then a measure of turnaround. Where this is positive, it shows a movement towards relative (re)centralization. It should be noted that a positive value does not necessarily imply positive growth in the second time period in the urban core. Table 19.3 shows the values for those FURs in the EU12 that experienced the greatest turnaround during the 1980s compared to the 1970s. The cities do not represent a random selection. There is a significant tendency for them to be in the medium-sized group ($x^2 = 4.74$, significant at 5 percent) and these are mainly cities abundant in urban amenities: Canterbury, Oxford, Cambridge, Ulm, and Freiburg.

The comparative performance of Oxford and Reading is illuminating. They are cities of similar size, close to each other in one of the most prosperous parts of southeast England. Both are within 90 km of London, with Reading nearer by 25 km and with better access both to central London and to London's Heathrow Airport. Both have highly skilled labor forces within their urban regions. Both experienced rapid economic and population growth during the 1970s and the 1980s. The FUR rate of population growth in those decades was 4.4 percent and 8.9 percent in Reading and 5.0 percent and 7.2 percent in Oxford. Both cities exhibited strong decentralization during the 1970s. In Reading the excess of hinterland over core growth was 17.5 percentage points; in Oxford it was 19.9 percentage points. During the 1980s, however, while Reading continued to decentralize sharply, with hinterland growth exceeding core growth by 14.3 percentage points, Oxford exhibited not only strong relative turnaround but significant absolute core growth. The growth in the hinterland was 4.3 percent less than in the core.

As the Joseph Rowntree Foundation's (1995) study showed, Oxford is a city with an unusual pattern of residential segregation in British or American terms. Higher income residents and higher occupational groups are concentrated in central areas; low-income and deprived households are concentrated in social housing in peripheral estates. Reading, although it also has a university, has an edge-of-town campus, and the city itself has grown from a nineteenth-century industrial town. Its downtown area is dominated by modern high-rise office buildings, and it is poorly supplied, certainly relative to Oxford or London, with urban amenities. Many of its entertainment and recreational facilities, including restaurants, theatres, and even nightclubs, are in its exurban hinterland. While Reading has become an ultra-low-density mini-City of London, Oxford has become Hampstead-amongst-the-spires.

The evidence of table 19.3, therefore, and the experience of Oxford and Reading, support the conclusion that while the balance of forces driving decentralization changed and weakened around 1980, and even created the potential for decentralization to reverse, recentralization is very far from inevitable. The situation became rather one in which the drive to decentralization weakened for nearly all cities but their experience became much more varied and depended on their initial endowments and their circumstances. The experience of individual cities depended partly on the structure of their economies and on the skills of their labor forces. It also depended on the character of their housing stock and on the location and supply of urban amenities and access to green amenities. Above all it depended on their institutional structure and starting positions. American cities, given the fiscal penalties they experience, the growing concentration of poorer households within them, and their locally supported efforts towards poverty relief, suffer all but insuperable disadvantages in generating recentralization. This is so even if their relative position in the 1980s was not as dire as it was during the 1970s. Given the difficulties of creating city-suburb coalitions to promote services and spread the tax burdens associated with poverty relief (Summers 1997) this disadvantage seems likely to remain.

To an extent both decentralization and recentralization are self-reinforcing because of the demand for proximity to location-specific neighborhood characteristics, including the mean income of a neighborhood's households. In the production of urban amenities, demand creates supply and additional supply feeds back to demand, because of its impact on residential choice and because some growing sectors of employment are locationally sensitive to the locational preferences of their skilled labor forces.

THE ROLE OF POLICY

These arguments also suggest an enhanced role for public policy, both positively and negatively. Policy cannot push water uphill. Not only could policy not stem the outflow of industrial jobs during the 1960s and 1970s, in the long term, as the experience of those cities that tried hardest to do so suggests, it was counterproductive for policy to attempt to stem the flow. The arguments of the previous section and the evidence of the substantial variation in trends since about 1980 suggest, however, that the competitive advantage of decentralized locations is now far less overwhelming and that policy can therefore have a more significant influence.

By negative policy is meant the role policies may unintentionally have in influencing either decentralization or recentralization. In this context policy in the United States seems uniquely effective in reinforcing decentralization. The two most obvious factors are transport and institutional and fiscal arrangements. The very low tax on gasoline and low level of support for public transport[3] mean that there is a higher relative cost to higher density living than is the case in Europe (or Japan). It also means that a more central location offers relatively less advantage in terms of labor market access. The apparent political impossibility of redrawing boundaries or creating metro area governmental units (Summers 1997), coupled with cities' responsibility for a substantial amount of welfare provision from the fiscal tools of local governments, mean that central city businesses and residents are likely to pay an ever-rising price for their locations. The general increase in income inequality experienced in most mature economies in the period 1975–95 exacerbated this. More transfers were justified. But it was only in the institutional context of American cities that this became a significant further incentive to decentralize.

Zoning policy in the United States also provides incentives for decentralization. In most cities there is no constraint on the supply of land for development because a new community can always be incorporated.[4] This, too, represents in international terms a uniquely balkanized arrangement. It reduces overall densities because of the incentive for communities, once they are established, to restrict internal densities, encouraging the incorporation of yet another suburban community. It also provides a framework within which edge cities can develop on greenfield sites.

Land use planning systems vary widely but always provide an influential framework promoting or restricting decentralization and influencing, often unintentionally, the form it takes. In the United Kingdom, for example, the aim of urban containment, whereby policy attempts to restrict development to the boundaries of existing settlements (most powerfully by the use of so-called Green Belts), is to restrict decentralization. In growing urban regions, however, it has the paradoxical effect of encouraging leapfrogging to existing settlements beyond the boundaries of the metro area. It thus helps to generate a form of concentrated deconcentration in high-density exurbs. The functional equivalent of edge cities in the United Kingdom are, as a result, redeveloped high-rise downtowns in satellite cities such as Reading. The land-use planning system in France, in contrast, tends to generate urban extension by development contiguous to the existing urban areas. The functional equivalents of edge cities in France tend to be purpose-planned developments on the fringe of the existing downtown, such as La Defense (in Paris), Eurolille (in Lille), or Part Dieu (in Lyon).

There may also be an increasing role for positive policy. By positive policy is meant interventions specifically designed to promote or discourage decentralization.[5] The role that housing policies played in revival in Glasgow (as table 19.3 demonstrates, the FUR with one of the strongest performances on relative turnaround in the EU12) has been emphasised by Maclennan (chapter 16 of this volume). If other elements of the analysis presented in this chapter are plausible, then successful housing policies that attract more highly skilled residents to the central city will also make it a more attractive location for some sectors of employment growth, particularly business services, education, health, R&D and FIRE. There may be yet another reinforcing element. Black et al. (1996) produce evidence which suggests that the use of the equity value held by owner-occupiers as a source of start-up capital is an important factor in influencing the probability of success of new businesses. If this is true, then attracting additional, better-educated owner-occupier residents will in turn influence the long-run rate of net new business formation in the central city. Similarly, the supply of urban amenities is more open to influence by policy than was the competitiveness of central locations for industrial use. The role that public policy plays in shaping transport infrastructure and the role that this infrastructure plays in determining the relative spatial pattern of accessibility provides another lever for policy to work on.

In this context a further difference influencing diverging patterns of urban decentralization between North America and Europe is the significance of high-speed rail. Because of the low density of population and employment in the United States there are few, if any, corridors where high-speed rail is likely to be sufficiently competitive to be built. In Europe it is already an established fact. Significant extensions to the network are under construction and more are planned. Just as the development of air travel and air freight was a factor driving decentralization, so high-speed rail will tend to favor recentralization. Access to airports is maximized in the suburban and exurban hinterland. With a few exceptions, such as Eurodisney, Ebbsfleet on the southeast fringe of London, and some airport interchanges, the limited access points to the high-speed rail network will be in traditional downtown areas. The evidence from experience in France is that high-speed rail dominates air travel to a distance of about 500 kms and continues to be competitive up to 800 or 900 kms. Insofar as an increasing proportion of business travel in Europe is likely to be by high-speed rail, those cities that are served will be subject to an additional recentralizing force. But as with the other factors favoring recentralization, this force will be selective. It will have no impact in cities such as Dublin, Liverpool, or Toulouse, which will not be connected to the network.

CONCLUSIONS

The conclusion would appear to be that progressive and incremental decentralization ceased to be a necessary fact of urban areas in mature economies sometime during the late 1970s or early 1980s. During the 1960s and 1970s the decentralization of industrial employment and labor forces was driven by an overwhelming competitive imperative. The 1990 conference on which this book was based took place against this background. The data that began to lead to a re-evaluation of the future trajectory of decentralization was then just beginning to become available. Moreover, national policy and the particular institutional circumstances of American cities, coupled with their inheritances, make them much less suitable candidates for recentralization than European cities. All observers are conditioned by their experience, and the experience of American observers did not favor recentralization. In many areas of social and economic life, patterns of change in the United States are a precursor of those in Europe and elsewhere in the developed world. In the context of urban decentralization and future urban form this seems not to be the case. Cities in the United States are more a special case.

That it is human institutions and the incentives they generate, not God, that created American cities and makes it so difficult for them to cease decentralizing was illustrated by Blandinières (1997). He presented a superb three-dimensional representation of the Paris metro region. Measured on the vertical axis was the price of quality-constant housing space. This was colored from red to blue according to the socioeconomic composition of each census tract. In this representation the center of Paris rises like a red Alpine peak of professional and managerial concentration in the most expensive space. To the south and east were the low blue plains inhabited by the unemployed and the unskilled. The socioeconomic composition of neighborhoods shades off in Paris continuously with the price of space. From the red peaks of the most chic inner-city neighborhoods it shades to the brown and yellow slopes of the comfortable outer core, and then to the shallow yellow and green slopes of the solid working-class suburbs until it finally reaches the blue flatlands of the dispossessed and excluded: those without the walls. This is the virtual mirror image of most American cities. It reflects an entirely different inherited spatial distribution of locationally fixed amenities and an entirely different set of institutionally constructed incentives.

The change in the balance of forces which has taken place since about 1980 does not therefore make recentralization inevitable in any country or city. The particular circumstances of many cities have led to continued decentralization. What we might reasonably have expected to happen was a widespread slowing of decentralization during the 1980s, and that seems to be what the data show, even for cities in the United States. More generally, urban development is likely to bring greater diversity in both patterns of change and in the physical form of cities in the future than in the middle decades of the twentieth century. Many cities, particularly those brought into existence by the Industrial Revolution with restricted service functions, are likely to continue to decentralize and even decline. This is even more likely if they are port cities or are not connected to the high-speed rail network. Thus in Europe, cities such as Liverpool, Duisburg, Le Havre, or Charleroi might reasonably be expected to continue to decentralize and decline. Other cities, such as some of those identified in table 19.3, may continue to centralize and grow. Some of the largest cites, such as London, Frankfurt, Berlin, Amsterdam, or Brussels, with highly developed service and control functions, may stabilize or even recentralize. In the United States, the whole balance is more tilted by institutional factors and by policies that have had the effect of encouraging decentralization than is the case in Europe.

The weakening of the competitive imperative for decentralization implies that future patterns of development are likely to be more varied across cities than in the past. Within particular cities over time, however, there may be more consistent patterns. From 1951 to 1981 individual cities tended to develop from stages of centralization to decentralization. Because of the interaction between cause and effect, however, the longer the trajectory of a particular city has been established, the more unlikely it will be to change. As decentralization in a particular city region extends outward to lower densities, so road transport gains an increasing advantage, and the whole city region becomes more car and truck dependent. This causes all types of economic activity to become yet more land extensive, which induces yet greater decentralization. At the same time a location in the core confers fewer advantages for either business or residence.

Those cities that recentralize (as there are some signs that London is doing again, after a reversal in the late 1980s and early 1990s)[6] will have new investment in their core, both in private buildings and in their public infrastructure, especially transport infrastructure. This will improve the relative competitiveness of more central locations. As owner occupation tends to extend, there will be increasing redevelopment of industrial sites and conversion of old buildings, which in their former state generated negative neighborhood effects. It will also improve urban amenities because of increased demand, and that will lead, perhaps, to an eventual increase in the net rate of business formation. Thus while urban development and form may become more varied over time, cross sectionally, particular cities may follow more consistent paths than in the past.

Notes

1. Reproduced from Cheshire 1995. For a definition of FURs see Cheshire, chapter 5 of this volume.

2. It is more conventional to talk about the location of the poor in the context of the incentive that welfare systems may give for the poor to concentrate where the systems are most generous. However, this ignores the fact that by definition the rich can always outbid the poor. If the socioeconomic composition of a neighborhood is an attribute which commands a price—and the evidence shows that it is (Cheshire and Sheppard, 1995)—then the rich can buy "more" of it. It is more consistent therefore to think of richer households buying into better neighborhoods rather than poorer households choosing to live in less desirable ones.

3. This is not to suggest that it would necessarily be appropriate to subsidize public transport more. The very low densities of American cities—reflecting, in part, the low price of gasoline and the lack of subsidy for public transport over the past seventy-five years—make public transport economically unattractive. But it is still true that the pattern of settlement would be different if past policies had been different.

4. There are a few minor and partial exceptions such as Portland, Ore.

5. Note "containment" policy in the UK does not attempt to discourage decentralization by altering incentive structures. It attempts to restrict it by fiat but in the process sets up unintended incentives which encourage it.

6. The most recent population data available for London (Office of National Statistics, 1998) show population increases between 1981 and 1996 of 6.2 percent in Inner London, 2.6 percent in Outer London, and 4.0 percent in Greater London as a whole.

References

Anas, A., and L. Moses. 1978. "Transportation and Land Use in the Mature Metropolis," in *The Mature Metropolis*, edited by C. L. Leven. Lexington, Mass: D.C. Heath.

Beale, C.L. 1975. *The Revival of Population Growth in Non-Metropolitan America*. Washington, D.C.: U.S. Department of Agriculture, ERS 605.

Berg, L. van den, R. Drewett, L. H. Klaassen, A. Rossi, and C. H. T. Vijverberg. 1982. *Urban Europe: A Study of Growth and Decline*. Oxford: Pergamon.

Berry, B.J.L. 1976. *Urbanization and Counterurbanization*. Beverly Hills, Calif.: Sage.

Black, J., D. De Meza, and D. Jeffreys. 1996. "House Prices, the Supply of Collateral and the Enterprise Economy." *Economic Journal* 106: 60–75.

Blandinières, J. P. 1997. "Global Conditions for Land Observatories' Implementation in France." Paper given to Lincoln Land Institute Conference on Land Prices, Land Information Systems and the Market for Land Information, November.

Blomquist, G. C., M. C. Berger, and J. P. Hoehn. 1988. "New Estimates of the Quality of Life in Urban Areas." *American Economic Review* 78: 89–107.

Bourne, L. S. 1993. "The Myth and Reality of Gentrification: A Commentary of Emerging Urban Forms." *Urban Studies* 30 (1): 183–89.

———. 1995. *Urban Growth and Population Redistribution in North America: a Diverse and Unequal Landscape*. University of Toronto, Centre for Urban and Community Studies Major Report 32.

Champion, A. G. 1989. *Counterurbanization: The Changing Pace and Nature of Population Deconcentration*. London: Edward Arnold.

Champion, A. G., and P. Congdon. 1987. "An Analysis of the Recovery of London's Population Change Rate." *Built Environment* 13 (4): 193–211.

Cheshire, P. C. 1987. *Economic Factors in Urban Change: European Prospects*. University of Reading Discussion Papers in Urban and Regional Economics, Series C. No 30.

———. 1995. "A New Phase of Urban Development in Western Europe? The Evidence for the 1980s." *Urban Studies* 32: 1045–63.

Cheshire, P. C., and I.R. Gordon. 1995. "Change and Spatial Specialisation within the South East's Economy." In *Territorial Competition in an Integrating Europe: Local Impact and Public Policy*, edited by Cheshire and Gordon. Aldershot, England: Avebury.

Cheshire, P. C., and D. G. Hay. 1986. "The Development of the European Urban System, 1971–81," in *The Future of the Metropolis: Economic Aspects*, edited by H. J. Ewers, J. B. Goddard, and H. Matzerath. Berlin: de Gruyter.

Cheshire, P. C., and S. Sheppard. 1995. "On the Price of Land and the Value of Amenities." *Economica* 62: 247–67.

Dangschat, J. S. 1993. "Berlin and the German Systems of Cities." *Urban Studies* 30 (6): 1025–51.

Evans, A. W., and G. R. Crampton. 1989. "Myth, Reality and Employment in London." *Journal of Transport Economics and Policy* 23(1): 89–108.

Frey, W. H. 1993. "The New Urban Revival in the United States." *Urban Studies* 30 (4/5): 741–77.

Furtado, A. 1997. "Regional Wage Differentials and Spatial Disparities in Europe—Evidence from Germany, Great Britain, Italy and Spain." Ph.D. *Thesis*, London School of Economics.

Garreau, J. 1991. *Edge City: Life on the New Frontier*. New York: Doubleday.

Greenwood, M. J., and R. Stock. 1990. "Patterns of Change in the Intrametropolitan Location of Population, Jobs and Housing: 1950 to 1980." *Journal of Urban Economics* 28: 243–76.

Gyourko, J. 1997. *Place- vs. People-Based Aid and the Role of an Urban Audit in a New Urban Strategy*. University of Pennsylvania, Wharton Real Estate Center, Working Paper 245.

Gyourko, J., and A. A. Summers. 1997. *A New Strategy for Helping Cities Pay for the Poor*. Washington, D.C.: Brookings Institution, Policy Brief 18.

Hall, P., and D. G. Hay. 1980. *Growth Centres in the European Urban System*. London: Heinemann Educational.

Jensen, M. J., and C. L. Leven. 1997. "Quality of Life in Central Cities and Suburbs." *Annals of Regional Science* 31: 431–49.

Joseph Rowntree Foundation. 1995. *Enquiry into Income and Wealth*. York: Joseph Rowntree Foundation.

Leven, C. L. 1978. *The Mature Metropolis*. Lexington, Mass: D.C. Heath.

Long, L., and D. DeAre. 1988. "U.S. Population Redistribution: A Perspective on the Nonmetropolitan Turnaround." *Population and Development Review* 14: 433–50.

Long, L., and A. Nucci. 1995. "The 'Clean Break' Revisited: Is US Population Again Deconcentrating?" Washington, D.C.: U.S. Bureau of the Census, mimeo.

Matthiessen, C. W. 1983. "Settlement Change in Denmark." In *Urban Policy and Urban Development in the 80s, Danish Experience in a European Context*, edited by C. W. Matthiessen. University of Copenhagen.

Office of National Statistics. 1998. *Regional Trends 33*: table 14.1.

Pack, J.R. 1995. *Poverty and Urban Public Expenditures*. University of Pennsylvania, Wharton Real Estate Center, Working Paper 197.

Pettengill, R. B., and J. S. Uppal. 1974. *Can Cities Survive? The Fiscal Plight of American Cities*. New York: St. Martin's Press.

Rowthorne, R. E., and J. R. Wells. 1987. *De-industrialization and Foreign Trade*. Cambridge: Cambridge University Press.

Summers, A. A. 1997. *Major Regionalization Efforts between Cities and Suburbs in the United States*. University of Pennsylvania, Wharton Real Estate Center, Working Paper 246.

Summers, A. A., and G. Ritter. 1996. *The Costs to Large Cities of Educating Poor Children*. University of Pennsylvania, Wharton Real Estate Center, draft working paper.

Thurston, L., and A. M. J. Yezer. 1994. "Causality in the Suburbanization of Population and Employment." *Journal of Urban Economics* 35: 105–18.

Vining, D. R., and A. Strauss. 1977. "A Demonstration That the Current Deconcentration of Population in the United States Is a Clean Break with the Past." *Environment and Planning A* 9: 751–58.

Vining, D. R., and T. Kontuly. 1978. "Population Dispersal from Major Metropolitan Regions: An International Comparison." *International Regional Science Review* 3: 49–73.

redistributive services, 327. *See also* public services
refrigeration, 90
Regional Contribution Agreements (RCAs), 435, 436
regional coordination, lack of, 51, 52
regional developmental programs, 300
regional economic growth rates, 467
"regional headquarters" cities, 31
regional nodal cities/centers, 64, 65
regional planning policies, 74
regional subsidies, 74
regionalism, 138
"regionalization" policies, 304
regulatory restrictions, impeding economic development, 4
Reich, Robert, 62
Reischauer, Robert D., 368n.22
rent controls, 517–518, 528–529, 564
rent cost, 204, 206, 372
rental housing, 49, 52, 517–518
  subsidized, 50
research and development (R&D), 497, 503–504
research and development (R&D) programs, 480, 482. *See also* technology development programs
research and development (R&D) sector, 578
residential densities, 19
residential integration, 440–441
residential segregation, 580. *See also* ethnic segregation
residualization, 535–536
resource allocation, 41
  among metropolitan areas, 41, 42, 46–47
  within metropolitan areas, 41, 43
resource-based industries, dependence on, 179
rest of the legally defined central city (RCC), 92, 94, 96

employment growth rates, 97–100, 104–108, 123, 125, 126, 128
population growth rates, 109–117, 130, 132, 135
"resurgence of the states," 483
retail employment, percentage of people in, 121, 122, 124, 126, 130, 132, 136
retail jobs/population ratio, 428, 429
retail trade employment, change in, 428
reurbanization, 551
revenue-raising capacity, 335, 344, 368n.25. *See also* fiscal condition of cities
Roback, Jennifer, 378, 403n.6, 404n.7
Rosen/Roback model, 371, 373–375
Rotterdam, 172, 173
Ruhr, Germany, 27, 28, 305, 315
rural counties, 320–321
rural populations, 220
rural renaissance, 287
rural-urban migration, 23–24, 30, 266
Rustbelt areas, 112, 114, 194

S

San Francisco, 72, 75
Schmandt, Jürgen, 481–482
"school reform," 33
schools. *See also* educational system
  urban, 362–365, 402, 403n.4
schools aid, state, 474n.6, 476n.26
Schwarz, Joshua, 372
science and technology programs. *See* technology development programs
Scotland, 530, 536, 570
  housing transactions, 528. *See also* Glasgow
segregation. *See* ethnic segregation; socioeconomic segregation
Senn, Lanfranco, 9, 11, 231

ABOUT THE EDITORS

Anita A. Summers is professor emerita of public policy and management and codirector of the Wharton Urban Decentralization Project in the Wharton School of the University of Pennsylvania, and has appointments in the real estate department and the graduate school of education. She was the chair of the department from 1983 to 1988, and was formerly head of the Urban Research Section of the Federal Reserve Bank of Philadelphia. She has published a number of articles on educational efficiency in the *American Economic Review*, the *Journal of Human Resources*, and *Advances in Applied Microeconomics*. She is the author (with Thomas F. Luce) of three books on economic development and public finance issues in the Philadelphia metropolitan area, published by the University of Pennsylvania Press in 1985, 1986, and 1987, and the author of a number of working papers on the design of a new federal urban policy in the United States. She is currently a participating scholar at the Center on Urban and Metropolitan Policy of the Brookings Institution, and a member of the Research Advisory Committee of the Pennsylvania Economy League.

Paul C. Cheshire has been professor of economic geography at the London School of Economics since 1995, having previously been professor of urban and regional economics at the University of Reading. He has been a consultant to numerous government and international organizations. Between 1983 and 1989 he directed a large-scale study, funded by the European Commission, of European urban and regional development. He is presently directing a study within the ESRC's Cities Initiative modeling urban growth and spatial interactions in Europe. His research interests include urban and regional systems, the economics of land use and land use planning, and the hedonic analysis of urban housing and land markets. His books include *Urban Problems in Western Europe: An Economic Analysis* (with D. G. Hay, 1989), *Territorial Competition in an Integrating Europe: Local Impact and Public Policy* (with I. R. Gordon, 1995), and *Regions in Rivalry:*

The Impacts of Territorial Competition (forthcoming), and he has also written numerous articles for professional journals.

Lanfranco Senn is professor of regional and urban economics at Bocconi University of Milan, where he is also director of the Research Center in Regional Economics, Transport, and Tourism (CERTET). He is chairman of a degree program in public administration and international organizations. He has taught in a number of Italian universities (Tret, Bari, and Bergamo). A former president of the Italian section of the Regional Science Association, he is also an expert on regional policies for the European Commission, and is a member of the board of RESER, a European network on services and space. He is president of the Scientific Committee of Gruppo CLAS, a major consulting firm in Italy, and is currently counselor to the Minister of Public Works and of Transport of the Italian government. He has written in the fields of regional and urban economics, input-output analysis, and service activities. He recently coedited and contributed to *Innovation Networks and Innovative 'Milieux': A Challenge for Regional Development,* with Denis Maillat and Michel Quevit.

Leo van den Berg is professor of regional and urban economics at the Erasmus University, Rotterdam. He is director of the European Institute for Comparative Urban Research (Euricur), and is scientific coordinator of the master's program in urban management. He is author or coauthor of a number of books, including *Urban Europe, A Study of Growth and Decline* (1982), *Urban Systems in a Dynamic Society* (1987), *Spacial Cycles* (1987), *Governing Metropolitan Regions* (1993), *Urban Tourism* (1995), *Metropolitan Organizing Capacity* (1997), *National Urban Policies in the European Union* (1998), and *The European High-Speed Train and Urban Development* (1998).

Anthony Downs has been a senior fellow at the Brookings Institution since 1977. Before that, he was for 17 years a member, and for four years chairman, of the Real Estate Research Corporation, a nationwide consulting firm specializing in real estate market studies, appraisals, urban policy studies, and demographic analyses. His fields include housing, real estate finance and location, urban affairs, urban planning, and race relations. He has published 13 books and more than 360 articles. He is the author of *An Economic Theory of Democracy, Inside Bureaucracy, Who Are the Urban Poor?, Opening Up the Suburbs, Neighborhoods and Urban Development,* and *Stuck in Traffic,* and coauthor of *Urban Decline and the Future of American Cities.*

Gianluigi Gorla is a research fellow at the University of Trento, Italy, where he teaches a course in spatial economics, and researcher at the department of economics at Bocconi University of Milan. His main research fields are urban and regional economics and policies. He has recently coedited (with Flavio Boscacci) *Local Competitive Economies.*

Joseph Gyourko is director of the Zell/Lurie Real Estate Center, and professor of real estate and finance, at the Wharton School of the

University of Pennsylvania. His research interests include real estate finance, local public finance, and urban economics. Professor Gyourko recently was named coeditor of *Real Estate Economics*, the journal of the American Real Estate and Urban Economics Association, and he serves on the editorial boards of the *Journal of Real Estate Finance and Economics*, the *Journal of Regional Science*, *Real Estate Finance*, and the *Journal of the Asian Real Estate Society*. Newly appointed as a nonresident senior fellow at the Brookings Institution, he is also a fellow of the Urban Land Institute and a member of the National Council of Real Estate Investment Fiduciaries.

Peter Hall is professor of planning at University College, London, and professor emeritus of city and regional planning at the University of California, Berkeley. He is the author or editor of over 30 books on problems of urban development and planning, including *Cities of Tomorrow* and *Cities in Civilization*. He is editor of the journal *Built Environment*.

Mark Alan Hughes graduated from Swarthmore College and holds a doctorate from the University of Pennsylvania. He is the author of numerous scholarly articles, including "Decentralization and Accessibility," which was published in the *Journal of the American Planning Association* and won the Association's National Planning Award in 1992. A former professor at Princeton University, Hughes has taught at Harvard, Swarthmore, and the University of Pennsylvania. Since 1994, he has been vice president for policy development at Public/Private Ventures in Philadelphia.

Helen F. Ladd is professor of public policy studies and economics at Duke University, where she is also director of graduate studies in public policy. An expert on state and local public finance, Professor Ladd has written extensively on the property tax, education finance, tax and expenditure limitations, intergovernmental aid, state economic development, and the fiscal problems of U.S. cities. In addition, she has coauthored books on discrimination in mortgage lending and the capitalization of property taxes and edited a volume on tax and expenditure limitations. Her most recent books (with John Yinger) are *America's Ailing Cities: Fiscal Health and the Design of Urban Policy* (Johns Hopkins University Press, 1989; updated edition, 1991), *Holding Schools Accountable: Performance-Based Reform in Education* (Brookings Institution, 1996), and *Local Government Tax and Land*

Use Policies in the United States: Understanding the Links (Edward Elgar, 1998).

Charles L. Leven is professor emeritus of economics at Washington University and distinguished professor of public policy at the University of Missouri–St. Louis. Previously he served on the faculty at Iowa State University, the University of Pennsylvania, and the University of Pittsburgh, and was an economist at the Federal Reserve Bank of Chicago. His most recent published papers include "Economics of Regional Decentralization: Lessons from U.S. Experience," "Quality of Life in Central Cities and Suburbs," and "Casino Gaming in Missouri: The Spending Displacement Effect and Gaming's Net Economic Impact." He is a past president of the Regional Science Association, a former distinguished fellow of the Southern Regional Science Association, and a recipient of the Walter Isard Award for Distinguished Scholarship in Regional Sciences.

Peter D. Linnemann is senior managing director of Equity International Properties, Ltd., and also serves as vice-chairman of Equity Group Investments, Inc. He is a leading real estate industry strategist, researcher, and market analyst. Dr. Linneman was the Albert Sussman Professor of Real Estate, Finance, and Public Policy at the Wharton School of the University of Pennsylvania. He served as director of the Wharton Real Estate Center for 13 years and was the founding chairman of the real estate department. He has published and consulted extensively in real estate, corporate strategy, and finance, and is one of the founding coeditors of the *Wharton Real Estate Review*.

Anaïs Loizillon is a policy and program analyst at Public/Private Ventures and is the author of several reports on critical policy issues facing Philadelphia's low-income neighborhoods. Her research on metropolitan labor markets, welfare reform, child welfare, and juvenile justice has been supported by the Pew Charitable Trusts, the Rockefeller Foundation, and the William Penn Foundation.

Michael I. Luger is professor of public policy analysis and management at the University of North Carolina at Chapel Hill. He serves as chairman of the Curriculum in Public Policy Analysis and as director of the university's Office of Economic Development. He has written extensively about urban and regional economics and development, infrastructure, and public policy. His most recent book (with Kenneth Temkin) is *The Cost of Red Tape: Regulation and the Price of Housing*, to be published in 1999 by Rutgers University Press.

Rainer Mackensen is professor emeritus of sociology at the Technical University of Berlin. His main fields of research are population and urban and regional studies. Before moving to Berlin in 1968, he worked as research director at the Social Research Institute of Münster University at Dortmund, Germany, and taught at the Ulm School of Design and at Münster University. He is a past president of the German Association of Futures Research and of the German Society of Population Research. He has published numerous books and articles, including *The Demography of the Later Phases of the Family Life Cycle* (with C. Höln and P. Greebenik) and *Population Movements in the European Community* (with W. Schwartz and M. Wingen).

Duncan Maclennan is the Mactaggart Chair of Land Economics and Finance at the University of Glasgow. He is director of the ESRC Cities Program, chairman of the JRF Area Regeneration Program, and a member of the Treasury Panel of Advisers on Public Services/Microeconomic Policy. He has been a member of the Board of Scottish Homes, which spends 300 million annually on housing and regeneration, since its inception in 1989. Professor Maclennan was made a C.B.E. in the Birthday Honours List of June 1997.

Edwin S. Mills is professor emeritus of real estate at the Kellogg Graduate School of Management, Northwestern University. He has held faculty positions in economics at Princeton and Johns Hopkins Universities and at the Massachusetts Institute of Technology. For 30 years, his teaching and research have been devoted to urban economics and real estate. He has written many books and papers on those subjects and is coauthor (with Bruce Hamilton) of *Urban Economics*, now in its fifth edition.

Dick Netzer is professor of economics and public administration at the Wagner Graduate School of Public Service of New York University. He has written and done research in urban economics and public finance for nearly 50 years, with extensive experience as a member of governmental policy making and advisory boards and commissions, especially in New York City and New York state.

John B. Parr is professor of regional and urban economics at the department of urban studies at the University of Glasgow and has held positions at a number of other institutions, including the University of Pennsylvania and the University of Washington. He has coauthored and coedited four volumes on urban structure and regional analysis and has published journal articles on regional development, the analysis of urban systems, and the spatial structure of the regional economy. He is currently a member of the management board of *Urban Studies* and serves on the editorial boards of three other journals on urban and regional analysis.

John M. Quigley is Chancellor's Professor of Economics and Public Policy at the University of California, Berkeley. His research specialties include the analysis of urban housing and labor markets and local public finance. He is the author of 10 books and a large collection of articles in scholarly journals on public finance and the urban economy. His latest book is a two-volume collection, *The Economics of Housing* (Edward Elgar, 1998).

Joseph Tracy is an assistant vice-president in the Domestic Research Department of the Federal Reserve Bank of New York. He has held academic positions in the economics departments at Yale University and Columbia University. His research focuses on labor and housing markets.